1971

MUIRHEAD LIBRARY OF PHILOSOPHY

An admirable statement of the aims of the Library of Philosophy was provided by the first editor, the late Professor J. H. Muirhead, in his description of the original programme printed in Erdmann's *History of Philosophy* under the date 1890. This was slightly modified in subsequent volumes to take the form of the following statement:

'The Muirhead Library of Philosophy was designed as a contribution to the History of Modern Philosophy under the heads: first of Different Schools of Thought—Sensationalist, Realist, Idealist, Intuitivist; secondly of different Subjects—Psychology, Ethics, Political Philosophy, Theology. While much had been done in England in tracing the course of evolution in nature, history, economics, morals and religion, little had been done in tracing the development of thought on these subjects. Yet "the evolution of opinion is part of the whole evolution".

'By the co-operation of different writers in carrying out this plan it was hoped that a thoroughness and completeness of treatment, otherwise unattainable, might be secured. It was believed also that from writers mainly British and American fuller consideration of English Philosophy than it had hitherto received might be looked for. In the earlier series of books containing, among others, Bosanquet's *History of Aesthetic*, Pfleiderer's *Rational Theology since Kant*, Albee's *History of English Utilitarianism*, Bonar's *Philosophy and Political Economy*, Brett's *History of Psychology*, Ritchie's *Natural Rights*, these objects were to a large extent effected.

'In the meantime original work of a high order was being produced both in England and America by such writers as Bradley, Stout, Bertrand Russell, Baldwin, Urban, Montague, and others, and a new interest in foreign works, German, French and Italian, which had either become classical or were attracting public attention, had developed. The scope of the Library thus became extended into something more international, and it is entering on the fifth decade of its existence in the hope that it may contribute to that mutual understanding between countries which is so pressing a need of the present time.'

The need which Professor Muirhead stressed is no less pressing today, and few will deny that philosophy has much to do with enabling us to meet it, although no one, least of all Muirhead himself, would regard that as the sole, or even the main, object of philosophy. As

Professor Muirhead continues to lend the distinction of his name to the Library of Philosophy it seemed not inappropriate to allow him to recall us to these aims in his own words. The emphasis on the history of thought also seemed to me very timely; and the number of important works promised for the Library in the very near future augur well for the continued fulfilment, in this and other ways, of the expectations of the original editor.

H. D. LEWIS

MUIRHEAD LIBRARY OF PHILOSOPHY

General Editor: H. D. Lewis
Professor of History and Philosophy of Religion in the University of London

Action by SIR MALCOLM KNOX
The Analysis of Mind by BERTRAND RUSSELL
Brett's History of Psychology edited by R. S. PETERS
Clarity is Not Enough by H. D. LEWIS
Coleridge as a Philosopher by J. H. MUIRHEAD
The Commonplace Book of G. E. Moore edited by C. LEWY
Contemporary American Philosophy edited by G. P. ADAMS and W. P. MONTAGUE
Contemporary British Philosophy first and second Series edited by J. H. MUIRHEAD
Contemporary British Philosophy third Series edited by H. D. LEWIS
Contemporary Indian Philosophy edited by RADHAKRISHNAN and J. H. MUIRHEAD 2nd edition
The Discipline of the Cave by J. N. FINDLAY
Doctrine and Argument in Indian Philosophy by NINIAN SMART
Essays in Analysis by ALICE AMBROSE
Ethics by NICOLAI HARTMANN translated by STANTON COIT 3 vols
The Foundations of Metaphysics in Science by ERROL E. HARRIS
Freedom and History by H. D. LEWIS
The Good Will: A Study in the Coherence Theory of Goodness by H. J. PATON
Hegel: A Re-examination by J. N. FINDLAY
Hegel's Science of Logic translated by W. H. JOHNSTON and L. G. STRUTHERS 2 vols
Hegel's Science of Logic translated by A. V. MILLER
History of Aesthetic by B. BOSANQUET 2nd edition
History of English Utilitarianism by E. ALBEE
History of Psychology by G. S. BRETT edited by R. S. PETERS abridged one volume edition 2nd edition
Human Knowledge by BERTRAND RUSSELL
A Hundred Years of British Philosophy by RUDOLF METZ translated by J. H. HARVEY, T. E. JESSOP, HENRY STURT
Ideas: A General Introduction to Pure Phenomenology by EDMUND HUSSERL translated by W. R. BOYCE GIBSON
Identity and Reality by EMILE MEYERSON
Imagination by E. J. FURLONG

Indian Philosophy by RADHAKRISHNAN 2 vols revised 2nd edition

Introduction to Mathematical Philosophy by BERTRAND RUSSELL 2nd edition

Kant's First Critique by H. W. CASSIRER

Kant's Metaphysic of Experience by J. H. PATON

Know Thyself by BERNADINO VARISCO translated by GUGLIELMO SALVADORI

Language and Reality by WILBUR MARSHALL URBAN

Lectures on Philosophy by G. E. MOORE

Lectures on Philosophy by G. E. MOORE edited by C. LEWY

Matter and Memory by HENRI BERGSON translated by N. M. PAUL and W. S. PALMER

Memory by BRIAN SMITH

The Modern Predicament by H. J. PATON

Natural Rights by D. G. RITCHIE 3rd edition

Nature, Mind and Modern Science by E. HARRIS

The Nature of Thought by BRAND BLANSHARD

On Selfhood and Godhood by C. A. CAMPBELL

Our Experience of God by H. D. LEWIS

Perception by DON LOCKE

The Phenomenology of Mind by G. W. F. HEGEL translated by SIR JAMES BAILLIE revised 2nd edition

Philosophy in America by MAX BLACK

Philosophical Papers by G. E. MOORE

Philosophy and Illusion by MORRIS LAZEROWITZ

Philosophy and Political Economy by JAMES BONAR

Philosophy and Religion by AXEL HÄGERSTROM

Philosophy of Space and Time by MICHAEL WHITEMAN

Philosophy of Whitehead by W. MAYS

The Platonic Tradition in Anglo-Saxon Philosophy by J. H. MUIRHEAD

The Principal Upanisads by RADHAKRISHNAN

The Problems of Perception by R. J. HIRST

Reason and Goodness by BLAND BLANSHARD

The Relevance of Whitehead by IVOR LECLERC

The Science of Logic by G. W. F. HEGEL

Some Main Problems of Philosophy by G. S. MOORE

Studies in the Metaphysics of Bradley by SUSHIL KUMAR SAXENA

The Theological Frontier of Ethics by W. G. MACLAGAN

Time and Free Will by HENRI BERGSON translated by F. G. POGSON

The Transcendence of the Cave by J. N. FINDLAY

Values and Intentions by J. N. FINDLAY

The Ways of Knowing: or the Methods of Philosophy by W. P. MONTAGUE

Muirhead Library of Philosophy

EDITED BY H. D. LEWIS

HEGEL'S SCIENCE OF LOGIC

HEGEL'S
SCIENCE OF LOGIC

TRANSLATED BY
A. V. MILLER

FOREWORD BY
PROFESSOR J. N. FINDLAY

LONDON · GEORGE ALLEN & UNWIN LTD
NEW YORK · HUMANITIES PRESS

PRINTED IN GREAT BRITAIN
in 11 on 12 point Imprint type
BY UNWIN BROTHERS LIMITED
WOKING AND LONDON

THIS TRANSLATION IS
DEDICATED TO THE MEMORY OF
FRANCIS SEDLÁK
1873–1935

FOREWORD

I am happy to recommend this new translation of Hegel's *Wissenschaft der Logik* by my friend Arnold Miller. His deep enthusiasm for, and passionate self-identification with the thought of Hegel has opened his eyes to the sense of many of the most difficult passages in the book, and has given his style some of the unfailing readability, the often homely charm, of the original. That he has been always wholly successful in rendering every passage would be too much to expect, but where he is dark, and his words doubtfully chosen, the darkness and doubtfulness are generally to be found in the original, and do not stem from a poor mastery of Hegel's thought, vocabulary and syntax. His book brings the pattern of the *Logic* across in English with astonishing faithfulness, and makes clear that, like all Hegel's writings, it represents the honest, if transforming, commerce of what can reasonably be called a world-mind with a whole world of detailed understanding and knowledge. The book will go far in dispelling the picture of Hegel as a magus of false dialectic. He will appear as the greatest of European thinkers, engaged in a self-critical enterprise which even he only half understood, whose most obscure, botched utterances are often worth many of the lucidities of modern philosophers. As a practical teacher, concerned to put Hegel across to English-speaking students, I am grateful to Mr Miller for his new translation.

J. N. FINDLAY
Clark Professor of Moral Philosophy
and Metaphysics
Yale University

TRANSLATOR'S PREFACE

It is now nearly forty years since the first complete translation of Hegel's *Wissenschaft der Logik* was published. With the current revival of interest in Hegel both in this country and across the Atlantic, there is perhaps a need for a more accurate rendering of this important work which is indispensable for an understanding of his system. The present translation is an attempt to satisfy this need and I have done my best to provide the student who is unfamiliar with German with a rendering which, I hope, is usefully close to Hegel's exposition. How far I have succeeded is, of course, for others to judge; but if I have in some measure made this key to Hegel's system more accessible to the student, I shall feel amply rewarded for my labours.

It is my hope that the translation will prove useful not only to professional students but also to the interested layman. As Mr G. R. G. Mure says in his *Introduction to Hegel* (p. 80), 'philosophy is no more the exclusive business of professionals than is art or religion. If there were not in every man, however intermittently he feels it, and however inadequately he interprets it, the nisus towards attaining a total and unreserved self-consciousness, there would be no professional philosophers.'

What the student chiefly requires for a fruitful study of Hegel is faith in the essential greatness of the human spirit and its ability to attain to a knowledge of absolute truth. This is what Hegel himself demanded of his students in his introductory lectures on the history of philosophy.

Most of the crasser errors and misconceptions about Hegel have been cleared away by the work of scholars such as Professor J. N. Findlay, Mr G. R. G. Mure, and Professor Kaufman, to name only a few, and the student will obtain valuable assistance from their writings. But above all, he must 'mark, learn, and inwardly digest' what Hegel himself has to say in his Prefaces and Introduction and, last but not least, in the chapter entitled 'With What Must the Science Begin?'. This chapter is of great importance for an understanding of the beginning of the *Science of Logic*, for in it Hegel has made it quite clear why he begins with *pure being*.

It may safely be said that the main obstacle to a grasp of the *Logic* is the fact that we are unaccustomed to dialectical thinking and are loth to make the effort to rid ourselves of the prejudices and presuppositions on which our ordinary thinking rests. We have always to be on our guard that we do not allow ourselves to rely solely upon the understanding, the abstractive intellect, which holds its concepts rigidly apart in isolation and overlooks their essential connectedness. This is what Hegel calls 'die Anstrengung des Begriffs', the effort demanded by the Notion for its comprehension.

The translation has been made from Lasson's edition of the *Wissenschaft der Logik*, published in 1923. I have been sparing in my use of capitals for Hegel's categories except where it was important to distinguish their technical meaning: thus 'Existence' and 'Appearance' with initial capitals stand for *Existenz* and *Erscheinung*, categories in the sphere of essence, and Hegel's *Begriff* and *Idee* I have translated by 'Notion' and 'Idea', always spelt with capitals. The usual translation of *Schein* by 'show' hardly does justice to Hegel's use of this term in his *Logic*, and I have translated it by 'illusory being'. '*Schein*', says Hegel (p. 395), 'consists solely in the sublatedness of being, in its nothingness; this nothingness it has in essence and apart from its nothingness, apart from essence, *Schein* is *not*.' And in the *Phenomenology of Spirit*[1] he says that '*Schein* is the name we give to being that is immediately in its own self a non-being'. 'Show' is too ambiguous and imprecise a term to render Hegel's meaning in this context.

In conclusion I wish to thank Professor J. N. Findlay for the encouragement he has given me to complete a task already begun before we had met.

A. V. MILLER

Whiteway,
Stroud,
Glos.
May, 1968.

---

[1] Hoffmeister's edition, 1952, p. 110.

CONTENTS

Volume Two: SUBJECTIVE LOGIC
or
THE DOCTRINE OF THE NOTION

VOLUME ONE

THE OBJECTIVE LOGIC

PREFACE TO THE FIRST EDITION

The complete transformation which philosophical thought in Germany has undergone in the last twenty-five years and the higher standpoint reached by spirit in its awareness of itself, have had but little influence as yet on the structure of logic.

That which, prior to this period, was called metaphysics has been, so to speak, extirpated root and branch and has vanished from the ranks of the sciences. The ontology, rational psychology, cosmology, yes even natural theology, of former times—where is now to be heard any mention of them, or who would venture to mention them? Inquiries, for instance, into the immateriality of the soul, into efficient and final causes, where should these still arouse any interest? Even the former proofs of the existence of God are cited only for their historical interest or for purposes of edification and uplifting the emotions. The fact is that there no longer exists any interest either in the form or the content of metaphysics or in both together. If it is remarkable when a nation has become indifferent to its constitutional theory, to its national sentiments, its ethical customs and virtues, it is certainly no less remarkable when a nation loses its metaphysics, when the spirit which contemplates its own pure essence is no longer a present reality in the life of the nation.

The exoteric teaching of the Kantian philosophy—that the understanding ought not to go beyond experience, else the cognitive faculty will become a theoretical reason which by itself generates nothing but fantasies of the brain—this was a justification from a philosophical quarter for the renunciation of speculative thought. In support of this popular teaching came the cry of modern educationists that the needs of the time demanded attention to immediate requirements, that just as experience was the primary factor for knowledge, so for skill in public and private life, practice and practical training generally were essential and alone necessary, theoretical insight being harmful even. Philosophy [*Wissenschaft*] and ordinary common sense thus co-operating to bring about the downfall of metaphysics, there was seen the strange spectacle of a cultured nation without metaphysics—like a temple richly ornamented in other respects but without a holy of holies. Theology, which in former times was the guardian of the speculative mysteries and of metaphysics (although this was subordinate to it) had given up this science in exchange for feelings, for what was popularly matter-of-fact, and for historical erudition. In keeping with this change, there vanished from the world those solitary souls who were sacrificed by their people and exiled from the world to the end that the eternal should be contemplated and served by lives devoted solely thereto—not for any practical gain but for the sake of blessedness; a disappearance which, in another context, can be regarded as essentially the same phenomenon as that previously mentioned. So that having got rid of the dark utterances of metaphysics, of the colourless communion of the spirit with itself, outer existence seemed to be transformed into the bright world of flowers—and there are no *black* flowers, as we know.

Logic did not fare quite so badly as metaphysics. That one *learns* from logic *how to think* (the usefulness of logic and hence its purpose, were held to consist in this—just as if one could only learn how to digest and move about by studying anatomy and physiology) this prejudice has long since vanished, and the spirit of practicality certainly did not intend for logic a better fate than was suffered by the sister science. Nevertheless, probably for the sake of a certain formal utility, it was still left a place among the sciences, and indeed was even retained as a subject of public instruction. However, this better lot concerns only the outer fate of logic, for its structure and contents have remained the same throughout a long inherited tradition, although in the course of being passed on the contents have become ever more diluted and attenuated; logic shows no traces so far of the new spirit which has arisen in the sciences no less than in the world of actuality. However, once the substantial form of the spirit has inwardly reconstituted itself, all attempts to preserve the forms of an earlier culture are utterly in vain; like withered leaves they are pushed off by the new buds already growing at their roots.

Even in the philosophical sphere this ignoring of the general change is beginning gradually to come to an end. Imperceptibly, even those who are opposed to the new ideas have become familiar with them and have appropriated them, and if they continue to speak slightingly of the source and principles of those ideas and to dispute them, still they have accepted their consequences and have been unable to defend themselves from their influence; the only way in which they can give a positive significance and a content to their negative attitude which is becoming less and less important, is to fall in with the new ways of thinking.

On the other hand, it seems that the period of fermentation with which a new creative idea begins is past. In its first manifestation, such an idea usually displays a fanatical hostility toward the entrenched systematization of the older principle; usually too, it is fearful of losing itself in the ramifications of the particular and again it shuns the labour required for a scientific elaboration of the new principle and in its need for such, it grasps to begin with at an empty formalism. The challenge to elaborate and systematize the material now becomes all the more pressing. There is a period in the culture of an epoch as in the culture of the individual, when the primary concern is the acquisition and assertion of the principle in its undeveloped intensity. But the higher demand is that it should become systematized knowledge.

Now whatever may have been accomplished for the form and the content of philosophy [*Wissenschaft*] in other directions, the science of logic which constitutes metaphysics proper or purely speculative philosophy, has hitherto still been much neglected. What it is exactly that I understand by this science and its standpoint, I have stated provisionally in the Introduction. The fact that it has been necessary to make a completely fresh start with this science, the very nature of the subject matter and the absence of any previous works which might have been utilized for the projected reconstruction of logic, may be taken into account by fair-minded critics, even though a labour covering many years has been unable to give this effort a greater perfection. The essential point of view is that what is involved is an altogether new concept of scientific procedure. Philosophy, if it would be science, cannot, as I have remarked elsewhere,[1] borrow its method from a subordinate science like mathematics, any more than it can remain satisfied with categorical assurances of inner intuition, or employ arguments based on grounds adduced by external reflection. On the contrary, it can be only the nature of the content itself which spontaneously develops itself in a scientific method of knowing, since it is at the same time the reflection of the content itself which first posits and *generates* its determinate character.

---

[1] *Phenomenology of Spirit*, Preface to the first edition. Strictly, the exposition is the cognition of the method and it has its place in logic itself. [1831.]

The understanding *determines*, and holds the determinations fixed; reason is negative and *dialectical*, because it resolves the determinations of the understanding into nothing; it is positive because it generates the universal and comprehends the particular therein. Just as the understanding is usually taken to be something separate from reason as such, so too dialectical reason is usually taken to be something distinct from positive reason. But reason in its truth is *spirit* which is higher than either merely positive reason, or merely intuitive understanding. It is the negative, that which constitutes the quality alike of dialectical reason and of understanding; it negates what is simple, thus positing the specific difference of the understanding; it equally resolves it and is thus dialectical. But it does not stay in the nothing of this result but in the result is no less positive, and in this way it has restored what was at first simple, but as a universal which is within itself concrete; a given particular is not subsumed under this universal but in this determining, this positing of a difference, and the resolving of it, the particular has at the same time already determined itself. This spiritual movement which, in its simple undifferentiatedness, gives itself its own determinateness and in its determinateness its equality with itself, which therefore is the immanent development of the Notion, this movement is the absolute method of knowing and at the same time is the immanent soul of the content itself. I maintain that it is this self-construing method alone which enables philosophy to be an objective, demonstrated science. It is in this way that I have tried to expound consciousness in the *Phenomenology of Spirit*. Consciousness is spirit as a concrete knowing, a knowing too, in which externality is involved; but the development of this object, like the development of all natural and spiritual life, rests solely on the nature of the pure essentialities which constitute the content of logic. Consciousness, as spirit in its manifestation which in its progress frees itself from its immediacy and external concretion, attains to the pure knowing which takes as its object those same pure essentialities as they are in and for themselves. They are pure thoughts, spirit thinking its own essential nature. Their self-movement is their spiritual life and is that through which philosophy constitutes itself and of which it is the exposition.

In the foregoing there is indicated the relation of the science which I call the *Phenomenology of Spirit*, to logic. As regards the external relation, it was intended that the first part of the *System of Science*[1] which contains the *Phenomenology* should be followed by a second part containing logic and the two concrete [*realen*] sciences, the Philosophy of Nature and the Philosophy of Spirit, which would complete the System of Philosophy. But the necessary expansion which logic itself has demanded has induced me to have this part published separately; it thus forms the first sequel to the *Phenomenology of Spirit* in an expanded arrangement of the system. It will later be followed by an exposition of the two concrete philosophical sciences mentioned. This first volume of the Logic contains as Book One the Doctrine of Being; Book Two, the Doctrine of Essence, which forms the second part of the first volume, is already in the press; the second volume will contain Subjective Logic or the Doctrine of the Notion.

Nuremberg, *March* 22, 1812.

[1] Bamberg and Würzburg, Göbhard, 1807. This title will not be repeated in the second edition which will be published next Easter. In place of the projected second part mentioned in the rest of the sentence, which was to contain all the other philosophical sciences, I have since brought out the *Encyclopaedia of the Philosophical Sciences*, the third edition of which appeared last year. [1831.]

PREFACE TO THE SECOND EDITION

When I undertook this fresh elaboration of the Science of Logic of which this is the first volume, I was fully conscious not only of the inherent difficulty of the subject matter and of its exposition, but also of the imperfection of its treatment in the first edition; earnestly as I have tried after many years of further occupation with this science to remedy this imperfection, I feel I still have reason enough to claim the indulgence of the reader. One title to such claim in the first instance may well be based on the fact that in the main there was available for the contents of the science only external material in the older metaphysics and logic. Though these two sciences have been universally and abundantly cultivated, the latter even up to our own day, the interest taken in the speculative side has been only slight; in fact, on the whole, the same material has been just repeated over and over again, sometimes being thinned out to the point of being trivial and superficial and sometimes more of the old ballast has been hauled out afresh and trailed along with logic. From such efforts, often purely mechanical, the philosophical import of the science could gain nothing. To exhibit the realm of thought philosophically, that is, in its own immanent activity or what is the same, in its necessary development, had therefore to be a fresh undertaking, one that had to be started right from the beginning; but this traditional material, the familiar forms of thought, must be regarded as an extremely important source, indeed as a necessary condition and as a presupposition to be gratefully acknowledged even though what it offers is only here and there a meagre shred or a disordered heap of dead bones.

The forms of thought are, in the first instance, displayed and stored in human *language*. Nowadays we cannot be too often reminded that it is *thinking* which distinguishes man from the beasts. Into all that becomes something inward for men, an image or conception as such, into all that he makes his own, language has penetrated, and everything that he has transformed into language and expresses in it contains a category—concealed, mixed with other forms or clearly determined as such, so much is logic his natural element, indeed his own peculiar *nature*. If nature as such, as the physical world, is contrasted with the

spiritual sphere, then logic must certainly be said to be the
supernatural element which permeates every relationship of man
to nature, his sensation, intuition, desire, need, instinct, and
simply by so doing transforms it into something human, even
though only formally human, into ideas and purposes. It is an
advantage when a language possesses an abundance of logical
expressions, that is, specific and separate expressions for the
thought determinations themselves; many prepositions and
articles denote relationships based on thought; the Chinese
language is supposed not to have developed to this stage or only
to an inadequate extent. These particles, however, play quite a
subordinate part having only a slightly more independent form
than the prefixes and suffixes, inflections and the like. It is much
more important that in a language the categories should appear
in the form of substantives and verbs and thus be stamped with
the form of objectivity. In this respect German has many advantages over other modern languages; some of its words even possess
the further peculiarity of having not only different but opposite
meanings so that one cannot fail to recognize a speculative spirit
of the language in them: it can delight a thinker to come across
such words and to find the union of opposites naïvely shown in the
dictionary as one word with opposite meanings, although this
result of speculative thinking is nonsensical to the understanding.
Philosophy therefore stands in no need of a special terminology;
true, some words have to be taken from foreign languages but
these have already acquired through usage the right of citizenship
in the philosophical realm—and an affected purism would be
most inappropriate where it was the distinctive meaning which
was of decisive importance. The advance of culture generally, and
of the sciences in particular, gradually brings into use higher
relationships of thought, or at least raises them to greater universality and they have thus attracted increased attention. This
applies even to the empirical and natural sciences which in general
employ the commonest categories, for example, whole and parts,
a thing and its properties, and the like. In physics, for example,
the category of force has become predominant, but more recently
the category of polarity which is the determination of a difference
in which the different terms are *inseparably* conjoined, has played
the leading part although it has been used inordinately in connection with all phenomena, even with light. It is a matter of

infinite importance that in this way an advance has been made beyond the form of *abstraction*, of identity, by which a specific concept, as, for example, force, acquires an independent self-subsistence, and that prominence and currency have been given to the *determinate* form, the difference, which is at the same time an inseparable element in the identity. Because of the fixed reality of natural objects the study of nature compels us to fix the categories which can no longer be ignored in her, although with complete inconsistency towards other categories which are also allowed to remain valid; and such study does not permit the further step of abstracting from the opposition and indulging in generalities as so easily happens in the intellectual sphere.

But while logical objects and their expressions may be thoroughly familiar to educated people it does not follow, as I have said elsewhere,[1] that they are intelligently apprehended; and to have to occupy oneself with what is familiar can even arouse impatience—and what is more familiar than just those determinations of thought which we employ on every occasion, which pass our lips in every sentence we speak? It is the purpose of this foreword to indicate the general features of the course followed by knowing in its advance beyond a mere acquaintance with its objects, of the relation of philosophical [*wissenschaftlichen*] thinking to this natural thinking. This much, together with what was contained in the earlier Introduction, will be sufficient to give a general idea of what is meant by logical cognition, the kind of preliminary general idea which is demanded in the case of any science prior to its exposition, that is, prior to the import of the science itself.

In the first place, we must regard it as an infinite step forward that the forms of thought have been freed from the material in which they are submerged in self-conscious intuition, figurate conception, and in our desiring and willing, or rather in ideational desiring and willing—and there is no human desiring or willing without ideation—and that these universalities have been brought into prominence for their own sake and made objects of contemplation as was done by Plato and after him especially by Aristotle; this constitutes the beginning of the intelligent apprehension of them. 'It was only', says Aristotle, 'after almost everything

---

[1] 'That with which we are simply familiar [*bekannt*], is for that very reason not intelligently apprehended [*erkannt*].' (Preface to the *Phenomenology of Spirit*.)

B

necessary and everything requisite for human comfort and inter-
course was available, that man began to concern himself with
philosophical knowledge.'[1] 'In Egypt', he had previously remarked,
'there was an early development of the mathematical sciences
because there the priestly caste at an early stage were in a position
to have leisure.'[2]

As a matter of fact, the need to occupy oneself with pure thought
presupposes that the human spirit must already have travelled a
long road; it is, one may say, the need of the already satisfied need
for the necessities to which it must have attained, the need of a
condition free from needs, of abstraction from the material of
intuition, imagination, and so on, of the concrete interests of
desire, instinct, will, in which material the determinations of
thought are veiled and hidden. In the silent regions of thought
which has come to itself and communes only with itself, the
interests which move the lives of races and individuals are hushed.
'In so many respects', says Aristotle in the same context, 'the
nature of man is in bondage; but this science, which is not studied
for its utility, is the only absolutely free science and seems therefore to be a more than human possession'.[3] Philosophical thinking
in general is still concerned with concrete objects—God, nature,
spirit; but logic is concerned only and solely with these thoughts
as thoughts, in their complete abstraction. For this reason it is
customary to include logic in the curriculum of youth, for youth
is not yet involved in the practical affairs of life, living at leisure
so far as they are concerned; and it is only for its own subjective
ends that it has to busy itself with acquiring the means to enable
it to become actively engaged with the objects of those practical
interests—and still theoretically even with these. Contrary to
Aristotle's view just mentioned, the science of logic is included in
these *means*; the study of logic is a preliminary labour to be carried
out in school and it is not until later that the serious business of
life and the pursuit of substantial ends begins. In life, the categories are *used*; from the honour of being contemplated for their
own sakes they are degraded to the position where they *serve* in
the creation and exchange of ideas involved in intellectual exercise
on a living content. First they serve as *abbreviations* through their
universality (for what a host of particulars of outer existence and
actions is embraced by a conception—battle, war, nation, ocean,

[1] *Metaph.*, A 2. 982b.   [2] *Ibid.*, A 1. 981.   [3] *Ibid.*, A 2. 982b.

or animal, for example—and in the conception of God or of love there is epitomized in the *simplicity* of such ideating an infinite host of ideas, actions, states, etc.!). Secondly, the categories serve for the more exact determination and discovery of *objective relations*; but in this process the import and purpose, the correctness and truth of the thought involved, are made to depend entirely on the subject matter itself and the thought determinations are not themselves credited with any active part in determining the content. Such a use of the categories, which above was called natural logic, is unconscious; and when in philosophical reflection the categories are assigned the role of serving as means, then thinking as such is treated as something subordinate to the other activities of mind. We do not indeed say of our feelings, impulses or interests that they serve us, rather do they count as independent forces and powers, so that to have this particular feeling, to desire and to will this particular thing and to be interested in it—just this, is what we are. But probably we are more conscious of obeying our feelings, impulses, passions, interests, not to mention habits, than of having them in our possession, still less, in view of our intimate union with them, of their being at our disposal. Such determinations of feeling and mind soon show themselves as *particular* in contrast to the *universality* which we are conscious ourselves of being and in which we have our freedom; and we are disposed to regard ourselves as caught up in these particular states and dominated by them. Consequently it is much more difficult to believe that the forms of thought which permeate all our ideas— whether these are purely theoretical or contain a matter belonging to feeling, impulse, will—are means for us, rather than that we serve them, that in fact they have us in their possession; what is there more in *us* as against them, how shall *we*, how shall *I*, set myself up as *more* universal than they, which are the universal as such? When we give ourselves up to a sensation, a purpose, an interest, and in it feel ourselves confined and unfree, the place into which we can withdraw ourselves back into freedom is this region of self-certainty, of pure abstraction, of thought. Or again, to speak of *things*, we call the *nature* or the *essence* of things their *notion*, and this is only for thought; but still less shall we say of the notions of things that we dominate them, or that the determinations of thought of which they are the complex are at our service; on the contrary, it is our thinking that must accommodate itself to them and our caprice or freedom ought not to want to mould them to suit itself. Since, therefore, subjective thought is our very own, innermost, act, and the objective notion of things constitutes their essential import, we cannot go outside this our act, we cannot stand above it, and just as little can we go beyond the nature of things. We can, however, disregard the latter determination; in so far as it coincides with the first it would yield a relation of our thoughts to the object [*Sache*], but this would be a valueless result because it would imply that the thing, the object, would be set up as a criterion for our notions and yet for us the object can be nothing else but our notions of it. The way in which the critical philosophy understands the relationship of these three terms is that we place our thoughts as a medium between ourselves and the objects, and that this medium instead of connecting us with the objects rather cuts us off from them. But this view can be countered by the simple observation that these very things which are supposed to stand beyond us and, at the other extreme, beyond the thoughts referring to them, are themselves figments of subjective thought, and as wholly indeterminate they are only a single thought-thing—the so-called thing-in-itself of empty abstraction.

Still, sufficient has been said of the point of view which no longer takes the determinations of thought to be only an instrument and a means; more important is the further point connected with it, namely that it is usual to regard them as an external form. The activity of thought which is at work in all our ideas, purposes, interests and actions is, as we have said, unconsciously busy (natural logic); what we consciously attend to is the contents, the objects of our ideas, that in which we are interested; on this basis, the determinations of thought have the significance of *forms* which are only attached to the content, but are not the content itself. But if the truth of the matter is what we have already stated and also is generally admitted, namely that the nature, the peculiar essence, that which is genuinely permanent and substantial in the complexity and contingency of appearance and fleeting manifestation, is the *notion* of the thing, the *immanent universal*, and that each human being though infinitely unique is so primarily because he is a *man*, and each individual animal is such individual primarily because it is an animal: if this is true, then it would be impossible to say what such an individual could still be if this foundation were removed, no matter how richly endowed the individual might be with other predicates, if, that is, this foundation can equally be called a predicate like the others. The indispensable foundation, the notion, the universal which is the thought itself, in so far as one can make abstraction from the general idea expressed by the word 'thought', cannot be regarded as *only* an indifferent form attached to a content. But these thoughts of everything natural and spiritual, even the substantial *content*, still contain a variety of determinatenesses and are still charged with the difference of a soul and a body, of the notion and a relative reality; the profounder basis is the soul [*Seele*] itself, the pure Notion which is the very heart of things, their simple life-pulse, even of the subjective thinking of them. To focus attention on this *logical* nature which animates mind, moves and works in it, this is the task. The broad distinction between the instinctive act and the intelligent and free act is that the latter is performed with an awareness of what is being done; when the content of the interest in which one is absorbed is drawn out of its immediate unity with oneself and becomes an independent object of one's thinking, then it is that spirit begins to be free, whereas when thinking is an instinctive activity, spirit is enmeshed in the bonds of its categories and is broken up into an infinitely varied material. Here and there in this mesh there are firm knots which give stability and direction to the life and consciousness of spirit; these knots or nodes owe their fixity and power to the simple fact that having been brought before consciousness, they are independent, self-existent Notions of its essential nature. The most important point for the nature of spirit is not only the relation of what it is *in itself* to what it is *actually*, but the relation of what it *knows itself* to be to what it actually is; because spirit is essentially consciousness, this self-knowing is a fundamental determination of its *actuality*. As impulses the categories are only instinctively active. At first they enter consciousness separately and so are variable and mutually confusing; consequently they afford to mind only a fragmentary and uncertain actuality; the loftier business of logic therefore is to clarify these categories and in them to raise mind to freedom and truth.

What we indicated as the beginning of the science [of logic]—a beginning which we have already recognized as having a high value both on its own account and as a condition of genuine knowledge—namely, the treatment of Notions generally and the moments of the Notion, that is, the determinations of thought, primarily as forms which are distinct from the matter of thought and only attached to it, this attitude directly reveals itself as intrinsically inadequate for the attainment of truth—and truth is the declared object and aim of logic. For, as such mere forms, as distinct from the content, they are assumed to be standing in a determination which stamps them as finite and makes them incapable of holding the truth which is in its own self infinite. In whatever respect the true may be associated with limitation and finitude, this is the aspect of its negation, of its untruth and unreality, that is, of its end, not of the affirmation which, as the true, it is. Faced with the baldness of the merely formal categories, the instinct of healthy common sense has, in the end, felt itself to be so much in the right that it has contemptuously abandoned acquaintanceship with them to the domain of school logic and metaphysics; at the same time, common sense fails to appreciate the value even of a proper awareness of these fragments and is quite unaware that in the instinctive thinking of natural logic, and still more in the deliberate rejection of any acquaintance with or knowledge of the thought determinations themselves, it is in bondage to unclarified and therefore unfree thinking. The simple basic determination or common form of the collection of such forms is *identity* which, in the logic of this collection, is asserted as the law of identity, as $A = A$, and as the principle of contradiction. Healthy common sense has so much lost its respect for the school which claims possession of such laws of truth and still busies itself with them that it ridicules it and its laws and regards anyone as insufferable who can utter truths in accordance with such laws: the plant is—a plant, science is—science. It has also formed an equally just estimate of the significance of the formulas which constitute the rules of syllogizing which in fact is a cardinal function of the understanding (although it would be a mistake not to recognize that these have their place in cognition where they must be obeyed); it knows that the formulas quite as well serve impartially error and sophistry and that however truth may be defined, they cannot serve higher, for example, religious truth—that generally speaking they concern only the correctness of the knowledge of facts, not truth itself.

The inadequacy of this way of regarding thought which leaves truth on one side can only be made good by including in our conception of thought not only that which is usually reckoned as belonging to the external form but the content as well. It is soon evident that what at first to ordinary reflection is, as content, divorced from form, cannot in fact be formless, cannot be devoid of inner determination; if it were, then it would be only vacuity, the abstraction of the thing-in-itself; that, on the contrary, the content in its own self possesses form, in fact it is through form alone that it has soul and meaning, and that it is form itself which is transformed only into the semblance of a content, hence into the semblance of something external to this semblance. With this introduction of the content into the logical treatment, the subject matter is not *things* but their *import*, the Notion of them. But in this connection we can be reminded that *there is* a multitude of Notions, a multitude of objects [*Sache*]. We have, however, already said how it is that restrictions are imposed on this multitude, that the Notion, simply as thought, as a universal, is the immeasurable abbreviation of the multitudes of particular things which are vaguely present to intuition and pictorial thought; but also *a* Notion is, first, in its own self *the* Notion, and this is only one and is the substantial foundation; secondly, *a* Notion is *determinate* and it is this determinateness in it which appears as content: but the determinateness of the Notion is a specific form of this substantial oneness, a moment of the form as totality, *of that same Notion* which is the foundation of the specific Notions. This Notion is not sensuously intuited or represented; it is solely an object, a product and content of *thinking*, and is the absolute, self-subsistent object [*Sache*], the logos, the reason of that which is, the truth of what we call things; it is least of all the logos which should be left outside the science of logic. Therefore its inclusion in or omission from this science must not be simply a matter of choice. When those determinations of thought which are only external forms are truly considered in themselves, this can only result in demonstrating their finitude and the untruth of their supposed independent self-subsistence, that their truth is the Notion. Consequently, the science of logic in dealing with the thought determinations which in general run through our mind instinctively and unconsciously—and even when they become part of the language do not become objects of our attention—will also be a reconstruction of those which are singled out by reflection and are fixed by it as subjective forms external to the matter and import of the determinations of thought.

No subject matter is so absolutely capable of being expounded with a strictly immanent plasticity as is thought in its own necessary development; no other brings with it this demand in such a degree; in this respect the Science of Logic must surpass even mathematics, for no subject matter has in its own self this freedom and independence. Such an exposition would demand that at no stage of the development should any thought-determination or reflection occur which does not immediately emerge at this stage and that has not entered this stage from the one preceding it—a requirement which is satisfied, after its fashion, in the process of mathematical reasoning. However, such an abstract perfection of exposition must, I admit, in general be dispensed with; the very fact that the science must begin with what is absolutely simple, that is, with what is most general and of least import, would restrict the exposition solely to these same quite simple expressions of the simple without any further addition of a single word; all that could properly be admitted would be negative considerations intended to ward off and banish any heterogeneous elements which otherwise might be introduced by pictorial thought or unregulated thinking. However, such intrusive elements in the simple immanent course of the development are themselves contingent, so that the effort to ward them off is itself tainted with this contingency; besides which it is futile to try to deal with *all* of them, lying as they do outside the subject matter, and in any case, any demand for a systematic disposal of such random reflections could only be partially satisfied. But the peculiar restlessness and distraction of our modern consciousness compel us to take some account of the more readily suggested reflections and opinions. A plastic discourse demands, too, a plastic receptivity and understanding on the part of the listener; but youths and men of such a temper who would calmly suppress *their own* reflections and opinions in which *original* thought is so impatient to manifest itself, listeners such as Plato feigned, who would attend only to the matter in hand, could have no place in a modern dialogue; still less could one count on readers of such a disposition. On the contrary, I have been only too often and too vehemently attacked by opponents who were incapable of making the simple reflection that their opinions and objections

contain categories which are presuppositions and which themselves need to be criticized first before they are employed.
Ignorance in this matter reaches incredible lengths; it is guilty of
the fundamental misunderstanding, the uncouth and uneducated
behaviour of taking a category which is under consideration for
something other than the category itself. This ignorance is the less
justifiable because this 'something other' consists of determinate
thoughts and concepts, and in a system of logic these other
categories must likewise have been assigned their own place and
must themselves have been subjected to critical examination
within the system. This ignorance is most obvious in the great
majority of the objections and attacks on the first Notions of logic,
being and nothing, and becoming which, itself a simple determination—the simplest analysis shows it to be so—contains the two
other determinations as moments. Thoroughness seems to require
that the beginning, as the foundation on which everything is built,
should be examined before anything else, in fact that we should
not go any further until it has been firmly established and if, on
the other hand, it is not, that we should reject all that follows.
This thoroughness at the same time has the advantage of guaran-
teering that the labour of thinking shall be reduced to a minimum;
it has before it, enclosed in this germ, the entire development and
reckons that it has settled the whole business when it has disposed
of the beginning which is the easiest part of the business, for it is
the simplest, the simple itself; it is the trifling effort of thought
required to do this which really recommends this 'thoroughness'
which is so satisfied with itself. This restriction to what is simple
gives scope for the free play of caprice which does not want to
remain simple but brings in its own reflections on the subject
matter. Having good right to occupy itself at first *only* with the
principle and in doing so not to concern itself with what lies
beyond it, this thoroughness actually proceeds to do the opposite
of this, for it does bring in what lies *beyond*, that is, categories
other than those which constitute the principle itself, other presuppositions and prejudices. Such presuppositions as that infinity
is different from finitude, that content is other than form, that
the inner is other than the outer, also that mediation is not
immediacy (as if anyone did not know such things), are brought
forward by way of information and narrated and asserted rather
than proved. But there is something stupid—I can find no other

B*

word for it—about this didactic behaviour; technically it is unjustifiable simply to presuppose and straightway assume such propositions; and, still more, it reveals ignorance of the fact that it is the requirement and the business of logical thinking to enquire into just this, whether such a finite without infinity is something true, or whether such an abstract infinity, also a content without form and a form without content, an inner by itself which has no outer expression, an externality without an inwardness, whether any of these is *something true* or *something actual*. But this education and discipline of thinking by which it acquires plasticity and by which the impatience of casual reflection is overcome, is procured solely by going further, by study and by carrying out to its conclusion the entire development.

Anyone who labours at presenting anew an independent structure of philosophical science may, when referring to the Platonic exposition, be reminded of the story that Plato revised his *Republic* seven times over. The remembrance of this, the comparison, so far as such may seem to be implied in it, should only urge one all the more to wish that for a work which, as belonging to the modern world, is confronted by a profounder principle, a more difficult subject matter and a material richer in compass, leisure had been afforded to revise it seven and seventy times. However, the author, in face of the magnitude of the task, has had to content himself with what it was possible to achieve in circumstances of external necessity, of the inevitable distractions caused by the magnitude and many-sidedness of contemporary affairs, even under the doubt whether the noisy clamour of current affairs and the deafening chatter of a conceit which prides itself on confining itself to such matters leave any room for participation in the passionless calm of a knowledge which is in the element of pure thought alone.

Berlin, *November* 7, 1831.

INTRODUCTION

GENERAL NOTION OF LOGIC

In no science is the need to begin with the subject matter itself, without preliminary reflections, felt more strongly than in the science of logic. In every other science the subject matter and the scientific method are distinguished from each other; also the content does not make an absolute beginning but is dependent on other concepts and is connected on all sides with other material. These other sciences are, therefore, permitted to speak of their ground and its context and also of their method, only as premises taken for granted which, as forms of definitions and such-like presupposed as familiar and accepted, are to be applied straightway, and also to employ the usual kind of reasoning for the establishment of their general concepts and fundamental determinations.

Logic, on the contrary, cannot presuppose any of these forms of reflection and laws of thinking, for these constitute part of its own content and have first to be established within the science. But not only the account of scientific method, but even the Notion itself of the science as such belongs to its content, and in fact constitutes its final result; what logic is cannot be stated beforehand, rather does this knowledge of what it is first emerge as the final outcome and consummation of the whole exposition. Similarly, it is essentially within the science that the subject matter of logic, namely, thinking or more specifically *comprehensive* thinking is considered; the Notion of logic has its genesis in the course of the exposition and cannot therefore be premised. Consequently, what is premised in this Introduction is not intended, as it were, to establish the Notion of logic or to justify its method scientifically in advance, but rather by the aid of some reasoned and historical explanations and reflections to make more accessible to ordinary thinking the point of view from which this science is to be considered.

When logic is taken as the science of thinking in general, it is understood that this thinking constitutes the *mere form* of a cognition, that logic abstracts from all *content* and that the so-called second *constituent* belonging to cognition, namely its *matter*, must come from elsewhere; and that since this matter is absolutely independent of logic, this latter can provide only the formal conditions of genuine cognition and cannot in its own self contain any real truth, nor even be the *pathway* to real truth because just that which is essential in truth, its content, lies outside logic.

But in the first place, it is quite inept to say that logic abstracts from all *content*, that it teaches only the rules of thinking without any reference to *what* is thought or without being able to consider its nature. For as thinking and the rules of thinking are supposed to be the subject matter of logic, these directly constitute its peculiar content; in them, logic has that second constituent, a matter, about the nature of which it is concerned.

But secondly, the conceptions on which the Notion of logic has rested hitherto have in part already been discarded, and for the rest, it is time that they disappeared entirely and that this science were grasped from a higher standpoint and received a completely changed shape.

Hitherto, the Notion of logic has rested on the separation, presupposed once and for all in the ordinary consciousness, of the *content* of cognition and its *form*, or of *truth* and *certainty*. First, it is assumed that the material of knowing is present on its own account as a ready-made world apart from thought, that thinking on its own is empty and comes as an external form to the said material, fills itself with it and only thus acquires a content and so becomes real knowing.

Further, these two constituents—for they are supposed to be related to each other as constituents, and cognition is compounded from them in a mechanical or at best chemical fashion—are appraised as follows: the object is regarded as something complete and finished on its own account, something which can entirely dispense with thought for its actuality, while thought on the other hand is regarded as defective because it has to complete itself with a material and moreover, as a pliable indeterminate form, has to adapt itself to its material. Truth is the agreement of thought with the object, and in order to bring about this agreement—for it does not exist on its own account—thinking is supposed to adapt and accommodate itself to the object.

Thirdly, when the difference of matter and form, of object and thought is not left in that nebulous indeterminateness but is taken more definitely, then each is regarded as a sphere divorced from the other. Thinking therefore in its reception and formation of material does not go outside itself; its reception of the material and the conforming of itself to it remains a modification of its own self, it does not result in thought becoming the other of itself; and self-conscious determining moreover belongs only to thinking. In its relation to the object, therefore, thinking does not go out of itself to the object; this, as a thing-in-itself, remains a sheer beyond of thought.

These views on the relation of subject and object to each other express the determinations which constitute the nature of our ordinary, phenomenal consciousness; but when these prejudices are carried out into the sphere of reason as if the same relation obtained there, as if this relation were something true in its own self, then they are errors the refutation of which throughout every part of the spiritual and natural universe is *philosophy*, or rather, as they bar the entrance to philosophy, must be discarded at its portals.

Ancient metaphysics had in this respect a higher conception of thinking than is current today. For it based itself on the fact that the knowledge of things obtained through thinking is alone what is really true in them, that is, things not in their immediacy but as first raised into the form of thought, as things *thought*. Thus this metaphysics believed that thinking (and its determinations) is not anything alien to the object, but rather is its essential nature, or that things and the thinking of them—our language too expresses their kinship—are explicitly in full agreement, thinking in its immanent determinations and the true nature of things forming one and the same content.

But *reflective* understanding took possession of philosophy. We must know exactly what is meant by this expression which moreover is often used as a slogan; in general it stands for the understanding as abstracting, and hence as separating and remaining fixed in its separations. Directed against reason, it behaves as ordinary common sense and imposes its view that truth rests on sensuous reality, that thoughts are *only* thoughts, meaning that it is sense perception which first gives them filling and reality and that reason left to its own resources engenders only figments of the brain. In this self-renunciation on the part of reason, the Notion of truth is lost; it is limited to knowing only subjective truth, only phenomena, appearances, only something to which the nature of the object itself does not correspond: knowing has lapsed into opinion.

However, this turn taken by cognition, which appears as a loss and a retrograde step, is based on something more profound on which rests the elevation of reason into the loftier spirit of modern philosophy. The basis of that universally held conception is, namely, to be sought in the insight into the necessary conflict of the determinations of the understanding with themselves. The reflection already referred to is this, to transcend the concrete immediate object and to determine it and separate it. But *equally* it must transcend these its *separating* determinations and straight-way *connect* them. It is at the stage of this connecting of the determinations that their conflict emerges. This connecting activity of reflection belongs in itself to reason and the rising above those determinations which attains to an insight into their conflict is the great negative step towards the true Notion of reason. But the insight, when not thorough-going, commits the mistake of thinking that it is reason which is in contradiction with itself; it does not recognize that the contradiction is precisely the rising of reason above the limitations of the understanding and the resolving of them. Cognition, instead of taking from this stage the final step into the heights, has fled from the unsatisfactoriness of the categories of the understanding to sensuous existence, imagining that in this it possesses what is solid and self-consistent. But on the other hand, since this knowledge is self-confessedly knowledge only of appearances, the unsatisfactoriness of the latter is admitted, but at the same time presupposed: as much as to say that admittedly, we have no proper knowledge of things-in-themselves but we do have a proper knowledge of them within the sphere of appearances, as if, so to speak, only the *kind of objects* were different, and one kind, namely things-in-themselves, did not fall within the scope of our knowledge but the other kind, phenomena, did. This is like attributing to someone a correct perception, with the rider that nevertheless he is incapable of perceiving what is true but only what is false. Absurd as this would be, it would not be more so than a true knowledge which did not know the object as it is in itself.

The criticism of the forms of the understanding has had the result already mentioned, that these forms do not apply to things-in-themselves. This can have no other meaning than that these forms are in themselves something untrue. But then if they are allowed to remain valid for subjective reason and experience, the criticism has not produced any alteration in them: they are left in the same shape for the subject knower as they formerly possessed for the object. If, however, they are inadequate for the thing-in-itself, still less must the understanding to which they are supposed to belong put up with them and rest content with them. If they cannot be determinations of the thing-in-itself, still less can they be determinations of the understanding to which one ought at least to concede the dignity of a thing-in-itself. The determinations of finite and infinite conflict in the same way, whether they are applied to time and space, to the world, or are determinations within the mind—just as black and white produce grey whether they are mixed on a canvas or on the palette. If our conception of the *world* is dissolved by the transference to it of the determinations of infinite and finite, still more is *spirit* itself, which contains both of them, inwardly self-contradictory and self-dissolving: it is not the nature of the material or the object to which they are applied or in which they occur that can make a difference for it is only through those determinations and in accordance with them that the object contains the contradiction.

The forms of objective thinking, therefore, have been removed by this criticism only from the thing; but they have been left in the subject just as they were originally. That is to say, this criticism did not consider these forms on their own merits and according to their own peculiar content, but simply took them as accepted starting points from subjective logic: so that there was no question of an immanent deduction of them as forms of subjective logic, still less of a dialectical consideration of them.

Transcendental idealism in its more consistent development, recognized the nothingness of the spectral thing-in-itself left over by the Kantian philosophy, this abstract shadow divorced from all content, and intended to destroy it completely. This philosophy also made a start at letting reason itself exhibit its own determinations. But this attempt, because it proceeded from a subjective standpoint, could not be brought to a successful conclusion. Later this standpoint, and with it too the attempt to develop the content of pure science, was abandoned.

But what is commonly understood by logic is considered without any reference whatever to metaphysical significance. This science in its present state has, it must be admitted, no content of a kind which the ordinary consciousness would regard as a reality and as a genuine subject matter. But it is not for this reason a *formal* science lacking significant truth. Moreover, the region of truth is not to be sought in that matter which is missing in logic, a deficiency to which the unsatisfactoriness of the science is usually attributed. The truth is rather that the insubstantial nature of logical forms originates solely in the way in which they are considered and dealt with. When they are taken as fixed determinations and consequently in their separation from each other and not as held together in an organic unity, then they are dead forms and the spirit which is their living, concrete unity does not dwell in them. As thus taken, they lack a substantial content—a matter which would be substantial in itself. The content which is missing in the logical forms is nothing else than a solid foundation and a concretion of these abstract determinations; and such a substantial being for them is usually sought outside them. But logical reason itself is the substantial or real being which holds together within itself every abstract determination and is their substantial, absolutely concrete unity. One need not therefore look far for what is commonly called a matter; if logic is supposed to lack a substantial content, then the fault does not lie with its subject matter but solely with the way in which this subject matter is grasped.

This reflection leads up to the statement of the point of view from which logic is to be considered, how it differs from previous modes of treatment of this science which in future must always be based on this, the only true standpoint.

In the *Phenomenology of Spirit*[1] I have exhibited consciousness in its movement onwards from the first immediate opposition of itself and the object to absolute knowing. The path of this movement goes through every form of the *relation of consciousness to the object* and has the Notion of science for its result. This Notion therefore (apart from the fact that it emerges within logic itself) needs no justification here because it has received it in that work; and it cannot be justified in any other way than by this emergence in consciousness, all the forms of which are resolved into this Notion as into their truth. To establish or explain the Notion of science ratiocinatively can at most achieve this, that a general idea

---

[1] Bamberg and Würzburg, 1807.

of the Notion is presented to our thinking and a historical knowledge of it is produced; but a definition of science—or more precisely of logic—has its proof solely in the already mentioned necessity of its emergence in consciousness. The definition with which any science makes an absolute beginning cannot contain anything other than the precise and correct expression of what is *imagined* to be the *accepted* and *familiar* subject matter and aim of the science. That precisely *this* is what is imagined is an historical asseveration in respect of which one can only appeal to such and such as recognized facts; or rather the plea can be advanced that such and such could be accepted as recognized facts. There will always be someone who will adduce a case, an instance, according to which something more and different is to be understood by certain terms the definition of which must therefore be made more precise or more general and the science too, must be accommodated thereto. This again involves argumentation about what should be admitted or excluded and within what limits and to what extent; but argumentation is open to the most manifold and various opinions, on which a decision can finally be determined only arbitrarily. In this method of beginning a science with its definition, no mention is made of the need to demonstrate the *necessity* of its *subject matter* and therefore of the science itself.

The Notion of pure science and its deduction is therefore pre-supposed in the present work in so far as the *Phenomenology of Spirit* is nothing other than the deduction of it. Absolute knowing is the *truth* of every mode of consciousness because, as the course of the *Phenomenology* showed, it is only in absolute knowing that the separation of the *object* from the *certainty of itself* is completely eliminated: truth is now equated with certainty and this certainty with truth.

Thus pure science presupposes liberation from the opposition of consciousness. It contains *thought in so far as this is just as much the object in its own self, or the object in its own self in so far as it is equally pure thought*. As science, truth is pure self-consciousness in its self-development and has the shape of the self, so that the absolute truth of being is the known Notion and the Notion as such is the absolute truth of being.

This objective thinking, then, is the content of pure science. Consequently, far from it being formal, far from it standing in need of a matter to constitute an actual and true cognition, it is its content alone which has absolute truth, or, if one still wanted to employ the word matter, it is the veritable matter—but a matter which is not external to the form, since this matter is rather pure thought and hence the absolute form itself. Accordingly, logic is to be understood as the system of pure reason, as the realm of pure thought. This realm is truth as it is without veil and in its own absolute nature. It can therefore be said that this content is the exposition of God as he is in his eternal essence before the creation of nature and a finite mind.

Anaxagoras is praised as the man who first declared that *Nous*, thought, is the principle of the world, that the essence of the world is to be defined as thought. In so doing he laid the foundation for an intellectual view of the universe, the pure form of which must be logic. What we are dealing with in logic is not a thinking *about* something which exists independently as a base for our thinking and apart from it, nor forms which are supposed to provide mere signs or distinguishing marks of truth; on the contrary, the necessary forms and self-determinations of thought are the content and the ultimate truth itself.

To get at least some idea of this, one must discard the prejudice that truth must be something tangible. Such tangibility is, for example, imported even into the Platonic Ideas which are in God's thinking, as if they are, as it were, existing things but in another world or region; while the world of actuality exists outside that region and has a substantial existence distinct from those Ideas and only through this distinction is a substantial reality. The Platonic Idea is the universal, or more definitely the Notion of an object; only in its Notion does something possess actuality and to the extent that it is distinct from its Notion it ceases to be actual and is a non-entity; the side of tangibility and sensuous self-externality belongs to this null aspect. But on the other side, one can appeal to the conceptions of ordinary logic itself; for it is assumed, for example, that the determinations contained in definitions do not belong only to the knower, but are determinations of the object, constituting its innermost essence and its very own nature. Or, if from given determinations others are inferred, it is assumed that what is inferred is not something external and alien to the object, but rather that it belongs to the object itself, that to the thought there is a correspondent being.

It is implied generally in the use of forms of the Notion, of judgement, syllogism, definition, division, etc., that they are not merely forms of self-conscious thinking but also of the objective understanding. *Thought* is an expression which attributes the determination contained therein primarily to consciousness. But inasmuch as it is said that understanding, reason, is in the objective world, that mind and nature have universal laws to which their life and changes conform, then it is conceded that the determinations of thought equally have objective value and existence.

The critical philosophy had, it is true, already turned metaphysics into logic but it, like the later idealism, as previously remarked, was overawed by the object, and so the logical determinations were given an essentially subjective significance with the result that these philosophies remained burdened with the object they had avoided and were left with the residue of a thing-in-itself, an infinite obstacle, as a beyond. But the liberation from the opposition of consciousness which the science of logic must be able to presuppose lifts the determinations of thought above this timid, incomplete standpoint and demands that they be considered not with any such limitation and reference but as they are in their own proper character, as logic, as pure reason.

Kant moreover considers logic, that is, the aggregate of definitions and propositions which ordinarily passes for logic, to be fortunate in having attained so early to completion before the other sciences; since Aristotle, it has not lost any ground, but neither has it gained any, the latter because to all appearances it seems to be finished and complete. Now if logic has not undergone any change since Aristotle—and in fact, judging by modern compendiums of logic the changes frequently consist mainly in omissions—then surely the conclusion which should be drawn is that it is all the more in need of a total reconstruction; for spirit, after its labours over two thousand years, must have attained to a higher consciousness about its thinking and about its own pure, essential nature. A comparison of the forms to which spirit has raised itself in the practical and religious sphere and in every branch of science both physical and mental, with the form presented by logic which is spirit's consciousness of its own pure essence, reveals so vast a difference that the utter inadequacy and unworthiness of the latter consciousness in comparison with the higher consciousness displayed in those other spheres cannot fail to strike the most superficial observer.

In point of fact the need for a reconstruction of logic has long been felt. In form and in content logic, as exhibited in the text-books, may be said to have fallen into contempt. It is still dragged in, but more from a feeling that one cannot dispense with logic altogether and because the tradition of its importance still sur-vives, rather than from a conviction that such commonplace content and occupation with such empty forms is valuable and useful.

The additions of psychological, pedagogic and even physio-logical material which logic received in the past have subsequently been recognized almost universally as disfigurements. A great part of these psychological, pedagogic and physiological observations, laws and rules, whether they occur in logic or anywhere else, must appear very shallow and trivial in themselves; and without exception all those rules such as, for example, that one must think out and test what one reads in books or hears by word of mouth, that when one's sight is not good one should help one's eyes by wearing spectacles—rules which in textbooks of so-called applied logic were solemnly set out in paragraphs and put forward as aids to the attainment of truth—these must strike everyone as super-fluous—except only the writer or teacher who finds difficulty in expanding by some means or other the otherwise scanty and life-less content of logic.[1]

Regarding this content, the reason why it is so dull and spiritless has already been given above. Its determinations are accepted in their unmoved fixity and are brought only into an external relation with each other. In judgements and syllogisms the operations are in the main reduced to and founded on the quantita-tive aspect of the determinations; consequently everything rests on an external difference, on mere comparison and becomes a completely analytical procedure and mechanical [begriffloses] calculation. The deduction of the so-called rules and laws, chiefly of inference, is not much better than a manipulation of rods of

---

[1] *Remark in first edition.* The latest treatment of this science which has recently appeared, *System of Logic by Fries*, returns to the anthropological foundations. The idea or opinion on which it is based is so shallow, both in itself and in its execution, that I am spared the trouble of taking any notice of this insignificant publication.

unequal lengths in order to sort and group them according to size—than a childish game of fitting together the pieces of a coloured picture puzzle. Consequently, this thinking has been equated, not incorrectly, with reckoning, and reckoning again with this thinking. In arithmetic, numbers are regarded as devoid of any concrete conceptual content, so that apart from their wholly external relationship they have no meaning, and neither in themselves nor in their interrelationships are thoughts. When it is calculated in mechanical fashion that three-fourths multiplied by two-thirds makes one-half, this operation contains about as much and as little thought as calculating whether in a logical figure this or that kind of syllogism is valid.

Before these dead bones of logic can be quickened by spirit, and so become possessed of a substantial, significant content, its method must be that which alone can enable it to be pure science. In the present state of logic one can scarcely recognize even a trace of scientific method. It has roughly the form of an empirical science. The empirical sciences have found for their own appropriate purposes their own peculiar method, such as it is, of defining and classifying their material. Pure mathematics, too, has its method which is appropriate for its abstract objects and for the quantitative form in which alone it considers them. I have said what is essential in the preface to the *Phenomenology of Spirit* about this method and, in general, the subordinate form of scientific method which can be employed in mathematics; but it will also be considered in more detail in the logic itself. Spinoza, Wolf, and others have let themselves be misled in applying it also to philosophy and in making the external course followed by Notion-less quantity, the course of the Notion, a procedure which is absolutely contradictory. Hitherto philosophy had not found its method; it regarded with envy the systematic structure of mathematics and, as we have said, borrowed it or had recourse to the method of sciences which are only amalgams of given material, empirical propositions and thoughts—or even resorted to a crude rejection of all method. However, the exposition of what alone can be the true method of philosophical science falls within the treatment of logic itself; for the method is the consciousness of the form of the inner self-movement of the content of logic. In the *Phenomenology of Spirit* I have expounded an example of this method in application to a more concrete object, namely to consciousness.[1] Here, we are dealing with forms of consciousness each of which in realizing itself at the same time resolves itself, has for its result its own negation—and so passes into a higher form. All that is necessary to achieve scientific progress—and it is essential to strive to gain this quite *simple* insight—is the recognition of the logical principle that the negative is just as much positive, or that what is self-contradictory does not resolve itself into a nullity, into abstract nothingness, but essentially only into the negation of its *particular* content, in other words, that such a negation is not all and every negation but the negation of a specific subject matter which resolves itself, and consequently is a specific negation, and therefore the result essentially contains that from which it results; which strictly speaking is a tautology, for otherwise it would be an immediacy, not a result. Because the result, the negation, is a *specific* negation it has a *content*. It is a fresh Notion but higher and richer than its predecessor; for it is richer by the negation or opposite of the latter, therefore contains it, but also something more, and is the unity of itself and its opposite. It is in this way that the system of Notions as such has to be formed—and has to complete itself in a purely continuous course in which nothing extraneous is introduced.

I could not pretend that the method which I follow in this system of logic—or rather which this system in its own self follows—is not capable of greater completeness, of much elaboration in detail; but at the same time I know that it is the only true method. This is self-evident simply from the fact that it is not something distinct from its object and content; for it is the inwardness of the content, the dialectic which it possesses within itself, which is the mainspring of its advance. It is clear that no expositions can be accepted as scientifically valid which do not pursue the course of this method and do not conform to its simple rhythm, for this is the course of the subject matter itself.

In conformity with this method, I would point out that the divisions and headings of the books, sections and chapters given in this work as well as the explanations associated with them, are made to facilitate a preliminary survey and strictly are only of *historical* value. They do not belong to the content and body of the science but are compilations of an external reflection which

---

[1] And subsequently to other concrete objects and corresponding departments of philosophy.

has already run through the whole of the exposition and consequently knows and indicates in advance the sequence of its moments before these are brought forward by the subject matter itself.

Similarly in the other sciences, such preliminary definitions and divisions are in themselves nothing else but such external indications; but even within the particular science they are not raised above this status. Even in logic, for example, we may be told perhaps that 'logic has two main parts, the theory of elements and methodology', then under the former there straightway follows perhaps the superscription, *Laws of Thought;* and then, *Chapter I: Concepts. First Section: Of the Clearness of Concepts,* and so on. These definitions and divisions, made without any deduction or justification, constitute the systematic framework and the entire connectedness of such sciences. Such a logic regards it as its vocation to talk about the necessity of *deducing* concepts and truths from principles; but as regards what it calls method, the thought of a deduction of it simply does not occur to it. The procedure consists, perhaps, in grouping together what is similar and making what is simple precede what is complex, and other external considerations. But as regards any inner, necessary connectedness, there is nothing more than the list of headings of the various parts and the transition is effected simply by saying *Chapter II*, or, *We now come to judgements*, and the like.

The superscriptions and divisions, too, which appear in this system are not themselves intended to have any other significance than that of a list of contents. Besides, the *immanent coming-to-be* of the distinctions and the *necessity* of their connection with each other must present themselves in the exposition of the subject matter itself for it falls within the spontaneous progressive determination of the Notion

That which enables the Notion to advance itself is the already mentioned *negative* which it possesses within itself; it is is this which constitutes the genuine dialectical element. Dialectic in this way acquires an entirely different significance from what it had when it was considered as a separate part of logic and when its aim and standpoint were, one may say, completely misunderstood. Even the *Platonic* dialectic, in the Parmenides itself and elsewhere even more directly, on the one hand, aims only at abolishing and refuting limited assertions through themselves, and, on the other hand, has for result simply nothingness. Dialectic is commonly regarded as an external, negative activity which does not pertain to the subject matter itself, having its ground in mere conceit as a subjective itch for unsettling and destroying what is fixed and substantial, or at least having for result nothing but the worthlessness of the object dialectically considered.

Kant rated dialectic higher—and this is among his greatest merits—for he freed it from the seeming arbitrariness which it possesses from the standpoint of ordinary thought and exhibited it as a *necessary function of reason*. Because dialectic was held to be merely the art of practising deceptions and producing illusions, the assumption was made forthwith that it is only a spurious game, the whole of its power resting solely on concealment of the deceit and that its results are obtained only surreptitiously and are a subjective illusion. True, Kant's expositions in the antinomies of pure reason, when closely examined as they will be at length in the course of this work, do not indeed deserve any great praise; but the general idea on which he based his expositions and which he vindicated, is the *objectivity of the illusion* and the *necessity of the contradiction* which belongs to the nature of thought determinations: primarily, it is true, with the significance that these determinations are applied by reason to *things in themselves*; but their nature is precisely what they are in reason and with reference to what is intrinsic or in itself. This result, grasped in its positive aspect, is nothing else but the inner negativity of the determinations as their self-moving soul, the principle of all natural and spiritual life. But if no advance is made beyond the abstract negative aspect of dialectic, the result is only the familiar one that reason is incapable of knowing the infinite; a strange result for—since the infinite is the Reasonable—it asserts that reason is incapable of knowing the Reasonable.

It is in this dialectic as it is here understood, that is, in the grasping of opposites in their unity or of the positive in the negative, that speculative thought consists. It is the most important aspect of dialectic, but for thinking which is as yet unpractised and unfree it is the most difficult. Such thinking, if it is still engaged in breaking itself of the habit of employing sensuously concrete terms and of ratiocination, must first practise abstract thinking, hold fast Notions in their *determinateness* and learn to cognize by means of them. An exposition of logic to this end would, in its method, have to keep to the division of the subject above-mentioned and with regard to the more detailed contents, to the definitions given for the particular Notions without touching on the dialectical aspect. As regards its external structure, such an exposition would resemble the usual presentation of this science, but it would also be distinguished from it with respect to the content and still would serve for practice in abstract thinking, though not in speculative thinking, a purpose which can never be realized by the logic which has become popular through the addition of psychological and anthropological material. It would give to mind the picture of a methodically ordered whole, although the soul of the structure, the method (which dwells in the dialectical aspect) would not itself appear in it.

Finally, with respect to education and the relation of the individual to logic, I would further remark that this science, like grammar, appears in two different aspects or values. It is one thing for him who comes to it and the sciences generally for the first time, but it is another thing for him who comes back to it from those sciences. He who begins the study of grammar finds in its forms and laws dry abstractions, arbitrary rules, in general an isolated collection of definitions and terms which exhibit only the value and significance of what is implied in their immediate meaning; there is nothing to be known in them other than themselves. On the other hand, he who has mastered a language and at the same time has a comparative knowledge of other languages, he alone can make contact with the spirit and culture of a people through the grammar of its language; the same rules and forms now have a substantial, living value. Through the grammar he can recognize the expression of mind as such, that is, logic. Similarly, he who approaches this science, at first finds in logic an isolated system of abstractions which, confined within itself, does not embrace within its scope the other knowledges and sciences. On the contrary, when contrasted with the wealth of the world as pictorially conceived, with the apparently real content of the other sciences, and compared with the promise of absolute science to unveil the essential being of this wealth, the inner nature of mind and the world, the truth, then this science in its abstract shape, in the colourless, cold simplicity of its pure determinations looks as if it could achieve anything sooner than the fulfilment of its promise and seems to confront that richness as an empty, insubstantial form. The first acquaintance with logic confines its significance to itself alone; its content passes only for a detached occupation with the determinations of thought, *along-side* which other scientific activities possess on their own account a matter and content of their own, on which logic may perhaps have a formal influence, though an influence which comes only from itself and which if necessary can of course also be dispensed with so far as the scientific structure and its study are concerned. The other sciences have on the whole discarded the correct method, that is, a sequence of definitions, axioms, theorems and their proofs, etc.; so-called natural logic now has its own validity in the sciences and manages to get along without any special knowledge of the nature of thought itself. But the matter and content of these sciences is held to be completely independent of logic and also has more appeal for sense, feeling, figurate conception, and practical interest of any kind.

At first, therefore, logic must indeed be learnt as something which one understands and sees into quite well but in which, at the beginning, one feels the lack of scope and depth and a wider significance. It is only after profounder acquaintance with the other sciences that logic ceases to be for subjective spirit a merely abstract universal and reveals itself as the universal which embraces within itself the wealth of the particular—just as the same proverb, in the mouth of a youth who understands it quite well, does not possess the wide range of meaning which it has in the mind of a man with the experience of a lifetime behind him, for whom the meaning is expressed in all its power. Thus the value of logic is only appreciated when it is preceded by experience of the sciences; it then displays itself to mind as the universal truth, not as a *particular* knowledge *alongside* other matters and realities, but as the essential being of all these latter.

Now although the mind is not conscious of this power of logic at the beginning of its study, it none the less receives within itself through such study the power which leads it into all truth. The system of logic is the realm of shadows, the world of simple essentialities freed from all sensuous concreteness. The study of this science, to dwell and labour in this shadowy realm, is the absolute culture and discipline of consciousness. In logic, consciousness is busy with something remote from sensuous intuitions and aims, from feelings, from the merely imagined world of figurate conception. Considered from its negative aspect, this business consists in holding off the contingency of ordinary thinking and the arbitrary selection of particular grounds—or their opposites—as valid.

But above all, thought acquires thereby self-reliance and independence. It becomes at home in abstractions and in progressing by means of Notions free from sensuous substrata, develops an unsuspected power of assimilating in rational form all the various knowledges and sciences in their complex variety, of grasping and retaining them in their essential character, stripping them of their external features and in this way extracting from them the logical element—or what is the same thing, filling the abstract basis of Logic acquired by study with the substantial content of absolute truth and giving it the value of a universal which no longer stands as a particular alongside other particulars but includes them all within its grasp and is their essence, the absolutely True.

GENERAL DIVISION OF LOGIC

From what has been said about the *Notion* of this science and where its justification is to be found, it follows that the general division of it here can only be *provisional*, can be given, as it were, only in so far as the author is already familiar with the science and consequently is *historically* in a position to state here in advance the main distinctions which will emerge in the development of the Notion.

Still, the attempt can be made to promote an understanding beforehand of what is requisite for such a division, even though in doing so we must have recourse to an application of the method which will only be fully understood and justified within the science itself. We must therefore point out at the start that we are presupposing that the division must be connected with the Notion, or rather must be implicit in the Notion itself. The Notion is not indeterminate but is in its own self determinate; the division, however, expresses this its determinateness as *developed*; it is the *judgement* of the Notion, not a judgement *about* some object or other picked up from outside, but the *judging*, that is, *determining*, of the Notion in its own self. The quality of being right-angled, acute-angled or equilateral, according to which

triangles are classified, is not implicit in the determinateness of
the triangle itself, that is, not in what is usually called the Notion
of the triangle, just as little as there is implicit in what passes
for the Notion of animal as such, or of the mammal, bird, etc.—
the determinations governing the classification into mammal,
bird, etc., and the subdivision of these classes into other species.
Such determinations are taken from elsewhere and are annexed
to such so-called Notion from outside. In the philosophical treatment of classification or division, the Notion itself must show
that it is itself the course of those determinations.

But in the Introduction, the Notion of logic was itself stated
to be the result of a preceding science, and so here, too, it is a
presupposition. In accordance with that result logic was defined as
the science of pure thought, the principle of which is *pure knowing*,
the unity which is not abstract but a living, concrete unity in
virtue of the fact that in it the opposition in consciousness between
a self-determined entity, a subject, and a second such entity, an
object, is known to be overcome; being is known to be the pure
Notion in its own self, and the pure Notion to be the true being.
These, then, are the two *moments* contained in logic. But now they
are known to be *inseparable*, not as in consciousness where each
also has a separate being of its own; it is solely because they are
at the same time known as *distinct* (yet not with an independent
being) that their unity is not abstract, dead and inert, but concrete.

This unity also constitutes the logical principle as *element*, so
that the development of the difference directly present in that
principle proceeds only *within* this element. For since the division
is, as we have said, the *judgement* of the Notion, the positing of
the determination already immanent in it, and therefore of the
difference, we must not understand this positing as a resolving
of that concrete unity back into its determinations as if these had
an independent self-subsistence, for this would be an empty
return to the previous standpoint, to the opposition of consciousness. This however has vanished; the said unity remains the element, and the distinctions of the division and of the development
no longer originate outside that element. Consequently the earlier
determinations (those used on the *pathway to truth*) such as subjectivity and objectivity, or even thought and being, or Notion and
reality, no matter from what standpoint they were determined,
have lost their independent and purely affirmative character and

are now *in their truth*, that is, in their unity, reduced to *forms*. In their difference, therefore, they themselves remain *implicitly* the whole Notion, and this, in the division, is posited only under its own specifications.

Thus what is to be considered is the whole Notion, firstly as the Notion *in the form of being*, secondly, as the *Notion*; in the first case, the Notion *is* only *in itself*, the Notion of reality or being; in the second case, it is the Notion as such, the Notion existing *for itself* (as it is, to name concrete forms, in thinking man, and even in the sentient animal and in organic individuality generally, although, of course, in these it is not *conscious*, still less *known*; it is only in inorganic nature that it is *in itself*). Accordingly, logic should be divided primarily into the logic of the Notion as *being* and of the Notion as *Notion*—or, by employing the usual terms (although these as least definite are most ambiguous) into 'objective' and 'subjective' logic.

But in accordance with the fundamental element of the immanent unity of the Notion, and hence with the inseparability of its determinations, these latter, when *distinguished* from each other in the positing of the Notion in its *difference*, must at least also stand in *relation* to each other. There results a sphere of *mediation*, the Notion as a system of *reflected determinations*, that is, of being in process of transition into the being-within-self or inwardness of the Notion. In this way, the Notion is not yet posited *as such* for itself, but is still fettered by the externality of immediate being. This is the doctrine of essence which stands midway between the doctrine of being and that of the Notion. In the general division of logic in the present work it has been included in objective logic because although essence is already the inwardness of being, the character of subject is to be expressly reserved for the Notion.

Recently Kant[1] has opposed to what has usually been called

[1] I would mention that in this work I frequently refer to the Kantian philosophy (which to many may seem superfluous) because whatever may be said, both in this work and elsewhere, about the precise character of this philosophy and about particular parts of its exposition, it constitutes the base and the starting-point of recent German philosophy and this its merit remains unaffected by whatever faults may be found in it. The reason, too, why reference must often be made to it in the objective logic is that it enters into detailed consideration of important, *more specific* aspects of logic, whereas later philosophical works have paid little attention to these and in some instances have only displayed a crude—not unavenged—contempt for them. The

logic another, namely, a *transcendental logic*. What has here been called objective logic would correspond in part to what with him is transcendental logic. He distinguishes it from what he calls general logic in this way, (α) that it treats of the notions which refer *a priori* to *objects*, and consequently does not abstract from the whole *content* of objective cognition, or, in other words, it contains the rules of the pure thinking of an *object*, and (β) at the same time it treats of the origin of our cognition so far as this cognition cannot be ascribed to the objects. It is to this second aspect that Kant's philosophical interest is exclusively directed. His chief thought is to vindicate the *categories* for self-conscious-ness as the *subjective ego*. By virtue of this determination the point of view remains confined within consciousness and its opposition; and besides the empirical element of feeling and intuition it has something else left over which is not posited and determined by thinking self-consciousness, a *thing-in-itself*, something alien and external to thought—although it is easy to perceive that such an abstraction as the thing-in-itself is itself only a product of thought, and of merely abstractive thought at that. If other disciples of Kant have expressed themselves concerning the determining of the *object* by the ego in this way, that the objectifying of the ego is to be regarded as an original and necessary act of consciousness, so that in this original act there is not yet the idea of the ego itself —which would be a conscousness of that consciousness or even an objectifying of it—then this objectifying act, in its freedom from the opposition of consciousness, is nearer to what may be taken simply for *thought* as such.[1] But this act should no longer be called

philosophizing which is most widespread among us does *not* go beyond the Kantian results, that Reason cannot acquire knowledge of any true content or subject matter and in regard to absolute truth must be directed to faith. But what with Kant is a result, forms the immediate starting-point in this philosophizing, so that the preceding exposition from which that result issued and which is a philosophical cognition, is cut away beforehand. The Kantian philosophy thus serves as a cushion for intellectual indolence which soothes itself with the conviction that everything is already proved and settled. Consequently for genuine knowledge, for a specific content of thought which is not to be found in such barren and arid complacency, one must turn to that preceding exposition.

[1] If the expression 'objectifying act of the ego' suggests other products of spirit, e.g. fantasy, it is to be observed that we are speaking of a determining of an object in so far as the elements of its content do *not* belong to feeling and intuition. Such an object is a *thought*, and to determine it means partly, first to produce it, partly, in so far as it is something presupposed, to have further thoughts about it, to develop it further by thought.

consciousness; consciousness embraces within itself the opposition of the ego and its object which is not present in that original act. The name consciousness gives it a semblance of subjectivity even more than does the term *thought*, which here, however, is to be taken simply in the absolute sense as *infinite* thought untainted by the finitude of consciousness, in short, *thought as such*.

Now because the interest of the Kantian philosophy was directed to the so-called *transcendental* aspect of the categories, the treatment of the categories themselves yielded a blank result; what they are in themselves without the abstract relation to the ego common to all, what is their specific nature relatively to each other and their relationship to each other, this has not been made an object of consideration. Hence this philosophy has not contributed in the slightest to a knowledge of their nature; what alone is of interest in this connection occurs in the Critique of Ideas. But if philosophy was to make any real progress, it was necessary that the interest of thought should be drawn to a consideration of the formal side, to a consideration of the ego, of consciousness as such, i.e. of the abstract relation of a subjective knowing to an object, so that in this way the cognition of the *infinite form*, that is, of the Notion, would be introduced. But in order that this cognition may be reached, that form has still to be relieved of the finite determinateness in which it is ego, or consciousness. The form, when thus thought out into its purity, will have within itself the capacity to *determine* itself, that is, to give itself a content, and that a *necessarily* explicated content—in the form of a system of determinations of thought.

The objective logic, then, takes the place rather of former *metaphysics* which was intended to be the scientific construction of the world in terms of *thoughts* alone. If we have regard to the final shape in the elaboration of this science, then it is first and immediately *ontology* whose place is taken by objective logic— that part of this metaphysics which was supposed to investigate the nature of *ens* in general; *ens* comprises both *being* and *essence*, a distinction for which the German language has fortunately preserved different terms. But further, objective logic also comprises the rest of metaphysics in so far as this attempted to comprehend with the forms of pure thought particular substrata taken primarily from figurate conception, namely the soul, the world and God; and the *determinations of thought* constituted what was *essential* in the mode of consideration. Logic, however, considers these forms free from those substrata, from the subjects of figurate conception; it considers them, their nature and worth, in their own proper character. Former metaphysics omitted to do this and consequently incurred the just reproach of having employed these forms *uncritically* without a preliminary investigation as to whether and how they were capable of being determinations of the thing-in-itself, to use the Kantian expression—or rather of the Reasonable. Objective logic is therefore the genuine critique of them—a critique which does not consider them as contrasted under the abstract forms of the *a priori* and the *a posteriori*, but considers the determinations themselves according to their specific content.

The subjective logic is the logic of the *Notion*, of essence which has sublated its relation to being or its illusory being [*Schein*], and in its determination is no longer external but is subjective—free, self-subsistent and self-determining, or rather it is the subject itself. Since subjectivity brings with it the misconception of contingency and caprice and, in general, characteristics belonging to the form of *consciousness*, no particular importance is to be attached here to the distinction of subjective and objective; these determinations will be more precisely developed later on in the logic itself.

Logic thus falls generally into objective and subjective logic, but more specifically it has three parts:

I   The logic of being,
II   The logic of essence, and
III The logic of the Notion.

BOOK ONE

THE DOCTRINE OF BEING

WITH WHAT MUST THE SCIENCE BEGIN?

It is only in recent times that thinkers have become aware of the difficulty of finding a beginning in philosophy, and the reason for this difficulty and also the possibility of resolving it has been much discussed. What philosophy begins with must be either *mediated* or *immediate*, and it is easy to show that it can be neither the one nor the other; thus either way of beginning is refuted.

The *principle* of a philosophy does, of course, also express a beginning, but not so much a subjective as an *objective* one, the beginning of *everything*. The principle is a particular determinate *content*—water, the one, *nous*, idea, substance, monad, etc. Or, if it refers to the nature of cognition and consequently is supposed to be only a criterion rather than an objective determination—thought, intuition, sensation, ego, subjectivity itself. Then here too it is the nature of the content which is the point of interest. The beginning as such, on the other hand, as something subjective in the sense of being a particular, inessential way of introducing the discourse, remains unconsidered, a matter of indifference, and so too the need to find an answer to the question, With what should the beginning be made? remains of no importance in face of the need for a principle in which alone the interest of the matter in hand seems to lie, the interest as to what is the *truth*, the *absolute ground*.

But the modern perplexity about a beginning proceeds from a further requirement of which those who are concerned with the dogmatic demonstration of a principle or who are sceptical about finding a subjective criterion against dogmatic philosophizing, are not yet aware, and which is completely denied by those who begin, like a shot from a pistol, from their inner revelation, from faith, intellectual intuition, etc., and who would be exempt from *method* and logic. If earlier abstract thought was interested in the principle only as content, but in the course of philosophical development has been impelled to pay attention to the other side, to the behaviour of the cognitive process, this implies that the *subjective* act has also been grasped as an *essential* moment of objective truth, and this brings with it the need to unite the method with the content, the form with the principle. Thus the principle ought also to be the beginning, and what is the first for thought ought also to be the first in the *process* of thinking.

Here we have only to consider how the *logical* beginning appears; the two sides from which it can be taken have already been named, to wit, either as a mediated result or as a beginning proper, as an immediacy. This is not the place to deal with the question apparently so important in present-day thought, whether the knowledge of truth is an immediate knowledge having a pure beginning, a faith, or whether it is a mediated knowledge. In so far as this can be dealt with *preliminarily* it has been done elsewhere.[1] Here we need only quote from it this, that there is nothing, nothing in heaven or in nature or mind or anywhere else which does not equally contain both immediacy and mediation, so that these two determinations reveal themselves to be *unseparated* and inseparable and the opposition between them to be a nullity. But as regards the philosophical discussion of this, it is to be found in every logical proposition in which occur the determinations of immediacy and mediation and consequently also the discussion of their opposition and their truth. Inasmuch as this opposition, as related to thinking, to knowing, to cognition, acquires the more concrete form of immediate or mediated *knowledge*, it is the nature of cognition simply as such which is considered within the science of logic, while the more concrete form of cognition falls to be considered in the philosophy of spirit and in the phenomenology of spirit. But to want the nature of cognition clarified *prior* to the science is to demand that it be considered *outside* the science; *outside* the science this cannot be accomplished, at least not in a scientific manner and such a manner is alone here in place.

The beginning is *logical* in that it is to be made in the element of thought that is free and for itself, in *pure knowing*. It is *mediated* because pure knowing is the ultimate, absolute truth of *consciousness*. In the Introduction it was remarked that the phenomenology of spirit is the science of consciousness, the exposition of it, and that consciousness has for result the *Notion* of science, i.e. pure knowing. Logic, then, has for its presupposition the science of manifested spirit, which contains and demonstrates the necessity, and so the truth, of the standpoint occupied by pure

---

[1] In my *Encyclop. of the Phil. Sciences*, 3rd edition, *Preliminary Notion*, Section 61 et seq.

knowing and of its mediation. In this science of manifested spirit the beginning is made from empirical, *sensuous* consciousness and this is *immediate* knowledge in the strict sense of the word; in that work there is discussed the significance of this immediate knowledge. Other forms of consciousness such as belief in divine truths, inner experience, knowledge through inner revelation, etc., are very ill-fitted to be quoted as examples of immediate knowledge as a little reflection will show. In the work just mentioned immediate consciousness is also the first and that which is immediate in the science itself, and therefore the presupposition; but in logic, the presupposition is that which has proved itself to be the result of that phenomenological consideration—the Idea as pure knowledge. *Logic is pure science*, that is, pure knowledge in the entire range of its development. But in the said result, this Idea has determined itself to be the certainty which has become truth, the certainty which, on the one hand, no longer has the object over against it but has internalized it, knows it as its own self—and, on the other hand, has given up the knowledge of itself as of something confronting the object of which it is only the annihilation, has divested itself of this subjectivity and is at one with its self-alienation.

Now starting from this determination of pure knowledge, all that is needed to ensure that the beginning remains immanent in its scientific development is to consider, or rather, ridding oneself of all other reflections and opinions whatever, simply to take up, *what is there before us.*

Pure knowing as concentrated into this unity has sublated all reference to an other and to mediation; it is without any distinction and as thus distinctionless, ceases itself to be knowledge; what is present is only *simple immediacy.*

Simple immediacy is itself an expression of reflection and contains a reference to its distinction from what is mediated. This simple immediacy, therefore, in its true expression is *pure being*. Just as *pure* knowing is to mean knowing as such, quite abstractly, so too pure being is to mean nothing but *being* in general: being, and nothing else, without any further specification and filling.

Here the beginning is made with being which is represented as having come to be through mediation, a mediation which is also a sublating of itself; and there is presupposed pure knowing as the outcome of finite knowing, of consciousness. But if no pre-supposition is to be made and the beginning itself is taken *immediately*, then its only determination is that it is to be the beginning of logic, of thought as such. All that is present is simply the resolve, which can also be regarded as arbitrary, that we propose to consider thought as such. Thus the beginning must be an *absolute*, or what is synonymous here, an *abstract* beginning; and so it *may not presuppose anything*, must not be mediated by anything nor have a ground; rather it is to be itself the ground of the entire science. Consequently, it must be purely and simply *an* immediacy, or rather merely *immediacy* itself. Just as it cannot possess any determination relatively to anything else, so too it cannot contain within itself any determination, any content; for any such would be a distinguishing and an inter-relationship of distinct moments, and consequently a mediation. The beginning therefore is *pure being*.

To this simple exposition of what is only directly involved in the simplest of all things, the logical beginning, we may add the following further reflections; yet these cannot be meant to serve as elucidations and confirmations of that exposition—this is complete in itself—since they are occasioned by preconceived ideas and reflections and these, like all other preliminary prejudices, must be disposed of within the science itself where their treatment should be awaited with patience.

The insight that absolute truth must be a result, and conversely, that a result presupposes a prior truth which, however, because it is a first, objectively considered is unnecessary and from the subjective side is not known—this insight has recently given rise to the thought that philosophy can only begin with a *hypothetical* and *problematical* truth and therefore philosophizing can at first be only a quest. This view was much stressed by Reinhold in his later philosophical work and one must give it credit for the genuine interest on which it is based, an interest which concerns the speculative nature of the philosophical *beginning*. The detailed discussion of this view is at the same time an occasion for intro-ducing a preliminary understanding of the meaning of progress in logic generally; for that view has a direct bearing on the advance; this it conceives to be such that progress in philosophy is rather a retrogression and a grounding or establishing by means of which we first obtain the result that what we began with is not something merely arbitrarily assumed but is in fact the *truth*, and also the *primary truth*.

It must be admitted that it is an important consideration—one which will be found in more detail in the logic itself—that the advance is a *retreat into the ground*, to what is *primary* and *true*, on which depends and, in fact, from which originates, that with which the beginning is made. Thus consciousness on its onward path from the immediacy with which it began is led back to absolute knowledge as its innermost *truth*. This last, the ground, is then also that from which the first proceeds, that which at first appeared as an immediacy. This is true in still greater measure of absolute spirit which reveals itself as the concrete and final supreme truth of all being, and which at the *end* of the development is known as freely externalizing itself, abandoning itself to the shape of an *immediate being*—opening or unfolding itself [*sich entschliessend*] into the creation of a world which contains all that fell into the development which preceded that result and which through this reversal of its position relatively to its beginning is transformed into something dependent on the result as principle. The essential requirement for the science of logic is not so much that the beginning be a pure immediacy, but rather that the whole of the science be within itself a circle in which the first is also the last and the last is also the first.

We see therefore that, on the other hand, it is equally necessary to consider as *result* that into which the movement returns as into its *ground*. In this respect the first is equally the ground, and the last a derivative; since the movement starts from the first and by correct inferences arrives at the last as the ground, this latter is a result. Further, the *progress* from that which forms the beginning is to be regarded as only a further determination of it, hence that which forms the starting point of the development remains at the base of all that follows and does not vanish from it. The progress does not consist merely in the derivation of an other, or in the effected transition into a genuine other; and in so far as this transition does occur it is equally sublated again. Thus the beginning of philosophy is the foundation which is present and preserved throughout the entire subsequent development, remaining completely immanent in its further determinations.

Through this progress, then, the beginning loses the one-sidedness which attaches to it as something simply immediate and abstract; it becomes something mediated, and hence the line of the scientific advance becomes a *circle*. It also follows that because that which forms the beginning is still undeveloped, devoid of content, it is not truly known in the beginning; it is the science of logic in its whole compass which first constitutes the completed knowledge of it with its developed content and first truly grounds that knowledge.

But because it is the *result* which appears as the absolute ground, this progress in knowing is not something provisional, or pro-blematical and hypothetical; it must be determined by the nature of the subject matter itself and its content. The said beginning is neither an arbitrary and merely provisional assumption, nor is it something which appears to be arbitrarily and tentatively pre-supposed, but which is subsequently shown to have been properly made the beginning; not as is the case with the constructions one is directed to make in connection with the proof of a theorem in geometry, where it becomes apparent only afterwards in the proof that one took the right course in drawing just those lines and then, in the proof itself, in beginning with the comparison of those lines or angles; drawing such lines and comparing them are not an essential part of the proof itself.

Thus the *ground*, the *reason*, why the beginning is made with pure being in the pure science [of logic] is directly given in the science itself. This pure being is the unity into which pure knowing withdraws, or, if this itself is still to be distinguished as form from its unity, then being is also the content of pure knowing. It is when taken in this way that this *pure being*, this absolute immediacy has equally the character of something absolutely mediated. But it is equally essential that it be taken only in the one-sided character in which it is pure immediacy, *precisely because* here it is the beginning. If it were not this pure indeter-minateness, if it were determinate, it would have been taken as something mediated, something already carried a stage further: what is determinate implies an other to a first. Therefore, it lies in the *very nature of a beginning* that it must be being and nothing else. To enter into philosophy, therefore, calls for no other preparations, no further reflections or points of connection.

We cannot really extract any further determination or *positive* content for the beginning from the fact that it is the beginning of philosophy. For here at the start, where the subject matter itself is not yet to hand, philosophy is an empty word or some assumed, unjustified conception. Pure knowing yields only this negative determination, that the beginning is to be *abstract*. If pure being is taken as the *content* of pure knowing, then the latter must stand back from its content, allowing it to have free play and not determining it further. Or again, if pure being is to be considered as the unity into which knowing has collapsed at the extreme point of its union with the object, then knowing itself has vanished in that unity, leaving behind no difference from the unity and hence nothing by which the latter could be determined. Nor is there anything else present, any content which could be used to make the beginning more determinate.

But the determination of *being* so far adopted for the beginning could also be omitted, so that the only demand would be that a pure beginning be made. In that case, we have nothing but the *beginning* itself, and it remains to be seen what this is. This position could also be suggested for the benefit of those who, on the one hand, are dissatisfied for one reason or another with the beginning with being and still more so with the resulting transition of being into nothing, and, on the other hand, simply know no other way of beginning a science than by *presupposing some general idea*, which is then *analysed*, the result of such analysis yielding the first specific concept in the science. If we too were to observe this method, then we should be without a particular object, because the beginning, as the beginning of *thought*, is supposed to be quite abstract, quite general, wholly form without any content; thus we should have nothing at all beyond the general idea of a mere beginning as such. We have therefore only to see what is contained in such an idea.

As yet there is nothing and there is to become something. The beginning is not pure nothing, but a nothing from which something is to proceed; therefore being, too, is already contained in the beginning. The beginning, therefore, contains both, being and nothing, is the unity of being and nothing; or is non-being which is at the same time being, and being which is at the same time non-being.

Further, in the beginning, being and nothing are present as *distinguished* from each other; for the beginning points to something else—it is a non-being which carries a reference to being as to an other; that which begins, as yet *is* not, it is only on the
c*

way to being. The being contained in the beginning is, therefore, a being which removes itself from non-being or sublates it as something opposed to it.

But again, that which begins already *is*, but equally, too, *is not* as yet. The opposites, being and non-being are therefore directly united in it, or, otherwise expressed, it is their *undifferentiated unity*.

The analysis of the beginning would thus yield the notion of the unity of being and nothing—or, in a more reflected form, the unity of differentiatedness and non-differentiatedness, or the identity of identity and non-identity. This concept could be regarded as the first, purest, that is, most abstract definition of the absolute—as it would in fact be if we were at all concerned with the form of definitions and with the name of the absolute. In this sense, that abstract concept would be the first definition of this absolute and all further determinations and developments only more specific and richer definitions of it. But let those who are dissatisfied with *being* as a beginning because it passes over into nothing and so gives rise to the unity of being and nothing, let them see whether they find this beginning which begins with the general idea of a *beginning* and with its analysis (which, though of course correct, likewise leads to the unity of being and nothing), more satisfactory than the beginning with being.

But there is a still further observation to be made about this procedure. The said analysis presupposes as familiar the idea of a beginning, thus following the example of other sciences. These presuppose their subject-matter and take it for granted that everyone has roughly the same general idea of it and can find in it the same determinations as those indicated by the sciences which have obtained them in one way or another through analysis, comparison and other kinds of reasoning. But that which forms the absolute beginning must likewise be something otherwise known; now if it is something concrete and hence is variously determined within itself, then this *internal relation* is presupposed as something known; it is thus put forward as an *immediacy* which, however, it is not; for it is a relation only as a relation of distinct moments, and it therefore contains *mediation* within itself. Further, with a concrete object, the analysis and the ways in which it is determined are affected by contingency and arbitrariness. Which determinations are brought out depends on what each person just *finds* in his own immediate, contingent idea. The relation contained in something concrete, in a synthetic unity, is *necessary* only in so far as it is not just given but is produced by the spontaneous return of the moments back into this unity—a movement which is the opposite of the analytical procedure, which is an activity belonging to the subject-thinker and external to the subject matter itself.

The foregoing shows quite clearly the reason why the beginning cannot be made with anything concrete, anything containing a relation *within itself*. For such presupposes an internal process of mediation and transition of which the concrete, now become simple, would be the result. But the beginning ought not itself to be already a first *and* an other; for anything which is in its own self a first *and* an other implies that an advance has already been made. Consequently, that which constitutes the beginning, the beginning itself, is to be taken as something unanalysable, taken in its simple, unfilled immediacy, and therefore *as being*, as the completely empty being.

If impatience with the consideration of the abstract beginning should provoke anyone to say that the beginning should be made not with the beginning, but straightway with the subject matter itself, well then, this subject matter is nothing else but the said empty being; for what this subject matter is, that will be explicated only in the development of the science and cannot be presupposed by it as known beforehand.

Whatever other form the beginning takes in the attempt to begin with something other than empty being, it will suffer from the defects already specified. Let those who are still dissatisfied with this beginning tackle the problem of avoiding these defects by beginning in some other way.

But we cannot leave entirely unmentioned an original beginning of philosophy which has recently become famous, the beginning with the *ego*. It came partly from the reflection that from the first truth the entire sequel must be derived, and partly from the requirement that the *first* truth must be something with which we are acquainted, and still more, something of which we are *immediately certain*. This beginning is, in general, not a contingent idea which can be differently constituted in different subjects. For the ego, this immediate consciousness of self, at first appears to be itself both an immediacy and also something much more familiar to us than any other idea; anything else known belongs to the ego, it is true, but is still a content distinguished from it and therefore contingent; the ego, on the contrary, is the simple certainty of its own self. But the ego as such is *at the same time* also concrete, or rather, the ego is the most concrete of all things—the consciousness of itself as an infinitely manifold world. Before the ego, this concrete Being, can be made the beginning and ground of philosophy, it must be disrupted—this is the absolute act through which the ego purges itself of its content and becomes aware of itself as an abstract ego. Only this pure ego now is *not* immediate, is not the familiar, ordinary ego of our consciousness to which the science of logic could be directly linked for everyone. That act, strictly speaking, would be nothing else but the elevation to the standpoint of pure knowing where the distinction of subject and object has vanished. But as thus *immediately* demanded, this elevation is a subjective postulate; to prove itself a genuine demand, the progression of the concrete ego from immediate consciousness to pure knowing must have been indicated and exhibited through the necessity of the ego itself. Without this objective movement pure knowing, even in the shape of intellectual intuition, appears as an arbitrary standpoint, or even as one of the empirical *states* of consciousness with respect to which everything turns on whether or not it is found or can be produced in each and every individual. But inasmuch as this pure ego must be essential, pure knowing, and pure knowing is not *immediately* present in the individual consciousness but only as posited through the absolute act of the ego in raising itself to that stand-point, we lose the very advantage which is supposed to come from this beginning of philosophy, namely that it is something thoroughly familiar, something everyone finds in himself which can form the starting point for further reflection; that pure ego, on the contrary, in its abstract, essential nature, is something unknown to the ordinary consciousness, something it does not find therein. Instead, such a beginning brings with it the disadvantage of the illusion that whereas the thing under discussion is supposed to be something familiar, the ego of empirical self-consciousness, it is in fact something far removed from it. When pure knowing is characterized as ego, it acts as a perpetual reminder of the subjective ego whose limitations should be forgotten, and it fosters the idea that the propositions and relations resulting from the further development of the ego are present and can already be found in the ordinary consciousness—for in fact it is this of which they are asserted. This confusion, far from clarifying the problem of a beginning, only adds to the difficulties involved and tends completely to mislead; among the uninitiated it has given rise to the crudest misunderstandings.

Further, as regards the *subjective* determinateness of the ego in general, it is true that pure knowing frees the ego from the restricted meaning imposed on it by the insuperable opposition of its object; but for this reason it would be *superfluous* at least to retain this subjective attitude and the determination of pure knowing as ego. This determination, however, not only introduces the disturbing ambiguity mentioned, but closely examined it also remains a subjective *ego*. The actual development of the science which starts from the ego shows that in that development the object has and retains the perennial character of an other for the ego, and that the ego which formed the starting-point is, therefore, still entangled in the world of appearance and is not the pure knowing which has in truth overcome the opposition of consciousness.

In this connection a further essential observation must be made, namely that although the ego could *in itself* or *in principle* [*an sich*] be characterized as pure knowing or as intellectual intuition and asserted as the beginning, we are not concerned in the science of logic with what is present only in *principle* or as something *inner*, but rather with the determinate reality *in thought* of what is inner and with the *determinateness* possessed by such an inner in this reality. But what, at the *beginning* of the science, is *actually present* of intellectual intuition—or of the eternal, the divine, the absolute, if its object be so named—cannot be anything else than a first, immediate, simple determination. Whatever richer name be given to it than is expressed by mere *being*, the consideration of such absolute must be restricted solely to the way in which it enters into our knowing as *thought* and is enunicated as such. True, intellectual intuition is the forcible rejection of mediation and the ratiocinative, external reflection; but what it enunciates above and beyond simple immediacy is something concrete, something which contains within itself diverse determinations. However, as we have remarked, the enunciation and exposition of such concrete beginning is a process of mediation which starts from *one* of the determinations and advances to the other, even though the latter returns to the first; it is a movement which at the same time may not be arbitrary or assertoric. Consequently, it is not the concrete something itself with which that exposition begins but only the simple immediacy from which the movement starts. And further, if something concrete is taken as the beginning, the conjunction of the determinations contained in it demand proof, and this is lacking.

If, therefore, in the expression of the absolute, or eternal, or God (and *God* has the absolutely undisputed right that the beginning be made with him)—if in the intuition or thought of these there is *implied more* than pure being—then this *more* must make its *appearance* in our knowing only as something *thought*, not as something imagined or figurately conceived; let what is present in intuition or figurate conception be as rich as it may, the determination which *first* emerges in knowing is simple, for only in what is simple is there nothing more than the pure beginning; only the immediate is simple, for only in the immediate has no advance yet been made from a *one* to an *other*. Consequently, whatever is intended to be expressed or implied beyond *being*, in the richer forms of representing the absolute or God, this is in the beginning only an empty word and only being; this simple determination which has no other meaning of any kind, this emptiness, is therefore simply as such the beginning of philosophy.

This insight is itself so simple that this beginning as such requires no preparation or further introduction; and, indeed, these preliminary, external reflections about it were not so much intended to lead up to it as rather to eliminate all preliminaries.

GENERAL DIVISION OF BEING

Being is determined, first, as against another in general;

Secondly, as immanently self-determining;

Thirdly, setting aside the preliminary character of this division, it is the abstract indeterminateness and immediacy in which it must be the beginning.

According to the first determination, *being* is classified as distinct from *essence*, for later in its development it proves to be in its totality only one sphere of the *Notion* and to this sphere as moment, it opposes another sphere.

According to the second determination, it is the sphere within which fall the determinations and the entire movement of its reflection. Here, *being* will posit itself in three determinations:

I as *determinateness* as such: *quality*
II as *sublated* determinateness: *magnitude, quantity*
III as *qualitatively* determined *quantity: measure.*

At this stage, this division is, as was remarked of these divisions generally in the *Introduction*, a preliminary statement; its determinations have first to arise from the movement of *being* itself and in so doing define and justify themselves. As regards the divergence of this classification from the usual presentation of the categories, namely, as *quantity, quality, relation* and *modality*—these moreover with Kant are supposed to be only titles for his categories though they are, in fact, themselves categories, only more general ones—this calls for no special comment here, as the entire exposition will show a complete divergence from the usual arrangement and significance of the categories.

This only perhaps can be remarked, that hitherto the determination of *quantity* has been made to precede *quality* and this—as is mostly the case—for no given reason. It has already been shown that the beginning is made with being *as such*, therefore, with qualitative being. It is easily seen from a comparison of quality with quantity that the former by its nature is first. For quantity is quality which has already become negative; *magnitude* is the determinateness which is no longer one with *being* but is already differentiated from it, sublated quality which has become indifferent. It includes the alterableness of being, although the category itself, namely being, of which it is the determination, is not altered by it. The qualitative determinateness, on the other hand, is one with its being: it neither goes beyond it nor is internal to it, but is its immediate limitedness. Quality therefore, as the *immediate* determinateness, is primary and it is with it that the beginning must be made.

Measure is a *relation*, but not relation in general, for it is the specific relation between *quality* and *quantity*; the categories which Kant includes under relation will come up for consideration in quite another place. Measure can also, if one wishes, be regarded as a modality; but since with Kant modality is supposed no longer to constitute a determination of the content, but to concern only the relation of the content to thought, to the subjective element, it is a quite heterogeneous relation and is not pertinent here.

The third determination of *being* falls within the section Quality, for as abstract immediacy it reduces itself to a single determinateness in relation to its other determinatenesses within its sphere.

Section One: Determinateness (Quality)

Being is the indeterminate *immediate;* it is free from determinateness in relation to *essence* and also from any which it can possess within itself. This reflectionless *being* is *being* as it is immediately in its own self alone.

Because it is indeterminate being, it lacks all quality; but *in itself*, the character of indeterminateness attaches to it only in contrast to what is *determinate* or qualitative. But *determinate* being stands in contrast to being in general, so that the very indeterminateness of the latter constitutes its quality. It will therefore be shown that the *first* being is in itself determinate, and therefore, *secondly*, that it passes over into *determinate being*—is *determinate being*—but that this latter as finite being sublates itself and passes over into the infinite relation of being to its own self, that is, *thirdly*, into *being-for-self*.

CHAPTER I

BEING

A. BEING

Being, pure being, without any further determination. In its indeterminate immediacy it is equal only to itself. It is also not unequal relatively to an other; it has no diversity within itself nor any with a reference outwards. It would not be held fast in its purity if it contained any determination or content which could be distinguished in it or by which it could be distinguished from an other. It is pure indeterminateness and emptiness. There is *nothing* to be intuited in it, if one can speak here of intuiting; or, it is only this pure intuiting itself. Just as little is anything to be thought in it, or it is equally only this empty thinking. Being, the indeterminate immediate, is in fact *nothing*, and neither more nor less than *nothing*.

B. NOTHING

Nothing, pure nothing: it is simply equality with itself, complete emptiness, absence of all determination and content—undifferentiatedness in itself. In so far as intuiting or thinking can be mentioned here, it counts as a distinction whether something or *nothing* is intuited or thought. To intuit or think nothing has, therefore, a meaning; both are distinguished and thus nothing *is* (exists) in our intuiting or thinking; or rather it is empty intuition and thought itself, and the same empty intuition or thought as pure being. Nothing is, therefore, the same determination, or rather absence of determination, and thus altogether the same as, pure *being*.

C. BECOMING

I. UNITY OF BEING AND NOTHING

Pure being and *pure nothing* are, therefore, the same. What is the truth is neither being nor nothing, but that being—does not pass over but has passed over—into nothing, and nothing into being. But it is equally true that they are not undistinguished from each other, that, on the contrary, they are not the same, that they are absolutely distinct, and yet that they are unseparated and inseparable and that each immediately *vanishes in its opposite*. Their truth is, therefore, this movement of the immediate vanishing of the one in the other: *becoming*, a movement in which both are distinguished, but by a difference which has equally immediately resolved itself.

Remark 1: *The Opposition of Being and Nothing in Ordinary Thinking*

Nothing is usually opposed to *something;* but the being of *something* is already determinate and is distinguished from another *something*; and so therefore the nothing which is opposed to the something is also the nothing of a particular something, a determinate nothing. Here, however, nothing is to be taken in its indeterminate simplicity. Should it be held more correct to oppose to being, *non-being* instead of nothing, there would be no objection to this so far as the result is conerned, for in *non-being* the relation to *being* is contained: both being and its negation are enunciated in a *single* term, nothing, as it is in becoming. But we are concerned first of all not with the form of opposition (with the form, that is, also of *relation*) but with the abstract, immediate negation: nothing, purely on its own account, negation devoid of any relations—what could also be expressed if one so wished merely by 'not'.

It was the *Eleatics*, above all Parmenides, who first enunicated the simple thought of *pure being* as the absolute and sole truth: *only being is, and nothing absolutely is not*, and in the surviving fragments of Parmenides this is enunciated with the pure enthusiasm of thought which has for the first time apprehended itself in its absolute abstraction. As we know, in the oriental systems, principally in Buddhism, *nothing*, the void, is the absolute principle. Against that simple and one-sided abstraction the deep-thinking Heraclitus brought forward the higher, total concept of *becoming* and said: *being* as little *is*, as nothing *is*, or, all *flows*, which means, all is a *becoming*. The popular, especially oriental proverbs, that all that exists has the germ of death in its very birth, that death, on the other hand, is the entrance into new life, express at bottom the same union of being and nothing. But these expressions have a substratum in which the transition takes place; being and nothing are held apart in time, are conceived as alternating in it, but are not thought in their abstraction and consequently, too, not so that they are in themselves absolutely the same.

Ex nihilo nihil fit—is one of those propositions to which great importance was ascribed in metaphysics. In it is to be seen either only the empty tautology: nothing is nothing; or, if *becoming* is supposed to possess an actual meaning in it, then, since from *nothing* only *nothing becomes*, the proposition does not in fact contain *becoming*, for in it nothing remains nothing. Becoming implies that nothing does not remain nothing but passes into its other, into being. Later, especially Christian, metaphysics whilst rejecting the proposition that out of nothing comes nothing, asserted a transition from nothing into being; although it understood this proposition synthetically or merely imaginatively, yet even in the most imperfect union there is contained a point in which being and nothing coincide and their distinguishedness vanishes. The proposition: out of nothing comes nothing, nothing is just nothing, owes its peculiar importance to its opposition to *becoming* generally, and consequently also to its opposition to the creation of the world from nothing. Those who maintain the proposition: nothing is just nothing, and even grow heated in its defence, are unaware that in so doing they are subscribing to the abstract pantheism of the *Eleatics*, and also in principle to that of Spinoza. The philosophical view for which 'being is only being, nothing is only nothing', is a valid principle, merits the name of 'system of identity'; this abstract identity is the essence of pantheism.

If the result that being and nothing are the same seems startling or paraodoxical in itself, there is nothing more to be said; rather should we wonder at this wondering which shows itself to be such a newcomer to philosophy and forgets that in this science there occur determinations quite different from those in ordinary consciousness and in so-called ordinary common sense—which is not exactly sound understanding but an understanding educated up to abstractions and to a belief, or rather a superstitious belief, in abstractions. It would not be difficult to demonstrate this unity of being and nothing in every example, in *every* actual thing or thought. The same must be said of *being* and *nothing*, as was said above about immediacy and mediation (which latter contains a reference to an other, and hence to *negation*), that nowhere in heaven or on earth is there anything which does not contain within itself both being and nothing. Of course, since we are speaking here of a particular *actual something*, those determinations are no longer present in it in the complete untruth in which they are as being and nothing; they are in a more developed determination, and are grasped, for example, as positive and negative, the former being posited, reflected being, the latter posited, reflected nothing; the positive contains as its abstract basis being, and the negative, nothing. Thus in God himself, *quality* (energy, creation, power, and so forth), essentially involves the determination of the negative—they are the producing of an *other*. But an empirical elucidation by examples of the said assertion would be altogether superfluous here. Since the unity of being and nothing as the primary truth now forms once and for all the basis and element of all that follows, besides *becoming* itself, all further logical determinations: determinate being, quality, and generally all philosophical Notions, are examples of this unity. But self-styled sound common sense, if it rejects the unseparatedness of being and nothing, may be set the task of trying to discover an example in which the one is found separated from the other (*something* from *limit* or *limitation*, or, as just mentioned, the infinite, God, from energy or activity). Only the empty figments of thought, being and nothing themselves are these separated things and it is these that are preferred by 'sound common sense' to the truth, to the unseparatedness of both which is everywhere before us.

We cannot be expected to meet on all sides the perplexities which such a logical proposition produces in the ordinary consciousness, for they are inexhaustible. Only a few of them can be mentioned. One source among others of such perplexity is that the ordinary consciousness brings with it to such an abstract logical proposition, conceptions of something concrete, forgetting that what is in question is not such concrete something but only the pure abstractions of being and nothing and that these alone are to be held firmly in mind.

Being and non-being are the same, therefore it is the same whether this house is or is not, whether these hundred dollars are part of my fortune or not. This inference from, or application of, the proposition completely alters its meaning. The proposition contains the pure abstractions of being and nothing; but the application converts them into a determinate being and a determinate nothing. But as we have said, the question here is not of determinate being. A determinate, a finite, being is one that is in relation to an other; it is a content standing in a necessary relation to another content, to the whole world. As regards the reciprocally determining context of the whole, metaphysics could make the— at bottom tautological—assertion that if a speck of dust were destroyed the whole universe would collapse. In the instances adduced against the proposition in question, something appears as not indifferent to whether it is or is not, not on account of being or non-being, but on account of its *content*, which brings it into relation with something else. If a specific content, any determinate being, is *presupposed*, then because it is *determinate*, it is in a manifold relationship with another content; it is not a matter of indifference to it whether a certain other content with which it is in relation is, or is not; for it is only through such relation that it essentially is what it is. The same is the case in the ordinary way of thinking (taking non-being in the more specific sense of such way of thinking as contrasted with actuality) in the context of which the being or the absence of a content, which, as determinate, is conceived as in relation to another, is not a matter of indifference.

This consideration involves what constitutes a cardinal factor in the Kantian criticism of the ontological proof of the existence of God, although here we are only interested in the distinction made in that proof between being and nothing generally, and *determinate* being or non-being. As we know, there was presupposed in that so-called proof the concept of a being possessing all realities, including therefore *existence*, which was likewise assumed as one of the realities. The main thesis of the Kantian criticism was that *existence* or being (these being taken here as synonymous) is not a *property* or a *real predicate*, that is to say, is not a concept of something which could be added to the *concept* of a thing. By this Kant means to say that being is not a determination of the content of a thing.[1] Therefore, he goes on to say, the possible does not contain more than the actual; a hundred actual dollars do not contain a whit more than a hundred possible

[1] Kant's *Critique of Pure Reason*, 2nd ed., pp. 628 sqq.

ones; that is, the content of the former has no other determination than has the content of the latter. If this content is considered as isolated, it is indeed a matter of indifference whether it is, or is not; it contains no distinction of being or non-being, this difference does not affect it at all. The hundred dollars do not diminish if they do not exist, or increase if they do. A difference must come only from elsewhere. 'On the other hand,' Kant reminds us, 'my fortune benefits more from a hundred actual dollars than from the mere concept of them or from their possibility. For in actuality, the *object* is not merely contained analytically in my concept, but is *added synthetically to my concept* (which is a determination of my state), although the hundred dollars in my thought are not themselves increased one whit by this being which they have apart from my concept.'

There are *presupposed* here two different states (to retain the Kantian expressions which are not free from a confused clumsiness): one, which Kant calls the concept (by which we must understand figurate conception), and another, the state of my fortune. For the one as for the other, my fortune and the figurate conception, a hundred dollars are a determination of a content or, as Kant expresses it, 'they are added to such a concept synthetically'; I as *possessor* of a hundred dollars or as not possessing them, or even I as *imagining* or not imagining them, is of course a different content. Stated more generally: the abstractions of being and nothing both cease to be abstractions if they acquire a determinate content; being is then reality, the determinate being of a hundred dollars; nothing is the negation, the determinate non-being of them. This determinate content itself, the hundred dollars, also grasped isolatedly in abstraction is unchanged the same in the one as it is in the other. But since, furthermore, being is taken as a state of my fortune, the hundred dollars stand in relation to this state, as regards which the determinateness which they are is not a matter of indifference; their being or non-being is only an *alteration*; they are transposed into the sphere of *determinate being*. When, therefore, it is urged against the unity of being and nothing that it is nevertheless not a matter of indifference whether anything (the hundred dollars) is, or is not, we practise the deception of converting the difference between whether I *have* or *have not* the hundred dollars into a difference between being and non-being—a deception based, as we have

shown, on the one-sided abstraction which ignores the determinate being present in such examples and holds fast merely to
being and non-being, just as, conversely, the abstract being and
nothing which should be apprehended is transformed into a
definite being and nothing, into a determinate being. *Determinate
being* is the first category to contain the real difference of being and
nothing, namely, *something* and *other*. It is this real difference
which is vaguely present in ordinary thinking, instead of abstract
being and pure nothing and their only imagined difference.

As Kant expresses it, 'through its existence something enters
into the context of the whole of experience, . . . we obtain thereby
an additional object of *perception* without anything being added
to our *concept* of the object'. As our explanation has shown, this
means simply that something, through its existence, just because
it is a determinate existence, is essentially in relationship with
others, including also a percipient subject. The concept of the
hundred dollars, says Kant, gains nothing by their being perceived. *Concept* here means the hundred dollars previously noted
as thought *in isolation*. As thus isolated they are, it is true, an
empirical content, but cut off, having no relationship with any
other content and possessing no determinate character relatively
to such; the form of identity-with-self strips them of any connection with an other, so that it is a matter of indifference whether
they are perceived or not. But this so-called *concept* of the hundred
dollars is a spurious concept; the form of simple self-relation does
not belong to such a limited, finite content itself; it is a borrowed
form attached to it by the subjective understanding; the being of
the hundred dollars is not self-related but alterable and perishable.

The thinking or figurate conception which has before it only a
specific, determinate being must be referred back to the pre-
viously-mentioned beginning of the science made by Parmenides
who purified and elevated his own figurate conception, and so,
too, that of posterity, to *pure thought*, to being as such and thereby
created the element of the science. What is the first in the *science*
had of necessity to show itself *historically* as the first. And we
must regard the Eleatic *One* or *being* as the first step in the knowledge of thought; water and suchlike material principles are
certainly *meant* to be the universal, but as material they are not
pure thoughts; numbers are neither the first simple, nor the self-

communing thought, but the thought which is wholly external to itself.

The reference back from *particular finite* being to being as such in its wholly abstract universality is to be regarded not only as the very first theoretical demand but as the very first practical demand too. When for example a fuss is made about the hundred dollars, that it does make a difference to the state of my fortune whether I *have* them or *not*, still more whether *I* am or not, or whether something else is or is not, then—not to mention that there will be fortunes to which such possession of a hundred dollars will be a matter of indifference—we can remind ourselves that man has a duty to rise to that abstract universality of mood in which he is indeed indifferent to the existence or non-existence of the hundred dollars, whatever may be their quantitative relation to his fortune, just as it ought to be a matter of indifference to him whether he is or is not, that is, in finite life (for a state, a determinate being is meant), and so on—*si fractus illabatur orbis, impavidum ferient ruinae* was said by a Roman, and still more ought the Christian to possess this indifference.

There remains still to be noted the immediate connection between, on the one hand, the elevation above the hundred dollars and finite things generally, and on the other, the ontological proof and the Kantian criticism of it we have cited. This criticism, through its popular example, has made itself universally plausible: who does not know that a hundred actual dollars are different from a hundred merely possible ones? that they make a difference to the state of my fortune? Because this difference is so obvious with the hundred dollars, therefore the concept, that is, the specific nature of the content as an empty possibility, and being, are different from each other; *therefore* the Notion of God too is different from his being, and just as little as I can extract from the possibility of the hundred dollars their actuality, just as little can I extract from the Notion of God his existence; but the onotological proof is supposed to consist of this extraction of the existence of God from his Notion. Now though it is of course true that Notion is different from being, there is a still greater difference between God and the hundred dollars and other finite things. It is the *definition of finite things* that in them the Notion is different from being, that Notion and reality, soul and body, are separable and hence that they are perishable and mortal; the abstract definition of God, on the other hand, is precisely that his Notion and his being are *unseparated* and *inseparable*. The genuine criticism of the categories and of reason is just this: to make intellect aware of this difference and to prevent it from applying to God the determinations and relationships of the finite.

Remark 2: *Defectiveness of the Expression 'Unity, Identity of Being and Nothing'*

Another contributory reason for the repugnance to the proposition about being and nothing must be mentioned; this is that the result of considering being and nothing, as expressed in the statement: being and nothing are one and the same, is incomplete. The emphasis is laid chiefly on their being one and the same, as in judgements generally, where it is the predicate that first states what the subject is. Consequently, the sense seems to be that the difference is denied, although at the same time it appears directly in the proposition; for this enunicates *both* determinations, being and nothing, and contains them as distinguished. At the same time, the intention cannot be that abstraction should be made from them and only the unity retained. Such a meaning would self-evidently be one-sided, because that from which abstraction is to be made is equally present and named in the proposition. Now in so far as the proposition: being and nothing are the same, asserts the identity of these determinations, but, in fact, equally contains them both as distinguished, the proposition is self-contradictory and cancels itself out. Bearing this in mind and looking at the proposition more closely, we find that it has a movement which involves the spontaneous vanishing of the proposition itself. But in thus vanishing, there takes place in it that which is to constitute its own peculiar content, namely, *becoming*.

The proposition thus *contains* the result, it is this *in its own self*. But the fact to which we must pay attention here is the defect that the result is not itself *expressed* in the proposition; it is an external reflection which discerns it therein. In this connection we must, at the outset, make this general observation, namely, that the proposition in the *form of a judgement* is not suited to express speculative truths; a familiarity with this fact is likely to remove many misunderstandings of speculative truths. Judgment is an *identical* relation between subject and predicate; in it we abstract from the fact that the subject has a number of determinatenesses other than that of the predicate, and also that the predicate is more extensive than the subject. Now if the content is speculative, the *non-identical* aspect of subject and predicate is also an essential moment, but in the judgement this is not expressed. It is the form of simple judgement, when it is used to express speculative results, which is very often responsible for the paradoxical and bizarre light in which much of recent philosophy appears to those who are not familiar with speculative thought.

To help express the speculative truth, the deficiency is made good in the first place by adding the contrary proposition: being and nothing are not the same, which is also enunciated as above. But thus there arises the further defect that these propositions are not connected, and therefore exhibit their content only in the form of an antinomy whereas their content refers to one and the same thing, and the determinations which are expressed in the two propositions are supposed to be in complete union—a union which can only be stated as an *unrest* of *incompatibles*, as a *movement*. The commonest injustice done to a speculative content is to make it one-sided, that is, to give prominence only to one of the propositions into which it can be resolved. It cannot then be denied that this proposition is asserted; *but the statement is just as false as it is true*, for once one of the propositions is taken out of the speculative content, the other must at least be equally considered and stated. Particular mention must be made here of that, so to speak, unfortunate word, 'unity'. Unity, even more than identity, expresses a subjective reflection; it is taken especially as the relation which arises from *comparison*, from external reflection. When this reflection finds the same thing in two *different objects*, the resultant unity is such that there is presupposed the complete *indifference* to it of the objects themselves which are compared, so that this comparing and unity does not concern the objects themselves and is a procedure and a determining external to them. Unity, therefore, expresses wholly *abstract* sameness and sounds all the more blatantly paradoxical the more the terms of which it is asserted show themselves to be sheer opposites. So far then, it would be better to say only *unseparatedness* and *inseparability*, but then the affirmative aspect of the relation of the whole would not find expression.

Thus the whole true result which we have here before us is *becoming*, which is not merely the one-sided or abstract unity of being and nothing. It consists rather in this movement, that pure being is immediate and simple, and for that very reason is equally pure nothing, that there *is* a difference between them, but a difference which no less sublates itself and is *not*. The result, therefore, equally asserts the difference of being and nothing, but as a merely fancied or imagined difference.

It is the common opinion that being is rather the sheer other of nothing and that nothing is clearer than their absolute difference, and nothing seems easier than to be able to state it. But it is equally easy to convince oneself that this is impossible, that it is *unsayable. Let those who insist that being and nothing are different tackle the problem of stating in what the difference consists.* If being and nothing had any determinateness by which they were distinguished from each other then, as has been observed, they would be determinate being and determinate nothing, not the pure being and pure nothing that here they still are. Their difference is therefore completely empty, each of them is in the same way indeterminate; the difference, then, exists not in themselves but in a third, in subjective *opinion*. Opinion, however, is a form of subjectivity which is not proper to an exposition of this kind. But the third in which being and nothing subsist must also present itself here, and it has done so; it is *becoming*. In this, being and nothing are distinct moments; becoming only *is*, in so far as they are distinguished. This third is an other than they; they subsist only in an other, which is equivalent to saying that they are not self-subsistent. Becoming is as much the subsistence of being as it is of non-being; or, their subsistence is only their being in a *one*. It is just this their subsistence that equally sublates their difference.

The challenge to distinguish between being and nothing also includes the challenge to say what, then, is being and what is nothing. Those who are reluctant to recognize either one or the other as only a *transition* of the one into the other, and who assert this or that about being and nothing, let them state *what* it is they are speaking of, that is, put forward a *definition* of being and nothing and demonstrate its correctness. Without having satisfied this first requirement of the ancient science whose logical rules they accept as valid and apply in other cases, all that they maintain about being and nothing amounts only to assertions which are scientifically worthless. If elsewhere it has been said

that existence, in so far as this at first is held to be synonymous
with being, is the *complement* to *possibility*, then this presupposes
another determination, possibility, and so being is not enunciated
in its immediacy, but in fact as not self-subsistent, as conditioned.
For being which is the outcome of *mediation* we shall reserve
the term: *Existence*. But one *pictures* being to oneself, perhaps in
the image of pure light as the clarity of undimmed seeing, and
then nothing as pure night—and their distinction is linked with
this very familiar sensuous difference. But, as a matter of fact,
if this very seeing is more exactly imagined, one can readily
perceive that in absolute clearness there is seen just as much, and
as little, as in absolute darkness, that the one seeing is as good
as the other, that pure seeing is a seeing of nothing. Pure light
and pure darkness are two voids which are the same thing.
Something can be distinguished only in determinate light or
darkness (light is determined by darkness and so is darkened
light, and darkness is determined by light, is illuminated
darkness), and for this reason, that it is only darkened light and
illuminated darkness which have within themselves the moment
of difference and are, therefore, *determinate* being.

Remark 3: *The Isolating of These Abstractions*
The unity, whose moments, being and nothing, are inseparable,
is at the same time different from them and is thus a third to
them; this third in its own most characteristic form is *becoming*.
Transition is the same as becoming except that in the former one
tends to think of the two terms, from one of which transition is
made to the other, as at rest, apart from each other, the transition
taking place *between* them. Now wherever and in whatever form
being and nothing are in question, this third must be present;
for the two terms have no separate subsistence of their own but
are only in becoming, in this third. But this third has many
empirical shapes, which are set aside or ignored by abstraction
in order to hold fast, each by itself, these its products, being and
nothing, and to show them protected against transition. Such
simple procedure of abstraction can be countered, equally simply,
by calling to mind the empirical existence in which that abstraction
is itself only a something having a determinate being. Or else it is
some other form of reflection which is supposed to effect the
separation of what is inseparable. Such determination carries

within itself its own opposite, and, without referring back and appealing to the nature of the thing itself, the determination of reflection can be refuted in its own self by taking it just as it presents itself and pointing out in it its own other. It would be lavour in vain to attempt to intercept all the shifts and turns of reflection and its arguments in order to cut off and render impossible to it all the evasions and digressions by which it conceals from itself its own self-contradiction. For this reason I, too, refrain from taking notice of many of the so-called objections and refutations which have been advanced against the proposition that neither being nor nothing truly *is*, but that their truth is only becoming. The intellectual training which alone can afford an insight into the nullity of such refutations, or rather spontaneously dispel such random fancies, is effected only by a critical knowledge of the forms of the understanding; but those who are most prolific with such objections straightway launch their reflections against the first propositions without first acquiring or having acquired, by a further study of logic, an awareness of the nature of these crude reflections.

We shall consider some of the results which appear when being and nothing are postulated in isolation from each other, each outside the sphere of the other, with the consequence that their transition is denied.

Parmenides held fast to *being* and was most consistent in affirming at the same time that *nothing* absolutely is not; only *being* is. As thus taken, entirely on its own, being is indeterminate, and has therefore no relation to an other; consequently, it seems that *from this beginning* no further *progress* can be made—that is, from this beginning itself—and that progress can only be achieved by linking it on to something extraneous, something *outside* it. Hence the progress made in affirming that being is the same as nothing appears as a second, absolute beginning—a transition which is independent of being and added to it from outside. If being had a determinateness, then it would not be the absolute beginning at all; it would then depend on an other and would not be immediate, would not be the beginning. But if it is indeterminate and hence a genuine beginning, then, too, it has nothing with which it could bridge the gap between itself and an other; it is at the same time the *end*. It is just as impossible for anything to break forth from it as to break into it; with Parmenides as with

Spinoza, there is no progress from being or absolute substance to the negative, to the finite. If, nevertheless, there is progress—which, as has been remarked, in the case of relationless, and so progress-less being can be accomplished only in an external manner—then this progress is a second, a fresh beginning. Thus Fichte's absolutely primary, unconditioned principle: A = A, is thesis; the second is antithesis. This latter is supposed to be *partly* conditioned, *partly* unconditioned (and so an internal contradiction). This is a progress by external reflection which, having negated the absolute with which it began—the antithesis is the negation of the first identity—straightway expressly converts its second *unconditioned* into a *conditioned*. But if there were any justification at all for the progress, that is, for sublating the first beginning, then this first would itself have to be of such a nature that an other could connect itself with it; and therefore it would have to be *determinate*. But neither *being*, nor even absolute substance, claims to be such: on the contrary. Being is the *immediate*, that which is still utterly *indeterminate*.

The most eloquent, perhaps forgotten, descriptions of the impossibility of advancing from an abstract first to something beyond it, and effecting a union of both, are made by Jacobi in support of his polemic against the Kantian *a priori* synthesis of self-consciousness in his *Treatise on the Undertaking of the Critical Philosophy to Bring Reason to Understanding*.[1] He states the problem thus: that there be demonstrated the originating or producing of a synthesis in a *pure* [unity], whether of consciousness, of space, or of time. 'Let space be one, time be one, consciousness be one . . . Now tell me how does any one of these three ones *purely* make itself into a manifold within itself . . . each is only a *one* and *no other;* a one and the same sort, a self-sameness without any distinction of one from the other; for these distinctions still slumber in the empty infinitude of the indeterminate from which each and everything determinate has yet to proceed! What brings *finitude* into those three infinities? What impregnates space and time *a priori* with number and measure and transforms them into a *pure manifold*? What brings *pure spontaneity* (ego) into oscillation? Whence does its pure vowel get its consonant, or rather how does its *soundless*, uninterrupted *sounding* interrupt itself and break off in order to gain at least a kind of 'self-sound'

[1] F. H. Jacobi, *Works*, vol. III.

(vowel), an *accent*?'[1] It is evident that Jacobi recognized very clearly the insubstantial nature, the *non ens*, of abstraction, whether so-called absolute (i.e. only abstract) space, or abstract time, or abstract pure consciousness, the ego; he remains fixed in such abstraction in order to maintain the impossibility of a transition to an other (the condition of a synthesis), and to the synthesis itself. The synthesis, which is the point of interest, must not be taken as a connection of determinations already *externally* there; the question is partly of the genesis of a second to a first, of a determinate to an indeterminate first principle, partly, however, of *immanent* synthesis, synthesis *a priori*—a self-subsistent, self-determined unity of distinct moments. *Becoming* is this immanent synthesis of being and nothing; but because synthesis suggests more than anything else the sense of an external bringing together of mutually external things already there, the name synthesis, synthetic unity, has rightly been dropped. Jacobi asks *how* does the pure vowel of the ego get its consonant, *what* brings determinateness into indeterminateness? The *what* would be easy to answer and has been answered by Kant in his own manner; but the question *how* means: in what peculiar manner, in what relationship, and so forth, and thus demands the statement of a particular category; but there can be no question here of a peculiar manner, of categories of the understanding. The very question *how* itself belongs to the bad habits of reflection, which demands comprehensibility, but at the same time presupposes its own fixed categories and consequently knows beforehand that it is armed against the answering of its own question. Neither has it with Jacobi the higher sense of a question concerning the *necessity* of the synthesis; for he remains, as has been said, fixed in the abstractions in order to maintain the impossibility of the synthesis. Especially graphic is his description of the procedure for reaching the abstraction of space. 'For a time I must try clean to forget that I ever saw, heard, touched or handled anything at all, myself expressly not excepted. Clean, clean, clean must I forget all movement, and precisely this *forgetting*, because it is hardest, I must make my greatest concern. Just as I have thought away everything in general, so I must also completely and entirely get rid of it, retaining nothing but the forcibly arrested intuition alone of infinite *immutable space*. I may not therefore *again think*

[1] F. H. Jacobi, *Works*, vol. III, p. 113.

into it my own self as something distinct from it and yet connected with it; I may not let myself be merely *surrounded* and *pervaded* by it: but I must wholly *pass over* into it, become one with it, transform myself into it; I must leave nothing over of myself but *this my intuition* itself, in order to contemplate it as a genuinely self-subsistent, independent, single and sole conception.'[1]

With this wholly abstract purity of continuity, that is, in-determinateness and vacuity of conception, it is indifferent whether this abstraction is called space, pure intuiting, or pure thinking; it is altogether the same as what the Indian calls Brahma, when for years on end, physically motionless and equally unmoved in sensation, conception, fantasy, desire and so on, looking only at the tip of his nose, he says inwardly only *Om, Om, Om,* or else nothing at all. This dull, empty consciousness, understood as consciousness, is—*being.*

In this void, Jacobi now continues, he experiences the opposite of what Kant assures him he should experience; he does not find himself to be a *many* and *manifold*, but rather a one devoid of all plurality and variety; indeed, 'I myself am the *impossibility*, the *annihilation* of all that is manifold and plural—*cannot* from my pure, absolutely simple, immutable being *produce again* or spook into myself even the least bit of anything . . . Thus all separatedness and juxtaposition, and all manifoldness and plurality based thereon, are revealed (in this purity) as a *sheer impossibility*.'[2]

This impossibility amounts to nothing else than the tautology: I hold fast to abstract unity and shut out all plurality and manifold-ness, confine myself to the differenceless and the indeterminate and shut my eyes to all that is differentiated and determinate. The Kantian *a priori* synthesis of self-consciousness, that is, the function of this unity to differentiate itself and in this differentia-tion to preserve itself, is attenuated by Jacobi into the same abstraction. That 'synthesis *in itself*', the 'original act of judge-ment', he converts one-sidedly into 'the *copula in itself*—an "is, is, is", without beginning or end and without what, who or which. This repetition of repetition *ad infinitum* is the sole business, function and product of the absolutely pure synthesis; it is itself empty, pure, absolute repetition itself.' Though, in fact, since there is no breaking off, that is, no negation or distinguishing in it, it is not a repetition but merely undifferentiated, simple being.

[1] F. H. Jacobi, *Works*, vol. III, p. 147. [2] *Ibid.*, p. 149.

D

But, then, is this still a synthesis if Jacobi omits precisely that which makes the unity a synthetic unity?

In the first place, it must be said that when Jacobi thus fixes himself in absolute or abstract space, time and consciousness, he places and fixes himself in this way in something which is *empirically* false; *there is*, that is, there is empirically present, no such space and time which is not spatially and temporally limited, or whose continuity is not filled by manifoldly limited determinate being and change, so that these limits and changes belong, unseparated and inseparable, to the nature of spatiality and temporality; similarly, consciousness is filled with determinate sensation, conception, desire and so on; it does not exist separated from some particular content. The empirical *transition*, moreover, is self-evident; consciousness can of course make empty space, empty time, and even empty consciousness itself or pure being, its object and content, but it does not stop at that; it goes beyond it or rather presses forward out of such a vacuity to a better content, that is, to a content which in some way or other is more concrete, and which to that extent is better and truer however bad it may be in other respects; just such a content is in general synthetic, this word being taken in its more general sense. Thus Parmenides has to reckon with illusion and opinion, the opposite of being and truth; Spinoza likewise, with attributes, modes, extension, movement, understanding, will, and so on. The synthesis contains and demonstrates the falsity of those abstractions; in it they are in unity with their other, not, therefore, as independently self-subsistent, not as absolute, but purely as relative.

The demonstration of the empirical nullity of empty space, and so forth, is not, however, what we are concerned with. Consciousness by making abstraction can, of course, fill itself with such indeterminates also and the abstractions thus held fast are the *thoughts* of pure space, pure time, pure consciousness, or pure being. It is the thought of pure space, etc.—that is, pure space, etc., *in its own self*—that is to be demonstrated as null: that it is as such already its own opposite, that its opposite has already penetrated into it, that it is already by itself the accomplished coming-forth-from-itself, a determinateness.

But this is found immediately in them. They are, as Jacobi profusely describes them, results of abstraction; they are expressly determined as *indeterminate* and this—to go back to its simplest form—is being. But it is this very *indeterminateness* which constitutes its determinateness; for indeterminateness is opposed to determinateness; hence as so opposed it is itself determinate or the negative, and the pure, quite abstract negative. It is this indeterminateness or abstract negation which thus has being present within it, which reflection, both outer and inner, enunciates when it equates it with nothing, declares it to be an empty product of thought, to be nothing. Or it can be expressed thus: because being is devoid of all determination whatsoever, it is not the (affirmative) determinateness which it is; it is not being but nothing.

In the pure reflection of the beginning as it is made in this logic with being as such, the transition is still concealed; because *being* is posited only as immediate, therefore *nothing* emerges in it only immediately. But all the subsequent determinations, like determinate being which immediately follows, are more concrete; in determinate being there is already *posited* that which contains and produces the contradiction of those abstractions and therefore their transition. When being is taken in this simplicity and immediacy, the recollection that it is the result of complete abstraction, and so for that reason alone is abstract negativity, nothing, is left behind, outside the science, which, within its own self, from *essence* onwards will expressly exhibit the said one-sided *immediacy* as a mediated immediacy where being is *posited* as *existence* and the mediating agent of this being is *posited* as *ground*.

In the light of such recollection, the transition from being into nothing can be represented, or, as it is said, *explained* and *made intelligible*, as something even easy and trivial; of course the being which is made the beginning of the science is *nothing*, for abstraction can be made from everything, and if abstraction is made from everything then *nothing* is left over. But, it may be continued, the beginning is thus not an affirmative, not being, but just nothing, and nothing is then also the *end*, at least as much as immediate being, and even more so. The shortest way is to let such reasoning take its course and then wait and see what is the nature of its boasted results. That *nothing* would be the result of such reasoning and that now the beginning should be made with nothing (as in Chinese philosophy), need not cause us to lift a finger, for before we could do so this nothing would no less have converted itself into being (see Section B above). But further, this abstraction from everything (which 'everything' nevertheless is an affirmative *being*) having been presupposed, then it must be understood more exactly; the result of making abstraction from all that is, is first of all abstract being, *being* as such; just as in the cosmological proof of the existence of God from the contingent being of the world, in which proof we rise above such contingent being, *being* is still taken up with us in our ascent and is determined as *infinite being*. Of course, one *can* also abstract from this pure being, being *can* be thrown in with the all from which abstraction has already been made; then nothing remains. Now if we want to forget the *thinking* of *nothing*, that is, its conversion into being, or are ignorant of it, we *can* proceed in the style of 'one *can*'; we can for example (God be praised!) also abstract from nothing (for the creation of the world, too, is an abstraction from nothing), and then what remains is not nothing, for it is just from this that we have made abstraction; we have in fact arrived at being again. This, 'one *can*', gives an external play of abstraction, in which the abstracting itself is only the one-sided activity of the negative. It is directly implied in this very form of 'one *can*', that for it being is just as indifferent as nothing, and that with the vanishing of either of them there is equally an arising of the other; but it is equally a matter of indifference whether one starts from the doing of nothing, or from nothing; for the former, that is the mere abstracting, has neither more nor less of truth in it than mere nothing has.

The dialectic employed by Plato in treating of the One in the *Parmenides* is also to be regarded rather as a dialectic of external reflection. Being and the One are both Eleatic forms which are the same thing. But they are also to be distinguished; and it is thus that Plato takes them in that dialogue. After removing from the One the various determinations of whole and parts, of being-within-itself, of being-in-another, etc., of shape, time, etc., he reaches the result that being does not belong to the One, for being belongs to any particular something only in one of these modes.[1] Plato next deals with the proposition: *the One is*, and we should refer to Plato himself to see how, starting from this proposition, he accomplishes the transition to the *non-being* of

[1] p. 141e., vol. III, ed. Steph.

the One. He does it by *comparing* the two determinations of the proposition put forward: *the One is*; it contains the One *and* being, and 'the One is' contains more than when we only say: the One. It is through their being *different* that the moment of negation contained in the proposition is demonstrated. It is evident that this course has a presupposition and is an external reflection.

Here the way in which the One is connected with being is such that being, which is supposed to be held fast abstractly *by itself*, is demonstrated in the simplest way and without any effort of thought, to be in a union which implies the contrary of what is supposed to be maintained. Being, taken as it is immediately, belongs to *a subject*, is something enunciated, has an empirical *existence* in general and stands therefore in the field of limitation and the negative. In whatever phrases or turns of speech understanding may express itself in attacking the unity of being and nothing and appealing to what immediately confronts us, it will find just in this very experience nothing but *determinate* being, being with a limitation or negation—that very unity which it rejects. The assertion of immediate being thus reduces to an empirical existence, and it cannot reject the *demonstration* of this because it is to the immediacy which is outside of thought that it wants to cling.

The same is the case with *nothing*, only contrariwise, and this reflection on it is familiar and has been made often enough. Nothing, taken in its immediacy, shows itself as affirmative, as *being*; for according to its nature it is the same as being. Nothing is thought of, imagined, spoken of, and therefore it *is*; in the thinking, imagining, speaking and so on, nothing has its being. But, further, this being is also distinguished from it; it is therefore said that although nothing is in thought or imagination, yet for that very reason it is not *nothing* that *is*, being does not belong to nothing as such, but only thought or imagination is this being. With this distinguishing it is equally not to be denied that nothing stands in *relationship* to a being; but in the relation, even though it contains the difference, there is present a unity with being. In whatever way nothing is enunciated or indicated, it shows itself connected with, or if you like in contact with a being, unseparated from a being, that is to say in a *determinate* being.

But when the presence of nothing in a determinate being is thus demonstrated, there still lingers on the thought of this difference of it from being, namely that the determinate being of nothing does not at all pertain to nothing itself, that nothing does not possess an independent being of its own, is not being as such. Nothing, it is said, is only the absence of being, darkness thus only the *absence* of light, cold only absence of heat, and so on. And darkness only has meaning in relation to the eye, in external comparison with the positive factor, light, and similarly cold is only something in our sensation; on the other hand, light and heat, like being, are objective, active realities on their own account, and are of quite another quality and dignity than this negative, than nothing. One can often find it put forward as a weighty reflection and an important piece of information that darkness is *only absence* of light, cold *only absence* of heat. About this acute reflection in this field of empirical objects, it can be empirically observed that darkness does in fact show itself active in light, determining it to colour and thereby imparting visibility to it, since, as was said above, just as little is seen in pure light as in pure darkness. Visibility, however, is effected in the eye, and the supposed negative has just as much a share in this as the light which is credited with being the real, positive factor; similarly, cold makes its presence known in water, in our sensations etc., and if we deny it so-called objective reality it is not a whit the worse for our doing so. But a further objection would be that here, too, as before, it is a negative with a determinate content that is spoken of, the argument is not confined to pure nothing, to which being, regarded as an empty abstraction, is neither inferior nor superior. But cold, darkness, and similar determinate negations are to be taken directly as they are by themselves and we shall then see what we have thereby effected in respect of their universal determination which has led them to be introduced here. They are supposed to be not just nothing but the nothing of light, heat, etc., of something determinate, of a content; thus they are a determinate, a contentful, nothing if one may so speak. But, as will subsequently appear, a determinateness is itself a negation, and so they are negative nothings; but a negative nothing is an affirmative something. The conversion of nothing through its determinateness (which previously appeared as a *determinate* being in a subject thinker, or in some other form) into an affirmative, appears to the consciousness which is fixed in the abstraction of the understanding as the acme of paradox;

the insight that the negation of the negation is something positive, simple as it is, or rather because of its very simplicity, appears as a triviality to which haughty understanding need pay no heed, although the correctness of the insight is admitted—and the insight is not only correct, but, because of the universality of such determinations, it has its infinite extension and universal application, so that it were indeed well to pay attention to it.

A further remark can be made about the determination of the transition of being and nothing into each other, namely that it is to be understood as it is without any further elaboration of the transition by reflection. It is immediate and quite abstract because the transient moments are themselves abstract, that is, because the determinateness of either moment by means of which they passed over into each other is not yet posited in the other; nothing is not yet *posited* in being, although it is true that being is *essentially* nothing, and *vice versa*. It is therefore inadmissible to employ more developed forms of mediation here and to hold being and nothing in any kind of relationship—the transition in question is not yet a relation. Thus is it impermissible to say: nothing is the *ground* of being, or being is the *ground* of nothing or nothing is the *cause* of being, and so forth; or, transition into nothing can only occur *under the condition* that something *is*, or into being only *under the condition* of non-being. The kind of connexion cannot be further determined without the connected *sides* being further determined at the same time. The connexion of ground and consequent, etc., has no longer merely being and nothing as the sides which it connects, but expressly being which is a ground, and something which, although merely posited and not self-subsistent, is yet not the abstract nothing.

Remark 4: Incomprehensibility of the Beginning
What has been said indicates the nature of the dialectic against the beginning of the world and also its end, by which the *eternity* of matter was supposed to be proved, that is, the dialectic against *becoming*, coming-to-be or ceasing-to-be, in general. The Kantian antinomy relative to the finitude or infinity of the world in space and time will be considered more closely under the Notion of quantitative infinity. This simple, ordinary dialectic rests on holding fast to the opposition of being and nothing. It is proved

in the following manner that a beginning of the world, or of anything, is impossible:

It is impossible for anything to begin, either in so far as it is, or in so far as it is not; for in so far as it is, it is not just beginning, and in so far as it is not, then also it does not begin. If the world, or anything, is supposed to have begun, then it must have begun in nothing, but in nothing—or nothing—is no beginning; for a beginning includes within itself a being, but nothing does not contain any being. Nothing is only nothing. In a ground, a cause, and so on, if nothing is so determined, there is contained an affirmation, a being. For the same reason, too, something cannot cease to be; for then being would have to contain nothing, but being is only being, not the contrary of itself.

It is obvious that in this proof nothing is brought forward against becoming, or beginning and ceasing, against this *unity* of being and nothing, except an assertoric denial of them and an ascription of truth to being and nothing, each in separation from the other. Nevertheless this dialectic is at least more consistent than ordinary reflective thought which accepts as perfect truth that being and nothing only *are* in separation from each other, yet on the other hand acknowledges beginning and ceasing to be equally genuine determinations; but in these it does in fact assume the unseparatedness of being and nothing.

With the absolute separateness of being from nothing presupposed, then of course—as we so often hear—beginning or becoming is something *incomprehensible*; for a presupposition is made which annuls the beginning or the becoming which yet is *again* admitted, and this contradiction thus posed and at the same time made impossible of solution, is called *incomprehensible*.

The foregoing dialectic is the same, too, as that which understanding employs the notion of *infinitesimal* magnitudes given by higher analysis. A more detailed treatment of this notion will be given later. These magnitudes have been defined as such that they *are* in their vanishing, not *before* their vanishing, for then they are finite magnitudes, or *after* their vanishing, for then they are nothing. Against this pure notion it is objected and reiterated that such magnitudes are *either* something *or* nothing; that there is no *intermediate state* between being and non-being ('state' is here an unsuitable, barbarous expression). Here too, the absolute separation of being and nothing is assumed. But against this it has been shown that being and nothing are, in fact, the same, or to use the same language as that just quoted, that *there is nothing which is not an intermediate state between being and nothing.* It is to the adoption of the said determination, which understanding opposes, that mathematics owes its most brilliant successes.

This style of reasoning which makes and clings to the false presupposition of the absolute separateness of being and non-being is to be named not dialectic but sophistry. For sophistry is an argument proceeding from a baseless presupposition which is uncritically and unthinkingly adopted; but we call dialectic the higher movement of reason in which such seemingly utterly separate terms pass over into each other spontaneously, through that which they are, a movement in which the presupposition sublates itself. It is the dialectical immanent nature of being and nothing themselves to manifest their unity, that is, becoming, as their truth.

2. MOMENTS OF BECOMING: COMING-TO-BE AND CEASING-TO-BE

Becoming is the unseparatedness of being and nothing, not the unity which abstracts from being and nothing; but as the unity of *being* and *nothing* it is this *determinate* unity in which there *is* both being and nothing. But in so far as being and nothing, each unseparated from its other, *is*, each *is not.* They *are* therefore in this unity but only as vanishing, sublated moments. They sink from their initially imagined *self-subsistence* to the status of *moments*, which are still *distinct* but at the same time are sublated.

Grasped as thus distinguished, each moment is in this *distinguishedness* as a unity with the *other*. Becoming therefore contains being and nothing as *two* such unities, *each* of which is itself a unity of being and nothing; the one is being as immediate and as relation to nothing, and the other is nothing as immediate and as relation to being; the determinations are of unequal values in these unities.

Becoming is in this way in a double determination. In one of them, *nothing* is immediate, that is, the determination starts from nothing which relates itself to being, or in other words changes into it; in the other, *being* is immediate, that is, the determination
D*

starts from being which changes into nothing: the former is coming-to-be and the latter is ceasing-to-be.

Both are the same, *becoming*, and although they differ so in direction they interpenetrate and paralyse each other. The one is *ceasing-to-be*: being passes over into nothing, but nothing is equally the opposite of itself, transition into being, coming-to-be. This coming-to-be is the other direction: nothing passes over into being, but being equally sublates itself and is rather transition into nothing, is ceasing-to-be. They are not reciprocally sublated —the one does not sublate the other externally—but each sublates itself in itself and is in its own self the opposite of itself.

3. SUBLATION OF BECOMING

The resultant equilibrium of coming-to-be and ceasing-to-be is in the first place *becoming* itself. But this equally settles into a stable unity. Being and nothing are in this unity only as vanishing moments; yet becoming as such *is* only through their distinguishedness. Their vanishing, therefore, is the vanishing of becoming or the vanishing of the vanishing itself. Becoming is an unstable unrest which settles into a stable result.

This could also be expressed thus: becoming is the vanishing of being in nothing and of nothing in being and the vanishing of being and nothing generally; but at the same time it rests on the distinction between them. It is therefore inherently self-contradictory, because the determinations it unites within itself are opposed to each other; but such a union destroys itself.

This result is the vanishedness of becoming, but it is not *nothing*; as such it would only be a relapse into one of the already sublated determinations, not the resultant of *nothing and being*. It is the unity of being and nothing which has settled into a stable oneness. But this stable oneness is being, yet no longer as a determination on its own but as a determination of the whole.

Becoming, as this transition into the unity of being and nothing, a unity which is in the form of being or has the form of the one-sided *immediate* unity of these moments, is *determinate being*.

Remark: The Expression 'To Sublate'
To sublate, and the *sublated* (that which exists ideally as a moment), constitute one of the most important notions in philosophy. It is

a fundamental determination which repeatedly occurs throughout the whole of philosophy, the meaning of which is to be clearly grasped and especially distinguished from *nothing*. What is sublated is not thereby reduced to nothing. Nothing is *immediate*; what is sublated, on the other hand, is the result of *mediation*; it is a non-being but as a *result* which had its origin in a being. It still has, therefore, *in itself* the *determinateness from which it originates.*

'*To sublate*' has a twofold meaning in the language: on the one hand it means to preserve, to maintain, and equally it also means to cause to cease, to put an end to. Even 'to preserve' includes a negative element, namely, that something is removed from its immediacy and so from an existence which is open to external influences, in order to preserve it. Thus what is sublated is at the same time preserved; it has only lost its immediacy but is not on that account annihilated. The two definitions of 'to sublate' which we have given can be quoted as two dictionary *meanings* of this word. But it is certainly remarkable to find that a language has come to use one and the same word for two opposite meanings. It is a delight to speculative thought to find in the language words which have in themselves a speculative meaning; the German language has a number of such. The double meaning of the Latin *tollere* (which has become famous through the Ciceronian pun: *tollendum est Octavium*) does not go so far; its affirmative determination signifies only a lifting-up. Something is sublated only in so far as it has entered into unity with its opposite; in this more particular signification as something reflected, it may fittingly be called a *moment*. In the case of the lever, weight and distance from a point are called its mechanical moments on account of the sameness of their effect, in spite of the contrast otherwise between something real, such as a weight, and something ideal, such as a mere spatial determination, a line.[1] We shall often have occasion to notice that the technical language of philosophy employs Latin terms for reflected determinations, either because the mother tongue has no words for them or if it has, as here, because its expression calls to mind more what is immediate, whereas the foreign language suggests more what is reflected.

The more precise meaning and expression which being and nothing receive, now that they are *moments*, is to be ascertained

[1] See *Encycl.* 3rd edition, Section 261, Remark.

from the consideration of determinate being as the unity in which they are preserved. Being is being, and nothing is nothing, only in their contradistinction from each other; but in their truth, in their unity, they have vanished as these determinations and are now something else. Being and nothing are the same; *but just because they are the same they are no longer being and nothing*, but now have a different significance. In becoming they were coming-to-be and ceasing-to-be; in determinate being, a differently determined unity, they are again differently determined moments. This unity now remains their base from which they do not again emerge in the abstract significance of being and nothing.

CHAPTER 2

DETERMINATE BEING

In considering determinate being the emphasis falls on its determinate character; the determinateness is in the form of *being*, and as such it is *quality*. Through its quality, something is determined as opposed to an other, as *alterable* and *finite*; and as negatively determined not only against an other but also in its own self. This its negation as at first opposed to the finite something is the *infinite*; the abstract opposition in which these determinations appear resolves itself into the *infinity* which is free from the opposition, into *being-for-self*.

The treatment of determinate being falls therefore into three parts:

    A. Determinate being as such
    B. Something and other, finitude
    C. Qualitative infinity.

A. DETERMINATE BEING AS SUCH

In determinate being (*a*) *as such*, its determinateness is first of all (*b*) to be distinguished as *quality*. This, however, is to be taken as well in the one determination of determinate being as in the other—as *reality* and *negation*. But in these determinatenesses determinate being is equally reflected into itself; and posited as such it is (*c*) *something*, a determinate being.

(*a*) *Determinate Being in General*

From becoming there issues determinate being, which is the simple oneness of being and nothing. Because of this oneness it has the form of *immediacy*. Its mediation, becoming, lies behind it; it has sublated itself and determinate being appears, therefore, as a first, as a starting-point for the ensuing development. It is first of all in the one-sided determination of *being*; the other determination, *nothing*, will likewise display itself and in contrast to it.

It is not mere being, but determinate being [*Dasein*], etymologically taken, being in a certain *place*; but the idea of space is
irrelevant here. Determinate being as the result of its becoming
is, in general, being with a non-being such that this non-being is
taken up into simple unity with being. *Non-being* thus taken up
into being in such a way that the concrete whole is in the form
of being, of immediacy, constitutes *determinateness* as such.

The *whole* is likewise in the form, that is, in the *determinateness*
of being, for being has likewise shown itself in becoming to be
only a moment—a sublated, negatively determined being; but it
is such *for us in our reflection*, it is not yet *posited* as such in its
own self. But the determinateness as such of determinate being is
the determinateness which is posited, and this is implied in the
expression *Dasein* [*there*-being or being which is *there*]. The two
are always to be clearly distinguished from each other; only that
which is *posited* in a Notion belongs in the dialectical development
of that Notion to its content; whereas the determinateness that is
not yet posited in the Notion itself belongs to our reflection,
whether it concerns the nature of the Notion itself or is an external
comparison. To draw attention to a determinateness of the latter
kind can only serve to elucidate or indicate in advance the course
which will be exhibited in the development itself. That the whole,
the unity of being and nothing, is in the one-sided determinateness
of being is an external reflection; but in the negation, in *something*
and *other* and so on, it will come to be *posited*. It was necessary
here to draw attention to the distinction referred to; but to take
account of all the remarks which may be prompted by reflection
would lead to the prolixity of anticipating what must yield itself
in the subject matter. Such reflections may facilitate a general
view and thereby an understanding of the development, but they
also have the disadvantage of appearing as unjustified assertions,
grounds and foundations for what is to follow. They should
therefore not be taken for more than they are supposed to be and
should be distinguished from what is a moment in the development of the subject matter itself.

Determinate being corresponds to *being* in the previous sphere,
but being is indeterminate and therefore no determinations issue
from it. *Determinate* being, however, is *concrete*; consequently a
number of determinations, distinct relations of its moments, make
their appearance in it.

(b) Quality

Because of the immediacy of the oneness of being and nothing in determinate being, they do not extend beyond each other; so far as determinate being is in the form of being, so far is it non-being, so far is it determinate. Being is not the *universal*, determinateness not the *particular*. Determinateness has not yet severed itself from being; and indeed it will no more sever itself from being, for the truth which from now on underlies them as ground is the unity of non-being with being; on this as ground all further determinations are developed. But the relation in which determinateness here stands to being is the immediate unity of both, so that as yet no differentiation of this unity is posited.

Determinateness thus isolated by itself in the form of *being* is *quality*—which is wholly simple and immediate. *Determinateness* as such is the more universal term which can equally be further determined as quantity and so on. Because of this simple character of quality as such, there is nothing further to be said about it.

Determinate being, however, in which nothing no less than being is contained, is itself the criterion for the one-sidedness of quality as a determinateness which is only *immediate* or only in the form of *being*. It is equally to be posited in the determination of nothing, when it will be posited as a differentiated, reflected determinateness, no longer as immediate or in the form of being. Nothing, as thus the determinate element of a determinateness, is equally something reflected, a *negation*. Quality, taken in the distinct character of *being*, is *reality*; as burdened with a negative it is *negation* in general, likewise a quality but one which counts as a deficiency, and which further on is determined as limit, limitation.

Both are determinate being, but in *reality* as quality with the accent on *being*, the fact is concealed that it contains determinateness and therefore also negation. Consequently, reality is given the value only of something positive from which negation, limitation and deficiency are excluded. Negation taken as mere deficiency would be equivalent to nothing; but it is a *determinate* being, a quality, only determined with a non-being.

Remark: Quality and Negation

Reality may seem to be a word of various meanings because it is used of different, indeed of opposed determinations. In philosophy one may perhaps speak of a *merely empirical* reality as of a worthless existence. But when it is said that thoughts, concepts, theories *have no reality*, this means that they do not possess *actuality*; *in itself* or in its notion, the idea of a Platonic Republic, for example, may well be true. Here the worth of the idea is not denied and it is left its place *alongside* the reality. But as against *mere* ideas, *mere* notions, the real alone counts as true. The sense in which, on the one hand, outer existence is made the criterion of the truth of a content is no less one-sided than when the idea, essential being, or even inner feeling is represented as indifferent to outer existence and is even held to be the more excellent the more remote it is from reality.

In connection with the term 'reality', mention must be made of the former metaphysical concept of God which, in particular, formed the basis of the so-called ontological proof of the existence of God. God was defined as the sum-total of all realities, and of this sum-total it was said that no contradiction was contained in it, that none of the realities cancelled any other; for a reality is to be taken only as a perfection, as an *affirmative* being which contains no negation. Hence the realities are not opposed to one another and do not contradict one another.

Reality as thus conceived is assumed to survive when all negation has been thought away; but to do this is to do away with all determinateness. Reality is quality, determinate being; consequently, it contains the moment of the negative and is through this alone the determinate being that it is. Reality, taken as we are supposed to take it, in the so-called *eminent sense* or as *infinite* —in the usual meaning of the word—is expanded into indeterminateness and loses its meaning. God's goodness is not to be goodness in the ordinary, but in the eminent sense; not different from justice but *tempered* by it (a mediatory expression used by Leibniz), just as, conversely, justice is tempered by goodness; and so goodness is no longer goodness, nor justice any more justice. Power is supposed to be tempered by wisdom, but in that case it is not power as such for it would be subject to wisdom; wisdom is supposed to be expanded into power, in which case it vanishes as the wisdom which determines the end and measure of things. The true Notion of the infinite and its *absolute* unity which will present itself later, is not to be understood as a *tempering*, a *reciprocal restricting* or a *mixing*; such a superficial conception of the relationship leaves it indefinite and nebulous and can satisfy only a Notion-less way of thinking. When reality, taken as a determinate quality as it is in the said definition of God, is extended beyond its determinateness it ceases to be reality and becomes abstract being; God as the *pure* reality in all realities, or as the sum total of all realities, is just as devoid of determinateness and content as the empty absolute in which all is one.

If, on the other hand, reality is taken in its determinateness, then, since it essentially contains the moment of the negative, the sum-total of all realities becomes just as much a sum-total of all negations, the sum-total of all contradictions; it becomes then straightway the absolute *power* in which everything determinate is absorbed; but reality itself *is*, only in so far as it is still confronted by a being which it has not sublated; consequently, when it is thought as expanded into realized, limitless power, it becomes the abstract nothing. The said reality in all realities, the being in all determinate being, which is supposed to express the concept of God, is nothing else than abstract being, which is the same as nothing.

Determinateness is negation posited as affirmative and is the proposition of Spinoza: *omnis determinatio est negatio.* This proposition is infinitely important; only, negation as such is formless abstraction. However, speculative philosophy must not be charged with making negation or nothing an ultimate: negation is as little an ultimate for philosophy as reality is for it truth.

Of this proposition that determinateness is negation, the unity of Spinoza's substance—or that there is only one substance—is the necessary consequence. *Thought* and *being* or extension, the two attributes, namely, which Spinoza had before him, he had of necessity to posit as one in this unity; for as determinate realities they are negations whose infinity is their unity. According to Spinoza's definition, of which more subsequently, the infinity of anything is its affirmation. He grasped them therefore as attributes, that is, as not having a separate existence, a self-subsistent being of their own, but only as sublated, as moments; or rather, since substance in its own self lacks any determination whatever, they are for him not even moments, and the attributes like the modes are distinctions made by an external intellect. Similarly, the substantiality of individuals cannot persist in the face of that proposition. The individual is a relation-to-self through its setting limits to everything else; but these limits are thereby also limits of itself, relations to an other, it does not possess its determinate being within itself. True, the individual is *more* than merely an entity bounded on all sides, but this *more* belongs to another sphere of the Notion; in the metaphysics of being, the individual is simply a determinate something, and in opposition to the independence and self-subsistence of such something, to the finite as such, determinateness effectively brings into play its essentially negative character, dragging what is finite into that same negative movement of the understanding which makes everything vanish in the abstract unity of substance.

Negation stands directly opposed to reality: further on, in the special sphere of reflected determinations, it becomes opposed to the *positive*, which is reality reflecting the negation—the reality in which the negative *has an illusory being* [*scheint*], the negative which in reality as such is still hidden.

Quality is especially a *property* only where, in an *external* relation, it manifests itself as an *immanent* determination. By properties of herbs, for instance, we understand determinations which not only are *proper* to something, but are the means whereby this something in its relations with other somethings *maintains* itself in its own peculiar way, counteracting the alien influences posited in it and making its own determinations *effective* in the other—although it does not keep this at a distance. The more stable determinatenesses, on the other hand, such as figure, shape, are not called properties, nor even qualities perhaps, because they are conceived as alterable, as not identical with the *being* [of the object].

'*Qualierung*' or '*Inqualierung*', an expression of Jacob Boehme's, whose philosophy goes deep, but into a turbid depth, signifies the movement of a quality (of sourness, bitterness, fieriness, etc.) within itself in so far as it posits and establishes itself in its negative nature (in its '*Qual*' or torment) from out of an other —signifies in general the quality's own internal unrest by which it produces and maintains itself only in conflict.

(c) Something

In determinate being its determinateness has been distinguished as quality; in quality as determinately present, there *is* distinction —of reality and negation. Now although these distinctions are

present in determinate being, they are no less equally void and
sublated. Reality itself contains negation, is determinate being,
not indeterminate, abstract being. Similarly, negation is determinate being, not the supposedly abstract nothing but posited
here as it is in itself, as affirmatively present [*als seiend*], belonging
to the sphere of determinate being. Thus quality is completely
unseparated from determinate being, which is simply determinate,
qualitative being.

This sublating of the distinction is more than a mere taking
back and external omission of it again, or than a simple return
to the simple beginning, to determinate being as such. The distinction cannot be omitted, for it *is*. What is, therefore, in fact
present is determinate being in general, distinction in it, and
sublation of this distinction; determinate being, not as devoid of
distinction as at first, but as *again* equal to itself through sublation
of the distinction, the simple oneness of determinate being
resulting from this sublation. This sublatedness of the distinction
is determinate being's *own* determinateness; it is thus *being-within-
self*: determinate being is *a determinate being*, a *something*.

Something is the *first negation of negation*, as simple self-
relation in the form of being. Determinate being, life, thought,
and so on, essentially determine themselves to become a determinate being, a living creature, a thinker (ego) and so on. This
determination is of supreme importance if we are not to remain
at the stage of determinate being, life, thought, and so on—also
the Godhead (instead of God)—as generalities. In our ordinary
way of thinking, *something* is rightly credited with reality. However, something is still a very superficial determination; just as
reality and negation, determinate being and its determinateness,
although no longer blank being and nothing, are still quite abstract
determinations. It is for this reason that they are the most current
expressions and the intellect which is philosophically untrained
uses them most, casts its distinctions in their mould and fancies
that in them it has something really well and truly determined.
The negative of the negative is, as *something*, only the beginning
of the subject [*Subjekt*]—being-within-self, only as yet quite
indeterminate. It determines itself further on, first, as *a being-for-
self* and so on, until in the Notion it first attains the concrete
intensity of the subject. At the base of all these determinations
lies the negative unity with itself. But in all this, care must be

taken to distinguish between the *first* negation as negation *in general*, and the second negation, the negation of the negation: the latter is concrete, *absolute* negativity, just as the former on the contrary is only *abstract* negativity.

Something is the negation of the negation in the form of *being*; for this second negation is the restoring of the simple relation to self; but with this, something is equally *the mediation of itself with itself*. Even in the simple form of *something*, then still more specifically in *being-for-self*, *subject*, and so on, self-mediation is present; it is present even in *becoming*, only the mediation is quite abstract. In *something*, mediation with self is *posited*, in so far as something is determined as a simple identity. Attention can be drawn to the presence of mediation in general, as against the principle of the alleged mere immediacy of knowledge, from which mediation is supposed to be excluded; but there is no further need to draw particular attention to the moment of mediation, for it is to be found everywhere, in every Notion.

This mediation with itself which something is *in itself*, taken only as negation of the negation, has no concrete determinations for its sides; it thus collapses into the simple oneness which is *being*. Something *is*, and *is*, then, also a determinate being; further, it is *in itself* also *becoming*, which, however, no longer has only being and nothing for its moments. One of these, being, is now determinate being, and, further, *a* determinate being. The second is equally a *determinate* being, but determined as a negative of the something—an *other*. Something as a *becoming* is a transition, the moments of which are themselves somethings, so that the transition is *alteration*—a becoming which has already become *concrete*. But to begin with, something alters only in its Notion; it is not yet *posited* as mediating and mediated, but at first only as simply maintaining itself in its self-relation, and its negative is posited as equally qualitative, as only an *other* in general.

B. FINITUDE

(*a*) Something *and* other are at first indifferent to one another; an other is also immediately a determinate being, a something; the negation thus falls outside both. Something is *in itself* as against its *being-for-other*. But the determinateness also belongs to its *in-itself* and is

(b) its *determination*; this equally passes over into *constitution* which, being identical with the determination, constitutes the immanent and at the same time negated being-for-other, the *limit* of the something. This limit is

(c) the immanent determination of the something itself, which latter is thus the *finite*.

In the first section, in which *determinate being* in general was considered, this had, as at first taken up, the determination of *being*. Consequently, the moments of its development, quality and something, equally have an affirmative determination. In this section, on the other hand, the negative determination contained in determinate being is developed, and whereas in the first section it was at first only negation in general, the *first* negation, it is now determined to the point of the *being-within-self* or the *inwardness* of the something, to the negation of the negation.

(a) *Something and an Other*

1. Something and other are, in the first place, both determinate beings or somethings.

Secondly, each is equally an other. It is immaterial which is first named and solely for that reason called *something*; (in Latin, when they both occur in a sentence, both are called *aliud*, or 'the one, the other', *alius alium*; when there is reciprocity the expression *alter alterum* is analogous). If of two things we call one A, and the other B, then in the first instance B is determined as the other. But A is just as much the other of B. Both are, in the same way, *others*. The word 'this' serves to fix the distinction and the something which is to be taken affirmatively. But 'this' clearly expresses that this distinguishing and signalizing of the one something is a subjective designating falling outside the something itself. The entire determinateness falls into this external pointing out; even the expression 'this' contains no distinction; each and every something is just as well a 'this' as it is also an other. By 'this' we *mean* to express something completely determined; it is overlooked that speech, as a work of the understanding, gives expression only to universals, except in the *name* of a single object; but the individual name is meaningless, in the sense that it does not express a universal, and for the same reason appears as something merely posited and arbitrary; just as proper names, too, can be arbitrarily assumed, given or also altered.

Otherness thus appears as a determination alien to the determinate being thus characterized, or as the other *outside* the one
determinate being; partly because a determinate being is determined as other only through being *compared* by a Third, and
partly because it is only determined as other on account of the
other which is outside it, but is not an other on its own account.
At the same time, as has been remarked, every determinate being,
even for ordinary thinking, determines itself as an other, so that
there is no determinate being which is determined only as such,
which is not outside a determinate being and therefore is not
itself an other.

Both are determined equally as something and as other, and
are thus the same, and there is so far no distinction between them.
But this self-sameness of the determinations likewise arises only
from external reflection, from the *comparing* of them; but the
other as at first posited, although an other in relation to the
something, is nevertheless also an other on its own account, apart
from the something.

Thirdly, therefore, the other is to be taken as isolated, as in
relation to itself, *abstractly* as the *other*; the τὸ ἕτερον of Plato,
who opposes it as one of the moments of totality to the One, and
in this way ascribes to the other a *nature* of its own. Thus the
other, taken solely as such, is not the other of something but the
other in its own self, that is, the other of itself. Such an other,
determined as other, is physical nature; it is the other of spirit.
This its determination is thus at first a mere relativity by which is
expressed, not a quality of nature itself, but only a relation external
to it. However, since spirit is the true something and nature,
consequently, in its own self is only what it is as contrasted with
spirit, the quality of nature taken as such is just this, to be the
other in its own self, that which is *external to itself* (in the determinations of space, time and matter).

The other simply by itself is the other in its own self, hence
the other of itself and so the other of the other—it is, therefore,
that which is absolutely dissimilar within itself, that which negates
itself, *alters* itself. But in so doing it remains identical with itself,
for that into which it alters is the other, and this is its sole determination; but what is altered is not determined in any different
way but in the same way, namely, to be an other; in this latter,
therefore, it only unites with its own self. It is thus posited as

reflected into itself with sublation of the otherness, as a self-identical something from which, consequently, the otherness, which is at the same time a moment of it, is distinct from it and does not appertain to the something itself.

2. Something *preserves* itself in the negative of its determinate being [*Nichtdasein*]; it is essentially *one* with it and essentially *not one* with it. It stands, therefore, in a *relation* to its otherness and is not simply its otherness. The otherness is at once contained in it and also still *separate* from it; it is a *being-for-other*.

Determinate being as such is immediate, without relation to an other; or, it is in the determination of *being*; but as including within itself non-being, it is *determinate* being, being negated within itself, and then in the first instance an other—but since at the same time it also preserves itself in its negation, it is only a *being-for-other*.

It preserves itself in the negative of its determinate being and is being, but not being in general, but as self-related in *opposition* to its relation to other, as self-equal in opposition to its inequality. Such a being is *being-in-itself*.

Being-for-other and being-in-itself constitute the two moments of the something. There are here present *two pairs* of determinations: 1. Something and other, 2. Being-for-other and being-in-itself. The former contain the unrelatedness of their determinateness; something and other fall apart. But their truth is their relation; being-for-other and being-in-itself are, therefore, the above determinations posited as *moments* of one and the same something, as determinations which are relations and which remain in their unity, in the unity of determinate being. Each, therefore, at the same time, also contains within itself its other moment which is distinguished from it.

Being and nothing in their unity, which is determinate being, are no longer being and nothing—these they are only outside their unity—thus in their unstable unity, in becoming, they are coming-to-be and ceasing-to-be. The being in something is *being-in-itself*. Being, which is self-relation, equality with self, is now no longer immediate, but is only as the non-being of otherness (as determinate being reflected into itself). Similarly, non-being as a moment of something is, in this unity of being and non-being, not negative determinate being in general, but an other, and more specifically—seeing that being is differentiated from it—at the same time a *relation* to its negative determinate being, a being-for-other.

Hence being-in-itself is, first, a negative relation to the negative determinate being, it has the otherness outside it and is opposed to it; in so far as something is *in itself* it is withdrawn from otherness and being-for-other. But secondly it has also present in it non-being itself, for it is itself the *non-being* of being-for-other.

But being-for-other is, first, a negation of the simple relation of being to itself which, in the first instance, is supposed to be determinate being and something; in so far as something is in an other or is for an other, it lacks a being of its own. But secondly it is not negative determinate being as pure nothing; it is negative determinate being which points to being-in-itself as to its own being which is reflected into itself, just as, conversely, being-in-itself points to being-for-other.

3. Both moments are determinations of what is one and the same, namely, the something. Something is *in itself* in so far as it has returned into itself out of the being-for-other. But something also has *in itself* (here the accent falls on *in*) or *within it*, a determination or circumstance in so far as this circumstance is outwardly *in it*, is a being-for-other.

This leads to a further determination. Being-in-itself and being-for-other are, in the first instance, distinct; but that something also has *within it* the same character that it is *in itself*, and, conversely, that what it is as being-for-other it also is in itself—this is the identity of being-in-itself and being-for-other, in accordance with the determination that the something itself is one and the same something of both moments, which, therefore, are undividedly present in it. This identity is already formally given in the sphere of determinate being, but more expressly in the consideration of *essence* and of the relation of *inner* and *outer*, and most precisely in the consideration of the Idea as the unity of the Notion and *actuality*. People fancy that they are saying something lofty with the expression 'in itself', as they do in saying 'the inner'; but what something is *only in itself*, is also *only* in *it*; 'in itself' is only an abstract, and so even external determination. The expressions: there is nothing *in it*, or, there is something *in it*, imply, though somewhat obscurely, that what is *in* a thing also belongs to the thing's *being-in-itself*, to its inner, true worth.

It may be observed that the meaning of the *thing-in-itself* is here revealed; it is a very simple abstraction but for some while it counted as a very important determination, something superior, as it were, just as the proposition that we do not know what things are in themselves ranked as a profound piece of wisdom. Things are called 'in themselves' in so far as abstraction is made from all being-for-other, which means simply, in so far as they are thought devoid of all determination, as nothings. In this sense, it is of course impossible to know *what* the *thing-in-itself* is. For the question: *what?* demands that *determinations* be assigned; but since the things of which they are to be assigned are at the same time supposed to be *things in-themselves*, which means, in effect, to be without any determination, the question is thoughtlessly made impossible to answer, or else only an absurd answer is given. The thing-in-itself is the same as that *absolute* of which we know nothing except that in it all is one. What is *in* these things-in-themselves, therefore, we know quite well; they are as such nothing but truthless, empty abstractions. What, however, the thing-in-itself is in truth, what truly is in itself, of this logic is the exposition, in which however something better than an abstraction is understood by 'in-itself', namely, what something is in its Notion; but the Notion is concrete within itself, is comprehensible simply as Notion, and as determined within itself and the connected whole of its determinations, is cognizable.

Being-in-itself, in the first instance, has being-for-other as its contrasted moment; but *positedness*, too, is contrasted with it. This expression, it is true, includes also being-for-other, but it specifically contains the already accomplished bending back of that which is not *in itself* into that which is its being-in-itself, in which it is *positive*. Being-in-itself is generally to be taken as an abstract way of expressing the Notion; *positing*, properly speaking, first occurs in the sphere of *essence*, of objective reflection; the *ground posits* that which is grounded by it; still more, the *cause produces* or *brings forth* an *effect*, a determinate being whose self-subsistence is *immediately* negated and which carries the meaning of having its matter [*Sache*], its being, in an other. In the sphere of being, determinate being only *proceeds* from *becoming*, or, with the something an other is posited, with the finite, the infinite; but the finite does not bring forth the infinite, does not *posit* it. In the sphere of being, the *self-determining* even of the Notion is at first only *in itself* or *implicit*—as such it is called a transition; and the reflected determinations of being such as something and other, or finite and infinite, although they essentially refer to each other or are as a being-for-other, they too count as *qualitative*, as existing on their own account; the other *is*, the finite ranks equally with the infinite as an immediate, affirmative being, standing fast on its own account; the meaning of each appears to be complete even without its other. On the other hand positive and negative, cause and effect, however much they may be taken as isolated from each other, are at the same time meaningless one without the other. There is *present in them* their showing or reflection in each other, the showing or reflection in each of its other. In the different spheres of determination and especially in the progress of the exposition, or more precisely in the progress of the Notion towards the exposition of itself, it is of capital importance always clearly to distinguish what is still *in itself* and what is *posited*, the determinations as they are in the Notion, and as they are as posited, or as being-for-other. This is a distinction which belongs only to the dialectical development and which is unknown to metaphysical philosophizing, which also includes the critical philosophy; the definitions of metaphysics, like its presuppositions, distinctions and conclusions, seek to assert and produce only what comes under the category of *being*, and that, too, of *being-in-itself*.

Being-for-other is, in the unity of the something with itself, identical with its *in-itself*; the being-for-other is thus present *in* the something. The determinateness thus reflected into itself is, therefore, again in the simple form of *being*, and hence is again a quality: *determination*.

(b) Determination, Constitution and Limit

The *in-itself* into which something is reflected into itself out of its being-for-other is no longer an abstract in-itself, but as negation of its being-for-other is mediated by the latter, which is thus its moment. It is not only the immediate identity of the something with itself, but the identity through which there is present *in* the the something that which it is *in itself*; being-for-other is present *in it* because the *in-itself* is the sublation of the being-for-other, has returned *out of* the being-for-other into itself; but equally, too, simply because it is abstract and therefore essentially burdened with negation, with being-for-other. There is present here not only quality and reality, determinateness in the form of simple being, but determinateness in the form of the *in-itself*; and the development consists in *positing* this determinateness as reflected into itself.

1. The quality which is constituted by the essential unity of the in-itself in the simple something with its other moment, the *presence in it* of its being-for-other, can be called the *determination* of the in-itself, in so far as this word in its exact meaning is distinguished from *determinateness* in general. Determination is affirmative determinateness as the in-itself with which something in its determinate being remains congruous in face of its entanglement with the other by which it might be determined, maintaining itself in its self-equality, and making its determination hold good in its being-for-other. Something *fulfils* its determination in so far as the further determinateness which at once develops in various directions through something's relation to other, is congruous with the in-itself of the something, becomes its filling. Determination implies that what something is *in itself*, is also *present in* it.

The *determination* of man is thinking reason; thought in general, thought as such, in his simple *determinateness*—by it he is distinguished from the brute; *in himself* he is thought, in so far as this is also distinguished from his being-for-other, from his own natural existence and sense-nature through which he is directly connected with his other. But thought is also present *in* him; man himself is thought, he actually exists as thinking, it is his concrete existence and actuality; and, further, since thought is in his determinate being and his determinate being is in thought, it is to be taken as *concrete*, as having content and filling; it is thinking reason and as such the *determination* of man. But even this determination again is only *in itself* as something which *ought* to be, that is it, together with the filling which is incorporated in its in-itself, is in the form of the in-itself in general, *in contrast to* the determinate being not incorporated in it, which at the same time still confronts it externally as immediate sense-nature and nature.

2. The filling of the in-itself with determinateness is also distinct from the determinateness which is only being-for-other and remains outside the determination. For in the sphere of quality, the differences in their sublated form as moments also retain the form of immediate, qualitative being relatively to one another.

That which something has *in it*, thus divides itself and is from this side an external determinate being of the something, which is also *its* determinate being, but does not belong to the something's in-itself. The determinateness is thus a *constitution*.

Constituted in this or that way, something is involved in external influences and relationships. This external connection on which the constitution depends, and the circumstance of being determined by an other, appears as something contingent. But it is the quality of something to be open to external influences and to have a *constitution*.

In so far as something alters, the alteration falls within its constitution; it is that *in* the something which becomes an other. The something itself preserves itself in the alteration which affects only this unstable surface of its otherness, not its determination.

Determination and constitution are thus distinguished from each other; something, in accordance with its determination, is indifferent to its constitution. But that which something has *in it*, is the middle term connecting them in this syllogism. Or, rather, the *being-in-the-something* showed itself as falling apart into these two extremes. The simple middle term is *determinateness* as such; to its identity belongs both determination and constitution. But determination spontaneously passes over into constitution, and the latter into the former. This is implied in what has been said already; the connection is more precisely this: in so far as that which something is *in itself* is also present *in it*, it is burdened with being-for-other; hence the determination is, as such, open to relationship to other. The determinateness is at the same time a moment, but contains at the same time the qualitative distinction of being different from the in-itself, of being the negative of the something, another determinate being. The determinateness which thus holds the other within it, being united with the in-itself, brings the otherness into the latter or into the determination, which, consequently, is reduced to constitution. Conversely, being-for-other isolated as constitution and posited by itself, is in its own self the same as the other as such, the other in its own self, that is, the other of itself; but thus it is *self-related* determinate being, the in-itself with a determinateness, and therefore a *determination*. Consequently, in so far as determination and constitution are also to be held apart, the latter, which appears to be grounded in something external, in an other in general, also *depends* on the former, and the determining from outside is at the same time determined by the something's own, immanent determination. But further, the constitution belongs to that which the something is in itself; something alters with its constitution.

This alteration of something is no longer the first alteration of something merely in accordance with its being-for-other; the first was only an implicit (*an sich seiende*) alteration belonging to the inner Notion; now alteration is also *posited* in the something. The something itself is further determined and the negation is posited as immanent in it, as its developed *being-within-self*.

In the first place, the transition of determination and constitution into each other is the sublation of their difference, resulting in the positing of determinate being or something in general; and since this latter results from that difference which equally includes within it qualitative otherness, there are *two* somethings which, however, are not opposed to each other only as others in general— for in that case this negation would still be abstract and would arise only from *comparing* them. But the negation is now *immanent* in the somethings. As *determinate beings* they are indifferent to each other, but this their affirmation is no longer immediate, each relates itself to itself only *by means of* the sublation of the otherness which, in the determination, is reflected into the in-itself.

Thus something *through its own nature* relates itself to the other, because otherness is posited in it as its own moment; its being-within-self includes the negation within it, by means of which alone it now has its affirmative determinate being. But the other is also qualitatively distinguished from this and is thus posited outside the something. The negation of its other is now[1] the quality of the something, for it is as this sublating of its other that it is something. It is only in this sublation that the other is really opposed to another determinate being; the other is only externally opposed to the *first* something, or rather, since in fact they are *directly* connected, that is in their Notion, their connection is this, that determinate being has *passed over* into otherness, something into other, and something is just as much an other as the other itself is. Now in so far as the being-within-self is the non-being of the otherness which is contained in it but which at the same time has a distinct being of its own, the some-

---

[1] Reading *nun* for *nur*.

thing is itself the negation, *the ceasing of an other in it*; it is posited as relating itself negatively to the other and in so doing preserving itself; this other, the being-within-self of the something as negation of the negation, is its *in-itself*, and at the same time this sublation is *present in it* as a simple negation, namely, as its negation of the other something external to it. There is a *single* determinateness of both, which on the one hand is identical with the being-within-self of the somethings as negation of the negation, and on the other hand, since these negations are opposed to one another as other somethings, conjoins and equally disjoins them through their own nature, each negating the other: this determinateness is *limit*.

3. Being-for-other is the indeterminate, affirmative community of something with its other; in the limit the *non-being*-for-other becomes prominent, the qualitative negation of the other, which is thereby kept apart from the something which is reflected into itself. We must observe the development of this Notion, which manifests itself, however, rather as an entanglement and a contradiction. This contradiction is at once to be found in the circumstance that the limit, as something's negation reflected into itself, contains *ideally* in it the moments of something and other, and these, as distinguished moments, are at the same time posited in the sphere of determinate being as really, *qualitatively distinct*.

(α) Something, therefore, is immediate, self-related determinate being, and has a limit, in the first place, relatively to an other; the limit is the non-being of the other, not of the something itself: in the limit, something limits its other. But the other is itself a something in general, therefore the limit which something has relatively to the other is also the limit of the other as a something, its limit whereby it keeps the first something as *its* other apart from it, or is a *non-being of that something*; it is thus not only non-being of the other, but non-being equally of the one and of the other something, consequently of the something as such.

But the limit is essentially equally the non-being of the other, and so something at the same time *is* through its limit. It is true that something, in limiting the other, is subjected to being limited itself; but at the same time its limit is, as the ceasing of the other in it, itself only the being of the something; *through the limit something is what it is, and in the limit it has its quality*. This relationship is the outward manifestation of the fact that the limit is simple negation or the *first* negation, whereas the other is, at the same time, the negation of the negation, the being-within-self of the something.

Something, as an immediate determinate being, is, therefore, the limit relatively to another something, but the limit is present in the something itself, which is a something through the mediation of the limit which is just as much the non-being of the something. Limit is the mediation through which something and other each as well *is*, as *is not*.

(*β*) Now in so far as something in its limit both *is* and *is not*, and these moments are an immediate, qualitative difference, the negative determinate being and the determinate being of the something fall outside each other. Something has its determinate being *outside* (or, as it is also put, on the *inside*) of its limit; similarly, the other, too, because it is a something, is outside it. Limit is the *middle between* the two of them in which they cease. They have their determinate being *beyond* each other and *beyond* their limit; the limit as the non-being of each is the other of both.

It is in accordance with this difference of something from its limit that the line appears as line only outside its limit, the point; the plane as plane outside the line; the solid as solid only outside its limiting surface. It is primarily this aspect of limit which is seized by pictorial thought—the self-externality of the Notion—and especially, too, in reference to spatial objects.

(*γ*) But further, something as it is outside the limit, the unlimited something, is only a determinate being in general. As such, it is not distinguished from its other; it is only determinate being and therefore has the same determination as its other; each is only a something in general, or each is an other; thus both are the *same*. But this their primarily immediate determinate being is now posited with the determinateness as limit, in which both are what they are, distinguished from each other. Limit is, however, equally their *common* distinguishedness, their unity and distinguishedness, like determinate being. This double identity of both, of determinate being and limit, contains this: that something has its determinate being only in the limit, and that since the limit and the determinate being are each at the same time the negative of each other, the something, which *is* only in its limit, just as much separates itself from itself and points beyond itself to its non-being, declaring this is to be its being and thus passing

over into it. To apply this to the preceding example and taking
first the determination that something is what it is only in its
limit: as thus determined, the point is therefore the limit of the
line, not merely in the sense that the line only ceases in the point,
and as a determinate being is outside it; neither is the line the
limit of the plane merely in the sense that the plane only ceases
in it—and similarly with surface as limit of the solid; on the
contrary, in the point the line also *begins*; the point is its absolute
beginning. Even when the line is represented as unlimited on
either side, or, as it is put, is produced to infinity, the point still
constitutes its *element*, just as the line is the element of the plane,
and the surface that of the solid. These limits are the *principle*
of that which they limit; just as one, for example as hundredth,
is the limit, but also the element, of the whole hundred.

The other determination is the unrest of the something in its
limit in which it is immanent, an unrest which is the *contradiction*
which impels the something out beyond itself. Thus the point is
this dialectic of its own self to become a line, the line the dialectic
to become a plane, and the plane the dialectic to become total
space. A second definition is given of line, plane and total space:
namely, that the line originates through the *movement* of the point,
the plane through the movement of the line, and so on. But this
movement of the point, line and so on, is regarded as something
contingent or as only thus imagined. This point of view is, however, really retracted in so far as the determinations from which
the line and so on are supposed to originate are their elements
and principles which, at the same time, are nothing else but their
limits; and so the origin is not considered as contingent or as
only thus imagined. That point, line and plane by themselves are
self-contradictory, are *beginnings* which spontaneously repel themselves from themselves, so that the point, through its Notion,
passes out of itself into the line, *moves in itself* and gives rise to the
line, and so on, lies in the Notion of limit which is immanent in
the something. The application itself, however, belongs to the
consideration of space; to give an indication of it here, the point
is the wholly abstract limit, *but in a determinate being*; this is taken
as still wholly abstract, it is so-called absolute, that is, abstract
space, a purely continuous asunderness. But the limit is not
abstract negation, but is *in this determinate being*, is a *spatial*
determinateness; the point is, therefore, spatial, the contradiction

of abstract negation and continuity, and is, therefore, the transition, the accomplished transition into the line, and so on; just as also, for the same reason, *there is* no such thing as a point, line or plane.

Something with its immanent limit, posited as the contradiction of itself, through which it is directed and forced out of and beyond itself, is the *finite*.

(c) Finitude

The being of something is determinate; something has a quality and in it is not only determined but limited; its quality is its limit and, burdened with this, it remains in the first place an affirmative, stable being. But the development of this negation, so that the opposition between its determinate being and the negation as its immanent limit, is itself the being-within-self of the something, which is thus in its own self only a becoming, constitutes the finitude of something.

When we say of things that *they are finite*, we understand thereby that they not only have a determinateness, that their quality is not only a reality and an intrinsic determination, that finite things are not merely limited—as such they still have determinate being outside their limit—but that, on the contrary, non-being constitutes their nature and being. Finite things *are*, but their relation to themselves is that they are *negatively* self-related and in this very self-relation send themselves away beyond themselves, beyond their being. They *are*, but the truth of this being is their *end*. The finite not only alters, like something in general, but it *ceases to be*; and its ceasing to be is not merely a possibility, so that it could be without ceasing to be, but the being as such of finite things is to have the germ of decease as their being-within-self: the hour of their birth is the hour of their death.

(α) The Immediacy of Finitude

The thought of the finitude of things brings this sadness with it because it is qualitative negation pushed to its extreme, and in the singleness of such determination there is no longer left to things an affirmative being *distinct* from their destiny to perish. Because of this qualitative singleness of the negation, which has gone back to the abstract opposition of nothing and ceasing-to-be as opposed to being, finitude is the most stubborn category of the understanding; negation in general, constitution and limit,

E

reconcile themselves with their other, with determinate being; and even nothing, taken abstractly as such, is given up as an abstraction; but finitude is the negation as *fixed in itself*, and it therefore stands in abrupt contrast to its affirmative. The finite, it is true, lest itself be brought into flux, it is itself this, to be determined or destined to its end, but *only* to its end—or rather, it is the refusal to let itself be brought affirmatively to its affirmative, to the infinite, and to let itself be united with it; it is therefore posited as inseparable from its nothing, and is thereby cut off from all reconciliation with its other, the affirmative. The determination or destiny of finite things takes them no further than their *end*. The understanding persists in this sadness of finitude by making non-being the determination of things and at the same time making it *imperishable* and *absolute*. Their transitoriness could only pass away or perish in their other, in the affirmative; their finitude would then be parted from them; but it is their unalterable quality, that is, their quality which does not pass over into its other, that is, into its affirmative; *it is thus eternal*.

This is a very important consideration; but certainly no philosophy or opinion, or understanding, will let itself be tied to the standpoint that the finite is absolute; the very opposite is expressly present in the assertion of the finite; the finite is limited, transitory, it is *only* finite, not imperishable; this is directly implied in its determination and expression. But the point is, whether in thinking of the finite one holds fast to the *being* of finitude and lets the *transitoriness* continue to be, or whether the *transitoriness* and the *ceasing-to-be cease to be*. But it is precisely in that view of the finite which makes *ceasing-to-be* the *final* determination of the finite, that this does not happen. It is the express assertion that the finite is irreconcilable with the infinite and cannot be united with it, that the finite is utterly opposed to the infinite. Being, absolute being, is ascribed to the infinite; confronting it, the finite thus remains held fast as its negative; incapable of union with the infinite, it remains absolute on its own side; from the affirmative, from the infinite, it would receive affirmation, and would thus cease to be; but a union with the infinite is just what is declared to be impossible. If it is not to remain fixed in its opposition to the infinite but is to cease to be, then, as we have already said, just this ceasing-to-be is its final determination, not the affirmative which would be only the ceasing to be of the ceasing-to-be. If, however, the finite is not to pass way in the affirmative, but its end is to be grasped as the *nothing*, then we should be back again at that first, abstract nothing which itself has long since passed away.

With this nothing, however, which is supposed to be *only* nothing, and which at the same time is granted an existence in thought, imagination or speech, there occurs the same contradiction as has just been indicated in connection with the finite, but with this difference, that in the case of that first nothing it only *occurs*, whereas in finitude it is *explicitly stated*. There it appears as subjective; here it is asserted that the finite *stands perpetually* opposed to the infinite, that what is in itself null *is*, and is *as* in itself null. We have to become conscious of this; and the development of the finite shows that, having this contradiction present within it, it collapses within itself, yet in doing so actually resolves the contradiction, that not only is the finite transitory and ceases to be, but that the ceasing-to-be, the nothing, is not the final determination, but itself ceases to be.

(β) *Limitation and the Ought*

This contradiction is, indeed, abstractly present simply in the circumstance that the *something* is finite, or that the finite is. But *something* or being is no longer abstractly posited but reflected into itself and developed as being-within-self which possesses a determination and a constitution, and, still more specifically, a limit which, as immanent in the something and constituting the quality of its being-within-self, is finitude. It is to be seen what moment are contained in this Notion of the finite something.

Determination and constitution showed themselves as *sides* for external reflection; but the former already contained otherness as belonging to the something's *in-itself*; the externality of the otherness is on the one hand in the something's own inwardness, on the other hand it remains, as externality, distinguished from it, it is still externality as such, but present *in* the something. But further, since the otherness is determined as *limit*, as itself negation of the negation, the otherness immanent in the something is posited as the connection of the two sides, and the unity with itself of the something which possesses both determination and constitution, is its relation turned towards its own self, the relation of its *implicit* determination to the limit immanent in the something, a relation in which this immanent limit is negated. The self-identical being-within-self thus relates itself to itself as its own non-being, but as negation of the negation, as negating the non-being which at the same time retains in it determinate being, for determinate being is the quality of its being-within-self. Something's own limit thus posited by it as a negative which is at the same time essential, is not merely limit as such, but *limitation*. But what is posited as negated is not limitation alone; the negation is two-edged, since what is posited by it as negated is the *limit*, and this is in general what is common to both something and other, and is also a determinateness of the *in-itself* of the determination as such. This *in-itself*, therefore, as the negative relation to its limit (which is also distinguished from it), to itself as limitation, is the *ought*.

In order that the limit which is in something as such should be a limitation, something must at the same time in its own self transcend the limit, it must in its own self *be related to the limit as to something which is not*. The determinate being of something lies inertly indifferent, as it were, *alongside* its limit. But something only transcends its limit in so far as it is the accomplished sublation of the limit, is the *in-itself* as negatively related to it. And since the limit is in the *determination* itself as a limitation, something transcends *its own self*.

The ought therefore contains the determination in double form: once as the *implicit* determination counter to the negation, and again as a non-being which, as a limitation, is distinguished from the determination, but is at the same time itself an implicit determination.

The finite has thus determined itself as the relation of its determination to its limit; in this relation, the determination is an ought and the limit is a *limitation*. Both are thus moments of the finite and hence are themselves finite, both the ought and the limitation. But only the limitation is *posited* as finite; the ought is limited only in itself, that is, for us. It is limited through its relation to the limit which is already immanent in the ought itself, but this its restriction is enveloped in the in-itself, for, in accordance with its determinate being, that is, its determinateness relatively to the limitation, it is posited as the in-itself.

What ought to be *is*, and at the same time *is not*. If it *were*, we could not say that it *ought* merely *to be*. The ought has, therefore, essentially a limitation. This limitation is not alien to it; that which *only* ought to be is the *determination*, which is now posited as it is in fact, namely, as at the same time only a determinateness.

The being-in-itself of the something in its determination reduces itself therefore to an *ought-to-be* through the fact that the same thing which constitutes its in-itself is in one and the same respect a *non-being*; and that, too, in this way, that in the being-within-self, in the negation of the negation, this in-itself as one of the negations (the one that negates) is a unity with the other, which at the same time is a qualitatively distinct limit, through which this unity is a *relation* to it. The limitation of the finite is not something external to it; on the contrary, its own determination is also its limitation; and this latter is both itself and also the ought-to-be; it is that which is common to both, or rather that in which both are identical.

But now further, the finite as the ought *transcends* its limitation; the same determinateness which is its negation is also sublated, and is thus its in-itself; its limit is also not its limit.

Hence as the *ought*, something is *raised above its limitation*, but conversely, it is only as the *ought* that it has its *limitation*. The two are inseparable. Something has a limitation in so far as it has negation in its determination, and the determination is also the accomplished sublation of the limitation.

Remark: The Ought

The ought has recently played a great part in philosophy, especially in connection with morality and also in metaphysics generally, as the ultimate and absolute concept of the identity of the in-itself or *self*-relation, and of the *determinateness* or limit.

'You can, because you ought'—this expression, which is supposed to mean a great deal, is implied in the notion of ought. For the ought implies that one is superior to the limitation; in it the limit is sublated and the in-itself of the ought is thus an identical self-relation, and hence the abstraction of 'can'. But conversely, it is equally correct that: 'you cannot, just because you ought.' For in the ought, the limitation as limitation is equally implied; the said formalism of possibility has, in the limitation, a reality, a qualitative otherness opposed to it and the relation of each to the other is a contradiction, and thus a 'cannot', or rather an impossibility.

In the ought the transcendence of finitude, that is, infinity, begins. The ought is that which, in the further development, exhibits itself in accordance with the said impossibility as the progress to infinity.

With respect to the form of the *limitation* and the *ought*, two prejudices can be criticized in more detail. First of all, great stress is laid on the limitations of thought, of reason, and so on, and it is asserted that the limitation *cannot* be transcended. To make such an assertion is to be unaware that the very fact that something is determined as a limitation implies that the limitation is already transcended. For a determinateness, a limit, is determined as a limitation only in opposition to its other in general, that is, in opposition to that which is *free from the limitation*; the other of a limitation is precisely the *being beyond* it. Stone and metal do not transcend their limitation because this is not a limitation *for them*. If, however, in the case of such general propositions framed by the understanding, such as that limitation cannot be transcended, thought will not apply itself to finding out what is implied in the Notion, then it can be directed to the world of actuality where such proportions show themselves to be completely unreal. Just because thought is *supposed* to be superior to actuality, to dwell apart from it in higher regions and therefore to be itself determined as an *ought-to-be*, on the one hand, it does not advance to the Notion, and, on the other hand, it stands in just as untrue a relation to actuality as it does to the Notion. Because the stone does not think, does not even feel, its limitedness is not a limitation *for it*, that is, is not a negation in it for sensation, imagination, thought, etc., which it does not possess. But even the stone, as a something, contains the distinction of its determination or in-itself and its determinate being, and to that extent it, too, transcends its limitation; the Notion which is implicit in it contains the identity of the stone with its other. If it is a base capable of being acted on by an acid, then it can be oxidized, and neutralized, and so on. In oxidation, neutralization and so on, it overcomes its limitation of existing only as a base; it transcends it, and similarly the acid overcomes its limitation of being an acid. This ought, the obligation to transcend limitations, is present in both acid and caustic base in such a degree that it is only by force that they can be kept fixed as (waterless, that is, purely non-neutral) acid and caustic base.

If, however, an existence contains the Notion not merely as an abstract in-itself, but as an explicit, self-determined totality, as instinct, life, ideation, etc., then in its own strength it overcomes the limitation and attains a being beyond it. The plant transcends the limitation of being a seed, similarly, of being blossom, fruit, leaf; the seed becomes the developed plant, the blossom fades away, and so on. The sentient creature, in the limitation of hunger, thirst, etc., is the urge to overcome this limitation and it does overcome it. It feels *pain*, and it is the privilege of the sentient nature to feel pain; it is a negation in its *self*, and the negation is determined as a *limitation* in its feeling, just because the sentient creature has the feeling of its *self*, which is the totality that transcends this determinateness. If it were not above and beyond the determinateness, it would not feel it as its negation and would feel no pain. But it is reason, thought, which is supposed to be unable to transcend limitation—reason, which is the *universal* explicitly beyond particularity *as such* (that is, *all* particularity), which is nothing but the overcoming of limitation! Granted, not every instance of transcending and being beyond limitation is a genuine liberation from it, a veritable affirmation; even the ought itself, and abstraction in general, is an imperfect transcending. However, the reference to the wholly abstract universal is a sufficient reply to the equally abstract assertion that limitation cannot be transcended, or, again, even the reference to the infinite in general is a sufficient refutation of the assertion that the finite cannot be transcended.

In this connection we may mention a seemingly ingenious fancy of Leibniz: that if a magnet possessed consciousness it would regard its pointing to the north as a determination of its will, as a law of its freedom. On the contrary, if it possessed consciousness and consequently will and freedom, it would be a thinking being. Consequently, space for it would be *universal*, embracing *every* direction, so that the single direction to the north would be rather a limitation on its freedom, just as much as being fixed to one spot would be a limitation for a man although not for a plant.

On the other hand, the ought is the transcending, but still only *finite transcending*, of the limitation. Therefore, it has its place and its validity in the sphere of finitude where it holds fast to being-in-itself in opposition to limitedness, declaring the former to be the regulative and essential factor relatively to what is null. Duty is an ought directed against the particular will, against self-seeking desire and capricious interest and it is held up as an ought to the will in so far as this has the capacity to isolate itself from the true. Those who attach such importance to the ought of morality and fancy that morality is destroyed if the ought is not recognized as ultimate truth, and those too who, reasoning from the level of the understanding, derive a perpetual satisfaction from being able to confront everything there is with an ought, that is, with a 'knowing better'—and for that very reason are just as loth to be robbed of the ought—do not see that as regards the finitude of their sphere the ought receives full recognition. But in the world of actuality itself, Reason and Law are not in such a bad way that they only *ought* to be—it is only the abstraction of the in-itself that stops at this—any more than the ought is in its own self perennial and, what is the same thing, that finitude is absolute. The philosophy of Kant and Fichte sets up the ought as the highest point of the resolution of the contradictions of Reason; but the truth is that the ought is only the standpoint which clings to finitude and thus to contradiction.

(γ) *Transition of the Finite into the Infinite*

The ought as such contains limitation, and limitation contains the ought. Their relation to each other is the finite itself which contains them both in its being-within-self. These moments of its determination are qualitatively opposed; limitation is determined as the negative of the ought and the ought likewise as the negative of limitation. The finite is thus inwardly self-contradictory; it sublates itself, ceases to be. But this its result, the negative as such, is (α) its very *determination*; for it is the negative of the negative. Thus, in ceasing to be, the finite has not ceased to be; it has become in the first instance only *another* finite which, however, is equally a ceasing-to-be as transition into another finite, and so on to *infinity*. But (β) closer consideration of this result shows that the finite in its ceasing-to-be, in this negation of itself has attained its being-in-itself, is *united with itself*. Each of its moments contains precisely this result; the ought transcends the limitation, that is, transcends itself; but beyond itself or its other, is only the limitation itself. The limitation, however, points directly beyond itself to its other, which is the ought; but this latter is the same duality of *being-in-itself* and *determinate being* as the limitation; it is the same thing; in going beyond itself, therefore, it equally only unites with itself. This *identity with itself*, the negation of negation, is affirmative being and thus the other of the finite, of the finite which is supposed to have the first negation for its determinateness; this other is the *infinite*.

C. INFINITY

The infinite in its simple Notion can, in the first place, be regarded as a fresh definition of the absolute; as indeterminate self-relation it is posited as *being* and *becoming*. The forms of *determinate being* find no place in the series of those determinations which can be regarded as definitions of the absolute, for the individual forms of that sphere are immediately posited only as determinatenesses, as finite in general. The infinite, however, is held to be absolute without qualification for it is determined expressly as negation of the finite, and reference is thus expressly made to limitedness in the infinite—limitedness of which being and becoming could perhaps be capable, even if not possessing or showing it—and the presence in the infinite of such limitedness is denied.

But even so, the infinite is not yet really free from limitation and finitude; the main point is to distinguish the genuine Notion of infinity from spurious infinity, the infinite of reason from the infinite of the understanding; yet the latter is the *finitized* infinite, and it will be found that in the very act of keeping the infinite pure and aloof from the finite, the infinite is only made finite.

The infinite is:

(a) in its *simple determination*, affirmative as negation of the finite

(b) but thus it is in *alternating determination* with the *finite*, and is the abstract, *one-sided* infinite

(c) the self-sublation of this infinite and of the finite, as a *single* process—this is the *true* or *genuine infinite*.

(a) The Infinite in General

The infinite is the negation of the negation, affirmation, *being* which has restored itself out of limitedness. The infinite *is*, and more intensely so than the first immediate being; it is the true being, the elevation above limitation. At the name of the infinite,

E*

the heart and the mind light up, for in the infinite the spirit is not merely abstractly present to itself, but rises to its own self, to the light of its thinking, of its universality, of its freedom.

The Notion of the infinite as it first presents itself is this, that determinate being in its being-in-itself determines itself as finite and transcends the limitation. It is the very nature of the finite to transcend itself, to negate its negation and to become infinite. Thus the infinite does not stand as something finished and complete above or superior to the finite, as if the finite had an enduring being *apart from* or *subordinate to* the infinite. Neither do *we* only, as subjective reason, pass beyond the finite into the infinite; as when we say that the infinite is the Notion of reason and that through reason we rise superior to temporal things, though we let this happen without prejudice to the finite which is in no way affected by this exaltation, an exaltation which remains external to it. But the finite itself in being raised into the infinite is in no sense acted on by an alien force; on the contrary, it is its nature to be related to itself as limitation,—both limitation as such and as an ought—and to transcend the same, or rather, as self-relation to have negated the limitation and to be beyond it. It is not in the sublating of finitude in general that infinity in general comes to be; the truth is rather that the finite is only this, through its own nature to become itself the infinite. The infinite is its *affirmative determination*, that which it truly is in itself.

Thus the finite has vanished in the infinite and what *is*, is only the *infinite*.

(*b*) *Alternating Determination of the Finite and the Infinite*
The infinite *is*; in this immediacy it is at the same time the *negation* of an other, of the finite. As thus in the form of simple being and at the same time as the *non-being* of an *other*, it has fallen back into the category of *something* as a determinate being in general— more precisely, into the category of something with a limit, because the infinite is determinate being reflected into itself, resulting from the sublating of determinateness in general, and hence is determinate being *posited* as distinguished from its determinateness. In keeping with this determinateness, the finite stands opposed to the infinite as a *real determinate being*; they stand thus in a qualitative relation, each *remaining* external to the other; the *immediate being* of the infinite resuscitates the *being* of

its negation, of the finite again which at first seemed to have vanished in the infinite.

But the infinite and the finite are not in these categories of relation only; the two sides are determined beyond the stage of being merely *others* to each other. Finitude, namely, is limitation posited as limitation; determinate being is posited with the *determination* to pass over into its *in itself*, to *become* infinite. Infinity is the nothing of the finite, it is what the latter is *in itself*, what it *ought to be*, but this ought-to-be is at the same time reflected into itself, is *realized*; it is a purely self-related, wholly affirmative being. In infinity we have the satisfaction that all determinateness, alteration, all limitation and with it the ought itself, are posited as vanished, as sublated, that the nothing of the finite is posited. As this negation of the finite the in-itself is determinate and thus, as negation of the negation, is affirmative within itself. But this affirmation as qualitative, is *immediate* self-relation, is *being*; and thus the infinite is reduced to the category of a being which has the finite confronting it as an other; its negative nature is posited as the simply *affirmative*, hence as the first and immediate negation. The infinite is in this way burdened with the opposition to the finite which, as an other, remains at the same time a determinate reality although in its in-itself, in the infinite, it is at the same time posited as sublated; this infinite is the non-finite—a being in the determinateness of negation. Contrasted with the finite, with the sphere of affirmative determinatenesses, of realities, the infinite is the indeterminate void, the beyond of the finite, whose being-in-itself is not present in its *determinate* reality.

The infinite as thus posited over against the finite, in a relation wherein they are as qualitatively distinct others, is to be called the *spurious infinite*, the infinite of the understanding, for which it has the value of the highest, the absolute Truth. The understanding is satisfied that it has truly reconciled these two, but the truth is that it is entangled in unreconciled, unresolved, absolute contradiction; it can only be brought to a consciousness of this fact by the contradictions into which it falls on every side when it ventures to apply and to explicate these its categories.

This contradiction occurs as a direct result of the circumstance that the finite remains as a determinate being opposed to the infinite, so that there are *two* determinatenesses; *there are* two worlds, one infinite and one finite, and in their relationship the infinite is only the *limit* of the finite and is thus only a determinate infinite, an *infinite which is itself finite.*

This contradiction develops its content into more explicit forms. The finite is real determinate being which persists as such even when transition is made to its non-being, to the infinite; this, as has been shown, has only the first, immediate negation for its determinateness relatively to the finite, just as the finite as opposed to that negation has, as negated, only the significance of an other and is, therefore, still [only] *something.* When, therefore, the understanding, raising itself above this finite world, ascends to its highest, to the infinite, this finite world remains for it on *this* side, so that the infinite is only set *above* or *beyond* the finite, is *separated* from it, with the consequence that the finite is separated from the infinite; each is *assigned* a *distinct* place—the finite as determinate being here, on *this* side, and the infinite, although the *in-itself* of the finite, nevertheless as a beyond in the dim, inaccessible distance, *outside* of which the finite is and remains.

As thus separated they are just as much essentially *connected* by the very negation which separates them. This negation which connects them—the *somethings* reflected into themselves—is the limit of the one relatively to the other, and that, too, in such a manner that each of them does not have the limit *in it* merely relatively to the other, but the negation is their *being-in-itself*; the limit is thus present in each on its own account, in separation from the other. But the limit is in the form of the first negation and thus both are limited, finite in themselves. However, each as affirmatively self-related is also the negation of its limit; each thus immediately repels the limit, as its non-being, from itself and, as qualitatively separated from it, posits it as *another being* outside it, the finite positing its non-being as this infinite and the infinite, similarly, the finite. It is readily conceded that there is a necessary transition from the finite to the infinite—necessary through the determination of the finite—and that the finite is raised to the form of being-in-itself, since the finite, although persisting as a determinate being, is at the same time *also* determined as *in itself* nothing and therefore as destined to bring about its own dissolution; whereas the infinite, although determined as burdened with negation and limit, is at the same time also determined as possessing *being-in-itself*, so that this abstraction of self-related affirmation constitutes its determination, and hence finite determinate being is not present in it. But it has been shown that the infinite itself attains affirmative being only *by means of* negation, as the negation of negation, and that when this its affirmation is taken as merely simple, qualitative being, the negation contained in it is reduced to a simple immediate negation and thus to a determinateness and limit, which then, as in contradiction with the being-in-itself of the infinite is posited as excluded from it, as not belonging to it, as, on the contrary, opposed to its being-in-itself, as the finite. As therefore each is in its own self and through its own determination the positing of its other, they are *inseparable*. But this their unity is *concealed* in their *qualitative* otherness, it is the *inner* unity which only lies at their base.

This determines the manner in which this unity is manifested: posited in *determinate being*, the unity is a changing or transition of the finite into the infinite, and vice versa; so that the infinite only *emerges* in the finite and the finite in the infinite, the other in the other; that is to say, each arises *immediately* and independently in the other, their connection being only an external one.

The process of their transition has the following detailed shape. We pass from the finite to the infinite. This transcending of the finite appears as an external act. In this void beyond the finite, what arises? What is the positive element in it? Owing to the inseparability of the infinite and the finite—or because this infinite remaining aloof on its own side is itself limited—there arises a limit; the infinite has vanished and its other, the finite, has entered. But this entrance of the finite appears as a happening external to the infinite, and the new limit as something that does not arise from the infinite itself but is likewise found as given. And so we are faced with a relapse into the previous determination which has been sublated in vain. But this new limit is itself only something which has to be sublated or transcended. And so again there arises the void, the nothing, in which similarly the said determinateness, a new limit, is encountered—*and so on to infinity*.

We have before us the alternating determination of the *finite* and the *infinite*; the finite is finite only in its relation to the ought or to the infinite, and the latter is only infinite in its relation to the finite. They are inseparable and at the same time mutually related as sheer others; each has in its own self the other of itself. Each is thus the unity of itself and its other and is in its determinateness *not* that which it itself is, and which its other is.

It is this alternating determination negating both its own self and its negation, which appears as the *progress to infinity*, a progress which in so many forms and applications is accepted as something ultimate beyond which thought does not go but, having got as far as this 'and so on to infinity', has usually reached its goal. This progress makes its appearance wherever *relative* determinations are pressed to the point of opposition, with the result that although they are in an inseparable unity, each is credited with a self-subsistent determinate being over against the other. The progress is, consequently, a *contradiction* which is not resolved but is always only enunciated as *present*.

What we have here is an abstract transcending of a limit, a transcending which remains incomplete because *it is not itself transcended*. Before us is the infinite; it is of course transcended, for a new limit is posited, but the result is rather only a return to the finite. This spurious infinity is in itself the same thing as the perennial ought; it is the negation of the finite it is true, but it cannot in truth free itself therefrom. The finite reappears *in the infinite itself* as its other, because it is only in its *connection* with its other, the finite, that the infinite is. The progress to infinity is, consequently, only the perpetual repetition of one and the same content, one and the same tedious *alternation* of this finite and infinite.

The infinity of the infinite progress remains burdened with the finite as such, is thereby limited and is itself *finite*. But this being so, the infinite progress would in fact be posited as the unity of the finite and the infinite; but this unity is not reflected on. Yet it is this unity alone which evokes the infinite in the finite and the finite in the infinite; it is, so to speak, the mainspring of the infinite progress. This progress is the *external* aspect of this unity at which ordinary thinking halts, at this perpetual repetition of one and the same alternation, of the vain unrest of advancing beyond the limit to infinity, only to *find* in this infinite a new limit in which, however, it is as little able to rest as in the infinite. This infinite has the fixed determination of a *beyond*, which cannot be reached, for the very reason that *it is not meant* to be reached, because the determinateness of the beyond, of the *affirmative* negation, is not let go. In accordance with this determination the infinite has the finite opposed to it as a being *on this side*, which is equally unable to raise itself into the infinite just because it has this determination of an *other*, of a *determinate being* which perpetually generates itself in its beyond, a beyond from which it is again distinct.

(c) *Affirmative Infinity*
In this alternating determination of the finite and the infinite from one to the other and back again, their truth is already implicitly *present*, and all that is required is to take up what is before us. This transition from one to the other and back again constitutes the external realization of the Notion. In this realization is *posited* the content of the Notion, but it is posited as *external*, as falling *asunder*; all that is required is to compare these different moments which yield the *unity* which gives the Notion itself; the *unity* of the infinite and the finite is—as has often been remarked already but here especially is to be borne in mind— the one-sided expression for the unity as it is in truth; but the elimination, too, of this one-sided determination must lie in the externalization of the Notion now before us.

Taken according to their first, only immediate determination, the infinite is only the *beyond* of the *finite*; according to its determination it is the negation of the finite; thus the finite is only that which must be transcended, the negation of itself in its own self, which is infinity. In *each*, therefore, there lies the *determinateness of the other*, although according to the standpoint of the infinite progress these two are supposed to be shut out from each other and only to follow each other alternately; neither can be posited and grasped without the other, the infinite not without the finite, nor the latter without the infinite. In *saying* what the infinite is, namely the negation of the *finite*, the latter is itself included in what is *said*; it cannot be dispensed with for the definition or determination of the infinite. One only needs to *be aware of what one is saying* in order to find the determination of the finite in the infinite. As regards the finite, it is readily conceded that it is the null; but its very nullity is the infinity from which it is thus inseparable. In this way of conceiving them, each may seem to be taken in its *connection* with its other. But if they are taken as *devoid of connection* with each other so that they are only joined by 'and', then each confronts the other as self-subsistent, as in its own self only affirmatively present. Let us see how they are constituted when so taken. The infinite, in that case, is *one of the two*; but as *only* one of the two it is itself finite, it is not the whole but only *one* side; it has its limit in what stands over against it; it is thus the *finite infinite*. There are present only *two finites*. It is precisely this holding of the infinite *apart* from the finite, thus giving it a *one-sided* character, that constitutes its finitude and, therefore, its unity with the finite. The finite, on the other hand, characterized as independent of and apart from the infinite, is that *self-relation* in which its relativity, its dependence and transitoriness is removed; it is the same self-subsistence and affirmation which the infinite is supposed to be.

The two modes of consideration at first seem to have a different determinateness for their point of departure, inasmuch as the former is supposed to be only the *connection* of the infinite and the finite, of each with its other, and the latter is supposed to hold them apart in complete separation from each other; but both modes yield one and the same result: the infinite and the finite viewed as *connected* with each other—the connection being only external to them but also essential to them, without which neither is what it is—each contains its own other in its own determination, just as much as each, taken *on its own account*, considered *in its own self*, has its other present within it as its own moment.

This yields the decried unity of the finite and the infinite—the unity which is itself the infinite which embraces both itself and finitude—and is therefore the infinite in a different sense from that in which the finite is regarded as separated and set apart from the infinite. Since now they must also be distinguished, each is, as has just been shown, in its own self the unity of both; thus we have two such unities. The common element, the unity of the two determinatenesses, as unity, posits them in the first place as negated, since each is supposed to be what it is in its distinction from the other; in their unity, therefore, they lose their qualitative nature—an important reflection for rebutting that idea of the unity which insists on holding fast to the infinite and finite in the quality they are supposed to have when taken in their separation from each other, a view which therefore sees in that unity *only* contradiction, but not also resolution of the contradiction through the negation of the qualitative determinateness of both; thus the unity of the infinite and finite, simple and general in the first instance, is falsified.

But further, since now they are also to be taken as distinct, the *unity* of the infinite which each of these moments is, is differently determined in each of them. The infinite determined as such, has present in it the finitude which is distinct from it; the former is the *in-itself* in this unity, and the latter is only determinateness, limit in it; but it is a limit which is the sheer other of the in-itself, is its opposite; the infinite's determination, which is the in-itself as such, is ruined by the addition of such a quality; it is thus a *finitized infinite*. Similarly, since the finite as such is only the negation of the in-itself, but by reason of this unity also has its opposite present in it, it is exalted and, so to say, infinitely exalted above its worth; the finite is posited as the *infinitized* finite.

Just as before, the simple unity of the infinite and finite was falsified by the understanding, so too is the double unity. Here too this results from taking the infinite in one of the two unities not as negated, but rather as the in-itself, in which, therefore, determinateness and limitation are not to be explicitly present, for these would debase and ruin it. Conversely, the finite is likewise held fast as not negated, although in itself it is null; so that in its union with the infinite it is exalted to what it is not and is thereby infinitized in opposition to its determination as finite, which instead of vanishing is perpetuated.

The falsification of the finite and infinite by the understanding which holds fast to a qualitatively distinct relation between them and asserts that each in its own nature is separate, in fact absolutely separate from the other, comes from forgetting what the Notion of these moments is for the understanding itself. According to this, the unity of the finite and infinite is not an external bringing together of them, nor an incongruous combination alien to their own nature in which there would be joined together determinations inherently separate and opposed, each having a simple affirmative being independent of the other and incompatible with it; but each is in its own self this unity, and this only as a *sublating* of its own self in which neither would have the advantage over the other of having an in-itself and an affirmative determinate being. As has already been shown, finitude *is* only as a transcending of itself; it therefore contains infinity, the other of itself. Similarly, infinity *is* only as a transcending of the finite; it therefore essentially contains its other and is, consequently, in its own self the other of itself. The finite is not sublated by the infinite as by a power existing outside it; on the contrary, its infinity consists in sublating its own self.

This sublating is, therefore, not alteration or otherness as such, not the sublating of a *something*. That in which the finite sublates itself is the infinite as the negating of finitude; but finitude itself has long since been determined as only the *non-being* of determinate being. It is therefore only *negation* which *sublates* itself in the *negation*. Thus infinity on *its* side is determined as the negative of finitude, and hence of determinateness in general, as the empty beyond; the sublating of itself in the finite is a return from an empty flight, a *negation* of the beyond which is in its own self a *negative*.

What is therefore present is the same negation of negation in each. But this is *in itself* self-relation, affirmation, but as return to itself, that is through the *mediation* which the negation of negation is. These are the determinations which it is essential to keep in view; but secondly it is to be noted that they are also *posited* in the infinite progress, and how they are posited in it, namely, as not yet in their ultimate truth.

In the first place, both the infinite and the finite are negated in the infinite progress; both are transcended in the same manner. Secondly, they are posited one after the other as distinct, each as positive on its own account. We thus compare these two determinations in their separation, just as in our comparison—an external comparing—we have separated the two modes of considering the finite and the infinite: on the one hand in their connexion, and on the other hand each on its own account. But the infinite progress expresses more than this; in it there is also posited the *connexion* of terms which are also distinct from each other, although at first the connexion is still only a transition and alternation; only a simple reflection on our part is needed to see what is in fact present.

In the first place, the negation of the finite and infinite which is posited in the infinite progress can be taken as simple, hence as separate and merely successive. Starting from the finite, the limit is transcended, the finite negated. We now have its beyond, the infinite, but in this the limit *arises* again; and so we have the transcending of the infinite. This double sublation, however, is partly only an external affair, an alternation of the moments, and partly it is not yet posited as a *single unity*; the transcending of each moment starts independently, is a fresh act, so that the two processes fall apart. But in addition there is also present in the infinite progress their *connexion*. First there is the finite, then this is transcended and this negative or beyond of the finite is the infinite, and then this negation is again transcended, so that there arises a new limit, a *finite* again. This is the complete, self-closing movement which has arrived at that which constituted the beginning; what arises is the *same* as that from which the movement *began*, that is, the finite is restored; it has therefore united *with itself*, has in its beyond only found *itself* again.

The same is the case with the infinite. In the infinite, the beyond of the limit, there arises only another limit which has the same fate, namely, that as finite it must be negated. Thus what is present again is the *same* infinite which had previously disappeared in the new limit; the infinite, therefore, through its sublating, through its transcending of the new limit, is not removed any further either from the finite—for the finite is only this, to pass over into the infinite—or from itself, for it has arrived *at its own self*.

Thus, both finite and infinite are this *movement* in which each returns to itself through its negation; they *are* only as *mediation* within themselves, and the affirmative of each contains the negative of each and is the negation of the negation. They are thus a *result*, and consequently not what they are in the determination of their *beginning*; the finite is not a *determinate being* on *its* side, and the infinite a *determinate being* or *being-in-itself* beyond the determinate being, that is, beyond the being determined as finite. The reason why understanding is so antagonistic to the unity of the finite and infinite is simply that it presupposes the limitation and the finite, as well as the in-itself, as *perpetuated*; in doing so it *overlooks* the negation of both which is actually present in the infinite progress, as also the fact that they occur therein only as moments of a whole and that they come on the scene only by means of their opposite, but essentially also by means of the sublation of their opposite.

If, at first, the return into self was considered to be just as much a return of the finite to itself as return of the infinite to itself, this very result reveals an error which is connected with the one-sidedness just criticized: first the finite and then the infinite is taken as the *starting point* and it is only this that gives rise to *two* results. It is, however, a matter of complete indifference which is taken as the beginning; and thus the difference which occasioned the *double* result disappears of itself. This is likewise explicit in the line—unending in both directions—of the infinite progress in which each of the moments presents itself in equal alternation, and it is quite immaterial what point is fixed on or which of the two is taken as the beginning. They are distinguished in it but each is equally only the moment of the other. Since both the finite and the infinite itself are moments of the progress they are *jointly or in common the finite*, and since they are equally together negated in it and in the result, this result as negation of the finitude of both is called with truth the infinite. Their difference is thus the *double* meaning which both have. The finite has the double meaning of being first, only the finite *over against* the infinite which stands opposed to it, and secondly, of being the finite and *at the same time* the infinite opposed to it. The infinite, too, has the double meaning of being *one* of these two moments— as such it is the spurious infinite—and also the infinite in which both, the infinite and its other, are only moments. The infinite, therefore, as now before us is, in fact, the process in which it is deposed to being only *one* of its determinations, the opposite of the finite, and so to being itself only one of the finites, and then raising this its difference from itself into the affirmation of itself and through this mediation becoming the *true* infinite.

This determination of the true infinite cannot be expressed in the *formula*, already criticized, of a *unity* of the finite and infinite; *unity* is abstract, inert self-sameness, and the moments are similarly only in the form of inert, simply affirmative being. The infinite, however, like its two moments, is essentially only as a *becoming*, but a becoming now *further determined* in its moments. Becoming, in the first instance, has abstract being and nothing for its determinations; as alteration, its moments possess determinate being, something and other; now, as the infinite, they are the finite and the infinite, which are themselves in process of becoming.

This infinite, as the consummated return into self, the relation of itself to itself, is *being*—but not indeterminate, abstract being, for it is posited as negating the negation; it is, therefore, also *determinate* being for it contains negation in general and hence determinateness. It *is* and *is there*, present before us. It is only the spurious infinite which is the *beyond*, because it is *only* the negation of the finite posited as *real*—as such it is the abstract, first negation; determined *only* as negative, the affirmation of *determinate* being is lacking in it; the spurious infinite, held fast as only negative, is even *supposed to be not there*, is supposed to be unattainable. However, to be thus unattainable is not its grandeur but its defect, which is at bottom the result of holding fast to the *finite* as such as a *merely affirmative being*. It is what is untrue that is unattainable, and such an infinite must be seen as a falsity. The image of the progress to infinity is the *straight line*, at the two limits of which alone the infinite is, and always only is where the line—which is determinate being—is not, and which goes *out beyond* to this negation of its determinate being, that is, to the indeterminate; the image of true infinity, bent back into itself, becomes the *circle*, the line which has reached itself, which is closed and wholly present, without *beginning* and *end*.

True infinity taken thus generally as *determinate* being which is posited as *affirmative* in contrast to the abstract negation, is *reality* in a higher sense than the former reality which was *simply* determinate; for here it has acquired a concrete content. It is not the finite which is the real, but the infinite. Thus reality is further determined as essence, Notion, Idea, and so on. It is, however, superfluous to repeat an earlier, more abstract category such as reality, in connexion with the more concrete categories and to employ it for determinations which are more concrete than it is in its own self. Such repetition as to say that essence, or the Idea, is the real, has its origin in the fact that for untrained thinking, the most abstract categories such as being, determinate being, reality, finitude, are the most familiar.

The more precise reason for recalling the category of reality here is that the negation to which it is opposed as the affirmative is here negation of the negation; as such it is itself opposed to that reality which finite determinate being is. The negation is thus determined as ideality; ideal being [*das Ideelle*][1] is the finite

---

[1] '*Das Ideale*' has a more precise meaning (of the beautiful and its associations) than '*das Ideelle*'; the former is not yet appropriate here and for this reason we have used the expression '*ideell*'. We do not make this distinction though when speaking of reality; the expressions '*reell*' and '*real*' are used practically synonymously and no interest is served by giving the words different shades of meaning. [Author's note.]

as it is in the true infinite—as a determination, a content, which is distinct but is not an *independent, self-subsistent* being, but only a *moment*. Ideality has this more concrete signification which is not fully expressed by the negation of finite determinate being. With reference to reality and ideality, however, the opposition of finite and infinite is grasped in such a manner that the finite ranks as the real but the infinite as the 'ideal' [*das Ideelle*]; in the same way that further on the Notion, too, is regarded as an 'ideal', that is, as a *mere* 'ideal', in contrast to determinate being as such which is regarded as the real. When they are contrasted in this way, it is pointless to reserve the term 'ideal' for the concrete determination of negation in question; in that opposition we return once more to the one-sidedness of the abstract negative which is characteristic of the spurious infinite, and perpetuate the affirmative determinate being of the finite.

TRANSITION

Ideality can be called the *quality* of infinity; but it is essentially the process of *becoming*, and hence a transition—like that of becoming in determinate being—which is now to be indicated. As a sublating of finitude, that is, of finitude as such, and equally of the infinity which is merely its opposite, merely negative, this return into self is *self-relation, being*. As this being contains negation it is *determinate*, but as this negation further is essentially negation of the negation, the self-related negation, it is that determinate being which is called *being-for-self*.

Remark 1: *The Infinite Progress*

The infinite—in the usual meaning of the spurious infinity—and the progress to infinity are, like the ought, the expression of a contradiction which is itself put forward as the final solution. This infinite is a first elevation of sensuous conception above the finite into thought, the content of which, however, is only nothing, that is, it is *expressly* in the form of not-being—a flight beyond limited being which does not inwardly collect itself and does not know how to bring the negative back to the positive. This *incomplete reflection* has completely before it both determinations of the genuine infinite: the *opposition* of the finite and infinite, and their *unity*, but it does not bring these two thoughts together;

the one inevitably evokes the other, but this reflection lets them only *alternate*. This alternation, the infinite progress, is exhibited whenever one remains fixed in the contradiction of the *unity* of two determinations and of their *opposition*. The finite is the sublating of itself, it includes within itself its negation, infinity— the *unity* of both; there is a movement away from the finite to the infinite, to the beyond of the finite—the *separation* of both; but beyond the infinite is another finite—the beyond; the infinite contains finitude—the *unity* of both; but this finite, too, is a negative of the infinite—the *separation* of both; and so on. Thus, in the causal relation, cause and effect are inseparable; a cause which had no effect would not be a cause, just as an effect which had no cause would no longer be an effect. This relation yields, therefore, the infinite progress of causes and effects; something is determined as cause, but as finite (and it is finite for the very reason that it is separated from its effect) it, too, has a cause, that is, it is also an effect; hence the *same thing* that was determined as cause is also determined as effect—the *unity* of cause and effect; now that which is determined as effect again has a cause, that is, the cause has to be separated from its effect and posited as a different something; but this fresh cause is itself only an effect— the *unity* of cause and effect; it has an other for its cause—the separation of both determinations, and so on to *infinity*.

Thus the progress can be put in the following more characteristic form. The assertion is made: the finite and infinite are a single unity; this false assertion must be corrected by the opposite: they are absolutely different and opposed to each other; this must be corrected again by declaring that they are inseparable, that the determination of each lies in the other, by the assertion of their unity, and so on to infinity. What is required in order to see into the nature of the infinite is nothing difficult: it is to be aware that the infinite progress, the developed infinite of the understanding, is so constituted as to be the *alternation* of the two determinations, of the *unity* and the *separation* of both moments and also to be aware that this unity and this separation are themselves inseparable.

The resolution of this contradiction is not the recognition of the equal correctness and equal incorrectness of the two assertions— this is only another form of the abiding contradiction—but the *ideality* of both, in which as distinct, reciprocal negations, they are only *moments*. The said monotonous alternation is actually the negation of their unity and also of their separation. In it, also actually, there is present what was pointed out above: that the beyond of the finite is the infinite, but equally beyond the infinite again the finite finds itself reborn; consequently, in this process the finite is united only with itself, and the same is true of the infinite—so that the same negation of the negation results in an affirmation, this result thus proving itself to be their truth and primary determination. In this being which is thus the *ideality* of the distinct moments, the contradiction has not vanished abstractly, but is resolved and reconciled, and the thoughts are not only complete, but they are also *brought together*. In this detailed example, there is revealed the specific nature of speculative thought, which consists solely in grasping the opposed moments in their unity. Each moment actually shows that it contains its opposite within itself and that in this opposite it is united with itself; thus the affirmative truth is this immanently active unity, the taking together of both thoughts, their infinity—the relation to self which is not immediate but infinite.

Thinkers have often placed the essence of philosophy in the answering of the question: how does the infinite go forth from itself and become finite? This, it is supposed, cannot be made comprehensible. In the course of this exposition the infinite, the Notion of which we have reached, will *further determine* itself and will show in all its varied forms what is demanded, that is, *how* (if we want so to express it) *the infinite becomes finite*. Here we are considering this question only in its immediacy and with respect to the meaning considered above which is usually attached to the infinite.

It is supposed that it depends altogether on the answering of this question *whether there is a philosophy*; and while people pretend that they are willing to let the decision rest on this, they also believe themselves to possess in the question itself a sort of puzzle, an invincible talisman, by which they are firmly secured against the answering of the question and consequently against philosophy and the entering of its portals. Even in other subjects, to understand how to put questions presupposes a certain education, and this holds good even more in the case of philosophical topics if one is to obtain a better answer than that the question is an idle one.

With such questions it is usually claimed as a reasonable assumption that the matter does not depend on the words, but that the point at issue can be understood from one or other of the ways in which the question is expressed. Expressions of sensuous conception like *going forth* and suchlike, which are used in the question, arouse the suspicion that they spring from the level of ordinary conception and that for the answer, too, conceptions which are current in everyday life are expected and in the form of a sensuous simile.

If instead of the infinite being as such is taken, then the *determining* of being, a negation or finitude in it, seems easier to understand. Being, it is true, is itself the indeterminate; but that it is the opposite of determinate being, this is not directly expressed in it. In the infinite, on the other hand, this is expressed; it is the *not*-finite. The unity of the finite and infinite thus seems to be directly excluded, and that is why incomplete reflection is most stubbornly opposed to this unity.

But it has been shown that it is at once evident without going into further detail about the determination of the finite and infinite, that the infinite as understood by said reflection, namely, as opposed to the finite, has in it its other, just because it is opposed to the finite, and therefore is already limited and itself finite— the spurious infinite. The answer, therefore, to the question: how does the infinite become finite? is this: that *there is not* an infinite which is first of all infinite and only subsequently has need to become finite, to go forth into finitude; on the contrary, it is on its own account just as much finite as infinite. The question assumes that the infinite, on the one side, exists by itself, and that the finite which has gone forth from it into a separate existence—or from whatever source it might have come—is in its separation from the infinite truly real; but it should rather be said that this separation is *incomprehensible*. Neither such a finite nor such an infinite has truth; and what is untrue is incomprehensible. But equally it must be said that they are comprehensible, to grasp them even as they are in ordinary conception, to see that in the one there lies the determination of the other, the simple insight into their inseparability, means to comprehend them; *this inseparability is their Notion*. But the separate self-subsistence of the said infinite and finite assumed in the question is an untrue content, and the question already implies an untrue connection between them. Instead, therefore, of answering the question, we must deny the false presuppositions contained in

it, that is, the question itself. The question as to the truth of the
said infinite and finite involves a change of standpoint and this
change will cause a recoil upon the first question of the embarrass-
ment it was intended to produce. This question of ours is something *new* for the reflection which is the source of the first question,
since such reflection does not contain the speculative interest
which, for its own sake and before it connects determinations,
sets out to ascertain whether these, as presupposed, are something
true. But in so far as the falsity of that abstract infinite, and of
the finite which equally is supposed to remain standing on *its*
side, is recognized, there is this to be said about the coming or
going forth of the finite from the infinite: the infinite goes forth
out of itself into finitude because, being grasped as an abstract
unity, it has no truth, no enduring being within it; and conversely
the finite goes *into* the infinite for the same reason, namely that
it is a nullity. Or rather it should be said that the infinite has
eternally gone forth into finitude, that, solely by itself and without
having its other present *within it*, the infinite no more *is* than
pure *being* is.

The question as to how the infinite goes forth to the finite
can contain still another presupposition, namely that the infinite
in itself includes the finite, hence is in itself the unity of itself and
its other, so that the difficulty is connected chiefly with the
separating of them, which is in opposition to the presupposed
unity of both. In this presupposition, the opposition which is
insisted on merely has another form; the *unity* and the *differentiation* are separated and isolated from each other. But if the former
is taken, not as the abstract indeterminate unity but, as it already
is in the presupposition, as the determinate unity of the finite
and the infinite, then the differentiation of both is already present
in it too—a differentiation which is thus at the same time not a
releasing of them into a separate self-subsistence, but which
leaves them as *ideal* moments in the unity. This *unity* of the
finite and infinite and the *distinction* between them are just as
inseparable as are finitude and infinity.

Remark 2: Idealism
The proposition that the finite is ideal [*ideell*] constitutes idealism.
The idealism of philosophy consists in nothing else than in
recognizing that the finite has no veritable being. Every philosophy

is essentially an idealism or at least has idealism for its principle, and the question then is only how far this principle is actually carried out. This is as true of philosophy as of religion; for religion equally does not recognize finitude as a veritable being, as something ultimate and absolute or as something underived, uncreated, eternal. Consequently the opposition of idealistic and realistic philosophy has no significance. A philosophy which ascribed veritable, ultimate, absolute being to finite existence as such, would not deserve the name of philosophy; the principles of ancient or modern philosophies, water, or matter, or atoms are *thoughts*, universals, ideal entities, not things as they immediately present themselves to us, that is, in their sensuous individuality— not even the water of Thales. For although this is also empirical water, it is at the same time also the *in-itself* or *essence* of al¹ other things, too, and these other things are not self-subsi. tent or grounded in themselves, but are *posited* by, are *derived* from, an *other*, from water, that is they are ideal entities. Now above we have named the principle or the universal the *ideal* (and still more must the Notion, the Idea, spirit be so named); and then again we have described individual, sensuous things as *ideal* in principle, or in their Notion, still more in spirit, that is, as sublated; here we must note, in passing, this twofold aspect which showed itself in connection with the infinite, namely that on the one hand the ideal is concrete, veritable being, and on the other hand the moments of this concrete being are no less ideal—are sublated in it; but in fact what is, is only the one concrete whole from which the moments are inseparable.

By the ideal [*dem Ideellen*] is meant chiefly the form of figurate conception and imagination, and what is simply *in* my conception, or *in* the Notion, or *in* the idea, *in* imagination, and so on, is called *ideal*, so that even fancies are counted as ideals— conceptions which are not only distinct from the real world, but are supposed to be essentially *not* real. In point of fact, the spirit is the *idealist* proper; in spirit, even as feeling, imagination and still more as thinking and comprehending, the content is not present as a so-called *real existence;* in the simplicity of the ego such external being is present only as sublated, it is *for me,* it is *ideally* in me. This subjective idealism, either in the form of the unconscious idealism of consciousness generally, or consciously enunciated and set up as a principle, concerns only the *form* of conception according to which a content is mine; in the systematic idealism of subjectivity this form is declared to be the only true exclusive form in opposition to the form of objectivity or reality, of the *external existence* of that content. Such idealism is [merely] formal because it disregards the *content* of imagination or thought, which content in being imagined or thought can remain wholly in its finitude. In such an idealism nothing is lost, just as much because the reality of such a finite content, the existence filled with finitude, is preserved, as because, in so far as abstraction is made from such finite reality, the content is supposed to be of no consequence *in itself*; and in it nothing is gained for the same reason that nothing is lost, because the ego, conception, spirit, remains filled with the same content of finitude. The opposition of the form of subjectivity and objectivity is of course one of the finitudes; but the *content*, as taken up in sensation, intuition or even in the more abstract element of conception, of thought, contains finitudes in abundance and with the exclusion of only one of the modes of finitude, namely, of the said form of subjective and objective, these finitudes are certainly not eliminated, still less have they spontaneously fallen away.

CHAPTER 3

BEING-FOR-SELF

In being-for-self, *qualitative* being finds its *consummation*; it is infinite being. The being of the beginning lacks all determination. Determinate being is sublated but only immediately sublated being. It thus contains, to begin with, only the first negation, which is itself immediate; it is true that being, too, is preserved in it and both are united in determinate being in a simple unity, but for that very reason they are in themselves still unequal to each other and their unity is not yet *posited*. Determinate being is therefore the sphere of difference, of dualism, the field of finitude. Determinateness is determinateness as such, in which being is only relatively, not absolutely determined. In being-for-self, the difference between being and determinateness or negation is posited and equalized; quality, otherness, limit—like reality, being-in-itself, the ought, and so on—are the imperfect embodiments of the negation in being in which the difference of both still lies at the base. Since, however, in finitude the negation has passed into infinity, into the *posited* negation of negation, it is simple self-relation and consequently in its own self the equalization with being, *absolutely determined being*.

Being-for-self is first, immediately *a* being-for-self—the One.

Secondly, the One passes into a *plurality of ones—repulsion*—and this otherness of the ones is sublated in their ideality—*attraction*.

Thirdly, we have the alternating determination of repulsion and attraction in which they collapse into equilibrium, and quality, which in being-for-self reached its climax, passes over into *quantity*.

A. BEING-FOR-SELF AS SUCH

We have arrived at the general Notion of being-for-self. All that is now necessary to justify our use of the term for this Notion is to demonstrate that the said Notion corresponds to the general idea associated with the expression, being-for-self. And so indeed it seems; we say that something is for itself in so far as it transcends otherness, its connexion and community with other, has repelled them and made abstraction from them. For it, the other has being only as sublated, as *its moment;* being-for-self consists in having so transcended limitation, its otherness, that it is, as this negation, the infinite *return* into itself. Consciousness, even as such, contains in principle the determination of being-for-self in that it *represents* to itself an object which it senses, or intuits, and so forth; that is, it has *within it* the content of the object, which in this manner has an 'ideal' being; in its very intuiting and, in general, in its entanglement with the negative of itself, with its other, consciousness is still only in the presence of its own self. Being-for-self is the polemical, negative attitude towards the limiting other, and through this negation of the latter is a reflected-ness-into-self, although *along* with this return of consciousness into itself and the ideality of the object, the *reality* of the object is *also* still preserved, in that it is *at the same time* known as an external existence. Consciousness thus belongs to the sphere of *Appearance*, or is the dualism, on the one hand of knowing an alien object external to it, and on the other hand of being for its own self, having the object ideally [*ideell*] present in it; of being not only in the presence of the other, but therein being in the presence of its own self. *Self-consciousness*, on the other hand, is being-for-self as *consummated* and *posited;* the side of connexion with an other, with an external object, is removed. Self-conscious-ness is thus the nearest example of the presence of infinity; granted, of an infinity which is still abstract, yet which, at the same time, is a very different concrete determination from being-for-self in general, the infinity of which has a determinateness which is still quite qualitative.

(a) Determinate Being and Being-for-self

As already mentioned, being-for-self is infinity which has collapsed into simple being; it is *determinate* being in so far as the negative nature of infinity, which is the negation of negation, is from now on in the explicit form of the *immediacy* of being, as only negation in general, as simple qualitative determinateness. But being, which in such determinateness is *determinate* being, is also at once distinct from being-for-self, which is only being-for-self in so far as its determinateness is the infinite one above-mentioned;

nevertheless, determinate being is at the same time also a moment of being-for-self; for this latter, of course, also contains being charged with negation. Thus the determinateness which in determinate being as such is an other, and a being-for-other, is bent back into the infinite unity of being-for-self, and the moment of determinate being is present in being-for-self as a *being-for-one*.

(b) Being-for-one

This moment expresses the manner in which the finite is present in its unity with the infinite, or is an ideal being [*Ideelles*]. In being-for-self, negation is not present as a determinateness or limit, or consequently as a relation to a determinate being which is for it an other. Now though this moment has been designated as *being-for-one*, there is as yet nothing present for which it would be—no *one*, of which it would be the moment. There is, in fact, nothing of the kind as yet fixed in being-for-self; that for which something (and here there is no something) would be, whatever the other side as such might be, is likewise a moment, is itself only a being-for-one, not yet a one. Consequently, what we have before us is still an undistinguishedness of the two sides which may be suggested by being-for-one; there is only *one* being-for-other, and because there is only *one*, this too is only a being-for-one; there is only the *one* ideality of that, for which or in which there is supposed to be a determination as moment, and of that which is supposed to be a moment in it. Being-for-one and being-for-self are, therefore, not genuinely opposed determinatenesses. If the difference is assumed for a moment and we speak of *a* being-for-self, then it is this itself which, as the sublatedness of otherness, relates itself to itself as the sublated other, and is therefore '*for one*'; it is related in its other only to its own self. Ideal being [*Ideelles*] is necessarily 'for one', but it is not for an other; the one for which it is, is only itself. The ego, therefore, spirit as such, or God, are 'ideal' because they are infinite; but as being for themselves they are not 'ideally' different from that which is 'for one'. For if they were, they would be only immediate existences, or, more precisely, determinate being and a being-for-other, because that which would be for them would be, not themselves but an other, if they were supposed to lack the moment of being 'for one'. God is, therefore, *for himself* in so far as he himself is that which is *for him*.

To be 'for self' and to be 'for one' are therefore not different meanings of ideality, but are essential, inseparable moments of it.

Remark: The German Expression, 'What For a Thing' (Meaning 'What Kind of a Thing')
The German expression for enquiring after the quality of anything —an expression which appears strange at first sight—'What for a thing [*was für ein Ding*]' something is, brings into prominence, in its reflection-into-self, the moment here considered. This expression is in its origin idealistic, since it does not ask what this thing A is for *another* thing B, not what this man is for another man; on the contrary, it asks what this thing, this man, is *for a thing, for a man*, so that this being-for-one has at the same time returned into this thing, into this man himself; in other words that *which is*, and that *for which* it is, are one and the same— an identity, such as ideality also must be considered to be.

Ideality attaches in the first place to the sublated determinations as distinguished from that *in which* they are sublated, which by contrast can be taken as the real. But thus the ideal is again one of the moments, and the real the other; but the significance of ideality is that both determinations are equally only *for one* and count only for *one*, which *one* ideality is, without distinction, reality. In this sense self-consciousness, spirit, God, is ideal as an infinite relation purely to self. Ego is for ego, both are the same, the ego is twice named, but so that each of the two is only a 'for-one', is ideal; spirit is only for spirit, God only for God, and this unity alone is God, God as spirit. Self-consciousness, however, as consciousness, enters into the difference *of itself* and of an *other*—or of its *ideality*, in which it produces conceptions, and of its *reality*, inasmuch as its conception has a determinate content which still has the side of being known as the unsublated negative, as a real, determinate being. However, to call thought, spirit, God, *only* an ideal being, presupposes the standpoint from which finite being counts as the real, and the ideal being or being-for-one has only a one-sided meaning.

In a previous Remark the principle of idealism was indicated and it was said that in any philosophy the precise question was, how far has the principle been carried through.[1] As to the manner in which it is carried through, a further observation may be made

[1] P. 155.

in connection with the category we have reached. This carrying through of the principle depends primarily on whether the finite reality still retains an independent self-subsistence alongside the being-for-self, but also on whether in the infinite itself the moment of *being-for-one*, a relationship of the ideal to itself as ideal, is posited. Thus the Eleatic Being or Spinoza's substance is only the abstract negation of all determinateness, without ideality being posited in substance itself. With Spinoza, as will be mentioned later, infinity is only the absolute *affirmation* of a thing, hence only the unmoved unity; consequently, substance does not even reach the determination of being-for-self, much less that of subject and spirit. The idealism of the noble Malebranche is in itself more explicit. It contains the following fundamental thoughts: because God includes within himself all eternal truths, the ideas and perfections of all things, so that they are *his* and his alone, we see them only in him; God awakens in us our sensations of objects by an action in which there is nothing sensuous, whereby we imagine to ourselves that we obtain not only the idea of the object which represents its essential nature, but also the sensation of its existence.[1] As then the eternal truths and Ideas (essentialities) of things are in God, are ideal, so also is their existence in God ideal, not an actual existence; though they are *our* objects, they are only *for one*. This moment of explicit and concrete idealism which is lacking in Spinozism is present here, in that absolute ideality is characterized as a *knowing*. Pure and profound as this idealism is, the above relations on the one hand still contain much that is indeterminate for thought and, on the other hand, their content is directly quite concrete (sin and salvation, etc., enter directly into them); the logical determination of infinity on which they would have to be based is not explicitly realized, and thus this lofty and rich idealism, though it is the product of a pure, speculative spirit, is still not the product of a pure, speculative thinking which alone can truly establish it.

The Leibnizian idealism lies more within the bounds of the abstract Notion. The ideating being, the monad, of Leibniz is essentially ideal [*Ideelles*]. Ideation is a being-for-self in which the determinatenesses are not limits, and consequently not a determinate being, but only moments. Ideation is also, it is true, a more concrete determination, but here it has no further signification

---

[1] *De la Recherche de la Vérité, Éclairc.* 'Sur la nature des idées' etc.

F

than that of ideality; for with Leibniz, even that which lacks consciousness is an ideating, percipient being. In this system, then, otherness is sublated; spirit and body, or the monads generally, are not others for one another, they do not limit one another and do not affect one another; all relationships generally which are based on a determinate being fall away. The diversity is only ideal and inner and in it the monad remains related only to itself; the alterations develop within the monad and are not relations of it to others. What is taken to be, in accordance with the real determination, a determinately existent relation of the monads to one another, is an independent, only *simultaneous becoming*, enclosed within the being-for-self of each of them. That there is a *plurality of monads*, that therefore they are also determined as others, does not concern the monads themselves; this is the reflection, external to them, of a third. They are not *in themselves others to one another;* the being-for-self is kept pure, and is free from the accompaniment of any real being. But herein lies, too, the inadequacy of this system. The monads are such ideating, percipient beings only *in themselves*, or *in God* as the monad of monads, or *even in the system*. Otherness is equally present, whether in the ideation itself or in whatever shape the third assumes which considers them as others, as a plurality. The plurality of their determinate being is only excluded, and that only momentarily, the monads being posited as not-others only by abstraction. If it is a third which posits their otherness, it is also a third which sublates it; but this *entire movement which gives them their ideality* falls outside them. Should it be pointed out that this movement of thought itself falls, nevertheless, only within an ideating monad, the reply must be that the very *content* of such thinking is *within itself external to itself*. The transition from the oneness of absolute ideality (the monad of monads) to the category of the abstract (connectionless) *plurality* of determinate being, is immediate and uncomprehended (it is effected through the image of creation); and the transition from this plurality back to the oneness is equally abstract. Ideality, ideation generally, remains something formal, as also does ideation raised to the form of consciousness. Just as consciousness is conceived as a one-sided form which is indifferent to its determination and content, in the above-mentioned fancy of Leibniz—namely, that the magnetic needle, if it possessed consciousness, would regard its direction to the north as freely determined by itself—so, too, ideality in the monads is a form remaining external to the plurality. Ideality is supposed to be immanent in them, their nature is supposed to be ideation; but their relationship is on the one hand their harmony, which does not fall within the sphere of their determinate being and is, consequently, pre-established; and on the other hand, this determinate being of theirs is not grasped as a being-for-other, or, further, as ideality, but is determined only as an abstract plurality; the ideality of the plurality and the further determination of it to harmony are not immanent in and proper to this plurality itself.

Other idealisms, as for example those of Kant and Fichte, do not go beyond the *ought* or the *infinite progress*, and remain in the dualism of determinate being and being-for-self. True, in these systems, the thing-in-itself or the infinite shock or resistance principle [*Anstoss*] enters directly into the ego and becomes only something *for it;* but it proceeds from a free otherness which is perpetuated as a negative being-in-itself. The ego is therefore undoubtedly determined as ideal [*das Ideelle*], as being for itself, as infinite self-relation; but the moment of *being-for-one* is not completed to the point where the beyond, or the direction to the beyond, vanishes.

(c) The One

Being-for-self is the simple unity of itself and its moment, being-for-one. There is before us only a single determination, the self-relation of the sublating. The *moments* of being-for-self have collapsed into the *undifferentiatedness* which is immediacy or being, but an *immediacy* based on the negating which is posited as its determination. Being-for-self is thus *a* being-for-self, and since in this immediacy its inner meaning vanishes, it is the wholly abstract limit of itself—the *one*.

Attention may be drawn in advance to the difficulty involved in the following exposition of the *development* of the one and to its cause. The *moments* which constitute the Notion of the one as a being-for-self fall *asunder* in the development. They are: (1) negation in general, (2) *two* negations, (3) two that are therefore the *same*, (4) sheer opposites, (5) self-relation, identity as such, (6) relation which is *negative* and yet to *its own self*. The reason for the separation of these moments here is that the form of *immediacy*, of *being* enters into being-for-self as *a* being-for-self; through this immediacy *each moment is posited* as a *distinct, affirmative determination,* and yet they are no less *inseparable.* Hence of each determination the opposite must equally be asserted; it is this contradiction, together with the abstract nature of the moments, which constitutes the difficulty.

B. THE ONE AND THE MANY

The one is the simple self-relation of being-for-self in which its moments have collapsed in themselves and in which, consequently, being-for-self has the form of *immediacy,* and its moments therefore now have a *determinate* being.

As self-relation of the *negative* the one is a process of determining—and as *self*-relation it is an infinite *self*-determining. But because being-for-self is now in the form of immediacy, these *differences* are no longer posited only as moments of one and the same self-determination, but as at the same time *affirmatively* present. The *ideality* of being-for-self as a totality thus reverts, in the first place, to *reality* and that too in its most fixed, abstract form, as the *one.* In the one, being-for-self is the *posited* unity of simple being and determinate being, as the absolute union of the relation to other and self-relation; but, further, the determinateness of being also stands *opposed* to the determination of the *infinite negation,* to the self-determination, so that what the one is *in itself* is now only *ideally present in it,* and the negative consequently is an other distinct from it. What shows itself to be *present* as distinct from the one is its own self-determining; the unity of the one with itself as thus distinguished from itself is reduced to a *relation,* and as a *negative* unity it is a negation of its own self as *other, exclusion* of the one as other from itself, from the one.

(a) The One in its own self

In its own self the one simply *is;* this its being is neither a determinate being, nor a determinateness as a relation to an other, nor is it a constitution; what it is, in fact, is the accomplished negation of this circle of categories. Consequently, the one is not capable of becoming an other: it is *unalterable.*

It is indeterminate but not, however, like being; its indeterminateness is the determinateness which is a relation to its own self, an absolute determinedness—*posited* being-within-self. As the one is in accordance with its Notion a self-related negation, it has difference in it—a turning away from itself to an other; but this movement is immediately turned back on itself, because it follows from this moment of self-determining that there is no other to which the one can go, and the movement has thus returned into itself.

In this simple immediacy the mediation of determinate being and of ideality itself, and with it all difference and manifoldness, has vanished. There is *nothing* in it; this *nothing*, the abstraction of self-relation, is here distinguished from the being-within-self itself; it is a *posited* nothing because this being-within-self no longer has the simple character of something but, as a mediation, has a concrete determination; but as abstract, though it is identical with the one, it is distinct from its determination. This nothing, then, posited as *in the one*, is the nothing as the *void*. The void is thus the *quality* of the *one* in its immediacy.

(b) The One and the Void

The one is the void as the abstract relation of the negation to itself. However, the void as the nothing is absolutely distinct from the simple immediacy, the also *affirmative* being of the one, and since they stand in one and the same relation, namely, that of the one, their difference is *posited;* but as distinct from the affirmative being of the one, the nothing as the void is *outside* it.

Being-for-self determined in this manner as the one *and* the void has again acquired a *determinate* being. The one and the void have negative relation to self for their common, simple base. The moments of being-for-self emerge from this unity, become external to themselves; through the *simple* unity of the moments there enters the determination of *being* and the unity thus reduces itself to being only *one* side, and so to a determinate being; and in this it is confronted by its other determination, the negation as such, likewise as a determinate being of the nothing, as the void.

Remark: Atomism

The one in this form of determinate being is the stage of the category which made its appearance with the ancients as the

atomistic principle, according to which the essence of things is
the atom and the void (το ἄτομον or τὰ ἄτομα καὶ τὸ κενόν). The
abstraction which has developed into this form has acquired a
greater determinateness than the *being* of Parmenides and the
becoming of Heraclitus. Lofty as is this abstraction, in that it
makes this simple determinateness of the one and the void the
principle of all things, deriving the infinite variety of the world
from this simple antithesis and boldly presuming to know the
former from the latter, it is equally easy for figurate conception
to picture *here* atoms and *alongside* them the void. It is, therefore,
no wonder that the atomistic principle has at all times been
upheld; the equally trivial and external relation of *composition*
which must be added to achieve a semblance of concreteness and
variety is no less popular than the atoms themselves and the void.
The one and the void is being-for-self, the highest qualitative
being-within-self, sunk back into complete *externality*; the
immediacy or being of the one, because it is the negation of all
otherness, is posited as being no longer determinable and alterable;
such therefore is its absolute, unyielding rigidity that all determination, variety, conjunction remains for it an utterly external
relation.

However, with the first thinkers the atomistic principle did not
remain in this externality but besides its abstraction had also a
speculative determination in the fact that the void was recognized
as the source of movement, which is an entirely different relation
of the atom and the void from the mere juxtaposition and mutual
indifference of these two determinations. That the void is the
source of movement has not the trivial meaning that something
can only move into an empty space and not into an already
occupied space, for in such a space it would not find any more
open room—understood in this sense, the void would be only the
presupposition or condition of movement, not its *ground*, just as
the movement itself, too, would be presupposed as already
existing, the essential point, its ground, being forgotten. The
view that the void constitutes the ground of movement contains
the profounder thought that in the negative as such there lies the
ground of becoming, of the unrest of self-movement—in which
sense, however, the negative is to be taken as the veritable
negativity of the infinite. The void is the *ground* of movement
only as the *negative* relation of the one to its *negative*, to the one,

that is to itself, which however is posited as having determinate being.

But in other respects, the further determinations of the ancients concerning the shape and position of the atoms and the direction of their movement, are arbitrary and external enough and, in addition, stand in direct contradiction to the basic determination of the atom. Physics with its molecules and particles suffers from the atom, this principle of extreme externality, which is thus utterly devoid of the Notion, just as much as does that theory of the State which starts from the particular will of individuals.

(c) Many Ones: Repulsion

The one and the void constitute the first stage of the determinate being of being-for-self. Each of these moments has negation for its determination and is at the same time posited as a determinate being; according to the former determination the one and the void are the *relation* of negation to negation as of an other to its other: the one is negation in the determination of being, and the void is negation in the determination of non-being. But the one is essentially self-relation only as related *negation*, that is, it is itself that which the void outside it is supposed to be. Each, however, is also *posited* as an affirmative *determinate being*, one as a being-for-self as such, the other an an unspecified determinate being in general, and each is related to the other as to *another determinate being*. The being-for-self of the one, is, however, essentially the ideality of determinate being and of other: it relates itself not to an other but only *to itself*. But since being-for-self is fixed as a one, as *affirmatively* for itself, as *immediately* present, its *negative* relation *to itself* is at the same time a relation to an *affirmative* being; and since the relation is just as much negative, that to which it relates itself remains determined as a *determinate being* and an *other;* as essentially *self*-relation, the other is not indeterminate negation as the void, but is likewise a *one*. The one is consequently a *becoming of many ones*.

Strictly, however, this is not really a *becoming*, for becoming is a transition of *being* into *nothing:* the one, on the other hand, becomes only one. The one, as related, contains the negative as a relation, has it therefore *within* it. Instead of a becoming, then, there is present first the immanent relation of the one itself; and secondly, since the relation is negative and the one is at the same time affirmatively present, the one repels itself *from itself*. The negative relation of the one to itself is *repulsion*.

This repulsion as thus the positing of *many ones* but through the one itself, is the one's own coming-forth-from-itself but to such outside it as are themselves only ones. This is repulsion according to its Notion, repulsion *in itself*. The second repulsion is different from it, it is what is immediately suggested to external reflection: repulsion not as the *generation* of ones, but only as the mutual repelling of ones presupposed as already *present*. We have now to see how the first repulsion, repulsion *in itself*, determines itself to the second, to external repulsion.

First of all we must establish what determinations are possessed by the many ones as such. As an explication of what the one is in itself, the becoming of the many, or the generation of the many, vanishes immediately; the products of the process are ones, and these are not for an other, but relate themselves infinitely to themselves. The one repels only *itself* from itself, therefore does not *become* but *already is*; and what is represented as repelled is likewise a *one*, a one that *is*. To repel and to be repelled applies equally to both, and makes no difference.

The ones are thus *presupposed* relatively to one another—*supposed* or *posited* by the repulsion of the one from itself; *pre*-supposed as *not* posited. Their positedness is sublated, and as related only to *themselves* they are *affirmative* beings relatively to one another.

Thus plurality appears not as an *otherness*, but as a determination completely external to the one. The one, in repelling itself, remains self-related, like that which to begin with is taken as repelled. That the ones are related to one another as *others*, are brought together into the determinateness of plurality, does not therefore concern the ones. If plurality were a relation of the ones themselves to one another then they would limit one another and there would be affirmatively present in them a being-for-other. Their relation—and this they have through their *implicit* unity—as here *posited* is determined as none: it is again the previously posited *void*. The void is their limit but a limit which is external to them, in which they are not to be *for one another*. The limit is that in which what are limited both *are* and *are not*: but the void is determined as pure non-being, and this alone constitutes their limit.

The repulsion of the one from itself is the explication of that which the one is in itself; but infinity as *explicated* is here the infinity which has *come forth from itself;* it has come forth from itself by virtue of the immediacy of the infinite, the one. It is a simple relating of the one to the one, and no less also the absolute absence of relation in the one; it is the former according to the simple, affirmative self-relation of the one, and the latter according to the self-same relation as negative. In other words, the plurality of the one is its own positing; the one is nothing but the *negative* relation of the one to itself, and this relation—and therefore the one itself—is the plural one. But equally, plurality is absolutely external to the one; for the one is, precisely, the sublating of otherness; repulsion is its self-relation and simple equality with itself. The plurality of ones is infinity as a contradiction which unconstrainedly produces itself.

Remark: The Monad of Leibniz.

We have previously referred to the Leibnizian idealism. We may add here that this idealism which started from the *ideating monad*, which is determined as being for itself, advanced only as far as the repulsion just considered, and indeed only to *plurality* as such, in which each of the ones is only for its own self and is indifferent to the determinate being and being-for-self of the others; or, in general, for the one, there are no others at all. The monad is, by itself, the entire closed universe; it requires none of the others. But this inner manifoldness which it possesses in its ideational activity in no way affects its character as a being-for-self. The Leibnizian idealism takes up the *plurality* immediately as something *given* and does not grasp it as a *repulsion* of the monads. Consequently, it possesses plurality only on the side of its abstract externality. The atomistic philosophy does not possess the Notion of ideality; it does not grasp the one as an ideal being, that is, as containing *within itself* the two moments of being-for-self and being-for-it, but only as a simple, dry, real being-for-self. It does, however, go beyond mere indifferent plurality; the atoms become further determined in regard to one another even though, strictly speaking, this involves an inconsistency; whereas, on the contrary, in that indifferent independence of the monads, plurality remains as a fixed *fundamental determination*, so that the connexion

F*

between them falls only in the monad of monads, or in the philosopher who contemplates them.

C. REPULSION AND ATTRACTION

(a) Exclusion of the One

The many ones have affirmative being; their determinate being or relation to one another is a non-relation, is external to them—the abstract void. But they themselves are now this negative relation to themselves as to *affirmatively present* others—the demonstrated contradiction, infinity posited in the immediacy of being. Thus repulsion now simply *finds immediately before* it that which is repelled by it. In this determination repulsion is an *exclusion*; the one repels from itself only the many ones which are neither generated nor posited by it. This mutual or all-round repelling is relative, is limited by the being of the ones.

The plurality is, in the first place, non-posited otherness, the limit is only the void, only that in which the ones *are not*. But in the limit they also *are*; they are in the void, or their repulsion is their *common relation*.

This mutual repulsion is the posited *determinate being* of the many ones; it is not their being-for-self, for according to this they would be differentiated as many only in a third, but it is their own differentiating which preserves them. They negate one another reciprocally, posit one another as being only *for-one*. But at the same time they equally *negate* this *being only for-one*; they *repel* this their *ideality* and *are*. Thus the moments which in ideality are absolutely united are separated. The one is, in its being-for-self, also *for-one*, but this one for which it is is its own self; its differentiation of itself is immediately sublated. But in plurality the differentiated one has a being; the being-for-one as determined in exclusion is, consequently, a being-for-other. Each is thus repelled by an other, is sublated and made into that which is not *for itself* but *for-one*, and that another one.

The being-for-self of the many ones shows itself, therefore, as their self-preservation through the mediation of their mutual repulsion in which they mutually sublate themselves and each posits the others as a mere being-for-other; but the self-preservation at the same time consists in repelling this ideality and in positing the ones as not being for-an-other. This self-preservation of the ones through their negative relation to one another is, however, rather their dissolution.

The ones not only *are*, but they maintain themselves through their reciprocal exclusion. Now in the first place that which should enable the ones to maintain their diversity in opposition to their being negated is their *being*, in fact, their being-*in-itself* as opposed to their relation-to-other; this being-in-itself is that they are *ones*. But *this is what they all are*; they are in their being-in-itself the *same* instead of this latter being the fixed point of their diversity. Secondly, their determinate being and their relation to one another, that is, their *positing of themselves as ones*, is the reciprocal negating of themselves; but this likewise is *one and the same* determination of them all, through which then they rather posit themselves as identical; similarly, because they are in themselves the same, their ideality, instead of being posited through others, is *their own*, and they therefore repel it just as little. Consequently, as regards both their being and their positing, they are only *one* affirmative unity.

This reflection that the ones, determined both as simply being and as inter-related, show themselves to be one and the same and indistinguishable, is a comparison made by us. But we have also to see what is *posited* in them in their *inter-relatedness*. They *are*—this is presupposed in this inter-relatedness—and they *are* only in so far as they reciprocally negate one another and at the same time hold themselves aloof from this their ideality, their negatedness, that is, negate this reciprocal negating. But they *are* only in so far as they negate; consequently, since this their negating is negated, their being is negated. It is true that since they *are*, they would not be negated by this negating, which for them is only something external; this negating by the other rebounds off them and touches only their surface. And yet it is only through this negating of the others that the ones return into themselves: they *are* only as this mediation, and this their return is their self-preservation and their being-for-self. Since their negating is ineffectual because of the resistance offered by the ones either as simply affirmative or as negating, they do not return into themselves, do not preserve themselves, and so are not.

The observation was made above that the ones are the same, each of them is a *one* like the other. This is not only a relating of them by us, an external bringing of them together; on the contrary, repulsion is itself a relating; the one which excludes the ones relates itself to them, to the ones, that is, to its own self. Hence the negative relationship of the ones to one another is only a *going-together-with-self*. This identity into which their repelling passes over is the sublating of their diversity and externality which they, as excluding, ought rather to maintain relatively to one another.

This positing of themselves by the many ones into a single one is *attraction*.

Remark: The unity of the One and the Many

Self-subsistence pushed to the point of the one as a being-for-self is abstract, formal, and destroys itself. It is the supreme, most stubborn error, which takes itself for the highest truth, manifesting in more concrete forms as abstract freedom, pure ego and, further, as Evil. It is that freedom which so misapprehends itself as to place its essence in this abstraction, and flatters itself that in thus being with itself it possesses itself in its purity. More specifically, this self-subsistence is the error of regarding as negative that which is its own essence, and of adopting a negative attitude towards it. Thus it is the negative attitude towards itself which, in seeking to possess its own being destroys it, and this its act is only the manifestation of the futility of this act. The reconciliation is the recognition that the object of this negative attitude is rather its own essence, and is only the *letting go* of the negativity of *its* being-for-self instead of holding fast to it.

It is an ancient proposition that the one is many and especially that the many are one. We may repeat here the observation that the truth of the one and the many expressed in propositions appears in an inappropriate form, that this truth is to be grasped and expressed only as a becoming, as a process, a repulsion and attraction—not as being, which in a proposition has the character of a stable unity. We have already mentioned and recalled the dialectic of Plato in the Parmenides concerning the derivation of the many from the one, namely, from the proposition: the one is. The inner dialectic of the Notion has been stated; it is easiest to grasp the dialectic of the proposition, that the many are one, as an external reflection; and it may properly be grasped externally here inasmuch as the object too, the many, are mutually external. It directly follows from this comparison of the many with one another that any one is determined simply like any other one; each is a one, each is one of the many, *is* by excluding the others— so that they are absolutely the same, there is present one and only one determination. This is the *fact*, and all that has to be done is to grasp this simple fact. The only reason why the understanding stubbornly refuses to do so is that it has *also* in mind, and indeed rightly so, the difference; but the existence of this difference is just as little excluded because of the said fact, as is the certain existence of the said fact in spite of the difference. One could, as it were, comfort understanding for the naïve manner in which it grasps the fact of the difference, by assuring it that the difference will also come in again.

(b) *The one One of Attraction*

Repulsion is the self-differentiating of the one, at first into many, whose negative relationship is without effect because they presuppose one another as affirmatively present; it is only the *ought-to-be* of ideality. In attraction, however, ideality is realized. Repulsion passes over into attraction, the many ones into *one* one. Both repulsion and attraction are in the first place distinct from each other, the former as the reality of the ones, the latter as their posited ideality. The relation of attraction to repulsion is such that the former has the latter for *presupposition*. Repulsion provides the material for attraction. If there were no ones there would be nothing to attract; the conception of a perpetual attraction, of an absorption of the ones, presupposes an equally perpetual production of them. Spatial attraction as pictorially conceived makes the flow of attracted ones proceed uninterruptedly; in place of the atoms which vanish in the centre of attraction, another multitude comes forth from the void, and so on to infinity if one wishes. If attraction were conceived as accomplished, the many being brought to the point of the one one, then there would be present only an inert one and no longer any attraction. The ideality present in attraction still also bears within itself the determination of the negation of itself, the many ones of which it is the relatedness: attraction is inseparable from repulsion.

In the first place, attraction belongs equally to each of the many ones as *immediately* present; none has any precedence over another; this would result in an equilibrium in attraction, or, strictly speaking, an equilibrium of attraction and repulsion itself, and an inert state of rest in which ideality would have no determinate being. But there can be no question here of a precedence of such a one over another, for this would presuppose a specific difference between them; rather is attraction the positing of the immediately present undifferentiatedness of the ones. It is only attraction itself that is a *positing* of a one distinct from other ones; these are only immediate ones which should maintain themselves through repulsion; but through their posited negation arises the one of attraction, which is consequently determined as mediated, the *one posited as one*. The first ones, as immediate, do not in their ideality return into themselves but have this ideality in another one.

The one one, however, is the realized ideality, posited in the one; it is attraction through the mediation of repulsion, and it contains this mediation within itself as *its determination*. Thus it does not absorb the attracted ones into itself as into a centre, that is, it does not sublate them abstractly. Since it contains repulsion in its determination, this latter at the same time preserves the ones as many in it; through its attracting, so to speak, it acquires something for itself, obtains an extension or filling. There is thus in it the unity of repulsion and attraction in general.

(c) *The Relation of Repulsion and Attraction*

The difference of the one and the many is now determined as the difference of their *relation* to one another, with each other, a relation which splits into two, repulsion and attraction, each of which is at first independent of the other and stands apart from it, the two nevertheless being essentially connected with each other. Their as yet indeterminate unity is to be more precisely ascertained.

Repulsion, as the basic determination of the one, appears first and as *immediate*, like its ones which although generated by repulsion are yet also posited as immediate. As such, repulsion is indifferent to attraction which is externally added to it as thus presupposed. Attraction on the other hand is not presupposed by repulsion in such a manner that the former is supposed to have no part in the positing and being of the latter, that is, as if repulsion were not already in its own self the negation of itself and the ones were not already in themselves negated. In this way we have repulsion abstractly on its own account and, similarly, attraction relatively to the ones as *affirmatively* present, has the side of an immediate determinate being and comes to them as an other.

If repulsion is thus taken merely by itself, then it is the dispersion of the many ones into somewhere undetermined, outside the sphere of repulsion itself; for repulsion is this, to negate the inter-relatedness of the many: the absence of any relation between them is the determination of the many taken abstractly. But repulsion is not merely the void; the ones, as unrelated, do not repel or exclude one another, this constitutes their determination. Repulsion is, although negative, still essentially *relation;* the mutual repulsion and flight is not a liberation from what is repelled and fled from, the one as excluding still remains *related* to what it excludes. But this moment of relation is attraction and thus is in repulsion itself; it is the negating of that abstract repulsion according to which the ones would be only self-related affirmative beings not excluding one another.

In starting, however, with the repulsion of the determinately present ones and so, too, with attraction posited as externally connected with it, the two determinations although inseparable are held apart as distinct; but it has been found that not merely is repulsion presupposed by attraction, but equally, too, there is a reverse relation of repulsion to attraction, and the former equally has its presupposition in the latter.

As thus determined they are inseparable and at the same time each is determined as an ought and a limitation relatively to the other. Their ought is their abstract determinateness in the form of the *in-itself;* but with this determinateness each is simply directed away from itself and relates itself to the *other*, and thus each *is* through the mediation of the *other* as *other*; their self-subsistence consists in the fact that in this mediation each is posited for the other as a *different* determining: repulsion as the positing of the many, attraction as the positing of the one, the latter as at the same time a negation of the many, and the former as a negation of their ideality in the one, so that attraction, too, is attraction only *through the mediation* of repulsion, just as repulsion is repulsion through the mediation of attraction. But the fact that in this interdependence the mediation of each through the other is rather negated, each of these determinations being a self-mediation, becomes evident after a closer consideration of them and brings them back to the unity of their Notion.

In the first place, that each presupposes *itself*, is related only to itself in its presupposition, this is already implied in the relationship between repulsion and attraction in their initially still relative character.

Relative repulsion is the mutual repelling of the *present* many ones which are supposed to be immediately *given*. But that *there are* many ones, this is repulsion itself; any presupposition which it might have is only its own positing. Further, the determination of *being* which might belong to the ones apart from the circumstance that they are posited—whereby they would be *already there*—belongs likewise to repulsion. The repelling is that whereby the ones manifest and maintain themselves as ones, whereby they *are* as such. Their being is repulsion itself, which is thus not a relative determinate being over against another such, but relates itself simply and solely to its own self.

Attraction is the positing of the one as such, of the real one, in contrast to which the many in their determinate being are determined as only ideal [*ideell*] and as vanishing. Attraction thus directly presupposes itself—in the determination, namely, of the other ones as ideal, which ones are otherwise supposed to be *for themselves*, repelling *others*, and therefore also any attracting one. Ideality, as opposed to this determination of repulsion, does not belong to the ones only through the relation to attraction; on the contrary, it is presupposed, it is the ideality *inherent* in the ones in that, as ones—including the one conceived as attracting—they are not distinguished from one another, are one and the same.

Further, this self-presupposing of the two determinations each for itself, means that each contains the other as a moment within it. The *self-presupposing* as such is the one's positing of itself in a one as the *negative* of itself—repulsion; and what is therein presupposed is *the same* as that which presupposes—attraction. That each is *in itself* only a moment, is the transition of each out of itself into the other, the self-negating of each in itself and the self-positing of each as its own other. The one as such, then, is a coming-out-of-itself, is only the positing of itself as its own other, as many; and the many, similarly, is only this, to collapse within itself and to posit itself as *its* other, as one, and in this very act to be related only to its own self, each continuing itself in its other. Thus there is already present in principle (*an sich*) the undividedness of the coming-out-of-itself (repulsion) and the self-positing as one (attraction). But in the relative repulsion and attraction, which presuppose immediate, *determinately* existent ones, it is *posited* that each is in its own self this negation of itself and is thus also the continuity of itself in its other. The repulsion of the determinately existent ones is the self-preservation of the one through the mutual repulsion of the others, so that (1) the other ones are negated *in it*—this is the side of its determinate being or of its being-for-other; but this is thus attraction as the ideality of the ones; and (2) the one is *in itself*, without relation to the others; but not only has being-in-itself as such long since passed over into being-for-self, but the one *in itself*, by its determination, is the aforesaid becoming of many ones. The *attraction* of the determinately existent ones is their ideality and the positing of the one, in which, accordingly, attraction as a negating and a generating of the one sublates itself, and as a positing of the one is in its own self the negative of itself, repulsion.

With this, the development of being-for-self is completed and has reached its conclusion. The one as *infinitely self*-related— infinitely, as the posited negation of negation—is the mediation in which it repels from itself its own self as its absolute (that is, abstract) *otherness*, (the *many*), and in relating itself negatively to this its non-being, that is, in sublating it, it is only self-relation; and one is only this *becoming* in which it is no longer determined as having a *beginning*, that is, is no longer posited as an immediate, affirmative being, neither is it as result, as having restored itself as the one, that is, the one as equally *immediate* and excluding; the process which it is posits and contains it throughout only as sublated. The sublating, at first determined as only a relative sublating of the *relation* to another determinately existent one—a relation which is thus itself not an indifferent repulsion and attraction—equally displays itself as passing over into the infinite relation of mediation through negation of the external relations of the immediate, determinately existent ones, and as having for result that very process of becoming which, in the instability of its moments, is the collapse, or rather going-together-with-itself, into simple immediacy. This being, in the determination it has now acquired, is *quantity*.

A brief survey of the moments of this *transition of quality into quantity* shows us that the fundamental determination of quality is being and immediacy, in which limit and determinateness are so identical with the being of something, that with its alteration the something itself vanishes; as thus *posited* it is determined as finite. Because of the immediacy of this unity, in which the *difference* has vanished but is *implicitly* present in the unity of *being* and *nothing*, the difference as *otherness* in general falls *outside* this unity. This relation to other contradicts the immediacy in which qualitative determinateness is self-relation. This otherness sublates itself in the infinity of being-for-self which makes explicit the difference (which in the negation of the negation is present in it) in the form of the one and the many and their relations, and has raised the qualitative moment to a genuine unity, that is, a unity which is no longer immediate but is posited as accordant with itself.

This unity is, therefore, (α) *being*, only as *affirmative*, that is *immediacy*, which is self-mediated through negation of the negation; being is posited as the unity which *pervades* its determinatenesses, limit, etc., which are posited in it as sublated; (β) *determinate being:* in such determination it is the negation or determinateness as a moment of affirmative being, yet determinateness no longer as immediate, but as reflected into itself, as related not to an other but to itself; a being determined simply *in itself*—the one; the otherness as such is itself a being-for-self; (γ) *being-for-self*, as that being which continues itself right through the determinateness and in which the one and the intrinsic determinedness is itself posited as sublated. The one is determined simultaneously as having gone beyond itself, and as *unity*; hence the one, the absolutely determined limit, is posited as the limit which is no limit, which is present in being but is indifferent to it.

Remark: The Kantian Construction of Matter from the Forces of Attraction and Repulsion

Attraction and repulsion, as we know, are usually regarded as *forces*. This determination of them and the relationships connected with it have to be compared with the Notions which have resulted from our consideration of them. Conceived as forces, they are regarded as self-subsistent and therefore as not connected with each other through their own nature; that is, they are considered not as moments, each of which is supposed to pass into the other, but rather as fixed in their opposition to each other. Further, they are imagined as meeting in a third, in *matter*, but not in such a manner that this unification is counted as their truth; on the contrary, each is regarded as a first, as being in and for itself, and matter, or its determinations, are supposed to be realized and produced by them. When it is said that matter has the forces *within itself*, they are understood to be so conjoined in this unity that they are at the same time presupposed as intrinsically free and independent of each other.

Kant, as we know, *constructed* matter from the forces of attraction and repulsion, or at least he has, to use his own words, set up the metaphysical elements of this construction. It will not be without interest to examine this construction more closely. This *metaphysical* exposition of a subject matter which not only itself but also in its determinations seemed to belong only to *experience* is noteworthy, partly because as an experiment with the Notion it at least gave the impulse to the more recent philosophy of nature, to a philosophy which does not make nature as given in sense-perception the basis of science, but which goes to the absolute Notion for its determinations; and partly because in many cases no advance is made beyond the Kantian construction which is held to be a philosophical beginning and foundation for physics.

Now it is true that matter as it exists for sense perception is no more a subject matter of logic than are space and its determinations. But the forces of attraction and repulsion, in so far as they are regarded as forces of empirical matter, are also based on the pure determinations here considered of the one and the many and their inter-relationships, which, because these names are most obvious, I have called repulsion and attraction.

Kant's method in the deduction of matter from these forces, which he calls a *construction*, when looked at more closely does not deserve this name, unless any exercise of reflection, even analytical reflection, is to be called a construction; and later philosophers of nature have in fact given the name of construction to the shallowest reasoning and the most baseless concoction of unbridled imagination and thoughtless reflection—and it is especially for the so-called factors of attraction and repulsion that such philosophers have shown a predilection.

For Kant's method is basically analytical, not constructive. He presupposes the idea of matter and then asks what forces are required to maintain the determinations he has presupposed. Thus, on the one hand, he demands the force of attraction because, properly speaking, through repulsion alone and without attraction matter could not exist;[1] and on the other hand he derives repulsion, too, from matter and gives as the reason that we think of matter as impenetrable, since it presents itself under this category to the sense of touch by which it manifests itself to us. Consequently, he proceeds, repulsion is at once thought in the *concept* of matter because it is immediately *given* therein, whereas attraction is added to the concept *syllogistically*. But these syllogisms, too, are based on what has just been said, namely, that matter which possessed repulsive force alone, would not exhaust our conception of matter. It is evident that this is the method of a cognition which reflects on experience, which first *perceives* the determinations in a phenomenon, then makes these the foundation, and for their so-called *explanation* assumes corresponding *basic elements* or *forces* which are supposed to produce those determinations of the phenomenon.

With respect to this difference as to the way in which cognition finds the forces of repulsion and attraction in matter, Kant further remarks that the force of attraction certainly just as much belongs to the concept of matter *'although it is not contained in it'*; this last expression is italicized by Kant. However, it is hard to perceive what this difference is supposed to be; for a determination which belongs to the concept of anything *must* be truly *contained in it*.

What causes the difficulty and gives rise to this vain subterfuge, is that Kant from the start one-sidedly attributes to the concept of matter only the determination of impenetrability, which we are supposed to perceive by the sense of touch, for which reason the force of repulsion as the holding off of an other from itself is immediately *given*. But if, further, the *existence* of matter is supposed to be impossible without attraction, then this assertion is based on a conception of matter taken from sense perception; consequently, the determination of attraction, too, must come within the range of sense perception. It is indeed easy to perceive that matter, besides its being-for-self, which sublates the being-for-other (offers resistance), has also a *relation* between its *self-*

[1] *Anfangsgr. der Naturwissensch.*, p. 53 *et seq.*

determined parts, a spatial *extension* and *cohesion*, and in rigidity and solidity the cohesion is very firm. Physics explains that the tearing apart, etc., of a body requires a force which shall be stronger than the mutual *attraction* of the parts of the body. From this observation reflection can just as directly derive the force of attraction or assume it as *given*, as it did with the force of repulsion. In point of fact, if we consider Kant's arguments from which the force of attraction is supposed to be deduced (the proof of the proposition that the possibility of matter requires a force of attraction as a second fundamental force, *loc. cit.*), it is apparent that their sole content is this, that through repulsion alone matter would not be *spatial*. Matter being presupposed as filling space, it is credited with continuity, the ground of which is assumed to be the force of attraction.

Now if the merit of such a construction of matter were at most that of an analysis (though a merit diminished by the faulty exposition), still the fundamental thought, namely, the derivation of matter from these two opposite determinations as its fundamental forces, must always be highly esteemed. Kant is chiefly concerned to banish the vulgar mechanistic way of thinking which stops short at the one determination of impenetrability, of self-determined and self-subsistent puncticity, and converts into something *external* the opposite determination, the *relation* of matter within itself or the relation of a plurality of matters, which in turn are regarded as particular ones—a way of thinking which, as Kant says, will admit no motive forces except pressure and thrust, that is, only action from without. This *external* manner of thinking always presupposes motion as already externally *present* in matter, and it does not occur to it to regard motion as something immanent and to comprehend motion itself in matter, which latter is thus assumed as, on its own account, motionless and inert. This stand-point has before it only ordinary mechanics, not immanent and free motion. It is true that Kant sublates this externality in so far as he makes attraction (the *relation* of matters to one another in so far as these are assumed as separated from one another, or matter generally in its self-externality) a *force of matter itself*; still, on the other hand, his two fundamental forces within matter remain external to and completely independent of each other.

The fixed difference of these two forces attributed to them

from that external standpoint is no less null than any other distinction must show itself to be which, in respect of its specific content, is made into something supposedly fixed; because these forces are only moments which pass over into each other, as we saw above when they were considered in their truth. I go on to consider these other distinctions as they are stated by Kant.

He defines the force of attraction as a penetrative force by which one bit of matter can act *directly* on the parts of another even beyond the area of contact; the force of repulsion, on the other hand, he defines as a surface force through which bits of matter can act on each other only in the common area of contact. The reason adduced that the latter can be only a surface force is as follows: 'The parts in *contact* each limit the sphere of action of the other, and the force of repulsion cannot move any more distant part except through the agency of the intervening parts; an immediate action of one part of matter on another passing right across these intervening parts by forces of expansion (which means here, forces of repulsion) is impossible.'[1]

But here we must remember that in assuming 'nearer' or 'more distant' parts of matter, the same distinction would likewise arise with respect to attraction, namely, that though one atom acted on another, yet a third, more distant atom (between which and the first atom, the second atom would be), would first enter into the sphere of attraction of the intervening atom nearer to it; therefore the first atom would not have an *immediate*, simple action on the third, from which it would follow that the action of the force of attraction, like that of repulsion, is equally mediated. Further, the *genuine penetration* of the force of attraction could of necessity consist only in this, that every part of matter was in and for itself attractive, not that a certain number of atoms behaved passively and only one atom actively. But we must at once remark with respect to the force of repulsion itself that in the passage quoted, 'parts in contact' are mentioned which implies *solidity* and *continuity* of a matter already *finished and complete* which would not permit the passage through it of a repelling force. But this solidity of matter in which parts are in *contact* and are no longer separated by the void already pre-supposes that the force of repulsion is sublated; according to the sensuous conception of repulsion which prevails here, parts

---

[1] See *Anfangsgr. der Naturwissensch. Erklärung und Zusätze*, p. 67.

in contact are to be taken as those which do not repel each other. It therefore follows, quite tautologically, that where repulsion is assumed to be *not*, there no repulsion can take place. But from this nothing else follows which could serve to determine the force of repulsion. However, reflection on the statement that parts in contact are in contact only in so far as they hold themselves *apart*, leads directly to the conclusion that the force of repulsion is not merely *on the surface* of matter but within the sphere which was supposed to be only a sphere of attraction.

Kant assumes further that 'through the force of attraction, matter only occupies space but does not fill it';[1] and 'because matter through the force of attraction does not fill space, this force can act across empty space since there is no intervening matter to limit it'. This distinction is much the same as the one mentioned above where a determination was supposed to belong to the concept of a thing but not to be contained in it; here, then, matter is supposed only to *occupy* a space but not to *fill* it. There it is repulsion, if we stop at the first determination of matter, through which the ones repel one another and so are only negatively related to one another, here that means, by empty space. Here, however, it is the force of attraction which keeps space empty; it does not fill space by its connection of the atoms, in other words, it keeps the atoms in a negative relation to one another. We see that Kant here unconsciously realizes what is implicit in the nature of the subject matter, when he attributes to the force of attraction precisely what, in accordance with the first determination, he attributed to the opposite force. While he was busy with establishing the difference between the two forces, it happened that one had passed over into the other. Thus through repulsion, on the other hand, matter is supposed to fill a space, and consequently through repulsion the empty space left by the force of attraction vanishes. In point of fact repulsion, in doing away with empty space, also destroys the negative relation of the atoms or ones, that is, their repulsion of one another; in other words, repulsion is determined as the opposite of itself.

To this effacing of the differences there is added the confusion arising from the fact that, as we observed at the beginning, Kant's exposition of the opposed forces is analytic; and whereas matter is supposed to be derived from its elements, it is presented through-

[1] *Ibid.*

out the entire discourse as already formed and constituted. In the definition of surface and penetrative force both are assumed as motive forces by means of which matter is supposed to be able to act in one or other of these ways. Here, therefore, they are represented as forces, not through which matter first comes into being but through which matter, as an already finished product, is only set in motion. But in so far as we are speaking of the forces through which different bodies act on one another and are set in motion, this is something quite different from the determination and relation which these forces were supposed to have as [constitutive] moments of matter.

The same opposition of attractive and repulsive forces is made by their more developed form of centripetal and centrifugal forces. These appear to offer an essential distinction, since in their sphere there is a fixed single one, a centre, in relation to which the other ones behave as *not for themselves*, so that the difference between the forces can be linked to this presupposed difference between a single central one and the others which are not independent relatively to it. But if they are to be used for explanation—for which purpose they are assumed to be (like the forces of repulsion and attraction) in an inverse quantitative ratio so that the one increases as the other decreases—then the phenomenon of the motion and its inequality ought to be the result of these forces which were assumed for the purpose of explanation. However, one need only examine the accounts (any of them will do) of a phenomenon like the unequal velocity of a planet in its orbit round the sun, based on the opposition of these forces, to become aware of the confusion which prevails in such explanations, and the impossibility of disentangling the magnitudes of the forces, so that the one which in the explanation is assumed to be decreasing can just as well be assumed to be increasing, and *vice versa*. To make this evident would require a lengthier exposition than could be given here; but what is necessary for this purpose is adduced later on in connection with the inverted relation.

Section Two: Magnitude (Quantity)

The difference between quantity and quality has been stated. Quality is the first, immediate determinateness, quantity is the determinateness which has become indifferent to being, a limit which is just as much no limit, being-for-self which is absolutely identical with being-for-other—a repulsion of the many ones which is directly the non-repulsion, the continuity of them.

Because that which is for itself is now posited as not excluding its other, but rather as affirmatively continuing itself into it, it is otherness in so far as *determinate being* again appears in this continuity and its determinateness is *at the same time* no longer in a simple self-relation, no longer an immediate determinateness of the determinately existent something, but is posited as self-repelling, as in fact having the relation-to-self as a determinateness in another something (which is *for itself*); and since they are *at the same time* indifferent, relationless limits reflected into themselves, the determinateness in general is outside itself, an absolutely *self-external* determinateness and an equally external something; such a limit, the indifference of the limit within itself and of the something to the limit, constitutes the *quantitative* determinateness of the something.

In the first place, *pure quantity* is to be distinguished from itself as a *determinate* quantity, from *quantum*. As the former, it is in the first place real being-for-self which has returned into itself and which as yet contains no determinateness: a compact, infinite unity which continues itself into itself.

Secondly, this develops a determinateness which is posited in it as one which is at the same time no determinateness, as only an *external* one. It becomes *quantum*. Quantum is indifferent determinateness, that is, a self-transcending, self-negating determinateness; as this otherness of otherness it relapses into the infinite progress. But the infinite quantum is the indifferent determinateness *sublated*, it is the restoration of quality.

Thirdly, quantum in a qualitative form is quantitative *ratio*. Quantum transcends itself only generally: in ratio, however, its transition into its otherness is such that this otherness in which it has its determination is at the same time posited, is another quantum. Thus quantum has returned into itself and in its otherness is related to itself.

At the base of this ratio there is still the externality of quantum; the quanta which are related to each other are *indifferent*, that is, they have their self-relation in such self-externality. The ratio is thus only a formal unity of quality and quantity. Its dialectic is its transition into their absolute unity, into *Measure*.

Remark: In something, its limit as quality is essentially its determinateness. If, however, by limit we mean quantitative limit, then when, for example, a field alters its limit it still remains what it was before, a field. If on the other hand its qualitative limit is altered, then since this is the determinateness which makes it a field, it becomes a meadow, wood, and so on. A red, whether brighter or paler, is still red; but if it altered its quality it would cease to be red, would become blue or some other colour. The determination of *magnitude* as quantum reached above, namely that it has a permanent substratum of being *which is indifferent to its determinateness*, can be found in any other example.

By magnitude *quantum* is meant, as in the examples cited, not quantity; and it is chiefly for this reason that this foreign term must be used.

The definition of magnitude given in mathematics likewise concerns quantum. A magnitude is usually defined as that which can be increased or diminished. But to increase means to make the magnitude more, to decrease, to make the magnitude less. In this there lies a *difference* of magnitude as such from itself and magnitude would thus be that of which the magnitude can be altered. The definition thus proves itself to be inept in so far as the same term is used in it which was to have been defined. Since the same term must not be used in the definition, the *more* and *less* can be resolved into an affirmative addition which, in accordance with the nature of quantum, is likewise external, and a subtraction, as an equally external negation. It is this *external* form both of reality and of negation which in general characterizes the nature of *alteration* in quantum. In that imperfect expression, therefore, one cannot fail to recognize the main point involved, namely the indifference of the alteration, so that the alteration's own *more* and *less*, its indifference to itself, lies in its very Notion.

CHAPTER I
QUANTITY

A. PURE QUANTITY

Quantity is sublated being-for-self; the repelling one which related itself only negatively to the excluded one, having passed over into relation to it, treats the other as identical with itself, and in doing so has lost its determination: being-for-self has passed over into attraction. The absolute brittleness of the repelling *one* has melted away into this *unity* which, however, as containing this one, is at the same time determined by the immanent repulsion, and as unity of the self-externality is unity with itself. Attraction is in this way the moment of *continuity* in quantity.

Continuity is, therefore, simple, self-same self-relation, which is not interrupted by any limit or exclusion; it is not, however, an *immediate* unity, but a unity of ones which possess being-for-self. The *asunderness of the plurality* is still contained in this unity, but at the same time as not differentiating or *interrupting* it. In continuity, the plurality is posited as it is in itself; the many are all alike, each is the same as the other and the plurality is, consequently, a simple, undifferentiated sameness. Continuity is this moment of self-sameness of the asunderness, the self-continuation of the different ones into those from which they are distinguished.

In continuity, therefore, magnitude immediately possesses the moment of *discreteness*—repulsion, as now a moment in quantity. Continuity is self-sameness, but of the Many which, however, do not become exclusive; it is repulsion which expands the self-sameness to continuity. Hence discreteness, on its side, is a coalescent discreteness, where the ones are not connected by the void, by the negative, but by their own continuity and do not interrupt this self-sameness in the many.

Quantity is the unity of these moments of continuity and discreteness, but at first it is so in the *form* of one of them, *continuity*, as a result of the dialectic of being-for-self, which has collapsed into the form of self-identical immediacy. Quantity is, as such, this simple result in so far as being-for-self has not yet developed its moments and posited them within itself. It *contains* them to begin with as being-for-self posited as it is in truth. The determination of being-for-self was to be a self-sublating relation-to-self, a perpetual coming-out-of-itself. But what is repelled is itself; repulsion is, therefore, the creative flowing away of itself. On account of the self-sameness of what is repelled, this distinguishing or differentiation is an uninterrupted continuity; and because of the coming-out-of-itself this continuity, without being interrupted, is at the same time a plurality, which no less immediately remains in its self-identicalness.

Remark 1: *The Conception of Pure Quantity*

Pure quantity has not as yet any limit or is not as yet quantum; and even in so far as it becomes quantum it is not bounded by limit but, on the contrary, consists precisely in not being bounded by limit, in having being-for-self within it as a sublated moment. The presence in it of discreteness as a moment can be expressed by saying that quantity is simply the omnipresent *real possibility* within itself of the one, but conversely that the one is no less absolutely continuous.

In thinking that is not based on the Notion, continuity easily becomes mere *composition*, that is, an *external* relation of the ones to one another, in which the one is maintained in its absolute brittleness and exclusiveness. But it has been shown that the one essentially and spontaneously (*an und für sich selbst*) passes over into attraction, into its ideality, and that consequently continuity is not external to it but belongs to it and is grounded in its very nature. It is just this *externality* of continuity for the ones to which atomism clings and which ordinary thinking finds it difficult to forsake. Mathematics, on the other hand, rejects a metaphysics which would make time *consist* of points of time; space in general—or in the first place the line—*consist* of points of space; the plane, of lines; and total space of planes. It allows no validity to such discontinuous ones. Even though, for instance, in determining the magnitude of a plane, it represents it as the *sum* of infinitely many lines, this discreteness counts only as a momentary representation, and the sublation of the discreteness is already implied in the *infinite* plurality of the lines, since the space which they are supposed to constitute is after all bounded.

It is the notion of pure quantity as opposed to the mere image of it that Spinoza, for whom it had especial importance, has in mind when he speaks of quantity as follows:

'*Quantitas duobus modis a nobis concipitur, abstracte scilicet sive superficialiter, prout nempe ipsam imaginamur; vel ut substantia, quod a solo intellectu fit. Si itaque ad quantitatem attendimus, prout in imaginatione est, quod saepe et facilius a nobis fit, reperietur finita, divisibilis et ex partibus conflata, si autem ad ipsam, prout in intellectu est, attendimus, et eam, quatenus substantia est, concipimus, quod difficillime fit,—infinita, unica et indivisibilis reperietur. Quod omnibus, qui inter imaginationem et intellectum distinguere sciverint, satis manifestum erit.*'[1]

More specific examples of pure quantity, if they are wanted, are space and time, also matter as such, light, and so forth, and the ego itself: only by quantity, as already remarked, is not to be understood quantum. Space, time and the rest, are expansions, pluralities which are a coming-out-of-self, a flowing which, however, does not pass over into its opposite, into quality or the one, but as a coming-out-of-self they are a perennial *self-production* of their unity.

Space is this absolute *self-externality* which equally is absolutely uninterrupted, a perpetual becoming-other which is self-identical; time is an absolute coming-out-of-itself, a generating of the one, (a point of time, the now) and immediately the annihilation of it, and again the continuous annihilation of this passing away; so that this spontaneous generating of non-being is equally a simple self-sameness and self-identity. As regards *matter* as quantity, among the seven surviving propositions of the first dissertation of Leibniz there is one, the second, which runs: *Non omnino improbabile est, materiam et quantitatem esse realiter idem.*[2] In fact, the distinction between these two concepts is simply this, that quantity is a determination of pure thought, whereas matter is the

---

[1] Eth. P. I. Prop, XV, Schol.: 'Quantity is conceived by us in two manners, to wit, abstractly and superficially, as an offspring of imagination or as a substance, which is done by the intellect alone. If, then, we look at quantity as it is in the imagination, which we often and very easily do, it will be found to be finite, divisible, and composed of parts; but if we look at it as it is in the intellect and conceive it, in so far as it is a substance, which is done with great difficulty, then as we have already sufficiently shown, it will be found to be infinite, without like, and indivisible. This, to all who know how to distinguish between the imagination and the intellect, will be quite clear.'

[2] Left-hand page of Part I of his works.

same determination in outer existence. The determination of pure quantity belongs also to the ego which is an absolute becoming-other, an infinite removal or all-round repulsion to the negative freedom of being-for-self which, however, remains utterly simple continuity—the continuity of universality or being-with-self uninterrupted by the infinitely manifold limits, by the content of sensations, intutions, and so forth. Those who reject the idea of plurality as a simple unity and besides the *Notion* of it, to wit, that each of the many is the same as every other, namely, a one of the many—since here we are not speaking of the many as further determined, as green, red, and so on, but of the many considered in and for itself—demand also a *representation* of this unity, will find plenty of instances in those continua which exhibit the deduced Notion of quantity as present in simple intutition.

Remark 2: The Kantian Antinomy of the Indivisibility and the Infinite Divisibility of Time, Space and Matter
It is the nature of quantity, this simple unity of discreteness and continuity, that gives rise to the conflict or antinomy of the infinite divisibility of space, time, matter, etc.

This antinomy consists solely in the fact that discreteness must be asserted just as much as continuity. The one-sided assertion of discreteness gives infinite or absolute dividedness, hence an indivisible, for principle: the one-sided assertion of continuity, on the other hand, gives infinite divisibility.

It is well known that the Kantian *Critique of Pure Reason* sets up four (cosmological) antinomies, the second of which deals with the antithesis constituted by the moments of quantity.

These Kantian antinomies will always remain an important part of the critical philosophy; they, more than anything else, brought about the downfall of previous metaphysics and can be regarded as a main transition into more recent philosophy since they, in particular, helped to produce the conviction of the nullity of the categories of finitude in regard to their *content*—which is a more correct method than the formal one of a subjective idealism, according to which their defect is supposed to be, not what they are in themselves, but only that they are subjective. But this exposition with all its merits is imperfect; its course is impeded and tangled, and also it is false in regard to its result, which presupposes that cognition has no other forms of thought than finite categories. In both respects these antinomies deserve a more exact critical appraisal which will not only throw more light on their standpoint and method but will also free the main point at issue from the useless form into which it has been forced.

In the first place, I remark that Kant wanted to give his four cosmological antinomies a show of competeness by the principle of classification which he took from his schema of the categories. But profounder insight into the antinomial, or more truly into the dialectical nature of reason demonstrates *any* Notion whatever to be a unity of opposed moments to which, therefore, the form of antinomial assertions could be given. Becoming, determinate being, etc., and any other Notion, could thus provide its particular antinomy, and thus as many antinomies could be constructed as there are Notions. Ancient scepticism did not spare itself the pains of demonstrating this contradiction or antinomy in every notion which confronted it in the sciences.

Further, Kant did not take up the antinomy in the Notions themselves, but in the already *concrete* form of cosmological determinations. In order to possess the antinomy in its purity and to deal with it in its simple Notion, the determinations of thought must not be taken in their application to and entanglement in the general idea of the world, of space, time, matter, etc; this concrete material must be omitted from consideration of these determinations which it is powerless to influence and which must be considered purely on their own account since they alone constitute the essence and the ground of the antinomies.

Kant's conception of the antinomies is that they are 'not sophisms but contradictions which reason must necessarily *come up against*' (a Kantian expression); and this is an important view. 'Reason, when it sees into the ground of the natural illusion of the antinomies is, it is true, no longer imposed on by them but yet continues to be deceived.' The Kantian solution, namely, through the so-called transcendental ideality of the world of perception, has no other result than to make the so-called conflict into something *subjective*, in which of course it remains still the same illusion, that is, is as unresolved, as before. Its genuine solution can only be this: two opposed determinations which belong necessarily to one and the same Notion cannot be valid each on its own in its one-sidedness; on the contrary, they are true only as sublated, only in the unity of their Notion.

The Kantian antinomies on closer inspection contain nothing more than the quite simple categorical assertion of *each* of the two opposed moments of a determination, each being taken on its own in isolation from the other. But at the same time this simple categorical, or strictly speaking assertoric statement is wrapped up in a false, twisted scaffolding of reasoning which is intended to produce a semblance of proof and to conceal and disguise the merely assertoric character of the statement, as closer consideration will show.

The relevant antinomy here concerns the so-called infinite divisibility of matter and rests on the antithesis of the moments of continuity and discreteness which are contained in the Notion of quantity.

The thesis of the same as expounded by Kant runs thus:

'Every composite substance in the world consists of simple parts, and nowhere does there exist anything but the simple or what is compounded from it.'

To the simple, the atom, there is here opposed the composite, which is a very inferior determination compared to the continuous. The substrate given to these abstractions, namely, substances in the world, here means nothing more than things as sensuously perceived and it has no influence on the antinomy itself; space or time could equally well be taken. Now since the thesis speaks only of composition instead of continuity it is really as it stands an analytical or *tautological* proposition. That the composite is not in its own self a one, but only something externally put together and *consisting of what is other than itself*, this is its immediate determination. But the other of the composite is the simple. It is therefore tautological to say that the composite consists of the simple. To ask of what something consists is to ask for an indication of something else, the compounding of which constitutes the said something. If ink is said to consist simply of ink, the meaning of the inquiry after the something else of which it consists has been missed and the question is not answered but only repeated. A further question then is whether that which is under discussion is supposed to *consist of something* or not. But the composite is simply that which is supposed to be a combination of something else. If, however, the simple which is the other of the composite is taken only as *relatively* simple and is itself composite, too, then the question still remains unanswered. What ordinary thinking has in mind is, perhaps, only some composite or other of which something or other, too, would be assigned as *its* simple, such particular something being composite on its own account. But what is under discussion here is the *composite as such.*

Now as regards the Kantian *proof* of the thesis this, like all the Kantian proofs of the rest of the antinomial propositions, makes the detour of being apagogic, a detour which will prove to be quite superfluous.

'Assume', he begins, 'that composite substances do not consist of simple parts; then if *all* composition were thought away no composite part and (since we have just assumed that there are no simple parts) no simple part—hence nothing at all—would remain; consequently, no substance would have been given.'

This conclusion is quite correct: if nothing but composite substances exist and all that is composite is thought away, then nothing whatever remains; this will be conceded, but this tauto-logical redundance could be omitted and the proof straightway begin with what follows, namely:

'Either it is impossible to think away all composition, or else there remains after such removal in thought something which is not composite, that is, the simple.

'In the first case, however, the composite again would not consist of substances (because with these, composition is only a contingent relation of substances[1] which, apart from such rela-tion, must still persist on their own account). Now since this case contradicts what was assumed, only the second case is left: namely, that all composite substances consist of simple parts.'

The very reason which is the main point, and in face of which all that precedes is completely superfluous, is mentioned by the way, in a parenthesis. The dilemma is this: either the composite persists, or else the simple. If the former, that is, the composite, persists, then what persists would not be substances, for com-position is for these only a contingent relation; but substances do persist, therefore, what persists is the simple.

It is clear that the apagogical detour could be omitted and the

---

[1] In addition to the redundance of the proof itself there is here also a redun-dance of language—'because *with these*' (namely the substances) 'composition is only a contingent relation of *substances*'.

G

thesis: 'composite substance consists of simple parts', could be directly followed by the reason: *because* composition is merely a *contingent* relation of substances, and is therefore external to them and does not concern the substances themselves. If the composition is in fact contingent then, of course, substances are essentially simple. But this contingency which is the sole point at issue is not proved but straightway assumed, and casually, too, in a parenthesis—as something self-evident or of secondary importance. True, it goes without saying that composition is a contingent and external determination; but if the point at issue were only a contingent togetherness instead of continuity, it would not be worth while constructing an antinomy about it—or rather it would not be possible to formulate one. Therefore, the assertion that the parts are simple is, as remarked, only a tautology.

The apagogical detour thus contains the very assertion which should result from it. The proof therefore can be put more concisely thus:

Let us assume that substances do not consist of simple parts but are only composite. But now all composition can be thought away (for it is only a contingent relation); after its removal, therefore, there are no substances left unless we assume that they consist of simple parts. But substances we must have for we have assumed them; *everything* is not meant to vanish, *something* must be left over, for we have presupposed something persistent which we called substance. Therefore this something must be simple.

To complete the whole, we have still to consider the conclusion which runs as follows:

'From this it follows, as a direct consequence, that all things in the world without exception are simple entities, that composition is only an external state of them, and that reason must think the elementary substances as simple entities.'

Here we see the externality, that is contingency, of composition put forward as a *consequence* after it had already been introduced parenthetically and used in the proof.

Kant strongly protests that he is not looking for sophisms in the conflicting statements of the antinomy for the purpose, as it were, of special pleading. But the defect of the proof in question is not so much that it is a sophism, as that its laboured, tortuous complexity serves no other purpose than to produce the merely outward semblance of a proof and partially to obscure the quite transparent fact that what was supposed to emerge as a consequence is, parenthetically, that on which the proof hinges; that there is no proof at all, but only an assumption.

The antithesis runs:

'No composite thing in the world consists of simple parts and nowhere in the world does there exist anything simple.'

The proof has equally an apagogical turn and, in a different way, is just as faulty as the previous one.

'Suppose', it runs, 'that a composite thing as a substance consists of simple parts. Because all *external* relation, and consequently all composition of substances, is possible only in *space*, therefore, the space occupied by the composite substance must consist of as many parts as those of which the composite substance consists. Now space does not consist of simple parts but of spaces. Therefore each part of the composite substance must occupy a space.'

'But the absolutely primary parts of everything composite are simple.'

'Therefore the simple occupies a space.'

'Now since every real thing that occupies a space comprises a manifold of mutually external parts and is consequently composite, consisting of substances, it would follow that the simple is a composite substance—which is self-contradictory.'

This proof can be called a whole *nest* (to use an expression elsewhere employed by Kant) of faulty procedure.

In the first place, its apagogical form is a groundless illusion. For the assumption that whatever is substantial is spatial, but that space does not consist of simple parts is a direct assertion which is made the immediate ground of what is to be proved, and with this there is an end to the proving of the antithesis.

Next, this apagogical proof begins with the proposition: 'that all composition from substances is an *external* relation', but oddly enough immediately forgets it. For it then goes on to conclude that composition is possible only in *space*, that space does not consist of simple parts, and that therefore the real thing occupying a space is composite. But once composition is assumed as an external relation, then spatiality itself (in which alone composition is supposed to be possible) is for that very reason an external relation for the substances, which does not concern them or affect their nature any more than anything else does that can be inferred from the determination of spatiality. For this very reason, the substances ought not to have been put into space.

Further, it is assumed that the space in which the substances here are placed does not consist of simple parts, because it is an intuition, that is, according to the Kantian definition, a representation which can only be given through a single object, and is not a so-called discursive concept. This Kantian distinction between intuition and concept has, as everyone knows, given rise to a deal of nonsense about the former, and to avoid the labour of comprehension the value and sphere of intuition have been extended to the whole field of cognition. What is pertinent here is just this, that space, and also intuition itself, must be grasped in terms of their *Notions* if, that is, we want really to *comprehend*. And thus the question would arise whether space, even though a simple continuity for intuition, ought not to be grasped, in accordance with its Notion, as consisting of simple parts, or whether it would be involved in the same antinomy which applied only to substance. As a matter of fact, if the antinomy is grasped abstractly, it concerns, as we remarked, quantity *as such*, and hence equally space and time.

But it is assumed in the proof that space does not consist of simple parts; this therefore ought to have been the reason for not placing the simple in this element which is incompatible with the nature of the simple. There is also involved here a clash between the continuity of space and composition; the two are confused with each other, the former being substituted for the latter (which results in a *quaternio terminorum* in the conclusion). With Kant, space has the express determination of being 'sole and single, its parts resting only on limitations, so that they do not precede the one, all-embracing space as, so to speak, its component parts from which it could be compounded'.[1] Here continuity is quite correctly and definitely predicated of space in denial of its composition from parts. On the other hand, in the argument the placing of substances in space is supposed to involve 'a manifold of mutually external parts' and, more particularly, 'consequently a composite'. Yet, as we have quoted, the way in which manifoldness is present in space is expressly intended to exclude composition and component parts antecedent to the unity of space.

[1] *Critique of Pure Reason*, 2nd edition, p. 39.

In the remark to the proof of the antithesis we are also expressly reminded of the other fundamental conception of the critical philosophy, namely, that we have a *notion* of bodies only as appearances or phenomena; as such, however, they necessarily presuppose space as the condition of the possibility of all outer appearance. If by substances we are meant here to understand only bodies as we see, touch, taste them, and so on, then we are not really discussing them as they are in their Notion but only as sensuously perceived. The proof of the antithesis, then, amounted in short to this: all our visual, tactile, and other experience shows us only what is composite; even the best microscopes and the keenest knives have not enabled us to *come across* anything simple. Then neither should reason expect to come across anything simple.

When we look more closely into the opposition of this thesis and antithesis, freeing their proofs from all pointless redundancy and tortuousness, we see that the proof of the antithesis dogmatically assumes *continuity* (by placing substances in space) and also that the proof of the thesis, by assuming that composition is the mode of relation of substances, dogmatically assumes the *contingency of this relation*, and hence assumes that substances are *absolute ones*. Thus the whole antinomy reduces to the separation of the two moments of quantity and the direct assertion of them as absolutely separate. When substance, matter, space, time, etc., are taken only as *discrete*, they are absolutely divided; their principle is the one. When they are taken as *continuous*, this one is only a sublated one; division remains a divisibility, it remains the *possibility* of division, as a possibility, without actually reaching the atom. Now even if we stop at the determination given in what has been said about these antitheses, then the moment of the atom is contained in continuity itself, for this is simply the possibility of division; just as said dividedness, discreteness, sublates all distinction of the ones—for each of the simple ones is what the other is—consequently, also contains their sameness and hence their continuity. Since each of the two opposed sides contains its other within itself and neither can be thought without the other, it follows that neither of these determinations, taken alone, has truth; this belongs only to their unity. This is the true dialectical consideration of them and also the true result.

Infinitely more ingenious and profound than this Kantian

antinomy are the dialectical examples of the ancient Eleatic school, especially those concerning motion, which likewise are based on the Notion of quantity and in it find their solution. To consider them here, too, would be too lengthy a business; they concern the Notions of space and time and can be dealt with at the same time as these subjects and in the history of philosophy. They reflect the greatest credit on the intelligence of their inventors; they have for *result* the pure being of Parmenides, in that in them is demonstrated the dissolution of all determinate being; they are thus in themselves the *flux* of Heraclitus. For this reason they deserve a more thorough consideration than the usual explanation that they are just sophisms; which assertion sticks to empirical perception, following the procedure of Diogenes (a procedure which is so illuminating to ordinary common sense) who, when a dialectician pointed out the contradiction contained in motion, made no effort to reason it out but, by silently walking up and down, is supposed to have referred to the evidence of sight for an answer. Such assertion and refutation is certainly easier to make than to engage in thinking and to hold fast and resolve by thought alone the complexities originating in thought, and not in abstruse thought either, but in the thoughts spontaneously arising in ordinary consciousness.

The solutions propounded by Aristotle of these dialectical forms merit high praise, and are contained in his genuinely speculative Notions of space, time and motion. To infinite divisibility (which, being imagined as actually carried out, is the same as infinite dividedness, as the atoms) on which is based the most famous of those proofs, he opposes continuity, which applies equally well to time as to space, so that the infinite, that is, *abstract* plurality is contained only *in principle* [*an sich*], as a *possibility*, in continuity. What is actual in contrast to abstract plurality as also to abstract continuity, is their concrete forms, space and time themselves, just as these latter are abstract relatively to matter and motion. What is *abstract* has only an implicit or potential being; it only *is* as a moment of something real. Bayle, who finds Aristotle's solution of the Zenonic dialectic '*pitoyable*',[1] does not understand the meaning of the statement that matter is only *potentially* infinitely divisible; he rejoins that if matter is infinitely divisible, then it *actually* contains an infinite

[1] P. Bayle: *Dictionnaire*, Article 'Zenon'.

number of parts, that, therefore, this infinite is not an infinite *en puissance* but an infinite that really and actually exists. On the contrary, divisibility itself even is only a possibility, not an *existing* of the parts, and the plurality as such is posited in the continuity only as a moment, as sublated. Acute understanding, in which Aristotle, too, is certainly unsurpassed, is not competent to grasp and to decide on speculative Notions, any more than the crudity of sensuous conception instanced above is adequate to refute the reasoning of Zeno. Such intellect commits the error of holding such mental fictions, such abstractions, as an infinite number of parts, to be something true and actual; but this sensuous consciousness does not let itself be brought beyond the empirical element to thought.

The Kantian solution of the antinomy likewise consists solely in the supposition that reason should not soar beyond sensuous perception and should take the world of appearance, the phenomenal world, as it is. This solution leaves the content of the antinomy itself on one side; it does not attain to the nature of the *Notion* of its determinations, each of which, isolated on its own, is null and is in its own self only the transition into its other, the unity of both being *quantity* in which they have their truth.

B. CONTINUOUS AND DISCRETE MAGNITUDE

1. Quantity contains the two moments of continuity and discreteness. It is to be posited in both of them as determinations of itself. It is already their *immediate* unity, that is, quantity is posited at first only in one of its determinations, continuity, and as such is continuous magnitude.

Or we may say that continuity is indeed one of the moments of quantity which requires the other moment, discreteness, to complete it. But quantity is a concrete unity only in so far as it is the unity of *distinct* moments. These, are, therefore, also to be taken as distinct, but are not to be resolved again into attraction and repulsion, but are to be taken as they are in their truth, each remaining in its unity with the other, that is, remaining the *whole*. Continuity is only coherent, compact unity as unity of the discrete; *posited* as such it is no longer only a moment but the whole of quantity, *continuous magnitude*.

2. *Immediate* quantity is continuous magnitude. But quantity is not an immediate at all; immediacy is a determinateness the sublatedness of which is quantity itself. It is, therefore, to be posited in the determinateness immanent in it, and this is the one. Quantity is *discrete magnitude*.

Discreteness is, like continuity, a moment of quantity but it is itself also the whole of quantity just because it is a moment in it, in the whole, and therefore as a distinct moment it does not stand outside the whole, outside its unity with the other moment. Quantity is in itself asunderness, and continuous magnitude is this asunderness continuing itself without negation as an internally self-same connectedness. But discrete magnitude is this asunderness as discontinuous, as interrupted. With this plurality of ones, however, we are not again in the presence of the plurality of atoms and the void, repulsion in general. Because discrete magnitude is quantity, its discreteness is itself continuous. This continuity in the discrete consists in the ones being the same as one another, or in having the same *unity*. Discrete magnitude is, therefore, the asunderness of the manifold one as self-same, not the manifold one in general but posited as the *many of a unity*.

Remark: The Usual Separation of These Magnitudes
In the usual ideas of continuous and discrete magnitude, it is overlooked that *each* of these magnitudes contains both moments, continuity and discreteness, and that the distinction between them consists only in this, that in one of the moments the determinateness is *posited* and in the other it is only *implicit*. Space, time, matter, and so forth are continuous magnitudes in that they are repulsions from themselves, a streaming forth out of themselves which at the same time is not their transition or relating of themselves to a qualitative other. They possess the absolute possibility that the one may be posited in them at any point—not the empty possibility of a mere otherness (as when it is said, it is possible that a tree might stand in the place of this stone), but they contain the principle of the one within themselves; it is one of the determinations which constitute them.

Conversely, in discrete magnitude continuity is not to be overlooked; this moment is, as has been shown, the one as unity.

Continuous and discrete magnitude can be regarded as *species* of quantity, provided that magnitude is posited, not under any external determinateness, but under the determinatenesses of its own moments; the ordinary transition from genus to species allows *external* characteristics to be attributed to the former according to some *external* basis of classification. And besides, continuous and discrete magnitude are not yet quanta; they are only quantity itself in each of its two forms. They are, perhaps, called magnitudes in so far as they have in common with quantum simply this—to be a determinateness in quantity.

C. LIMITATION OF QUANTITY

Discrete magnitude has first the one for its principle; secondly, it is a plurality of ones; and thirdly, it is essentially continuous; it is the one as at the same time sublated, as *unity*, the continuation of itself as such in the discreteness of the ones. Consequently, it is posited as *one* magnitude, the determinateness of which is the one which, in this posited and determinate being is the *excluding* one, a limit in the unity. Discrete magnitude as such is immediately not limited; but as distinguished from continuous magnitude it is a determinate being, a something, with the one as its determinateness and also as its first negation and limit.

This limit, which is related to the unity and is the negation *in it*, is also, as the one, self-related; it is thus the enclosing, encompassing limit. Limit here is not at first distinguished from its determinate being as something, but, as the one, is immediately this negative point itself. But the being which here is limited is essentially a continuity, by virtue of which it passes beyond the limit, beyond this one, to which it is indifferent. Real discrete quantity is thus *a* quantity, or quantum—quantity as a determinate being and a something.

Since the one which is a limit includes within itself the many ones of discrete quantity, it equally posits them as sublated within it; and because it is a limit of continuity simply as such, the distinction between continuous and discrete magnitude is here of no significance; or, more correctly, it is a limit to the continuity of the one as much as of the other; *both* undergo transition into quanta.

CHAPTER 2

QUANTUM

Quantum, which to begin with is quantity with a determinateness or limit in general is, in its complete determinateness, number. Quantum differentiates itself *secondly*, into (*a*) *extensive* quantum, in which the limit is a limitation of the determinately existent plurality; and (*b*) intensive quantum or *degree*, the determinate being having made the transition into being-for-self. Intensive quantum as both *for itself* and at the same time immediately *outside itself*—since it is an indifferent limit—has its determinateness in an other. As this manifest contradiction of being determined simply within itself yet having its determinateness outside it, pointing outside itself for it, quantum posited as being in its own self external to itself, passes over *thirdly*, into *quantitative infinity*.

A. NUMBER

Quantity is quantum, or has a limit, both as continuous and as discrete magnitude. The difference between these two kinds has here, in the first instance, no immediate significance.

The very nature of quantity as sublated being-for-self is *ipso facto* to be indifferent to its limit. But equally, too, quantity is not unaffected by the limit or by being a quantum; for it contains within itself as its own moment the one, which is absolutely determined and which, therefore, as posited in the continuity or unity of quantity, is its limit, but a limit which remains what it has become, simply a one.

This one is thus the principle of quantum, but as the one of *quantity*. Hence, first, it is continuous, it is a *unity*; secondly, it is discrete, a plurality of ones, which is implicit in continuous, or explicit in discrete magnitude, the ones having equality with one another, possessing the said continuity, the same unity. Thirdly, this one is also a negation of the many ones as a simple limit, an excluding of its otherness from itself, a determination of itself in opposition to *other* quanta. Thus the one is (α) *self-relating*, (β) *enclosing* and (γ) *other-excluding* limit.

Quantum completely posited in these determinations is *number*. The complete positedness lies in the existence of the limit as a *plurality* and so in its distinction from the unity. Consequently, number appears as a discrete magnitude, but in the unity it equally possesses continuity. It is, therefore, also quantum in its complete *determinateness*, for in it the limit is present as a specific *plurality* which has for its principle the one, the absolutely determinate. Continuity, in which the one is present only *in principle*, as a sublated moment—posited as a unity—is the form of indeterminateness.

Quantum, merely as such, is limited generally; its limit is an abstract, simple determinateness of it. But in quantum as number, this limit is posited as *manifold within itself*. It contains the many ones which constitute its determinate being, but does not contain them in an indeterminate manner, for the determinateness of the limit falls in them; the limit excludes other determinate being, that is, other pluralities and the ones it encloses are a specific aggregate, the *amount*—which is the form taken by discreteness in number—the other to which is the *unit*, the continuity of the amount. *Amount* and *unit* constitute the *moments* of number.

As regards amount, we must see more closely how the many ones of which it *consists* are present in the limit; it is correct to say of amount that it *consists* of the many, for the ones are in it not as sublated but as *affirmatively present*, only posited with the excluding limit to which they are indifferent. This, however, is not indifferent to them. In the sphere of determinate being, the relation of the limit to it was primarily such that the determinate being persisted as the affirmative on this side of its limit, while the limit, the negation, was found outside on the border of the determinate being; similarly, the breaking-off [in the counting] of the many ones and the exclusion of other ones appears as a determination falling outside the enclosed ones. But in the qualitative sphere it was found that the limit pervades the determinate being, is co-extensive with it, and consequently that it lies in the nature of something to be limited, that is, finite. In the quantitative sphere a number, say a hundred, is conceived in such a manner that the hundredth one alone limits the many to make them a hundred. In one sense this is correct; but on the other hand none of the hundred ones has precedence over any other for they are only equal—each is equally the hundredth;

thus they all belong to the limit which makes the number a hundred and the number cannot dispense with any of them for its determinateness. Hence, relatively to the hundredth one, the others do not constitute a determinate being that is in any way different from the limit, whether they are outside or inside it. Consequently, the number is not a plurality over against the enclosing, limiting one, but itself constitutes this limitation which is a specific quantum; the many constitute a number, a two, a ten, a hundred, and so on.

Now the limiting one is the number as determined relatively to other numbers, as distinguished from them. But this distinguishing does not become a qualitative determinateness but remains quantitative, falling only within the comparing *external* reflection; the number, as a one, remains returned into itself and indifferent to others. This *indifference* of a number to others is an essential determination of it and constitutes the implicit determinedness of the number, but also the number's own externality. Number is thus a *numerical* one as the absolutely determinate one, which at the same time has the form of simple immediacy and for which, therefore, the relation to other is completely external. Further, one as a *number* possesses *determinateness* (in so far as this is a relation to other) as the moments of itself contained within it, in its difference of unit and amount; and amount is itself a plurality of ones, that is, this absolute externality is in the one itself. This contradiction of number or of quantum as such within itself is the quality of quantum, in the further determinations of which this contradiction is developed.

Remark 1: *The Species of Calculation in Arithmetic; Kant's Synthetic Propositions* a priori *of Intuition*

Spatial magnitude and numerical magnitude are usually regarded as two species, the former being on its own account a determinate magnitude just as much as the latter; their difference is held to consist only in the different determinations of continuity and discreteness, but as quantum they stand on the same level. In spatial magnitude, geometry has, in general, continuous magnitude for its subject matter while the subject matter of arithmetic is the discrete magnitude of number. But with this dissimilarity of their subject matter, the manner and completeness of their limitation or determinedness is also different. Spatial magnitude possesses only limitation generally; if it is to be considered as a thoroughly determinate quantum then *number* is required. Geometry as such does not *measure* spatial figures (it is not mensuration), but only *compares* them. In its definitions, too, the determinations are in part derived from the *equality* of the sides and angles, or from *equidistance*. Thus the circle, because it is based solely on the *equidistance* of all possible points in it from a centre, does not require number for its determination. These determinations based on equality or inequality are genuinely geometrical. But they are not sufficient, and for other figures, for example, the triangle or rectangle, number is requisite; this in its principle, the one, contains a *self*-determinedness, it is determined without the aid of an other and therefore not through comparison. It is true that in the point, spatial magnitude has a determinateness corresponding to the one; but the point, in becoming external to itself, becomes an other, becomes the line; because it is essentially only a *spatial* one, it becomes in the *relation* a continuity in which the nature of the point, the self-determinedness, the one, is sublated. In so far as the self-determinedness is supposed to be preserved in the self-externality, the line must be represented as an aggregate of ones, and to the *limit* must be imparted the determination of the *many* ones, that is, the magnitude of the line—and similarly of other spatial determinations—must be taken as a number.

Arithmetic considers number and its figures; or rather does not consider them but operates with them. For number is the determinateness which is indifferent, inert; it must be actuated from without and so brought into a relation. The modes of relation are the species of calculation. In arithmetic they are presented *seriatim* and it is clear that one depends on the other; but the thread which links the progressive stages is not made prominent in arithmetic. However, the systematic arrangement justly claimed for the presentation of these elements in the text-books is readily provided by the determinations of number itself stemming from its Notion. These cardinal determinations will be briefly noted here.

Number has for its principle the one and is, therefore, simply an aggregate externally put together, a purely analytic figure devoid of any inner connectedness; and because it is produced in this merely external manner all calculation is the production of quite externally given. The postulate that 5 be added to 7, bears the same relation to the postulate of simply counting, as does the postulate that a straight line be produced to the postulate that a straight line be drawn.

Just as meaningless as the expression 'synthesis', is its characterization as occurring *a priori*. Counting is not, of course, determined by sensation which, according to Kant's definition of intuition is all that remains over for the *a posteriori*, and counting is certainly an activity based on abstract intuiting, that is, an intuiting determined by the category of the one, and in which abstraction is made from all other determinations of sensation, no less than from concepts, too. The *a priori* is altogether too vague a characterization; feeling, determined as impulse, sense, and so on, has in it the *a priori* moment, just as much as space and time, in the shape of spatial and temporal existence, is determined *a posteriori*.

We may add in this connection that Kant's assertion of the synthetic nature of the foundations of pure geometry is equally without any solid basis. He admits that several are really analytic but only adduces one in support of his assertion that they are synthetic, namely, the axiom that the straight line is the shortest line between two points. 'For my notion of straightness contains nothing pertaining to magnitude, but only a quality; the notion of the shortest is, therefore, wholly an addition and cannot be inferred from any analysis of the notion of a straight line; we must therefore have recourse to intuition here which alone makes the synthesis possible.' But here again the question is not of a notion of straightness as such but of a straight line, and this is already something spatial and intuited. The determination (or, if you like, the concept) of the straight line is, after all, none other than that the line is absolutely simple, that is, in coming out of itself (the so-called movement of the point) the line is purely self-related, and its extension does not involve any alteration in its determination, or reference to another point or line outside itself; it is a simple direction purely internal to the line. This simplicity is indeed its quality, and should it seem difficult to define the straight line analytically this would be due solely to the simplicity and self-relation of the determination, and merely because reflection thinks of determining primarily in terms of a plurality, a determining through something else. But there is no inherent difficulty whatever in grasping this determination of the simplicity of extension within the line, of the absence of determination by anything else; Euclid's definition contains nothing else than this simplicity. But now the transition of this quality to the quantitative determination (of the shortest) which is supposed to constitute the synthetic element is wholly analytical. As spatial, the line is quantity in general; the simplest in terms of quantum is the *least;* and this predicated of a line is the *shortest.* Geometry can accept these determinations as a corollary to the definition; but Archimedes in his books on the sphere and cylinder[1] did the appropriate thing in making the said determination of a straight line into an axiom, in just as correct a sense as Euclid included the determination concerning parallel lines among the axioms, for the development of this determination into a definition would have required determinations not immediately spatial in character but of a more abstract qualitative kind, like simplicity, sameness of direction, and the like just mentioned. These ancients gave even to their sciences a plastic character, confining their exposition strictly to the peculiarity of their subject matter and therefore excluding what would have been heterogeneous to it.

Kant's notion of synthetic *a priori* judgements—the notion of something differentiated which equally is inseparable, of an identity which is in its own self an inseparable difference, belongs to what is great and imperishable in his philosophy. Of course, this notion is also present in intuition since it is the Notion itself and everything is implicitly the Notion; but the determinations selected in those examples do not exhibit it. On the contrary, number and counting is an identity and the creating of an identity which is wholly and solely external, only a superficial synthesis, a unity of ones which are, in fact, posited as inherently not identical with one another but as external, each separate on its own account; the determination of the straight line as being the shortest between two points is based rather on the moment of a merely abstract identity possessing no difference within itself.

I return from this digression to addition itself. The negative species of calculation corresponding to it, subtraction, is similarly the wholly analytical separation into numbers which, as in

---

[1] See Hauber's translation, p. 4.

But the perversity of employing mathematical categories for the determination of what belongs to the method or content of the science of philosophy is shown chiefly by the fact that, in so far as mathematical forms signify thoughts and distinctions based on the Notion, this their meaning has indeed first to be indicated, determined and justified in philosophy. In the concrete philosophical sciences philosophy must take the logical element from logic, not from mathematics; it can only be an expedient of philosophical incapacity which, instead of going to philosophy for the logical element, has recourse to the shapes assumed by the logical element in other sciences, many of which shapes are only adumbrations of that element, others even defective forms of it. Apart from this, the mere application of such borrowed forms is an external procedure; the application itself must be preceded by an awareness not only of their meaning but of their value, too, and such awareness can come only from reflecting on them, not from the authority of mathematics. But logic itself is such awareness and it strips these forms of their particularity which it renders superfluous and unnecessary; it is logic which rectifies these forms and alone procures for them their justification, meaning and value.

As for the supposed primary importance of number and calculation in an *educational* regard, the truth of the matter is clearly evident from what has been said. Number is a non-sensuous object, and occupation with it and its combinations is a non-sensuous business; in it mind is held to communing with itself and to an inner abstract labour, a matter of great though one-sided importance. For, on the other hand, since the basis of number in only an external, thoughtless difference, such occupation is an unthinking, mechanical one. The effort consists mainly in holding fast what is devoid of the Notion and in combining it purely mechanically. The content is the empty one; the substantial content of moral and spiritual life in its various forms on which, as the noblest aliment, education should nurture the young mind, is to be supplanted by the blank one or unit; when such exercise is made the prime interest and occupation, the only possible outcome must be to dull the mind and to empty it of both form and substance. Calculation being so much an external and therefore mechanical business, it has been possible to construct machines which perform arithmetical operations with complete accuracy. A knowledge of just this one fact about the nature of calculation is sufficient for an appraisal of the idea of making calculation the principal means for educating the mind and stretching it on the rack in order to perfect it as a machine.

B. EXTENSIVE AND INTENSIVE QUANTUM

(a) Their Difference
1. We have seen that quantum has its determinateness as limit in *amount*. Within itself quantum is discrete, a plurality which has no being distinct from its limit, nor is the limit external to it. Quantum thus then with its limit, which is in its own self a plurality, is *extensive magnitude*.

Extensive and *continuous* magnitude are to be distinguished from each other; the direct opposite of the former is not discrete but *intensive* magnitude. Extensive and intensive magnitudes are determinatenesses of the quantitative *limit* itself, whereas quantum is identical with its limit; continuous and discrete magnitudes, on the other hand, are determinations of magnitude *in itself*, that is, of quantity as such, in so far as in quantum abstraction is made from the limit. Extensive magnitude has the moment of continuity present within itself and in its limit, for its many is altogether continuous; the limit as negation appears, therefore, in this *equality* of the many as a limiting of the oneness. Continuous magnitude is quantity as continuing itself without regard to any limit and in so far as it is conceived as having a limit, this is simply a limitation *free from any posited discreteness*. Quantum as only continuous magnitude is not yet truly determined as being for itself because it lacks the one (in which being-for-selfness is implied) and number. Similarly, a discrete magnitude is immediately only a differentiated many in general; were this as such supposed to have a limit, it would be only an aggregate, that is, would be only indefinitely limited; before it can be a specific quantum, the many must be compressed into a one and thereby posited as identical with the limit. Continuous and discrete magnitude, taken simply as *quanta* have each posited in it only one of the two sides which together make quantum fully determined and a *number*. This latter is immediately an *extensive quantum*—the *simple* determinateness which is essentially an *amount*, but an amount of one and the same *unit*; extensive quantum is distinguished from number only by this, that in number the determinateness is expressly posited as a plurality.

2. However, the determinateness of something in terms of number does not require it to be distinguished from another numerically determined something, as if both were necessary to the determinateness of the first; and this is because the determinateness of magnitude as such is a limit determinate by itself, indifferent and related simply to itself; and in number the limit is posited as included in the one, which is a being-for-self, and it has *within itself* the externality, the relation to other. Further, this many of the limit itself is, like the many as such, not unequal within itself but continuous; each of the many is the same as the others; consequently, the many as a plural asunderness or discreteness does not constitute the determinateness as such. This many, therefore, spontaneously collapses into its continuity and becomes a simple oneness. Amount is only a moment of number, but *as an aggregate of numerical ones*, it does *not* constitute the determinateness of number; on the contrary, these ones as indifferent and self-external are sublated in number which has returned into itself; the externality which constituted the ones as a plurality vanishes in the one as a relation of number to its own self.

Consequently the limit of quantum, which as extensive had its real determinateness in the self-external amount, passes over into *simple determinateness*. In this simple determination of the limit, quantum is intensive magnitude; and the limit or determinateness which is identical with the quantum is now also thus posited as unitary—*degree*.

The degree is thus a specific magnitude, a quantum; but at the same time it is not an aggregate or plural *within itself;* it is a plurality only in principle (*eine Mehrheit*), for plurality has been brought together into a simple, *unitary* determination, determinate being has returned into being-for-self. The determinateness of degree must, it is true, be expressed by a *number*, the completely determined form of quantum, but the number is not an *amount* but unitary, only a degree. When we speak of ten or twenty degrees, the quantum that has that number of degrees is the tenth or twentieth degree, not the amount and sum of them—as such, it would be an extensive quantum—but it is only *one* degree, the tenth or twentieth. It contains the determinateness implied in the amount ten or twenty, but does not contain it as a plurality but is number as a *sublated* amount, as a *unitary* determinateness.

3. In number, quantum is posited in its complete determinateness; but as intensive quantum, as in number's being-for-self, it is posited as it is in its Notion or in itself. That is to say, the form of self-relation which it has in degree is at the same time *the externality of the degree to its own self*. Number, as an extensive quantum, is a numerical plurality and so has the externality within itself. This externality, as simply a plurality, collapses into undifferentiatedness and sublates itself in the numerical one, in its self-relation. Quantum, however, has its determinateness as an amount; it contains this, as we have already seen, even though the amount is no longer posited in it. Degree, therefore, which, as in its own self unitary, no longer has *within* itself this external otherness, has it *outside* itself and relates itself to it as to its determinateness. A plurality external to the degree constitutes the determinateness of the simple limit which the degree is for itself. In extensive quantum amount, in so far as it was supposed to be present in the number, was so only as sublated; now it is determined as placed outside the number. Number as a one, being posited as self-relation reflected into itself, excludes from itself the indifference and externality of the amount and is self-relation *as relation through itself to an externality*.

In this, quantum has a reality conformable to its Notion. The *indifference* of the determinateness constitutes its quality, that is, the determinateness which is in its own self a self-external determinateness. Accordingly, degree is a unitary quantitative determinateness *among* a plurality of such intensities which, though differing from each other, each being only a simple self-relation, are at the same time essentially interrelated so that each has its determinateness in this continuity with the others. This relation of degree through itself to its other makes ascent and descent in the scale of degrees a continuous progress, a flux, which is an uninterrupted, indivisible alteration; none of the various distinct degrees is separate from the others but each is determined only through them. As a self-related determination of quantity, each degree is indifferent to the others; but it is just as much implicitly related to this externality, it is only through this externality that it is what it is; its relation to itself is, in short, the non-indifferent relation to externality, and in this it has its quality.

(b) Identity of Extensive and Intensive Magnitude

Degree is not external to itself within itself. Nevertheless, it is not the *indeterminate* one, the principle of number as such, which is not amount save in the negative sense of not being any particular amount. Intensive magnitude is primarily a unitary one of a plurality; there are many degrees, but they are determined neither as a simple one nor as a plurality, but only in the relation of this self-externality, or in the identity of the one and the plurality. If, therefore, the many as such are indeed outside the simple, unitary degree, nevertheless the determinateness of the degree consists in its relation to them; it thus contains amount. Just as twenty, as an extensive magnitude, contains the twenty ones as discrete within it, so does the specific degree contain them as the continuity which this determinate plurality simply is; it is the *twentieth* degree, and is the twentieth degree only by virtue of this amount, which as such is outside it.

The determinateness of intensive magnitude is, therefore, to be considered from two sides. Intensive magnitude is determined by *other* intensive quanta and is continuous with its otherness, so that its determinateness consists in this relation to its otherness. Now in the first place, in so far as it is a *simple* determinateness it is determinate *relatively* to other degrees; it excludes them from itself and has its determinateness in this exclusion. But, secondly, it is determinate in its own self; this it is in the amount as its *own* amount, not in the amount as excluded, nor in the amount of other degrees. The twentieth degree contains the twenty within itself; it is not only determined as distinguished from the nineteenth, twenty-first, and so on, but its determinateness is its *own* amount. But in so far as the amount is its own—and the determinateness is at the same time essentially an amount—the degree is an extensive quantum.

Extensive and intensive magnitude are thus one and the same determinateness of quantum; they are only distinguished by the one having amount within itself and the other having amount outside itself. Extensive magnitude passes over into intensive magnitude because its many spontaneously collapse into oneness, outside which the many stand. But conversely, this unitary degree has its determinateness only in the amount, and that too in its *own* amount; as indifferent to the differently determined intensities it has within itself the externality of the amount; and so intensive magnitude is equally essentially an extensive magnitude.

With this identity, the *qualitative something* makes its appearance, for the identity is the unity which is self-related through the *negation of its differences*; these differences, however, constitute the determinate being of the quantitative determinateness; this negative identity is therefore *a something*, and a something which is indifferent to its quantitative determinateness. *Something* is a quantum; but now the qualitative determinate being, as it is in itself, is posited as indifferent to quantum. Quantum, number as such, and so forth, could be spoken of without any mention of its having a something as substrate. But the something now confronts these its determinations, through the negation of which it is *mediated* with itself, as *existing for itself* and, since it has a quantum, as something which has an extensive and an intensive quantum. Its one determinateness which it has as quantum is posited in the differentiated moments of *unit* and *amount*; this determinateness is not only *in itself* one and the same, but its positing in these differences as extensive and intensive quantum is the return into this unity which, as negative, is the something posited as indifferent to it.

Remark 1: *Examples of This Identity*

Extensive and intensive quantum are usually distinguished in the ordinary conception of them as *kinds of magnitude*, as if some objects had only intensive, others only extensive magnitude. In addition, we have the conception of a philosophical science of Nature in which what is a plurality or *extensive*—for example, in the fundamental property of matter to occupy space, and in other concepts too—is converted into something *intensive*, meaning thereby that the intensive aspect as *dynamic* is the true determination; density, or the specific filling of space, for example, must essentially be understood *not* as a certain *aggregate* and *amount* of material parts in a quantum of space, but as a certain degree of the space-filling *force* of matter.

There are two kinds of determinations to be distinguished here. In what has been called the conversion of the mechanical into the dynamic point of view, there occurs the concept of *separately*

existing, independent parts, which are only externally combined
into a whole, and the concept of *force* which is distinct from this.
In the occupation of space, what is regarded on the one hand as
only an aggregate of atoms external to one another, is on the
other hand regarded as the expression of an underlying simple
force. But these relations of whole and parts, of force and its
expression, which here stand opposed to each other, do not
belong in this section; they will be considered in their proper
place later on. But this much may be remarked here, that though
the relation of force and its expression which corresponds to intensive magnitude is in the first instance truer than that of whole and
parts, yet this does not make force, as intensive, any less one-sided;
also *expression,* the externality of extensive magnitude, is equally
inseparable from force; so that *one and the same content* is equally present in the two forms, both in intensive and in extensive magnitude.

The other determinateness which occurs here is the *quantitative*
as such, which, as extensive quantum, is sublated and transformed
into degree, the supposedly true determination; but it has been
shown that degree equally contains the former determinateness,
so that the two forms are essential to each other; consequently,
every existence exhibits its quantitative character just as much as
an extensive as an intensive quantum.

Consequently everything, in so far as it manifests a quantitative
character, serves as an example of this. Number itself necessarily
has this double form immediately within it. It is an amount in
so far as it is an extensive magnitude; but number is also one, a
ten, a hundred, and as such it is on the threshold of transition
into an intensive magnitude, seeing that in this unity the plurality
has become simple. One is *in itself* an extensive magnitude, it
can be represented as an arbitrary amount of parts. Thus the
tenth, the hundredth, is this simple, intensive magnitude which
has its determinateness in the plurality lying outside it, that is,
in extensive magnitude. Number is a ten, a hundred and at the
same time the tenth, hundredth, in the system of numbers; both
are the same determinateness.

In the circle the one is called degree because the determinateness
of any part of the circle derives essentially from the many parts
outside it; that is, it is determined as only one of a fixed amount of
such ones. As a mere spatial magnitude, the degree of the circle
is only an ordinary number; taken as degree, it is intensive

magnitude which has a meaning only as determined by the amount of degrees into which the circle is divided, just as number generally has meaning only in the number series.

The magnitude of a more concrete object exhibits its dual aspects of being extensive and intensive, in the dual determinations of its real being, in one of which it appears as an outer being but in the other as an inwardness. Thus, for example, a mass as weight is an extensive magnitude, in so far as it constitutes an amount of pounds, hundredweights, etc., and an intensive magnitude in so far as it exerts a certain pressure; the magnitude of the pressure is a simple number, a degree, which is specified by its place in a scale of degrees. As exerting pressure, mass is manifested as a being-within-self, as a subject to which belongs a difference of intensive magnitude. Conversely, that which exerts this *degree* of pressure is capable of displacing a certain *amount* of pounds, etc., and its magnitude is measured by this.

Again, heat has a degree; this degree, whether it be the tenth, twentieth and so on, is a simple sensation, something subjective. But this degree is equally present as an *extensive* magnitude, as the expansion of a fluid, of mercury in a thermometer, of air, or sound, and so on. A higher degree of temperature expresses itself as a longer column of mercury, or as a narrower sound-cylinder; it heats a larger space in the same way as a lower degree heats only a smaller space.

The higher note is, as more intensive, at the same time a greater number of vibrations, and a louder note, to which we ascribe a higher *degree*, is audible in a larger space. A larger surface can be coloured with a more intensive colour than with a weaker colour used in the same way; or again a *brighter* object (another kind of intensity) is visible at a greater distance than one less bright, and so forth.

Similarly in the spiritual sphere, high intensity of character, of talent or genius, is bound up with a correspondingly far-reaching reality in the outer world, is of widespread influence, touching the real world at many points. The profoundest Notion also has the most universal significance and application.

Remark 2: *The determination of degree as applied by Kant to the soul*

The determinateness of intensive quantum has been applied by

Kant in a peculiar way to a metaphysical determination of the soul. In his criticism of metaphysical propositions about the soul, which he calls paralogisms of pure reason, he comes to consider the inference from the simplicity of the soul to its permanence. He counters this argument by saying 'that even if we admit the simple nature of the soul since, namely, it does not contain a plurality of separate parts and therefore no extensive magnitude, yet we cannot deny to it, any more than to any other existent thing, an intensive magnitude, that is, a *degree* of reality in respect of all its faculties, indeed, in respect of all that constitutes its existence; this *degree* can diminish through all the infinitely many smaller degrees so that although the postulated substance cannot be reduced to nothing by division (into parts), it can be so reduced by a gradual lessening (*remissio*) of its powers. For *consciousness* itself has, at any moment, a degree which can always be diminished, and the same must therefore also be true of its faculty of being aware of itself and thus of all the other faculties'.[1] In rational psychology, which is an abstract metaphysics, the soul is considered not as spirit but as a merely immediate being, as a soul-thing. Kant thus has the right to apply the category of quantum to it 'as to any other existent thing', and in so far as this immediate being is determined as simple, to apply to it the category of intensive quantum. *Being* does, of course, belong to spirit, but its intensity is wholly different from that of intensive quantum; indeed, its intensity is such that in it the form of merely immediate being and all its categories are sublated. What should have been admitted was the elimination not only of the category of extensive quantum but that of quantum altogether. But a further advance has still to be made, namely, to understand how existence, consciousness, finitude, *is* in the eternal nature of spirit and proceeds from it without spirit thereby becoming a thing.

(c) *Alteration of Quantum*

The difference between extensive and intensive quantum is indifferent to the determinateness of quantum as such. But in general quantum is determinateness posited as sublated, the indifferent limit, the determinateness which is equally the negation of itself. In extensive magnitude this difference is developed; but intensive magnitude is the *existence* of this externality which

---

[1] *Critique of Pure Reason*, p. 414.

quantum is within itself. This difference, as internally self-contradictory, is posited as being the simple, *self-related* determinateness which is the negation of itself, having its determinateness not within itself but in another quantum.

A quantum, therefore, in accordance with its quality, is posited in absolute continuity with its externality, with its otherness. Therefore, not only *can* it transcend every quantitative determinateness, not only *can* it be altered, but it is *posited* that it *must* alter. The quantitative determinateness continues itself into its otherness in such a manner that the determination has its being only in this continuity with an other; it is not a *simply affirmative* limit, but a limit which *becomes*.

The one is infinite or self-related negation, hence the repulsion of itself from itself. The quantum, too, is infinite and is posited *as* self-related negativity; it repels itself from itself. But the quantum is a *determinate* one, the one which has passed over into determinate being and limit; it is, therefore, the repulsion of the determinateness from itself, not the producing of that which is the same as itself as in the repulsion of the one, but the producing of its otherness; it is now the express character of quantum to *impel itself beyond itself* and to become an other. In consists in undergoing increase or decrease; it is in its own self the externality of the determinateness.

Thus quantum impels itself beyond itself; this other which it becomes is in the first place itself a quantum; but it is quantum as a limit which does not stay, but which impels itself beyond itself. The limit which again arises in this beyond is, therefore, one which simply sublates itself again and impels itself beyond to a further limit, *and so on to infinity*.

C. QUANTITATIVE INFINITY

(a) *Its Notion*

Quantum alters and becomes another quantum; the further determination of this alteration, namely, that it goes on to infinity, lies in the circumstance that quantum is established as being immanently self-contradictory. Quantum becomes an other; but it *continues* itself into its otherness; the other is thus also a quantum. This, however, is not only the other of a particular quantum, but of quantum itself, the negative of quantum as limited; hence it

H

is the unlimitedness of quantum, its *infinity*. Quantum is an ought-to-be; it is by implication determined as being for itself, and this being-determined-for-itself is rather the being-determined-in-an-other, and, conversely, it is the sublation of being-determined-in-an-other, is an *indifferent* subsisting for itself.

In this way, finitude and infinity each acquire in themselves a dual, and indeed, an opposite meaning. The quantum is *finite*, in the first place simply as limited, and secondly, as impelled beyond itself, as being determined in an other. But the *infinity* of quantum is first, its unlimitedness, and secondly, its returnedness into itself, its indifferent being-for-self. If we now compare these moments with each other, we find that the determination of the finitude of quantum, the impulse to go beyond itself to an other in which its determination lies, is equally the determination of the infinite; the negation of the limit is the same impulsion beyond the determinateness, so that in this negation, in the infinite, quantum possesses its final determinateness. The other moment of infinity is the being-for-self which is indifferent to the limit; but the limiting of quantum itself is such that quantum is explicitly indifferent to its limit, and hence to other quanta and to its *beyond*. In quantum, finitude and infinity (the spurious infinity supposedly separate from the finite) each already has within it the moment of the other.

The difference between the qualitative and quantitative infinite is that in the former the finite and infinite are *qualitatively* opposed and the transition of the finite into the infinite, or the relation of each to the other, lies only in the *in-itself*, in their Notion. Qualitative determinateness, as an immediacy, is related to otherness essentially as to an alien being; it is not *posited* as having its negation, its other *within* it. Quantity, on the other hand, is, as such, *sublated* determinateness; it is *posited* as being unlike and indifferent to itself, consequently as alterable. Therefore the qualitative finite and infinite stand absolutely, that is abstractly, opposed to each other; their unity is their underlying *inner* relation; and therefore the finite continues itself into its other only *implicitly*, not *affirmatively*. The quantitative finite, on the other hand, is *self*-related in its infinite, in which it has its absolute determinateness. This their relation is displayed in the first place in the *quantitative infinite progress*.

(b) The Quantitative Infinite Progress

The progress to infinity is in general the expression of contradiction, here, of that which is implicit in the quantitative finite, or quantum as such. It is the reciprocal determining of the finite and infinite which was considered in the sphere of quality, with the difference that, as just remarked, in the sphere of quantity the limit in its own self dispatches and continues itself into its beyond and hence, conversely, the quantitative infinite too is posited as having quantum within it; for quantum in its self-externality is also its own self, its externality belongs to its determination.

Now the *infinite progress* is only the *expression* of this contradiction, *not its resolution*; but because the one determinateness is continued into its other, the progress gives rise to the show of a solution in a union of both. As at first posed, it is the *problem* of attaining the infinite, not the actual reaching of it; it is the perpetual *generation* of the infinite, but it does not get beyond quantum, nor does the infinite become positively present. It belongs to the Notion of quantum to have a *beyond* of itself. This beyond is first, the abstract moment of the *non-being* of quantum: the vanishing of quantum is its own act; it is thus related to its *beyond* as to its infinity, in accordance with the *qualitative* moment of the opposition. Secondly, however, quantum is continuous with its beyond; quantum consists precisely in being the other of itself, in being external to itself; this externality is, therefore, no more an other than quantum itself; the *beyond* or the infinite is, therefore, itself *a quantum*. In this way, the beyond is recalled from its flight and the infinite is attained. But because the infinite now affirmatively present is again a quantum, what has been posited is only a fresh limit; this, too, as a quantum, has again fled from itself, is as such beyond itself and has repelled itself into its non-being, into its own beyond, and as it thus repels itself into the beyond, so equally does the beyond perpetually become a quantum.

The continuity of quantum with its other produces the conjunction of both in the expression of an infinitely great or infinitely small. Since both still bear the character of quantum they remain alterable, and the absolute determinateness which would be a being-for-self is, therefore, not attained. This *self-externality* of the determination is posited in the dual infinite—which is opposed to itself as a 'more' and a 'less'—in the infinitely great and infinitely small. In each, the quantum is *maintained* in perpetual opposition to its beyond. No matter how much the quantum is increased, it shrinks to insignificance; because quantum is related to the infinite as to its non-being, the opposition is *qualitative*; the increased quantum has therefore gained nothing from the infinite, which is now, as before, the non-being of quantum. In other words, the increase of quantum brings it no *nearer* to the infinite; for the difference between quantum and its infinity is essentially *not* a quantitative difference. The expression 'the infinitely great' only throws the contradiction into sharper relief; it is supposed to be *great*, that is, a quantum, and *infinite*, that is, not a quantum. Similarly, the infinitely small is, as small, a quantum, and therefore remains absolutely, that is, qualitatively, too great for the infinite and is opposed to it. In both, there remains the contradiction of the infinite progress which in them should have reached its goal.

This infinity which is perpetually determined as the beyond of the finite is to be described as the *spurious quantitative infinite*. Like the qualitative spurious infinite, it is the perpetual movement to and fro from one term of the lasting contradiction to the other, from the limit to its non-being, and from this back again to the limit. It is true that in the quantitative progress the movement is not simply towards an abstract *other* in general, but towards an explicitly different quantum; but this remains in the same way opposed to its negation. The progress, too, is therefore not a real advance but a repetition of one and the same thing, a positing, a sublating, and then again a positing and again a sublating, an impotence of the negative, for what it sublates is continuous with it, and in the very act of being sublated returns to it. Thus there are two terms, the bond between which is such that they simply flee from each other; and in fleeing from each other they cannot become separated but are joined together even in their flight from each other.

Remark 1: *The High Repute of the Progress to Infinity*
The spurious infinite, especially in the form of the quantitative progress to infinity which continually surmounts the limit it is powerless to remove, and perpetually falls back into it, is commonly held to be something sublime and a kind of divine worship, while in philosophy it has been regarded as ultimate. This

progression has often been the theme of tirades which have been admired as sublime productions. As a matter of fact, however, this *modern* sublimity does not magnify the *object*—rather does this take flight—but only the *subject* which assimilates such vast quantities. The hollowness of this exaltation, which in scaling the ladder of the quantitative still remains subjective, finds expression in its own admission of the futility of its efforts to get nearer to the infinite goal, the attainment of which must, indeed, be achieved by a quite different method.

In the following tirades of this kind it is also stated what becomes of such exaltation and how it finishes. Kant, for example, at the close of the *Critique of Practical Reason*, represents it as sublime 'when the subject raises himself in thought above the place he occupies in the world of sense, reaching out to infinity, to stars beyond stars, worlds beyond worlds, systems beyond systems, and then also to the limitless times of their periodic motion, their beginning and duration. Imagination fails before this progress into the infinitely remote, where beyond the most distant world there is a still more distant one, and the past, however remote, has a still remoter past behind it, the future, however distant, a still more distant future beyond it; thought fails in the face of this conception of the immeasurable, just as a dream, in which one goes on and on down a corridor which stretches away endlessly out of sight, finishes with falling or fainting.'

This exposition, besides giving a concise yet rich description of such quantitative exaltation, deserves praise mainly on account of the truthfulness with which it states how it fares finally with this exaltation: thought succumbs, the end is falling and faintness. What makes thought succumb, what causes falling and faintness, is nothing else but the wearisome repetition which makes a limit vanish, reappear, and then vanish again, so that there is a perpetual arising and passing away of the one after the other and of the one in the other, of the beyond in the here and now, and of the here and now in the beyond, giving only the feeling of the *impotence* of this infinite or this ought-to-be, which *would* be master of the finite and *cannot*.

Also Haller's description of eternity, called by Kant terrifying, is usually specially admired, but often just not for that very reason which constitutes its true merit:

'I heap up monstrous numbers,
Pile millions upon millions,
I put aeon upon aeon and world upon world,
And when from that awful height
Reeling, again I seek thee,
All the might of number increased a thousandfold
Is still not a fragment of thee.
I remove them and thou liest wholly before me.'

When this heaping and piling up of numbers is regarded as
what is valuable in a description of eternity, it is overlooked that
the poet himself declares this so-called terrifying journey into
the beyond to be futile and empty, and that he closes by saying
that only by giving up this empty, infinite progression can the
genuine infinite itself become present to him.

There have been astronomers who liked to pride themselves on
the sublimity of their science because it had to deal with an
innumerable host of stars, with such immeasurable spaces and
times in which distances and periods, already vast in themselves,
serve as units which, in whatever multiples taken, are again
abbreviated to insignificance. The shallow astonishment to which
they surrender themselves, the absurd hopes of wandering in
another life from one star to another and into immeasurable space
to acquire fresh facts *of the same kind*, this they declare to be a
cardinal factor in the excellence of their science—a science which
is admirable not on account of such quantitative infinitude but,
on the contrary, on account of the relations of *measure* and the
laws which reason recognizes in these objects and which are the
infinite of reason in contrast to that other, irrational infinite.

To the infinity of outer, sensuous intuition, Kant opposes the
other infinite, when 'the individual withdraws into his invisible
ego and opposes the absolute freedom of his will as a pure ego to
all the terrors of fate and tyranny, and starting with his immediate
surroundings, lets them vanish before him, and even what seems
enduring, worlds upon worlds, collapse into ruins, and, alone,
knows *himself as equal to himself*'.

The ego in being thus alone with itself is, it is true, the reached
beyond; it has *come to itself*, is *with* itself, here and now; the
absolute negativity which in the progress beyond the quantum of
sense was only a flight, in pure self-consciousness becomes

affirmative and present. But this pure ego, because it has fixed itself in its abstraction and emptiness, has determinate reality, the fulness of the universe of nature and mind, confronting it as a beyond. We are faced with that same contradiction which lies at the base of the infinite progress, namely a returnedness-into-self which is at the same time immediately an out-of-selfness, a relation to its other as to its non-being; and this relation remains a *longing*, because on the one side is the unsubstantial, untenable void of the ego fixed as such by the ego itself, and on the other, the fulness which though negated remains present, but is fixed by the ego as its beyond.

On these two sublimes Kant remarks 'that admiration (for the first, outer) and reverence (for the second, inner) do indeed stimulate inquiry but cannot be a substitute for their defect'. Thus he declares those exaltations to be unsatisfying for reason, which cannot stop at them and the feelings associated with them, nor can it let the beyond and the void rank as ultimate.

But it is specially in its application to morality that the infinite progress has been taken as ultimate. The just quoted antithesis of finite and infinite in the shape of the manifold world and the ego raised to its freedom, is primarily qualitative. The ego in its self-determining forthwith proceeds to determine nature and to liberate itself therefrom; it thus connects itself through itself with its other which, as an external reality, is manifold and quantitative. The relation to the quantitative becomes itself quantitative; the negative relation of the ego to it, the power of the ego over the non-ego, over sense and outer nature, is consequently so conceived that morality can and ought continually to increase, and the power of sense continually to diminish. But the perfect adequacy of the will to the moral law is placed in the unending progress to infinity, that is, is represented as an *absolutely unattainable* beyond, and this very unattainableness is supposed to be the true sheet-anchor and fitting consolation; for morality is supposed to be a struggle, but such it can be only if the will is inadequate to the moral law which thus becomes a sheer beyond for it.

In this opposition, ego and non-ego or the pure will and the moral law, and nature and the sensuousness of the will, are presupposed as completely self-subsistent and mutually indifferent. The pure will has its own appropriate law which stands in an essential relationship to the sphere of sense; and nature and sense on *its* side has laws which neither stem from nor are conformable to the will nor, although distinct from it, have they even in principle an essential connection with it but are determined independently, are finished and complete in themselves. At the same time, however, both are moments of *one and the same simple being*, the ego; the will is determined as the negative in relation to nature so that the will only *is* in so far as there is a sphere distinct from it which it sublates, but with which it thereby comes into contact and by which it is itself affected. Nature itself and nature as the sensuous sphere of man, as an independent system of laws, is indifferent to limitation by an other; it preserves itself in this process of limitation, enters into the relation as an independent factor and limits the will of law just as much as this limits it. The two processes comprise a single act: the self-determining of the will with the sublating of the otherness of nature, and the positing of this otherness as continuing itself as a reality in the process of being sublated, so that the otherness is not sublated. The contradiction involved in this is not resolved in the infinite progress: on the contrary, it is represented and affirmed as unresolved and unresolvable; the conflict of morality and sense is represented as the ultimate, absolute relation.

This standpoint which is powerless to overcome the qualitative opposition between the finite and infinite and to grasp the idea of the true will which is substantial freedom, has recourse to *quantity* in order to use it as a mediator, because it is sublated quality, the difference which has become indifferent. But since both members of the antithesis remain implied as qualitatively distinct, the fact is rather that each is straightway made indifferent to this alteration because it is *as quanta* that they are related to each other. Nature is determined by the ego, sense by the will of the good; the alteration produced in sense by the will is only a quantitative difference, one which leaves sense itself unchanged.

In the more abstract exposition of the Kantian philosophy, or at least of its principles, namely in Fichte's *Theory of Science*, the infinite progress in the same way constitutes the foundation and the ultimate. In this exposition, the first axiom, ego = ego, is followed by a second, independent of it, the opposition of the non-ego; the relation between the two is also directly assumed as a *quantitative* difference, that is, the non-ego is *partly* determined by the ego, and *partly* not. In this way, the non-ego is continued into its non-being in such wise that in its non-being it remains opposed as something not sublated. Consequently, after the contradictions contained in this have been developed in the system, the final result is that relationship which formed the beginning: the non-ego remains an infinite obstacle [*Anstoss*], an absolute other; the final relation of the non-ego and the ego to each other is the infinite progress, a longing and aspiration—the same contradiction with which the system began.

Because the quantitative is determinateness posited as sublated it was thought that much, or rather everything, had been gained for the unity of the absolute, for the one substantiality, when opposition generally had been reduced to a merely quantitative difference. That all opposition is only quantitative was for some time a cardinal thesis of recent philosophy; the opposed determinations have the same nature, the same content; they are real sides of the opposition in so far as each of them has within it both determinations, both factors of the opposition, only that on one side one of the factors *preponderates*, on the other side the other, that is, one of the factors, a material substance or activity, is present in a *greater quantity* or in an *intenser degree* in one side than in the other. But in so far as substances or activities are presupposed, the quantitative difference rather confirms and completes their externality and indifference to each other and to their unity. The difference of the *absolute* unity is supposed to be only quantitative; the quantitative, it is true, is immediate, sublated determinateness, but only the imperfect, as yet only *first*, negation, not the infinite, not the *negation* of the negation. When *being* and *thought* are represented as quantitative determinations of absolute substance they too, as quanta, become completely external to each other and unrelated as, in a subordinate sphere, do carbon, nitrogen, etc. It is a third, an external reflection, which abstracts from their difference and recognizes their unity, but a unity which is *inner, implicit* only, not *for itself*. This unity is, therefore, in fact conceived only as a first, *immediate* unity, or only as *being*, which in its quantitative difference *remains* like itself, but does not of itself *posit* itself as like itself; hence it is not grasped as a negation of the negation, as an infinite unity. Only in the qualitative opposition does the posited infinitude,

H*

being-for-self, emerge and the quantitative determination itself pass over into the qualitative, as we shall presently find.

Remark 2: *The Kantian Antinomy of the Limitation and Non-limitation of the World in Time and Space*

It was remarked above that the Kantian antinomies are expositions of the opposition of finite and infinite in a *more concrete* shape, applied to more specific substrata of conception. The antinomy there considered contained the opposition of qualitative finitude and infinitude. In another, the *first* of the four cosmological antinomies, it is the conflict arising rather from the quantitative limit which is considered. I shall therefore proceed to examine this antinomy here.

It concerns the limitation or non-limitation of the world in time and space. This antithesis could be considered equally well with reference to time and space themselves, for whether time and space are relations of things themselves or are only forms of intuition, the antinomy based on limitation or non-limitation in them is not affected thereby.

The detailed analysis of this antinomy will likewise show that both statements and equally their proofs (which, like those already considered, are conducted apagogically) amount to nothing more than the two simple opposite assertions: (1) there is a limit, and (2) the limit must be transcended.

The thesis is:

'The world has a beginning in time and is also enclosed within spatial limits.'

That part of the proof which concerns time assumes the opposite:

'The world has no beginning in time; therefore, up to *any given point of time*, an eternity has elapsed and consequently an infinite series of successive states of things in the world has *passed away*. Now the infinity of a series consists precisely in the impossibility of ever *completing* it by successive synthesis. Therefore an infinite world series which has passed away is impossible and consequently a beginning of the world is a necessary condition of its existence—which was to be proved.'

The other part of the proof which concerns space is based on time. To comprehend a spatially infinite world would require an infinite time and this time must be regarded as having already

elapsed in so far as the world in space is to be regarded not as
gradually coming to be but as completely given. But it was
shown of time in the first part of the proof that it is impossible to
assume an infinite time as elapsed.

But it is at once evident that it was unnecessary to make the
proof apagogical, or even to carry out a proof at all, since the
basis of the proof itself is the direct assertion of what was to be
proved. Namely, there is assumed some or any *given point of
time* up to which an eternity has elapsed (eternity here has only
the trivial meaning of a simply endless time). Now a given point
of time means nothing else than a definite limit in time. In the
proof therefore, a limit of time is *presupposed* as actual; but
that is just what *was to be proved*. For the thesis is, that the
world has a beginning in time.

There is only this difference, that the *assumed* limit of time is a
now as end of the time already elapsed, but the limit which is to
be proved is a now as beginning of a future. But this difference
is immaterial. The now is taken as the point in which an infinite
series of successive states of things in the world is supposed to
have *passed away*, therefore as end, a *qualitative* limit. If this *now*
were considered to be merely a quantitative limit which flows
on and which not only must be transcended but *is* only as the
transcending of itself, then the infinite time series would not have
passed away in it, but would continue to flow on, and so the
argument of the proof would vanish. On the other hand, if the
point of time is assumed as a qualitative limit for the past, in
which case it is also a *beginning* for the future (for each point of
time is *in itself* the connection of the past and the future), then
it is also an *absolute*, that is, abstract *beginning* for the future—and
it was this that was to be proved. The fact that its future and this
its beginning is already preceded by a past does not affect the
argument; because this point of time is a qualitative limit—and
that it is to be taken as qualitative is implied in the description of
it as *completed*, elapsed, and therefore as not continuing—therefore
in it time is *broken off* and the past lacks a connection with this
time which could only be called future with reference to that
past and, consequently, without such connection is only time
as such, which has an absolute beginning. But if—as is, then, the
case—it were related to the past through the now, the given
point of time, and were thus determined as a future, then this

point of time, too, regarded from the other side, would not be a limit; the infinite time series would continue itself in what was called future and would not be, as was assumed, *completed*.

In truth, time is pure quantity; the *point of time* in which it is supposed to be interrupted, which is employed in the proof, is really only the *self-sublating* being-for-self of the now. All that the proof does is to represent the absolute limit of time asserted in the thesis as a *given point of time*, and then straightway to assume it as a completed, that is, abstract point—a popular determination which sensuous conception readily lets pass as a *limit*, thus allowing as an *assumption* in the proof what had been put forward as the thing to be proved.

The antithesis runs:

'The world has no beginning and no limits in space but is infinite with reference both to time and space.'

The proof likewise assumes the opposite:

'The world has a beginning. Since the beginning is an existence preceded by a time in which the thing is not, there must have been a preceding time in which the world was not, that is, an empty time. Now no originating of anything is possible in an empty time; because no part of such a time possesses *in itself* and in preference to any other, any distinguishing condition of existence or non-existence. In the world, therefore, many groups of things can indeed begin, but the world itself can have no beginning and with respect to past time is infinite.'

This apagogical proof, like the others, contains the direct and unproved assertion of what it was supposed to prove. That is, it first assumes a beyond of the existing world, an empty time; but it also equally *continues* the existence of the world beyond itself into this empty time which is thereby sublated, with the result that the existence of the world is continued into infinity. The world is an existence; the proof *presupposes* that this existence *comes into being* and that the coming-to-be has an *antecedent condition* which is in time. But the antithesis itself consists in the very fact that there is no unconditioned existence, no absolute limit, but that the existence of the world always requires an *antecedent condition*. Thus, what was to be proved is found as an assumption in the proof. Further, the *condition* is sought in empty time, which means in effect that it is taken as temporal and therefore as an existence and as limited. Altogether, then, the assumption is made that the world as an existence presupposes another conditioned existence in time, and so on, therefore, to infinity. The proof regarding the infinity of the world in *space* is the same. Apagogically, the spatial finiteness of the world is assumed; 'this (the world) would therefore exist in an empty unlimited space and would stand in a relation to it; but such a relation of the world to *no* object is a nullity'.

Here, too, what was supposed to be proved is directly presupposed in the proof. It is directly assumed that the spatially limited world exists in an empty space and is supposed to stand in a *relation* to it, that is, there must be a movement out beyond it—on the one hand into the void, into the beyond and non-being of the world, but on the other hand, in order that it be in *relation* with its beyond, that is, *continue* itself into it, the beyond must be imagined as filled with the existence of the world. The infinity of the world in space which is asserted in the antithesis is nothing else than, on the one hand, empty space, and on the other the *relation* of the world to it, that is, the continuity of the world in empty space or the filling of space—which contradiction, namely, space as simultaneously empty and also filled, is the infinite progress of existence in space. This very contradiction, the relation of the world to empty space, is directly made the basis of the proof.

The thesis and antithesis and their proofs therefore represent nothing but the opposite assertions, that a *limit is*, and that the limit equally is only a *sublated* one; that the limit has a beyond, with which however it stands in *relation*, and beyond which it must pass, but that in doing so there arises another such limit, which is no limit.

The *solution* of these antinomies, as of those previously mentioned, is transcendental, that is, it consists in the assertion of the ideality of space and time as forms of intuition—in the sense that the world is *in its own self* not self-contradictory, not self-sublating, but that it is only *consciousness* in its intuition and in the relation of intuition to understanding and reason that is a self-contradictory being. It shows an excessive tenderness for the world to remove contradiction from it and then to transfer the contradiction to spirit, to reason, where it is allowed to remain unresolved. In point of fact it is spirit which is so strong that it can endure contradiction, but it is spirit, too, that knows how to resolve it. But the so-called world (whether it be called an objective, real world or, according to transcendental idealism, a subjective intuition and a sphere of sense determined by the categories of the understanding) is never and nowhere without contradiction, but it is unable to endure it and is, therefore, subject to coming-to-be and ceasing-to-be.

(c) The Infinity of Quantum

1. The infinite quantum as infinitely great or infinitely small is itself implicitly the infinite progress; as great or small it is a quantum and at the same time it is the non-being of quantum. The infinitely great and infinitely small are therefore pictorial conceptions which, when looked at more closely, turn out to be nebulous shadowy nullities. But in the infinite progress, this contradiction is explicitly present and with it that which is the nature of quantum which, as an intensive magnitude, has attained its reality and now in its determinate being is *posited* as it is in its *Notion*. It is this identity which we have now to consider.

Quantum as degree is unitary, self-related and determinate within itself. Through this unitary nature, the otherness and determinateness in quantum are sublated, so that the determinatenesss is external to it; it has it determinateness outside it. This its self-externality is in the first place the *abstract non-being* of quantum generally, the spurious infinity. But, further, this non-being is also quantitative and this continues itself into its non-being, for it is in its externality that quantum has its determinateness; this its externality is, therefore, itself equally a quantum; this non-being of quantum, infinity, is thus limited, that is, this beyond is sublated, is itself determined as quantum which, therefore, in its negation is with itself.

But this is what quantum as such is *in itself*. For it is *itself* just by being external to itself; externality constitutes that whereby it is quantum and is with itself. In the infinite progress, therefore, the *Notion* of quantum is *posited*.

Let us take the progress at first in its abstract determinations as we find them; then in it we have the sublating of quantum, but equally too of its beyond, therefore the negation of quantum as well as the negation of this negation. Its truth is their unity in which they are, but only as moments. It is the resolution of the contradiction of which it is the expression, and its immediate significance is, therefore, the restoration of the Notion of quantity, namely, that quantity is an indifferent or external limit. In the infinite progress as such, the only reflection usually made is that every quantum, however great or small, must be capable of vanishing, of being surpassed; but not that this self-sublating of quantum, the beyond, the spurious infinite itself also vanishes.

Even the *first* sublation, the negation of quality as such whereby quantum is posited, is *in principle* [*an sich*] the sublating of the negation—the quantum is sublated qualitative limit, hence sublated negation—but at the same time it is this only *in principle*; it is *posited* as a determinate being, and then its negation is fixed as the infinite, as the beyond of quantum, which remains on this side as an *immediate*; thus the infinite is determined only as a *first* negation and it appears as such in the infinite progress. But we have seen that in this something more is present, the negation of the negation, or that which the infinite in truth is. We regarded this previously as the restoration of the *Notion* of quantity; this restoration means in the first place, that its determinate being has received a more precise determination; we now have quantum determined in conformity with its Notion, which is different from quantum in its immediacy; externality is now the opposite of itself, posited as a moment of quantity itself—quantum is posited as having its determinateness in another quantum by means of its non-being, of infinity; that is, it is *qualitatively* that which it is. However, this comparison of the *Notion* of quantum with its determinate being belongs more to our reflection, to a relationship which is not yet present here. The immediately following determination is that the quantum has reverted to *quality*, is from now on qualitatively determined. For its peculiarity, its quality, is the externality, the indifference of the determinateness; and quantum is now posited as being in fact *itself* in its externality, as self-related therein, in simple unity with itself, that is, *qualitatively* determined. This qualitative moment is still more closely determined, namely as being-for-itself; for the self-relation to which it has attained has proceeded from mediation, from the negation of the negation. Quantum has infinity, self-determinedness, no longer outside it but within itself.

The infinite, which in the infinite progress has only the empty meaning of a non-being, of an unattained but sought beyond, is

in fact nothing else than *quality*. Quantum as an indifferent limit
goes out beyond itself to infinity; in doing so it seeks nothing else
than to be determined for itself, the qualitative moment, which,
however, is thus only an ought-to-be. Its indifference to limit, and
hence its lack of an explicit determinateness of its own and its
passage away from and beyond itself, is that which makes quantum
what it is; this its passage into the beyond is to be negated and
quantum is to find in the infinite its absolute determinateness.

Quite generally: quantum is sublated quality; but quantum is
infinite, goes beyond itself, is the negation of itself. Thus its passage
beyond itself is, therefore, *in itself* the negation of the negated
quality, the restoration of it; and thus quantum is explicitly
determined as possessing as its *own moment*, the externality which
formerly appeared as a beyond.

Quantum is thus posited as repelled from itself, with the result
that there are two quanta which, however, are sublated, are only
as moments of *one unity*, and this unity is the determinateness of
quantum. Quantum as thus *self-related* as an indifferent limit in
its externality and therefore posited as qualitative, is *quantitative
ratio*. In the ratio, quantum is external to itself, is distinguished
from itself; this its externality is the relation of one quantum
to another, each of which has meaning only in this its relation
to its other; and this relation constitutes the determinateness of
the quantum, which is as such a unity. It has in this unity not
an indifferent, but a qualitative, determination; in this its externality it has returned into itself, and in it quantum is that
which it is.

*Remark 1: The Specific Nature of the Notion of the Mathematical
Infinite*

The mathematical infinite has a twofold interest. On the one hand
its introduction into mathematics has led to an expansion of the
science and to important results; but on the other hand it is
remarkable that mathematics has not yet succeded in justifying its
use of this infinite by the Notion (Notion taken in its proper
meaning). Ultimately, the justifications are based on the *correctness
of the results* obtained with the aid of the said infinite, which
correctness is proved on quite other grounds: but the justifications
are not based on the clarity of the subject matter and on the

operation through which the results are obtained, for it is even admitted that the operation itself is incorrect.

This alone is in itself a bad state of affairs; such a procedure is unscientific. But it also involves the drawback that mathematics, being unaware of the nature of this its instrument because it has not mastered the metaphysics and critique of the infinite, is unable to determine the scope of its application and to secure itself against the misuse of it.

But in a philosophical respect the mathematical infinite is important because underlying it, in fact, is the notion of the genuine infinite and it is far superior to the ordinary so-called *metaphysical infinite* on which are based the objections to the mathematical infinite. Often, the science of mathematics can only defend itself against these objections by denying the competence of metaphysics, asserting that it has nothing to do with that science and does not have to trouble itself about metaphysical concepts so long as it operates consistently within its own sphere. Mathematics has to consider not what is true in itself but what is true in its own domain. Metaphysics, though disagreeing with the use of the mathematical infinite, cannot deny or invalidate the brilliant results obtained from it, and mathematics cannot reach clearness about the metaphysics of its own concept or, therefore, about the derivation of the modes of procedure necessitated by the use of the infinite.

If it were solely the difficulty of the Notion as such which troubled mathematics, it could ignore it without more ado since the Notion is more than merely the statement of the essential determinatenesses of a thing, that is, of the determinations of the understanding: and mathematics has seen to it that these determinatenesses are not lacking in precision; for it is not a science which has to concern itself with the concepts of its objects and which has to generate their content by explicating the concept, even if this could be effected only by ratiocination. But mathematics, in the method of its infinite, finds a radical contradiction to that very method which is peculiar to itself and on which as a science it rests. For the infinitesimal calculus permits and requires modes of procedure which mathematics must wholly reject when operating with finite quantities, and at the same time it treats these infinite quantities as if they were finite and insists on applying to the former the same modes of operation which are valid for the latter; it is a cardinal feature in the development of this science that it has succeeded in applying to *transcendental* determinations and their treatment the form of ordinary calculation.

Mathematics shows that, in spite of the clash between its modes of procedure, results obtained by the use of the infinite completely agree with those found by the strictly mathematical, namely, geometrical and analytical method. But in the first place, this does not apply to every result and the introduction of the infinite is not for the sole purpose of shortening the ordinary method but in order to obtain results which this method is unable to secure. Secondly, success does not by itself justify the mode of procedure. This procedure of the infinitesimal calculus shows itself burdened with a seeming inexactitude, namely, having increased finite magnitudes by an infinitely small quantity, this quantity is in the subsequent operation in part retained and in part ignored. The peculiarity of this procedure is that in spite of the admitted inexactitude, a result is obtained which is not merely fairly close and such that the difference can be ignored, but is perfectly exact. In the operation itself, however, which precedes the result, one cannot dispense with the conception that a quantity is not equal to nothing, yet is so inconsiderable that it can be left out of account. However, what is to be understood by mathematical determinateness altogether rules out any distinction of a greater or lesser degree of exactitude, just as in philosophy there can be no question of greater or less probability but solely of Truth. Even if the method and use of the infinite is justified by the result, it is nevertheless not so superfluous to demand its justification as it seems in the case of the nose to ask for a proof of the right to use it. For mathematical knowledge is scientific knowledge, so that the proof is essential; and even with respect to results it is a fact that a rigorous mathematical method does not stamp all of them with the mark of success, which in any case is only external.

It is worth while considering more closely the mathematical concept of the infinite together with the most noteworthy of the attempts aimed at justifying its use and eliminating the difficulty with which the method feels itself burdened. The consideration of these justifications and characteristics of the mathematical infinite which I shall undertake at some length in this Remark will at the same time throw the best light on the nature of the true Notion itself and show how this latter was vaguely present as a basis for those procedures.

The usual definition of the mathematical infinite is that it is a magnitude than which there is no greater (when it is defined as the infinitely great) or no smaller (when it is defined as the infinitely small), or in the former case is greater than, in the latter case smaller than, any given magnitude. It is true that in this definition the true Notion is not expressed but only, as already remarked, the same contradiction which is present in the infinite progress; but let us see what is implicitly contained in it. In mathematics a magnitude is defined as that which can be increased or diminished; in general, as an indifferent limit. Now since the infinitely great or small is that which cannot be increased or diminished, it is in fact no longer a quantum as such.

This is a necessary and direct consequence. But it is just the reflection that quantum (and in this remark quantum as such, as we find it, I call finite quantum) is sublated, which is usually not made, and which creates the difficulty for ordinary thinking; for quantum in so far as it is infinite is required to be thought as sublated, as something which is not a quantum but yet retains its quantitative character.

To quote Kant's opinion of the said definition which he finds does not accord with what is understood by an infinite whole: 'According to the usual concept, a magnitude is infinite beyond which there can be no greater (i.e. greater than the *amount* contained therein of a given unit); but there can be no greatest amount because one or more units can always be added to it. But our concept of an infinite whole does not represent *how great* it is and it is not therefore the concept of a *maximum* (or a minimum); this concept rather expresses only the *relation* of the whole to an arbitrarily assumed unit, with respect to which the relation is greater than any number. According as this assumed unit is greater or smaller, the infinite would be greater or smaller. The infinity, however, since it consists solely in the *relation* to this given unit, would always remain the same, although of course the absolute magnitude of the whole would not be known through it.'[1]

Kant objects to infinite wholes being regarded as a maximum, as a *completed* amount of a given unit. The maximum or minimum

[1] Observation on the 'Thesis of the First Cosmological Antinomy', in the *Critique of Pure Reason*.

as such still appears as a quantum, an amount. Such a conception cannot avert the conclusion, adduced by Kant, which leads to a greater or lesser infinite. And in general, so long as the infinite is represented as a quantum, the distinction of greater or less still applies to it. This criticism does not however apply to the Notion of the genuine mathematical infinite, of the infinite difference, for this is no longer a finite quantum.

Kant's concept of infinite, on the other hand, which he calls truly transcendental is 'that the successive synthesis of the unit in the measurement of a quantum *can never* be completed'. A quantum as such is presupposed as given; by synthetizing the *unit* this is supposed to be converted into an amount, into a definite assignable quantum; but this synthesis, it is said, can never be completed. It is evident from this that we have here nothing but an expression of the progress to infinity, only represented *transcendentally*, i.e. properly speaking, subjectively and psychologically. True, in itself the quantum is supposed to be completed; but transcendentally, namely in the *subject* which gives it a *relation* to a unit, the quantum comes to be determined only as incomplete and as simply burdened with a *beyond*. Here, therefore, there is no advance beyond the contradiction contained in quantity; but the contradiction is distributed between the object and the subject, limitedness being ascribed to the former, and to the latter the progress to infinity, in its spurious sense, beyond every assigned determinateness.

On the other hand, it was said above that the character of the mathematical infinite and the way it is used in higher analysis corresponds to the Notion of the genuine infinite; the comparison of the two determinations will now be developed in detail. In the first place, as regards the true infinite quantum, it was characterized as *in its own self* infinite; it is such because, as we have seen, the finite quantum or quantum as such and its *beyond*, the spurious infinite, are *equally* sublated. Thus the sublated quantum has returned into a simple unity and self-relation; but not merely like the extensive quantum which, in passing into intensive quantum, has its determinateness only *in itself* [or *implicitly*] in an external plurality, towards which, however, it is indifferent and from which it is supposed to be distinct. The infinite quantum, on the contrary, contains within itself first externality and secondly the negation of it; it is thus no longer any finite quantum, not a quantitative determinateness which would have a *determinate being* as *quantum*; it is simple, and therefore only a *moment*. It is a quantitative determinateness in *qualitative* form; its infinity consists in its being a *qualitative determinateness*. As such moment, it is in essential unity with its other, and *is* only as determined by this its other, i.e. it has meaning solely with reference to that which stands in *relation* to it. *Apart from this relation* it is a *nullity*—simply because quantum as such is indifferent *to the relation*, yet in the relation is supposed to be an *immediate*, inert determination. As only a moment, it is, *in the relation*, not an independent, indifferent something; the quantum in its infinity is a *being-for-self*, for it is at the same time a quantitative determinateness only in the form of a *being-for-one*.

The Notion of the infinite as abstractly expounded here will show itself to be the basis of the mathematical infinite and the Notion itself will become clearer if we consider the various stages in the expression of a quantum *as moment of a ratio*, from the lowest where it is still also a quantum as such, to the higher where it acquires the meaning and the expression of a properly infinite magnitude.

Let us then first take quantum in the relation where it is a fractional number. Such fraction, $\frac{2}{7}$ for example, is not a quantum like 1, 2, 3, etc.; although it is an ordinary finite number it is not an immediate one like the whole numbers but, as a fraction, is directly determined by two other numbers which are related to each other as amount and unit, the unit itself being a specific amount. However, if we abstract from this more precise determination of them and consider them solely as quanta in the qualitative relation in which they are here, then 2 and 7 are indifferent quanta; but since they appear here only as *moments*, the one of the other, and consequently of a third (of the quantum which is called the exponent), they directly count no longer simply as 2 and 7 but only according to the *specific relationship* in which they stand to each other. In their place, therefore, we can just as well put 4 and 14, or 6 and 21, and so on to infinity. With this, then, they begin to have a qualitative character. If 2 and 7 counted as mere quanta, then 2 is just 2 and nothing more, and 7 is simply 7; 4, 14, 6, 21 etc., are completely different from them and, as only immediate quanta, cannot be substituted for them. But in so far as 2 and 7 are not to be taken as such immediate quanta their indifferent limit is sublated; on this side therefore they contain the moment of infinity, since not only are they no longer merely 2 and 7, but their quantitative determinateness remains—but as one which is in itself qualitative, namely in accordance with their significance as moments in the ratio. Their place can be taken by infinitely many others without the value of the fraction being altered, by virtue of the determinateness possessed by the ratio.

However, the representation of infinity by a fractional number is still imperfect because the two sides of the fraction, 2 and 7, can be taken out of the relation and are ordinary, indifferent quanta; their connection as moments of the ratio is an external circumstance which does not directly concern them. Their relation, too, is itself an ordinary quantum, the exponent of the ratio.

The *letters* with which general arithmetic operates, the next universality into which numbers are raised, do not possess the property of having a specific numerical value; they are only general symbols and indeterminate possibilities of any specific value. The fraction $\frac{a}{b}$ seems, therefore, to be a more suitable expression of the infinite, since a and b, taken out of their relation to each other, remain undetermined, and taken separately, too, have no special peculiar value. However, although these letters are posited as indeterminate magnitudes their meaning is to be some finite quantum. Therefore, though they are the general representation of number, it is only of a *determinate number*, and the fact that they are in a ratio is likewise an inessential circumstance and they retain their value outside it.

If we consider more closely what is present in the ratio we find that it contains the following two determinations: first it is a quantum, secondly, however, this quantum is not immediate but contains qualitative opposition; at the same time it remains therein a determinate, indifferent quantum by virtue of the fact that it returns into itself from its otherness, from the opposition, and so also is infinite. These two determinations are represented in the following familiar form developed in their difference from each other.

The fraction $\frac{2}{7}$ can be expressed as $0 \cdot 285714 \ldots$ $\frac{1}{1-a}$ as $1 + a + a^2 + a^3$ etc. As so expressed it is an infinite series; the fraction itself is called the sum, or *finite expression* of it. A comparison of the two expressions shows that one of them, the infinite series, represents the fraction no longer as a ratio but from that side where it is a quantum as an *aggregate* of units added together, as an amount. That the magnitudes of which it is supposed to consist as amount are in turn decimal fractions and therefore are themselves ratios, is irrelevant here; for this circumstance concerns the particular kind of *unit* of these magnitudes, not the magnitudes as constituting an *amount*. Just as a multi-figured integer in the decimal system is reckoned essentially as an *amount*, and the fact that it consists of *products* of a number and of the number ten and powers of ten is ignored. Similarly here, it is irrelevant that there are fractions other than the example taken of $\frac{2}{7}$ which, when expressed as decimal fractions, do not give an infinite series; but they can all be so expressed in a numerical system based on another unit.

Now in the infinite series, which is supposed to represent the fraction as an amount, the aspect of the fraction as a ratio has vanished and with it there has vanished too the aspect which, as we have already shown, makes the fraction *in its own self* infinite. But this infinity has entered in another way; the series, namely, is itself infinite.

Now the nature of this infinity of the series is self-evident; it is the spurious infinity of the progression. The series contains and exhibits the contradiction of representing that which is a relation possessing a *qualitative* nature, as devoid of relation, as a mere *quantum*, as an amount. The consequence of this is that the amount which is expressed in the series always lacks something, so that in order to reach the required determinateness, we must always go further than the terms already posited. The law of the progression is known, it is implicit in the determination of the quantum contained in the fraction and in the nature of the form in which it is supposed to be expressed. By continuing the series the amount can of course be made as accurate as *required*; but representation by means of the series continues to remain only an *ought-to-be*; it is burdened with a *beyond* which cannot be sublated, because to express as an *amount* that which rests on a *qualitative* determinateness is a *lasting contradiction*.

In this infinite series, this inexactitude is actually present, whereas in the genuine mathematical infinite there is only an appearance of inexactitude. These two kinds of mathematical infinite are as little to be confounded as are the two kinds of philosophical infinite. In representing the genuine mathematical infinite, *the form of series* was used originally and it has recently again been invoked; but this form is not necessary for it. On the contrary, the infinite of the infinite series is essentially different from the genuine infinite as the sequel will show. Indeed the form of infinite series is even inferior to the fractional expression.

For the infinite series contains the spurious infinity, because what the series is meant to express remains an *ought-to-be* and what it does express is burdened with a beyond which does not vanish and *differs* from what was meant to be expressed. It is infinite not because of the terms actually expressed but because they are incomplete, because the *other* which essentially belongs to them is beyond them; what is really present in the series, no matter how many terms there may be, is only something finite, in the proper meaning of that word, posited as finite, i.e., as something *which is not what it ought to be*. But on the other hand, what is called the *finite expression* or the *sum* of such a series lacks nothing; it contains that complete value which the series only seeks; the *beyond* is recalled from its flight; what it is and what it ought to be are not separate but the same.

What distinguishes these two is more precisely this, that in the infinite series the *negative* is *outside* its terms which are present only *qua* parts of the *amount*. On the other hand, in the finite expression which is a ratio, the *negative* is immanent as the *reciprocal* determining of the sides of the ratio and this is an accomplished return-into-self, a self-related unity as a negation of the negation (*both* sides of the ratio are only *moments*), and consequently has *within it* the determination of infinity. Thus the usually so-called *sum*, the $\frac{2}{7}$ or $\frac{1}{1-a}$ is in fact a ratio; and this so-called *finite expression* is the truly *infinite expression*. The infinite *series*, on the other hand, is in truth a *sum*; its purpose is to represent in the form of a sum what is in itself a ratio, and the existing terms of the series are not terms of a ratio but of an aggregate. Furthermore, the series is in fact the *finite expression;* for it is the incomplete aggregate and remains essentially deficient. According to what is really present in it, it is a specific quantum, but at the same time it is less than what it ought to be; and then, too, what it lacks is itself a specific quantum; this missing part is in fact that which is called infinite in the series, from the merely formal point of view that it is something lacking, a *non-being;* with respect to its content it is a finite quantum. Only what is actually present in the series, plus what is lacking, together constitute the amount of the fraction, the specific quantum which the series also *ought* to be but is not capable of being. The word *infinite*, even as used in infinite series, is commonly fancied to be something lofty and exalted; this is a kind of superstition, the superstition of the understanding; we have seen how, on the contrary, it indicates only a deficiency.

We may further remark that the existence of infinite series which cannot be summed is an external and contingent circumstance with respect to the form of series as such. They contain a higher kind of infinity than do those which can be summed, namely an incommensurability, or the impossibility of representing the quantitative ratio contained in them as a quantum, even in the form of a fraction; but the *form of series* as such which they have contains the same determination of spurious infinity that is present in the series capable of summation.

The terminological inversion we have just noticed in connection with the fraction and its expression as a series, also occurs when the *mathematical* infinite—not the one just named but the genuine infinite—is called the *relative* infinite, while the ordinary *meta-physical*—by which is understood the abstract, spurious infinite—is called *absolute*. But in point of fact it is this metaphysical infinite which is merely relative, because the negation which it expresses is opposed to a limit only in such a manner that this limit *persists* outside it and is not sublated by it; the mathematical infinite, on the contrary, has within itself truly sublated the finite limit because the *beyond* of the latter is united with it.

It is primarily in this sense, in which it has been demonstrated that the so-called sum or finite expression of an infinite series is rather to be regarded as the infinite expression, that Spinoza opposes the concept of true infinity to that of the spurious and illustrates it by examples. It will shed most light on his concept if I follow up this exposition with what he says on the subject.

He starts by defining the infinite as the absolute affirmation of any kind of natural existence, the finite on the contrary as a determinateness, as a negation. That is to say, the absolute affirmation of an existence is to be taken as its relation to itself, its not being dependent on an *other*; the finite, on the other hand, is negation, a ceasing-to-be in the form of a *relation* to an *other* which begins *outside* it. Now the absolute affirmation of an existence does not, it is true, exhaust the notion of infinity; this implies that infinity is an affirmation, not as immediate, but only as restored by the reflection of the *other* into itself, or as negation of the negative. But with Spinoza, substance and its absolute unity has the form of an inert [*unbewegte*] unity, i.e. of a unity which is not self-mediated, of a fixity or rigidity in which the Notion of the negative unity of the self, i.e. subjectivity, is still lacking.

The mathematical example with which he illustrates the true infinite[1] is a space between two unequal circles which are not concentric, one of which lies inside the other without touching it. It seems that he thought highly of this figure and of the concept which it was used to illustrate, making it the motto of his *Ethics*. 'Mathematicians conclude', he says, 'that the inequalities possible in such a space are infinite, not from the infinite *amount* of parts, for its size is *fixed* and *limited* and I can assume larger and smaller such spaces, but because the nature of the fact surpasses every determinateness.' It is evident that Spinoza rejects that conception of the infinite which represents it as an amount or as a series which is not completed, and he points out that here, in the space of his example, the infinite is not beyond, but actually present and complete; this space is bounded, but it is infinite 'because the nature of the fact surpasses every determinateness', because the determination of magnitude contained in it cannot at the same time be represented as a quantum, or in Kant's words already quoted, the *synthesis* cannot be completed to form a (discrete) quantum. How in general the opposition of continuous and discrete quantum leads to the infinite, will be shown in detail in a later Remark. Spinoza calls the infinite of a series the infinite of the imagination; on the other hand, the infinite as self-relation he calls the infinite of thought, or *infinitum actu*. It is, namely, *actu*, *actually* infinite because it is complete and present within itself. Thus the series $0 \cdot 285714 \ldots$ or $1 + a + a^2 + a^3 \ldots$ is the infinite merely of imagination or supposition; for it has no

[1] *Epist. XXIX.*

actuality, it definitely lacks something; on the other hand $\frac{2}{7}$ or $\frac{1}{1-a}$ is *actually* not only what the series is in its developed terms, but is, in addition, what the series lacks, what it only *ought to be*. The $\frac{2}{7}$ or $\frac{1}{1-a}$ is equally a finite magnitude like Spinoza's space enclosed between two circles, with its inequalities, and can like this space be made larger or smaller. But this does not involve the absurdity of a larger or smaller infinite; for this quantum of the whole does not concern the relation of its moments, *the nature of the fact*, i.e. the qualitative determination of magnitude; what is *actually present* in the infinite series is equally a finite quantum, but it is also still deficient. *Imagination* on the contrary stops short at quantum as such and does not reflect on the qualitative relation which constitutes the ground of the existing incommensurability.

The incommensurability which lies in Spinoza's example embraces in general the functions of curved lines and more precisely, leads to the infinite which mathematics has introduced with such functions, in general, with the *functions of variable magnitudes*. This infinite is the *genuine mathematical* qualitative infinite which Spinoza also had in mind. We shall now consider this determination here in detail.

First of all, as regards the category of *variability* which is accorded such importance and which embraces the magnitudes related in these functions, it is to be noted that these magnitudes are not supposed to be variable in the way that the two numbers 2 and 7 are in the fraction $\frac{2}{7}$: their place can equally well be taken by 4 and 14, 6 and 21, and by other numbers *ad infinitum* without altering the value of the fraction; and still more in $\frac{a}{b}$ can a and b be replaced by any arbitrary number without altering what $\frac{a}{b}$ is intended to express. Now in the sense that in the place, too, of x and y of a function, there can be put an infinite, i.e. inexhaustible, multitude of numbers, a and b are just as much variable magnitudes as the said x and y. The expression 'variable magnitudes' is therefore very vague and ill-chosen for those determinations of magnitude whose interest and manner of treatment lie in something quite distinct from their mere variability.

In order to make clear wherein lies the true character of those moments of a function with which higher analysis is concerned, we must once more run through the stages to which we have already drawn attention. In $\frac{2}{7}$ or $\frac{a}{b}$, 2 and 7 are each independent determinate quanta and the relation is not essential to them; a and b likewise are intended to represent quanta which remain what they are even outside the relation. And further, $\frac{2}{7}$ and $\frac{a}{b}$ are each a fixed quantum, a quotient; the ratio constitutes an amount, the unit of which is expressed by the denominator and the amount of these units by the numerator, or conversely; even if 4 and 14, and so on, are substituted for 2 and 7, the ratio, also as a quantum, remains the same. But now in the function $\frac{y^2}{x} = p$, for example, this is essentially changed; here, it is true that x and y can stand for definite quanta, but only x and y^2 have a determinate quotient, not x and y. Hence not only are these *sides* of the ratio x and y, not any determinate quanta, but, secondly, their ratio is not a fixed quantum (nor is such a quantum meant as in the case of a and b), not a fixed quotient, but this quotient is, *as a quantum*, absolutely *variable*. But this is solely because x has a relation, not to y, but to the *square* of y. The relation of a magnitude to a *power* is not a *quantum*, but essentially a *qualitative* relation; the power-relation is the feature which is to be regarded as the fundamental determination. But in the function of the straight line y $= ax$, $\frac{y}{x} = a$ is an ordinary fraction and quotient; consequently this function is only *formally* a function of variable magnitudes, or x and y here are what a and b are in $\frac{a}{b}$, that is, they are not in that determination in which the differential and integral calculus considers them. On account of the *special* nature of the variable magnitudes in this mode of consideration, it would have been fitting to have introduced both a special name for them and other *symbols* than those generally used for *unknown quantities* in any finite equation, determinate or indeterminate; for there is an essential difference between those magnitudes and such quanta which are merely unknown, but are in themselves completely determined or are a definite range of determinate quanta. It is, too, only because of a lack of awareness of what constitutes the peculiar interest of higher analysis and of what has led to the need for and invention of the differential calculus, that functions of the first degree and the equation of the straight line are themselves included in the treatment of this calculus; such formalism originates partly, too, in the mistake of imagining that the intrinsically correct demand for the *generalization* of a method has been fulfilled when the *specific* determinateness on which the need for the calculus is based is omitted, as if in this domain we were concerned only with *variable magnitudes*. A great deal of formalism would, indeed, have been avoided if it had been perceived that the calculus is concerned not with variable magnitudes as such but with *relations of powers*.

But there is still another stage where the peculiar character of the mathematical infinite becomes prominent. In an equation in which x and y are determined primarily by a power-relation, x and y as such are still supposed to signify quanta; now this significance is altogether and completely lost in the so-called *infinitesimal differences*. Dx, dy, are no longer quanta, nor are they supposed to signify quanta; it is solely in their relation to each other that they have any meaning, *a meaning merely as moments*. They are no longer *something* (something taken as a quantum), not finite differences; but neither are they *nothing;* not empty nullities. Apart from their relation they are pure nullities, but they are intended to be taken only as moments of the relation, as *determinations* of the differential co-efficient $\dfrac{dx}{dy}$.

In this concept of the infinite, the quantum is genuinely completed into a qualitative reality; it is posited as actually infinite; it is sublated not merely as this or that quantum but as quantum generally. But the quantitative determinateness *remains* as *element* of the principle of the quanta, or, as has also been said, the quanta remain *in their first concept*.

It is this concept which has been the target for all the attacks made on the fundamental determination of the mathematics of this infinite, i.e. of the differential and integral calculus. Failure to recognize it was the result of incorrect ideas on the part of mathematicians themselves; but it is the inability to justify the object as *Notion* which is mainly responsible for these attacks. But mathematics, as we remarked above, cannot evade the Notion here; for, as mathematics of the infinite, it does not confine itself to the *finite* determinateness of its objects (as in ordinary mathematics, which considers and relates space and number and their determinations only according to their finitude); on the contrary, when it treats a determination taken from ordinary mathematics, it converts it into an identity with its opposite, e.g. converting a curved line into a straight one, the circle into a polygon, etc. Consequently, the operations which it allows itself to perform in the differential and integral calculus are in complete contradiction with the nature of merely finite determinations and their relations and would therefore have to be justified solely by the *Notion*.

Although the mathematics of the infinite maintained that these quantitative determinations are vanishing magnitudes, i.e. magnitudes which are no longer any particular quantum and yet are not nothing but are still a *determinateness* relatively to an other, it seemed perfectly clear that such an *intermediate state*, as it was called, between being and nothing does not exist. What we are to think of this objection and the so-called intermediate state, has already been indicated above in Remark 4 to the category of becoming. The unity of being and nothing is, of course, not a *state*; a state would be a determination of being and nothing into which these moments might be supposed to have lapsed only by accident, as it were, into a diseased condition externally induced through erroneous thinking; on the contrary, this mean and unity, the vanishing or equally the becoming is alone their *truth*.

Further, it has been said that what is infinite is not *comparable* as something greater or smaller; therefore there cannot be a relation between infinites according to orders or dignities of the infinite, although in the science of infinitesimals these distinctions do occur. Underlying this objection already mentioned is always the idea that here we are supposed to be dealing with *quanta* which are compared *as* quanta, that determinations which are no longer quanta no longer have any relationship to each other. But the truth is rather that that which has being *solely* in the ratio is not a quantum; the nature of quantum is such that it is supposed to have a completely indifferent existence apart from its ratio, and its difference from another quantum is supposed not to concern its own determination; on the other hand the qualitative is what it is only in its distinction from an other. The said infinite magnitudes, therefore, are not merely comparable, but they exist only as moments of comparison, i.e. of the ratio.

I will adduce the most important definitions of this infinite which have been given in mathematics. From these it will be clear that the thought underlying them accords with the Notion developed here, but that the originators of the definitions did not establish the thought as Notion and found it necessary in the application to resort again to expedients which conflict with their better cause.

The thought cannot be more correctly determined than in the way Newton has stated it. I eliminate here those determinations which belong to the idea of motion and velocity (from which, mainly, he took the name of *fluxions*) because in them the thought does not appear in its proper abstraction but as concrete and mixed with non-essential forms. Newton explains that he understands by these fluxions not *indivisibles* (a form which was used by earlier mathematicians, Cavalieri[1] and others and which involves the concept of an intrinsically determinate quantum), but *vanishing divisibles;* also not sums and ratios of determinate parts but the *limits (limites)* of *sums* and *ratios.*[2] It may be objected that vanishing magnitudes do not have a *final ratio*, because the ratio before it vanishes is not final, and when it has vanished is no longer a ratio. But by the ratio of vanishing magnitudes is to be understood not the ratio *before which* and *after which* they vanish, but *with which* they vanish (*quacum evanescunt*). Similarly, the *first* ratio of nascent magnitudes is that *with which* they become.

Newton did what the scientific method of his time demanded, he only explained what was to be understood by an expression; but that such and such is to be understood by it is, properly speaking, a subjective presumption, or a historical demand, without any indication that such a concept is in itself absolutely necessary or that there is truth in it. However, what has been quoted shows that the concept put forward by Newton corresponds to the way in which infinite quantity resulted from the reflection of quantum

---

[1] Cavalieri, Francesco Bonaventura, 1598–1647, Professor of Mathematics at Bologna: *Geometria Indivisibilium Continuorum Nova*, 1635; *Exercitationes Geometricae*, 1647.

[2] *Princ. Mathem. Phil. Nat.* L.I. Lemma XI. Schol.

into itself in the exposition above. By magnitudes is understood magnitudes in their vanishing, i.e. which are no longer quanta; also, not ratios of determinate parts, but the *limits of the ratio*. The meaning is, therefore, that with the vanishing of the quanta individually, the sides of the ratio, there also vanishes the ratio itself in so far as it is a quantum; the limit of the quantitative ratio is that in which it both is and is not, or, more precisely, in which the quantum has vanished, with the result that the ratio and its sides are preserved, the former only as a qualitative relation of quantity and the latter similarly as qualitative moments of quantity. Newton goes on to add that from the fact that there are final ratios of vanishing magnitudes, it must not be inferred that there are final magnitudes, *indivisibles*. For this would mean a leap again from the abstract ratio to its sides as supposedly having an independent value of their own as indivisibles outside their relation, as something which would be a one, something devoid of any relation at all.

To prevent such a misunderstanding, he again points out that *final ratios* are not ratios of *final magnitudes*, but are limits to which the ratios of the magnitudes decreasing without limit are nearer than any *given*, i.e. finite, difference; the ratios, however, do not exceed these limits, for if they did they would become nullities. In other words, *final magnitudes* could have been taken to mean, as already said, indivisibles or ones. But the definition of the final ratio excludes the conception both of the indifferent one which is devoid of any relation, and of the finite quantum. If the required determination had been developed into the Notion of a quantitative determination which is purely a moment of the ratio, there would have been no need for the *decreasing without limit* into which Newton converts the quantum and which only expresses the progress to infinity, or for the determination of divisibility which no longer has any immediate meaning here.

As regards the preservation of the ratio in the vanishing of the quanta, there is found elsewhere, as in Carnot,[1] the expression that *by virtue of the law of continuity*, the vanishing magnitudes still retain the ratio from which they come, before they vanish.

---

[1] Carnot, Lazare Nicolas Marguerite, Count, 1753–1823, 'organizer of victory' in the republican armies, equally important as politician and soldier until his banishment in 1815, died at Magdeburg: *Réflexions sur la Métaphysique du Calcul Infinitésimal*, 1797.

This conception expresses the true nature of the matter, if the continuity of the quantum is not understood to be the continuity which it has in the infinite progress where the quantum is continued in its vanishing in such a manner that in its *beyond* there arises only a finite quantum again, only a fresh term of the series; but a *continuous* progress is always imagined as one in which values are passed through, values which are still finite quanta. On the other hand, where the transition is made into the true infinite it is the ratio that is continuous; so *continuous* is it, so completely is it preserved, that the transition may be said to consist solely in throwing into relief the pure ratio and causing the non-relational determination—i.e. that a quantum which is a side of the ratio is still a quantum outside this relation—to vanish. This purification of the quantitative ratio is thus analogous to grasping an empirical reality in terms of its Notion. The empirical reality is thereby raised above itself in such a way that its Notion contains the same characteristic features as it has itself, but these are grasped in their essentiality and are taken *into the unity* of the Notion in which they have lost their indifferent, Notion-less existence.

The other form of Newton's exposition of the magnitudes in question is equally interesting, namely, as generative magnitudes or principles. A *generated magnitude* (*genita*) is a product or quotient, such as a root, rectangle, square, also the sides of rectangles and squares—in general, a *finite magnitude*. 'Such a magnitude being considered as variable, increasing or decreasing in ceaseless motion and flux, he gives its momentary increments or decrements the name of moments. But these are not to be taken for particles of a definite magnitude (*particulae finitae*): such would not themselves be *moments* but magnitudes *generated* from moments. Rather are they to be understood as the nascent *principles* or *beginnings* of finite magnitudes.' Here the quantum is distinguished from itself: as a product or a real being [*Daseiendes*], and in its becoming (or as nascent), in its beginning and principle, that is to say, in its Notion, or, what is here the same thing, in its qualitative determination: in the latter the quantitative differences, the infinite increments or decrements, are only moments; only that which has becoming at its back has passed over into the indifference of determinate being and into externality, i.e. is quantum. But if on the one hand the philosophy of the

I

true Notion must acknowledge these determinations of the infinite with respect to increments or decrements, on the other hand it must be observed that the very forms of increments etc. fall *within* the category of immediate quantum and of the continuous progress to which we have referred; in fact the conceptions of increment, growth or increase of x by dx or i, and so on, are to be regarded as the fundamental vice in these methods—the permanent obstacle to disengaging the determination of the qualitative moment of quantity in its purity from the conception of the ordinary quantum.

The conception of *infinitesimals* which is implicit, too, in the increment or decrement itself, is much inferior to the above determinations. The nature of these magnitudes is supposed to be such that they may be *neglected*, not only in comparison with finite magnitudes, but also their higher orders in comparison with their lower, and even the products of several in comparison with a single one. With Leibniz, this demand to neglect is more strikingly prominent than with previous inventors of methods relating to these infinitesimals in which this call to neglect also occurs. It is chiefly this call to neglect which, along with a gain in facility, has given this calculus the appearance of inexactitude and express incorrectness in its method of procedure. Wolf has tried to make this neglect intelligible in his own way of popularizing things, i.e. by polluting the pure Notion and setting in its place incorrect sensuous conceptions. For example, he compares the neglect of infinitesimals of higher orders relatively to lower with the procedure of a surveyor who, in measuring the height of a mountain is no less accurate if meanwhile the wind has blown away a grain of sand from the top; or with the neglect of the height of houses or towers when calculating lunar eclipses.[1]

Even if ordinary common sense in fairness allows such inexactitude, all geometricians reject this conception. It is quite obvious that in the science of mathematics there cannot be any question of such empirical accuracy; mathematical measuring by operations of the calculus or by geometrical constructions and proofs is altogether different from land-surveying, from the measuring of empirical lines, figures etc. Besides, by comparing the result obtained by a strictly geometrical method with that

[1] *Element. Mathes. univ. Tom. I. El. Analys. math. P. II. C.I. s. Schol.*

obtained by the method of infinite differences, analysts demonstrate that the one is the same as the other and that there is absolutely no question of a greater or lesser degree of exactness. And it is self-evident that an absolutely exact result could not emerge from an inexact method. Yet on the other hand again, the *method itself* cannot do without this omission of what is regarded as insignificant, despite its protestations against the way this omission is justified. And this is the difficulty which engages the efforts of the analysts to make intelligible and to remove the inherent inconsistency.

It is especially Euler's[1] conception of the matter which must be cited here. He adopts the general Newtonian definition and insists that the differential calculus considers the *ratios of the increments* of a magnitude, but that the *infinite difference* as such is to be considered as wholly *nil*.[2] How this is to be understood is clear from the foregoing; the infinite difference is a nil only of quantum, not a qualitative nil, but as a nil of quantum it is a pure moment of the ratio only. It is not a *quantitative* difference; but for that reason it is, on the one hand, altogether wrong to speak of those moments which are called infinitesimals, also as increments or decrements and as *differences*. This description implies that something is *added to* or *subtracted from* the initially given finite magnitude, that a subtraction or addition, an arithmetical, external operation takes place. But it is to be noticed that the transition of the function of the variable magnitude into its differential is of a quite different nature; as we have made clear, it is to be considered as a reduction of the finite function to the qualitative relation of its quantitative determinations. On the other hand, the error becomes obvious when it is said that the increments by themselves are zeros, that only their ratios are considered; for a zero no longer has any determinateness at all. This conception then, does get as far as the negative of the quantum and gives definite expression to it, but at the same time it does not grasp this negative in its positive significance of qualitative determinations of quantity which, if they were torn out of the ratio and regarded as quanta, would be only zeros.

---

[1] Euler, Leopold, 1707–1783, Professor at St Petersburg, at Berlin, and again at St Petersburg: *Introductio in Analysin Infinitorum*, 1748; *Institutiones Calculi Differentialis*, 1755; *Institutiones Calculi Integralis*, 1768–1794.

[2] *Institut. Calc. different. P.I.C. III.*

The opinion of Lagrange[1] on the idea of limits or final ratios is that although one can well imagine the ratio of two magnitudes so long as they remain finite, this ratio does not present any clear and definite concept to the intellect as soon as its terms become simultaneously zero. And the understanding must, indeed, transcend this merely negative side on which the terms of the ratio are quantitatively zero, and must grasp them positively, as qualitative moments. But we cannot regard as satisfactory Euler's further remarks[2] with regard to this conception of his in which he tries to show that two so-called infinitesimals which are supposed to be nothing else but zeros, nevertheless stand in a relation to each other, for which reason they are denoted by symbols other than zero. He tries to base this on the difference between the arithmetical and geometrical ratio: in the former, we have an eye to the difference, in the latter, to the quotient, so that although in the former there is no difference between two zeros, this is not so in the geometrical ratio; if $2 : 1 = 0 : 0$ then from the nature of proportion it follows that, because the first term is twice as great as the second, the third is also twice as great as the fourth; thus according to proportion, $0 : 0$ is to be taken as the ratio of $2 : 1$. Even in common arithmetic n. $0 = 0$ and therefore $n : 1 = 0 : 0$. But it is just because $2 : 1$ or $n : 1$ is a relation of quanta that there cannot be any corresponding ratio or expression of $0 : 0$.

I refrain from citing any further instances since those already considered show clearly enough that the genuine Notion of the infinite is, in fact, implied in them, but that the specific nature of that Notion has not been brought to notice and grasped. Consequently, in the actual application of the method of infinitesimals, the genuine Notion of the infinite cannot exercise any influence; on the contrary, there is a return of the finite determinateness of quantity and the operation cannot dispense with the conception of a quantum which is merely *relatively small*. The calculus makes it necessary to subject the so-called infinitesimals to ordinary arithmetical operations of addition and so on, which are based on the nature of finite magnitudes, and therefore to

---

[1] Lagrange, Jos. Louis, 1736–1812, Euler's successor at Berlin, then Professor at the *École Polytechnique* in Paris: *Théorie des Fonctions Analytiques*, 1797, *Introduction*.

[2] *op. cit.*, Section 84 *sqq.*

regard them momentarily as finite magnitudes and to treat them as such. It is for the calculus to justify its procedure in which it first brings them down into this sphere and treats them as increments or differences, and then neglects them as quanta after it had just applied forms and laws of finite magnitudes to them.

I will proceed to cite the main features of the attempts of the geometricians to remove these difficulties.

The older analysts had little scruples in the matter, but the moderns directed their efforts mainly towards bringing the differential calculus back to the evidence of a *strictly geometrical method* and in it to attain to the *rigour of the proofs of the ancients* (Lagrange's expressions) in mathematics. But since the principle of infinitesimal analysis is of a higher nature than the principle of the mathematics of finite magnitudes, that kind of *evidence* had perforce to be dispensed with, just as philosophy, too, cannot lay claim to that obviousness which belongs to the natural sciences, e.g. natural history—and just as eating and drinking are reckoned a more intelligible business than thinking and understanding. Accordingly, we shall deal only with the efforts to attain to the rigour of proof of the ancients.

Some have attempted to dispense altogether with the concept of the infinite, and without it to achieve what seemed to be bound up with its use. Lagrange speaks, e.g., of the method devised by Landen,[1] saying that it is purely analytical and does not employ infinitesimal differences, but starts with different values of variable magnitudes and subsequently equates them. He also gives it as his opinion that in this method, the differential calculus loses its own peculiar advantages, namely simplicity of method and facility of operation. This is, indeed, a procedure which in some measure corresponds to the starting-point of Descartes' tangential method of which detailed mention will be made later. This much, we may remark here, is generally evident, that the general procedure in which different values of variable magnitudes are assumed and subsequently equated, belongs to another department of mathematical treatment than that to which the method of the differential calculus itself belongs; and that the peculiar nature of the simple relation (to be considered in detail further on) to which its actual, concrete determination reduces, namely,

[1] Landen, John, English mathematician, 1719–1790: *Mathematical Lucubrations*, 1755, etc.

of the derived function to the original, is not brought into prominence.

The earlier of the moderns, Fermat,[1] Barrow,[2] and others for example, who at first used infinitesimals in that application which was subsequently developed into the differential and integral calculus, and then Leibniz, too, and those following him including Euler, always frankly believed that they were entitled to omit the products of infinitesimal differences and their higher powers, solely on the ground that they *vanish relatively* to the lower order. This is for them the sole basis of the fundamental principle, namely the determination of that which is the differential of a product or a power, *for the entire theoretical teaching reduces to this*. The rest is partly the mechanism of development and partly application, in which however as we shall later on see, the more important, or rather the sole, interest is to be found. With respect to the present topic, we need only mention here what is elementary, that on the same ground of *insignificance*, the cardinal principle adopted in relation to curves is that the elements of the curves, namely the *increments* of abscissa and ordinate, have the *relation* to each other of *subtangent* and *ordinate*; for the purpose of obtaining similar triangles, the arc which forms the third side of a triangle to the two increments of the *characteristic* triangle (as it rightly used to be called), is regarded as a straight line, as part of the tangent and one of the increments therefore as reaching to the tangent. By these assumptions those determinations are, on the one hand, raised above the nature of finite magnitudes, but on the other hand, a method which is valid only for finite magnitudes and which does not permit the omission of anything on the ground of insignificance, is applied to moments now called infinitesimal. With such a mode of procedure, the difficulty which encumbers the method remains in all its starkness.

We must mention here a remarkable procedure of Newton[3]—the invention of an ingenious device to remove the arithmetically incorrect omission of the products of infinitesimal differences or higher orders of them in the finding of differentials. He finds the differentials of products—from which the differentials of quotients,

[1] Fermat, Pierre de, 1601–1665: *Varia Opera Mathematica*, 1679.

[2] Barrow, Isaac, 1630–1677, Professor at Cambridge: *Lectiones Geometricae*, 1669; *Lectiones Opticae*, 1674.

[3] *Princ. Math. phil. nat.* Lib. II Lemma II, after Propos. VII.

powers, etc., can then be easily derived—in the following way. The product of x and y, when each is taken as reduced by *half* of its infinitesimal difference, becomes $xy - \dfrac{xdy}{2} - \dfrac{ydx}{2} + \dfrac{dxdy}{4}$; but if x and y are made to increase by the same amount, it becomes $xy + \dfrac{xdy}{2} + \dfrac{ydx}{2} + \dfrac{dxdy}{4}$. Now when the first product is subtracted from the second, $ydx + xdy$ remains as a surplus and this is said to be the surplus of the increase by a whole dx and dy, for this increase is the difference between the two products; it is therefore the differential of xy. Clearly, in this procedure, the term which forms the chief difficulty, the product of the two infinitesimal differences, cancels itself out. But in spite of the name of Newton it must be said that such an operation although very elementary, is incorrect; it is not true that $\left(x + \dfrac{dx}{2}\right)\left(y + \dfrac{dy}{2}\right) - \left(x - \dfrac{dx}{2}\right)\left(y - \dfrac{dy}{2}\right) = (x + dx)(y + dy) - xy$. It can only have been the need to establish the all-important fluxional calculus which could bring a Newton to deceive himself with such a proof.

Other forms which Newton employed in the derivation of differentials are bound up with concrete meanings of the elements and their powers, meanings relating to motion. About the use of the *serial form* which also characterizes his method, it suggests itself to say that it is always possible to obtain the required degree of accuracy by adding more terms and that the omitted terms are *relatively insignificant*, in general, that the result is only an *approximation;* though here too he would have been satisfied with this ground for omission as he is in his method of solving equations of higher degree by approximation, where the higher powers arising from the substitution in the given equation of any ascertained, still inexact term, are omitted on the crude ground of their relative smallness.[1]

The error into which Newton fell in solving a problem by omitting essential, higher powers, an error which gave his opponents the occasion of a triumph of their method over his, and the true origin of which has been indicated by Lagrange in his recent investigation of it[2] demonstrates the formalism and

---

[1] See Lagrange: *Équations Numériques*, p. 125.
[2] *Théorie des fonct. analyt.* 3me P., Ch. IV.

uncertainty which still prevailed in the use of this instrument. Lagrange shows that Newton made the mistake because he omitted the term of the series containing that power on which the specific problem turned. Newton had kept to the formal, superficial principle of omitting terms on account of their relative smallness. For example, it is well known that in mechanics the terms of the series in which the function of a motion is developed are given a *specific meaning*, so that the first term or the first function refers to the moment of velocity, the second to the accelerating force and the third to the resistance of forces. Here, then, the terms of the series are not to be regarded merely as *parts* of a sum, but rather as *qualitative moments of a whole determined by the concept*. In this way, the omission of the rest of the terms belonging to the spuriously infinite series acquires an altogether different meaning from omission on the ground of their relative smallness.[1] The error in the Newtonian solution

---

[1] Both considerations are found set simply side by side in the application by Lagrange of the theory of functions to mechanics in the chapter on rectilinear motion (*Théorie des fonct.* 3me P. Ch. I, art. 4). The space passed through, considered as a function of the time elapsed, gives the equation $x = ft$; this,

developed as $f(t + \delta)$ gives $ft + \delta f't + \dfrac{\delta 2}{2} f''t + $, etc.

Thus the space traversed in the period of time is represented in the formula as $= \delta f't + \dfrac{\delta 2}{2} f''t + \dfrac{\delta 3}{2 \cdot 3} f'''t + $, etc. The motion by means of which this space has been traversed is (it is said) *therefore*—i.e. because the analytical development gives several, in fact infinitely, many terms—*composed* of various partial motions, of which the spaces corresponding to the time will be $\delta f't$, $\dfrac{\delta 2}{2} f''t$, $\dfrac{\delta 3}{2 \cdot 3} f'''dt$, etc. The first partial motion is, in known motion, the formally uniform one with a velocity designated by $f't$, the second is uniformly accelerated motion derived from an accelerative force proportional to $f''t$. 'Now since the remaining terms do not refer to any simple known motion, it is not necessary to take them specially into account and we shall show that they may be abstracted from in determining the motion at the beginning of the point of time.' This is now shown, but of course only by *comparing* the series *all* of whose terms belonged to the determination of the magnitude of the space traversed in the period of time, with the equation given in *art.* 3 for the motion of a falling body, namely $x = at + bt^2$ in which only these two terms occur. But this equation has itself received this form only because the *explanation given* to the terms produced by the *analytical development* is presupposed; this presupposition is that the uniformly accelerated motion is *composed* of a formally uniform motion continued with the velocity attained in the preceding period of time, and of an increment (the a in $s = at^2$, i.e. the empirical co-efficient) which is arose, *not* because terms of the series were neglected only as *parts of a sum*, but because the *term containing the qualitative determination*, which is the essential point, was ignored.

In this example, the procedure is made to depend on the qualitative *meaning*. In this connection the general assertion can at once be made that the whole difficulty of the principle would be removed if the *qualitative* meaning of the principle were stated and the operation were made to depend on it—in place of the formalism which links the determination of the differential only to that which gives the problem its *name*, to the *difference* as such between a function and its variation after its variable magnitude has received an *increment*. In this sense, it is obvious that the differential of x^n is completely exhausted by the first term of the series which results from the expansion of $(x + dx)^n$. Thus the omission of the rest of the terms is not on account of their relative smallness; and so there is no assumption of an inexactitude, an error or mistake which could be compensated or rectified by another error—a point of view from which Carnot in particular justifies the ordinary method of the infinitesimal calculus. Since what is involved is not a *sum* but a *relation*, the differential is completely given *by the first term*; and where further terms, the differentials of higher orders, are required, their determination involves not the continuation of a series as a *sum*, but the *repetition* of one and the same *relation* which alone is desired and which is thus already *completely* given in the *first term*. The need for the *form* of a *series*, its summation and all that is connected with it, must then be wholly separated from the said *interest of the relation*.

The explanations of the methods of infinitesimal magnitudes given by Carnot, contain a most lucid exposition of what is essential in the ideas referred to above. But in passing to the practical application itself, there enter more or less the usual ideas about the infinite smallness of the omitted terms *relatively* to the others. He justifies the method, not by the nature of the procedure itself, but by the fact that the *results* are correct, and by the *advantages* of a simplification and shortening of the calculus which follow the introduction of *imperfect* equations, as he calls

ascribed to the force of gravity—a distinction which has no existence or basis whatever in the nature of the thing itself, but is only the falsely physicalized expression of what issues from the assumed analytical treatment.

I*

them, i.e. those in which such an arithmetically incorrect omission has occurred.

Lagrange, as is well known, reverted to Newton's original method, that of series, in order to be relieved of the difficulties inherent in the idea of the infinitely small and in the method of first and final ratios and limits. The advantages of his functional calculus as regards precision, abstraction and generality, are sufficiently recognized; we need mention only what is pertinent here, that it rests on the fundamental principle that the difference, without becoming zero, can be assumed so small that each term of the series is greater than the sum of all the following terms. This method, too, starts from the categories of *increment* and *difference* of the function, the variable magnitude of which receives the *increment*, thereby bringing in the troublesome series of the original function; also in the sequel the terms to be omitted are considered only as constituting a *sum*, while the reason for omitting them is made to consist in the relativity of their *quantum*. And so here, too, on the one hand, the principle of the omission is not brought back to the point of view exemplified in some applications, where (as was remarked above) terms of the series are supposed to have a specific *qualitative* significance, and terms are neglected *not* because of their quantitative insignificance but because they are not qualitatively significant; and then, on the other hand, the omission itself has no place in the essential point of view which, as regards the so-called differential coefficient, only becomes specifically prominent with Lagrange, in the so-called *application* of the calculus, as will be more fully considered in the following remark.

The demonstrated *qualitative character as such* of the form of magnitude here under discussion in what is called the infinitesimal, is found most directly in the category of *limit of the ratio* referred to above and the carrying out of which in the calculus has been developed into a characteristic method. Lagrange criticizes this method as lacking ease in application and he claims that the expression *limit* does not present any definite idea; this second point we will take up here and examine more closely what is stated about its analytical meaning. Now the idea of limit does indeed imply the true category of the *qualitatively* determined relation of variable magnitudes above-mentioned; for the forms of it which occur, dx and dy, are supposed to be taken simply and solely as moments of $\frac{dy}{dx}$, and $\frac{dy}{dx}$ itself must be regarded as a single indivisible symbol. That the mechanism of the calculus, especially in its application, thus loses the advantage it derived from the separation of the sides of the differential coefficient, this we will pass over here. Now the said limit is to be *limit* of a given function; it is to assign to this function a certain value determined by its mode of derivation. But with the mere category of limit we should not have advanced beyond the scope of this Remark, which is to demonstrate that the infinitely small which presents itself in the differential calculus as dx and dy, does not have merely the negative, empty meaning of a non-finite, non-given magnitude, as when one speaks of 'an infinite multitude', 'to infinity', and the like, but on the contrary has the specific meaning of the qualitative nature of what is quantitative, of a moment of a ratio as such. This category, however, merely as such, still has no relation to that which is a given function and does not itself enter into the treatment of such a function or into the use to be made of that determination; thus the idea of limit, too, confined to this its demonstrated character, would lead nowhere. But the very expression 'limit' implies that it is a limit of *something*, i.e. that it expresses a certain value which lies in the function of a variable magnitude; and we must examine the nature of this concrete rôle. It is supposed to be the limit of the *ratio* between the two *increments* by which the two variable magnitudes connected in an equation (one of which is regarded as a function of the other), are supposed to have been *increased;* the increase is taken here as quite undetermined and so far no use is made of the infinitely small. But the way in which this limit is found involves the same inconsistencies as are contained in the other methods. This way is as follows: if $y = fx$, then when y becomes $y + k$, fx is to change into $fx + ph + qh^2 + rh^3$ and so on; thus $k = ph + qh^2$, etc., and $\frac{k}{h} = p + qh + rh^2$, etc. Now if k and h vanish, the right-hand side of the equation also vanishes with the exception of p; now p is supposed to be the limit of the ratio of the two increments. It is clear that while h, as a quantum, is equated with o, $\frac{k}{h}$ nevertheless is not at the same time equal to $\frac{o}{o}$ but is supposed still to remain a ratio. Now the idea of *limit* is supposed to have the advantage of avoiding the inconsistency here involved; p is, at the same time, supposed to be not the actual ratio, which would be $\frac{o}{o}$, but only that specific value to which the ratio can *infinitely approximate*, i.e. can approach so near that the difference can be smaller than any given difference. The more precise meaning of *approximation* with respect to the terms which are supposed really to approach each other will be considered later. But that a quantitative difference, the definition of which is that it not only *can*, but *shall* be smaller than any given difference, is no longer a quantitative difference, this is self-evident, as self-evident as anything can be in mathematics; but we still have not got away from $\frac{dy}{dx} = o$. If on the other hand $\frac{dy}{dx} = p$, i.e. is assumed to be a definite quantitative ratio as in fact it is, then conversely there is a difficulty about the presupposition which equates h with o, a presupposition which is indispensable for obtaining the equation $\frac{k}{h} = p$. But if it be granted that $\frac{k}{h} = o$, (and when $h = o$, k is in fact automatically $= o$, for k, the increment of y, depends entirely on the existence of the increment h), then the question would arise, what p—which is a quite definite quantitative value—is supposed to be. To this there is at once an obvious answer, the simple, meagre answer that it is a coefficient derived in such and such a way—the first function, derived in a certain specific manner, of an original function. If we content ourselves with this—and Lagrange did, in fact, do so in practice—then the general part of the science of the differential calculus, and straightway this one particular form of it called the *theory of limits* would be rid of the increments and of their infinite or arbitrary smallness—spared too, the difficulty of getting rid again of all the terms of a series other than the first, or rather only the coefficient of the first, which inevitably follow on the introduction of these increments; in addition it would also be purged of those formal categories connected with them, especially of the infinite, of infinite approximation and, too, the categories, here equally empty, of continuous magnitude[1] which, moreover,

---

[1] The category of continuous or fluent magnitude enters with the consideration of the external and empirical variation of magnitudes—which are brought
by an equation into the relation in which one is a function of the other; but

like *nisus*, becoming, occasion of a variation, are deemed necessary. But it would then be required to show what other *meaning* and *value p* has—apart from the meagre definition, quite adequate for the theory, that it is simply a function derived from the expansion of a binomial—i.e. what *relationships* it embodies and what further *use* can be made of them mathematically; this will be the subject of Remark 2. But first we shall proceed to discuss the confusion which the conception of *approximation* currently used in expositions of the calculus, has occasioned in the understanding of the true, qualitative determinateness of the relation which was the primary interest concerned.

It has been shown that the so-called infinitesimals express the vanishing of the sides of the ratio as quanta, and that what remains is their quantitative relation solely as qualitatively determined; far from this resulting in the loss of the qualitative relation, the fact is that it is just this relation which results from the conversion of finite into infinite magnitudes. As we have seen, it is in this that the entire nature of the matter consists. Thus in the *final ratio*, for example, the quanta of abscissa and ordinate vanish; but the sides of this ratio essentially remain, the one an element of the ordinate, the other an element of the abscissa. This vanishing being represented as an infinite approximation, the previously distinguished ordinate is made to pass over into the other ordinate, and the previously distinguished abscissa into the other abscissa; but essentially this is not so, the ordinate does not pass over into the abscissa, neither does the abscissa pass into the ordinate. To continue with this example of variable magnitudes, the element

since the scientific object of the differential calculus is a *certain relation* (usually expressed by the differential co-efficient), the specific nature of which may equally well be called a *law*, the mere continuity is a heterogeneous aspect of this specific nature, and besides is in any case an abstract and here empty category seeing that nothing whatever is said about the law of continuity. Into what formal definitions one may be led in these matters can be seen from the penetrating exposition by my respected colleague, Prof. Dirksen (Dirksen, Enno Heeren, 1792–1850, Professor of Mathematics at Berlin: *Analytische Darstellung der Variationsrechnung*, 1823) of the fundamental determinations used in the deduction of the differential calculus, which forms an appendix to the criticism of some recent works on this science (*Jahrb. f. wissensch. Kritik*, 1827, No. 153 *sqq.*). The following definition is actually quoted (*op. cit.*, p. 1251): 'A continuous magnitude, a continuum, is any magnitude thought of as in a state of becoming such that this becoming takes place not by leaps but by an uninterrupted progress.' This is surely tautologically the same as what was to be defined.

of the ordinate is not to be taken as the *difference of one ordinate from another ordinate*, but rather as the difference or *qualitative* determination of magnitude relatively to the *element of the abscissa*; the principle of the one variable magnitude relatively to that of the other is in reciprocal relation with it. The difference, as no longer a difference of finite magnitudes, has ceased to be manifold within itself; it has collapsed into a simple intensity, into the determinateness of one qualitative moment of a ratio relatively to the other.

This is the nature of the matter but it is obscured by the fact that what has just been called an element, for example, of the ordinate, is grasped as a difference or increment in such a way that it is only the difference between the quantum of one ordinate and the quantum of another ordinate. And so the limit here does not have the meaning of ratio; it counts only as the final value to which another magnitude of a similar kind continually approximates in such a manner that it can differ from it by as little as we please, and that the final *ratio* is a ratio of *equality*. The infinite difference is thus the fluctuation of a difference of one quantum from another quantum, and the qualitative nature according to which dx is essentially *not* a determination of the ratio relatively to x, but to dy, comes to be overlooked. Dx^2 is permitted to vanish relatively to dx, but even more does dx vanish relatively to x; but this means in truth: it has a *relation only to dy*. In such expositions, geometricians are mainly concerned to make intelligible the *approximation* of a magnitude to its limit and to keep to this aspect of the difference of quantum from quantum, how it is no difference and yet still is a difference. But all the same, approximation is a category which of itself says nothing and explains nothing; dx already has approximation behind it; it is neither near nor nearer; and 'infinitely near', itself means the negation of nearness and approximation.

Now since this implies that the increments or infinitesimals have been considered only from the side of the quantum which vanishes in them, and only as a limit, it follows that they are grasped as *unrelated* moments. From this would follow the inadmissible idea that it is allowed in the final ratio to equate, say abscissa and ordinate, or even sine, cosine, tangent, versed sine, and what not. This idea seems at first to prevail when the arc is treated as a tangent; for the *arc*, too, is certainly *incommensurable* with the *straight line*, and its element is, in the first place, of another *quality* than the element of the straight line. It seems even more absurd and inadmissible than the confusing of abscissa, ordinate, versed sine, cosine, etc., when *quadrata rotundis*, when part of an arc, even though an infinitely small part, is taken to be a part of the tangent and so treated as a straight line. However, this treatment differs essentially from the confusion we have decried; it is justified by the circumstance that in the triangle which has for its sides the element of an arc and the elements of its abscissa and ordinate, the *relation is the same* as if this element of the arc were the element of a straight line, of the tangent; the *angles* which constitute the *essential relation*, i.e. that which remains to these elements when abstraction is made from the finite magnitudes belonging to them, are the same. This can also be expressed as the transition of straight lines which are infinitely small, into curved lines, and their relation in their infinity as a relation of curves. Since, according to its definition, a straight line is the *shortest* distance between two points, its difference from the curved line is based on the determination of *amount*, on the *smaller* amount of what is differentiated in this manner, a determination, therefore, of a *quantum*. But this determination vanishes in the line when it is taken as an intensive magnitude, as an infinite moment, as an element, and with it, too, its difference from the curved line which rested merely on the difference of quantum. As infinite, therefore, the straight line and arc no longer retain any quantitative relation nor consequently, on the basis of the assumed definition, any qualitative difference from each other either; on the contrary, the former passes into the latter.

Analogous, although also distinct from, the equating of heterogeneous forms is the assumption that *infinitely small parts* of the same whole are *equal* to each other; an assumption in itself indefinite and completely indifferent, but which, applied to an object heterogeneous within itself, i.e. an object whose quantitative determination is essentially non-uniform, produces the peculiar inversion contained in that proposition of higher mechanics which states that infinitely small parts of a curve are traversed in *equal*, infinitely small times in a *uniform* motion, inasmuch as this is asserted of a motion in which in equal *finite*, i.e. existent, parts of time, *finite*, i.e. existent, *unequal* parts of the curve are traversed, of a motion therefore which exists as non-uniform and is assumed as such. This proposition is the expression in words of what is supposed to be the significance of an analytical term obtained in the above-mentioned development of the formula relating to a motion which is non-uniform but otherwise conforms to a law. Earlier mathematicians sought to express in words and propositions and to exhibit in geometrical tables the results of the newly invented infinitesimal calculus (which moreover always had to do with concrete objects), chiefly in order to use them for theorems susceptible of the ordinary method of proof. The terms of a mathematical formula into which analytical treatment resolved the *magnitude* of the object, of motion, for instance, acquired there an *objective* significance, such as velocity, force of acceleration, and so on; in accordance with this meaning they were supposed to furnish correct propositions, physical laws; their objective connections and relations, too, were supposed to be determined in accordance with the analytical connection. A particular example is that in a uniformly accelerated motion there is supposed to exist a special velocity proportional to the times, but that to this velocity there constantly accrues an increment from the force of gravity. In the modern, analytical form of mechanics such propositions are put forward simply as results of the calculus, without enquiry whether by themselves and in themselves they have a *real* significance, i.e. one to which there is a corresponding physical existence and whether such meaning can be demonstrated. The difficulty of making intelligible the connection of such forms when they are taken in the real meaning alluded to, for example the transition from said simply uniform velocity to a uniformly accelerated velocity, is held to be completely eliminated by the analytical treatment in which such connection is a simple result of the authority now established once and for all of the operations of the calculus. It is announced as a triumph of science that by means of the calculus alone, laws are found *transcending experience*, that is, propositions about existence which have no existence. But in the earlier, still naïve period of the infinitesimal calculus, the aim was to assign to those forms and propositions represented in geometrical diagrams a real meaning of their own and to make that meaning plausible, and to apply the forms and propositions bearing such meaning in the proof of the main propositions concerned.[1]

[1] See Newton's proof of his fundamental proposition of the theory of gravitation in *Princ. mathem. philosophiae naturalis*, lib. I, Sect. II, Prop. I, and

It cannot be denied that in this field much has been accepted as proof, especially with the aid of the nebulous conception of the infinitely small, for no other reason than that the result was always already known beforehand, and that the proof which was so arranged that the result did emerge, at least produced the illusion of a framework of proof, an illusion which was still preferred to mere belief or knowledge from experience. But I do not hesitate to regard this affectation as nothing more than mere jugglery and window-dressing, and I include in this description even Newton's proofs, especially those belonging to what has just been quoted, for which Newton has been extolled to the skies and exalted above Kepler, namely that *he* demonstrated mathematically what Kepler had discovered *merely empirically*.

The empty scaffolding of such proofs was erected in order to prove physical laws. But mathematics is altogether incapable of proving quantitative determinations of the physical world in so far as they are laws based on the *qualitative nature* of the moments [of the subject matter]; and for this reason, that this science is not philosophy, does *not start from the Notion*, and therefore the qualitative element, in so far as it is not taken lemmatically from experience, lies outside its sphere. The desire to uphold the honour of mathematics, that all its propositions ought to be *rigorously proved*, has often caused it to forget its limits; thus it seemed against its honour to acknowledge simply experience as the source and sole proof of empirical propositions. Consciousness has since then developed a more instructed view of the matter; so long, however, as consciousness is not clearly aware of the distinction between what is mathematically demonstrable and what can come only from another source, between what are only terms of an analytical expansion and what are physical existences, scientific method cannot be developed into a rigorous and pure attitude in this field. Without doubt, however, the same justice will be done to that framework of Newtonian proof as was done to another baseless and artificial Newtonian structure of optical experiments and conclusions derived from them. Applied mathematics is still full of a similar concoction of experiment and

cf. Schubert's *Astronomy*—1st ed., vol. III. B, Section 20, where it is admitted that the position is not *exactly* as Newton assumes, i.e. at that point which is the nerve of the proof. (Schubert, Friedrich Theodor von, 1758–1825, Director of the Observatory at St Petersburg: *Lehrbuch der theoretischen Astronomie*, 1798; *Populäre Astronomie*, 3 vols., 1804–1810.)

reflection; but just as one part after another of Newtonian optics long since began to be ignored in practice by the science—with the inconsistency however that all the rest although in contradiction was allowed to stand—so, too, it is a fact that already some of those illusory proofs have fallen into oblivion or have been replaced by others.

Remark 2: *The Purpose of the Differential Calculus Deduced from its Application*

In the previous Remark we considered on the one hand the specific nature of the notion of the infinitesimal which is used in the differential calculus, and on the other the basis of its introduction into the calculus; both are abstract determinations and therefore in themselves also easy. The so-called *application*, however, presents greater difficulties, but also the more interesting side; the elements of this *concrete* side are to be the object of this Remark. The whole method of the differential calculus is complete in the proposition that $dx^n = nx^{n-1}dx$, or $\dfrac{f(x + i) - fx}{i} = P$, that is, is equal to the *coefficient* of the first term of the binomial $x + d$, or $x + i$, developed according to the powers of dx or i. There is no need to learn anything further: the development of the next forms, of the differential of a product, of an exponential magnitude and so on, follows mechanically; in little time, in half an hour perhaps—for with the finding of the differential the converse the finding of the original function from the differential, or integration, is also given—one can be in possession of the whole theory. What takes longer is simply the effort to understand, to make intelligible, how it is that, after having so easily accomplished the *first stage* of the task, the finding of the said differential, analytically, i.e. purely arithmetically, by the expansion of the function of the variable after this has received the form of a binomial by the addition of an increment; how it is that the *second stage* can be correct, namely the omission of all the terms except the first, of the series arising from the expansion. If all that were required were only this coefficient, then with its determination all that concerns the theory would, as we have said, be settled and done with in less than half an hour and the omission of the further terms of the series (with the determination of the first function, the determination of the second, third, etc., is also accomplished) far from causing any difficulty, would not come into question since they are completely irrelevant.

We may begin by remarking that the method of the differential calculus shows on the face of it that it was not invented and constructed for its own sake. Not only was it not invented for its own sake as another mode of analytical procedure; on the contrary, the arbitrary omission of terms arising from the expansion of a function is absolutely contrary to all mathematical principles, it being arbitrary in the sense that the *whole* of this development is nevertheless assumed to belong *completely* to the matter in hand, this being regarded as the *difference* between the developed function of a variable (after this has been given the form of a binomial) and the original function. The need for such a mode of procedure and the lack of any internal justification at once suggest that the origin and foundation must lie elsewhere. It happens in other sciences too, that what is placed at the beginning of a science as its elements and from which the principles of the science are supposed to be derived is not self-evident, and that it is rather in the sequel that the *raison d'être* and proof of those elements is to be found. The course of events in the history of the differential calculus makes it plain that the matter had its origin mainly in the various so-called tangential methods, in what could be considered ingenious devices; it was only later that mathematicians reflected on the nature of the method after it had been extended to other objects, and reduced it to abstract formulae which they then also attempted to raise to the status of *principles*.

We have shown that the specific nature of the notion of the so-called infinitesimal is the *qualitative* nature of determinations of quantity which are related to each other primarily as quanta; to this was linked the empirical investigation aimed at demonstrating the presence of this specific nature in the existing descriptions and definitions of the infinitesimal in so far as this is taken as an infinitesimal difference and the like. This was done only in the interest of the abstract nature of the notion as such; the next question would be as to the nature of the transition from this to the mathematical formulation and application. To this end we must first pursue our examination of the theoretical side, the specific nature of the notion, which will not prove wholly unfruitful in itself; we must then consider the relation of the theoretical side to its application; and in both cases we must

demonstrate, so far as it is relevant here, that the general conclusions are at the same time adequate to the purpose of the
differential calculus and to the way in which the calculus brings
about its results.

First, it is to be remembered that the mathematical form of
the determinateness of the notion under discussion has already
been stated in passing. The specifically qualitative character of
quantity is first indicated in the quantitative *relation* as such; but
it was already asserted in anticipation when demonstrating the
so-called kinds of reckoning (see the relative Remark), that it is
the *relation of powers* (still to be dealt with in its proper place) in
which number, through the equating of the moments of its
Notion, unit and amount, is posited as returned into itself, thereby
receiving into itself the moment of infinity, of being-for-self, i.e.
of being self-determined. Thus, as we have already said, the
express qualitative nature of quantity is essentially connected with
the forms of powers, and since the specific interest of the differential
calculus is to operate with qualitative forms of magnitude, its
own peculiar subject matter must be the treatment of forms of
powers, and the whole range of problems, and their solutions,
show that the interest lies solely in the treatment of determinations
of powers as such.

This foundation is important and at once puts in the forefront
something definite in place of the merely formal categories of
variable, continuous or infinite magnitudes or even of functions
generally; yet it is still too general, for other operations also have
to do with determinations of powers. The raising to a power,
extraction of a root, treatment of exponential magnitudes and
logarithms, series, and equations of higher orders, the interest
and concern of all these is solely with relations which are based
on powers. Undoubtedly, these together constitute a system of the
treatment of powers; but which of the various relations in which
determinations of powers can be put is the peculiar interest and
subject matter of the differential calculus, this is to be ascertained
from the calculus itself, i.e. from its so-called applications. These
are, in fact, the core of the whole business, the actual procedure
in the mathematical solution of a certain group of problems; this
procedure was earlier than the theory or general part and was
later called application only with reference to the subsequently
created theory, the aim of which was to draw up the general

method of the procedure and, as well, to endow it with first principles, i.e. with a justification. We have shown in the preceding Remark the futility of the search for principles which would clarify the method as currently understood, principles which would really solve the contradiction revealed by the method instead of excusing it or covering it up merely by the insignificance of what is here to be omitted (but which really is required by mathematical procedure), or, by what amounts to the same thing, the possibility of infinite or arbitrary approximation and the like. If from the practical part of mathematics known as the differential calculus the general features of the method were to be abstracted in a manner different from that hitherto followed, then the said principles and the concern about them would also show themselves to be superfluous, just as they reveal themselves to be intrinsically false and permanently contradictory.

If we investigate this peculiarity by simply taking up what we find in this part of mathematics, we find as its subject matter:

(*a*) Equations in which any number of magnitudes (here we can simply confine ourselves to *two*) are combined into a qualitative whole in such a way that first, these equations have their determinateness in *empirical magnitudes* which are their fixed limits, and also in the kind of connection they have with these limits and with each other as is generally the case in an equation; but since there is only one equation for both magnitudes (similarly, relatively more equations for more magnitudes, but always fewer than the number of magnitudes), these equations belong to the class of indeterminate equations; and secondly, that one aspect of the determinateness of these magnitudes is that they are—or at least one of them is—present in the equation in a *higher power* than the first.

Before proceeding further, there are one or two things to be noticed about this. The first is that the magnitudes, as described under the first of the above two headings, have simply and solely the character of *variables* such as occur in the problems of *indeterminate* analysis. Their value is undetermined, but if one of them does receive a completely determined value, i.e. a numerical value, from outside, then the other too, is determined, so that one is a *function* of the other. Therefore, in relation to the specific quantitative determinateness here in question, the categories of variable magnitudes, functions and the like are, as we have already said, merely *formal*, because they are still too general to contain that specific element on which the entire interest of the differential calculus is focused, or to permit of that element being explicated by analysis; they are in themselves simple, unimportant, easy determinations which are only made difficult by importing into them what they do not contain in order that this may then be derived from them—namely, the specific determination of the differential calculus. Then as regards the so-called *constant*, we can note that it is in the first place an indifferent empirical magnitude determining the variables only with respect to their empirical quantum as a limit of their minimum and maximum; but the nature of the connection between the constants and the variables is itself a significant factor in the nature of the particular function which these magnitudes are. Conversely, however, the constants themselves are also functions; in so far as a straight line, for example, has the meaning of being the *parameter* of a parabola, then this meaning is that it is the function $\frac{y^2}{x}$; and in the expansion of the binomial generally, the constant which is the coefficient of the first term of the development is the sum of the roots, the coefficient of the second is the sum of the products, in pairs, and so on; here, therefore, the constants are simply functions of the roots. Where, in the integral calculus, the constant is determined from the given formula, it is to that extent treated as a function of this. Further on we shall consider these coefficients in another character than that of functions, their meaning in the concrete object being the focus of the whole interest.

Now the difference between variables as considered in the differential calculus, and in their character as factors in indeterminate problems, must be seen to consist in what has been said, namely, that at least one of those variables (or even all of them), is found in a power higher than the first; and here again it is a matter of indifference whether they are all of the same higher power or are of unequal powers; their specific indeterminateness which they have here consists solely in this, that in *such a relation of powers they are functions of one another*. The alteration of variables is in this way *qualitatively* determined, and hence *continuous*, and this continuity, which again is itself only the purely formal category of an *identity*, of a determinateness which is preserved and remains self-same in the alteration, has here its determinate meaning, solely, that is, in the power-relation, which does not have a quantum for its exponent and which forms the *non-quantitative*, permanent determinateness of the ratio of the variables. For this reason it should be noted, in criticism of another formalism, that the first power is only a power in relation to higher powers; *on its own*, x is merely any indeterminate quantum. Thus there is no point in differentiating for their own sakes the equations $y = ax + b$ (of the straight line), or $s = ct$ (of the plain uniform velocity); if from $y = ax$, or even $ax + b$,

we obtain $a = \dfrac{dy}{dx}$, or from $s = ct$, $\dfrac{ds}{dt} = c$, then $a = \dfrac{y}{x}$ is equally

the determination of the tangent, or $\dfrac{s}{t}$ that of velocity simply as

such. The latter is given the form of $\dfrac{dy}{dx}$ in the context of what

is said to be the development of the uniformly accelerated motion; but, as already remarked, the presence in the system of such a motion, of a moment of simple, merely uniform velocity, i.e. a velocity which is not determined by the higher power of one of the moments of the motion is itself an empty assumption based solely on the routine of the method. Since the method starts from the conception of the increment which the variable is supposed to acquire, then of course a variable which is only a function of the first power can also receive an increment; when now in order to find the differential we have to subtract the difference of the second equation thus produced from the given equation, the meaninglessness of the operation becomes apparent, for, as we have remarked, the equation for the so-called increments, both before and after the operation, is the same as for the variables themselves.

(b) What has been said determines the nature of the equation which is to be treated; we have now to indicate what is the interest on which the treatment of the equation is focused. This consideration can yield only known results, in a form found especially in Lagrange's version; but I have made the exposition completely elementary in order to eliminate the heterogeneous determinations associated with it. The basis of treatment of an equation of this kind shows itself to be this, that the power is taken as being *within itself* a relation or a *system of relations*. We said above that power is number which has reached the stage where it *determines its own alteration*, where its moments of unit and amount are identical—as previously shown, *completely* identical first in the square, *formally* (which makes no difference here) in higher powers. Now power is *number* (magnitude as the more general term may be preferred, but it is *in itself* always number), and hence a *plurality*, and also is represented as a *sum*; it can therefore be directly analysed into an arbitrary amount of numbers which have no further determination relatively to one another or to their sum, other than that together they are equal to the sum. But the power can also be split into a *sum* of differences which are determined by the *form of the power*. If the power is taken as a sum, then its radical number, the root, is also taken as a sum, and arbitrarily after manifold divisions, which manifoldness, however, is the indifferent, empirically quantitative element. The sum which the root is supposed to be, when reduced to its simple determinateness, i.e. to its genuine universality, is the *binomial*; all further increase in the number of terms is a mere *repetition* of the same determination and therefore meaningless.[1] The sole point of importance here is the *qualitative determinateness* of the terms resulting from the *raising to a power* of the root taken as a sum, and this determinateness lies solely in the alteration which the potentiation is. These terms, then, are wholly *functions of potentiation and of the power*. Now this representation of number as a *sum* of a *plurality* of terms which are functions of potentiation, and the finding of the *form* of such functions and also this *sum* from the plurality of those terms, in so far as this must depend solely on that form, this constitutes, as we know, the special theory of *series*. But in this connexion it is essential to distinguish another object of interest, namely the *relation of the fundamental magnitude* itself (whose determinateness, since it is a complex, i.e. here an equation, includes *within itself* a power) *to the functions of its potentiation*. This relation, taken in complete

---

[1] It springs solely from the formalism of that *generality* to which analysis perforce lays claim when, instead of taking $(a + b)^n$ for the expansion of powers, it gives the expression the form of $(a + b + c + d \ldots)^n$ as happens too in many other cases; such a form is to be regarded as, so to speak, a mere affectation of a show of generality; the matter itself is exhausted in the binomial. It is through the expansion of the binomial that the *law* is found, and it is the law which is the genuine universality, not the external, mere *repetition* of the law which is all that is effected by this $a + b + c + d \ldots$

abstraction from the previously mentioned interest of the *sum*, will show itself to be the sole standpoint yielded by the practical aspect of the science.

But first, another determination must be added to what has been said, or rather, one which is implied in it must be removed. It was said that the variable into the determination of which power enters is regarded as within itself a sum, in fact a system of terms in so far as these are functions of the potentiation, and that thus the root, too, is regarded as a sum and in the simply determined form of a binomial: $x^n = (y + z)^n = (y + ny^{n-1} z + \ldots)$. This exposition started from the *sum* as such for the expansion of the power, i.e. for obtaining the functions of its potentiation; but what is concerned here is not a *sum* as such, or the *series* arising from it; what is to be taken up from the sum is only the *relation*. The *relation* as such of the magnitudes is, on the one hand, all that remains after abstraction is made from the *plus* of a sum as such, and on the other hand, all that is needed for finding the functions produced by the expansion of the power. But such relation is already determined by the fact that here the object is an equation, $y^m = ax^n$, and so already a *complex* of several (variable) magnitudes which contains a power determination of them. In this complex, each of these variables is posited simply as in *relation* to the others with the meaning, one could say, of a *plus* implicit in it—as a function of the other variables; their character, that of being functions of one another, gives them this determination of a *plus* which, however, for that same reason, is wholly *indeterminate*—not an increase or an increment, or anything of that nature. Yet even this abstract point of view we could leave out of account; we can quite simply stop at the point where the variables in the equation having received the form of functions of one another, such functions containing a relation of powers, the functions of *potentiation* are then also compared with one another—these second functions being determined simply and solely by the potentiation itself. To treat an equation of the powers of its variables as a relation of the functions developed by potentiation can, in the first place, be said to be just a *matter of choice* or a *possibility*; the *utility* of such a transformation has to be indicated by some further *purpose* or use; and the sole reason for the transformation was its utility. When we started above from the representation of these functions of potentiation of a variable which is taken as a *sum complex within itself*, this served only partly to indicate the nature of such functions, but partly also to show the way in which they are found.

What we have here then is the ordinary analytical development which for the purpose of the differential calculus is operated in this way, that an increment dx or i is given to the variable and then the power of the binomial is developed by the terms of the series belonging to it. But the so-called increment is supposed to be not a quantum but only a *form*, the whole value of which is that it *assists* the development; it is admitted—most categorically by Euler and Lagrange and in the previously mentioned conception of limit—that what is wanted is only the resulting power determinations of the variables, the so-called *coefficients*, namely, of the increment and its powers, according to which the series is ordered and to which the different coefficients belong. On this we could perhaps remark that since an increment (which has no quantum) is assumed only for the sake of the development, it would be most appropriate to take 1 (the one) for that purpose, for in the development this always occurs only as a factor; the factor one, therefore, fulfils the purpose, namely, that the increment is not to involve any quantitative determinateness or alteration; on the other hand, dx, which is burdened with the false idea of a quantitative difference, and other symbols like i with the mere show—pointless here—of generality, always have the appearance and pretension of a quantum and its powers; which pretension then involves the trouble that they must nevertheless be removed and left out. In order to retain the form of a series expanded on the basis of powers, the designations of the exponents as indices could equally well be attached to the one. But in any case, abstraction must be made from the series and from the determination of the coefficients according to their place in the series; the relation between all of them is the same; the second function is derived from the first in exactly the same manner as this is from the original function, and for the function counted as second, the first derived function is itself original. But the essential point of interest is not the series but simply and solely the determination of the power resulting from the expansion in its relation to the variable which for the *power determination is immediate*. It should not therefore be defined as the *coefficient* of the *first* term of the development, for it is *first* only in relation to the other terms following it in the series, and a power such as that of an increment, like the series itself, is here out of place; instead, the simple expression: derived function of a power, or as was said above: function of potentiation of a magnitude, would be preferable—the knowledge of the way in which the derivation is taken to be a development included within a power being presupposed.

Now if the strictly mathematical beginning in this part of analysis is nothing more than the finding of the function determined by the expansion of the power, the further question is what is to be done with the relation so obtained, where has it an application and use, or indeed, for what *purpose* are such functions sought. It is the finding of relations in *a concrete subject matter* which can be reduced to such a function that has given the differential calculus its great interest.

But as regards the applicableness of the relation, we need not wait for conclusions to be drawn from particular applications themselves, the answer follows directly and automatically from the nature of the matter which we have shown to consist in the form possessed by the moments of powers: namely, the expansion of the powers, which yields the functions of their potentiation, contains (ignoring any more precise determination) in the first place, simply the *reduction* of the magnitude to the next lower power. This operation is therefore *applicable* in the case of those objects in which there is also present such a difference of power determinations. Now if we reflect on the specific nature of space, we find that it contains the three dimensions which, in order to distinguish them from the abstract differences of height, length and breadth, we can call *concrete*—namely, line, surface and total space; and when they are taken in their simplest forms and with reference to self-determination and consequently to analytical dimensions, we have the straight line, plane surface and surface taken as a square, and the cube. The straight line has an empirical quantum, but with the plane there enters the qualitative element, the determination of power; further modifications, e.g. the fact that this also happens in the case of plane curves, we need not consider, for we are concerned primarily with the distinction in general. With this there arises, too, the *need to pass from a higher power to a lower, and vice versa*, when, for example, linear determinations are to be derived from given equations of the plane, or vice versa. Further, the *motion* in which we have to consider the quantitative relation of the space traversed to the time elapsed, manifests itself in the different determinations of a motion which is simply uniform, or uniformly accelerated, or alternately uniformly accelerated and uniformly retarded, and thus a self-returning motion; since these different kinds of motion are expressed in accordance with the quantitative relation of their moments, of space and time, their equations contain different determinations of powers, and when it is necessary to determine one kind of motion, or a spatial magnitude to which one kind of motion is linked, from another kind of motion, the operation also involves the passage from one power-function to another, either higher or lower. These two examples may suffice for the purpose for which they are cited.

The appearance of arbitrariness presented by the differential calculus in its applications would be clarified simply by an awareness of the nature of the spheres in which its application is permissible and of the peculiar need for and condition of this application. But now the further point of interest within these spheres themselves is to know between what *parts* of the subject matter of the mathematical problem such a relation occurs as is posited peculiarly by the differential calculus. First, it must be observed that there are two kinds of relation. The operation of depotentiating an *equation* considered according to the derivative functions of its variables, yields a result which, *in itself*, is no longer truly an equation but a *relation*; this relation is the subject matter of the *differential calculus proper*. This also gives us, secondly, the relation of the higher power form (the original equation) itself to the lower (the derivative). This second relation we must ignore for the time being; it will prove to be the special subject matter of the *integral calculus*.

Let us start by considering the first relation; for the determination of its moment (to be taken from the application, in which lies the interest of the operation) we shall take the simplest example from curves determined by an equation of the second degree. As we know, the relation of the co-ordinates is given *directly* by the equation in a power form. From the fundamental determination follow the determinations of the other straight lines connected with the co-ordinates, tangent, subtangent, normal, and so on.

But the equations between these lines and the co-ordinate are *linear* equations; the wholes with respect to which these lines are determined as parts, are right-angled triangles formed by *straight* lines. The transition from the original equation which contains the power form, to said linear equations, involves now the above-mentioned transition from the original function (which is an *equation*), to the derived function (which is a *relation*, a relation, that is, between certain lines contained in the curve). The problem consists in finding the connection between the *relation* of these lines and the *equation* of the curve.

It is not without interest, as regards the historical element, to remark this much, that the first discoverers could only record their findings in a wholly empirical manner without being able to account for the operation, which remained a completely external affair. It will be sufficient here to refer to Barrow, to him who was Newton's teacher. In his *lect. Opt. et Geom.*, in which he treats problems of higher geometry according to the method of indivisibles, a method which, to begin with, is distinct from the characteristic feature of the differential calculus, he also puts on record[1] his procedure for determining tangents—'because his friends urged him to do so'. To form a proper idea of how this procedure is formulated simply as an *external rule*, in the same style as the 'rule of three', or better still the so-called 'test by casting out nines', one must read Barrow's own exposition. He draws the tiny lines afterwards known as the increments in the characteristic triangle of a curve and then gives the instruction, in the form of a mere *rule, to reject as superfluous* the terms which, as a result of the expansion of the equations, appear as powers of the said increments or as products (*etenim isti termini nihilum valebunt*); similarly, the terms which contain only magnitudes to be found in the original equation are to be rejected (the subsequent subtraction of the original equation from that formed with the increments); and finally, for the increments of the ordinate and abscissa, the ordinate itself and the subtangent respectively are to be substituted. The procedure, if one may say so, can hardly be set forth in a more schoolmasterlike manner; the latter substitution is the assumption of the proportionality of the increments of the ordinate and the abscissa with the ordinate and the subtangent, an assumption on which is based the determination of

[1] *Lect. X.*

the tangent in the ordinary differential method; in Barrow's rule this assumption appears in all its naïve nakedness. A simple way of determining the subtangent was found; the artifices of Roberval and Fermat have a similar character. The method for finding maximal and minimal values from which Fermat started rests on the same basis and the same procedure. It was a mathematical craze of those times to find so-called *methods*, i.e. rules of that kind and to make a secret of them—which was not only easy, but in one respect even necessary, for the same reason that it was easy—namely, because the inventors had found only an empirical, external rule, not a method, i.e. nothing derived from established principles. Leibniz accepted such so-called methods from his contemporaries and so did Newton who got them directly from his teacher; by generalizing their form and applicableness they opened up new paths for the sciences, but at the same time they also felt the need to wrest free the procedure from the shape of merely external rules and to try to procure for it the necessary justification.

If we analyse the method more closely, we find the genuine procedure to be as follows. Firstly the power forms (of the variables of course) contained in the equation are reduced to their first functions. But the *value* of the terms of the equation is thereby *altered*; there is now no longer an equation, but instead only a *relation* between the first function of the one variable and the first function of the other. Instead of $px = y^2$ we have $p : 2y$, or instead of $2ax - x^2 = y^2$, we have $a - x : y$, the relation which later came to be designated $\dfrac{dy}{dx}$. Now the equation represents a curve; but this relation, which is completely dependent on it and derived from it (above, according to a mere *rule*), is, on the contrary, a linear relation with which certain lines are in proportion: $p : 2y$ or $a - x : y$ are themselves relations of straight line of the curve, of the co-ordinates and parameters. *But with all this, nothing is as yet known.* The interest centres on finding that the *derived relation* applies to *other* lines connected with the curve, on finding the equality of two relations. And so there is, secondly, the question, which are the straight lines determined by the nature of the curve, standing in such a relation? But this is just what *was already known*: namely, that the relation so obtained is the relation of the ordinate to the subtangent. This the ancients

had found in an ingenious geometrical manner; what the moderns
have discovered is the empirical procedure of so preparing the
equation of the curve that it yields that first relation of which it
was already known that it is equal to a relation containing the
line (here the subtangent) which is to be determined. Now on
the one hand, this preparation of the equation—the differentiation
—has been methodically conceived and executed; but on the
other hand the imaginary increments of the co-ordinates and an
imaginary characteristic triangle formed by them and by an
equally imaginary increment of the tangent, have been invented
in order that the proportionality of the ratio found by lowering
the degree of the equation to the ratio formed by the ordinate
and subtangent, may be represented, not as something only
empirically accepted as an already familiar fact, but as something
demonstrated. However, in the said form of rules, the already
familiar fact reveals itself absolutely and unmistakably as the
sole occasion and respective justification of the assumption of the
characteristic triangle and the said proportionality.

Now Lagrange rejected this pretence and took the genuinely
scientific course. We have to thank his method for bringing into
prominence the real point of interest for it consists in separating
the two transitions necessary for the solution of the problem and
treating and proving each of them separately. One part of this
solution (for the more detailed statement of the process we shall
confine ourselves to the example of the elementary problem of
finding the subtangent), the theoretical or general part, namely,
the finding of the *first function* from the given equation of the
curve, is dealt with separately; the result is a *linear relation*, a
relation therefore of straight lines occurring in the system determined by the curve. The other part of the solution now is the
finding of those lines in the curve which stand in this relation.
Now this is effected in a direct manner[1] i.e., without the characteristic triangle, which means that there is no assumption of
infinitely small arcs, ordinates and abscissae, the last two being given
the significance of dy and dx, that is, of being sides of that relation,
and at the same time directly equating the infinitely small ordinate
and abscissa with the ordinate and subtangent themselves. A line
(and a point, too), is determined only in so far as it forms the side
of a triangle and the determination of a point, too, falls only in

[1] *Théorie des Fonct. Anal.*, II. P. II Chap.

such triangle. This, it may be mentioned in passing, is the fundamental proposition of analytical geometry from which are derived the co-ordinates of that science, just as (it is the same standpoint) in mechanics it gives rise to the parallelogram of forces, for which very reason the many efforts to find a proof of this latter are quite unnecessary. The subtangent, now, is made to be the side of a triangle whose other sides are the ordinate and the tangent connected to it. The equation of the latter, as a straight line, is $p = aq$ (the determination does not require the additional term, $+ b$ which is added only on account of the fondness for generality);—the determination of the *ratio* $\frac{p}{q}$ falls within a, the coefficient of q which is the respective first function (derivative) of the equation, but may simply be considered only as $a = \frac{p}{q}$ being, as we have said, the essential determination of the straight line which is applied as tangent to the curve. But the first function (derivative) of the equation of the curve is equally the determination of a straight line; seeing then that the co-ordinate p of the first straight line and y, the co-ordinate of the curve, are assumed to be identical (so that the point at which the curve is touched by the first straight line assumed as tangent is also the starting point of the straight line determined by the first function of the curve), the problem is to show that this second straight line coincides with the first, i.e. is a tangent; or, algebraically expressed, that since $y = fx$ and $p = Fq$, and it is assumed that $y = p$ and hence that $fx = Fq$, therefore $f'x = F'q$. Now in order to show that the straight line applied as a tangent and the straight line determined by the first function of the equation coincide, and that therefore the latter is a tangent, Descartes has recourse to the *increment i* of the abscissa and to the increment of the ordinate determined by the expansion of the function. Thus here, too, the objectionable increment also makes its appearance; but its introduction for the purpose indicated and its rôle in the expansion of the function must be carefully distinguished from the previously mentioned employment of the increment in finding the differential equation and in the characteristic triangle. Its employment here is justified and necessary because it falls within the scope of geometry, the geometrical determination of a tangent as such implying that between it and the curve with which it has a point in common, no other straight line can be drawn which also passes through the said point. For, as thus determined, the quality of tangent or not-tangent is reduced to a *quantitative difference*, that line being the tangent of which simply *greater smallness* is predicated with respect to the determination in point. This seemingly only relative smallness contains no empirical element whatever, i.e. nothing dependent on a quantum as such; in virtue of the nature of the formula it is explicitly qualitative if the difference of the moments on which the magnitude to be compared depends is a difference of powers. Since this difference becomes that of i and i^2 and i (which after all is meant to signify a number) is then to be conceived as a fraction, i^2 is therefore *in itself* and *explicitly* smaller than i, so that the very conception of an *arbitrary* magnitude in connection with i is here superfluous and in fact out of place. For the same reason the demonstration of the greater smallness has nothing to do with an infinitesimal, which thus need not be brought in here at all.

I must also mention the tangential method of Descartes, if only for its beauty and its fame—well-deserved but nowadays mostly forgotten; it has, moreover, a bearing on the nature of equations and this, again, calls for a further remark. Descartes expounds this independent method, in which the required linear determination is likewise found from the same derivative function, in his geometry which has proved to be so fruitful in other respects too[1]; in it he has taught the great basis of the nature of equations and their geometrical construction, and also of the application of analysis, thereby greatly widened in its scope, to geometry. With him the problem took the form of drawing straight lines perpendicularly to given points on a curve as a method for determining the subtangent, etc. One can understand the satisfaction he felt at his discovery, which concerned an object of general scientific interest at that time and which is so purely geometrical and therefore was greatly superior to the mere rules of his rivals, referred to above. His words are as follows: '*J'ose dire que c'est ceci le problème le plus utile et le plus général, non seulement que je sache, mais même que j'aie jamais désiré de savoir en géometrie.*' He bases his solution on the analytic equation of the right-angled triangle formed by the ordinate of the point on the curve to which the required straight line in the problem

[1] Liv. II (p ·357 *sqq. Œuvres Compl.*, ed. Cousin, Tom. V).

K

is to be drawn perpendicularly, by this same straight line (the normal), and thirdly, by that part of the axis which is cut off by the ordinate and the normal (the subnormal). Now from the known equation of a curve, the value of either the ordinate or the abscissa is substituted in the said triangle, the result being an equation of the second degree (and Descartes shows how even curves whose equations contain higher powers reduce to this); in this equation, only *one* of the variables occurs, namely, as a square and in the first degree—a quadratic equation which at first appears as a so-called impure equation. Descartes now makes the reflection that if the assumed point on the curve is imagined to be a point of intersection of the curve and of a circle, then this circle will also cut the curve in another point and we shall then get for the unequal xs thus produced, two equations with the same constants and of the same form, or else only *one* equation with unequal values of x. But the equation only becomes *one* for the one triangle in which the hypotenuse is perpendicular to the curve or is the normal, the case being conceived of in this way, that the two points of intersection of the curve and the circle are made to coincide and the circle is thus made to touch the curve. But in that case it is also true that the x or y of the quadratic equation no longer have *unequal* roots. Now since in a quadratic equation with two equal roots the coefficient of the term containing the unknown in the first power is twice the single root, we obtain an equation which yields the required determinations. This procedure must be regarded as the brilliant device of a genuinely analytical mind, in comparison with which the dogmatically assumed proportionality of the subtangent and the ordinate with the postulated infinitely small, so-called increments, of the abscissa and ordinate drops into the background.

The final equation obtained in this way, in which the coefficient of the second term of the quadratic equation is equated with the double root or unknown, is the same as that obtained by the method of the differential calculus. The differentiation of $x^2 - ax - b = 0$ yields the new equation $2x - a = 0$; or $x^3 - px - q = 0$ gives $3x^2 - p = 0$. But it suggests itself here to remark that it is by no means self-evident that such a derivative equation is also correct. We have already pointed out that an equation with two variables (which, just because they are variables, do not lose their character of being unknown quantities) yields only a *proportion*;

and for the simple reason stated, namely, that when the functions
of potentiation are substituted for the powers themselves, the
value of both terms of the equation is altered and it is not yet
known whether an equation still exists between them with their
values thus altered. All that the equation $\frac{dy}{dx} = P$ expresses is that
P is a *ratio* and no other real meaning can be ascribed to dy/dx.
But even so, we still do not know of this ratio $= P$, to what other
ratio it is equal; and it is only such equation or *proportionality*
which gives a value and meaning to it. We have already mentioned
that this meaning, which was called the application, was taken
from another source, empirically; similarly, in the case of the
equations here under discussion which have been obtained by
differentiation, it is from another source that we must know
whether they have equal roots in order that we may learn whether
the equation thus obtained is still correct. But this fact is not
expressly brought to notice in the textbooks; it is disposed of,
certainly, when an equation with one unknown, reduced to zero,
is straightway equated with y, with the result, of course, that
differentiation yields a $\frac{dy}{dx}$, i.e. only a ratio. The functional calculus,
it is true, is supposed to deal with functions of potentiation and
the differential calculus with differentials; but it by no means
follows from this alone that the magnitudes from which the
differentials or functions of potentiation are taken, are themselves
supposed to be *only* functions of *other* magnitudes. Besides, in the
theoretical part, in the instruction to derive the differentials, i.e.
the functions of potentiation, there is no indication that the
magnitudes which are to be subjected to such treatment are
themselves supposed to be functions of other magnitudes.

Further, with regard to the omission of the constant when
differentiating, we may draw attention to the fact that the omission
has here the meaning that the constant plays no part in the
determination of the roots if these are equal, the determination
being exhausted by the coefficient of the second term of the
equation: as in the example quoted from Descartes where the
constant is itself the square of the roots, which therefore can be
determined from the constant as well as from the coefficients—
seeing that, like the coefficients, the constant is simply a function
of the roots of the equation. In the usual exposition, the omission

of the so-called constants (which are connected with the other terms only by *plus* and *minus*) results from the mere mechanism of the process of differentiation, in which to find the differential of a compound expression only the variables are given an increment, and the expression thereby formed is subtracted from the original expression. The meaning of the constants and of their omission, in what respect they are themselves functions and, as such, are or are not of service, are not discussed.

In connection with the omission of constants we may make a similar observation about the *names* of differentiation and integration as we did before about the expressions finite and infinite: that is, that the character of the operation in fact belies its name. To differentiate denotes that differences are posited, whereas the result of differentiating is, in fact, to reduce the dimensions of an equation, and to omit the constant is to remove from the equation an element in its determinateness. As we have remarked, the roots of the variables are made equal, and therefore their *difference* is *cancelled*. In integration, on the other hand, the constant must be added in again and although as a result the equation is integrated, it is so in the sense that the previously cancelled *difference* of the roots is restored, that is, what was posited as equal is differentiated again. The ordinary expression helps to obscure the essential nature of the matter and to set everything in a point of view which is not only subordinate but even alien to the main interest, the point of view, namely, of the infinitely small difference, the increment and the like, and also of the mere difference as such between the given and the derived function, without any indication of their specific, i.e. qualitative, difference.

Another important sphere in which the differential calculus is employed is *mechanics*. The *meanings* of the distinct power functions yielded by the elementary equations of its subject matter, *motion*, have already been mentioned in passing; at this point, I shall proceed to deal with them directly. The equation, i.e. the mathematical expression, for simply uniform motion, $c = \dfrac{s}{t}$, or $s = ct$, in which the spaces traversed are proportional to the times elapsed in accordance with an empirical unit c (the magnitude of the velocity), offers no meaning for differentiation: the coefficient c is already completely determined and known, and no further expansion of powers is possible. We have already noticed how $s = at^2$, the equation of the motion of a falling body, is analysed; the first term of the analysis, $\frac{ds}{dt} = 2at$ is translated into language, and also into existence, in such a manner that it is supposed to be a factor in a *sum* (a conception we have long since abandoned), to be one part of the motion, which part moreover is attributed to the force of inertia, i.e. of a simply uniform motion, in such a manner that in *infinitely small* parts of time the motion is *uniform*, but in *finite* parts of time, i.e. in actually existent parts of time, it is non-uniform. Admittedly, $fs = 2at$; and the meaning of a and t themselves is known and so, too, the fact that the motion is determined as of uniform velocity; since $a = \frac{s}{t^2}$, $2at$ is equal simply to $\frac{2s}{t}$. But knowing this we are not a whit wiser; it is only the erroneous assumption that $2at$ is a part of the motion regarded as a *sum*, that gives the false appearance of a physical proposition. The factor itself, a, the empirical unit—a simple quantum—is attributed to gravity; but if the category of 'force of gravity' is to be employed then it ought rather to be said that the whole, $s = at^2$, is the effect, or, better, the law, of gravity. Similarly with the proposition derived from $\frac{ds}{dt} = 2at$, that *if* gravity ceased to act, the body, with the velocity reached at the *end* of its fall, would cover twice the distance it had traversed, in the same period of time as its fall. This also implies a metaphysics which is itself unsound: the *end* of the fall, or the *end* of a period of time in which the body has fallen, is itself still a period of time; if it were *not*, there would be assumed a state of *rest* and hence no velocity, for velocity can only be fixed in accordance with the space traversed *in a period* of time, not at its *end*. When, however, the differential calculus is applied without restriction in other departments of physics where there is no motion at all, as for example in the behaviour of light (apart from what is called its propagation in space) and in the application of quantitative determinations to colours, and the first function of a quadratic function here is also called a velocity, then this must be regarded as an even more illegitimate formalism of inventing an existence.

The motion represented by the equation $s = at^2$ we find, says Lagrange, empirically in falling bodies; the next simplest motion would be that whose equation were $s = ct^3$, but no such motion is found in Nature; we do not know what significance the co-efficient c could have. Now though this is indeed the case, there is nevertheless a motion whose equation is $s^3 = at^2$—Kepler's law of the motion of the bodies of the solar system; the significance here of the first derived function $\dfrac{2at}{3s^2}$ and the further direct treatment of this equation by differentiation, the development of the laws and determinations of that absolute motion *from this starting point*, must indeed present an interesting problem in which analysis would display a brilliance most worthy of itself.

Thus the application of the differential calculus to the elementary equations of motion does not of itself offer any *real* interest; the formal interest comes from the general mechanism of the calculus. But another significance is acquired by the analysis of motion in connection with the determination of its trajectory; if this is a curve and its equation contains higher powers, then transitions are required from rectilinear functions, as functions of potentiation, to the powers themselves; and since the former have to be obtained from the original equation of motion containing the factor of time, this factor being eliminated, the powers must at the same time be reduced to the lower functions of development from which the said linear equations can be obtained. This aspect leads to the interesting feature of the other part of the differential calculus.

The aim of the foregoing has been to make prominent and to establish the simple, specific nature of the differential calculus and to demonstrate it in some elementary examples. Its nature has been found to consist in this, that from an equation of power functions the coefficient of the term of the expansion, the so-called first function, is obtained, and the *relation* which this first function represents is demonstrated in moments of the concrete subject matter, these moments being themselves determined by the equation so obtained between the two relations. We shall also briefly consider the principle of the *integral calculus* to see what light is thrown on its specific, concrete nature by the application of the principle. The view of the integral calculus has been simplified and more correctly determined merely by the fact that it is no longer taken to be a *method of summation* in which it appeared essentially connected with the form of series; the method was so named in contrast to differentiation where the increment counts as the essential element. The problem of this calculus is, in the first instance, like that of the differential calculus, theoretical or rather formal, but it is, as everyone knows, the converse of the latter. Here, the starting point is a function which is considered as *derived*, as the coefficient of the first term arising from the expansion of an equation as yet unknown, and the problem is to find the original power function from the derivative; what would be regarded in the natural order of the expansion as the original function is here derived, and the function previously regarded as derived is here the given, or simply original, function. Now the formal part of this operation seems to have been accomplished already in the differential calculus in which the transition and the relation of the original to the derived function in general has been established. Although in doing this it is necessary in many cases to have recourse to the *form of series* simply in order to obtain the function which is to be the starting point and also to effect the transition from it to the original function, it is important to remember that this form as such has nothing directly to do with the peculiar principle of integration.

The other part of the problem of the calculus appears in connection with its formal operation, namely the *application* of the latter. But this now is itself the *problem*: namely, to find the *meaning* in the above-mentioned sense, possessed by the original function of the given function (regarded as first) of a particular subject matter; it might seem that this doctrine, too, was in principle already finally settled in the differential calculus; but a further circumstance is involved which prevents the matter from being so simple. In the differential calculus, namely, it was found that the linear relation is obtained from the first function of the equation of a curve, so that it is also known that the integration of this relation gives the equation of the curve in the relation of abscissa and ordinate; or, if the equation for the area enclosed by the curve were given, then we should be supposed to know already from the differential calculus that the meaning of the first function of such equation would be that it represented the ordinate as a function of the abscissa, and therefore the equation of the curve.

The problem now is to determine which of the moments determining the subject matter is *given* in the equation itself; for the analytical treatment can only start from what is given and then pass on to the other moments of the subject matter. What is given is, for example, not the equation of an area enclosed by the curve, nor, say, of the figure resulting from its rotation; nor again of an arc of the curve, but only the relation of the abscissa and ordinate in the equation of the curve itself. Consequently, the transitions from those determinations to this equation itself cannot yet be dealt with in the differential calculus; the finding of these relations is reserved for the integral calculus.

But further, it has been shown that the differentiation of an equation of several variables yields the derived function or differential coefficient, not as an equation but only in the form of a ratio; the problem is then to find in the moments of the given subject matter a second *ratio* that is equal to this first *ratio* which is the *derived* function. By contrast, the object of the integral calculus is the relation itself of the *original* to the *derived* function, which latter is here supposed to be given; so that the problem concerns the *meaning* to be assigned to the sought-for original function in the subject matter of the given first derived function; or rather, since this *meaning*, for example, the area enclosed by a curve or the rectification of a curve represented as a straight line, already finds expression in the statement of the problem, to show that an original function has that meaning, and which is the *moment* of the subject matter which must be assumed for this purpose as the initial function of the derived function.

Now the usual method makes the matter easy for itself by using the idea of the infinitesimal difference; for the quadrature of curves, an infinitely small rectangle, a product of the ordinate into the element, i.e. the infinitesimal bit of the abscissa, is taken for the trapezium one of whose sides is the infinitely small arc opposite to the infinitesimal bit of the abscissa; the product is now integrated in the sense that the integral is the sum of the infinitely many trapezia or the area to be determined—namely, the *finite* magnitude of this element of the area. Similarly, from an infinitely small element of the arc and the corresponding ordinate and abscissa, the ordinary method forms a right-angled triangle in which the square of the arc element is supposed to be equal to the sum of the squares of the two other infinitely small elements, the integration of this giving the length of the arc itself as a finite quantity.

This procedure rests on the general discovery on which this field of analysis is based, in this instance, namely, that the quadrated curve, or the rectified arc, stands to a certain function given by the equation of the curve, in the relation of the so-called original function to its derivative. The aim of the integral calculus is this: when a certain part of a mathematical object (e.g. of a curve) is assumed to be the derived function, which other part of the object is expressed by the corresponding original function? It is known that when the function of the *ordinate* given by the equation of the curve is taken as the *derived* function, the corresponding original function gives the quantitative expression for the *area* of the curve cut off by this ordinate; and, when a *certain tangential* determination is identified with the derived function, the corresponding original function expresses the length of the *arc* belonging to this tangential determination, and so on. But the method which employs the infinitesimal, and operates with it mechanically, simply makes use of the discovery that these relations—the one of an original function to its derivative and the other of the magnitudes of two parts or elements of the mathematical object—form a proportion, and spares itself the trouble of demonstrating the truth of what it simply presupposes as a fact. The singular merit here of mathematical acumen is to have found out from results already known elsewhere, that certain specific aspects of a mathematical object stand in the relationship to each other of the original to the derived function.

Of these two functions it is the derived function or, as it has been defined, the function of potentiation, which here in the integral calculus is *given* relatively to the original, which has first to be found by integration. But the derived function is not directly given, nor is it at once evident which part or element of the mathematical object is to be correlated with the derived function in order that by reducing this to the original function there may be found that other part or element, whose magnitude is required to be determined. The usual method, as we have said, begins by representing certain parts of the object as infinitely small in the form of derived functions determinable from the originally given equation of the object simply by differentiation (like the infinitely small abscissae and ordinates in connection with the rectification of a curve); the parts selected are those which can be brought into a certain relation (one established in

K*

elementary mathematics) with the subject matter of the problem
(in the given example, with the arc) this, too, being represented as
infinitely small, and from this relation the magnitude required
to be known can be found from the known magnitude of the
parts originally taken. Thus, in connection with the rectification
of curves, the three infinitely small elements mentioned are
connected in the equation of the right-angled triangle, while for
the quadrature of curves, seeing that area is taken arithmetically
to be simply the product of lines, the ordinate and the infinitely
small abscissa are connected in the form of a product. The
transition from such so-called elements of the area, the arc, etc.,
to the magnitude of the total area or the whole arc itself, passes
merely for the ascent from the infinite expression to the finite
expression, or to the *sum* of the infinitely many elements of which
the required magnitude is supposed to consist.

It is therefore merely superficial to say that the integral calculus
is simply the converse, although in general the more difficult,
problem of the differential calculus; the *real* interest of the integral
calculus concerns almost exclusively the relation between the
original and the derived function in the concrete subject matter.

Even in this part of the calculus, Lagrange did not smooth
over the difficulties of its problems simply by making those direct
assumptions. It will help to elucidate the nature of the matter in
hand if here, too, we indicate the details of his method in one or
two examples. The declared object of his method is, precisely,
to provide an independent *proof* of the fact that between particular
elements of a mathematical whole, for example, of a curve, there
exists a relation of the original to the derived function. Now this
proof cannot be effected in a direct manner because of the nature
of the relation itself in this domain; in the mathematical object
this relation connects terms which are *qualitatively* distinct,
namely, curves with straight lines, linear dimensions and their
functions with plane or surface dimensions and their functions,
so that the required determination can only be taken as the mean
between a *greater* and a *less*. Consequently, there spontaneously
enters again the form of an increment with a *plus* and *minus* and
the energetic '*développons*' is here in place; but we have already
pointed out that here the increments have only an arithmetical,
finite meaning. From the development of the condition that the
required magnitude is greater than the one easily determinable

limit and smaller than the other, it is then deduced that, e.g. the function of the ordinate is the derived, first function of the function of the area.

Lagrange's exposition of the rectification of curves in which he starts from the principle of Archimedes is interesting because it provides an insight into the *translation* of the Archimedean method into the principle of modern analysis, thus enabling us to see into the inner, true meaning of the procedure which in the other method is carried out mechanically. The mode of procedure is necessarily analogous to the one just indicated. The principle of Archimedes, that the arc of a curve is greater than its chord and smaller than the sum of the two tangents drawn through the end points of the arc and contained between these points and the point of intersection of the tangents, gives no direct equation, but simply *postulates* an endless alternation between terms determined as too great or too small, the successive terms always being still too great or too small but within ever narrower limits of inaccuracy; its translation into the modern analytical form, however, takes the form of finding an expression which is *per se* a simple fundamental equation. Now whereas the formalism of the infinitesimal directly presents us with the equation $dz^2 = dx^2 + dy^2$, Lagrange's exposition, starting from the basis indicated, demonstrates that the length of the arc is the original function to a derived function whose characteristic term is itself a function coming from the relation of a derived function to the original function of the ordinate.

Because in Archimedes' method, as well as later in Kepler's treatment of stereometric objects, the idea of the infinitesimal occurs, this has often been cited as an authority for the employment of this idea in the differential calculus, although what is peculiar and distinctive in it has not been brought specifically to notice. The infinitesimal signifies, strictly, the negation of quantum as quantum, that is, of a so-called *finite* expression, of the completed determinateness possessed by quantum as such. Similarly, in the subsequent celebrated methods of Valerius[1] and Cavalieri, among others, which are based on the treatment of the *relations* of geometrical objects, the fundamental principle is that the *quantum* as such of the objects concerned, which are primarily considered

---

[1] Valerius, Lucas, died 1618 at Rome, called by Galileo the Archimedes of his time: *De Quadratura Parabolae Per Simplex Falsum*.

only in their constituent relations, is for this purpose to be left out of account, the objects thus being taken as *non-quantitative*. However, in these methods the affirmative aspect as such which is veiled by the merely negative determination fails to be recognized or brought to notice—that aspect namely which above presented itself abstractly, as the *qualitative* determinateness of quantity, and more precisely, as lying in the relation of powers; and also, since this relation itself embraces a number of more precisely determined relations such as that of a power and the function of its development; these also, in turn, are supposed to be based on and derived from the general and negative determination of the same infinitesimal. In the exposition of Lagrange just noticed, the specific affirmative aspect which is implied in Archimedes' method of developing the problem is brought to notice with the result that the procedure which is burdened with an unlimited progression is given its proper limit. The greatness of the modern invention *per se* and its capacity to solve previously intractable problems and to treat in a simple manner those previously soluble, is to be ascribed solely to the discovery of the relation of the original to the so-called derived functions and of those parts of a mathematical whole which stand in such a relation.

What has been said may suffice to signalize that distinctive relation of magnitudes which is the subject matter of the particular kind of calculus under discussion. It was possible to confine our exposition to simple problems and the methods of solving them; it would neither have been expedient as regards the determination of the Notion, which determination is here our sole concern, not would it have lain in the author's power to have reviewed the entire compass of the so-called application of the differential and integral calculus, and by reference of all the respective problems and their solutions to what we have demonstrated to be the principle of the calculus, to have carried out completely the induction that the application is based upon this principle. But sufficient evidence has been produced to show that just as each particular mode of calculation has as its subject matter a specific determinateness or relation of magnitude, such relation constituting addition, multiplication, the raising to powers and extraction of roots, and operations with logarithms and series, and so on, so too has the differential and integral calculus; the subject matter proper to this calculus might be most appropriately named the relation between a power function and the function of its expansion or potentiation, because this is what is most readily suggested by an insight into the nature of the subject matter. Logarithms, circular functions and series are of course also employed in the calculus, especially for the purpose of making expressions more amenable for the operations necessary for deriving the original function from the functions of expansion; but they are only used in the same way that the other forms of calculation such as addition, etc., are also used in the calculus. The differential and integral calculus has, indeed, a more particular interest in common with the form of series namely, to determine those functions of expansion which in the series are called co-efficients of the terms; but whereas the calculus is concerned only with the relation of the original function to the coefficient of the first term of its expansion, the series aims at exhibiting in the form of a sum, groups of the terms arranged according to powers which have these coefficients. The infinite which is associated with infinite series, the indeterminate expression of the negative of quantum in general, has nothing in common with the affirmative determination belonging to the infinite of this calculus. Similarly, the infinitesimal in the shape of the *increment*, by means of which the expansion is given the form of a series, is only an external means for the expansion, and the sole meaning of its so-called infinity is to have no other meaning beyond its significance as such means; the series, which in fact is not what is wanted, produces an excess, the elimination of which causes the unnecessary trouble. The method of Lagrange, who preferred to use the form of series again, is also burdened with this difficulty; although it is through his method, in what is called the *application*, that what is truly characteristic of the calculus is brought to notice, for, without forcing the forms of dx, dy and so on, *into the objects*, it is directly demonstrated to which part of the object the determinateness of the derived function (function of expansion) belongs; and thus it is evident that the matter in hand here is not the form of series.[1]

[1] In the critique quoted above (*Jahrb. für wissensch. Krit.*, II Bd. 1827, Nr. 155, 6 *sqq.*), are to be found interesting views of a profound scholar in this science, Herr Spehr; (Spehr, Friedrich Wilhelm, 1799–1833, a Brunswick mathematician: *Vollständiger Lehrbegriff der reinen Kombinationslehre*, 1824.) they are quoted from his *Neue Prinzipien des Fluentenkalkuls*, Brunswick, 1826, and concern a factor which has materially contributed to what is obscure and

Remark 3: *Further Forms Connected With the Qualitative Determinateness of Magnitude*

It has been shown that the infinitesimal of the differential calculus is, in its affirmative meaning, the *qualitative* determinateness of magnitude; and, more precisely, that it is present in the calculus not merely as a power determinateness in general but specifically as the relation of a power function to the power derived from the expansion of the function. But the qualitative determinateness is also present in another, so to speak, weaker form and this form, together with the use and the meaning of the infinitely small in this connection, are to be the subject matter of this Remark.

In making the foregoing our starting point we must, in this respect, first of all recollect that from the *analytical* side, the different power determinations appear in the first place as only formal and quite homogeneous, that they signify *numerical* magnitudes which as such do not possess that qualitative difference from each other. But in the application to spatial objects, the qualitative determinateness of the analytic relation is fully manifested as the transition from linear to planar determinations, from determinations of straight lines to those of curves, and so on. This application further involves that spatial objects, which by their nature are given in the form of *continuous* magnitudes, are

unscientific in the differential calculus and they agree with what we have said about the general character of the *theory* of this calculus. 'Purely arithmetical investigations,' he says, 'admittedly those which have a primary bearing on the differential calculus, have not been separated from the differential calculus proper, and in fact, as with Lagrange, have even been taken to be the calculus itself whilst this latter was regarded as only the application of them. These arithmetical investigations include the rules of differentiation, the derivation of Taylor's theorem, etc., and even the various methods of integration. But the case is quite the reverse, for it is precisely those applications which form the subject matter of the differential calculus proper, all those arithmetical developments and operations being *presupposed by the calculus* from analysis.' We have shown how, with Lagrange, it is just the separation of the so-called application from the procedure of the general part which starts from series, which serves to bring to notice the characteristic subject matter of the differential calculus. It is strange, however, that the author, who realizes that it is just these applications which form the subject matter of the differential calculus proper, should get involved in the formal metaphysics (adduced in that work) of *continuous magnitude, becoming, flow*, etc., and should want to add even fresh ballast to the old; these determinations are *formal*, in that they are only general categories which do not indicate just what is the *specific nature* of the subject matter, this having to be learned and abstracted from the concrete theory, that is, the applications.

taken to be *discrete*, the plane therefore as a multitude of lines, the line as a multitude of points, and so on. The sole interest of this procedure is to determine the points and the lines themselves into which the lines and planes respectively have been resolved, in order that from such determination, progress can be made analytically, that is, strictly speaking, arithmetically; these starting points for the required magnitudes are the *elements* from which the function and equation for the *concrete*, that is, the *continuous* magnitude, is to be derived. For the problems where the employment of this procedure is chiefly indicated, it is requisite that the element forming the starting point should be *self-determined*—in contrast to the *indirect* method which, on the contrary, can begin only with *limits* between which lies the self-determined element as the *goal* towards which the method advances. But then the result in both methods comes to the same thing if what can be found is only the law for progressively determining the required magnitude without the possibility of reaching the perfect, that is, so-called finite, determination demanded. To Kepler is ascribed the honour of first having thought of this reversal of the process and of having made the discrete the starting point. His explanation of how he understands the first proposition in Archimedes' cyclometry expresses this quite simply. Archimedes' first proposition, as we know, is that a circle is equal to a right-angled triangle having one of the sides enclosing the right angle equal to the diameter and the other to the circumference of the circle. Now Kepler takes the meaning of this proposition to be that the *circumference* of the circle has as many parts as it has *points*, that is, an infinite number, each of which can be regarded as the base of an isosceles triangle, and so on; he thus gives expression to the resolution of the continuous into the form of the discrete. The expression 'infinite' which occurs here is still far removed from the definition it is supposed to have in the differential calculus. When now a determinateness, a function, has been found for such discrete elements, they are supposed to be summed up, to be essentially elements of the continuous. But since a sum of points does not make a line, or a sum of lines a plane, the points are already directly taken as linear and the lines as planar. But because these linear elements are at the same time supposed not to be lines, which they would be if they were taken as quantum, they are represented as being infinitely small. What is discrete can only be *externally* summed up, the moments of such sum retaining the meaning of the discrete one (unit); the analytic transition from these ones is made only to their *sum* and is not simultaneously the geometrical transition from the point to the line or from the line to the plane, and so on; therefore the element which is determined as point or line is at the same time also given the quality of being linear or planar respectively in order that the sum, as a sum of little lines, may become a line, or as a sum of little planes may become a plane.

It is the need to acquire this moment of qualitative transition and to have recourse for this purpose to the infinitely small, which must be regarded as the source of all the conceptions which, though they are meant to resolve this difficulty, constitute in themselves the greatest difficulty. Before one could dispense with this expedient, it would have to be possible to show that the analytic procedure itself which appears as a mere *summation*, in fact already contains a *multiplication*. But this involves a fresh assumption which forms the basis in this application of arithmetical relations to geometrical figures: the assumption, namely, that arithmetical multiplication is also for the geometrical determination a transition into a higher dimension—that the arithmetical multiplication of magnitudes spatially determined as *lines* also produces a plane from the linear determination; three times four linear feet gives twelve linear feet, but three linear feet times four linear feet gives twelve superficial feet and, in fact, square feet, since the unit in both factors as discrete quantities is the same. The multiplication of lines by lines at first sight appears meaningless in so far as multiplication concerns simply numbers, i.e. is an alteration of a subject matter that is perfectly homogeneous with what it passes over into, with the product, only the *magnitude* being altered. On the other hand, what was called multiplication of a line as such by a line—it has been called *ductus lineae in lineam*, like *plani in planum*, and is also *ductus puncti in lineam*—is an alteration not merely of magnitude, but of magnitude as a *qualitative* determination of spatial character, of a dimension; the transition of the line into a plane must be understood as the *self-externalization* of the line, and similarly the self-externalization of the point is a line, and of the plane a whole space [volume]. This is the same as the representation of the line as the *motion* of a point, and so forth; but motion includes a determination of time and thus appears in this representation rather as merely a contingent, external alteration of state. The transition must be grasped from the standpoint of the Notion which was expressed as a self-externalization—the qualitative alteration which arithmetically is the multiplication of unit (point, etc.) by amount (line, etc.). We may here further remark that with the self-externalization of the plane, which would appear as a multiplication of the plane by a plane, there is seemingly a difference between the arithmetical and geometrical operations such that the self-externalization of the plane as *ductus plani in planum* would give arithmetically a multiplication of a two-dimensional factor by another such, and consequently a four-dimensional product which, however, is reduced by the geometrical determination to three. Although on the one hand number, because its principle is the one, yields the fixed determination for the external, quantitative element, yet equally, the result of operating with it is formal. Taken as a numerical determination 3×3 when it reproduces itself is $3 \times 3 \times 3 \times 3$; but this same magnitude as a plane, when it reproduces itself, is restricted to $3 \times 3 \times 3$, because space, represented as an expansion outwards from the point, from the merely abstract limit, has its true limit as a *concrete* determinateness beyond the line in the third dimension. The difference referred to could prove itself effective as regards free motion in which one side, the spatial side has a geometrical significance (in Kepler's law, $s^3 : t^2$) and the other, the temporal side, is an arithmetical determination.

It will now be evident, without further comment, how the qualitative element here considered differs from the subject of the previous Remark. There, the qualitative element lay in the determinateness of power; here, like the infinitely small, it is only the factor as arithmetically related to the product, or as the point to the line or the line to the plane, and so on. Now the qualitative transition which has to be made from the discrete (into which continuous magnitude is imagined to be resolved), to the continuous, is effected as a process of summation.

But that the alleged pure summation does in fact include a multiplication and therefore the transition from linear to planar dimensions, this comes to view most simply in the way in which, for example, it is shown that the area of a trapezium is equal to the product of the sum of the two opposite parallel lines and half the height. This height is represented as being merely the *amount* of a multitude of *discrete* magnitudes which must be summed up. These magnitudes are lines which lie parallel between the said limiting parallels; there are infinitely many of them for they are supposed to constitute the plane, and yet are lines which therefore, in order to possess the character of a plane, must at the same time be posited with negation. In order to escape the difficulty that a sum of lines is supposed to give a plane, the lines are directly assumed to be planes but also as *infinitely narrow*, for they have their determination solely in the linear quality of the parallel limits of the trapezium. As parallel and bounded by the other pair of rectilinear sides of the trapezium, these lines can be represented as the terms of an arithmetical progression, having a simply uniform difference which does not, however, require to be determined, and whose first and last terms are these two parallel lines; as we know, the sum of such a series is the *product* of the parallels and half the *amount* or *number* of terms. This last quantum is called *amount* or *number* simply and solely with reference to the conception of infinitely many lines; it is simply the specific magnitude of something which is *continuous*—the height. It is clear that what is called a sum is at the same time a *ductus lineae in lineam*, a *multiplication* of lines by lines, and so according to the above determination the result is something having the quality of a plane. In the simplest case of any rectangle *AB,* each of the two factors is a simple magnitude; but even in the further, still elementary example of the trapezium, only one of the factors is simple as half of the height. The other, on the contrary, is determined by a progression; it is also linear but its specific magnitude is more complex; and since it can be expressed only by a series, the problem of summing it is called analytical, i.e. arithmetical; but the geometrical moment in it is multiplication, the qualitative element of the transition from the dimension of line to that of plane; the one factor was taken to be *discrete* only for the arithmetical determination of the other; by itself it is, like the other, the magnitude of a line.

But the method of representing planes as sums of lines is also often employed when multiplication as such is not used to produce the result. This happens when the problem is to indicate the magnitude in the equation not as a quantum but as a proportion.

It is, for example, a familiar way of showing that the area of a circle bears the same proportion to the area of an ellipse, the major axis of which is the diameter of the circle, as the major axis does to the minor axis, each of these areas being taken as the *sum* of the relative *ordinates*; each ordinate of the ellipse is to the corresponding ordinate of the circle as is the minor to the major axis; therefore, it is concluded, the *sums* of the ordinates, i.e. the *areas*, are also in the same proportion. Those who want to avoid here the representation of an area as a sum of lines resort to the usual, quite unnecessary expedient of making the ordinates into *trapezia* of infinitely small breadth; since the equation is only a proportion, only one of the two linear elements of the plane comes into the comparison. The other, the abscissa axis, is assumed as equal in ellipse and circle, as a factor therefore arithmetically equal to 1, and consequently the proportion depends solely on the relation of the one determining moment. The two dimensions are necessary to the *representation* of a plane, but the quantitative determination required to be indicated in this proportion affects only the *one* moment; to be swayed by the representation of a plane, or to help it out by adding the idea of *sum* to this *one* moment, is really to fail to recognize the essential mathematical element here involved.

The foregoing exposition also contains the criterion for Cavalieri's method of indivisibles referred to above which equally is justified by it and does not need to be helped out by the infinitely small. These indivisibles are lines when he is considering a plane, and squares or plane circles when he is considering a pyramid or a cone, etc. The base line or basic plane which is assumed as determined, he calls the *regula*; it is the constant, and with reference to a series it is its first or last term. The indivisibles are regarded as parallel with the *regula* and therefore as having the same determination as this with respect to the figure. Now Cavalieri's general fundamental proposition is 'that all figures, both plane and solid, are *proportionate* to all their indivisibles, these being compared with each other collectively and, if there is a common proportion in the figures, distributively'.[1] For this purpose, he compares in figures of the *same* base and height, the proportions between lines drawn parallel to the base and *equidistant* from it; all such lines in a figure have

[1] *Exerc. Geometr.*, VI: in the later work: *Exerc.*, I, p. 6.

one and the same determination and constitute its whole content. In this way, too, Cavalieri proves for example the elementary proposition that parallelograms of equal height are proportional to their bases; any two lines drawn equidistant from and parallel to the base in both figures are in the same proportion as the base lines and so therefore are the whole figures. The lines do not in fact constitute the whole content of the figure as *continuous*, but only the content in so far as it is to be arithmetically *determined*; it is the line which is the element of the content and through it alone must be grasped the specific nature of the figure.

This leads us to reflect on the difference which exists with respect to that feature into which the determinateness of a figure falls; this is either the *height*, as here, or an *external limit*. Where this determinateness is an external limit, it is admitted that the *continuity* of the figure, so to speak, *follows upon* the equality or the proportion of the limit; for example, the equality of figures which *coincide* follows from the fact that their boundaries coincide. But in parallelograms of equal height and base, only the latter determinateness is an external limit; the height (not the parallelism as such), on which is based the second main determination of the figures, their *proportion*, introduces a second principle of determination additional to the external limits. Euclid's proof of the equality of parallelograms having the same height and base reduces them to triangles, to *continuous* figures *limited externally*; in Cavalieri's proof, primarily in that of the proportionality of parallelograms, the limit is simply a *quantitative determinateness as such*, which is explicated in every pair of lines drawn at the same distance from each other in both figures. These lines, which are equal or in an equal ratio with the base, taken *collectively* give figures standing in the same ratio. The conception of an *aggregate* of lines is incompatible with the continuity of the figure; the essential determinateness is completely exhausted by a consideration of the lines alone. Cavalieri frequently answers the objection that the conception of indivisibles involves the comparison of lines or planes as if they were infinite in *amount*;[1] he makes the correct distinction that he does not compare their *amount*, which we do not know (and which is, as we have remarked, merely an empty idea assumed in support of the theory), but only the *magnitude*, i.e. the the quantitative determinateness as such which

[1] *Geom.*, Lib. II. Prop. I. Schol.

is equal to the space occupied by these lines; because this space is enclosed within limits, its magnitude too is enclosed within the same limits; *the continuous figure is nothing other than the indivisibles themselves,* he says; if it were something apart from them it would not be comparable; but it would be absurd to say that bounded continuous figures were not comparable with each other.

It is evident that Cavalieri means to distinguish what belongs to the *outer existence* of the continuous figure from what constitutes its *determinateness*; it is the latter alone to which we must attend when comparing the continuous or constructing theorems about it. The categories he employs in this connection, namely that the continuous is *composed* or *consists* of indivisibles, and the like, are of course inadequate since they demand at the same time the intuition of the continuous or, as already said, its outer existence; instead of saying that 'the continuous is nothing other than the indivisibles themselves', it would be more correct and also directly self-explanatory to say that the quantitative determinateness of the continuous is none other than that of the indivisibles themselves. Calvalieri does not support the erroneous conclusion that there are greater and lesser infinites which is drawn *by the schools* from the idea that the indivisibles constitute the continuous; further on[1] he gives expression to his quite definite awareness that his method of proof by no means forces on him the idea that the continuous is composed of indivisibles; continuous figures follow only the *proportion* of the indivisibles. He says he has taken the aggregate of indivisibles not as an apparent infinity for the sake of an *infinite* number of lines or planes, but in so far as they possess a specific kind of limitedness. But then, in order to remove this stumbling block, he does not spare himself the trouble of proving the principal proportions of his geometry (in the seventh book specially added for this purpose) in a way which remains free from any admixture of infinity. This method reduces the proofs to the usual form of the *coincidence* of figures above mentioned, i.e. as remarked, to the conception of determinateness as an external spatial limit.

About this form of coincidence, we may add that it is, on the whole, a so to speak childish aid for sense perception. In the elementary theorems about triangles, two traingles are represented side by side; of their six component parts, three are

[1] *Geom.*, Lib. VII. Praef.

assumed equal to the corresponding three of the other triangle and it is then shown that such triangles are congruent, i.e. that the remaining three parts of each triangle are also equal to those of the other triangle—because by virtue of the equality of the first three parts, the triangles *coincide*. If we take the matter more abstractly, then it is just because of this equality of each pair of corresponding parts in both triangles that there is only *one* triangle before us; in this it is assumed that three parts are *already determined* and from this follows the *determinateness* of the three remaining parts. In this way, the determinateness is exhibited as completed in the three parts; hence for the determinateness as such, the three remaining parts are a superfluity, the superfluity of sensuous existence, i.e. of the intuition of continuity. Expressed in this form, the qualitative determinateness stands out in its distinction from what is given in intuition, from the whole as continuous within itself; the form of coincidence does not bring this distinction to notice.

With parallel lines and with parallelograms there enters, as we have observed, another factor, partly the equality of the angles only and partly the height of the figures, from which latter their external limits, the sides of the parallelograms, are distinct. This gives rise to uncertainty whether in these figures, besides the determinateness of one side, the base, which is an external limit, we are to take for the other determinateness, the other external limit, namely the other side of the parallelogram, or else the height. In the case of two such figures having the same base and height, one of them being rectangular and the other having very acute angles (the opposite angles therefore being very obtuse), the latter triangle can easily look greater than the former, when its long side is taken as the determinant and, as in Cavalieri's method, the *planes* are compared according to the *aggregate* of parallel lines intersecting them; the *longer* side can be regarded as a potentiality of *more* lines than is given by the vertical side of the rectangle. Such a conception, however, is no argument against Cavalieri's method; the *aggregate* of parallel lines imagined in the two parallelograms, for the purpose of comparison, also presupposes the equidistance of the lines from each other or from the base; from which it follows that the height, and not the other side of the parallelogram, is the other determining moment. But the case is different again when the comparison is between two parallelograms having the same height and base but not lying in the same plane and making different angles with a third plane; here, the parallel sections which arise, when the third plane is imagined as cutting through the parallelograms and moving parallel to itself are no longer equidistant from each other and the two planes are unequal. Cavalieri is very careful to draw attention to this distinction which he defines as the difference between a *transitus rectus* and a *transitus obliquus* of the indivisibles and thus prevents a superficial misunderstanding which could arise on this point.[1] I remember that an objection to indivisibles by Tacquet,[2] an acute geometer who was also working at this time on new methods, concerns this very point: it is referred to in the above-mentioned work of Barrow[3] who also uses the method of indivisibles, although with him it is tainted with the assumption (which he passed on to his pupil Newton and other contemporary mathematicians including Leibniz, too), that a curvilinear triangle, like the so-called characteristic triangle, may be equated with a rectilinear triangle if both are infinitely, that is, *very* small. The difficulty raised by Tacquet likewise concerns the question which line, in the calculation of conical and spherical surfaces, should be taken as the basis of determination in the method based on the employment of the discrete. Tacquet's objection to the method of indivisibles is that in the calculation of the *surface* of a right-angled cone, this atomistic method represents the triangle of the cone to be composed of straight *lines* parallel to the base and perpendicular to the axis, which are at the same time *radii of the circles* of which the *surface* of the cone consists. Now if this surface is defined as a sum of the circumferences and this sum is determined from the number of their radii, i.e. from the length of the axis or the height of the cone, then, says Tacquet, such a result clashes with the truth formerly taught and demonstrated by Archimedes. Now Barrow counters this by showing that to determine the surface it is not the axis but the *side* of the triangle of the cone which must be taken as the line the revolution of which generates the surface; consequently, it is this line and not the axis which must be assumed as the specific magnitude for the aggregate of the circumferences.

[1] Both in *Exercit.*, I n, XII *sqq.* and in *Geometr.*, I. II.

[2] Tacquet, Andr., 1611–1660, Professor in the Jesuit College at Antwerp: *Cylindricorum Et Annularium*, Libri V, 1651-9.   [3] *Lect. Geom.*, II, p. 21.

Objections and uncertainties of this kind have their origin solely in the indefinite idea employed of the *infinite* aggregate of points of which the line (or of lines of which the plane) is supposed to consist; this idea obscures the essential determinateness of the magnitude of the lines or planes.

The intention of these Remarks has been to bring to notice the *affirmative* meanings which, in the various applications of the infinitely small in mathematics, remain so to speak in the background, and to lift them out of the nebulosity in which that category, merely negatively held, has concealed them. In infinite series, as in Archimedes' cyclometry, the meaning of the infinite is nothing more than this: that the law determining the series being known, but the so-called *finite*—i.e. arithmetical—expression not being given, the reduction of the arc to the straight line cannot be effected; this incommensurability is their qualitative difference. The qualitative difference between the discrete and the continuous generally, equally contains a negative determination which makes them appear as incommensurable and introduces the infinite in the sense that the continuous which is to be taken as discrete, is no longer to possess, as continuous, any quantum. The continuous which is to be taken arithmetically as a *product*, is therefore posited as in its own self discrete, i.e. it is analysed into the elements which are its factors and in these lies its quantitative determinateness; just because they are these factors or elements, they are of a lower dimension, and as powers are concerned, are of a lower power than the magnitude of which they are the elements or factors. This difference appears arithmetically as a purely quantitative one, that of the root and power, or whatever degree of powers it may be; however, if the expression is to be taken only quantitatively, for example, $a : a^2$ or $d.a^2 = 2a : a^2 = 2 : a$, or for the law of descent of a falling body, $t : a^2$, then it yields the meaningless ratios of $1 : a$, $2 : a$, $1 : at$; in supersession of their merely quantitative aspect, the sides would have to be held apart by their different qualitative significance, as $s = at^2$, the magnitude in this way being expressed as a quality, as a function of the magnitude of another quality. Here then, we are faced merely with a quantitative determinateness; there is no difficulty in operating with this in accordance with its own manner and no objection can be offered if the magnitude of one line is multiplied by the magnitude of another;

but the multiplication of these same magnitudes at the same time results in the qualitative alteration of the transition from line into plane; and to that extent a negative determination comes into play. It is this that occasions the difficulty, a difficulty which is resolved by an insight into its peculiarity and into the simple nature of the matter; but the introduction of the infinite which is meant to remove the difficulty only serves to aggravate it and prevent its solution.

CHAPTER 3

THE QUANTITATIVE RELATION OR QUANTITATIVE RATIO

The infinity of quantum has been determined to the stage where it is the negative beyond of quantum, which beyond, however, is contained within the quantum itself. This beyond is the qualitative moment as such. The infinite quantum as the unity of both moments, of the quantitative and qualitative determinateness, is in the first instance a *ratio*.

In the ratio, quantum no longer has merely an indifferent determinateness but is qualitatively determined as simply related to its beyond. It continues itself into its beyond; this, in the first place, is simply *another* quantum. But they are essentially related to each other not as external quanta, but the determinateness of each consists in this relation to the other. In this their otherness they have thus returned into themselves; what each is, it is in the other; the other constitutes the determinateness of each. The flight of quantum away from and beyond itself has now therefore this meaning, that it changed not merely into an other, or into its abstract other, into its negative beyond, but that in this other it reached its determinateness, finding *itself* in its beyond, which is another quantum. The *quality* of quantum, the specific nature of its Notion, is its externality as such, and in ratio the quantum is now *posited* as having its determinateness in its externality, in another quantum, and as being in its beyond what it is.

They are quanta which stand to each other in the relation just described. This *relation* is itself also a magnitude; the quantum is not only *in* a ratio, but it is itself *posited as a ratio*; there is only a *single* quantum and this has the said qualitative determinateness *within itself*. As such ratio, it is a self-enclosed totality and indifferent to limit, and it expresses this by containing within itself the externality of its determining and by being in this externality related only to itself. It is therefore, in its own self infinite.

Ratio as such is:

1. *direct* ratio. In this, the qualitative moment does not yet emerge explicitly as such; its mode is still only that of quantum, namely, to be posited as having its determinateness in its very externality. The quantitative ratio is in itself the contradiction of externality and self-relation, of the affirmative being of quanta and their negation; next, it is sublated

2. in the *indirect* or *inverse* ratio, in which is posited the negation of one of the quanta with the alteration of the other, and the alterableness of the direct relation itself;

3. in the *ratio of powers*, however, the unity which in its difference is self-related, vindicates itself as a simple self-production of the quantum; this qualitative moment itself, when finally posited in a simple determination and as identical with the quantum, becomes *measure*.

About the nature of the following ratios, much has been anticipated in the preceding Remarks concerning the infinite of quantity, i.e., the qualitative moment in it; it only remains therefore to expound the abstract Notion of these ratios.

A. THE DIRECT RATIO

1. In the ratio which, as immediate, is *direct*, the determinateness of either quantum lies reciprocally in the determinateness of the other. There is only *one* determinateness or limit of both and this is itself a quantum, namely, the *exponent* of the ratio.

2. The exponent is any quantum; but it is *self-related* in its own externality and a qualitatively determined quantum only in so far as it has within itself its own difference, its beyond and its otherness. This difference of quantum present within it is, however, the difference of unit and amount, unit being a being which is determined as for-itself, and amount the indifferent fluctuation of the determinateness, the external indifference of quantum. Unit and amount were at first *moments* of quantum; now, in the ratio, in the realisation so far of quantum, each of its moments appears as a quantum on its own, and as a determination of its existence—as a limiting of the otherwise merely external, indifferent determinateness of quantity.

The exponent is this difference as a simple determinateness, i.e. it has immediately within it the significance of both determinations. It is *first* of all a quantum. As such it is amount; if the one side of the ratio which is taken as unit is expressed numerically as one—and it counts only as such—then the other, the amount, is the quantum of the exponent itself. *Secondly*, it is simple determinateness as the qualitative moment of the sides of the ratio. When the quantum of one side is determined, the other, too, is determined by the exponent and it is quite immaterial how the first is determined; it no longer has any significance as a determinate quantum on its own, but can equally well be any other quantum without altering the value of the ratio, which depends solely on the exponent. The one which is taken as unit always remains unit however great it becomes, and the other, no matter how great it, too, becomes in consequence, must remain the *same* amount of that unit.

3. The two therefore constitute strictly only *one* quantum; the one has relatively to the other only the value of unit, not of amount, the other only that of amount; consequently, *according to the specific nature of their Notion*, they themselves are *not complete quanta*. But this incompleteness is a negation in them and a negation, not as regards their alterableness generally in virtue of which one of them (and it can be either of the two) can assume any possible magnitude, but as regards the determination that when one is altered the other is increased or diminished by the same amount; this means, as has been shown, that the quantum of only one of them, the unit, is altered, while the other side, the amount, remains the same quantum *of units*; but the former too still *counts* only as a unit no matter how it is altered as quantum. Thus each side is only one of the two moments of quantum and the independence which belongs to the peculiar character of quantum is in principle *negated*; in this qualitative relationship they are to be *posited* as *negative* relatively to each other.

The exponent ought to be the complete quantum, since the determination of *both* sides coincides in it; but in fact, even as quotient it has the value only of amount or of unit. There is nothing to determine which side of the ratio must be taken as unit or which as amount; if the quantum B is measured in terms of quantum A as unit, then the quotient C is the amount of such units; but if A is itself taken as amount, the quotient C is the unit which to the amount A is required for the quantum B. This quotient therefore is, as exponent, not posited as what it ought to be—the determinant of the ratio, or the ratio's qualitative unity. It is only posited as this in so far as it has the value of being the *unity of both moments*, of unit and amount. True, these sides are present as quanta as they should be in the explicated quantum, in the ratio; but at the same time they have only the value proper to them as sides of the ratio, namely to be *incomplete* quanta and to count only as one of those qualitative moments. They must therefore be posited with this their negation and thus there arises a more developed form of the ratio, one which corresponds more to its character, a ratio in which the exponent has the significance of the product of the sides. As thus determined, it is the *inverse* ratio.

B. INVERSE RATIO

1. The ratio as now before us is the *sublated* direct relation. At first, the ratio was *immediate* and therefore not yet truly determinate; the determinateness it now possesses is such that the exponent counts as a product, as a unity of unit and amount. As we have already seen, the exponent as immediate could equally well be taken either as unit or as amount; it was then also only a simple quantum and therefore, by choice, an amount; one side was the unit, to be taken as a numerical one, of which the other side is a fixed amount and, at the same time, the exponent; the quality of this latter, therefore, was simply that this quantum is taken as fixed, or rather that this fixed quantum has the meaning only of quantum.

Now in the inverse ratio the exponent as quantum is likewise immediate and is any quantum assumed as fixed. But this quantum is not a *fixed amount* to the *one* of the other quantum in the *ratio*; this ratio, which previously was fixed, is now on the contrary posited as alterable; if in place of the unit on one side of the ratio another quantum is taken, then the other side is no longer the *same amount* of units of the first side. In the direct ratio this unit is only the common element of both sides; as such, it continues itself into the other side, into the amount; and the amount itself taken by itself, or the exponent, is indifferent to the unit.

But now the ratio is so determined that the amount as such is altered relatively to the other side of the ratio, to the unit; when another quantum is taken for the unit, the quantum of amount also is altered. Consequently, although the exponent is also only an immediate quantum arbitrarily assumed as fixed, it is not preserved as such in the side of the ratio, but this side, and with it the direct ratio of the sides, is alterable. In the ratio, then, as now before us, the exponent as the determining quantum is posited as negative towards itself as a quantum of the ratio, and hence as qualitative, as a limit—with the result that the qualitative moment is manifested independently and in distinct contrast to the quantitative moment. In the direct ratio, the *alteration* of the two sides is only the one alteration of the quantum which is taken as unit, the common element of both sides; by as many times as the one side is increased or diminished, so also is the other: the ratio itself is not affected by this alteration which is external to it. In the indirect ratio on the other hand, although the alteration, in keeping with the indifferent quantitative moment is also arbitrary, it is *confined within the ratio*, and this arbitrary quantitative fluctuation, too, is limited by the negative determinateness of the exponent as by a limit.

2. We have now to consider more closely this qualitative nature of the inverse ratio, more particularly in its realisation, and to unravel the entanglement of the affirmative moment with the negative which is contained in it. The indirect or inverse ratio is quantum posited as a qualitative quantum, i.e., displaying itself as self-determining, as a limit of itself within itself. As such, the quantum is, *first*, an immediate magnitude as a *simple* determinateness, the *whole* as a quantum simply affirmatively present. But secondly, this immediate *determinateness* is also a *limit*; for that purpose the quantum is differentiated into two quanta which in the first instance are mutually related as others; but the quantum as their qualitative and, moreover, complete determinateness is the unity of unit and amount, a product of which the two quanta are the factors. Thus on the one hand the exponent of their ratio is in them identical with itself and is their affirmative moment which constitutes them quanta; on the other hand the exponent, as the negation posited in them, is the *unity* in them, so that although each is in the first place simply an immediate, limited quantum, it is at the same time limited in such a manner that it is only *in principle* [*an sich*] identical with its other. Thirdly,

the exponent as the simple determinateness is the negative unity of this differentiation of itself into two quanta and is the limit of their reciprocal limiting.

In conformity with these determinations, each of the two moments has its *limit* within the exponent, and since this is their specified unity each is the negative of the other; one of them becomes as many times smaller as the other becomes greater, the magnitude of each depending on its containing the magnitude which the other lacks. Each in this way continues itself *negatively* into the other; to the extent that each is amount, the amount of the other is cancelled, and each is what it is only through the negation or limit posited in it by the other. In this manner each also *contains* the other and is measured by it, for each is supposed to be only that quantum which the other is not; the magnitude of the other is an indispensable factor in the value of each and is therefore inseparable from it.

This continuity of each in the other constitutes the moment of *unity* through which they are in ratio—the moment of the *one* determinateness, of the simple limit which is the exponent. This unity, the whole, constitutes the *in-itself*, the *principle* of each, from which their *actual* magnitude is distinct; in accordance with the latter, each only *is* to the extent that it takes from the other a part of their common in-itself, the whole. But it can take from the other only as much as will make its own self equal to this in-itself; it has its maximum in the exponent which in accordance with the stated second determination is the limit of their reciprocal limiting. And since each is a moment of the ratio only in so far as it limits the other and is simultaneously limited by it, it loses this its determination in making itself equal to its in-itself; for in so doing not only does the *other* magnitude become zero, but it vanishes itself, since what it is supposed to be is not a mere quantum as such, but only quantum as such moment of a ratio. Thus each side is the contradiction between its determination as the in-itself, i.e. as unity of the whole, which is the exponent, and its determination as moment of the ratio; this contradiction is *infinity* again in a fresh, peculiar form.

The exponent is a *limit* of the sides of its ratio within which they increase and decrease relatively to each other; but they cannot become equal to the exponent because of the latter's affirmative determinateness as quantum. As thus the limit of their reciprocal limiting, the exponent, is (α) their beyond, to which they *infinitely* approximate but which they cannot reach. This infinity in which they approach their beyond is the spurious infinity of the infinite progress; it is itself finite, is bounded by its opposite, by the finitude of each side and of the exponent itself and is consequently only *approximation*. But (β) the spurious infinity is here also *posited* as what it is *in truth*, namely, as only the *negative moment* in general, in accordance with which the exponent is the *simple limit* of the differentiated quanta of the ratio as their in-itself; their finitude, as their simple alterableness, is related to this in-itself which, however, remains absolutely distinct from them as their negation. This infinity, then, to which these quanta can only approximate is likewise *affirmatively* present and actual—the simple quantum of the exponent. In it is reached the beyond with which the sides of the ratio are burdened; it is *implicitly* [*an sich*] the unity of both, and so implicitly the other side of each; for each has only as much value as the other has not, the whole determinateness of each thus resides in the other, and this their in-itself as an affirmative infinity is simply the exponent.

3. The outcome of this, however, is the transition of the inverse ratio into a different determination from that which it had at first. This consisted in an immediate quantum being also related to another quantum in such a way that its increase is proportional to the decrease of the other, that it is what it is through a negative relationship with the other; also, a third magnitude is the common limit of this their fluctuating increase. This fluctuation here is their distinctive character—in contrast to the qualitative moment as a *fixed* limit; they have the character of *variable* magnitudes, for which the said fixed limit is an infinite beyond.

But the determinations which have emerged and which we have to summarize are not only that this infinite beyond is at the same time some present finite quantum or other, but that its fixity—which constitutes it such infinite beyond relatively to the quantitative moment, and which is the qualitative moment of being only as abstract self-relation—has developed as a mediation of itself with itself in its other, in the finite terms of the ratio. The general result can be indicated by saying that the whole, as exponent, is the limit of the reciprocal limiting of both terms and is therefore posited as *negation of the negation*, hence as infinity, as an *affirmative* relation to itself. More specifically the exponent, simply as product, is *implicitly* the unity of unit and amount, but as each term is only one of these two moments, the exponent also includes them within itself and in them is *implicitly* related to itself. But in the inverse ratio, the difference has developed into the *externality* of quantitative being, and the qualitative moment is not merely the fixity of the exponent, or merely the immediate inclusion in it of the two moments of unit and amount, but is the identification of the exponent with itself in its *self-external otherness*. It is this determination which stands out as result in these moments as explicated. The exponent, namely, is found to be the in-itself which is realized in the simple alterableness of its moments as quanta; the indifference of their magnitudes in their alteration is displayed as an infinite progress, the basis of which is that in their indifference their determinateness is to have their value in the value of the other. Hence (α), in accordance with the affirmative aspect of the quantum, each is *implicitly* the whole of the exponent. Similarly (β), the quanta have for their negative moment, for their reciprocal limiting, the magnitude of the exponent; their limit is that of the exponent. The fact that they no longer have any other immanent limit, a fixed immediacy, finds expression in the infinite progress of their determinate being and of their limitation, in the negation of every particular value. This negation is, accordingly, the *negation* of the self-externality of the exponent which is displayed in the moments of the ratio; and the exponent, which is itself a simple quantum and is also differentiated into quanta, is, therefore, posited as preserving itself and uniting with itself in the negation of the indifferent existence of the quanta, thus being the determinant of its self-external otherness.

The ratio is now specified as the *ratio of powers*.

C. THE RATIO OF POWERS

1. The quantum which, in its otherness, is identical with itself and which determines the beyond of itself, has reached the stage of being-for-self. As a qualitative totality—for it posits itself as *developed*—it has for its moments the determinations of the Notion of number, unit and amount; in the inverse ratio, the latter is still a plurality determined not by the unit itself as such, but from elsewhere, by a Third; but now it is posited as determined

L

only by the unit. This is the case in the ratio of powers where the unit, which in its own self is amount, is also amount relatively to itself as unit. The otherness, the amount of units, is the *unit* itself. The power is a plurality of units each of which is this same plurality. The quantum as an indifferent determinateness undergoes alteration; but in so far as this alteration is a raising to a power, this its otherness is limited purely by itself. Thus in the power, quantum is posited as returned into itself; it is at once its own self and also its otherness.

The *exponent* of this ratio is no longer an immediate quantum as it is in the direct ratio and also in the inverse ratio. In the ratio of powers it is of a wholly *qualitative* nature—this *simple* determinateness that the amount is the unit itself, that the quantum in its otherness is *identical* with itself. In this is also contained the *quantitative* aspect of its nature, namely, that the limit or negation is not present simply affirmatively as an immediacy, but that the determinate being [of the quantum] is posited as continued into its otherness; for the truth of quality is just this, to be quantity, immediate determinateness as sublated.

2. The ratio of powers appears at first to be an external alteration to which any quantum can be subjected; but it has a closer connection with the *Notion* of quantum: namely, that in the determinate being into which it has developed in the ratio of powers, quantum has reached its Notion and has completely realized it. This ratio is the display of what quantum is *in itself* and it expresses that determinateness or *quality* of quantum which is its distinctive feature. Quantum is the *indifferent* determinateness, i.e., *posited* as *sublated*, determinateness as a limit which is equally no limit, which continues itself into its otherness and so remains identical with itself therein. In the ratio of powers this quality of quantum is *posited*; quantum itself determines its otherness, its going beyond itself into another quantum.

Comparing the progressive realization of quantum in the preceding ratios, we see that the quality of quantum as the posited difference of itself from itself is simply this: to be a ratio. As a direct ratio it is at first only the simple or unmediated form of such posited difference, so that its self-relation which it has as exponent, in contrast to its differences, counts only as the fixity of an amount of the unit. In the inverse ratio, the quantum is negatively determined as relating itself to itself—to itself as a negation of itself in which, however, it has its value; as an affirmative relation to itself it is an exponent which, as quantum, is only *in principle* the determinant of its moments. But in the ratio of powers, quantum is present in the difference as *its own difference from itself*. The *externality* of the determinateness is the quality of quantum and this externality is now posited in conformity with the Notion of quantum, as the latter's own self-determining, as its relation to its own self, as its *quality*.

3. But with the *positing* of quantum in conformity with its Notion, it has undergone transition into another determination; or, as we may also express it, its *determination* is now also a *determinateness*, what quantum is *in principle* it is now also *in reality*. It is *quantum* in so far as the externality or indifference of its determining (as it is said, it is that which can be increased or decreased) counts and is posited only *simply* or *immediately*; it has become the other of itself, namely, quality—in so far as this externality is now *posited* as mediated by quantum itself, and thus as moment of itself—so that *in this very externality quantum is self-related*, is *being* as quality.

At first, then, quantity as such appears in opposition to quality; but quantity is itself *a* quality, a purely self-related determinateness distinct from the determinateness of its other, from quality as such. But quantity is not only *a* quality; it is the truth of quality itself, the latter having exhibited its own transition into quantity. Quantity, on the other hand, is in its truth the externality which is no longer indifferent but has returned into itself. It is thus quality itself in such a manner that apart from this determination there would no longer be any quality as such. The *positing* of the totality requires the *double* transition, not only of the one determinateness into its other, but equally the transition of this other, its return, into the first. The first transition yields the identity of both, but at first only *in itself* or in principle; quality is contained in quantity, but this is still a one-sided determinateness. That the converse is equally true, namely, that quantity is contained in quality and is equally only a sublated determinateness, this results from the second transition—the return into the first determinateness. This observation on the necessity of the *double* transition is of great importance throughout the whole compass of scientific method.

Quantum is now no longer an indifferent or external determination but as such is sublated and is quality, and is that by virtue of which something is what it is; this is the truth of quantum, to be Measure.

Remark

In the Remarks above on the quantitative infinite, it was shown that this infinite and also the difficulties associated with it have their origin in the *qualitative* moment which makes its appearance in the sphere of quantity, and also how the qualitative moment of the ratio of powers in particular is the source of various developments and complexities. It was shown that the chief obstacle to a grasp of the Notion of this infinite is the stopping short at its merely negative determination as the negation of quantum, instead of advancing to the simple affirmative determination which is the qualitative moment. The only further remark to be made here concerns the intrusion of quantitative forms into the pure qualitative forms of thought in philosophy. It is the relationship of powers in particular which has been applied recently to the determinations of the Notion. The Notion in its immediacy was called the *first power* or *potence*; in its otherness or difference, in the determinate being of its moments, the *second power*; and in its return into itself or as a totality, the *third power*. It is at once evident that *power* as used thus is a category which essentially belongs to quantum—these *powers* do not bear the meaning of the *potentia*, the δύναμις of Aristotle. Thus, the relationship of powers expresses determinateness in the form or difference which has reached its truth, but difference as it is in the *particular Notion* of quantum, not as it is in the Notion as such. In quantum, the negativity which belongs to the nature of the Notion is still far from being posited in the determination proper to the Notion; differences which are proper to quantum are superficial determinations for the Notion itself and are still far from being determined as they are in the Notion. It was in the infancy of philosophic thinking that numbers were used, as by Pythagoras, to designate universal, essential distinctions—and first and second power, and so on are in this respect not a whit better than numbers. This was a preliminary stage to comprehension in the element of pure thought; it was not until after Pythagoras that thought determinations themselves were discovered, i.e., became *on their own account* objects for consciousness. But to retrogress from such determinations to those of number is the action of a thinking which feels its own incapacity, a thinking which, in opposition to current philosophical culture which is accustomed to thought determinations, now also makes itself ridiculous by pretending that this impotence is something new, superior, and an advance.

There is as little to be said against the expression *power* when it is used only as a *symbol*, as there is against the use of numbers or any other kind of symbols for Notions—but also there is just as much to be said against them as against all symbolism whatever in which pure determinations of the Notion or of philosophy are supposed to be represented. Philosophy needs no such help either from the world of sense or from the products of the imagination, or from subordinate spheres in its own peculiar province, for the determinations of such spheres are unfitted for higher spheres and for the whole. This unfitness is manifest whenever categories of the finite are applied to the infinite; the current determinations of force, or substantiality, cause and effect, and so on, are likewise only symbols for expressing, for example, vital or spiritual relationships, i.e. they are untrue determinations for such relationships; and still more so are the powers of quantum and degrees of powers, both for such and for speculative relationships generally. If numbers, powers, the mathematical infinite, and such-like are to be used not as symbols but as forms for philosophical determinations and hence themselves as philosophical forms, then it would be necessary first of all to demonstrate their philosophical meaning, i.e. the specific nature of their Notion. If this is done, then they themselves are superfluous designations; the determinateness of the Notion specifies its own self and its specification alone is the correct and fitting designation. The use of those forms is, therefore, nothing more than a convenient means of evading the task of grasping the determinations of the Notion, of specifying and of justifying them.

Section Three: Measure

Abstractly expressed, in measure quality and quantity are united. *Being* as such is an immediate identity of the determinateness with itself. This immediacy of the determinateness has sublated itself. *Quantity* is being which has returned into itself in such a manner that it is a simple self-identity as indifference to the determinateness. But this indifference is only the externality of having the determinateness not in its own self but in an other. Thirdly, we now have self-related externality; as self-related it is also a *sublated* externality and has within itself the difference from itself—the difference which, as an externality is the *quantitative*, and as taken back into itself is the *qualitative*, moment.

In transcendental idealism the categories of quantity and quality are followed, after the insertion of relation, by *modality*, which may therefore be mentioned here. This category has there the meaning of being the relation of the object to thought. According to that idealism thought generally is essentially external to the thing-in-itself. In so far as the other categories have only the transcendental character of belonging to consciousness, but to the *objective* element of it, so modality as the category of relation to the subject, to this extent contains relatively the determination of *reflection*-into-self; i.e. the objectivity which belongs to the other categories is lacking in the categories of modality; these, according to Kant, do not in the least add to the concept as a determination of the object but only express the relation to the faculty of cognition.[1] The categories which Kant groups under modality—namely, possibility, actuality and necessity—will occur later in their proper place; Kant did not apply the infinitely inportant form of triplicity—with him it manifested itself at first only as a formal spark of light—to the genera of his categories (quantity, quality, etc.), but only to their species which, too, alone he called categories. Consequently he was unable to hit on the third to quality and quantity.

With Spinoza, the *mode* is likewise the third after substance and attribute; he explains it to be the *affections* of substance, or that element which is in an other through which it is comprehended. According to this concept, this third is only externality as such;

[1] *Critique of Pure Reason*, 2nd ed., pp. 99, 266.

as has already been mentioned, with Spinoza generally, the rigid nature of substance lacks the return into itself.

The observation here made extends generally to those systems of pantheism which have been partially developed by thought. The first is being, the one, substance, the infinite, essence; in contrast to this abstraction the second, namely, all determinateness in general, what is only finite, accidental, perishable, nonessential, etc. can equally abstractly be grouped together; and this is what usually happens as the next step in quite formal thinking. But the connection of this second with the first is so evident that one cannot avoid grasping it as also in a unity with the latter; thus with Spinoza, the attribute is the whole substance, but is apprehended by the intellect which is itself a limitation or mode; but in this way the mode, the non-substantial generally, which can only be grasped through an other, constitutes the other extreme to substance, the third generally. Indian pantheism, too, in its monstrous fantasies has in an abstract way received this development which runs like a moderating thread through its extravagances; a point of some interest in the development is that Brahma, the one of abstract thought, progresses through the shape of Vishnu, particularly in the form of Krishna, to a third form, that of Siva. The determination of this third is the mode, alteration, coming-to-be and ceasing-to-be—the field of externality in general. This Indian trinity has misled to a comparison with the Christian and it is true that in them a common element of the nature of the Notion can be recognized; but it is essential to gain a more precise consciousness of the difference between them; for not only is this difference infinite, but it is the true, the genuine infinite which constitutes it. This third principle is, according to its determination, the dispersal of the unity of substance into its opposite, *not the return of the unity to itself*—not spirit but rather the non-spiritual. In the true trinity there is not only unity but union, the conclusion of the syllogism is a unity possessing *content* and *actuality*, a unity which in its wholly concrete determination is spirit. This principle of the mode and of alteration does not, it is true, altogether exclude the unity; in Spinozism, for example, it is precisely the mode as such which is untrue; substance alone is true and to it everything must be brought back. But this is only to submerge all content in the void, in a merely formal unity lacking all content. Thus Siva, too, is again the great whole, not distinct from Brahma, but Brahma himself. In other words, the difference and the determinateness only vanish again but are not preserved, are not sublated, and the unity does not become a concrete unity, neither is the disunity reconciled. The supreme goal for man placed in the sphere of coming-to-be and ceasing-to-be, of modality generally, is submergence in unconsciousness, unity with Brahma, annihilation; the Buddhist Nirvana, Nibbana etc., is the same.

Now although the mode as such is abstract externality, indifference to qualitative and quantitative determinations, and in essence the external and unessential elements are not supposed to count, it is still, on the other hand, admitted in many cases that everything depends on the kind and manner of the mode; such an admission means that the mode itself is declared to belong essentially to the substantial nature of a thing, a very indefinite connection but one which at least implies that this external element is not so abstractly an externality.

Here the mode has the specific meaning of measure. Spinoza's mode, like the Indian principle of change, is the measureless. The Greek awareness, itself still indeterminate, that everything has a measure—even Parmenides, after abstract being, introduced necessity as the ancient limit by which all things are bounded—is the beginning of a much higher conception than that contained in substance and in the difference of the mode from substance.

Measure in its more developed, more reflected form is necessity; fate, Nemesis, was restricted in general to the specific nature of measure, namely, that what is presumptuous, what makes itself too great, too high, is reduced to the other extreme of being brought to nothing, so that the mean of measure, mediocrity is restored. 'The absolute, God, is the *measure* of all things' is not more intensely pantheistic than the definition: 'The absolute, God, is *being*,' but it is infinitely truer. Measure, it is true, is an external kind and manner of determinateness, a more or less, but at the same time it is equally reflected into itself, a determinateness which is not indifferent and external but intrinsic; it is thus *the concrete truth of being*. That is why mankind has revered measure as something inviolable and sacred.

The Idea of *essence*, namely, to be self-identical in the immediacy of its determined being, is already immanent in measure; so that the immediacy is thus reduced by this self-identity to

L*

something mediated, which equally is mediated only through this externality, but is a mediation *with itself*—that is, reflection, the determinations of which *are*, but in this being are nothing more than moments of their negative unity. In measure, the qualitative moment is quantitative; the determinateness or difference is indifferent and so is no difference, is sublated. This nature of quantity as a return-into-self in which it is qualitative constitutes that being-in-and-for-itself which is essence. But measure is only *in itself* or in its Notion essence; this *Notion* of measure is not yet posited. Measure, still as such, is itself the *immediate [seiende]* unity of quality and quantity; its moments are determinately present as a quality, and quanta thereof; these moments are at first inseparable only in principle [*an sich*], but do not yet have the significance of this reflected determination. The development of measure contains the differentiation of these moments, but at the same time their *relation*, so that the identity which they are *in themselves* becomes their relation to each other, i.e. is *posited*. The significance of this development is the realization of measure in which it posits itself as in relation with itself, and hence as a moment. Through this mediation it is determined as sublated; its immediacy and that of its moments vanishes; they are reflected. Measure, having thus *realized* its own Notion, has passed into essence.

At first, measure is only an *immediate* unity of quality and quantity, so that: (1), we have a quantum with a qualitative significance, a *measure*. The progressive determining of this consists in *explicating* what is only *implicit* in it, namely, the difference of its moments, of its qualitatively and quantitatively determined being. These moments further develop themselves into wholes of measure which as such are *self-subsistent*. These are essentially in relationship with each other, and so measure becomes (2), a *ratio* of specific quanta having the form of self-subsistent measures. But their self-subsistence also rests essentially on quantitative relation and quantitative difference; and so their self-subsistence becomes a transition of each into the other, with the result that measure perishes in the *measureless*. But this beyond of measure is the negativity of measure only in principle; this results (3), in the positing of the *indifference* of the determinations of measure, and the positing of real measure—real through the negativity contained in the indifference—as an *inverse ratio of measures*

which, as self-subsistent qualities, are essentially based only on
their quantity and on their negative relation to one another,
thereby demonstrating themselves to be only moments of their
truly self-subsistent unity which is their reflection-into-self and
the positing thereof, *essence*.

The development of measure which has been attempted in the
following chapters is extremely difficult. Starting from immediate,
external measure it should, on the one hand, go on to develop
the abstract determination of the *quantitative* aspects of natural
objects (a mathematics of nature), and on the other hand, to
indicate the connection between this determination of measure
and the *qualities* of natural objects, at least in general; for the
specific proof, derived from the Notion of the concrete object, of
the *connection* between its qualitative and quantitative aspects,
belongs to the special science of the concrete. Examples of this
kind concerning the law of falling bodies and free, celestial motion
will be found in the *Encyclop. of the Phil. Sciences*, 3rd ed.,
Sections 267 and 270, Remark. In this connection the general
observation may be made that the different forms in which
measure is realized belong also to different spheres of natural
reality. The complete, abstract indifference of developed measure,
i.e. the *laws* of measure, can only be manifested in the sphere of
mechanics in which the concrete bodily factor is itself only *abstract*
matter; the qualitative differences of such matter are essentially
quantitatively determined; space and time are the purest forms
of externality, and the multitude of matters, masses, intensity of
weight, are similarly external determinations which have their
characteristic determinateness in the quantitative element. On
the other hand, such quantitative determinateness of abstract
matter is deranged simply by the plurality of conflicting qualities
in the inorganic sphere and still more even in the organic world.
But here there is involved not merely a conflict of qualities, for
measure here is subordinated to higher relationships and the
immanent development of measure tends to be reduced to the
simple form of immediate measure. The limbs of the animal
organism have a measure which, as a simple quantum, stands in a
ratio to the other quanta of the other limbs; the proportions of
the human body are the fixed ratio of such quanta. Natural
science is still far from possessing an insight into the connection
between such quantities and the organic functions on which they

wholly depend. But the readiest example of the reduction of an immanent measure to a merely externally determined magnitude is *motion*. In the celestial bodies it is free motion, a motion which is determined solely by the Notion and whose quantitative elements therefore equally depend solely on the Notion (see above); but such free motion is reduced by the living creature to arbitrary or mechanically regular, i.e. a wholly abstract, formal motion.

And in the realm of spirit there is still less to be found a characteristic, free development of measure. It is quite evident, for example, that a republican constitution like that of Athens, or an aristocratic constitution tempered by democracy, is suitable only for States of a certain size, and that in a developed civil society the numbers of individuals belonging to different occupations stand in a certain ratio to one another; but all this yields neither laws of measure nor characteristic forms of it. In the spiritual sphere as such there occur differences of *intensity* of character, *strength* of imagination, sensations, general ideas, and so on; but the determination does not go beyond the indefiniteness of *strength* or *weakness*. How insipid and completely empty the so-called laws turn out to be which have been laid down about the relation of strength and weakness of sensations, general ideas, and so on, comes home to one on reading the psychologies which occupy themselves with such laws.

CHAPTER I

SPECIFIC QUANTITY

Qualitative quantity in the *first* place an immediate, *specific quantum*. *Secondly*, this quantum as relating itself to another becomes a quantitative specifying, a sublating of the indifferent quantum. This measure is so far a *rule* and contains the two moments of measure distinguished; namely, the intrinsic quantitative determinateness and the external quantum. In this distinction, however, these two sides become qualities and the rule becomes a relation between them; consequently measure exhibits itself *thirdly*, as a relation of qualities. These at first have a single measure, but this is further specified within itself into distinct measures.

A. THE SPECIFIC QUANTUM

1. Measure is the simple relation of the quantum to itself, its own determinateness within itself; the quantum is thus qualitative. At first, as an immediate measure it is an immediate quantum, hence just some specific quantum or other; equally immediate is the quality belonging to it, some specific quality or other. The quantum as this no longer indifferent limit but as a self-related externality, is thus itself quality, and although distinguished from it does not transcend it, neither does the quality transcend the quantum. It is thus the determinateness which has returned into simple identity with itself, one with the specific determinate being, just as this latter is one with its quantum.

If it is desired to make a proposition out of the determination in question, it can be expressed thus: all that exists has a measure. Everything that exists has a magnitude and this magnitude belongs to the nature of the something itself; it constitutes its specific nature and its being-within-self. Something is not indifferent to this magnitude, so that if this were altered it would continue to be what it is; on the contrary, an alteration of the magnitude would alter the quality of the something. Quantum, as measure, has ceased to be a limit which is no limit; it is now the determination of the thing, which is destroyed if it is increased or diminished beyond this quantum.

A measure taken as a standard in the usual meaning of the word is a quantum which is arbitrarily assumed as the *intrinsically determinate* unit relatively to an external amount. Such a unit can, it is true, also be in fact an intrinsically determinate unit, like a foot and suchlike original measures; but in so far as it is also used as a standard for other things it is in regard to them only an external measure, not their original measure. Thus the diameter of the earth or the length of a pendulum may be taken, each on its own account, as a specific quantum; but the selection of a particular fraction of the earth's diameter or of the length of the pendulum, as well as the degree of latitude under which the latter is to be taken for use as a standard, is a matter of choice. But for other things such a standard is still more something external. These have further specified the general specific quantum in a particular way and have thereby become particular things. It is therefore foolish to speak of a *natural* standard of things. Moreover, a universal standard ought only to serve for *external* comparison; in this most superficial sense in which it is taken as a *universal measure* it is a matter of complete indifference what is used for this purpose. It ought not to be a fundamental measure in the sense that it forms a scale on which the natural measures of particular things could be represented and from which, by means of a rule, they could be grasped as specifications of a universal measure, i.e. of the measure of their universal body. Without this meaning, however, an absolute measure is interesting and significant only as a *common element*, and as such is a universal not in itself but only by agreement.

This immediate measure is a simple quantitative determination as, for example, the size of organic beings, of their limbs etc. But everything that exists has a size which makes it what it is, and in general enables it to have an external reality. As a quantum it is an indifferent magnitude open to external determination and capable of increase and decrease. But as a measure it is also distinguished from itself as a quantum, as such an indifferent determination, and is a limitation of that indifferent fluctuation about a limit.

Since the quantitative determinateness of anything is thus twofold —namely, it is that to which the quality is tied and also that which can be varied without affecting the quality—it follows that the destruction of anything which has a measure takes place through the alteration of its quantum. On the one hand this destruction appears as *unexpected*, in so far as the quantum can be changed without altering the measure and the quality of the thing; but on the other hand, it is made into something quite easy to understand through the idea of *gradualness*. The reason why such ready use is made of this category to render conceivable or to *explain* the disappearance of a quality or of something, is that it seems to make it possible almost to watch the disappearing with one's eyes, because quantum is posited as the external limit which is by its nature alterable, and so *alteration* (of quantum only) requires no explanation. But in fact nothing is explained thereby; the alteration is at the same time essentially the transition of one quality into another, or the more abstract transition of an existence into a negation of the existence; this implies another determination than that of gradualness which is only a decrease or an increase and is a one-sided holding fast to quantity.

2. The sudden conversion into a change of quality of a change which was apparently merely quantitative had already attracted the attention of the ancients who illustrated in popular examples the contradictions arising from ignorance of this fact; they are familiar under the names of 'the bald' and 'the heap'. These *elenchi* are, according to Aristotle's explanation, ways in which one is compelled to say the opposite of what one had previously asserted. The question was asked: does the pulling out of a single hair from the head or from a horse's tail produce baldness, or does a heap cease to be a heap if a grain is removed? An answer in the negative can be given without hesitation since such a removal constitutes only a quantitative difference, a difference moreover which is itself quite insignificant; thus a hair, a grain, is removed and this is repeated, only one of them being removed each time in accordance with the answer given. At last the qualitative change is revealed; the head or the tail is bald, the heap has disappeared. In giving the said answer, what was forgotten was not only the repetition, but the fact that the individually insignificant quantities (like the individually insignificant disbursements from a fortune) *add up* and the total constitutes the qualitative whole, so that finally this whole has vanished; the head is bald, the purse is empty.

The dilemma, the contradiction which results therefrom, is not a sophism in the usual sense of the word; for such contradiction is not a sham or a deception. The real mistake is committed by the assumed Other (i.e. our ordinary consciousness), the mistake, namely, of assuming a quantity to be only an indifferent limit, i.e. of assuming that it is just a quantity in the specific sense of quantity. This assumption is refuted by the truth to which it is brought —to wit, that quantity is a moment of measure and is connected with quality. What is refuted is the error of one-sidedly holding fast to the abstract determinateness of quantum. Therefore these examples, too, are not a pointless or pedantic joke but have their own correctness; they are the product of a mentality which is interested in the phenomena which occur in thinking.

Quantum, when it is taken as an indifferent limit, is the aspect of an existence which leaves it open to unsuspected attack and destruction. It is the cunning of the Notion to seize on this aspect of a reality where its quality does not seem to come into play; and such is its cunning that the aggrandizement of a State or of a fortune, etc., which leads finally to disaster for the State or for the owner, even appears at first to be their good fortune.

3. Measure in its immediacy is an ordinary quality with a specific magnitude attaching to it. Now that aspect of the quantum according to which it is an indifferent limit which can be exceeded without altering the quality, is also distinguished from its other aspect according to which it is qualitative and specific. Both are quantitative determinations of one and the same thing; but because of the initial immediacy of measure, this distinction is also to be taken as immediate, and therefore both aspects also have a distinct existence. The existence of measure, then, which is *intrinsically* determinate magnitude, is in its behaviour towards the existence of the alterable, external aspect, a sublating of its indifference, a *specifying* of measure.

B. SPECIFYING MEASURE

This is first a rule, a measure which is external with reference to mere quantum. Secondly it is a specific quantity which determines the external quantum, and thirdly *both sides*, as *qualities* of a specific quantitative determinateness, are related to one another as *one* measure.

(a) The Rule

The rule or standard, which has already been mentioned, is in the first place an intrinsically determinate magnitude which is a unit with reference to a quantum having a particular existence in a something other than the something of the rule; this other something is *measured* by the rule, i.e. is determined as an amount of the said unit. This *comparison* is an *external* act, the unit itself being an arbitrary magnitude which in turn can equally be treated as an amount (the foot as an amount of inches). But measure is not only an external rule; as a specifying measure its nature is to be related in its own self to an other which is a quantum.

(b) Specifying Measure

Measure is a specific determining of the *external*, i.e. indifferent magnitude which is now posited by some other existence in general in the measurable something; true, this latter is itself a quantum but, as distinguished from it, it is the qualitative side determining the merely indifferent, external quantum. The measurable something has in it this side of being-for-other to which the indifferent increasing and decreasing is proper. This immanent measuring standard is a quality of the something to which is opposed the same quality in another something; but in the latter something the quality is at first only relative, the quantum having no significance as a measure in relation to the other something which is determined as the standard of measuring.

Something, in so far as it is a measure within itself, has the magnitude of its quality altered from outside itself; it does not accept this externally imposed alteration as an arithmetical amount: its measure reacts against it, behaves towards the amount as an intensive quantum and assimilates it in a characteristic way; it alters the externally imposed alteration, makes this quantum into a different one and through this specifying shows itself to be *self*-determined in this externality. This *specifically assimilated* amount is itself a quantum which is also dependent on the other, or is for it only an *external* amount. Consequently the specified amount is also alterable, but is not therefore a quantum as such but the external quantum specified in a constant manner. The determinate being of measure is thus a *ratio*, the specific element of which is in general the *exponent* of this ratio.

When considering *intensive* and *extensive* quantum we found that it is the *same* quantum which is present, once in the form of intensity and again in the form of extension. In this difference the quantum lying at the base suffers no alteration, the difference being only an outer form. In the specifying measure, on the contrary, the quantum is taken in the first instance in its immediate magnitude, but in the second instance it is taken through the exponent of the ratio in another amount.

The exponent which constitutes the specific element can at first seem to be a fixed quantum, as a quotient of the ratio between the external and the qualitatively determined quantum. But as such, it would be nothing but an external quantum; the exponent here must be understood as nothing else but the qualitative moment itself which specifies the quantum as such. As we have already seen, the strictly immanent qualitative form of the quantum is solely its determination as a *power*. It must be such a determination which constitutes the ratio and which here, as the intrinsic determination of the quantum, confronts the quantum as externally constituted. The principle of the quantum is the numerical *one* which constitutes its intrinsic determinedness, and the mode of relation of the numerical one is external; and the alteration which is specified only by the nature of the immediate quantum as such, consists by itself in the addition of such a numerical one and then another and so on. If in this way the alteration of the external quantum is an arithmetical progression, the specifying reaction of the qualitative nature of measure produces another series which is related to the first, increases and decreases with it, but not in a ratio determined by a numerical exponent but in a number of incommensurable ratios, according to a determination of powers.

Remark

To cite an example, *temperature* is a *quality* in which these two sides of external and specified quantum are distinguished. As a quantum it is an external temperature, and that too, of a body as a general medium, and it is assumed that the alteration of the temperature proceeds on the scale of an arithmetical progression, increasing or decreasing uniformly. On the other hand, the particular bodies in the medium differ in the way they absorb the temperature, for through their immanent measure they determine it as received from outside themselves and the change of temperature in any one of them does not correspond in a direct ratio with that of the medium or of the other bodies among themselves. Different bodies compared at one and the same temperature give the numerical ratios of their specific heats, of their thermal capacities. But the thermal capacities of bodies vary in different temperatures and associated with this is a change in the specific shape. Thus a particular specification is manifested in the increase or decrease of temperature. The ratio of the temperature, taken as external, to the temperature of a specific body which is at the same time dependent on the former temperature, has no fixed exponent; the increase or decrease of this heat does not proceed uniformly with the increase or decrease of the external heat. Here a temperature is assumed which is purely external and whose changes are merely external or purely quantitative. But the temperature is itself the temperature of the air or some other specific temperature. The ratio, therefore, if looked at more closely, would strictly speaking have to be taken not as the ratio of a merely quantitative quantum to a qualitative one, but as the ratio of two specific quanta. In fact, the determining of the specifying ratio has now advanced to the stage where the moments of measure not only consist of a quantitative side and a side qualifying the quantum, both being sides of one and the same quality, but are related to each other as two qualities which are in themselves measures.

(c) *Relation of the two Sides as Qualities*
1. The qualitative, intrinsically determinate side of the quantum exists only as a relation to the externally quantitative side; as a specifying of the latter it is a sublating of its externality through which quantum as such is. This qualitative side thus has a quantum for its presupposition and its starting point. But this quantum is also qualitatively distinguished from the quality itself; this difference between them is now to be posited in the *immediacy* of being as such, in which determination measure still is. The two sides are thus qualitatively related and each is on its own account a qualitative determinate being; and the one quantum which at first was only a formal quantum indeterminate in itself, is the quantum of a something and of its quality, and also—now that the connection between them is determined as a measure—the specific magnitude of these qualities. These qualities are related

to each other according to their determination as measures—
which determination is their exponent. But they are already
implicitly related to each other in the *being-for-self* of measure;
the quantum in its dual character is both external and specific so
that each of the distinct quantities possesses this twofold determination and is at the same time inseparably linked with the other;
it is in this way alone that the qualities are determined. They are
therefore not only simply determinate beings existing for each
other but they are posited as inseparable and the specific magnitude
connected with them is a qualitative unity—a single determination
of measure in which, in accordance with their Notion, they are
implicitly bound up with each other. Measure is thus the *immanent*
quantitative relationship of *two* qualities to each other.

2. In measure there enters the essential determination of
variable magnitude, for measure is quantum as sublated, and
therefore no longer what, as quantum, it is supposed to be, but
quantum and something else; this something else is the qualitative
element and, as we have seen, is nothing else than its relation of
powers. In immediate measure this alteration is not yet posited;
it is only an arbitrary, single quantum to which a quality is bound.
In the specifying of measure (the preceding determination),
which is an alteration of the merely external quantum by the
qualitative element, there is posited the distinction between the
two specific magnitudes and hence generally the plurality of
measures in a common, external quantum. It is in this distinguishedness of the quantum from itself that it first shows itself
to be a real [*daseiendes*] measure; for it now appears as a determinate being which is both one and the same (e.g. the constant
temperature of the medium), and also quantitatively varied (in
the different temperatures of the bodies present in the medium).
This distinguishedness of the quantum in the different qualities
(the different bodies) gives a further form of measure, that in
which the two sides are mutually related as qualitatively determinate quanta. This can be called *realized measure*.

Magnitude, simply as magnitude, is alterable, for its determinateness is a limit which is at the same time no limit, so that
the alteration concerns only a particular quantum, the place of
which is taken by another. But the genuine alteration is that of
the quantum as such; when understood in this way, we have the
interesting determination of the variable magnitude in higher

mathematics; here we must not stop short at the merely formal determination of *variability* in general, neither must we introduce any determination other than the simple determination of the Notion according to which the *other of quantum is only quality*. The genuine determination, therefore, of real variable magnitude is that it is magnitude qualitatively determined, that is, as has been sufficiently demonstrated, determined by a ratio of powers. In this variable magnitude the fact is *posited* that what counts is not quantum as such but quantum determined in accordance with its other, i.e. qualitatively determined.

The two sides thus related have, in keeping with their abstract aspect as qualities generally, some particular significance—for example, space and time. Taken at first simply as specific magnitudes in their ratio as measures, one of them is an amount which increases and decreases in an external arithmetical progression, the other is an amount which is specifically determined by the first, which for it is unit. Now if each were only just a particular quality, that element of difference would be lacking which, with regard to their character as quantities, would indicate which of them was to be taken as merely externally quantitative and which as varying according to the specifying of its magnitude. If, for example, they are related as root and square, it is immaterial which is regarded as increasing or decreasing merely externally in arithmetical progression, and which, on the other hand, as specifically determining the other quantum.

But the difference between the qualities is not undefined, for as moments of *measure* the specifying of measure must be present in them. The next determinateness of the qualities themselves is that one is *extensive*—is in its own self externality—the other is *intensive*, the being-within-self or negative relatively to the other. Accordingly, the former of the quantitative moments is amount, and the latter is unit; in the simple direct ratio the former is to be taken as the dividend, the latter as divisor, and in the specifying ratio the former as the power or the becoming-other, the latter as the root. In so far as we still *count* here, i.e. still reflect on the external quantum (which is thus the quite contingent specific magnitude, the empirical amount), the alteration, too, being likewise taken as an external, arithmetical progression, then this falls on the side of the unit, of the intensive quality; the external, extensive side, on the other hand, is to be represented as altering in the specified series. But the direct ratio $\left(\text{like velocity as such, } \dfrac{s}{t}\right)$ is here reduced to the merely formal determination which has no existence except as an intellectual abstraction; and even though in the ratio of root and square (as in $s = at^2$) the root is to be taken as an empirical quantum varying in an arithmetical progression, and the other side is to be taken as specified, yet the higher realization of the qualifying of the quantitative, a realization more in harmony with the Notion, is that in which both sides are related to each other in higher determinations of powers (as is the case in $s^3 = at^2$).

Remark

The exposition here of the connection between the qualitative nature of something and its quantitative determination has its application in the already indicated example of motion. First of all, in *velocity* as the direct ratio of space traversed and time elapsed, the magnitude of time is taken as denominator while that of space is taken as numerator. If velocity as such is only a ratio of the space and time in a motion, it is immaterial which of the two moments is to be considered as amount or as unit. Space, however, like weight in specific gravity, is an external, real whole as such— hence amount—whereas time, like volume, is the ideal, negative factor, the side of unity. But here there essentially belongs the more important ratio, that which holds between the magnitudes of space and time in *free motion*; at first, in the still conditioned motion of a falling body where the time factor is determined as a root and the space factor as a square, or in the absolutely free motion of the celestial bodies where the period of revolution is lower by one power than the distance from the sun, the former being a square and the latter a cube. Fundamental relationships of this kind rest on the nature of the interrelated qualities of space and time and on the kind of relation in which they stand, either as a mechanical motion, i.e. as an unfree motion which is not determined by the Notion of the moments of space and time, or as the descent of a falling body, i.e. as a conditionally free motion, or as the absolutely free celestial motion. These kinds of motion, no less than their laws, rest on the development of the Notion of their moments, of space and time, since these qualities as such (space and time) prove to be in themselves, i.e. in their Notion, *inseparable* and their quantitative relationship is the being-for-self of measure, is only *one* measure-determination.

In regard to the absolute relations of measure, it is well to bear in mind that the mathematics of nature, if it is to be worthy of the name of science, must be essentially the science of measures— a science for which it is true much has been done empirically, but little as yet from a strictly scientific, that is, philosophical point of view. Mathematical principles of natural philosophy—as Newton called his work—if they are to fulfil this description in a profounder sense than that accorded to them by Newton and by the entire Baconian species of philosophy and science, must contain things of quite a different character in order to bring light into these still obscure regions which are, however, worthy in the highest degree of consideration. It is a great service to ascertain the empirical numbers of nature, e.g. the distances of the planets from one another; but it is an infinitely greater service when the empirical quanta are made to disappear and they are raised into a universal form of determinations of quantity so that they become moments of a *law* or of measure—immortal services which Galileo for the descent of falling bodies and Kepler for the motion of the celestial bodies have achieved. The laws they discovered they have proved in this sense, that they have shown the whole compass of the particulars of observation to correspond to them. But yet a still higher *proof* is required for these laws; nothing else, that is, than that their quantitative relations be known from the qualities or specific Notions of time and space that are correlated. Of this kind of proof there is still no trace in the said mathematical principles of natural philosophy, neither is there any in the subsequent works of this kind. It has already been remarked in connection with the show of mathematical proofs of certain relationships in nature, a show based on the misuse of the infinitely small, that it is absurd to try to demonstrate such proofs on a strictly mathematical basis, i.e. neither empirically nor from the standpoint of the Notion. These proofs *presuppose* their theorems, those very laws, from experience; what they succeed in doing is to reduce them to abstract expressions and convenient formulae. Undoubtedly the time will come when, with a clearer under- standing of what mathematics can accomplish and has accom- plished, the entire, real merit of Newton as against Kepler—the sham scaffolding of proofs being discarded—will clearly be seen to be restricted to the said transformation of Kepler's formula[1] and to the elementary analytical treatment accorded to it.

C. BEING-FOR-SELF IN MEASURE

1. In the form of specified measure just considered, the quantitative element of both sides is qualitatively determined (both in the ratio of powers); hence they are moments of *one* measure-determinateness of qualitative nature. At the same time, however, the two sides are so far posited only as immediate, *merely different* qualities, which do not themselves stand in the same relationship as their quantitative determinatenesses; that is, they cannot be said to have no meaning or existence *outside* that relationship, as is the case in the determinateness of quantity as a ratio of powers. The qualitative element thus masks itself, specifying not itself but the quantitative determinateness; only in the latter is it *posited*, remaining on its own account an *immediate* quality as such which, beside the fact that it explicitly differentiates the magnitude and beside its relation to its other, still has an independent determinate being of its own. Thus space and time, apart from that specification contained in their quantitative determinateness in the descent of a falling body, or in the absolutely free motion, count as space in general and time in general, space having an enduring existence of its own apart from and without time, and time flowing on its own independently of space.

This immediacy of the qualitative element as against its specific measure relation is, however, just as much bound up with a quantitative immediacy and with the indifference of this *quantitative* aspect in it towards this its relation; the immediate quality has also a merely *immediate quantum*. Consequently, the specific measure has also a side which is, to begin with, subject to external alteration in the sense of a merely arithmetical progression unaffected by the specific measure and in which falls the external, hence only empirical, determinateness of magnitude. Quality and quantum as thus also appearing outside the specific measure are at the same time correlated with it; immediacy is a moment

---

[1] See *Encyclopaedia of the Philosophical Sciences*, Remark on Section 270, on the transformation of Kepler's $\dfrac{S^3}{T^2}$ into Newton's $\dfrac{S^2 \times S}{T^2}$, the fraction $\dfrac{S}{T^2}$ being called the law of gravity.

of those sides which themselves belong to measure. Thus the immediate qualities also belong to measure, are likewise in relation and stand in a quantitative relationship which, as outside the specified determination, the ratio of powers, is itself only a direct ratio and an immediate measure. This conclusion and its import is to be indicated in more detail.

2. Even though the immediately determined quantum as such is, in virtue of its being a moment of measure, established as in itself determinable by the Notion, it is still with reference to the specific measure an externally given quantum. But the immediacy which is thus posited is the negation of the qualitative deter-mination of measure; this has already been demonstrated in respect of the sides of this determination of measure which for that reason appeared as independent qualities. Such negation and the return to the immediate determination of quantity lies in the qualitatively determined relation, for the relation of distinct terms as such implies their correlation as *one* determinateness which latter, in distinction from the determination of the relation, is here in the sphere of quantity a quantum. As a negation of the distinct qualitatively determined sides, this exponent is a being-for-self or absolute determinedness; but it is such being-for-self only *in principle* [*an sich*]; as a determinate being it is a simple immediate quantum which is the quotient or exponent of a direct ratio between the sides of the measure, but in general is the unit appearing as empirical, in the quantitative side of measure. In the motion of falling bodies the spaces traversed are proportional to the squares of the elapsed times, $s = at^2$. This is the specifically determined relation of space and time, a ratio of powers. The other, the direct ratio, would concern space and time as mutually indifferent qualities; it is supposed to be the ratio of the space traversed to the *first* unit of time. The same co-efficient a remains in all the following units of time—the *unit* being an ordinary quantum, while the *amount* is determined by the specifying measure. This unit at the same time counts as the exponent of that direct ratio which belongs to the imaginary, spurious velocity i.e. the merely formal velocity which is not specifically determined by the Notion. Such a velocity does not exist here, any more than the one previously mentioned which is supposed to accrue to the falling body at the *end* of a unit of time. That velocity was ascribed to the *first* unit of time in the motion of a falling body; but this

so-called unit of time is itself only an assumed unit and has as such
atomic point no real being. The beginning of the motion—the
alleged smallness of it could make no difference—is straightway a
magnitude and one specified by the law of descent of a falling body.
The said empirical quantum is attributed to the force of gravity,
on the supposition that this force itself has no connection with
the actual specification, with the ratio of powers characteristic of a
determination of measure. The *immediate* moment, that in the
motion of a falling body the amount of some fifteen spatial units,
taken as feet, is traversed in a unit—the so-called *first* unit—of
time, a second, is an immediate measure, like the measurements
of the limbs of the human body, the distances and diameters of
the planets and so forth. The determination of such a measure
falls elsewhere than in the qualitative measure determination
itself, here in the law of descent of a falling body; however, the
concrete sciences have so far failed to throw any light on the basis
of determination of such numbers, which are only immediate and
consequently are the empirical embodiment of a measure. Here
we are concerned only with the determinateness specified by the
Notion, namely, that the said empirical co-efficient constitutes
the moment of *being-for-self* in the measure-determination, and
that too only in so far as this moment is *unexplicated* [*an sich*],
and hence an immediacy. The second moment is the *developed*
side of this being-for-self, the specific measure determinateness of
the sides. In the motion of falling, a motion which is still half-
conditioned and half-free, gravity, according to this second
moment, is to be regarded as a force of nature, so that the relationship expressed by the law of descent of a falling body is determined
by the nature of space and time, and consequently the said specification, namely, the ratio of powers, falls within gravity; the
above-mentioned simple direct ratio expresses only a mechanical
relationship between space and time in the [merely] formal
velocity which is externally produced and determined.

3. Measure has now acquired the character of a specified
quantitative relation which, as qualitative, has in it the ordinary
external quantum; but this is not a quantum in general, but
essentially a determinant of the relation as such; hence in the
sense of an exponent, and by virtue of the immediacy of its
determination, of a fixed exponent, namely that of the already
mentioned direct ratio between the same qualities whose quantita-

tive relationship is at the same time specifically determined by the ratio. This direct ratio is, so to speak, anticipated and assumed as given in the example used of a measure, namely the law of descent of a falling body; but still, as we remarked, it does not *exist* in this motion. The fact, however, that the two sides of measure are themselves measures, the one immediate and external, and the other immanently specified, both being contained within the unity of measure itself, means that measure is now further determined, is *realised*. As this unity, measure contains the relation in which the magnitudes are determined and posited as differently specified by the nature of the qualities; its determinateness is accordingly wholly immanent and self-subsistent, and has at the same time collapsed into the being-for-self of an immediate quantum, the exponent of a direct ratio. The self-determination of the relation is thus *negated*, for in this its other it has its final, explicit determinateness; and conversely, the immediate measure which is supposed to be in its own self qualitative, possesses in truth such qualitative determinateness only in the other side of the relation. This negative unity is a *real being-for-self*, the category of a *something* as a unity of qualities which are related as measures—a completely *self-subsistent* something. The two sides which have presented themselves as distinct relations also immediately possess a twofold existence; or, to put it more explicitly, a self-subsistent whole of this kind, just because it is a real being-for-self, is at the same time a repulsion into *distinct self-subsistent* somethings whose qualitative nature and subsistence (materiality) lies in their measure determinateness.

CHAPTER 2

REAL MEASURE

Measure is now determined as a correlation of measures which constitute the quality of distinct self-subsistent somethings—or *things*. The relations of measure just considered concern abstract qualities like space and time; those now about to be considered are exemplified in specific gravity and later on in chemical properties, i.e. in determinations characteristic of *material* existence. Space and time are also moments of such measures but their relationship no longer depends simply on their own nature because they are now subordinated to further determinations. Among the determining moments in sound, for example, there is the *time* in which a number of vibrations occur, and the *spatial* element of length and thickness of the vibrating body; but the magnitudes of those ideal moments are determined externally. Space and time are no longer in a relation of powers but in the ordinary direct relation, harmony being reduced to a quite external simplicity of numbers whose relations can be grasped with the utmost ease and hence afford a satisfaction falling entirely within the element of sensation since there is an absence for spirit of figurate conception, fantasy, abstract thought, and the like. In that the sides which now constitute the measure relation are themselves measures, but at the same time real somethings, their measures are, in the first place, immediate measures and as regards their relations, direct relations. It is the inter-relationship of such relations that is now to be considered in its progressive determination.

Measure, as now real measure, is first, a self-subsistent measure of a material thing which is related to others and in this relation specifies them and with them their self-subsistent materiality. This specification as an external relating to a plurality of others in general, produces other relations and hence other measures; and the specific self-subsistence does not continue as a single direct relation but passes over into a specific determinateness which is a series of measures. Secondly, the direct relations thus produced are in themselves determinate and exclusive measures (elective affinities); but because the difference between them is also only quantitative, the progressive determination of the relations presents itself as in part a merely externally quantitative development which, however, is also interrupted by qualitative relationships and forms a *nodal line* of specific self-subsistent measure relations. Thirdly, however, in this development measure gives place to the *measureless* as such, and more specifically to the *infinity* of measure. In this, the self-exclusive and self-subsistent measures are one with each other, and the self-subsistent measure enters into a negative relation with itself.

A. THE RELATION OF SELF-SUBSISTENT MEASURES

Measures now are no longer merely immediate but self-subsistent, because they have become in themselves relations of measures which are themselves specified; and thus in this being-for-self are physical somethings, in the first instance, material things. The whole, which is a relation of such measures is, however, (*a*) first, itself *immediate;* thus the two sides which are determined as such self-subsistent measures exist apart in particular things and their *combination* is effected *externally*; (*b*) but what the self-subsistent material things are *qualitatively*, they are only in virtue of their *quantitative* determination as measures; hence through this same quantitative connection with others they are determined as *differently* specified in regard to them (so-called *affinity*), namely, as *members of a series* of such quantitative relationships; (*c*) at the same time, this *indifferent*, manifold inter-relationship finishes by converting itself into *exclusive* being-for-self—so-called *elective affinity*.

(*a*) Combination of Two Measures

Something is immanently determined as a measure relation of quanta which also possess qualities and the something is the connection of these qualities. One of them is the *being-within-self* or *inwardness* of the something by virtue of which it is a real being-for-self, a material thing (such as, taken intensively, weight, or in its extensive aspect, the multiplicity of *material* parts); the other quality is the *externality* of this inwardness (the abstract, ideal element of space). These qualities are quantitatively determined and their correlation constitutes the qualitative nature of the material something—e.g. the ratio of weight to volume: specific gravity. The volume, the ideal aspect, is to be taken as unit, but the intensive aspect, which manifests quantitatively and in comparison with the former as an extensive magnitude, as a plurality of independent ones, is to be taken as amount. The purely qualitative relation of the two specific magnitudes, that is, as a ratio of powers, has vanished, because with the self-subsistence of the material thing immediacy has returned and in this the specific magnitude is an ordinary quantum whose relation to the other side is likewise determined as the ordinary exponent of a direct ratio.

This exponent is the specific quantum of the something, but it is an immediate quantum and this is determined—and with it the specific nature of such something—only in the *comparison* with other exponents of such ratios. The exponent constitutes the specific intrinsic determinedness, the inner characteristic measure of something; but because this its measure rests on a quantum, it too is only an external, indifferent determinateness, with the consequence that the something, in spite of its inner determination as a measure, is alterable. The other to which it can, as alterable, enter into relation is not a material plurality, quantum in general— this it can withstand through its specific intrinsic determinedness —but it is a quantum which is at the same time also an exponent of such a specific ratio. Two things with different internal measures stand in relation and enter into combination—such as two metals of different specific gravities (the combination in question would not be, for example, of a metal and water); but what other kind of homogeneity is required to make possible such a combination will not be considered here. Now on the one hand, each of the two measures, just because it is a measure, preserves itself in the alteration which it ought to suffer through the externality of the quantum, but on the other hand this self-preservation is itself a negative relation towards this quantum, a specification of it; and since the quantum is the exponent of the measure relation, the self-preservation is an alteration of the measure itself and moreover a reciprocal specification.

As purely quantitatively determined, the compound would be a mere addition of the two magnitudes of the one quality and the two magnitudes of the other, e.g., the sum of the two weights and of the two volumes in the case of a compound of two material substances of different specific gravities; thus not only the weight of the mixture would remain equal to the said sum, but also the space occupied by the mixture would be equal to the sum of the said spaces. But this is true only of the weight of the mixture, which is equal to the sum of the weights before the combination; addition applies to that quality which, as a real being-for-self, has acquired a fixed determinate being with a permanent immediate quantum—the weight of the material thing, or, what counts as the same from the quantitative point of view, the number or amount of material parts. The exponents however are subject to alteration since they are the expression of the qualitative aspect of the compound, of its being-for-self in the form of measure relations; and since the quantum as such suffers contingent external alteration by an increase which is summed, the being-for-self at the same time displays itself as negating this externality. Because this immanent determining of the quantitative element cannot, as we have seen, be manifested in the weight, it displays itself in the other quality which is the ideal side of the relation. From the point of view of sense perception it may appear remarkable that the mixing of two specifically different material substances should be followed by an alteration—usually a diminution—in the sum of the two volumes, for it is space itself which constitutes the subsistence of matter in its external separated existence. But this subsistence in face of the negativity immanent in the being-for-self lacks intrinsic being, it is subject to alteration. In this manner space is posited as what it truly is, an ideal being [*das Ideelle*].

Not only, then, is one of the qualitative sides posited as alterable but measure itself—and so too the qualitative nature of the something based on it—has shown that it is unstable in its own self and, like the quantum as such, has its determinateness in other measure relations.

(b) Measure as a Series of Measure Relations

(1) If two things forming a compound body owed their respective specific natures only to a simple qualitative determination, they would only destroy each other when combined. But a thing which is an immanent measure relation is self-subsistent; it is therefore also capable of combining with another such thing. But in being reduced to an element of this unity, it preserves itself through

the persistence of its indifferent, quantitative character and at the same time functions as a specifying moment of a new measure relation. Its quality is masked in the quantitative element and is thus also indifferent towards the other measure, continuing itself in it and in the newly formed measure. The exponent of the new measure is itself only some quantum or other, an external determinateness, and its indifference finds expression in the fact that the specifically determined thing effects, in association with other such measures, precisely similar neutralizations of the reciprocal measure relations; it is in only one measure relation formed by itself and another specifically determined thing that its specific peculiarity is not expressed.

(2) This combination with a number of others which are likewise measures within themselves, yields different ratios which therefore have different exponents. The self-subsistent measure has the exponent of its intrinsic determinedness only in the comparison with others; its neutrality with the others, however, consititutes its real comparison with them; it is its comparison with them through its own self. But the exponents of these ratios differ and the qualitative exponent of the self-subsistent measure is thus represented as the *series* of these *different amounts* of which it is the *unit*, i.e. as a series whose members are in a specific relationship to others. The qualitative exponent, as one immediate quantum, expresses only one relation. The distinctive character of the self-subsistent measure finds its true expression in the characteristic series of exponents which it, taken as unit, forms with other such self-subsistent measures; for one of these measures when brought into relation with the rest of them and taken as unit forms another series. Now it is the interrelationship of the members of such a series that constitutes the qualitative aspect of the self-subsistent measure.

At first, it seems that a self-subsistent measure which forms a series of exponents with a series of such measures, is distinguished from another measure—outside this series—with which it is *compared*, by the fact that this other measure forms another series of exponents with the members of the first series. But in this way these two measures would *not be comparable*, because each is thus regarded as unit with respect to its exponents, and between the two series arising from this relation there is no *specified difference*. The two measures which, as self-subsistent, are supposed to be compared are at first contra-distinguished only as quanta; in order to determine their relation, an independent unit common to them both is required. This specific unit is to be sought, as has been indicated, only in that feature which embodies the specific determinate being of the measures to be compared, i.e. in the ratio which the exponents of the ratios of the members of the series have to each other. This ratio of the exponents themselves is, however, such independent and actually specific unit only in so far as the members of the series together have it as a *constant* ratio to both measures; in that way it can be *their common unit*. It is this alone, therefore, which makes it possible to compare the two self-subsistent measures which were assumed to be not reciprocally neutralising measures, but indifferent to each other. Each of them taken separately and apart from the comparison is the unit of the ratio it forms with the opposite members, which are the amounts relatively to that unit and which thus represent the series of exponents. But conversely, this series is the unit for the two measures which when compared with each other are related as quanta; as such they are themselves different amounts of the unit just indicated.

But further, those measures which together with the two, or rather indefinitely many self-subsistent measures of the first series—measures which are compared only with each other—yield a series of exponents of the ratios between the members of that series, are similarly in themselves self-subsistent measures, each being a specific something with its own intrinsic measure ratio. Each of these then is similarly to be taken as unit so that they have a series of exponents in the two, or rather indefinitely many members of the first series which are compared merely among themselves, and these exponents are the numbers resulting from comparison among themselves of the measures just named; and conversely, the comparative numbers of the measures which are now also to be taken singly as self-subsistent are the series of exponents for the members of the first series. In this way, both sides are series in which each number is firstly simply a unit to the opposite series in which it has its self-determined character as a series of exponents; secondly, each number is itself one of the exponents for each member of the opposite series; and thirdly, it is a comparative number for the other numbers of its series and as such amount, which belongs to it also as an exponent, it has its own specifically determined unit in the opposite series.

M

3. In this form of relationship there is a return to the particular kind of way in which quantum is posited as self-determined, i.e., as degree: namely, it is simple or unitary, but it has its quantitative determinateness in a quantum existing outside it, which is a circle of quanta. In measure, however, this external aspect is not merely a quantum and a circle of quanta, but a series of numerical ratios and it is in the entirety of these that the self-determinedness of measure lies. As is the case in the being-for-self of quantum as degree, the nature of the self-subsistent measure is converted into this externality of itself. Its self-relation is in the first place an *immediate* relation and therefore its indifference to an other consists only in the quantum. It is into this externality therefore that its qualitative side falls and its *relationship to its other* becomes that quantitative mode of relationship which constitutes the specific determination of this self-subsistent measure, a mode which is determined just as much by the other as by the measure itself; and this other is a series of quanta and the measure is reciprocally a quantum. But this relation in which two specific measures specify themselves in a third something, the exponent, also implies that the one has not passed into the other; that therefore there is not only *one* negation, but that *both* are posited as negative in the relation, and since in this each preserves itself as indifferent towards the other *its negation* is also in turn *negated*. This their qualitative unity is thus a self-subsistent *exclusive* unit. It is only as exclusive that the exponents, which are primarily comparative numbers of the members of the series, have in them their genuinely specific determinateness relatively to one another, and their difference thus acquires a qualitative nature. But this difference has a quantitative basis: first, the self-subsistent measure is related to a *plurality* of its qualitatively other side only because in this relationship it is, at the same time, indifferent; secondly, the neutral relationship, in virtue of its quantitative aspect, is now not simply an alteration but is posited as a negation of the negation and as an exclusive unit. Consequently, the *affinity* of a self-subsistent measure with the measures of the other side is no longer an indifferent relationship but an *elective affinity*.

(c) *Elective Affinity*

The expression *elective* affinity used here and the terms *neutrality* and *affinity* employed in the preceding paragraphs, refer to the *chemical* relationship. For a chemical substance has its specific determinateness essentially in its relation to its other and exists only as this difference from it. Furthermore, this specific relation is bound up with quantity and is at the same time the relation, not only to a single other but to a series of specifically different others opposed to it. The combinations with this series are based on a so-called affinity with *every* member of the series; but along with this indifference each member is at the same time exclusive towards the others and it is this correlation of opposed determinations which we have still to consider. It is, however, not only in the sphere of chemistry that the specific relation is represented in a circle of combinations; the individual note, too, only has meaning in relationship and combination with another note and with a series of others. The harmony or disharmony in such a circle of combinations constitutes its qualitative nature which is at the same time based on quantitative ratios; these form a series of exponents and are the ratios of the two specific ratios which each of the combined notes is in its own self. The individual note is the key of a system, but again it is equally an individual member in the system of every other key. The harmonies are exclusive elective affinities whose characteristic quality is equally dissolved again in the externality of a merely quantitative progression. What it is, however, that constitutes the principle of a measure for those affinities which (whether chemical or musical or what else) are elective affinities between and in opposition to the others, will be the subject of a further Remark in connection with chemical affinity; but this higher question is very closely bound up with the specific nature of the strictly qualitative aspect and belongs to the particular concrete natural sciences.

Inasmuch as the member of a series has its qualitative unity in its relation to all the members of an opposite series, whose members however are distinguished only by the quantum required for neutralizing them with the member of the first series, the more specific determinateness in this multiple affinity is likewise only quantitative. In elective affinity as an exclusive, qualitative correlation, the relationship is rid of this quantitative difference. The next determination which offers itself is this; that in accordance with the difference of the amounts, that is, of *extensive* magnitude, of the substances of the one series required for the neutralization of a substance in the other series, the elective affinity of the latter substance would also be directed towards the substances of the first series with all of which it has an affinity. The exclusion which would thereby be established in the form of a *firmer* holding together against other possibilities of combination, would appear, thus transformed, in a proportionately greater *intensity* in virtue of the previously demonstrated identity of the forms of extensive and intensive magnitude, the quantitative determinateness being one and the same in both forms. However, this sudden conversion of the one-sided form of extensive magnitude into its other, intensive form, makes no difference to the nature of the fundamental determination, which is one and the same quantum; consequently, no real exclusion would, in fact, result therefrom and there could take place equally well either only one combination, or a combination of an indefinite number of substances, provided that the portions of them entering into the combination corresponded to the required quantum in accordance with the ratios existing between them.

The combination which we have also called neutralization, however, is not only the form of intensity; the exponent is essentially a measure determination and therefore exclusive. In this aspect of exclusive relations, numbers have lost their continuity with one another and their fluid combinatory nature; the relationship is one of *more* or *less*, which acquires a negative character and the *preference* which one exponent has over another does not remain confined to the quantitative determinateness. But equally, too, there co-exists this other aspect which again makes it a matter of indifference that a substance receives the neutralizing quantum from several substances of the opposed series and from each according to its specific ratio relatively to the others; the exclusive, negative relation is thus at the same time adversely affected by the quantitative aspect. The effect of this is an actual conversion of an indifferent, merely quantitative relationship into a qualitative one, and conversely, a transition from a specifically determined relation into a merely external one—a series of relations which are sometimes of a merely quantitative nature and sometimes are specific relations and measures.

Remark: Berthollet on Chemical Affinity and Berzelius's Theory of it

Chemical substances are the most characteristic examples of those measures which, as moments of a measure, are characterized solely by their relationship to other such measure moments. Acids and alkalis or bases generally, appear to be intrinsically determinate things just as they are; but the fact is that they are incomplete elements of bodies, constituents which strictly speaking do not exist for themselves but only as a tendency to get rid of their isolatedness by combining with another constituent. Further, the difference in virtue of which they are *self-subsistent*, does not consist in this immediate quality but in the peculiar quantitative mode of the relationship. This, namely, is not restricted to the chemical opposition of acid and alkali or base in general, but is a specific *measure of saturation* and consists in the specific determinateness of the quantity of the substances which neutralize each other. This specific quantity required for saturation constitutes the qualitative nature of a substance; it makes it what it is on its own account and the number which expresses this is essentially one of several exponents for an opposed unit. A substance of this kind has a so-called affinity with another. If this connection remained of a purely qualitative nature, then, as in the case of the magnetic poles or positive and negative electricity, the one determinateness would be only the negative of the other and both sides would not at the same time show themselves to be indifferent towards each other. But because the connection has also a quantitative side, each of these substances is capable of neutralizing itself with *more* than one and is not restricted only to the one to which it is opposed. It is not only an acid and an alkali or base which are in relation, but acids and alkalis or bases which are related to one another. They are specifically distinguished from each other primarily according to whether one acid, for example, requires a greater amount of an alkali for its saturation than another acid does. But the independent, self-determined character of the substances is displayed in the exclusiveness of the relation between the affinities, one having a preference over another in that one acid can by itself enter into combination with any alkali, and conversely. Thus the cardinal difference between two acids consists in one of them having a closer affinity to a base than the other, i.e., in a so-called elective affinity.

The law of the chemical affinities of acids and alkalis has been discovered and it states that if two neutral solutions are mixed resulting in dissociation followed by two new compounds, these products, too, are neutral. From this it follows that the amounts of two alkaline bases required for the saturation of an acid must be in the same ratio to saturate another acid; and in general, when for one alkali, taken as unit, the series of numerical ratios has been determined in which the various acids saturate it, then this series is the same for any other alkali, though the different alkalis must be taken in different amounts relatively to one another—amounts which again on their part form a similar fixed series of exponents for each of the opposite acids since they are related to any one acid in the same ratio as to any other. Fischer[1] was the first to extract these series in their simplicity from the works of Richter,[2] and Berthollet.[3] Since that was written, our knowledge of the numerical ratios of mixtures of chemical elements has been greatly expanded in every direction and to consider it here would be a digression, all the more so because this empirical expansion which is in part only hypothetical remains confined within the same group of concepts. We may however add a few remarks on the categories employed here and also on the views about chemical elective affinity itself and its relation to the quantitative aspect as well as the attempt to base this on specific physical qualities.

It is well known that Berthollet modified the general conception of elective affinity by the concept of the activity of a *chemical mass*. This modification does not affect the quantitative ratios of the chemical laws of saturation themselves, but its effect on the qualitative moment of exclusive elective affinity as such is not only to weaken it but rather to eliminate it, and this is a point that must not be overlooked. If two acids act on an alkali and the one which has a greater affinity for it is also present in the requisite amount for saturating it, then according to the concept of elective affinity this is the only saturation which occurs; the other acid remains quite inactive and is excluded from the neutral combination. According to the concept of the activity of a *chemical mass*, on the other hand, each of the two acids is active in a proportion which is composed of the amounts of the acids present and their

[1] Fischer, Ernst Gottfried, 1754–1831. Professor of Physics at Berlin, Member of the Academy.

[2] Richter, Jeremiah Benjamin, 1762–1807. Bergassessor in Berlin. See his observations to the translation of Berthollet's treatise on *The Laws of Affinity in Chemistry*, p. 232.

[3] Berthollet, Claude Louis, Count, 1748–1822: *Statique Chimique*, I Part p. 134 *sqq*. Professor at the Polytechnic School in Paris.

saturation capacity or so-called affinity. Berthollet's investigations have indicated in greater detail the circumstances in which the activity of the chemical mass is nullified and one acid (the one with a stronger affinity) appears to expel and to *exclude* the action of the other acid (with a weaker affinity) that is, appears to be active in the sense of elective affinity. He has shown that this exclusion takes place in certain *circumstances*, such as strength of cohesion, or the insolubility in water of the salts formed, but the qualitative *nature* of the agents as such does not come into play; and the action of these circumstances can in turn be nullified by other circumstances, for example, by temperature. With the removal of these obstacles the chemical mass enters unimpeded into activity and what appeared as a purely qualitative exclusion, as an elective affinity, proves to depend only on external modifications.

It is Berzelius[1] principally who should be heard further on this subject although in his *Textbook of Chemistry* he does not put forward anything original or more specific on the matter. The views of Berthollet are taken up and repeated literally, only decked out in the metaphysics peculiar to an uncritical reflection, the categories of which are therefore all that offer themselves for a more detailed consideration. The theory goes beyond the limits of experience and, on the one hand, invents sensuous images such as are not given in experience and on the other hand, applies categories of thought, in both cases making itself a subject for logical criticism. We propose therefore to hear what he has to say about the theory in the *Textbook* itself. Now there we read 'that one *must imagine* that in a uniformly mixed liquid, each *atom* of the dissolved substance is *surrounded* by an *equal number* of *atoms* of the solvent; and if several substances are dissolved together they must *share between them* the *interstices* between the atoms of the solvent, so that with a uniform mixture of the liquid there is produced a *symmetry in the arrangement* of the atoms such that *all the atoms* of the individual substances are *uniformly arranged in relation to the atoms* of the other bodies; it could therefore be said that the solution is characterized by *symmetry in the arrangement* of the atoms, and the combination by the fixed proportions.'[2] This is then illustrated by an example of compounds formed when

[1] Berzelius, Johann Jakob, Baron von, 1779–1848: *Textbook of Chemistry*, 3 volumes, 1808–1828. From 1807 Professor of Chemistry at Stockholm.
[2] Vol. III, Section 1, Wöhler's translation, pp. 82 *sqq*.

sulphuric acid is added to a solution of copper chloride; but the example certainly does not demonstrate that *atoms* exist; neither does it show that a number of atoms of the dissolved substances *surround* atoms of the fluid, nor that free atoms of the two acids *arrange themselves around* the atoms which remain combined (with the copper oxide), nor that there exists a *symmetry* in their *position and arrangement*, nor that interstices between the atoms exist—and least of all that the dissolved substances *share among themselves* the *interstices* between the atoms of the solvent. This would mean that the atoms of the dissolved substances take up their positions where the solvent is *not*—for the interstices between the atoms of the solvent are spaces *empty* of it—and hence that the dissolved substances are *not* present in the solvent, but rather are *outside* it, even if the solvent is arranged around them or they around it, and it is also certain therefore that they are not dissolved by it. One fails therefore to see why it is *necessary* to form such conceptions which are not empirically demonstrated, are in essence directly self-contradictory and are not corroborated in any other way. Corroboration could be provided only by a consideration of these conceptions themselves, i.e. by metaphysics, which is logic; but this cannot confirm them any more than experience can—on the contrary! For the rest, Berzelius admits what was also said above, that Berthollet's propositions are not opposed to the theory of fixed proportions, although he does add that they are also not opposed to the views of the corpuscular theory, i.e. the ideas mentioned above of atoms, of the filling of the interstices of the solvent by the atoms of the solid substances, and so on; this latter baseless metaphysics however, has essentially nothing to do with the proportions of saturation as such.

Hence, what finds specific expression in the laws of saturation concerns only the amount of units themselves quantitative (not atoms), of a substance with which the quantitative *unit* (equally not an atom) of another substance chemically distinct from the first, is neutralised; the difference between them consists solely in these different proportions. When Berzelius, then, notwithstanding the fact that his theory of proportions is wholly and solely a determination of *amounts*, nevertheless also speaks of *degrees* of affinity[1] in explaining Berthollet's *chemical mass* as the sum of the *degree of affinity*, from the given quantity of the active

[1] For example, on p. 86.

substance—although Berthollet is more consistent for he uses the expression *capacité de saturation*—then he himself lapses into the form of *intensive* magnitude; but it is this form which is the characteristic feature of the so-called *dynamic* philosophy which earlier on he calls 'the speculative philosophy of certain German schools',[1] and emphatically rejects in favour of the excellent 'corpuscular theory'. He there states of this dynamic philosophy that it assumes that the elements *interpenetrate* one another in their chemical combination, and that neutralization consists in this *mutual interpenetration*; this means nothing else than that the chemically different particles, which are interrelated as a plurality, collapse into the simplicity of an *intensive* magnitude, a fact which also finds expression as a diminution of volume. In the corpuscular theory, on the other hand, even the atoms which are chemically *combined* are supposed to be preserved in the interstices, i.e. *outside* one another (juxtaposition); in such a relationship which is one of merely extensive magnitude, of a perpetuated *amount*, a *degree* of affinity has no meaning. In the same place it is stated that for the dynamic view the phenomena of specific proportions came as something quite unforeseen; but this would be only an external, historical circumstance, apart from the fact that Richter's stoechiometric series in Fischer's compilation of them were already known to Berthollet and are quoted in the first edition of this *Logic* which proves the nullity of the categories on which the old, like the would-be new, corpuscular theory is based. But Berzelius is in error when he judges that if 'the dynamic view' had prevailed, the phenomena of specific proportions would have remained 'for ever' unknown—meaning that this view is incompatible with the determinateness of proportions. This is, in any case, only a determinateness of quantity, no matter whether in an extensive or an intensive form; so that even Berzelius, much as he adheres to the first of these forms, that of aggregate or amount [*Menge*], himself makes use of the conception of degrees of affinity.

Since in this way affinity is reduced to a quantitative difference, it is sublated as *elective* affinity; but the *exclusive* factor which occurs in it is ascribed to *circumstances*, i.e. to determinations which appear as something external to the affinity, to cohesion, insolubility of the compounds formed, and so on. A partial

---

[1] P. 29, *loc. cit.*

M*

comparison may be made between this conception and the manner of considering the effect of gravity on a moving pendulum. Through gravity the pendulum necessarily passes into a state of rest; but this intrinsic effect of gravity itself is treated as a merely concomitant circumstance of the external resistance of the air, the thread and so on, and it is ascribed solely to *friction* instead of to gravity. Here it makes no difference to the nature of the *qualitative* element present in elective affinity whether this is manifested in the form of these circumstances taken as its conditions, and is so interpreted. With the qualitative aspect as such there begins a new order, the specifying of which is no longer only a matter of quantitative difference.

Now although the *chemical* affinity in a series of quantitative ratios has thus been accurately distinguished from *elective* affinity which occurs as a qualitative determinateness whose behaviour in no way coincides with the order of that series, this distinction in turn gets utterly confused by the way in which electrical action has recently been coupled with chemical action; and the hope that this supposedly profounder principle would throw light on the most important relation, that of measure, has met with complete disappointment. We need not here consider more closely this theory in which the phenomena of electricity and chemistry are completely *identified*, since it concerns the physical nature of substances and not merely their measure relations and it calls for mention only in so far as the distinctive character of the determinations of measure is confused by it. The theory as such must be dubbed shallow, for shallowness consists in omitting the difference between distinct terms and then treating them as identical. As for affinity, chemical processes being thus identified with electrical, and also with the phenomena of fire and light, this is reduced 'to neutralisation of opposite electricities'. It is almost comical to find the identification of electricity and chemical action expounded in the following manner: 'it is true that electrical phenomena explain the action of bodies at a greater or lesser distance, their *attraction* before combination (i.e. a behaviour which is not yet chemical) and the *fire*(?) caused by this combination, but they throw no light on the cause of the combination which persists with such strength *after* the opposite electrical condition has been destroyed;'[1] that is to say, the theory tells us

P. 63, *loc. cit.*

that electricity is the cause of the chemical action, but about the
specifically chemical nature of the chemical process electricity
tells us nothing. Chemical difference as such being thus reduced
to the opposition of positive and negative electricity, the different
affinities of the agents on either side are determined as the order
of two series of electro-positive and electro-negative substances.
In identifying electricity and chemical action it is overlooked that
the former generally (and its neutralization) is *transient* and
remains *external* to the quality of substances, whereas chemical
action, especially in the process of neutralization, embraces and
alters the entire qualitative nature of substances. Equally transient
within electricity is its opposition of positive and negative; this is
so unstable that it is dependent on the most trivial outer circumstances and cannot be compared with the definiteness and fixity
of the opposition between acids, for example, and metals, and so
on. The alterations which can be produced by chemical action
under extremely powerful influences, e.g., of a raised temperature
are not comparable with the superficial nature of the opposition in
electricity. Also the further distinction *within the series* of each of
the two sides, between a more or less positive-electrical or more or
less negative-electrical disposition is quite uncertain and entirely
unconfirmed. But it is on the basis of the 'electrical dispositions'
of these series of substances that 'the electro-chemical system
is to be set up, which above all would be best fitted to provide
an idea of chemistry'[1]: these series are now quoted; but what
their nature really is, is indicated in the remark 'that this is
approximately the order of these substances, but so little investigation has been made into this matter, that as yet *nothing really
certain* can be ascertained about this relative order.'[2] Both the
numerical ratios of the series of affinities (first made by Richter)
as well as the extremely interesting reduction by Berzelius of the
combinations of two substances to the simplicity of a few quantitative ratios, are absolutely independent of that hypothetical
electro-chemical hotch-potch. If the experimental method has
been the correct guiding star in the theory of proportions and its
universal expansion since Richter, then the mixing of these great
discoveries with the so-called corpuscular theory, a desert lying
away from the path of experience, forms all the greater contrast
with it; only this beginning, the abandoning of the principle of

[1] Berzelius, *op. cit.*, p. 84 *sq.*   [2] P. 67.

experience, could be the reason for taking up again and developing that idea introduced earlier, especially by Ritter,[1] namely, the setting up of fixed classifications of electro-positive and electro-negative substances, which classifications were also supposed to have a chemical significance.

Even if the opposition of electro-positive and electro-negative substances were more in keeping with the facts than it is, then the nullity of this assumed basis of chemical affinity soon shows itself even experimentally and this again leads to further inconsistencies. It is admitted that two so-called electro-negative substances such as sulphur and oxygen combine in a much more intimate way than, e.g. oxygen and copper, although the latter is electro-positive.[2] Here therefore, the basis for the affinity founded on the general opposition of positive and negative electricity must give place to a mere *more* or *less* within one and the same series of electrical quality. From this it is now inferred that the *degree of affinity* of the substances depends therefore not only on their specific *unipolarity* (with what hypothesis this determination is connected is irrelevant here; it is significant here only for the 'either' of the positive and the 'or' of the negative); the degree of affinity must be derived mainly from the *intensity* of their *polarity* generally. At this point then, the consideration of affinity passes on to the relationship of *elective* affinity which is our chief concern; let us see then what the result now is for this subject. It is at once admitted that the *degree* of this polarity, if this does not exist merely in our imagination, does not seem to be a *constant quality* but to depend very much on temperature;[3] so that, after all, the result turns out to be not only that every chemical action is therefore at bottom an electrical phenomenon, but also that what seems to be an effect of so-called elective affinity is brought about *only* by an electrical polarity which in certain substances is present in greater strength than in others. The conclusion then after all this meandering in hypothetical conceptions, is that we are left with the category of *greater intensity*, which is the same *formal* determination as elective affinity in general; and since the latter is made to depend on a greater intensity of electrical polarity, it is not a whit nearer to being put on a physical basis than it was

----

[1] Ritter, Johann Wilhelm, 1776–1810: *Das Elektrische System der Körper*, 3 volumes, 1805–1806. Member of the Academy of Munich.
[2] P. 73, *loc. cit.*   [3] *loc. cit.*, p. 73

before. But even what is here supposed to be determined as a greater specific intensity is subsequently reduced to the modifications demonstrated by Berthollet which have already been cited.

The merit and fame which Berzelius has earned by his theory of proportions, which has been extended to all chemical relations, ought not as such to be made a reason for not setting forth the weaknesses of this theory; but a more particular reason for doing so must be the circumstance that such merit in one aspect of a science, as with Newton, tends to become an *authority* for a baseless structure of spurious categories which is attached to it and that it is just this kind of metaphysics which is proclaimed and echoed too with the greatest pretension.

Apart from the forms of measure relation connected with chemical and elective affinity, others too can be considered with respect to quantities which are specified into a system. Chemical substances form a system of relations with respect to saturation; saturation itself rests on the specific proportion in which the reciprocal amounts of two substances, each of which has a particular material existence, combine with each other. But there are also measure relations the moments of which are inseparable and cannot be displayed in a separate and distinct existence of their own. These are what we called earlier on, *immediate self-subsistent* measures and which are displayed in the *specific gravities* of substances. They are a ratio within the substances of weight to volume; the exponent of the ratio, which is the expression of the difference between one specific gravity and another, is a definite quantum only as a result of *comparison*. This is a relationship external to the substances in an external reflection, and is not founded on the one substance's own qualitative behaviour towards another contrasted substance. The problem would be to recognize the exponents of the ratios of the series of specific gravities as a *system* based on a *rule* which would specify a merely arithmetical plurality into a series of harmonic nodes. The same demand would apply to our knowledge of the series of chemical affinities already mentioned. But the accomplishment of this task still lies a long way ahead, as far ahead as the problem of grasping the numbers of the relative distances of the planets from the sun as elements in a system of measure.

Although at first specific gravities do not seem to have any qualitative relationship to one another, yet they likewise enter into a qualitative relation. When substances are chemically combined, or even form only amalgams or synsomates, there occurs also a *neutralization* of the specific gravities. We mentioned earlier on the fact that the volume of a mixture, even a mixture of substances remaining really indifferent chemically to each other, is not of the same magnitude as the sum of the volumes of the substances before mixing. There is a reciprocal modification in the mixture of the quantum of specific gravity with which the substances enter into the relation and in this way they indicate their qualitative behaviour towards each other. Here the quantum of specific gravity is expressed not merely as a fixed *comparative number*, but as a *numerical ratio* which can be varied; and the exponents of the mixtures give series of measures the specifying principle of which is other than the numerical ratios of the specific gravities of the substances in combination. The exponents of these ratios are not exclusive determinations of measure; their progress is continuous but it contains an immanent specifying law which is distinct from the formally progressive ratios in which the amounts are combined and makes the former progress incommensurable with the latter.

B. NODAL LINE OF MEASURE-RELATIONS

The last determination of the measure relation was that being specific it is *exclusive*; the neutrality is exclusive because it is a *negative* unity of the distinct moments. For the relation of this *self-subsistent* unity, of the elective affinity to the other neutralities, no further principle of specification has offered itself; the specification resides only in the quantitative determination of affinity in general, according to which the amounts which neutralize themselves are specific and therefore stand opposed to other relative elective affinities of their moments. But further, because the fundamental determination is quantitative, the *exclusive* elective affinity also continues itself into the opposed neutralities; and this continuity is not only an external relation of the different ratios of the neutralities in the form of a comparison, but the neutrality is, as such, *separable into the moments* which united to produce it, since it is as self-subsistent somethings that these enter into relation indifferently with one or the other of the opposite series, although combining in different, specifically determined amounts. This measure, based on such a relation, is thus infected with its own indifference; it is in its own self something external and alterable in its relation to itself.

The relation *to itself* of the measure relation is distinct from its externality and alterableness which represent its quantitative aspect. As related to itself in contrast to these, it is an affirmatively present [*seiende*], qualitative foundation—a permanent, material substrate which, as also the continuity of the measure *with itself* in its externality, must contain in its quality the principle of the specification of this externality referred to above.

Now the exclusive measure as thus more precisely determined is external to itself in its being-for-self and hence repels itself from itself, positing itself both as another measure relation and also as another, merely quantitative, relation; it is determined as in itself a specifying unity which produces measure relations within itself. These relations differ from the affinities of the kind above-mentioned in which a self-subsistent measure relates itself to self-subsistent measures of a different quality and to a series of such. They take place in *one and the same* substrate within the same moments of the neutrality; the self-repelling measure develops other, merely quantitatively different relations which likewise form affinities and measures, alternating with those which remain only *quantitatively* different. They form in this way a nodal line of measures on a scale of more and less.

Here we have a measure relation, a self-subsistent reality which is qualitatively distinguished from others. Such a being-for-self, because it is at the same time essentially a relation of quanta, is open to externality and to quantitative alteration; it has a range within which it remains indifferent to this alteration and does not change its quality. But there enters a point in this quantitative alteration at which the quality is changed and the quantum shows itself as specifying, so that the altered quantitative relation is converted into a measure, and thus into a new quality, a new something. The relation which has taken the place of the first is determined by this, partly according to the qualitative identity of the moments which are in affinity, and partly according to the quantitative continuity. But because the difference falls into this quantitative aspect, the relation between the new something and its predecessor is one of indifference; their difference is the external one of quantum. The new something has therefore not emerged from or developed out of its predecessor but directly from itself, that is, from the inner specifying unity which has not yet entered into existence. The new quality or new something is subjected to the same progressive alteration, and so on to infinity.

Since the progress from one quality [to another] is in an uninterrupted continuity of the quantity, the ratios which approach a specifying point are, quantitatively considered, only distinguished by a more and a less. From this side, the alteration is *gradual*. But the gradualness concerns merely the external side of the alteration, not its qualitative aspect; the preceding quantitative relation which is infinitely near the following one is still a different qualitative existence. On the qualitative side, therefore, the gradual, merely quantitative progress which is not in itself a limit, is absolutely interrupted; the new quality in its merely quantitative relationship is, relatively to the vanishing quality, an indifferent, indeterminate other, and the transition is therefore a *leap*; both are posited as completely external to each other. People fondly try to make an alteration *comprehensible* by means of the gradualness of the transition; but the truth is that gradualness is an alteration which is merely indifferent, the opposite of qualitative change. In gradualness too, the connection of the two realities, whether these are taken to be states or self-subsistent things, is eliminated; gradualness necessarily implies that neither of the two is the limit of the other but that each is completely external to the other. In this way there is eliminated the very factor which is necessary for an *understanding* of change, although little enough is required for that purpose.

Remark: Examples of Such Nodal Lines; the Maxim, 'Nature Does Not Make Leaps'

The system of natural numbers already shows a nodal line of qualitative moments which emerge in a merely external succession. It is on the one hand a merely quantitative progress and regress, a perpetual adding or subtracting, so that each number has the same *arithmetical* relation to the one before it and after it, as these have to their predecessors and successors, and so on. But the numbers so formed also have a *specific* relation to other numbers preceding and following them, being either an integral multiple of one of them or else a power or a root. In the musical scale which is built up on quantitative differences, a quantum gives rise to an harmonious relation without its own relation to those on either side of it in the scale differing from the relation between these again and their predecessors and successors. While successive notes seem to be at an ever-increasing distance from the keynote, or numbers in succeeding each other arithmetically seem only to become other numbers, the fact is that there suddenly emerges a *return*, a surprising accord, of which no hint was given by the quality of what immediately preceded it, but which appears as an *actio in distans*, as a connection with something far removed. There is a sudden interruption of the succession of merely indifferent relations which do not alter the preceding specific reality or do not even form any such, and although the succession is continued quantitatively in the same manner, a specific relation breaks in *per saltum*.

Such qualitative nodes and leaps occur in chemical combinations when the mixture proportions are progressively altered; at certain points in the scale of mixtures, two substances form products exhibiting particular qualities. These products are distinguished from one another not merely by a more or less, and they are not already present, or only perhaps in a weaker degree, in the proportions close to the nodal proportions, but are bound up with these nodes themselves. For example, different oxides of nitrogen and nitric acids having essentially different qualities are formed only when oxygen and nitrogen are combined in certain specific proportions, and no such specific compounds are formed by the intermediate proportions. Metal oxides, e.g. the lead oxides, are formed at certain quantitative points of oxidation and are distinguished by colours and other qualities. They do not pass gradually into one another; the proportions lying in between these nodes do not produce a neutral or a specific substance. Without having passed through the intervening stages, a specific compound appears which is based on a measure relation and possesses characteristic qualities. Again, water when its temperature is altered does not merely get more or less hot but passes through from the liquid into either the solid or gaseous states; these states do not appear gradually; on the contrary, each new state appears as a leap, suddenly interrupting and checking the gradual succession of temperature changes at these points. Every birth and death, far from being a progressive gradualness, is an

interruption of it and is the leap from a quantitative into a qualitative alteration.

It is said, *natura non facit saltum*; and ordinary thinking when
it has to grasp a coming-to-be or a ceasing-to-be, fancies it has
done so by representing it as a *gradual* emergence or disappearance.
But we have seen that the alterations of being in general are not
only the transition of one magnitude into another, but a transition
from quality into quantity and *vice versa*, a becoming-other
which is an interruption of gradualness and the production of
something qualitatively different from the reality which preceded
it. Water, in cooling, does not gradually harden as if it thickened
like porridge, gradually solidifying until it reached the consistency
of ice; it suddenly solidifies, all at once. It can remain quite fluid
even at freezing point if it is standing undisturbed, and then a
slight shock will bring it into the solid state.

In thinking about the gradualness of the coming-to-be of
something, it is ordinarily assumed that what comes to be is
already sensibly or *actually in existence*; it is not yet perceptible
only because of its smallness. Similarly with the gradual disappearance of something, the *non-being* or the other which takes
its place is likewise assumed to be *really there*, but not yet obser-
vable, and *there*, too, not in the sense of being implicitly or ideally
contained in the first something, but *really there*, only not obser-
vable. In this way, coming-to-be and ceasing-to-be lose all
meaning; that is to say, the form of the in-itself, the inner being
of something before it actually exists, is transformed into a
smallness of an outer existence, and the essential difference,
that of the Notion, is converted into an external difference of mere
magnitude. The attempt to explain coming-to-be or ceasing-to-be
on the basis of the gradualness of the alteration is tedious like any
tautology; what comes to be or ceases to be is assumed as already
complete and in existence beforehand and the alteration is turned
into a mere change of an external difference, with the result that
the explanation is in fact a mere tautology. The intellectual
difficulty attendant on such an attempted explanation comes from
the qualitative transition from something into its other in general,
and then into its opposite; but the *identity* and the *alteration* are
misrepresented as the indifferent, external determinations of the
quantitative sphere.

In the moral sphere, in so far as it is considered under the categories of being, there occurs the same transition from quantity into quality and different qualities appear to be based on a difference of magnitude. It is through a more and less that the measure of frivolity or thoughtlessness is exceeded and something quite different comes about, namely crime, and thus right becomes wrong and virtue vice. Thus states, too, acquire through their quantitative difference, other things being assumed equal, a distinct qualitative character. With the expansion of the state and an increased number of citizens, the laws and the constitution acquire a different significance. The state has its own measure of magnitude and when this is exceeded this mere change of size renders it liable to instability and disruption under that same constitution which was its good fortune and its strength before its expansion.

C. THE MEASURELESS

The exclusive measure, even in its realised being-for-self, remains burdened with the moment of quantitative determinate being and is therefore open to movement up and down a scale of fluctuating ratios. Something, or a quality, based on such a ratio is impelled beyond itself into the *measureless* and is destroyed by the mere alteration of its magnitude. Magnitude is that side of determinate being through which it can be caught up in a seemingly harmless entanglement which can destroy it.

The abstract measureless is the quantum as such which lacks an inner significance and is only an indifferent determinateness which does not alter the measure. Measure in the nodal line of measures is at the same time posited as specifying and the abstract measureless raises itself into a qualitative determinateness; the new measure relation into which the original one passes is, with respect to this, measureless, but in its own self it is equally a quality on its own account. Thus there is posited the alternation of specific existences with one another and of these equally with relations remaining merely quantitative—and so on *ad infinitum*. What therefore is present in this transition is both the negation of the specific relations and the negation of the quantitative progress itself—the *infinite* which is *for itself*. The *qualitative* infinite, as simply a determinate being, was the eruption of the infinite in the finite as an *immediate transition* and vanishing of the latter in its beyond. The *quantitative* infinite on the other hand is, simply by virtue of its determinateness, the *continuity* of the quantum, a continuity of it into its be*yond*. The qualitative finite *becomes* the infinite; the quantitative finite is in its own self its beyond and *points beyond itself*. But this infinity of the specification of measure *posits* both the qualitative and the quantitative as *sublating* themselves in each other, and hence posits their first, immediate *unity*, which is measure as such, as returned into itself and therefore as itself *posited*. The transition of the qualitative, of one specific existence, into another, is such that all that occurs is an alteration of the specific magnitude of a ratio. Hence the alteration of the qualitative itself into the qualitative is posited as an external and indifferent change, as a coming together with itself; moreover, the quantitative, in being converted into the qualitative, into that which is determined in and for itself, sublates itself. This unity which thus continues itself into itself in its alternating measures is the truly persisting, self-subsistent material substance or thing.

What therefore is present here is (α) one and the same thing which is posited as the perennial substrate of its differentiations. This severance of being from its determinateness begins already in quantum as such; under the category of *magnitude*, a thing is indifferent to its affirmative determinateness. In measure, the thing itself is already in itself the unity of its qualitative and quantitative moments, the two moments which constitute the element of difference within the general sphere of being and of which one is the beyond of the other; in this way the perennial substrate has directly in its own self the determination of affirmative infinity. (β) This self-sameness of the substrate is *posited* in the fact that the qualitative self-subsistent measures into which the specifying unity is dispersed consist only of quantitative differences, so that the substrate continues itself into this differentiation of itself; (γ) in the infinite progress of the nodal series there is posited the continuation of the qualitative moment into the quantitative progress as into an indifferent alteration, but equally too, there is posited the negation of the qualitative moment contained therein and hence of the merely quantitative externality too. The quantitative reference beyond itself to an other which is itself quantitative perishes in the emergence of a measure relation, of a quality; and the qualitative transition is sublated in the very fact that the new quality is itself only a quantitative relation. This transition of the qualitative and the quantitative into each other proceeds on the basis of their unity, and the meaning of this process is only to *show* or to *posit* the *determinate being* of such a substrate underlying the process, a substrate which is their unity.

In the series of self-subsistent measure relations the one-sided members of the series are immediately qualitative somethings (specific gravities or chemical substances, bases, alkalis, or acids for example), and then their neutralizations (by which must also be understood here the compounds of substances of different specific gravity) are self-subsistent and even exclusive measure relations, self-determined and mutually indifferent totalities of determinate being. Now such relations are determined only as nodal points of one and the same substrate. Consequently, the measures and the self-subsistent things posited with them are reduced to *states*. The alteration is only change of a *state*, and the *subject* of the transition is posited as remaining the *same* in the process.

Surveying the progressive determinations which measure has passed through we can summarise them as follows. Measure is, in the first instance, only the immediate unity of quality and quantity as an ordinary quantum which is, however, specific. As thus a specific quantity which is related not to another but to itself, it is essentially a *ratio*. It therefore also contains its moments as sublated and undivided within itself; as is always the case in a Notion, the difference in the ratio is present in such a manner that each of its moments is itself a unity of quality and quantity. The difference therefore is real and yields a number of measure relations which, as formal totalities in themselves, are self-subsistent. The two series formed by the sides of these ratios are the same constant arrangement for each individual member which, as belonging to one side, enters into relationship with all the members of the opposite series. This unity as a mere *arrangement* is still quite external, and although it shows itself to be an immanent specifying unity of a self-subsistent measure distinguished from its specifications, it is not yet the free Notion which alone gives its differences an immanent determination: it is as yet only a substrate, a material, and for its differentiation into totalities, i.e., into differences embodying the nature of the unchanged substrate, it is dependent solely on the external, quantitative determination which shows itself at the same time as a difference of quality. In this unity of the substrate with itself the measure determination is sublated and its quality is an external state determined by the quantum. This process is equally the progressive determination of measure in its realization and also the reduction of measure to the status of a moment.

CHAPTER 3

THE BECOMING OF ESSENCE

A. ABSOLUTE INDIFFERENCE

Being is the abstract equivalence [*Gleichgültigkeit*]—for which, since it is to be thought of by itself as *being*, the expression indifference [*Indifferenz*] has been employed—in which there is supposed to be as yet no determinateness of any kind; pure quantity is indifference as open to all determinations provided that these are external to it and that quantity has no immanent connection with them; but the indifference which can be called absolute is the indifference which, *through the negation* of every determinateness of being, i.e., of quality, quantity, and their at first immediate unity, measure, is a process of *self-mediation* resulting in a simple unity. Any determinateness it still possesses is only a *state*, i.e. something qualitative and external which has the indifference for a *substrate*.

But what has thus been determined as qualitative and external is only a vanishing determinateness; quality as thus external to being is the opposite of itself and as such is only the sublation of itself. In this manner, the determinateness is still only posited in the substrate as an empty differentiation. But it is just this empty differentiation which is indifference itself as a result; and indifference is thus concrete, a mediation-with-self through the negation of every determination of being. As this mediation it contains negation and relation, and what was called state is its immanent, self-related differentiation; it is precisely externality and its vanishing which make the unity of being into indifference and they are therefore *within* this indifference, which therewith ceases to be only a substrate and *in its own self* only abstract.

B. INDIFFERENCE AS INVERSE RATIO OF ITS FACTORS

We have now to see how this determination of indifference is posited within the indifference itself and how the latter is therewith posited as being for itself.

1. The reduction of measure relations which at first ranked as self-subsistent measures, establishes their common substrate;

this is their continuation into one another and hence the indivisible self-subsistent measure which is *wholly* present in its differentiations. For this difference, there are present the determinations of quality and quantity which the measure contains, and everything turns solely on how these are posited in it. This, however, is determined by the fact that the substrate is in the first place a result and only *in principle* [*an sich*] a mediation; but because this mediation is not yet posited as such *in the measure itself*, this latter is in the first place a substrate and with respect to determinateness, *indifference*.

Consequently, at first it is essentially the merely quantitative external difference which is present in it; there are two distinct quanta of one and the same substrate which in this way would be their *sum* and therefore would itself be determined as quantum. But the indifference is this fixed measure, the implicit, absolute limit, only in *relation* to those differences in such a manner that it would not be in its own self a quantum or opposed in any way, either as a sum or even as an exponent, to other quanta whether sums or indifferences. It is only the abstract determinateness which falls into the indifference; the two quanta, in order that they may be posited in it as moments, are variable, indifferent, greater or smaller relatively to one another. Bounded however by the fixed limit of their sum, they are related to each other not externally but negatively, and this now is the qualitative determination of their relationship. They are consequently *inversely proportional*. This relation is distinguished from the earlier formal inverted relation or inverse ratio by the fact that here the whole is a real substrate and each of the two sides is posited as having to be itself *in principle* [*an sich*] this whole.

According to the stated qualitative determinateness, the difference is present, further, as *two qualities*, one of which is sublated by the other; but because both are held in a unity which they together constitute, neither is separable from the other. The substrate itself, as an indifference, is likewise in itself the unity of both qualities; therefore each side of the relation, too, contains both sides within itself and is distinguished from the other side only by a more of the one quality and a less of the other, and *vice versa*. The one quality is through its quantum only *preponderant* in the one side, and so, too, the other quality in the other side.

Consequently each side is in its own self an inverted relation. As formal, this relation recurs in the two distinct sides. These sides thus continue themselves into each other also in respect of their qualitative determinations; each quality is self-related in the other and is present in each of the two sides, only in a different quantum. Their quantitative difference is that indifference in accordance with which they continue themselves into each other and this continuation as the self-sameness of the qualities is in each of the two unities. The sides, however, each as the whole of the two determinations and hence containing the indifference itself, are thus at the same time posited as self-subsistent relatively to each other.

2. As this indifference, being is now the specification of measure no longer in its immediacy, but measure as developed in the manner just indicated; it is *indifference* first as *in itself*, the whole of the determinations of being which are resolved into this unity and secondly, as a *determinate being*, as a totality of the posited realization, in which the moments themselves are implicitly the totality of the indifference, borne by this latter as their unity. But because the unity is only an *indifference*, and hence is held fast only as an *implicit* unity, and the moments are not yet explicitly *self-determined*, i.e. are not yet determined as sublating themselves into a unity *within themselves* and *through one another*, what is here present is simply the *indifference* of the unity itself *towards itself* as a developed determinateness.

This self-subsistent measure as thus indivisible is now to be considered in more detail. It is immanent in all its determinations and in them remains in unity with itself and unaffected by them; but (α) as remaining *implicitly* the totality, it possesses the determinatenesses which are sublated in it, only as groundlessly *emerging* in it. The *implicit* being of the indifference and this *real* being of the latter are unconnected; the determinatenesses show themselves in the indifference in an immediate manner and the indifference is wholly present in each of them. Consequently, the difference between them is posited in the first place as sublated, therefore as only *quantitative*, but not as the self-repulsion of the indifference, and the indifference is not posited as self-determining but as being determinate and determined only *externally*. (β) The two moments are in an inverted quantitative relation—a to and fro in the scale of magnitude; but this fluctuation is determined

not by the indifference, which is just the indifference of this
fluctuation, but is determined herewith only externally. The
principle of determination resides not in the indifference, but in
something lying outside it. The absolute, as indifference, has in
this aspect the second defect of the *quantitative* form, namely
that the determinateness of the difference is not determined by the
absolute itself; just as it has the first defect in the fact that the
differences simply *emerge* in it, that is to say, the absolute's
positing is immediate in character, is not the mediation of the
absolute with itself. (γ) The quantitative determinateness of the
moments which are now *sides* of the relation constitutes this mode
of their *subsistence*; through this indifference their determinate
being is freed from the transition of the qualitative sphere. But in
distinction from this their real being, they have an implicit
subsistence in the fact that they are *in themselves* the indifference
itself, each being itself the unity of the two *qualities* into which the
qualitative moment splits itself. The difference between the two
sides is restricted to this, that one quality is posited in the one side
with a more and in the other with a less, and the other quality
similarly, but conversely. Hence each side is in its own self the
totality of the indifference. Each of the two qualities taken singly
on its own account also remains the same sum which the indifference is; it continues itself out of the one side into the other
and is not bounded by the quantitative limit which is thereby
posited in it. In consequence of this the determinations come into
immediate opposition and this develops itself into a contradiction
which we have now to consider.

3. Namely, each quality enters *within* each side into relation to
the other, and does so in such a manner that, as has been determined, this relation too is to be only a quantitative difference.
If the two qualities are self-subsistent—taken, say, as if they were
sensuous things independent of each other—then the whole
determinateness of indifference falls asunder; their unity and
totality would be empty names. But they are at the same time
expressly determined as comprised in a single unity, as inseparable,
each as having meaning and reality only in this one qualitative
relation to the other. But now, *because their quantitativity is simply
and solely of this qualitative nature, each reaches only as far as the
other*. If the qualities are regarded simply as distinct quanta, then
the one would reach beyond the other and would have in its *more*

an indifferent determinate being which the other would not have. But in their qualitative connectedness, each is only in so far as the other is. From this it follows that they are in *equilibrium*; that by as much as the one increases or decreases, the other likewise would increase or decrease and in the same proportion.

Therefore on the basis of their *qualitative* connection there can be no question of a *quantitative* difference or of a *more* of the one quality. The more by which *one* of the correlated moments would exceed the *other* would only be a baseless determination, or else this *more would only be the other itself again*; but in this their equality, both would have vanished, for their determinate being was supposed to be based solely on the inequality of their quantum. Each of these hypothetical factors vanishes, whether it is supposed to be *beyond* or *equal to* the other. This vanishing appears to quantitative conception as a disturbance of the equilibrium so that the one factor becomes greater than the other; thus there is posited the sublating of the quality of the other and its lack of any support. One factor becomes preponderant as the other diminishes with an accelerated velocity and is overpowered by the first, which therefore constitutes itself the sole self-subsistent quality; but this being so, there are no longer two specific moments and factors but only the one whole.

This unity thus posited as the totality of the process of determining, in which it is itself determined as indifference, is a contradiction in every respect; it therefore has to be *posited* as sublating this its contradictory nature and acquiring the character of a self-determined, self-subsistent being which has for its result and truth not the unity which is merely indifferent, but that immanently negative and absolute unity which is called essence.

Remark: Centripetal and Centrifugal Force
The relationship of a whole which is supposed to have its determinateness in the quantitative difference of two factors determined qualitatively against each other, is applied to the elliptical motion of the celestial bodies. This example exhibits primarily only two qualities in inverse relation to each other, not two sides, each of which is itself the unity of both and their inverse relation. The fact, the inverse relation, rests on a firm empirical foundation, but the theoretical explanation of it involves a consequence which is overlooked, namely the destruction of the basic fact; or if, as is

proper, the fact is retained it escapes notice that the theory proves to be meaningless in face of the fact. The ignoring of this consequence allows the fact and the theory conflicting with it to exist calmly side by side. The simple fact is that in the elliptical motion of the celestial bodies their velocity is accelerated as they approach perihelion and retarded as they approach aphelion. The quantitative side of this fact has been accurately ascertained by the untiring diligence of observation, and further, it has been reduced to its simple law and formula. Hence all that can properly be required of a theory has been accomplished; but to reflective understanding this did not appear sufficient. For the purpose of a so-called explanation of the phenomenon and its law a centripetal and a centrifugal force are assumed as qualitative moments of the curvilinear motion. Qualitatively, their difference consists in the opposed direction of the moments, and quantitatively, the moments being determined as unequal, in the fact that as the one increases the other is supposed to decrease, and *vice versa*; then further, that their relationship is reversed again so that after a period during which the centripetal force has been increasing and the centrifugal force decreasing, a point is reached where the former decreases and the latter increases.[1] But this way of representing the matter is contradicted by the essentially qualitative relation between their respective determinatenesses which makes their separation from each other completely out of the question. Each has meaning only with reference to the other; consequently, in so far as the one had an excess over the other, to that extent it would have no relation to it and the other would no longer exist. If it is assumed that one of them is at one time greater than the other, being *related* to it as the greater to the smaller, then what was said above applies, namely, that the greater would acquire absolute preponderance and the other would vanish; the other would be posited as a vanishing moment without any support; and nothing would be altered by supposing the vanishing to take place only gradually any more than by supposing that by as much as the vanishing moment decreases in magnitude the other increases, for the latter, too, is destroyed with the former, since it is what it is, only in so far as the other is. It requires but little

---

[1] In the first edition the following sentence is added here: 'I have elucidated this subject in an earlier dissertation and have demonstrated the futility of this distinction and the explanations based on it.'

consideration to see that if, for example, as is alleged, the body's centripetal force increases as it approaches perihelion, while the centrifugal force is supposed to decrease proportionately, the latter *would no longer be able* to tear the body away from the former and to set it again at a distance from its central body; on the contrary, for once the former has gained the preponderance, the other is overpowered and the body is carried towards its central body with accelerated velocity. Just as conversely, if the centrifugal force gains the upper hand when infinitely near to aphelion, it is equally contradictory that now, in the aphelion itself, it should be overpowered by the weaker force. Further, it is evident that it would be an *alien* force which effected this reversal; and this means that this alternation of accelerated and retarded velocity of the motion *cannot be ascertained* or, as it is said, *explained* from the assumed determination of the factors although these have been assumed for the express purpose of explaining this difference. The conclusion which follows from the vanishing of one or the other direction and hence of the elliptical motion altogether, is ignored and concealed because of the undeniable fact that this motion does go on and pass from the accelerated into the retarded velocity. The assumed transformation of the weakness of the centripetal force in aphelion into a preponderant strength over the centrifugal force, and conversely in perihelion, implies first the conclusion arrived at above, namely, that each side of the inverse relation is in its own self the whole inverse relation; for the side of the motion from aphelion to perihelion (when the centripetal force is supposed to be preponderant) is still supposed to contain the centrifugal force which, however, diminishes as the other increases, while on the side of the retarded motion the centrifugal force is assumed to be present in that same inverse relation in an ever-increasing preponderance over the centripetal force. Consequently, on neither side has either force vanished but only become increasingly smaller up to the point of its transformation into a preponderance over the other. All that recurs then on either side is the defect characteristic of this inverse relation, namely, either each force is credited with an independent self-subsistence, the pair being merely *externally* associated in a motion (as in the parallelogram of forces), in which case the unity of the Notion, the nature of the thing itself, is left out of account; or else, since each is qualitatively related to the other by the Notion, neither can attain an indifferent independent subsistence in face of the other, a subsistence supposedly imparted to it by a *more*. The form of intensity, the so-called dynamic factor, does not help, because this too has its determinateness in quantum and consequently can express only as much force (which is the measure of its existence) as is opposed to it by the opposite force. Secondly, this sudden change round from a preponderance into its opposite implies the alternation of the qualitative determination of positive and negative; an increase in the one means an equivalent loss in the other. In the theory, the inseparable qualitative connectedness of this qualitative opposition is distorted into a *succession in time*; but it fails thereby to give an *explanation* of this alternation and more particularly of this distortion itself. The semblance of unity which is still implied in the increasing of one side with an equivalent decreasing of the other vanishes here completely; what is alleged is a merely *external* succession of the sides which only contradicts what is necessarily implied in their qualitative connectedness, namely that with the preponderance of one side the other must disappear.

The same relationship has been applied to the forces of attraction and repulsion for the purpose of explaining the different *densities* of bodies; and the inverse ratio of sensibility and irritability has also been invoked to explain from the inequality of these factors of *life* the various determinations of the whole and of health and also the variety of living species. This mode of explanation was supposed to form a basis for the natural philosophy of physiology, nosology and also zoology, but the confused hotchpotch of nonsense in which it became entangled through the uncritical use of these determinations of the Notion soon led to the abandonment in these spheres of this formalism which, however, is practised without restraint in the other sciences, particularly in physical astronomy.

Since absolute indifference may seem to be the fundamental determination of Spinoza's *substance*, we may add that this is indeed the case in so far as in both every determination of being, like every further concrete differentiation of thought and extension and so forth, is posited as vanished. If we stop short at the abstraction [of substance] then it is a matter of complete indifference what something looked like in reality before it was swallowed up in this abyss. But when substance is conceived as indifference, it is tied up with the need for determining it and for taking this determining into consideration; it is not to remain Spinoza's substance, the sole determination of which is the negative one that everything is absorbed in it. With Spinoza, the moment of difference—attributes, thought and extension, then the modes too, the affections, and every other determination—is introduced quite empirically; it is intellect, itself a mode, which is the source of the differentiation. The relationship of the attributes to substance and to one another is not specified further than that they express the whole of substance, and their content, the order of things as extended and as thoughts, is the same. But by the determination of substance as indifference, the *difference* too, comes to be reflected on; whereas with Spinoza, the difference is an external, and more precisely a quantitative difference *only by implication*, now it is *posited* as such. The indifference does indeed, like substance, remain immanent in the differentiated moments, but only abstractly so, only *implicitly*; the difference is *not* immanent in the indifference, for as quantitative it is rather the opposite of immanence, and the quantitative indifference is rather the self-externality of the unity. Thus the difference is also not grasped qualitatively; substance is not determined as self-differentiating, not as subject. The immediate consequence with respect to the category of indifference itself is that in it the difference of quantitative or qualitative determination falls apart as we found in the explication of indifference; it is the *dissolution of measure*, in which both moments were directly posited as one.

C. TRANSITION INTO ESSENCE

Absolute indifference is the final determination of *being* before it becomes essence; but it does not attain to essence. It reveals itself as still belonging to the sphere of being through the fact that, determined as *indifferent*, it still contains difference as an *external*, quantitative determination; this is its *determinate being*, contrasted with which absolute indifference is determined as being only *implicitly* the absolute, not the absolute grasped as *actuality*. In other words, it is *external reflection* which stops short at conceiving the differences *in themselves* or in the absolute as *one and the same*, thinking of them as only indifferently distinguished, not as intrinsically distinct from one another. The further step which requires to be made here is to grasp that this reflection of the differences into their unity is not merely the product of the *external* reflection of the subjective thinker, but that it is the very nature of the differences of this unity to sublate themselves, with the result that their unity proves to be absolute negativity, its indifference to be just as much indifferent *to itself*, to its own indifference, as it is indifferent to otherness.

But we are already familiar with this self-sublating of the determination of indifference; in the development of its positedness, this determination has shown itself to be from every aspect a contradiction. It is *in itself* the totality in which every determination of being is sublated and contained; it is thus the substrate, but at first only in the one-sided determination of the in-itself, and consequently the differences, namely, the quantitative difference and the inverse ratio of factors, are present in it only in an *external* manner. As thus the contradiction of itself and its determinedness, of its implicit determination and its posited determinateness, it is the negative totality whose determinatenesses have sublated themselves in themselves and in so doing have sublated this fundamental one-sidedness of theirs, their [merely] implicit being [*Ansichsein*]. The result is that indifference is now posited as what it in fact is, namely a simple and infinite, negative relation-to-self, its inherent incompatibility with itself, a repelling of itself from itself. The process of determining and being determined is not a transition, nor an external alteration, nor an emergence of determinations in the indifference, but is its own self-relating which is the negativity of itself, of its [merely] implicit being.

Now these repelled determinations do not possess themselves, do not emerge as self-subsistent or external determinations, but first, *as moments* belonging to the *implicit* unity, they are not expelled from it but are borne by it as the substrate and are filled solely by it; secondly, as determinations which are immanent in the *explicated* unity, they *are* only through their repulsion from themselves. The being of the determinations is no longer simply *affirmative* as in the entire sphere of being, but is now a sheer *positedness*, the determinations having the fixed character and significance of being *related* to their unity, each consequently being related to its other and with negation; this is the mark of their relativity.

Thus we see that being in general and the being or immediacy of the distinct determinatenesses, no less than the *implicit being*, has vanished and the unity is *being*, an *immediate presupposed* totality such that it is this *simple self-relation only as a result of the sublating of this presupposition*, and this presupposedness and immediate being is itself only a moment of its repelling, the original self-subsistence and self-identity *is* only as the *resulting coming together with itself*. Being, in its determining, has thus determined itself to essence, a being which, through the sublating of being, is a simple *being-with-itself*.

BOOK TWO

THE DOCTRINE OF ESSENCE

The Doctrine of Essence

The truth of *being* is *essence*.

Being is the immediate. Since knowing has for its goal knowledge of the true, knowledge of what being is *in and for itself*, it does not stop at the immediate and its determinations, but penetrates it on the supposition that at the back of this being there is something else, something other than being itself, that this background constitutes the truth of being. This knowledge is a mediated knowing for it is not found immediately with and in essence, but starts from an other, from being, and has a preliminary path to tread, that of going beyond being or rather of penetrating into it. Not until knowing *inwardizes*, *recollects* [*erinnert*] itself out of immediate being, does it through this mediation find essence. The German language has preserved essence in the past participle [*gewesen*] of the verb *to be;* for essence is past—but timelessly past—being.

When this movement is pictured as the path of knowing, then this beginning with being, and the development that sublates it, reaching essence as a mediated result, appears to be an activity of knowing external to being and irrelevant to being's own nature.

But this path is the movement of being itself. It was seen that being inwardizes itself through its own nature, and through this movement into itself becomes essence.

If, therefore, the absolute was at first defined as *being*, now it is defined as *essence*. Cognition certainly cannot stop short at manifold *determinate being*, nor yet at *being*, *pure being;* the reflection that immediately forces itself on one is that this *pure being*, the *negation* of everything finite, presupposes an *internalization*, a *recollection* [*Erinnerung*] and movement which has purified immediate, determinate being to pure being. Being is accordingly determined as essence, as a being in which everything determinate and finite is negated. It is thus the *indeterminate*, simple unity from which what is determinate has been eliminated in an *external manner;* the determinate element itself was external to this unity and, after this elimination, still remains confronting it; for it has not been sublated in itself but only relatively, only in relation to this unity. We have already mentioned that if essence is defined as the *sum total of all realities*, then these realities likewise are subordinate to the nature of the determinateness and to the abstractive reflection and this sum total reduces to empty oneness. Essence is in this way only a product, an artefact. *External* negation—and this is what abstraction is—only shifts the determinatenesses of being *away* from what is left over as Essence; it only puts them, so to speak, elsewhere, leaving them the affirmative character they possessed before. But in this way, essence is neither *in itself* nor *for itself;* what it is, it is through an other, the external, abstractive reflection; and it is for an other, namely for abstraction and, in general, for the simply affirmative being [*das Seiende*] that remains confronting it. Its character, therefore, is to lack all determinate character, to be inherently lifeless and empty.

But essence as it has here come to be, is what it is through a negativity which is not alien to it but is its very own, the infinite movement of being. It is being that is *in itself and for itself;* it is absolute *being-in-itself* in that it is indifferent to every determinateness of being, and otherness and relation-to-other have been completely sublated. But it is not only this being-in-itself; as mere being-in-itself it would be only the abstraction of pure essence; but it is equally essentially *being-for-self;* it is itself this negativity, the self-sublating of otherness and determinateness.

Essence as the completed return of being into itself is thus at first indeterminate essence. The determinatenesses of being are sublated in it; they are contained in essence *in principle* [*an sich*] but are not *posited in it*. Absolute essence in this simple equality with itself has *no determinate being;* but it must develop determinate being, for it is both *in itself* and *for itself*, i.e. it *differentiates* the determinations which are *implicit* [*an sich*] in it. Because it is self-repelling or indifferent to itself, *negative* self-relation, it sets itself over against itself and is infinite being-for-self only in so far as it is at one with itself in this its own difference from itself. This determining then is of a different nature from the determining in the sphere of being, and the determinations of essence have a different character from the determinatenesses of being. Essence is absolute unity of being-in-itself and being-for-itself; consequently its determining remains within this unity and is neither a becoming nor a transition, nor are the determinations themselves an *other* as other, or relations *to other;* they are self-subsistent, but at the same time only in their association with each other in this unity. Since essence is at first simple negativity, it now has to posit in its *own* sphere the determinateness that is only *implicit* in it, in order to give itself determinate being and then being-for-self.

In the *whole* of logic, essence occupies the same place as quantity does in the sphere of being; absolute indifference to limit. But quantity is this indifference in an *immediate* determination, and the limit is present in it as an immediately external determinateness, quantity passes over into quantum; the external limit is necessary to quantity and is *affirmatively present* in it [*ist an ihr seiend*]. In essence, on the other hand, the determinateness is not a simple immediacy but is present only as *posited* by essence itself; it is not free, but is present only as *connected* with its unity. The negativity of essence is *reflection;* and the determinations are *reflected*, posited by essence itself and remaining in essence as sublated.

Essence stands between *being* and *Notion;* it constitutes their mean, and its movement is the *transition* from being into the Notion. Essence is being-in-and-for-itself, but in the determination of being-in-itself; for the general determination of essence is to have proceeded from being, or to be the *first negation of being*. Its movement consists in positing within itself the negation or determination, thereby giving itself *determinate being* and becoming as infinite being-for-self what it is in itself. It thus gives itself its *determinate being* that is *equal* to its being-in-itself and becomes *Notion*. For the Notion is the absolute that in its determinate being is absolute, or is in and for itself. But the determinate being which essence gives itself is not yet determinate being as in and for itself, but as *given* by essence to itself, or as *posited*, and is consequently still distinct from the determinate being of the Notion.

At first, essence *shines* or *shows within itself*, or is reflection; secondly, it *appears;* thirdly, it *manifests* itself. In its movement, essence posits itself in the following determinations:

I. As *simple* essence, essence in itself, which in its determinations remains within itself

II. As emerging into determinate being, or in accordance with its Existence and *Appearance*

III. As essence that is one with its Appearance, as *actuality*.

this utility, of necessity a matter of this matter of this quantity... is how far indispensable as being..... the several... determined... [illegible faded text]... far in itself, a... it... [illegible]... itself in respect of use, and thus... into... [illegible]

In the matters of... capital... subject... terms... quantities... in the... capital... into... this. The quantity is... indifferent... capital... remarkable... [illegible] measure... of the... is... in... [illegible] considerable, as... determined... effect... quantity... [illegible]... terms... the quantity... return... effort is necessary in... may... be... quantity... return... it is, so... it... strength. In... case... most... the... [illegible]... ness is not... simple... quantity... in... respect only as... sence itself... is not only... in... respect... it can... conceived... no utility. The... measure... is a... new conception... and... the... [illegible] relations are... related... as the... [illegible]... and... remaining... in... respect as all that.

It may be... on... to... see also... and... [illegible]... it... [illegible]... there means, and... [illegible]... is the... from... being... for... the... [illegible]... is... setting... and... Its... itself... [illegible]... [illegible] of being... itself, the... particular... another... of... experience... to have... [illegible]... from... before... to be... the... true... nature of... being... [illegible]... relation... instances... in... feeling... within... itself, the... [illegible]... or... determination, that... is... [illegible]... as... that... there... it... remaining indifferent... itself... [illegible]... that... it... a... itself. In this show... that it... determination... from... this... respect... to... be... being... in... itself... and... because... for... the... [illegible] in... the... objective... of... being... [illegible]... itself... is... another... in... itself... [illegible]... the... determinately... being... when... it... this... [illegible]... a... we... only... infinity... being... in... itself, but... so... only... by... conceived... in... itself... as... posited... and... consequently... still... [illegible]... from... the... [illegible]... being... of... the... process.

And... it... [illegible]... how... that... which... itself... is... transient... is... secondly, then, given... this... it... [illegible]... itself, in... its... movement... because... being... itself... in... the... [illegible]... of... [illegible].

I. So... there... are... [illegible]... in... itself... exhibit... in... its... determination.

II. A... simple... [illegible] determinate... being, as... in... accordance with its... determination... and... [illegible].

III. As... second... that... being... with... its... percentage, as... another.

Section One: Essence as Reflection Within Itself

Essence issues from being; hence it is not immediately in and for itself but is a *result* of that movement. Or if essence is taken at first as an immediacy, then it is a specific determinate being confronted by another such; it is only *essential*, as opposed to *unessential*, determinate being. But essence is being that has been sublated in and for itself; what confronts it is only *illusory* being [*Schein*]. The illusory being, however, is essence's own positing.

Essence is first *reflection*. Reflection determines itself and its determinations are a positedness which is at the same time reflection-into-self.

Secondly, we have to consider these *determinations of reflection* or essentialities.

Thirdly, essence as the reflection-into-self of its determining converts itself into *ground* and passes over into *Existence* and *Appearance*.

CHAPTER I

ILLUSORY BEING [SCHEIN]

Essence that issues from being seems to confront it as an opposite; this immediate being is, in the first instance, the *unessential*.

But secondly, it is more than merely unessential being, it is essenceless being, it is *illusory being*.

Thirdly, this illusory being is not something external to or other than essence; on the contrary, it is essence's own illusory being. The showing of this illusory being within essence itself is *reflection*.

A. THE ESSENTIAL AND THE UNESSENTIAL

Essence is *sublated being*. It is simple equality with itself, but only in so far as it is the *negation* of the sphere of being in general. Essence thus has immediacy confronting it as an immediacy from which it has become and which in this sublating has preserved and maintained itself. In this determination, essence itself is *simply affirmative [seiendes]*, immediate essence, and being is only a negative *in relation to* essence, not in and for itself; therefore essence is a *determinate* negation. In this way, being and essence are again related to each other as *others; for each has a being, an immediacy*, and these are indifferent to each other, and with respect to this being, being and essence are equal in value.

But at the same time, being, as contrasted with essence, is the unessential; in relation to essence, it has the determination of sublated being. Yet in so far as it is only related to essence simply as an other, essence is not strictly essence but only a differently determined being, the *essential*.

The distinction of essential and unessential has caused essence to relapse into the sphere of *determinate being*, since essence in its initial phase is determined as immediate, simply affirmative [seiendes] essence and hence only as *other* over against being. The sphere of determinate being is thereby made the base, and the fact that the being in this determinate being is being-in-and-for-itself, is a further determination external to determinate being itself; and conversely, while essence is indeed being-in-and-for-itself, it is so only in relation to an other, in a *specific* reference. Accordingly, in so far as the distinction is made of an essential and an unessential side in something [*Dasein*], this distinction is *externally* posited, a separation of one part of it from another that does not affect the something itself, a division which has its origin in a *third*. Such a division does not settle what is essential and what is unessential. It originates in some external standpoint and consideration and the same content can therefore be regarded now as essential and again as unessential.

Closer consideration shows that when essence is characterized as essential only relatively to what is unessential, it is because it is taken only as sublated being or determinate being. In this way, essence is only the *first* negation, or the negation which is a *determinateness* through which being becomes only determinate being, or the latter becomes only an other. But essence is the absolute negativity of being; it is being itself, but not determined only as an other, but being that has sublated itself both as immediate being and also as immediate negation, as negation that is infected with otherness. Thus being, or determinate being, has not preserved itself as an other—for we are in the sphere of essence—and the immediate that is still distinguished from essence is not merely an unessential determinate being but the immediate that is *in and for itself* a nullity; it is only a *non-essence, illusory* being.

B. ILLUSORY BEING

1. *Being is illusory being*. The being of illusory being consists solely in the sublatedness of being, in its nothingness; this nothingness it has in essence and apart from its nothingness, apart from essence, illusory being is *not*. It is the negative posited as negative.

Illusory being is all that still remains from the sphere of being. But it seems still to have an immediate side that is independent of essence and to be simply an other of essence. The other contains in general the two moments of determinate being and negated determinate being. Since the unessential no longer has a being, all that remains to it of otherness is the pure moment of negated determinate being; illusory being is this *immediate*, negated determinate being in the determinateness of being, in such wise that it has determinate being only in relation to an other, only in its negated determinate being; the non-self-subsistent which *is* only in its negation. All that is left to it, therefore, is the pure determinateness of *immediacy*; it is *reflected* immediacy, that is, immediacy which *is* only by means of its negation and which, when contrasted with its *mediation*, is nothing but the empty determination of the immediacy of negated determinate being.

Thus *illusory being* is the phenomenon of scepticism, and the Appearance of idealism, too, is such an *immediacy*, which is not a something or a thing, in general, not an indifferent being that would still be, apart from its determinateness and connexion with the subject. Scepticism did not permit itself to say 'It is'; modern idealism did not permit itself to regard knowledge as a knowing of the thing-in-itself; the illusory being of scepticism was supposed to lack any foundation of being, and in idealism the thing-in-itself was not supposed to enter into knowledge. But at the same time scepticism admitted a multitude of determinations of its illusory being, or rather its illusory being had for content the entire manifold wealth of the world. In idealism, too, Appearance embraces within itself the range of these manifold determinatenesses. This illusory being and this Appearance are *immediately* thus manifoldly determined. This content, therefore, may well have no being, no thing or thing-in-itself at its base; it remains on its own account as it is; the content has only been transferred from being into an illusory being, so that the latter has within itself those manifold determinatenesses, which are immediate, simply affirmative [*seiende*], and mutually related as others. Illusory being is, therefore, itself *immediately* determinate. It can have this or that content; whatever content it has, illusory being does not posit this itself but has it immediately. The various forms of idealism, Leibnizian, Kantian, Fichtean, and others, have not advanced beyond being as determinateness, have not advanced beyond this immediacy, any more than scepticism did. Scepticism permits the content of its illusory being to be *given* to it; whatever content it is supposed to have, for scepticism it is *immediate*. The *monad* of Leibniz evolves its ideas and representations out of itself; but it is not the power that generates and binds them together, rather do they arise in the monad like bubbles; they are indifferent and immediate over against one another and the same in relation to the monad itself. Similarly, the Kantian Appearance is a *given* content of perception; it presupposes affections, determinations of the subject, which are immediate relatively to themselves and to the subject. It may well be that the infinite obstacle [*Anstoss*] of Fichte's idealism has no underlying thing-in-itself, so that it becomes purely a determinateness in the ego; but for the ego, this determinateness which it appropriates and whose externality it sublates is at the same time *immediate*, a *limitation* of the ego, which it can transcend but which has in it an element of indifference, so that although the limitation is in the ego, it contains an *immediate* non-being of the ego.

2. Illusory being, therefore, contains an immediate presupposition, a side that is independent of essence. But it does not have to be shown that illusory being, in so far as it is distinct from essence, sublates itself and withdraws into essence; for being in its totality has withdrawn into essence; illusory being is in itself a nullity; all that has to be shown is that the determinations which distinguish it from essence are determinations of essence itself, and further, that this *determinateness of essence* which illusory being is, is sublated in essence itself.

It is the immediacy of *non-being* that constitutes illusory being; but this non-being is nothing else but the negativity of essence present within it. In essence, being is non-being. Its intrinsic *nothingness* is the *negative nature of essence itself*. But the immediacy or indifference which this non-being contains is essence's own absolute being-in-itself. The negativity of essence is its equality with itself or its simple immediacy and indifference. Being has preserved itself in essence in so far as the latter in its infinite negativity has this equality with itself; it is through this that essence itself is being. The immediacy of the determinateness in illusory being over against essence is consequently nothing other than essence's own immediacy; but the immediacy is not simply affirmative [*seiend*], but is the purely mediated or reflected immediacy that is illusory being—being, not *as* being, but only as the determinateness of being as opposed to mediation; being as a moment.

These two moments, namely the nothingness which yet is and the being which is only a moment, or the implicit negativity and the reflected immediacy that constitute *the moments of illusory being*, are thus *the moments of essence itself*. What we have here is not an illusory show of being *in* essence, or an illusory show of essence *in* being; the illusory being in essence is not the illusory being of an other, but is illusory being *per se, the illusory being of essence itself*.

Illusory being is essence itself in the determinateness of being. Essence has an illusory being because it is *determinate* within itself and thereby distinguished from its absolute unity. But equally this determinateness is absolutely sublated in its own self. For essence is the self-subsistent, which *is* as self-mediated through its negation, which negation essence itself is; it is therefore the identical unity of absolute negativity and immediacy. The negativity is negativity *per se;* it is its relation to itself and is thus in itself immediacy; but it is negative self-relation, a negating that is a repelling of itself, and the intrinsic immediacy is thus negative or *determinate* in regard to it. But this determinateness is itself absolute negativity, and this determining which is, as determining, immediately the sublating of itself, is a return-into-self.

Illusory being is the negative that has a being, but in an *other*, in its negation; it is a non-self-subsistent being which is in its own self-sublated and null. As such, it is the negative returned into itself, non-self-subsistent being as in its own self not self-subsistent. This *self-relation* of the negative or of non-self-subsistent being is its *immediacy;* it is an *other* than the negative itself; it is its determinateness over against itself; or it is the negation directed against the negative. But negation directed against the negative is purely *self*-related negativity, the absolute sublating of the determinateness itself.

The *determinateness*, therefore, which illusory being is in essence is infinite determinateness; it is the purely *self*-coincident negative; it is thus the determinateness which as such is self-subsistent and indeterminate. Conversely, the self-subsistent, as self-related *immediacy*, is equally sheer determinateness and moment and *is* only as self-related negativity. This negativity that is identical with immediacy and immediacy that is thus identical with negativity, is *essence*. Illusory being, therefore, is essence itself, but essence in a determinateness, in such wise, however, that this is only a moment of essence and *essence* is the reflection of itself within itself.

In the sphere of being, there *arises* over against being as an *immediacy*, non-being, which is likewise an *immediacy*, and their truth is *becoming*. In the sphere of essence, we have first essence opposed to the unessential, then essence opposed to illusory being, that is, to the unessential and to illusory being as the remainder of being. But both essence and illusory being, and also the difference of essence from them, derive solely from the fact that essence is at first taken as an *immediate*, not as it is in itself, *namely*, not as an immediacy that *is* as pure mediation or absolute negativity. The first immediacy is thus only the *determinateness* of immediacy. The sublating of this determinateness of essence, therefore, consists simply and solely in showing that the unessential is only illusory being and that the truth is rather that essence contains the illusory being within itself as the infinite immanent movement that determines its immediacy as negativity and its negativity as immediacy, and is thus the reflection of itself within itself. Essence in this its self-movement is *reflection*.

C. REFLECTION

Illusory being is the same thing as *reflection;* but it is reflection as *immediate*. For illusory being that has withdrawn into itself and so is estranged from its immediacy, we have the foreign word *reflection*.

Essence is reflection, the movement of becoming and transition that remains internal to it, in which the differentiated moment is determined simply as that which in itself is only negative, as illusory being. At the base of becoming in the sphere of being, there lies the determinateness of being, and this is relation to *other*. The movement of reflection, on the other hand, is the other as the *negation in itself*, which has a being only as self-related negation. Or, since the self-relation is precisely this negating of negation, the *negation as negation* is present in such wise that it has its being in its negatedness, as illusory being. Here, therefore, the other is not *being with a negation*, or limit, but *negation with the negation*. But the *first*, over against this other, the immediate or being, is only this very equality of the negation with itself, the negated negation, absolute negativity. This equality with itself, or *immediacy*, is consequently not a *first* from which the beginning was made and which passed over into its negation; nor is it an affirmatively present substrate that moves through reflection; on the contrary, immediacy is only this movement itself.

Consequently, becoming is essence, its reflective movement, is the *movement of nothing to nothing, and so back to itself*. The transition, or becoming, sublates itself in its passage; the *other* that in this transition comes to be, is not the non-being of a being, but the nothingness of a nothing, and this, to be the negation of a nothing, constitutes being. Being only *is* as the movement of nothing to nothing, and as such it is essence; and the latter does not *have* this movement *within it*, but is this movement as a being that is itself absolutely illusory, pure negativity, outside of which there is nothing for it to negate but which negates only its own negative, which latter *is* only in this negating.

This pure absolute reflection that is the movement from nothing to nothing determines itself further.

It is first, *positing reflection*.

Secondly, it forms the starting point of the presupposed immediate and is thus *external reflection*.

But thirdly, it sublates this presupposition; and since reflection in sublating the presupposition *at the same time* presupposes it, it is *determining reflection*.

(a) Positing Reflection

Illusory being is nothingness or the essenceless; but this nothingness or the essenceless does not have its being in an *other* in which its illusory being is reflected: on the contrary, its being is its own equality with itself. This interchange of the negative with itself has determined itself as the absolute reflection of essence.

This self-related negativity of essence is therefore the negating of its own self. Hence it is just as much *sublated* negativity as it is negativity; or it is itself both the negative, and simple equality with itself or immediacy. It consists, therefore, in *being itself* and *not itself* and that, too, in a single unity.

In the first place, reflection is the movement of nothing to nothing and is the negation that coincides with itself. This coincidence with itself is, in general, simple equality-with-self, immediacy. But this coincidence is not a transition of the negation into equality-with-self as into its otherness: on the contrary, reflection is transition as sublating of the transition; for reflection is immediate coincidence of the negative *with itself*. This coincidence is thus first, equality-with-self or immediacy; but secondly, this immediacy is the equality of *the negative* with itself, hence self-negating equality, the immediacy that is in itself the negative, the negative of itself, that consists in being that which it is not.

The self-relation of the negative is, therefore, its return into itself; it is immediacy as the sublating of the negative; but immediacy simply and solely *as* this relation or as *return from a negative*, and hence a self-sublating immediacy. This is *posited being* or *positedness*, immediacy purely and simply as *determinateness* or as self-reflecting. This immediacy which *is* only as *return* of the negative into itself, is that immediacy which constitutes the determinateness of illusory being and which previously seemed to be the starting point of the reflective moment. But this immediacy, instead of being able to form the starting point is, on the contrary, immediacy only as the return or as reflection itself. Reflection therefore is the movement that starts or returns only in so far as the negative has already returned into itself.

It is a *positing* in so far as it is immediacy as a returning movement; for there is no other on hand, either an other *from* which or *into* which immediacy returns; it is, therefore, only as a returning movement, or as the negative of itself. Furthermore, this immediacy is the sublated negation and the sublated return-into-self. Reflection, as sublating the negative, is a sublating of *its other*, of immediacy. Since, therefore, it is immediacy as a returning movement, as a coincidence of the negative with itself, it is equally a negative of the negative as negative. Thus it is a *presupposing*. Or immediacy, as a returning movement, is only the negative of itself, only this, to be *not* immediacy; but reflection is the sublating of the negative of itself, it is a coincidence with itself; it therefore sublates its positing, and since in its positing it sublates its positing, it is a presupposing. Reflection, in its presupposing, determines the return-into-self as the negative of itself, as that, the sublating of which is essence. The presupposing is the manner in which it relates itself to itself, but to itself as the negative of itself; only thus is it the self-relating negativity that remains internal to itself. Immediacy presents itself simply and solely as a return and is that negative which is the illusory being of the beginning, the illusory being which is negated by the return. Accordingly, the return of essence is its self-repulsion. In other words, reflection-into-self is essentially the presupposing of that from which it is the return.

It is only when essence has sublated its equality-with-self that it is equality-with-self. It presupposes itself and the sublating of this presupposition is essence itself; conversely, this sublating of its presupposition is the presupposition itself. Reflection therefore *finds before it* an immediate which it transcends and from which it is the return. But this return is only the presupposing of what reflection finds before it. What is thus found only *comes to be* through being *left behind;* its immediacy is sublated immediacy. Conversely, the sublated immediacy is the return-into-self, the *coming-to-itself* of essence, simple, self-equal being. Hence this coming-to-itself is the sublating of itself and is the self-repelling, presupposing reflection, and its self-repelling is the coming-to-itself of reflection.

It follows, therefore, from the foregoing considerations that the reflective movement is to be taken as an *absolute recoil* upon itself. For the presupposition of the return-into-self—that from which essence *comes*, and *is* only as this return—is only in the return itself. The transcending of the immediate from which reflection starts is rather the outcome of this transcending; and the transcending of the immediate is the arrival at it. The movement, as an advance, immediately turns round upon itself and only so is self-movement—a movement which comes from itself in so far as *positing* reflection is *presupposing*, but, as *presupposing* reflection, is simply *positing* reflection.

Thus reflection is itself and its non-being, and is only itself, in that it is the negative of itself, for only thus is the sublating of the negative at the same time a coincidence with itself.

The immediacy that reflection, as a process of sublating, presupposes for itself is purely and simply a *positedness*, an immediacy that is *in itself* sublated, that is not distinct from the return-into-self and is itself only this movement of return. But at the same time it is determined as negative, as immediately *opposed* to something, therefore to an other. Thus reflection is *determinate;* and since, in accordance with this determinateness, it *has* a presupposition and starts from the immediate as its other, it is *external reflection.*

(b) External Reflection

Reflection, as absolute reflection, is essence that reflects its illusory being within itself and presupposes for itself only an illusory being, only positedness; as presupposing reflection, it is immediately only positing reflection. But external or real reflection presupposes itself as sublated, as the negative of itself. In this determination it is doubled: it is what is presupposed, or reflection-into-self, which is the immediate; and also it is reflection that is negatively self-related; it is related to itself as to its non-being.

External reflection therefore *presupposes* a being, *first*, not in the sense that its immediacy is only positedness or a moment, but, on the contrary, that this immediacy is self-relation and the determinateness is only a moment. Its relationship to its presupposition is such that the latter is the negative of reflection, but so that this negative *as* negative is sublated. Reflection in its positing, immediately sublates its positing and thus has an *immediate presupposition*. It therefore *finds* this before it as something from which it starts, and from which it is first the return-into-self, the negating of this its negative. But the fact that what is thus presupposed is a negative or is posited does not concern it; this determinateness belongs only to the positing reflection, but in the presupposing the positedness is present only as sublated. The determinations posited by the external reflection in the immediate are to that extent external to the latter. This external reflection in the sphere of being was the infinite; the finite ranked as the first, as the real; as the foundation, the abiding foundation, it forms the starting point and the infinite is the reflection-into-self over against it.

This external reflection is the syllogism in which are the two extremes, the immediate and reflection-into-self; the middle term of the syllogism is the connection of the two, the determinate immediate, so that one part of the middle term, immediacy, belongs only to one of the extremes, the other, determinateness or negation, belongs only to the other extreme.

But a closer consideration of the action of external reflection shows it to be secondly, a positing of the immediate, which consequently becomes the negative or the determinate; but external reflection is immediately also the sublating of this its positing; for it *pre*supposes the immediate; in negating, it is the negating of this its negating. But in doing so it is immediately equally a *positing*, a sublating of the immediate negatively related to it, and this immediate from which it seemed to start as from something alien, *is* only in this its beginning. In this way, the immediate is not only *in itself*—that means, for us, or in external reflection—*identical* with reflection, but this identicalness is *posited*. For the immediate is determined by reflection as its negative or its other, but it is reflection itself that negates this determining. Hence the externality of reflection over against the immediate is sublated; its positing in which it negates itself, is the union of itself with its negative, with the immediate, and this union is the immediacy of essence itself. The fact is, therefore, that external reflection is not external, but is no less the immanent reflection of immediacy itself; in other words, the outcome of positing reflection is essence in and for itself. Reflection is thus *determining reflection*.

Remark

Reflection is usually taken in a subjective sense as the movement of the faculty of judgement that goes beyond a given immediate conception and seeks universal determinations for it or compares such determinations with it. Kant opposes *reflective judgement* to *determining judgement*.[1] He defines the faculty of judgement in general as the ability *to think the particular as subsumed under the universal. If the universal is given* (the rule, principle, law), then the faculty of judgement that subsumes the particular under it is *determinative*. But if only the particular is given *for which the universal is to be found*, then judgement is merely *reflective*. Here, then, to reflect is likewise to go beyond an immediate to the universal. On the one hand, it is only through this reference of the immediate to its universal that it is determined as a particular; by itself, it is only an individual or an immediate, simply affirmative being [*unmittelbares Seiendes*]. On the other hand, that to which it is referred is its universal, its rule, principle, law, in general, that which is reflected into itself, is self-related, essence or the essential.

But what is under discussion here is neither reflection at the level of consciousness, nor the more specific reflection of the understanding, which has the particular and the universal for its determinations, but of reflection generally. That reflection to which Kant ascribes the search for the universal of a given particular is clearly also only *external* reflection, which is related

[1] *Critique of Judgement, Introduction*, p. xxiii *sq.*

to the immediate as to something given. But in external reflection there is also implicit the notion of absolute reflection; for the universal, the principle or rule and law to which it advances in its determining, counts as the essence of that immediate which forms the starting point; and this immediate therefore counts as a nullity, and it is only the return from it, its determining by reflection, that is the positing of the immediate in accordance with its true being. Therefore, what reflection does to the immediate, and the determinations which issue from reflection, are not anything external to the immediate but are its own proper being.

It was external reflection, too, that recent philosophy had in mind when, as was the fashion for a while, it ascribed everything bad to reflection generally, regarding it and all its works as the polar opposite and hereditary foe of the absolute method of philosophizing. And intellectual reflection, in so far as it operates as external reflection, does in fact start from something immediately given which is alien to it, regarding itself as a merely formal activity which receives its content and material from outside and which, by itself, is only the movement conditioned by that content and material. Further, as will become more evident as soon as we come to consider determining reflection, the *reflected determinations* are of a different kind from the merely immediate determinations of being. The latter are more readily granted to be transient, merely relative and standing in relation to other; but the reflected determinations have the form of being-in-and-for-self. This makes them count as *essential*, and instead of passing over into their opposites they appear rather as absolute, free, and indifferent towards each other. Consequently, they are stubbornly opposed to their movement, their *being* is their self-identity in their determinateness, in accordance with which, even though they presuppose each other, they maintain themselves completely separate in this relation.

(c) Determining Reflection

Determining reflection is in general the unity of *positing* and *external* reflection. This is to be considered in more detail.

1. External reflection starts from immediate being, *positing* reflection from nothing. External reflection, when it determines, posits an other—but this is essence—in the place of the sublated being; but the determination thus posited is not put in the place

of an other; the positing has no presupposition. But that is why it is not the completed, determining reflection; the determination that it posits is consequently *only* something posited; it is an immediate, but not as equal to itself but as negating itself; it has an absolute relation to the return-into-self; it *is* only in reflection-into-self, but it is not this reflection itself.

What is *posited* is consequently an other, but in such a manner that the equality of reflection with itself is completely preserved; for what is posited *is* only as sublated, as a relation to the return-into-self. In the *sphere of being*, *determinate being* was the being in which negation was present, and being was the immediate base and element of this negation, which consequently was itself immediate. In the *sphere of essence*, *positedness* corresponds to determinate being. It is likewise a determinate being but its base is being as essence or as pure negativity; it is a determinateness or negation, not as affirmatively present [*seiend*] but immediately as sublated. *Determinate being is merely posited being or positedness;* this is the proposition of essence about determinate being. Positedness stands opposed, on the one hand, to determinate being, and on the other, to essence, and is to be considered as the middle term which unites determinate being with essence, and conversely, essence with determinate being. Accordingly, when it is said that a determination is *only* a positedness, this can have a twofold meaning; it is a positedness as opposed to determinate being or as opposed to essence. In the former meaning, determinate being is taken to be superior to positedness and the latter is ascribed to external reflection, to the subjective side. But in fact positedness is the superior; for as positedness, determinate being is that which it is in itself, a negative, something that is simply and solely related to the return-into-self. It is for this reason that positedness is *only* a positedness with respect to essence, as the negation of the accomplished return-into-self.

2. Positedness is not yet a determination of reflection; it is only determinateness as negation in general. But the positing is now in unity with external reflection; the latter is, in this unity, an absolute presupposing, that is, the repelling of reflection from itself, or the positing of the determinateness *as determinateness of itself*. Consequently, positedness is, as such, negation; but, as presupposed, it is also reflected into itself. Positedness is thus a *determination of reflection*.

The determination of reflection is distinct from the determinateness of being, from quality. The latter is immediate relation to other in general; positedness, too, is a relation to other, but to reflectedness-into-self. Negation as quality, is negation simply as *affirmative [seiend]*; being constitutes its ground and element. The determination of reflection, on the other hand, has for this ground reflectedness-into-self. Positedness fixes itself into a determination precisely because reflection is equality-with-self in its negatedness; its negatedness is consequently itself a reflection-into-self. Here the determination persists not through *being* but through its equality with itself. Because being, which supports quality, is not equal to the negation, quality is unequal within itself and hence a transitory moment vanishing in the other. The determination of reflection, on the other hand, is positedness *as* negation, negation which has negatedness as its ground; it is therefore not unequal within itself, and hence is *essential*, not transitory determinateness. It is *the equality of reflection with itself* that possesses the negative only as negative, as sublated or posited being, that enables the negative to persist.

By virtue of this reflection-into-self the determinations of reflection appear as free essentialities floating in the void without attracting or repelling one another. In them the determinateness has established and infinitely fixed itself through the relation-to-self. It is the determinate that has brought into subjection its transitoriness and its mere positedness, or has bent back its reflection-into-other into reflection-into-self. These determinations hereby constitute determinate illusory being as it is in essence, essential illusory being. Because of this, *determining reflection* is reflection that has come forth from itself; the equality of essence with itself has perished in the negation, which is the dominant factor.

In the determination of reflection, therefore, there are two sides which at first are distinguished from one another. First, the determination is positedness, negation as such; secondly, it is reflection-into-self. As positedness, it is negation as negation; this accordingly is already its unity with itself. But at first, it is this only *in itself* or *in principle [an sich]*, or, it is the immediate as sublating itself in its own self, as the other of itself. To this extent, reflection is an immanent determining. In the process, essence does not go outside itself; the differences are simply *posited*, taken back into essence. But according to the other side, they are not posited but reflected into themselves; the negation *as* negation is in an equality with itself, is not reflected into its other, into its non-being.

3. Now since the determination of reflection is as much a reflected relation within itself as it is positedness, this fact immediately throws more light on its nature. For as positedness, it is negation as such, a non-being over against an other, namely, *over against* absolute reflection-into-self, or over against essence. But as self-relation it is reflected into itself. This its reflection and the above positedness are distinct; its positedness is rather its sublatedness; but its reflectedness-into-self is its subsistence. In so far, therefore, as it is the positedness that is at the same time reflection-into-self, the determinateness of reflection is *the relation to its otherness within itself*. It is not an affirmative [*seiende*], quiescent determinateness, which would be related to an other in such a way that the related term and its relation are distinct from each other, the former a being-within-self, a something that excludes its other and its relation to this other from itself; on the contrary, the determination of reflection is in its own self the *determinate side* and the *relation* of this determinate side as determinate, that is, to its negation. Quality, through its relation, passes over into an other; in its relation its alteration begins. The determination of reflection, on the other hand, has taken its otherness back into itself. It is *positedness*, negation, which however bends back into itself the relation to other, and negation which is equal to itself, the unity of itself and its other, and only through this is an *essentiality*. It is, therefore, positedness, negation; but as reflection-into-self it is at the same time the sublatedness of this positedness, infinite self-relation.

CHAPTER 2

THE ESSENTIALITIES OR DETERMINATIONS OF REFLECTION

Reflection is determinate reflection; hence essence is determinate essence, or it is *an essentiality.*

Reflection is *the showing of the illusory being of essence within essence itself [das Scheinen des Wesens in sich selbst].* Essence, as infinite return-into-self, is not immediate but negative simplicity; it is a movement through distinct moments, absolute self-mediation. But it reflects itself into these its moments which consequently are themselves determinations reflected into themselves.

Essence is at first, simple self-relation, pure *identity.* This is its determination, but as such it is rather the absence of any determination.

Secondly, the proper determination is *difference*, a difference that is, on the one hand, external or indifferent, *diversity* in general, and on the other, is opposed diversity or *opposition.*

Thirdly, as *contradiction*, the opposition is reflected into itself and withdraws into its *ground.*

Remark

The *categories of reflection* used to be taken up in the form of *propositions*, in which they were asserted to be *valid for everything.* These propositions ranked as *the universal laws of thought* that lie at the base of all thinking, that are absolute in themselves and incapable of proof, but are immediately and incontestably recognized and accepted as true by all thinking that grasps their meaning.

Thus the essential category of identity is enunciated in the proposition: everything is identical with itself, A = A. Or negatively: A cannot at the same time be A and not A.

In the first place, there is no apparent reason why only these simple determinations of reflection should be grasped in this particular form, and not also the other categories, such as all the determinatenesses of the sphere of being. We should then have the propositions, for example: everything *is*, everything has a *determinate being*, and so on, or: everything has a *quality*, *quantity*, etc. For being, determinate being, and so forth, are, simply as logical categories, predicates of *everything*. According to its etymology and Aristotle's definition, category is what is predicated or asserted of the existent. But a determinateness of being is essentially a transition into its opposite; the negative of any determinateness is as necessary as the latter itself; as immediate determinatenesses, each is directly confronted by the other. Consequently, if these categories are put in the form of such propositions, then the opposite propositions equally appear; both present themselves with equal necessity and, as immediate assertions, are at least equally correct. The one, therefore, would demand proof as against the other, and consequently these assertions could no longer be credited with the character of immediately true and incontestable propositions of thought.

The determinations of reflection, on the contrary, are not of a qualitative kind. They are self-related, and so are at the same time determinations removed from determinateness against an other. Further, in that they are determinatenesses which are in themselves *relations*, to that extent they already contain within themselves the propositional form. For the difference between proposition and judgement is mainly that in the former the *content* constitutes the *relation* itself or is a *specific relation*. The judgement, on the contrary, transfers the content to the predicate as a universal determinateness which is for itself and is distinct from its relation, the simple copula. When a proposition is to be converted into a judgement, then the specific content—if, for example it is a verb—is changed into a participle, in order to separate in this way the determination itself and its relation to a subject. For the determinations of reflection, on the contrary, as positedness reflected into itself, the propositional form itself lies immediately at hand. Only, since they are enunciated as universal *laws of thought*, they still require a subject of their relation, and this subject is: *everything*, or an *A*, which equally means each and every existent.

On the one hand, this propositional form is a superfluity; the determinations of reflection are to be considered in and for themselves. Further, these propositions are defective in that they have for subject, *being*, *everything*. In this way, they resuscitate being and enunciate the categories of reflection—identity, and so on—of the something as a quality which something has in it, not in the speculative sense, but meaning that something as subject persists in such a quality as *simply affirmative* [*als seiendes*], not that it has passed over into identity, and so on, as into its truth and its essence.

But lastly, although the determinations of reflection have the form of equality-with-self and therefore of being unrelated to an other and without opposition, yet they are *determinate against* one another, as we shall find on closer examination of them, or as is immediately evident from the categories of identity, difference, and opposition; their form of reflection, therefore, does not exempt them from transition and contradiction. The *several propositions* which are set up as *absolute laws of thought*, are, therefore, more closely considered, *opposed to one another*, they contradict one another and mutually sublate themselves. If everything is *identical* with itself, then it is not *different*, not *opposed*, has no *ground*. Or, if it is assumed that *no two things are the same*, that is, everything is *different* from everything else, then *A* is not equal to *A*, nor is *A* opposed to *A*, and so on. The assumption of any of these propositions rules out the assumption of the others. The thoughtless consideration of them enumerates them *one after the other*, so that there does not appear to be any relation between them; it has in mind merely their reflectedness-into-self, ignoring their other moment, *positedness* or their *determinateness* as such which sweeps them on into transition and into their negation.

A. IDENTITY

1. Essence is simple immediacy as sublated immediacy. Its negativity is its being; it is self-equal in its absolute negativity, through which otherness and relation-to-other has vanished in its own self into pure equality-with-self. Essence is therefore simple identity-with-self.

2. This identity-with-self is the *immediacy* of reflection. It is not that equality-with-self that *being* or even *nothing* is, but the equality-with-self that has brought itself to unity, not a restoration of itself from an other, but this pure origination from and within itself, *essential* identity. Consequently, it is not *abstract* identity or has not arisen through a relative negating which had taken place outside it, merely separating off the distinguished moment

but otherwise leaving it afterwards as *simply affirmative* [*seiend*] as it was before. On the contrary, being and every determinateness of being has sublated itself not relatively, but in its own self: and this simple negativity of being in its own self is identity itself. So far, then, identity is still in general the same as essence.

Remark 1: Abstract Identity

Thinking that keeps to external reflection and knows of no other thinking but external reflection, fails to attain to a grasp of identity in the form just expounded, or of essence, which is the same thing. Such thinking always has before it only abstract identity, and apart from and alongside it, difference. In its opinion, reason is nothing more than a loom on which it externally combines and interweaves the warp, of say, identity, and then the woof of difference; or, also, again proceeding analytically, it now extracts especially identity and *then also again* obtains difference alongside it, is now a positing of likeness and *then also again* a positing of unlikeness—likeness when *abstraction* is made from difference, and unlikeness when abstraction is made from the positing of likeness. These assertions and opinions about what reason does must be completely set aside, since they are in a certain measure merely *historical*; the truth is rather that a consideration of everything that is, shows that *in its own self* everything is in its self-sameness different from itself and self-contradictory, and that in its difference, in its contradiction, it is self-identical, and is in its own self this movement of transition of one of these categories into the other, and for this reason, that each is in its own self the opposite of itself. The Notion of identity, that it is simple self-related negativity, is not a product of external reflection but has come from being itself. Whereas, on the contrary, that identity that is aloof from difference, and difference that is aloof from identity, are products of external reflection and abstraction, which arbitrarily clings to this point of indifferent difference.

2. This identity is, in the first instance, essence itself, not yet a determination of it, reflection in its entirety, not a distinct moment of it. As absolute negation it is the negation that immediately negates itself, a non-being and difference that vanishes in its arising, or a distinguishing by which nothing is distinguished, but which immediately collapses within itself. The distinguishing is the positing of non-being as non-being of the other. But the non-

being of the other is sublation of the other and therewith of the distinguishing itself. Here, then, distinguishing is present as self-related negativity, as a non-being which is the non-being of itself, a non-being which has its non-being not in another but in its own self. What is present, therefore, is self-related, reflected difference, or pure, *absolute difference*.

In other words, identity is the reflection-into-self that is identity only as internal repulsion, and is this repulsion as reflection-into-self, repulsion which immediately takes itself back into itself. Thus it is identity as difference that is identical with itself. But difference is only identical with itself in so far as it is not identity but absolute non-identity. But non-identity is absolute in so far as it contains nothing of its other but only itself, that is, in so far as it is absolute identity with itself.

Identity, therefore, is *in its own self* absolute non-identity. But it is also the *determination* of identity as against non-identity. For as reflection-into-self it posits itself as its own non-being; it is the whole, but, as reflection, it posits itself as its own moment, as positedness, from which it is the return into itself. It is only as such moment of itself that it is identity as such, as *determination* of simple equality with itself in contrast to absolute difference.

Remark 2: First Original Law of Thought

In this remark, I will consider in more detail identity as the law of identity which is usually adduced as the first law of thought.

This proposition in its positive expression $A = A$ is, in the first instance, nothing more than the expression of an empty *tautology*. It has therefore been rightly remarked that this law of thought has *no content* and leads no further. It is thus the empty identity that is rigidly adhered to by those who take it, as such, to be something true and are given to saying that identity is not difference, but that identity and difference are different. They do not see that in this very assertion they are themselves saying that *identity is different*; for they are saying that *identity is different* from difference; since this must at the same time be admitted to be the nature of identity, their assertion implies that identity, not externally, but in its own self, in its very nature, is this, to be different. But further, they do not see that, by clinging to this unmoved identity which has its opposite in difference, they thereby convert it into a one-sided determinateness which, as such, has no truth. It is admitted that the law of identity expresses only a one-sided determinateness, that it contains only *formal truth*, a truth which is *abstract, incomplete*. In this correct judgement, however, it is immediately implied that *truth is complete only in the unity of identity with difference*, and hence consists only in this unity. When asserting that this identity is imperfect, the perfection one has vaguely in mind is this totality, measured against which the identity is imperfect; but since, on the other hand, identity is rigidly held to be absolutely separate from difference and in this separation is taken to be something essential, valid, true, then the only thing to be seen in these conflicting assertions is the failure to bring together these thoughts, namely, that identity as abstract identity is essential, and that as such it is equally imperfect: the lack of awareness of the negative movement which, in these assertions, identity itself is represented to be. Or, when it is said that identity is *essential identity as separation* from difference, or *in the separation from difference*, then this is directly the expressed truth about it, namely, that identity consists in being *separation* as such, or in being essential *in separation*, that is, it is *nothing for itself* but is a moment of *separation*.

Now as regards other confirmation of the absolute *truth of the law* of identity, this is based on *experience* in so far as appeal is made to the experience of every consciousness; for anyone to whom this proposition $A = A$, *a tree is a tree*, is made, immediately admits it and is satisfied that the proposition as immediately self-evident requires no further confirmation or proof.

On the one hand, this appeal to experience, that the proposition is universally admitted by everyone, is a mere manner of speaking. For it is not pretended that the experiment with the abstract proposition $A = A$ has been made on every consciousness. The appeal, then, to actually carried-out experiment is not to be taken seriously; it is only the *assurance* that if the experiment were made, the proposition would be universally admitted. But if what were meant were not the abstract proposition as such, but its *concrete application* from which the former were supposed first to be *developed*, then the assertion of its universality and immediacy would consist in the fact that every consciousness would *treat it as fundamental*, even in every utterance it made, or that it lies *implicitly* in every utterance. But the *concrete* and the *application* are, in fact, precisely the *connexion* of the simple *identical* with *a manifold* that is *different* from it. Expressed as a proposition, the concrete would at first be a synthetic proposition. From the concrete itself or its synthetic proposition, abstraction could indeed extract by analysis the proposition of identity; but then, in fact, it would not have left *experience* as it is, but *altered* it; for the fact is that *experience* contains identity in unity with difference and is the *immediate refutation* of the assertion that abstract identity as such is something true, for the exact opposite, namely, identity only in union with difference, occurs in every experience.

On the other hand, the experiment with the pure law of identity is made only too often, and it is shown clearly enough in this experiment what is thought of the truth it contains. If, for example, to the question "What is a plant?" the answer is given "A plant is— a plant", the truth of such a statement is at once admitted by the entire company on whom it is tested, and at the same time it is equally unanimously declared that the statement says *nothing*. If anyone opens his mouth and promises to state what God is, namely God is—God, expectation is cheated, for what was expected was a *different determination*; and if this statement is absolute truth, such absolute verbiage is very lightly esteemed; nothing will be held to be more boring and tedious than conversation which merely reiterates the same thing, or than such talk which yet is supposed to be truth.

Looking more closely at this tedious effect produced by such truth, we see that the beginning, 'The plant is—,' sets out to say *something*, to bring forward a further determination. But since only the same thing is repeated, the opposite has happened, *nothing* has emerged. Such *identical* talk therefore *contradicts itself*. Identity, instead of being in its own self truth and absolute truth, is consequently the very opposite; instead of being the unmoved simple, it is the passage beyond itself into the dissolution of itself.

In the *form of the proposition*, therefore, in which identity is expressed, there lies *more* than simple, abstract identity; in it, there lies this pure movement of reflection in which the other appears only as illusory being, as an immediate vanishing; *A is*, is a beginning that hints at something different to which an advance is to be made; but this different something does not materialize; *A is—A*; the difference is only a vanishing; the movement returns into itself. The propositional form can be regarded as the hidden necessity of adding to abstract identity the more of that movement. And so an A, or a plant, or some other kind of substrate, too, is added which, as a useless content, is of no significance; but it constitutes the difference which seems to be accidentally associated with it. If instead of A or any other substrate, identity itself is taken—identity is identity—then equally it is admitted that also in its place any other substrate could be taken. Consequently, if the appeal is to be made to what experience[1] shows, then it shows that this identity is nothing, that it is negativity, the absolute difference from itself.

The other expression of the law of identity: *A cannot at the same time be A and not–A*, has a negative form; it is called the *law of contradiction*. Usually no justification is given of how the *form of negation* by which this law is distinguished from its predecessor, comes to identity. But this form is implied in the fact that identity, as the pure movement of reflection, is simple negativity which contains in more developed form the second expression of the law just quoted. *A* is enunciated, and a *not–A*, the pure other of *A*; but it only shows itself in order to vanish. In this proposition, therefore, identity is expressed—as negation of the negation. *A* and *not–A* are distinguished, and these distinct terms are related to one and the same *A*. Identity, therefore, is here represented as *this distinguishedness in one relation* or as *simple difference in the terms themselves*.

From this it is evident that the law of identity itself, and still more the law of contradiction, is not merely of *analytic* but of *synthetic* nature. For the latter contains in its expression not merely empty, simple equality-with-self, and not merely the other of this *in general*, but, what is more, *absolute inequality*, *contradiction per se*. But as has been shown, the law of identity itself contains the movement of reflection, identity as a vanishing of otherness.

What emerges from this consideration is, therefore, first, that the law of identity or of contradiction which purports to express merely abstract identity in contrast to difference as a truth, is not a law of thought, but rather the opposite of it; secondly, that these laws contain *more* than is *meant* by them, to wit, this opposite, absolute difference itself.

----

[1] Reading *Erfahrung* for *Erscheinung*.

B. DIFFERENCE

(a) Absolute Difference

Difference is the negativity which reflection has within it, the nothing which is said in enunciating identity, the essential moment of identity itself which, as negativity of itself, determines itself and is distinguished from difference.

1. This difference is difference *in and for itself*, *absolute difference*, the *difference of essence*. It is difference in and for itself, not difference resulting from anything external, but *self-related*, therefore *simple* difference. It is essential to grasp absolute difference as *simple*. In the absolute difference of *A* and *not-A* from each other, it is the *simple not* which, as such, constitutes it. Difference itself is the simple Notion. Two things are *different*, it is said, *in that* they, etc. '*In that*' is, in one and the same respect, in the same ground of determination. It is the *difference of reflection*, not the *otherness of determinate being*. One determinate being and another determinate being are posited as falling apart, each of them, as determined against the other, has an *immediate being* for itself. The *other of essence*, on the contrary, is the other in and for itself, not the other as other of an other, existing outside it but simple determinateness in itself. In the sphere of determinate being, too, otherness and determinateness proved to be of this nature, to be simple determinateness, identical opposition; but this identity revealed itself only as the *transition* of one determinateness into the other. Here, in the sphere of reflection, difference appears as reflected difference, which is thus posited as it is in itself.

2. Difference in itself is self-related difference; as such, it is the negativity of itself, the difference not of an other, but *of itself from itself*; it is not itself but its other. But that which is different from difference is identity. Difference is therefore itself and identity. Both together constitute difference; it is the whole, and its moment. It can equally be said that difference, as simple, is no difference; it is this only when it is in relation with identity; but the truth is rather that, as difference, it contains equally identity and this relation itself. Difference is the whole and its own *moment*, just as identity equally is its whole and its moment. This is to be considered as the essential nature of reflection and as the *specific, original ground of all activity and self-movement*. Difference and

O

also identity, make themselves into a moment or a positedness because, as reflection, they are negative relation-to-self.

Difference as thus unity of itself and identity, is *in its own self determinate* difference. It is not transition into an other, not relation to an other outside it: it has its other, identity, within itself, just as identity, having entered into the determination of difference, has not lost itself in it as its other, but preserves itself in it, is its reflection-into-self and its moment.

3. Difference possesses both moments, identity and difference; both are thus a *positedness*, a determinateness. But in this positedness each is *self-relation*. One of them, identity, is itself immediately the moment of reflection-into-self; but equally, the other is difference, difference in itself, reflected difference. Difference, in that it has two moments that are themselves reflections-into-self, is *diversity*.

(b) Diversity

1. Identity *falls apart* within itself into diversity because, as absolute difference, it posits itself as its own negative within itself, and these its moments, namely, itself and the negative of itself, are reflections-into-self, are self-identical; or, in other words, precisely because identity itself immediately sublates its negating and in its *determination is reflected into itself*. The distinguished terms *subsist* as indifferently different towards one another because each is self-identical, because identity constitutes its ground and element; in other words, the difference is what it is, only in its very opposite, in identity.

Diversity constitutes the otherness as such of reflection. The other of determinate being has for its ground immediate *being* in which the negative subsists. But in reflection it is self-identity, reflected immediacy, that constitutes the subsistence of the negative and its indifference.

The moments of difference are identity and difference itself. They are [merely] diverse when they are reflected into themselves, that is, when they are *self-related*; as such, they are *in the determination of identity*, they are only relation-to-self; the identity is not related to the difference, nor is the difference related to the identity; as each moment is thus only *self*-related, they are *not determined* against one another. Now because in this manner they are not different in themselves, the *difference* is *external* to them. The *diverse* moments are, therefore, mutually related, not as identity and difference, but merely as simply *diverse* moments, that are indifferent to one another and to their determinateness.

2. In diversity, as the indifference of difference, reflection has become, in general, *external* to itself; difference is merely a *posited* or sublated being, but it is itself the total reflection. When considered more closely, both identity and difference, as has just been demonstrated, are reflections, each of which is unity of itself and its other; each is the whole. Consequently, the determinateness in which they are *only* identity or *only* difference, is sublated. Therefore they are not qualities, because through the reflection-into-self, their determinateness is at the same time only a negation. What is present, therefore, is this duality, *reflection-into-self* as such, and determinateness as negation or *positedness*. Positedness is the reflection that is external to itself; it is the negation as negation—and so therefore *in itself* or *implicity*, the self-related negation and reflection-into-self, but only implicitly; it is relation to the negation as something external to it.

Thus the reflection that is implicit, and external reflection, are the two determinations into which the moments of difference, namely, identity and difference, posited themselves. They are these moments themselves in so far as they have now determined themselves. *Reflection in itself* is identity, but determined as being indifferent to difference, not as simply not possessing difference, but as being self-identical in its relationship with it; it is *diversity*. It is identity that has so reflected itself into itself that it is really the *one* reflection of the two moments into themselves; both are reflections-into-self. Identity is this one reflection of both, which contains difference only as an indifferent difference and is simply diversity. *External reflection*, on the other hand, is their *determinate* difference, not as an absolute reflection-into-self, but as a determination to which the [merely] implicit reflection is indifferent; difference's two moments, identity and difference itself, are thus externally posited determinations, not determinations in and for themselves.

Now this external identity is *likeness*, and external difference, *unlikeness*. *Likeness*, it is true, is identity, but only as a positedness, an identity that is not in and for itself. Similarly, *unlikeness* is difference, but as an external difference that is not in and for itself the difference of the unlike itself. Whether or not something is like something else does not concern either the one or the other; each of them is only self-referred, is in and for itself what it is; identity or non-identity, as likeness or unlikeness, is the verdict of a third party distinct from the two things.

3. External reflection relates what is diverse to likeness and unlikeness. This relation, which is a *comparing*, passes to and fro between likeness and unlikeness. But this relating to likeness and unlikeness, back and forth, is external to these determinations themselves; also, they are related not to one another but each, by itself, to a third. In this alternation, each stands forth immediately on its own. External reflection is, as such, external to itself; the *determinate* difference is the negated absolute difference. Therefore it is not simple, not reflection-into-self; on the contrary, it has this outside it. Its moments, therefore, fall asunder and are related also as mutually external to the reflection-into-self confronting them.

In the self-alienated reflection, therefore, likeness and unlikeness appear as mutually unrelated, and in relating them to *one and the same* thing, it separates them by the introduction of '*in so far*', of *sides* and *respects*. The diverse, which are one and the same, to which both likeness and unlikeness are related, are therefore, *from one side* like one another, but *from another side* are unlike, and *in so far* as they are like, they are not unlike. *Likeness* is related only to itself, and similarly *unlikeness* is only unlikeness.

But by this separation of one from the other they merely sublate themselves. The very thing that was supposed to hold off contradiction and dissolution from them, namely, that something is *like* something else *in one respect, but is unlike it in another*—this holding apart of likeness and unlikeness is their destruction. For both are determinations of difference; they are relations to one another, the one being what the other is not; like is not unlike and unlike is not like; and both essentially have this relation and have no meaning apart from it; as determinations of difference, each is what it is as *distinct* from its other. But through this mutual indifference, likeness is only self-referred, and unlikeness similarly is self-referred and a reflective determination on its own; each, therefore, is like itself; the difference has vanished, since they cannot have any determinateness over against one another; in other words, each therefore is only likeness.

This indifferent point of view or external difference thus

sublates itself and is in its own self the negativity of itself. It is the negativity that belongs to the comparer in the act of comparing. The comparer goes from likeness to unlikeness and from this back to likeness, and therefore lets the one vanish in the other and is, in fact, *the negative unity of both*. This unity, in the first instance, lies beyond the compared and also beyond the moments of the comparison as a subjective act falling outside them. But, as we have seen, this negative unity is, in fact, the very nature of likeness and unlikeness. The independent self-reference which each of them is, is in fact the self-reference that sublates their distinctiveness and so, too, themselves.

From this side, likeness and unlikeness, as moments of external reflection and as external to themselves, vanish together in their likeness. But further, this their *negative* unity is also *posited* in them; they have, namely the [merely] *implicit* reflection outside them, or are the likeness and unlikeness of a *third party*, of an other than they. And so likeness is not like itself; and unlikeness, as unlike not itself but something else unlike it, is itself likeness. The like and the unlike are therefore *unlike themselves*. Consequently each is this reflection: likeness, that it is itself and unlikeness, and unlikeness, that it is itself and likeness.

Likeness and unlikeness formed the side of *positedness* as against the compared or the diverse which had determined itself as the [merely] *implicit* reflection contrasted with them. But this positedness as thus determined has equally lost its determinateness as against them. But likeness and unlikeness, the determinations of external reflection, are just this merely implicit reflection which the diverse as such is supposed to be, the merely indeterminate difference of the diverse. The *implicit* reflection is self-relation without the negation, abstract self-identity, and so simply positedness itself. The merely diverse, therefore, passes over through positedness into negative reflection. The diverse is the merely posited difference, therefore the difference that is no difference, and therefore in its own self the negation of itself. Thus likeness and unlikeness themselves, that is, positedness, returns through indifference or the implicit reflection back into the negative unity with itself, into the reflection which the difference of likeness and unlikeness in its own self is. Diversity, whose *indifferent* sides are just as much simply and solely *moments* of one negative unity, is *opposition*.

Remark: The Law of Diversity

Diversity, like identity, is expressed in its own law. And both these laws are held apart as indifferently different, so that each is valid on its own without respect to the other.

All things are different, or: there are no two things like each other. This proposition is, in fact, opposed to the law of identity, for it declares: *A* is distinctive, therefore *A* is also not *A*; or: *A* is unlike something else, so that it is not simply A but rather a specific *A*. *A*'s place in the law of identity can be taken by any other substrate, but A as distinctive (*als Ungleiches*] can no longer be exchanged with any other. True, it is supposed to be distinctive, not *from itself*, but only *from another*; but this distinctiveness is its own determination. As self-identical *A*, it is indeterminate; but as determinate it is the opposite of this; it no longer has only self-identity, but also a negation and therefore a difference of itself from itself within it.

That everything is different from everything else is a very superfluous proposition, for things in the plural immediately involve manyness and wholly indeterminate diversity. But the proposition that no two things are completely like each other, expresses more, namely, *determinate* difference. Two things are not merely two—numerical manyness is only one-and-the-sameness—but they are different *through a determination*. Ordinary thinking is struck by the proposition that no two things are like each other—as in the story of how Leibniz propounded it at court and caused the ladies to look at the leaves of trees to see whether they could find two alike. Happy times for metaphysics when it was the occupation of courtiers and the testing of its propositions called for no more exertion than to compare leaves! The reason why this proposition is striking lies in what has been said, that *two*, or numerical manyness, does not contain any *determinate* difference and that diversity as such, in its abstraction, is at first indifferent to likeness and unlikeness. Ordinary thinking, even when it goes on to a determination of diversity, takes these moments themselves to be mutually indifferent, so that one without the other, the *mere likeness* of things *without unlikeness*, suffices to determine whether the things are different even when they are only a numerical many, not unlike, but simply different without further qualification. The law of diversity, on the other hand, asserts that things are different from one another through unlikeness, that the determination of unlikeness belongs to them just as much as that of likeness, for determinate difference is constituted only by both together.

Now this proposition that unlikeness must be predicated of all things, surely stands in need of proof; it cannot be set up as an immediate proposition, for even in the ordinary mode of cognition a proof is demanded of the combination of different determinations in a synthetic proposition, or else the indication of a third term in which they are mediated. This proof would have to exhibit the passage of identity into difference, and then the passage of this into determinate difference, into unlikeness. But as a rule this is not done. We have found that diversity or external difference is, in truth, reflected into itself, is difference in its own self, that the indifferent subsistence of the diverse is a mere positedness and therefore not an external, indifferent difference, but a *single* relation of the two moments.

This involves the dissolution and nullity of the *law of diversity*. Two things are not perfectly alike; so they are at once alike and unlike; alike, simply because they are things, or just two, without further qualification—for each is a thing and a one, no less than the other—but they are unlike *ex hypothesi*. We are therefore presented with this determination, that both moments, likeness and unlikeness, are different in one and the same thing, or that the difference, while falling asunder, is at the same time one and the same relation. This has therefore passed over into *opposition*.

The *togetherness* of both predicates is held asunder by the '*in so far*', namely, when it is said that two things are alike *in so far* as they are not unlike, or on one *side* or in one *respect* are alike, but on another *side* or in another *respect* are unlike. The effect of this is to remove the unity of likeness and unlikeness from the thing, and to adhere to what would be the thing's own reflection and the merely implicit reflection of likeness and unlikeness, as a reflection external to the thing. But it is this reflection that, in *one and the same activity*, distinguishes the two sides of likeness and unlikeness, hence contains both in one activity, lets the one show, be reflected, in the other. But the usual tenderness for things, whose only care is that they do not contradict themselves, forgets here as elsewhere that in this way the contradiction is not resolved but merely shifted elsewhere, into subjective or external reflection generally, and this reflection in fact contains in one unity as sublated and mutually referred, the two moments which are enunciated by this removal and displacement as a mere *positedness*.

(c) Opposition

In opposition, the *determinate reflection*, difference, finds its completion. It is the unity of identity and difference; its moments are different in one identity and thus are *opposites*.

Identity and *difference* are the moments of difference held within itself; they are *reflected* moments of its unity. But *likeness* and *unlikeness* are the self-alienated reflection; their self-identity is not merely the indifference of each towards the other distinguished from it, but towards being-in-and-for-self as such, an identity-with-self over against the identity that is reflected into itself; it is therefore the *immediacy* that is not reflected into itself. The positedness of the sides of the external reflection is accordingly a *being*, just as their non-positedness is a *non-being*.

Closer consideration shows the moments of opposition to be positedness reflected into itself or determination in general. Positedness is likeness and unlikeness; these two reflected into themselves constitute the determinations of opposition. Their reflection-into-self consists in this, that each is in its own self the unity of likeness and unlikeness. Likeness is only in the reflection that compares on the basis of unlikeness, and therefore is mediated by its other, indifferent moment; similarly, unlikeness is only in the same reflective relationship in which likeness is. Therefore each of these moments is, in its determinateness, the whole. It is the whole in so far as it also contains its other moment; but this its other is an indifferent, *simple affirmative* moment; thus each contains reference to its non-being, and is only reflection-into-self or the whole, as essentially connected with its non-being.

This self-*likeness* reflected into itself that contains within itself the reference to unlikeness, is the positive; and the unlikeness that contains within itself the reference to its non-being, to likeness, is the negative. Or, both are a positedness; now in so far as the differentiated determinateness is taken as a differentiated *determinate self-reference* of positedness, the opposition is, on the one hand, *positedness* reflected into its likeness to itself and on the other hand, *positedness* reflected into its unlikeness to itself—the positive and the negative. The positive is positedness as reflected into self-likeness; but what is reflected is positedness, that is, the negation as negation, and so this reflection-into-self has reference-to-other for its determination. The negative is positedness as reflected into unlikeness; but the positedness is unlikeness itself, and this reflection is therefore the identity of unlikeness with itself and absolute self-reference. Each is the whole; the positedness reflected into likeness-to-self contains unlikeness, and the positedness reflected into unlikeness-to-self also contains likeness.

The positive and the negative are thus the sides of the opposition that have become self-subsistent. They are self-subsistent in that they are the reflection of the *whole* into themselves, and they belong to the opposition in so far as this is the *determinateness* which, as a whole, is reflected into itself. On account of their self-subsistence, they constitute the *implicitly* determined opposition. Each is itself and its other; consequently, each has *its determinateness* not in an other, but *in its own self*. Each is self-referred, and the reference to its other is only a self-reference. This has a twofold aspect: each is a reference to its non-being as a sublating of this otherness within it; thus its non-being is only a moment in it. But on the other hand positedness here has become a being, an indifferent subsistence; consequently, the other of itself which each contains is also the non-being of that in which it is supposed to be contained only as a moment. Each therefore *is*, only in so far as its *non-being is*, and is in an identical relationship with it.

The determinations which constitute the positive and negative consist, therefore, in the fact that the positive and negative are, in the first place, absolute *moments* of the opposition; their subsistence is inseparably *one* reflection; it is a single mediation in which each *is* through the non-being of its other, and so *is* through its other or its own non-being. Thus they are simply *opposites*; in other words, *each* is only the opposite of the other, the one is not as yet positive, and the other is not as yet negative, but both are negative to one another. In the first place, then, each *is, only in so far as the other is*; it is what it is, through the other, through its own non-being; it is only a *positedness*; secondly, it is, *in so far as the other is not*; it is what it is, through the non-being of the other; it is *reflection-into-self*. But these two are the *one* mediation of the opposition as such, in which they are simply only *posited moments*.

Further, however, this mere positedness is simply reflected into

O*

itself; in accordance with this moment of *external reflection* the positive and negative are *indifferent* to that first identity in which they are only moments; in other words, since that first reflection is the positive's and negative's own reflection into themselves, each is in its own self its positedness, so each is indifferent to this its reflection into its non-being, to its own positedness. The two sides are thus merely different, and in so far as their being determined as positive and negative constitutes their positedness in relation to one another, each is not in its own self so determined but is only determinateness in general. Therefore, although one of the determinatenesses of positive and negative belongs to each side, they can be changed round, and each side is of such a kind that it can be taken equally well as positive as negative.

But thirdly, the positive and negative are not only something posited, not merely an indifferent something, but their *positedness*, or the *reference-to-other in a unity which they are not themselves, is taken back* into each. Each is in its own self positive and negative; the positive and negative are the determination of reflection in and for itself; it is only in this reflection of opposites into themselves that they are positive and negative. The positive has within itself the reference-to-other in which the determinateness of the positive is; similarly, the negative is not a negative as contrasted with an other, but likewise possesses within itself the determinateness whereby it is negative.

Thus each [the positive as well as the negative] is a self-subsistent, independent unity-with-self. The positive is, indeed, a positedness, but in such wise that for it the positedness is only positedness as sublated. It is the *not-opposite*, the sublated opposition, but as a side of the opposition itself. As positive, something is, of course, determined with reference to an otherness, but in such a manner that its nature is to be *not* something posited; it is the reflection-into-self that negates the otherness. But the other of itself, the negative, is itself no longer a positedness or moment, but a self-subsistent *being*; thus the negating reflection of the positive is immanently determined as *excluding* from itself this its *non-being*.

The negative, as such absolute reflection, is not the immediate negative but the negative as a sublated positedness, the negative in and for itself, which is based positively on itself. As reflection-into-self it negates its relationship to other; its other is the positive, a self-subsistent being; consequently, its negative relation to it is to exclude it. The negative is the independently existing opposite contrasted with the positive, which is the determination of the sublated opposition—the self-based *whole opposition* opposed to the self-identical positedness.

The positive and negative are therefore not merely *implicitly* [*an sich*] positive and negative, but explicitly and actually so [*an und für sich*]. They are *implicitly* positive and negative in so far as one makes abstraction from their exclusive relation to other and only takes them in accordance with their determination. Something is *in itself* positive or negative when it is supposed to be so determined not merely *relatively to an other*. But when the positive and negative are taken, not as positedness, and therefore not as opposites, then each is the immediate, *being* and *non-being*. But the positive and negative are moments of opposition; their in-itself constitutes merely the form of their reflectedness-into-self. Something is *in itself* positive, apart from the relation to the negative; and something is *in itself* negative, apart from the relation to the positive;[1] in this determination, one clings merely to the abstract moment of this reflectedness. But the positive or negative *in itself* essentially implies that to be an opposite is not merely a moment, does not stem from comparison, but is a determination belonging to the sides of the opposition themselves. They are therefore not positive or negative *in themselves* apart from the relation to other; on the contrary, *this relation*—an exclusive relation—constitutes their determination or in-itself; in it, therefore, they are at the same time explicitly and actually [*an und für sich*] positive or negative.

Remark: Opposite Magnitudes of Arithmetic
Here is where we must take a look at the notion of the positive and negative as it is employed in *arithmetic*. There it is assumed as known; but because it is not grasped in its determinate difference, it does not avoid insoluble difficulties and complications. We have just found the two *real* determinations of the positive and negative—apart from the simple notion of their opposition—namely, *first*, that the base is a merely different, immediate existence whose simple reflection-into-self is distinguished from its positedness, from the opposition itself. This opposition,

[1] Reading '*positive*' for '*negative*'.

therefore, is not regarded as having any truth in and for itself, and though it does belong to the different sides, so that each is simply an opposite, yet, on the other hand, each side exists indifferently on its own, and it does not matter which of the two opposites is regarded as positive or negative. But secondly, the positive is the positive in and for itself, the negative in and for itself the negative, so that the different sides are not mutually indifferent but this their determination is true in and for itself. These two forms of the positive and negative occur in the very first applications of them in arithmetic.

In the first instance, $+a$ and $-a$ are simply opposite magnitudes; a is the *implicit* [*ansichseiende*] *unity* forming their common base; it is indifferent to the opposition itself and serves here, without any further notion, as a dead base. True, $-a$ is defined as the negative, and $+a$ as the positive, but the one is just as much an *opposite* as the other.

Further, a is not merely the *simple* unity forming the base but, as $+a$ and $-a$, it is the reflection of these opposites into themselves; there are present *two different a's*, and it is a matter of indifference which of them one chooses to define as the positive or negative; both have a separate existence and are positive.

According to the first aspect, $+y-y = 0$; or in $-8+3$, the 3 positive units are negative in the 8. The opposites are cancelled in their combination. An hour's journey to the east and the same distance travelled back to the west, cancels the first journey; an amount of liabilities reduces the assets by a similar amount, and an amount of assets reduces the liabilities by the same amount. At the same time, the hour's journey to the east is not in itself the positive direction, nor is the journey west the negative direction; on the contrary, these directions are indifferent to this determinateness of the opposition; it is a third point of view outside them that makes one positive and the other negative. Thus the liabilities, too, are not in and for themselves the negative; they are the negative only in relation to the debtor; for the creditor, they are his positive asset; they are an amount of money or something of a certain value, and this is a liability or an asset according to an external point of view.

The opposites certainly cancel one another in their relation, so that the result is zero; but there is also present in them *their identical relation*, which is indifferent to the opposition itself;

in this manner they constitute a one. Just as we have pointed out that the sum of money is only one sum, that the a in $+a$ and $-a$ is only one a, and that the distance covered is only one distance, not two, one going east and the other going west. Similarly, an ordinate y is the same on which ever side of the axis it is taken; so far, $+y - y = y$; it is only the one ordinate and it has only one determination and law.

But again, the opposites are not only a single indifferent term, but *two* such. For as opposites, they are also reflected into themselves and thus exist as distinct terms.

Thus in $-8 + 3$ there are altogether eleven units present; $+y$ and $-y$ are ordinates on opposite sides of the axis, where each is an existence indifferent to this limit and to their opposition; thus $+y - y = 2y$.—Also the distance travelled east and west is the sum of a twofold effort or the sum of two periods of time. Similarly, in economics, a quantum of money or of wealth is not only this one quantum as a means of subsistence but is double: it is a means of subsistence both for the creditor and for the debtor. The wealth of the state is computed not merely as the total of ready money plus the value of property movable and immovable, present in the state; still less is it reckoned as the sum remaining after deduction of liabilities from assets. For capital, even if its respective determinations of assets and liabilities nullified each other, remains first, positive capital, as $+a - a = a$; and secondly, since it is a liability in a great number of ways, being lent and re-lent, this makes it a very much multiplied capital.

But not only are opposite magnitudes, on the one hand, merely opposite as such, and on the other hand, real or indifferent: for although quantum itself is being with an indifferent limit, yet the intrinsically positive and the intrinsically negative also occur in it. For example, a, when it bears no sign, is meant to be taken as positive if it has to be defined. If it were intended to become merely an opposite as such, it could equally well be taken as $-a$. But the positive sign is given to it immediately, because the positive on its own has the peculiar meaning of the immediate, as self-identical, in contrast to opposition.

Further, when positive and negative magnitudes are added and subtracted, they are counted as positive or negative on their own account and not as becoming positive or negative in an external manner merely through the relation of addition and subtraction.

In $8 - (-3)$ the first minus means opposite to 8, but the second minus (-3), counts as opposite *in itself*, apart from this relation.

This becomes more evident in multiplication and division. Here the positive must essentially be taken as the *not-opposite*, and the negative, on the other hand, as the opposite, not both determinations equally as only opposites in general. The textbooks stop short at the notion of opposite magnitudes as such in the proofs of the behaviour of the signs in these two species of calculation; these proofs are therefore incomplete and entangled in contradiction. But in multiplication and division *plus* and *minus* receive the more determinate meaning of the positive and negative in themselves, because the relation of the factors—they are related to one another as unit and amount—is not a mere relation of increasing and decreasing as in the case of addition and subtraction, but is a qualitative relation, with the result that *plus* and *minus*, too, are endowed with the qualitative meaning of the positive and negative. Without this determination and merely from the notion of opposite magnitudes, the false conclusion can easily be drawn that if $-a$ times $+a = -a^2$, conversely $+a$ times $-a = +a^2$. Since one factor is amount and the other unity, and the one which comes first usually means that it takes precedence, the difference between the two expressions $-a$ times $+a$ and $+a$ times $-a$ is that in the former $+a$ is the unit and $-a$ the amount, and in the latter the reverse is the case. Now in the first case it is usually said that if I am to take $+a$ $-a$ times, then I take $+a$ not merely a times but also in the opposite manner, $+a$ times $-a$; therefore since it is *plus*, I have to take it negatively, and the product is $-a^2$. But if, in the second case, $-a$ is to be taken $+a$ times, then $-a$ likewise is not to be taken $-a$ times but in the opposite determination, namely $+a$ times. Therefore it follows from the reasoning in the first case, that the product must be $+a^2$. And similarly in the case of division.

This is a necessary conclusion in so far as *plus* and *minus* are taken only as simply opposite magnitudes: in the first case the *minus* is credited with the power of altering the plus; but in the second case the *plus* was not supposed to have the same power over the *minus*, notwithstanding that it is no less an *opposite* determination of magnitude than the latter. In point of fact, the *plus* does not possess this power, for it is to be taken here as qualitatively determined against the *minus*, the factors having a qualitative relationship to one another. Consequently, the negative here is the intrinsically opposite as such, but the positive is an indeterminate, indifferent sign in general; it is, of course, also the negative, but the negative of the other, not in its own self the negative. A determination as negation, therefore, is introduced solely by the negative, not by the positive.

And so $-a$ times $-a$ is also $+a^2$, because the negative a is to be taken not merely in the opposite manner (in that case it would have to be taken as multiplied by $-a$), but because it is to be taken negatively. But the negation of negation is the positive.

C. CONTRADICTION

1. Difference as such contains its two sides as *moments*; in diversity they fall *indifferently* apart; in opposition as such, they are sides of the difference, one being determined only by the other, and therefore only moments; but they are no less determined within themselves, mutually indifferent and mutually exclusive: the *self-subsistent determinations of reflection.*

One is the positive, the other the negative, but the former as the intrinsically positive, the latter as the intrinsically negative. Each has an indifferent self-subsistence of its own through the fact that it has within itself the relation to its other moment; it is thus the whole, self-contained opposition. As this whole, each is mediated with itself *by its other* and *contains* it. But further, it is mediated with itself by the *non-being of its other*; thus it is a unity existing on its own and it *excludes* the other from itself.

The self-subsistent determination of reflection that contains the opposite determination, and is self-subsistent in virtue of this inclusion, at the same time also excludes it; in its self-subsistence, therefore, it excludes from itself its own self-subsistence. For this consists in containing within itself its opposite determination— through which alone it is not a relation to something external— but no less immediately in the fact that it is itself, and also excludes from itself the determination that is negative to it. It is thus *contradiction*.

Difference as such is already *implicitly* contradiction; for it is the *unity* of sides which are, only in so far as they are *not one*—and it is the *separation* of sides which are, only as separated *in the same relation*. But the positive and negative are the *posited* contradiction because, as negative unities, they are themselves the positing of themselves, and in this positing each is the sublating of itself and the positing of its opposite. They constitute the determining reflection as *exclusive*; and because the excluding of the sides is a single act of distinguishing and each of the distinguished sides in excluding the other is itself the whole act of exclusion, each side in its own self excludes itself.

If we consider the two determinations of reflection on their own, then the positive is *positedness* as reflected *into likeness to itself*, positedness that is not a relation to an other, a subsistence, therefore, in so far as positedness is *sublated* and *excluded*. But with this, the positive makes itself into the *relation of a non-being—* into a *positedness*. It is thus the contradiction that, in positing identity with itself by *excluding* the negative, it makes itself into the *negative* of what it excludes from itself, that is, makes itself into its opposite. This, as excluded, is posited as free from that which excludes it, and therefore as reflected into itself and as itself exclusive. The exclusive reflection is thus a positing of the positive as excluding its opposite, so that this positing is immediately the positing of its opposite which it excludes.

This is the absolute contradiction of the positive, but it is immediately the absolute contradiction of the negative; the positing of each is a *single* reflection. The negative, considered on its own over against the positive, is positedness as reflected *into unlikeness to itself*, the negative as negative. But the negative is itself the unlike, the non-being of an opposite; therefore its reflection into its unlikeness is rather its relation to itself. Negation *in general* is the negative as quality, or *immediate* determinateness; but the negative *as negative*, is related to the negative of itself, to its opposite. If this negative is only taken as identical with the first, then it, too, like the first, is merely immediate; and so they are not taken as mutual opposites and therefore not as negatives; the negative is not an immediate at all. But now, since it is also just as much a fact that each is the same as its opposite, this relation of the unlike is just as much their identical relation.

This is therefore the same contradiction that the positive is, namely, positedness or negation as self-relation. But the positive is only *implicitly* this contradiction, whereas the negative is the contradiction *posited*; for the latter, in virtue of its reflection-into-self which makes it a negative in and for itself or a negative that is identical with itself, is accordingly determined as a non-identical, as excluding identity. The negative is this, to be *identical with itself in opposition to identity*, and consequently, through its excluding reflection to exclude itself from itself.

The negative is, therefore, the whole opposition based, as opposition, on itself, absolute difference that *is not related to an other*; as opposition, it excludes identity from itself—but in doing so excludes itself; for as *self-relation* it is determined as the very identity that it excludes.

2. *Contradiction resolves itself.* In the self-excluding reflection we have just considered, positive and negative, each in its self-subsistence, sublates itself; each is simply the transition or rather the self-transposition of itself into its opposite. This ceaseless vanishing of the opposites into themselves is the *first unity* resulting from contradiction; it is the null.

But contradiction contains not merely the negative, but also the positive; or, the self-excluding reflection is at the same time *positing* reflection; the result of contradiction is not merely a nullity. The positive and negative constitute the *positedness* of the self-subsistence. Their own negation of themselves sublates the *positedness* of the self-subsistence. It is this which in truth perishes in contradiction.

The reflection-into-self whereby the sides of opposition are converted into self-subsistent self-relations is, in the first instance, their self-subsistence as *distinct* moments; as such they are only *implicitly* this self-subsistence, for they are still opposites, and the fact that they are *implicitly* self-subsistent constitutes their positedness. But their excluding reflection sublates this positedness, converts them into explicitly self-subsistent sides, into sides which are self-subsistent not merely *implicitly* or *in themselves* but through their negative relation to their opposite; in this way, their self-subsistence is also posited. But further, through this their positing, they make themselves into a positedness. *They destroy themselves* in that they determine themselves as self-identical, yet in this determination are rather the negative, an identity-with-self that is a relation-to-other.

However, this excluding reflection, looked at more closely, is not merely this formal determination. It is an *implicit* self-subsistence and is the sublating of this positedness, and it is only through this sublating that it becomes explicitly and in fact a self-subsistent unity. True, through the sublating of otherness or positedness, we are again presented with positedness, the negative of an other. But in point of fact, this negation is not merely the first, immediate relation-to-other again, not positedness as a sublated immediacy, but as a sublated positedness. The excluding reflection of self-subsistence, being exclusive, converts itself into a positedness, but is just as much a sublating of its positedness. It is a sublating self-relation; in this, it first sublates the negative, and secondly, posits itself as a negative, and it is only this negative that it sublates; in sublating the negative, it posits and sublates itself at the same time. In this way, the *exclusive determination itself* is that *other* of itself whose negation it is; consequently, the sublating of this positedness is not again a positedness as the negative of an other, but is a uniting with itself, the positive unity with itself. Self-subsistence is thus through *its own* negation a unity returned into itself, since it returns into itself through the negation of *its own* positedness. It is the unity of essence, being identical with itself through the negation, not of an other, but of itself.

3. According to this positive side, in which the self-subsistence in opposition, as the excluding reflection, converts itself into a positedness which it no less sublates, opposition is not only *destroyed* [*zugrunde gegangen*] but has withdrawn *into its ground*. The excluding reflection of the self-subsistent opposition converts this into a negative, into something posited; it thereby reduces its primarily self-subsistent *determinations*, the positive and negative, to the status of *mere* determinations; and the positedness, being thus made into a positedness, has simply returned into its unity with itself; it is *simple essence*, but essence as *ground*. Through the sublating of its inherently self-contradictory determinations, essence has been restored, but with this determination, that it is the excluding unity of reflection—a simple unity that determines itself as a negative, but in this positedness is immediately like itself and united with itself.

In the first place, therefore, the self-subsistent opposition through its contradiction *withdraws* into ground; this opposition is the *prius*, the immediate, that forms the starting point, and the sublated opposition or the sublated positedness is itself a positedness. Thus *essence as ground is a positedness*, something that has become. But conversely, what has been posited is only this, that opposition or positedness is a sublated positedness, only is *as* positedness. Therefore essence as ground is the excluding reflection in such wise that it makes its own self into a positedness, that the opposition from which we started and which was the immediate, is the merely posited, determinate self-subsistence of essence, and that opposition is merely that which sublates itself within itself, whereas essence is that which, in its determinateness, is reflected into itself. Essence as ground excludes *itself* from itself, it posits *itself*; its positedness—which is what is excluded—is only *as* positedness, as identity of the negative with itself. This self-subsistent is the negative *posited* as negative; it is self-contradictory and therefore remains immediately in essence as in its ground.

The resolved contradiction is therefore ground, essence as unity of the positive and negative. In opposition, the determination has attained to self-subsistence; but ground is this completed self-subsistence; in it, the negative is self-subsistent essence, but as a negative; as self-identical in this negativity, ground is just as much the positive. Opposition and its contradiction is, therefore, in ground as much abolished as preserved. Ground is essence as positive identity-with-self, which, however, at the same time relates itself to itself as negativity, and therefore determines itself and converts itself into an excluded positedness; but this positedness is the whole self-subsistent essence, and essence is ground, as self-identical and positive in this its negation. The self-contradictory, self-subsistent opposition was therefore already itself ground; all that was added to it was the determination of unity-with-self, which results from the fact that each of the self-subsistent opposites sublates itself and makes itself into its opposite, thus falling to the ground [*zugrunde geht*]; but in this process it at the same time only unites with itself; therefore, it is only in falling to the ground [*in seinem Untergange*], that is, in its positedness or negation, that the opposite is really the essence that is reflected into and identical with itself.

Remark 1: Unity of Positive and Negative
The positive and negative are the same. This expression stems from *external reflection* in so far as this draws a *comparison* between these two determinations. But it is not an external comparison that should be drawn between them any more than between any

other categories; rather must they be considered in themselves, that is, we have to consider what their own reflection is. But we have found that each is essentially the mere show or illusory being of itself in the other and is itself the positing of itself as the other.

But the superficial thinking that does not consider the positive and negative as they are in and for themselves, can, of course, be referred to comparison in order to bring to its notice the untenability of these distinguished sides which it assumes to be fixed in their opposition to one another. Even a slight experience in reflective thinking will make it apparent that if something has been defined as positive and one moves forward from this basis, then straightway the positive has secretly turned into a negative, and conversely, the negatively determined into a positive, and that reflective thinking gets confused and contradicts itself in these determinations. Unfamiliarity with their nature imagines this confusion to be an error that ought not to happen, and ascribes it to a subjective mistake. This transition also, in fact, remains a mere confusion when there is no awareness of the necessity of the transformation. But even for external reflection, it is a simple consideration that, in the first place, the positive is not an immediately identical, but on the one hand is an opposite to a negative, having meaning only in this relation, so that the negative itself is contained *in its* notion; on the other hand, that it is in its own self the self-related negation of mere positedness or the negative, is therefore itself *absolute negation* within itself. Similarly, the negative which stands over against the positive, has meaning only in this relation to its other; it therefore contains this *in its notion*. But the negative also has a *subsistence of its own* apart from this relation to the positive; it is self-identical; but as such it is itself that which the positive was supposed to be.

The opposition between the positive and negative is taken chiefly in the sense that the former (although etymologically it expresses *positedness*) is supposed to be an objective, and the latter a subjective that stems only from an external reflection and is no concern of the objective, which exists in and for itself and for which the subjective does not exist at all. Indeed, if the negative expresses nothing else but the abstraction of a subjective caprice or a determination of an external comparison, then of course it does not exist for the objective positive, that is, this is not related in its own self to such empty abstraction; but in that case the determination that it is a positive is likewise merely external to it. Thus, to take an example of the fixed opposition of these reflective determinations, light as such is reckoned as the pure positive and darkness as the pure negative. But light essentially possesses in its infinite expansion and in its power to promote growth and to animate, the nature of absolute negativity. Darkness, on the other hand, as a non-manifold or as the non-self-differentiating womb of generation, is the simply self-identical, the positive. It is taken as the pure negative in the sense that, as the mere absence of light, it simply does not exist for it, so that light, in its relation with darkness, is supposed to be in relation, not with an other but purely with itself, darkness therefore simply vanishing before it. But it is a familiar fact that light is dimmed to grey by darkness; and besides this merely quantitative alteration it suffers also the qualitative change of being determined to colour by its relation to darkness. Thus, for example *virtue* too is not without conflict; rather is it the supreme, finished conflict; as such it is not merely the positive, but is absolute negativity; also it is virtue not only in comparison with vice, but is *in its own self* opposition and conflict. Or again, *vice* is not merely the *lack* of virtue—innocence, too, is this lack—nor is it distinct from virtue only for an external reflection; on the contrary, it is in its own self opposed to it, it is *evil*. Evil consists in being self-poised in opposition to the good; it is a positive negativity. But innocence, being neither good nor evil, is indifferent to both determinations, is neither positive nor negative. But at the same time this lack must also be taken as a determinateness: on the one hand, it is to be considered as the positive nature of something; on the other, it is related to an opposite, and every nature emerging from its innocency, from its indifferent self-identity, spontaneously relates itself to its other and thereby falls to the ground or, in the positive sense, withdraws into its ground. Truth also is the positive as the knowing that agrees with the object; but it is only this likeness to itself in so far as the knower has put himself into a negative relation with the other, has penetrated the object and sublated the negation which it is. *Error* is a positive, as an opinion asserting what is not in and for itself, an opinion that is aware of itself and asserts itself. But ignorance is either indifferent to truth and error, and therefore neither positively nor negatively determined, its determination stemming from external reflection; or else as objective, as a nature's own determination, it is the impulse that is directed against itself, a negative that contains a positive direction within it. It is of the greatest importance to perceive and to bear in mind this nature of the reflective determinations we have just considered, namely, that their truth consists only in their relation to one another, that therefore each in its very Notion contains the other; without this knowledge, not a single step can really be taken in philosophy.

Remark 2: The Law of the Excluded Middle

The determination of opposition has also been made into a law, the so-called law of the excluded middle: *something is either A or not-A; there is no third.*

This law implies first, that everything is an *opposite*, is *determined* as either positive or negative. An important proposition, which has its necessity in the fact that identity passes over into difference, and this into opposition. Only it is usually not understood in this sense, but usually means nothing more than that, of all predicates, either this particular predicate or its non-being belongs to a thing. The opposite means here merely the lack [of a predicate], or rather *indeterminateness*; and the proposition is so trivial that it is not worth the trouble of saying it. When the determinations sweet, green, square are taken—and all predicates are meant to be taken—and then it is said that spirit is either sweet or not sweet, green or not green, and so on, this is a triviality leading nowhere. The determinateness, the predicate, is referred to something; the proposition asserts that the something is determined; now it ought essentially to imply this: that the determinateness further determine itself, become an intrinsic determinateness, become opposition. Instead of this, however, it merely passes over, in the trivial sense just mentioned, from the determinateness into its non-being in general, back to indeterminateness.

The law of the excluded middle is also distinguished from the laws of identity and contradiction considered above; the latter of these asserted that there is nothing that is *at once A and not-A.* It implies that there *is* nothing that is *neither A nor not-A*, that there is not a third that is indifferent to the opposition. But in fact the third that is indifferent to the opposition *is given* in the law itself, namely, *A* itself is present in it. This *A* is neither $+A$

nor $-A$, and is equally well $+A$ as $-A$. The something that was supposed to be either $-A$ or not A is therefore related to both $+A$ and not-A; and again, in being related to A, it is supposed *not* to be related to not-A, nor to A, if it is related to not-A. The something itself, therefore, is the third which was supposed to be excluded. Since the opposite determinations in the something are just as much posited as sublated in this positing, the third which has here the form of a dead something, when taken more profoundly, is the unity of reflection into which the opposition withdraws as into ground.

Remark 3: The Law of Contradiction

If, now, the first determinations of reflection, namely, identity, difference and opposition, have been put in the form of a law, still more should the determination into which they pass as their truth, namely, contradiction, be grasped and enunciated as a law: *everything is inherently contradictory*, and in the sense that this law in contrast to the others expresses rather the truth and the essential nature of things. The contradiction which makes its appearance in opposition, is only the developed nothing that is contained in identity and that appears in the expression that the law of identity says *nothing*. This negation further determines itself into difference and opposition, which now is the posited contradiction.

But it is one of the fundamental prejudices of logic as hitherto understood and of ordinary thinking, that contradiction is not so characteristically essential and immanent a determination as identity; but in fact, if it were a question of grading the two determinations and they had to be kept separate, then contradiction would have to be taken as the profounder determination and more characteristic of essence. For as against contradiction, identity is merely the determination of the simple immediate, of dead being; but contradiction is the root of all movement and vitality; it is only in so far as something has a contradiction within it that it moves, has an urge and activity.

In the first place, contradiction is usually kept aloof from things, from the sphere of being and of truth generally; it is asserted that *there is nothing that is contradictory*. Secondly, it is shifted into subjective reflection by which it is first posited in the process of relating and comparing. But even in this reflection, it does not really exist, for it is said that the *contradictory* cannot be *imagined* or *thought*. Whether it occurs in actual things or in reflective thinking, it ranks in general as a contingency, a kind of abnormality and a passing paroxysm of sickness.

Now as regards the assertion that *there is* no contradiction, that it does not exist, this statement need not cause us any concern; an absolute determination of essence must be present in every experience, in everything actual, as in every notion. We made the same remark above in connexion with the *infinite*, which is the contradiction as displayed in the sphere of being. But common experience itself enunciates it when it says that at least *there is* a *host* of contradictory things, contradictory arrangements, whose contradiction exists not merely in an external reflection but in themselves. Further, it is not to be taken merely as an abnormality which only occurs here and there, but is rather the negative as determined in the sphere of essence, the principle of all self-movement, which consists solely in an exhibition of it. External, sensuous motion itself is contradiction's immediate existence. Something moves, not because at one moment it is here and at another there, but because at one and the same moment it is here and not here, because in this 'here', it at once is and is not. The ancient dialecticians must be granted the contradictions that they pointed out in motion; but it does not follow that therefore there is no motion, but on the contrary, that motion is *existent* contradiction itself.

Similarly, internal self-movement proper, *instinctive urge* in general, (the appetite or *nisus* of the monad, the entelechy of absolutely simple essence), is nothing else but the fact that something is, in one and the same respect, *self-contained and* deficient, *the negative of itself*. Abstract self-identity is not as yet a livingness, but the positive, being in its own self a negativity, goes outside itself and undergoes alteration. Something is therefore alive only in so far as it contains contradiction within it, and moreover is this power to hold and endure the contradiction within it. But if an existent in its positive determination is at the same time incapable of reaching beyond its negative determination and holding the one firmly in the other, is incapable of containing contradiction within it, then it is not the living unity itself, not ground, but in the contradiction falls to the ground [*zugrunde geht*]. *Speculative thinking* consists solely in the fact that thought holds fast contradiction, and in it, its own self, but does not allow itself to be dominated by it as in ordinary thinking, where its determinations are resolved by contradiction only into other determinations or into nothing.

If the contradiction in motion, instinctive urge, and the like, is masked for ordinary thinking, in the simplicity of these determinations, contradiction is, on the other hand, immediately represented in the *determinations of relationship*. The most trivial examples of above and below, right and left, father and son, and so on *ad infinitum*, all contain opposition in each term. That *is* above, which is *not* below; 'above' is specifically just this, not to be 'below', and only *is*, *in so far as* there is a 'below'; and conversely, each determination implies its opposite. Father is the other of son, and son the other of father, and each only *is* as this other of the other; and at the same time, the one determination only is, in relation to the other; their being is a *single* subsistence. The father also has an existence of his own apart from the son-relationship; but then he is not father but simply man; just as above and below, right and left, are each also a reflection-into-self and are something apart from their relationship, but then only places in general. Opposites, therefore, contain contradiction in so far as they are, in the same respect, negatively related to one another or *sublate each other* and are *indifferent* to one another. Ordinary thinking when it passes over to the moment of the *indifference* of the determinations, forgets their negative unity and so retains them merely as 'differents' in general, in which determination right is no longer right, nor left left, etc. But since it has, in fact, right and left before it, these determinations are before it as self-negating, the one being in the other, and each in this unity being not self-negating but indifferently for itself.

Therefore though ordinary thinking everywhere has contradiction for its content, it does not become aware of it, but remains an external reflection which passes from likeness to unlikeness, or from the negative relation to the reflection-into-self, of the distinct sides. It holds these two determinations over against one another and has in mind *only them*, but not their *transition*, which is the essential point and which contains the contradiction. *Intelligent* reflection, to mention this here, consists, on the contrary, in grasping and asserting contradiction. Even though it does not express the Notion of things and their relationships and has for its material and content only the determinations of ordinary thinking, it does bring these into a relation that contains their contradiction and allows *their Notion to show or shine through* the contradiction. Thinking reason, however, sharpens, so to say, the blunt difference of diverse terms, the mere manifoldness of pictorial thinking, into *essential* difference, into *opposition*. Only when the manifold terms have been driven to the point of contradiction do they become active and lively towards one another, receiving in contradiction the negativity which is the indwelling pulsation of self-movement and spontaneous activity [*Lebendigkeit*].

We have already remarked that the basic determination in the ontological proof of the existence of God is *the sum total of all realities*. It is usually shown, first of all, that this determination is *possible* because it is free from *contradiction*, reality being taken only as reality without any limitation. We remarked that this sum total thus becomes simple indeterminate being, or if the realities are, in fact, taken as a plurality of determinate beings, into the sum-total of all negations. More precisely, when the difference of reality is taken into account, it develops from difference into opposition, and from this into contradiction, so that in the end the sum total of all realities simply becomes absolute contradiction within itself. Ordinary—but not speculative—thinking, which abhors contradiction, as nature abhors a vacuum, rejects this conclusion; for in considering contradiction, it stops short at the one-sided *resolution* of it into *nothing*, and fails to recognise the positive side of contradiction where it becomes *absolute activity* and absolute ground.

In general, our consideration of the nature of contradiction has shown that it is not, so to speak, a blemish, an imperfection or a defect in something if a contradiction can be pointed out in it. On the contrary, every determination, every concrete thing, every Notion, is essentially a unity of distinguished and distinguishable moments, which, by virtue of the *determinate, essential difference*, pass over into contradictory moments. This contradictory side of course resolves itself into nothing, it withdraws into its negative unity. Now the thing, the subject, the Notion, is just this negative unity itself; it is inherently self-contradictory, but it is no less the *contradiction resolved*: it is the *ground* that contains and supports its determinations. The thing, subject, or Notion, as reflected into itself in its sphere, is its resolved contradiction, but its entire sphere is again also *determinate, different*; it is thus a finite sphere and this means a *contradictory* one. It is not itself the resolution of this higher contradiction but has a higher sphere for its negative unity, for its ground. Finite things, therefore, in their indifferent multiplicity are simply this, to be contradictory and *disrupted within themselves and to return into their ground*. As will be demonstrated later, the true inference from a finite and contingent being to an absolutely necessary being does not consist in inferring the latter from the former as from a being that *is and remains the ground*; on the contrary, the inference is from a being that, as is also directly implied in *contingency*, is only in a state of collapse and is *inherently self-contradictory*; or rather, the true inference consists in showing that contingent being in its own self withdraws into its ground in which it is sublated, and further, that by this withdrawal it posits the ground only in such a manner that it rather makes itself into a positedness. In ordinary inference, the *being* of the finite appears as ground of the absolute; because the finite is, therefore the absolute is. But the truth is that the absolute is, because the finite is the inherently self-contradictory opposition, because it is *not*. In the former meaning, the inference runs thus: the being of the finite is the being of the absolute; but in the latter, thus: the non-being of the finite is the being of the absolute.

CHAPTER 3

GROUND

Essence determines itself as ground.

Just as *nothing* is at first in simple immediate unity with *being*, so here too the simple identity of essence is at first in immediate unity with its absolute negativity. Essence is only this its negativity, which is pure reflection. It is this pure negativity as the return of being into itself; as such, it is *determined in itself*, or for us, as ground in which being is dissolved. But this determinateness is not posited *by essence itself*; in other words, essence is not ground except in so far as it has itself posited this its determinateness. Its reflection, however, consists in its *positing* and *determining* itself as that which it is *in itself*, as a negative. The positive and negative constitute that determination of essence in which essence is lost in its negation. These self-subsistent determinations of reflection sublate themselves, and the determination that has fallen to the ground [*zugrunde gegangene*] is the true determination of essence.

Consequently, ground is itself *one of the reflected determinations* of essence; but it is the last of them, or rather the meaning of this determination is merely that it is a sublated determination. The reflected determination, in falling to the ground, acquires its true meaning, namely, to be within itself the absolute recoil upon itself, that is to say, the positedness that belongs to essence is only a sublated positedness, and conversely, only self-sublating positedness is the positedness of essence. Essence, in determining itself as ground, is determined as the non-determined; its determining is only the sublating of its being determined. Essence, in being determined thus as self-sublating, has not proceeded from another, but is, in its negativity, self-identical essence.

In so far as the determination of a first, an immediate, is the starting point of the advance to ground (through the nature of the determination itself which sublates itself or falls to the ground), ground is, in the first instance, determined by that first. But this determining is, on the one hand, as a sublating of the determining, only the restored, purified or manifested identity of essence which the reflected determination is *in itself*; on the other hand it is this negating movement as a determining that first posits that reflected determinateness which appeared as immediate, but which is posited only by the self-excluding reflection of ground and therein is posited as only a posited or sublated determination. Thus essence, in determining itself as ground, proceeds only from itself. As *ground*, therefore, it posits itself *as essence*, and it is in positing itself as essence that its determining consists. This positing is the reflection of essence, a reflection which in its determining *sublates* itself, on that side is a *positing*, on this side is *the* positing *of essence*, hence both in a single act.

Reflection is *pure mediation* in general, ground is *real mediation* of essence with itself. The former, the movement of nothing through nothing back to itself, is the reflection of *itself* in an other; but because the opposition in the reflection has not as yet any self-subsistence, the one that reflects is not a positive, nor is the *other* in which it is reflected a negative. Both are substrates, strictly speaking, only of imagination; they are not as yet self-related determinations. Pure mediation is only *pure relation*, without any related terms. Determining reflection, it is true, posits determinations that are self-identical, but at the same time they are only *determinate relations*. Ground, on the other hand, is real mediation because it contains reflection as sublated reflection; it is essence that, through its non-being, *returns into* and *posits itself*. In accordance with this moment of sublated reflection, the posited receives the determination of *immediacy*, of an immediate that, apart from the relation, or its illusory being, is self-identical. This immediate is *being* which has been restored by essence, the non-being of reflection through which essence mediates itself. Essence returns into itself as a negating activity; therefore in its return into itself, it gives itself determinateness, which is for this very reason the self-identical negative, sublated positedness, and consequently is equally an *affirmative being* [*seiendes*] as the identity of essence with itself as ground.

Ground is first, *absolute ground*, in which essence is, in the first instance, a substrate for the ground relation; but it further determines itself as *form* and *matter* and gives itself a *content*.

Secondly, it is a *determinate ground* as ground of a determinate content; in that the ground relation in its realization as such becomes external to itself, it passes over into *conditioning* mediation.

Thirdly, ground presupposes a condition; but the condition no less presupposes the ground; the unconditioned is their unity, the *fact in itself*, which through the mediation of the conditioning relation passes over into Existence.

Remark: The Law of Ground

Ground, like the other determinations of reflection, has been expressed in the form of a law; everything has its sufficient ground. This means in general nothing else but: what *is*, is not to be regarded as a merely *affirmative immediate* [*seiendes Unmittelbares*], but as something *posited*; we must not stop at immediate determinate being or determinateness as such, but must go back from this into its ground, in which reflection it is a sublated being and is in and for itself. In the law of ground, therefore, the essential character of reflection-into-self in contrast to mere being is expressed. To add that the ground must be *sufficient* is really quite superfluous for it is self-evident; that for which the ground is not sufficient would not have a ground, but everything is supposed to have a ground. Leibniz, however, who had the principle of the sufficient ground very much at heart and even made it the basis of his entire philosophy, associated with it a profounder meaning and more important concept than is usually connected with it when no advance is made beyond the immediate expression; although even with this meaning, the law must be considered important, for it declares being as such in its immediacy to be untrue and essentially something posited, and ground is declared to be the true immediate. But Leibniz opposed the *sufficiency* of ground mainly to causality in its strict sense as the mechanical mode of action. Since this is an altogether external activity, restricted as regards content to a single determinateness, the determinations posited by it are *externally* and *contingently conjoined*; partial determinations are comprehended by their causes, but their *connexion*, which constitutes the essential feature of an existent, is not contained in causes belonging to the sphere of mechanism. This relationship in which the whole is an essential unity, lies only in the *Notion*, in *end*. Mechanical causes are not sufficient for this unity because their basis is not end as the unity of the determinations. Accordingly, by sufficient ground, Leibniz understood one that was also sufficient for this unity and which therefore comprehended not merely causes, but *final causes*. But this is not yet the proper place for this determination of ground; *teleological* ground is a property of the Notion and of mediation by the Notion, which is reason.

A. ABSOLUTE GROUND

(a) Form and Essence

The determination of reflection, in so far as it withdraws into ground, is a first, an immediate determinate being in general, which forms the starting point. But determinate being still has only the meaning of positedness and essentially *presupposes* a ground—in the sense that it does not really *posit* a ground, that this positing is a sublating of itself, that really it is the immediate that is the posited, and ground the not-posited. As we have seen, this presupposing is positing that recoils on that which posits: ground, as the determination that has been sublated, is not indeterminate; it is essence determined through itself, but *determined* as *undetermined*, or as a sublated positedness. *Ground is essence that in its negativity is identical with itself.*

The *determinateness* of essence as ground is therefore twofold, that of *ground* and the *grounded*. It is first, essence as ground, *determined* as essence over against positedness, determined, that is, as a *not-positedness*. Secondly, it is the grounded, the immediate, which however is not in and for itself; it is positedness *qua* positedness. This, therefore, is likewise self-identical, but is the identity of the negative with itself. The self-identical negative and the self-identical positive is *now one and the same identity*. For ground is the identity of the positive or even of positedness, too, with itself; the grounded is positedness *qua* positedness, but this its reflection-into-self is the identity of the ground. This simple identity is therefore not itself ground, for ground is essence *posited* as the not-posited *over against positedness*. As the unity of this determinate identity (of the ground) and of the negative identity (of the grounded), it is *essence as such* as distinguished from its *mediation*.

This mediation, compared with the preceding reflection from which it has proceeded, is *first*, not pure reflection, which is not distinguished from essence and is the negative, consequently also does not as yet contain the independence of the determinations. In ground as sublated reflection, however, these determinations do persist. Nor is it determining reflection, whose determinations have an essential self-subsistence; for this has fallen to the ground [*zugrunde gegangen*] in the ground, in whose unity the determinations are only posited ones. This mediation of the ground is therefore the unity of the pure and the determining reflection; their determinations or the posited, has a subsistence, and conversely, their subsistence is a posited. Because this their subsistence is itself a posited or has a determinateness, they are distinguished from their simple identity, and constitute the *form as against essence*.

Essence *has* a form and determinations of the form. It is only as ground that it has a fixed immediacy or is a *substrate* [*Substrat*]. Essence as such is one with its reflection and inseparable from the movement of reflection itself. Consequently, it is not essence through which the reflective movement runs; nor is essence a first from which reflection begins. This circumstance makes the exposition of reflection in general more difficult; for we cannot really say that *essence* withdraws into itself, that *essence* inwardly reflects itself, because it is not *before* or *in* its movement, and this has no substrate on which it runs its course. A related determination only makes its appearance in ground conformably to the moment of sublated reflection. But essence as related substrate is determinate essence; by virtue of this positedness it essentially contains form. The form determinations, on the other hand, are now determinations *as in essence*; *the latter lies at their base* as the indeterminate which, in its determination, is indifferent towards them; in it they have their reflection-into-self. The determinations of reflection ought to have their subsistence within themselves and to be self-subsistent; but their self-subsistence is their dissolution; they have it in an other; but this dissolution is itself this self-identity or the ground of their subsistence that they give to themselves.

To form belongs in general everything *determinate*; it is a form determination in so far as it is something posited and consequently distinct from *that of which* it is the form; determinateness as *quality* is one with its substrate, with being; being is the immediately determinate that is not yet distinct from its determinateness—or which in it is not yet reflected into itself, and this determinateness, therefore, is a simply affirmative [*seiende*], not yet a posited, one. Further, the form-determinations of essence, as determinatenesses of reflection, are, in their more precise determinateness, the moments of reflection considered above, *identity* and *difference*, the latter partly as diversity, partly as *opposition*. But, again, the *ground relation* also belongs to form since, although it is the sublated determination of reflection, essence is thereby made into something posited. On the other hand, the identity possessed by ground does not belong to form, for in this, positedness as sublated and positedness as such— ground and the grounded—is a single reflection that constitutes essence as the *simple substrate* which is the *subsisting* of form. But this subsistence is *posited* in ground; or this essence is essentially determinate and is thus once again the moment of ground-relation and form. This is the absolute reciprocal relation of form and essence, that essence is this simple unity of ground and grounded, but in this very unity is itself determined, or a negative, and distinguishes itself as substrate from form, but thus at the same time itself becomes ground and moment of form.

Form is therefore the completed whole of reflection; it also contains this determination of reflection, namely, to be a sublated determination; consequently, as well as being a unity of its determining, it is also just as much *related* to its sublatedness, *to an other* which is not itself form, but form is *in it*. As essential self-related negativity over against this simple negative, form is the positing and determining principle; simple essence, on the other hand, is the indeterminate and *inactive* substrate in which the form-determinations subsist and are reflected into themselves. External reflection usually does not go beyond this distinction of essence and form; the distinction is necessary, but this distinguishing is itself their unity, just as this basic unity is essence which repels itself from itself and makes itself into a positedness. Form is absolute negativity or negative absolute self-identity through which precisely essence is not being but essence. This identity, taken abstractly, is essence as against form; just as negativity, taken abstractly, as positedness, is the single determination of form. But the determination, as we have seen, is, in its truth, the total, self-related negativity which, therefore, as this identity is in its own self simple essence. Consequently, form has in its own identity essence, just as essence has in its negative nature absolute form. The question cannot therefore be asked, *how form is added to essence*, for it is only the reflection of essence into essence itself

P

[*das Scheinen desselben in sich selbst*], essence's own immanent reflection. Form is in its own self equally the reflection that returns into itself, or identical essence; in its determining, form makes the determination into positedness as positedness. It does not therefore determine essence as if truly presupposed by the latter and as if separate from it, for thus it is the unessential determination of reflection that hastens without pause to destruction; on the contrary, it is itself the ground of its sublating or the identical connexion of its determinations. To say that form determines essence means, therefore, that form in its distinguishing sublates this very distinguishing and is the self-identity which essence is as the subsistence of the determination; it is the contradiction of being sublated in its positedness and of persisting in this sublatedness; it is accordingly ground as the essence that, in being determined or negated, is identical with itself.

These distinctions of form and essence are therefore only *moments* of the simple form relation itself. But they are to be more closely considered and held fast. The determining form is self-related as a sublated positedness, and is therefore related to its identity as to an other. It posits itself as sublated; in doing so it *presupposes* its identity; according to this moment, essence is the indeterminate for which form is an other. As such, it is not essence, which is in its own self absolute reflection, but is *determined* as formless identity; it is *matter*.

(b) Form and Matter

Essence becomes matter in that its reflection is determined as relating itself to essence as to the formless indeterminate. Matter is therefore the differenceless identity which is essence, with the determination of being the other of form. It is consequently the real *basis* or substrate of form, because it constitutes the reflection-into-self of the form-determinations, or the self-subsistent element to which the latter are related as to their positive subsistence.

1. If abstraction is made from every determination, from all form of anything, what is left over is indeterminate matter. Matter is a sheer *abstraction*. (Matter cannot be seen, felt, and so on—what is seen, felt, is a *determinate matter*, that is, a unity of matter and form.) This abstraction from which matter proceeds is, however, not merely an *external* removal and sublating of form,

rather does form, as we have seen, spontaneously reduce itself to this simple identity.

Further, form *presupposes* a matter to which it relates itself. But the two are not on that account simply present as externally and contingently opposite to one another; neither matter nor form is self-originated, or, in another terminology, *eternal*. Matter is that which is indifferent to form, but this indifference is the *determinateness* of self-identity into which form withdraws as into its basis. Form *presupposes* matter in the very fact that it posits itself as sublated and consequently relates itself to this its identity as to an other. Conversely, form is presupposed by matter; for the latter is not simple essence, which is immediately itself absolute reflection, but it is essence determined as the positive, that is, essence that only is as sublated negation. But from the other side, because form posits itself as matter only in so far as it sublates, hence *presupposes*, matter, matter is also determined as a *groundless* subsistence. Equally matter is not determined as the ground of form; but since matter posits itself as the abstract identity of the sublated form determination, it is not identity as ground, and, in so far, form is groundless relatively to it. Form and matter alike are accordingly determined as being not posited by one another, as not being the ground of one another. Matter is rather the identity of the ground and the grounded, as a basis which stands over against this form relation. This their common determination of indifference is the determination of matter as such and constitutes, too, the mutual connexion of both. Similarly, the determination of form to be the relation of the two as distinct sides, is also the other moment of their mutual relationship. Matter, the indifferently determinate, is the *passive* side over against form as the *active* side. The latter, as the self-related negative is the internal contradiction: it is self-resolving, self-repelling and self-determining. It relates itself to matter and is *posited* as relating itself to this its subsistence as to an other. Matter, on the other hand, is posited as being related only to itself and as indifferent to other; but it is *implicitly* related to form; for it contains sublated negativity and is matter only through this determination. It is related to form as to an *other* only because form is not posited in it, because it is only *implicitly* form. Matter contains form locked up within it and is absolute susceptibility to form only because it has form absolutely within itself, only because form is its implicit determination. *Matter must therefore be formed,* and form must materialize itself, must give itself in matter self-identity or subsistence.

2. Hence form determines matter, and matter is determined by form. Now because form itself is absolute identity-with-self and therefore contains matter within it, and equally, because matter in its pure abstraction or absolute negativity possesses within itself form, therefore the action of form on matter and the passivity of matter in its determining by form is, in effect, only *the removal of the illusion* of their *indifference* and distinguishedness. This relation of the determining is thus the mediation of each with itself through its own non-being; but these two mediations are one movement and the restoration of their original identity—the inwardizing of their outwardness. [*Entäusserung.*]

At first, form and matter *presuppose* one another. As we have seen, this simply means that the one essential unity is negative self-relation which thus sunders itself into essential identity, determined as the indifferent basis, and into essential difference or negativity, as the determining form. That unity of essence and form that confront one another as form and matter, is the *absolute ground* that *determines* itself. The relation, in differentiating itself, becomes by virtue of the fundamental identity of the different sides, reciprocal presupposition.

Secondly, form as self-subsistent is, besides, the self-sublating contradiction; but it is also posited as such, for it is at the same time both self-subsistent and essentially related to an other; it thus sublates itself. Since it is itself two-sided, this sublating, too, has a double aspect: first, it sublates *its self-subsistence*, converts itself into something *posited*, into something that is in an other, and this its other is matter. Secondly, it sublates its determinateness relatively to matter, its relation to it, and consequently its *positedness*, and in doing so gives itself a *subsistence*. Since form sublates its positedness, this its reflection is its own identity into which it passes; but since, at the same time, it divests itself of this identity and opposes itself to itself as matter, this reflection of the positedness into itself is a union with a matter in which it obtains a subsistence; in this union, therefore, it is just as much united with matter *as an other*—in accordance with the first aspect whereby it converts itself into something posited—as also, in that other, it is united *with its own identity*.

Thus the *activity of form* through which matter is determined consists in a negative bearing of form towards itself. But, conversely, in doing so, form also bears itself negatively towards matter; yet this activity by which matter is determined is just as much a movement belonging to form itself. Form is free from matter, but it sublates this its self-subsistence; but its self-subsistence is matter itself, for in this it has its essential identity. Therefore the conversion of itself into something posited is the same thing as its making matter into something determinate. But looked at from the other side, form is at the same time divested of its own identity, and matter is its other; and to this extent, matter is also not determined, since form sublates its own self-subsistence. But matter is self-subsistent only as against form; the negative, in sublating itself, also sublates the positive. Form, therefore, having sublated itself, the determinateness which matter has as against form also disappears, namely, to be an indeterminate subsistence.

This, which appears as *activity of form*, is also no less a *movement belonging to matter itself*. The *implicit* determination of matter or what it *ought* to be, is its absolute negativity. Through this, matter is not related to form simply as to an other: on the contrary, this external other is the form that lies concealed within matter itself. Matter is the same internal contradiction that form contains, and this contradiction, like its resolution, is only *one*. But matter is internally contradictory because, as indeterminate self-identity, it is also absolute negativity; it therefore sublates itself internally and its identity disintegrates in its negativity and the latter obtains from the former its subsistence. Therefore matter, in being determined by form as by something external, thereby achieves its determination, and the externality of the relationship both for form and matter consists in the fact that each, or rather their original unity, in its positing is at the same time *presupposing*, with the result that the relation to itself is at the same time a relation to itself as sublated, or a relation to its other.

Thirdly, through this movement of form and matter, their original unity is, on the one hand, restored, and on the other hand, it is now a posited unity. Matter is just as much *self*-determined, as this determining is for it an external activity of the form; conversely, form determines only itself or has within itself the matter that is determined by it, just as much as in its determining it relates itself to an other; and both, the activity of form and the movement of matter, are the same, save that the former is an activity, that is, negativity as posited, whereas the latter is a movement or becoming, negativity as an *implicit* determination. The result is accordingly the unity of implicit being or the in-itself, and positedness. Matter is as such determinate or necessarily has a form, and form is simply material, subsistent form.

Form, in so far as it presupposes a matter as its other, is *finite*. It is not ground but only the active principle. Similarly, matter, in so far as it presupposes form as its non-being, is *finite* matter; just as little is it ground of its unity with form, but only the basis for form. But this finite matter as well as the finite form has no truth; each relates itself to the other, in other words, only their unity is their truth. Into this unity both these determinations withdraw and therein sublate their self-subsistence: this unity thus demonstrates itself to be their ground. Matter is therefore ground of its form-determination only in so far as it is not matter as matter, but the absolute unity of essence and form; similarly, form is ground of the subsistence of its determinations only in so far as it is the same one unity. But this one unity as absolute negativity, and more specifically, as exclusive unity is, in its reflection, presupposing; or, there is but a single activity: form in its positing both preserves itself, as posited, in the unity, and also repels itself from itself; it is related to itself as itself and also to itself as an other. Or, the process by which matter is determined by form is the mediation of essence as ground with itself in a unity, through its own self and through the negation of itself.

Formed matter, or the form that has a subsistence, is now not only this absolute unity of the ground with itself, but also the *posited* unity. It is the movement just considered in which absolute ground has exhibited its moments as at the same time self-sublating and therefore also as posited. Or the restored unity, in uniting with itself has just as much repelled and determined itself; for since its unity is the outcome of negation, it is also a negative unity. It is therefore the unity of form and matter as their basis, but as their *determinate basis*, which is formed matter, but which is at the same time indifferent to form and matter, these being sublated and unessential determinations. It is *content*.

(c) Form and Content

At first, form stands opposed to essence; it is then the simple ground relation, and its determinations are the ground and the grounded. Secondly, it stands opposed to matter; it is then determining reflection, and its determinations are the reflected determination itself and the subsistence of the determination. Lastly, it stands opposed to content; and then its determinations are again form itself and matter. What was previously the self-identical—at first ground, then simple subsistence, and finally matter—comes under the dominance of form and is once more one of its determinations.

The content is, first, a form and a matter which belong to it and are essential; it is their unity. But since this unity is at the same time a *determinate* or *posited* unity, the content stands opposed to the form; this constitutes the *positedness* and is the unessential over against the content. The latter is therefore indifferent to form; form embraces both form as such and also matter; and the content therefore has a form and a matter of which it is the substrate, and which are to the content a mere positedness.

The content is, secondly, the identical element in form and matter, so that these would be only indifferent external determinations. They are positedness in general which, however, in the content has withdrawn into its unity or its ground. The identity of the content with itself is, therefore, first that identity which is indifferent to the form; but secondly, it is the identity *of the ground*. The ground has, in the first instance, vanished in the content; but the content is at the same time the negative reflection of the form-determinations into themselves; therefore its unity which is, at first, only the unity that is indifferent to the form, is also the formal unity or the *ground relation* as such. The content has, therefore, the latter for its *essential* form, and the *ground* conversely has a *content*.

The content of the ground is, therefore, the ground that has returned into its unity with itself; ground is at first the essence that in its positedness is self-identical; as different from and indifferent to its positedness it is indeterminate matter; but as content it is also formed identity and this form becomes ground relation because the determinations of its opposition are also posited as negated in the content. Further, the content is *determinate* in its own self; not merely like matter as the indifferent in general but as formed matter, so that the determinations of form have a material indifferent subsistence. On the one hand, content is the essential identity of ground with itself in its positedness; on the other hand, it is the posited identity over against the ground relation; this positedness, which is present in this identity as a form-determination, stands over against the free positedness, that is to say, over against the form as a whole relation of ground and grounded; this form is the total positedness that has returned into itself, and the former is therefore only positedness as immediate, *determinateness* as such.

The ground has thereby simply converted itself into determinate ground, and the determinateness itself is twofold: first, that of form, and secondly, that of content. The former is its determinateness of being external to the content as such which is indifferent to this relation. The latter is the determinateness of the content possessed by the ground.

B. THE DETERMINATE GROUND

(a) Formal Ground

The ground has a determinate content. The determinateness of the content is, as we have seen, the *substrate* for the form, the simple *immediate* over against the *mediation* of the form. The ground is negatively self-related identity, which thereby makes itself into *positedness;* it is negatively related to *itself*, in that it is self-identical in this its negativity; this identity is the substrate or the content, which in this way constitutes the indifferent or positive unity of the ground relation and is the *mediating principle* of this unity.

In this content, the determinateness of the ground and the grounded over against one another has at first vanished. But the mediation is further a *negative* unity. The negative element in the above indifferent substrate is the latter's *immediate determinateness* whereby the ground has a determinate content. But then this negative element is the negative relation of the form to itself. On the one hand, what has been posited sublates itself and withdraws into its ground; but the ground, the essential self-subsistence, relates itself negatively to itself and makes itself into a positedness. This negative mediation of the ground and the grounded is the characteristic mediation of the form as such, *formal mediation*. Now both sides of the form, because each passes over into the other, mutually posit themselves as sublated in *one identity*; in doing so they at the same time *presuppose* this identity. It is the determinate content to which, therefore, the formal mediation is related through itself as to the positive mediating principle. This content is the identical element of both, and since they are distinguished, but each in its difference is relation to the other, it is their subsistence, the subsistence of *each* as the *whole* itself.

It follows from the above that what is present in the determinate ground is this: first, a determinate *content* is considered from *two sides* in so far as it is posited first as *ground* and again as the *grounded*. The content itself is indifferent to this form; in both it is simply one determination only. Secondly, the ground itself is just as much a moment of the form as that which is posited by it; this is its *identity in respect of the form*. It does not matter which of the two determinations is made the first, whether the transition is made from the posited to the other as ground, or from the one as ground to the other as the posited. The grounded considered on its own is the sublating of itself; through this it makes itself on the one hand into a posited, and is at the same time a positing of the ground. The same movement is the ground as such, it makes itself into a posited and thereby becomes the ground of something, that is, in this movement it is present both as a posited and also first as ground. The posited is the ground that there is a ground, and conversely the ground is therefore a posited. The mediation begins just as much from the one as from the other, each side is just as much ground as posited, and each is the whole mediation or the whole form. Furthermore the whole form itself is, as the self-identical, the *substrate* of the determinations which are the two sides of the ground and the grounded, and thus form and content are themselves one and the same identity.

Because of this identity of the ground and the grounded, both as regards content and form, the ground is *sufficient* (the sufficiency of the ground being restricted to this relationship); *there is nothing in the ground that is not in the grounded*, and *there is nothing in the grounded that is not in the ground*. When we ask for a ground, we want to see the *same* determination that is content, double, once in the form of something posited, and again in the form of a determinate being reflected into itself, of essentiality.

Now since in the determinate ground, the ground and the grounded are each the whole form, and their content, though

P*

determinate, is one and the same, it follows that there is as yet no real determination of the sides of the ground, they have no distinct content; the determinateness is as yet only simple, it has not yet passed over into the sides; what is present is the determinate ground at first in its pure form, the *formal ground*. Because the content is only this simple determinateness which does not possess within itself the form of the ground-relation, this determinateness is the self-identical content, indifferent to the form, which is external to it; the content is other than the form.

Remark: Formal Method of Explanation From Tautological Grounds

When reflection, in dealing with determinate grounds, sticks to that form of the ground we have reached here, then the assignment of a ground remains a mere formalism and empty tautology which expresses in the form of reflection-into-self, of essentiality, the same content that is already present in the form of an immediate being, of a being considered as posited. Such an assigning of grounds is therefore accompanied by the same emptiness as the talk which restricts itself to the law of identity. The sciences, especially the physical sciences, are full of tautologies of this kind which constitute as it were a prerogative of science. For example, the ground of the movement of the planets round the sun is said to be the *attractive* force of the earth and sun on one another. As regards content, this expresses nothing other than what is contained in the phenomenon, namely the relation of these bodies to one another, only in the form of a determination reflected into itself, the form of force. If one asks what kind of a force the attractive force is, the answer is that it is the force that makes the earth move round the sun; that is, it has precisely the same content as the phenomenon of which it is supposed to be the ground; the relation of the earth and sun in respect of motion is the identical substrate of the ground and the grounded. When a crystalline form is explained by saying that it has its ground in the particular arrangement which the molecules form with one another, the fact is that the existent crystalline form is this very arrangement that is adduced as ground. In ordinary life, these aetiologies, which are the prerogative of the sciences, count for what they are, tautological empty talk. To answer the question, why is this person going to town, with the reason, the ground, that it is because there is an attractive force in the town which urges him in that direction, is to give the kind of reply that is sanctioned in the sciences but outside them is counted absurd. Leibniz objected to the Newtonian force of attraction that it was the same kind of occult quality that the scholastics used for the purpose of explanation. Rather is it the opposite objection which must be made to it, namely, that it is a too familiar quality; for it has no other content than the phenomenon itself. What commends this mode of explanation is precisely its great clarity and intelligibility; for there is nothing clearer or more intelligible than that, for example, a plant has its ground in a vegetative, that is, plant-producing force. It could be called an *occult* quality only in the sense that the ground is supposed to have *another content* than the thing to be explained, and such a ground is not adduced; the force used for the purpose of explanation is of course a concealed or occult ground in so far as the kind of ground demanded is *not* adduced. Something is no more explained by this formalism than the nature of a plant is known when I say that it is a plant; or that it has its ground in a plant-producing force; this statement with all its clarity can therefore be called a very *occult* mode of explanation.

Secondly, as regards form, in this mode of explanation the two opposite directions of the ground relation are present without being apprehended in their determinate relation. The ground is, on the one hand, ground as the reflection-into-self of the determination of the content of the phenomenon which it grounds, on the other hand, it is the posited. It is that from which the phenomenon is to be understood; but *conversely*, it is the ground that is inferred from the phenomenon and the former is understood from the latter. The main business of this reflection consists, namely, in finding the grounds from the phenomenon, that is, converting the immediate phenomenon into the form of reflected being; consequently the ground, instead of being in and for itself and self-subsistent, is, on the contrary, the posited and derived. Now since in this procedure the ground is derived from the phenomenon and its determinations are based on it, the phenomenon certainly flows quite smoothly and with a favourable wind from its ground. But in this way, knowledge has not advanced a step; its movement is confined within a difference of form which this same procedure inverts and sublates. Accordingly one of the main difficulties in the study of the sciences in which this method prevails comes from this perverse method of premising as ground what is in fact derived, and then actually placing in the consequents the ground of these supposed grounds. The exposition begins with grounds which are placed in mid-air as principles and primary concepts; they are simple determinations devoid of any necessity in and for themselves; what follows is supposed to be based on them. Therefore he who aims to penetrate such sciences must begin by instilling his mind with these grounds, a distasteful business for reason because it is asked to treat what is groundless as a valid foundation. Success comes most easily when, without much reflection, the principles are simply accepted as *given* and one then proceeds to use them as fundamental rules of one's understanding. Without this method one cannot make a start; nor without it can any progress be made. But progress is hindered by the fact that it reveals how the method counteracts itself: it proposes to demonstrate in the consequent what is derived, but in fact it is only in the derived that the grounds of the above presuppositions are contained. Also because the consequent shows itself to be the phenomenon from which the ground was derived, this relation in which the phenomenon is presented awakens a distrust of the exposition of it; for the relation presents itself not as expressed in its immediacy but as a support for the ground. But because this again is derived from the phenomenon one demands rather to see it in its immediacy in order to be able to derive the ground from it. In such an exposition, therefore, one does not know how to take either ground or phenomenon. Uncertainty is increased, especially if the exposition is not rigorously consistent but is more *honest*, by the fact that one comes across traces and features of the phenomenon which point to more and different things than are contained in the principles alone. Lastly, confusion becomes still greater when reflected and merely hypothetical determinations are mingled with immediate determinations of the phenomenon itself, and the former are spoken of as though they belonged to immediate experience. Many who come to these sciences with an honest belief may well imagine that molecules, empty interstices, centrifugal force, the ether, the single, separate ray of light, electrical and magnetic *matter*, and a host of other such things which are spoken of as though they had an immediate existence, are things or relations actually present *in perception*. They serve as primary grounds for something else, are enunciated as actualities and confidently applied; one lets them count as such in good faith before coming aware that they are, on the contrary, determinations inferred from that of which they are supposed to be the grounds, hypotheses and fictions derived from an uncritical reflection. In fact, one finds oneself in a kind of witches' circle in which determinations of real being and determinations of reflection, ground and grounded, phenomena and phantoms, run riot in indiscriminate company and enjoy equal rank with one another.

Along with the formal business of this mode of explanation from grounds, we at the same time hear it repeated—in spite of all the explaining based on well-known forces and matters—that we *do not know* the *inner nature* (*Wesen*) of these forces and matters themselves. This amounts only to a confession that this assigning of grounds is itself completely inadequate; that something quite different from such grounds is required. Only then it is not apparent why this trouble is taken with such explaining, why the something quite different is not sought for, or at least why this mode of explanation is not set aside and the facts left to speak for themselves.

(b) Real Ground

As we have seen, the determinateness of the ground is partly determinateness of the *substrate* or determination of the content, and partly the otherness in the *ground-relation* itself, namely, the distinction between the content and form; the relation of ground and grounded comes to be an external form imposed on the content which is indifferent to these determinations. But in point of fact the two are not external to one another; for the content is this, to be the *identity* of the *ground* with itself in the *grounded*, and of the *grounded* in the *ground*. The side of the ground has shown that it is itself a posited, and the side of the grounded that it is itself ground; each is in itself this identity of the whole. But because they belong at the same time to the form and constitute the form's determinate difference each is, *in its determinateness*, the identity of the whole with itself. Consequently each has a *distinctive content* of its own. Or, considered from the side of the content, because this is the identity *of the ground-relation* with itself, it essentially possesses this difference of the form within itself, and then is, as ground, other than what it is as grounded.

Now since ground and grounded have a distinctive content, the ground relation has ceased to be formal; the retreat into the ground and the emergence from it of the posited is no longer a tautology; the *ground* is realized. Therefore when we ask for a ground, we really demand that the content of the ground be a different determination from that of the phenomenon whose ground we are seeking.

Now this relation is further determined. Namely, in so far as the two sides have a different content, they are indifferent to one another; each is an immediate, self-identical determination. Further, in their relationship as ground and grounded, the ground, in being reflected into the other as into its positedness, is reflected into itself; the content, therefore, possessed by the side of the ground, is equally in the grounded; the latter, as the posited, has its self-identity and subsistence only in the ground. But apart from this content of the ground, the grounded now also has its own distinctive content and is accordingly the *unity* of a *twofold* content. Now this, as the unity of distinct sides, is indeed their negative unity, but because the determinations of the content are mutually indifferent, the unity is only their empty, intrinsically contentless relation, not their mediation; a *one* or a *something* as an external combination of them.

Therefore in the real ground relation, what is present is twofold: first, the determination of the content, which is ground, is in continuity with itself in the positedness, so that it constitutes the simple identical element of the ground and the grounded; the grounded thus completely contains within itself the ground, their relation is an undifferentiated essential compactness. Therefore, what more is added in the grounded to this simple *essence*, is only an unessential form, external determinations of the content which, as such, are free from the ground and are an immediate manifoldness. Of this unessential side, therefore, the essential is not the ground, nor is it ground of the *relation* of both to one another in the grounded. It is a positively identical that indwells the grounded, but does not posit itself therein in any difference of form, but, as self-related content, is an indifferent positive *substrate*. Secondly, what is combined with this substrate in the something is an indifferent content, but as the unessential side. The main thing is the *relation* of the substrate and the unessential manifoldness. But because the related determinations are an indifferent content, this relation is also *not ground*; true, one of them is determined as essential and the other as unessential or posited content, but as self-related content this form is external to both. The *one of the something* that constitutes their relation is therefore not a form relation but only an external bond which does not contain the unessential manifold content as *posited*; it is therefore likewise only a *substrate*.

Ground, in determining itself as real, consequently breaks up, on account of the diversity of content which constitutes its reality, into external determinations. The two relations, the *essential content* as the simple *immediate identity* of the ground and grounded, and then the *something* as relation of the diversified content, are *two different substrates*; the self-identical form of the ground, namely, that the something is, on the one hand, essential and, on the other hand, posited, has vanished; the ground relation has thus become *external* to itself.

Consequently there is now an external ground which brings the diversified content into combination and determines which is ground and which is posited by the ground; this determination does not lie in the double-sided content itself. The real ground is therefore *relation to an other*, on the one hand, of the content to another content, on the other hand, of the ground relation itself (of the form) to an other, namely, to an *immediate*, to something not posited by it.

Remark: Formal Method of Explanation From a Ground Distinct From That Which is Grounded

The formal ground-relation contains only one content for ground and grounded; in this identity lies their necessity, but at the same time their tautology. Real ground contains a diversified content; but this brings with it the contingency and externality of the ground relation. On the one hand, that which is considered as the essential and therefore as the fundamental determination, is not the ground of the other determinations connected with it. On the other hand, it is also undetermined which of the several determinations of the content of a concrete thing ought to be taken as essential and as ground; hence the choice between them is free. Thus in the former respect, for example, the ground of a house is its foundation; this is the ground by virtue of the *gravity* which is inherent in sensuous matter and which is the purely identical principle in both ground and the house which is grounded. Now that there is in heavy matter such a distinction as that of a foundation and a modification distinct from it through which it constitutes a house, this fact is a matter of complete indifference to the heavy matter itself; its relation to other determinations of the content, of the end, of the furnishing of the house, and so on, is external to it; consequently, though it is indeed the foundation, it is not the ground of these determinations. Gravity, which is the ground for a house standing, is no less also the ground for a stone falling; the stone has this ground, gravity, within it; but that the stone has a further determination of its content by virtue of which it is not merely something heavy but a stone, this is external to gravity; further, it is something else that has caused the stone to be placed beforehand at a distance from the body upon which it falls; similarly time, space, and their relation, which is motion, are another content than gravity and can be conceived of without it (as the saying is), and consequently are not essentially posited by it. Gravity is also equally the ground which makes a projectile describe a trajectory opposite to that of a falling body. From the variety of determinations of which it is the ground, it is clear that something else is also required to make it the ground of this or some other determination.

When it is said of nature, that it is the *ground of the world*, what is called nature is, on the one hand, one with the world, and the world is nothing but nature itself. But they are also different, nature being rather the indeterminate, or at least is determinate only in the universal differences which are laws, the self-identical essence of the world, and before nature can be the world a multiplicity of determinations must be externally added to it. But these do not have their ground in nature as such; on the contrary, nature is indifferent to them as contingencies. It is the same relationship as when God is characterized as the ground of nature. As ground, he is its essence; nature contains this essence and is identical with it; but nature has yet a further manifoldness which is distinct from the ground itself and is the third in which these two distinct sides are conjoined; that ground is neither ground of the manifoldness distinguished from it nor of its connexion with it. The cognition of nature is therefore not from God as ground, for as ground he would only be nature's universal essence, and nature as a determinate essence is not contained in the ground.

Because of this diversity of the content of the ground, or strictly speaking of the substrate, and of what is connected with it in the grounded, the assigning of real grounds is just as much a formalism as the formal ground itself. In the latter, the self-identical content is indifferent to the form; in real ground this is equally true. Now the result of this is, further, that the real ground does not itself indicate which of the manifold determinations ought to be taken as essential. *Something* is a *concrete* of manifold determinations which show themselves to be equally fixed and permanent in it. One as much as another can therefore be determined as ground, namely, as *essential*, compared with which the other is then only a posited. This links up with what has already been mentioned, namely, from the fact that in one case a determination is present as ground of another, it does not follow that this other is posited with it in another case or at all. Punishment, for example, has various determinations: it is retribution, a deterrent example as well, a threat used by the law as a deterrent, and also it brings the criminal to his senses and reforms him. Each of these different determinations has been considered the *ground of punishment*, because each is an essential determination, and therefore the others, as distinct from it, are determined as merely contingent relatively to it. But the one which is taken as ground is still not the whole punishment itself; this concrete also contains those others which, whilst associated with the ground in the punishment, do not have their ground in the latter. Again, an official has an aptitude for his office, as an individual has relationships with others, has a circle of acquaintances, a particular character, made an appearance in such and such circumstances and on such and such occasions, and so on. Each of these attributes can be, or can be regarded as, the ground for his holding his office; they are a diverse content which is joined together in a third; the form, in which they are determined as being either essential or posited in relation to one another, is external to the content. Each of these attributes is essential to the official because through it he is the specific individual that he is; in so far as the office can be regarded as an external, posited determination, each can be determined as ground relatively to it, but also conversely, they can be regarded as posited and the office as their ground. How they are *actually* related, that is, in the individual case, this is a determination external to the ground relation and to the content itself; it is a *third* that imparts to them the form of ground and grounded.

So in general anything can have a variety of grounds; each determination of its content, as self-identical, pervades the whole and can therefore be considered essential; the door is wide open to innumerable *aspects*, that is, determinations, lying *outside* the thing itself, on account of the contingency of their mode of connexion. Therefore whether a ground has this or that *consequent* is equally contingent. Moral motives, for example, are *essential determinations* of the ethical nature, but what follows from them is at the same time an externality distinct from them, which follows and also does not follow from them; it is only through a third that it is attached to them. More accurately this is to be understood in this way, that *if* the moral motive is a ground, it is *not* contingent to it whether it has or has not a consequent or a grounded, but it is contingent whether it is or is not made a ground at all. But again, since the content which is the consequent of the moral motive, if this has been made the ground, has the nature of externality, it can be immediately sublated by another externality. Therefore an action may, or may not, issue from a moral motive. Conversely, an action can have various grounds; as a concrete, it contains manifold essential determinations, each of which can therefore be assigned as ground. The search for and assignment of grounds, in which argumentation mainly consists, is accordingly an endless pursuit which does not reach a final determination; for any and every thing one or more good grounds can be given, and also for its opposite; and a host of grounds can exist without anything following from them. What Socrates and Plato call *sophistry* is nothing else but argumentation from grounds; to this, Plato opposes the contemplation of the Idea, that is, of the subject matter in and for itself or in its *Notion*. Grounds are taken only from *essential* determinations of a content, *essential* relationships and aspects, and of these every subject matter, just like its opposite, possesses several; in their form of essentiality, one is as valid as another; because it does not embrace the whole extent of the subject matter, each is a one-sided ground, the other particular sides having on their part particular grounds, and none of them exhausts the subject matter which constitutes their *togetherness* [*Verknüpfung*] and contains them all; none is a *sufficient* ground, that is, the Notion.

(c) *The Complete Ground*

1. In real ground, ground as content and ground as relation are

only *substrates*. The former is only *posited* as essential and as ground; the relation is the *something* of the grounded as the indeterminate substrate of a varied content, a 'togetherness' of it which is not its own reflection but an external and therefore only posited reflection. Hence the real ground-relation is rather the ground as sublated; consequently it constitutes rather the side of the *grounded* or of *positedness*. But as positedness, the ground itself has now withdrawn into its ground; it is now a grounded and this has *another ground*. In consequence, the latter so determines itself that, first, it is that which is *identical* with the real ground as its grounded; in conformity with this determination both sides have one and the same content; and the two determinations of the content and the 'togetherness' in the something are likewise present in the new ground. But secondly, the new ground into which that merely posited, external 'togetherness' has sublated itself is, as its reflection-into-self, the *absolute relation* of the two determinations of the content.

In consequence of the real ground itself having withdrawn into its ground, the identity of ground and grounded, or formal ground, is restored in it. The resultant ground-relation is therefore the *complete* ground relation, which embraces both formal and real ground and which mediates the determinations of the content which, in the latter, confront one another as immediate.

2. The ground-relation has thus determined itself more precisely in the following manner. First, something has a ground; it contains the *determination of the content* which is the *ground*, and, in addition a *second* determination, one which is *posited* by the ground. But each is an indifferent content, so that the one determination is not in its own self ground, nor is the other in its own self that which is grounded by the first; the fact is, that in the immediacy of the content, this *relation* is a sublated or posited relation and has, as such, its ground in *another*. This second relation, as different only in respect of form, has the same content as the first, namely, the two determinations of the content, but it is their *immediate* 'togetherness'. However, the determinations thus connected constitute a simply varied content, and are therefore determined as indifferent to one another; consequently, this relation is not their truly absolute relation in which one of the determinations would be self-identical in positedness, and the other only this positedness of the same self-identical determination. On the contrary, they are

supported by a something which constitutes their merely immediate, not reflected, relation which is, therefore, only a relative ground in relation to the 'togetherness' in the other something. The *two somethings* are therefore the two distinct relations of the content which have been brought to view. They stand in the identical ground-relation of form; they are one and the same *whole content*, namely, the two determinations of the content and their relation; they are distinguished only by the kind of this relation, which in the one is an immediate, in the other a posited relation; through this, they are distinguished one from the other as ground and grounded only *in respect of form*. Secondly, this ground-relation is not merely formal, but also real. The formal ground passes over into real ground as we have seen; the moments of form are reflected into themselves; they are a self-subsistent content, and the ground relation also contains one peculiar *content as ground*, and *another* as *grounded*. The content, in the first instance, constitutes the *immediate* identity of the two sides of the formal ground which thus have one and the same content. But it also has form within it and is thus a twofold *content* which has the nature of ground and grounded. One of the two determinations of the two somethings is therefore determined as being, not merely common to them as in an external comparison, but as being their identical substrate and the foundation of their relation. As against the other determination of the content, this determination is essential and is the ground of the other which is posited, namely, in the something, of which the grounded determination is the relation. In the first something, which is the ground-relation, this second determination of the content is immediately and *in itself* connected with the first. But the other something only contains the one *in itself* as that in which it is immediately identical with the first something, but the other as the determination posited in it. The former determination of the content is its ground by virtue of its being *originally* connected with the other determination in the first something.

The *ground-relation* of the determinations of the content in the second something is thus *mediated* by the first, implicit relation of the first something. The inference is as follows: in one something, the determination B is implicitly connected with determination A; therefore, in the second something to which only the one determination A immediately belongs, B is also linked with A. In the second something, not only is this second determination a mediated one, but the fact that its immediate determination is ground is also mediated, namely, by its original connexion with *B* in the first something. This connexion is thus the ground of ground *A*, and the *whole* ground-relation is, in the second something, a posited or a grounded.

3. Real ground shows itself to be the *self-external reflection* of ground; the complete mediation of ground is the restoration of its self-identity. But since this self-identity has thereby also acquired the externality of real ground, the formal ground-relation in this unity of itself and real ground is just as much self-positing as self-*sublating* ground; the ground-relation mediates itself with itself *through its negation*. First, ground as the *original relation*, is the relation of immediate content-determinations. The ground-relation, being essential form, its sides are determined as sublated or as moments. Therefore, as form of *immediate* determinations, it is self-identical relation at the same time that it is the relation of its negation; hence it is ground, not in and for itself, but as relation to the *sublated* ground-relation. Secondly, the sublated relation or the immediate which, in the original and the posited relation, is the identical *substrate*, is likewise not in and for itself real ground; on the contrary, it is posited as being ground through that original connexion.

The ground-relation in its totality is therefore essentially *presupposing* reflection; the formal ground presupposes the *immediate* content determination and this, as real ground, presupposes form. Ground is therefore form as an immediate 'togetherness' but in such a manner that the form repels itself from itself and rather presupposes immediacy, in which it is related to itself as to an other. This immediate is the content determination, the simple *ground*; but as this, namely, as ground, it is equally repelled from itself and likewise is related to itself as to an other. Thus the total ground-relation has determined itself to be *conditioning mediation*.

C. CONDITION

(a) The Relatively Unconditioned

1. Ground is the immediate, and the grounded the mediated. But it is positing reflection; as such it makes itself into a positedness

and is presupposing reflection; thus it relates itself to itself as to a sublated moment, to an immediate by which it is itself mediated. This mediation, as the progress from the immediate to the ground, is not an external reflection but, as we have seen, the native act of the ground itself, or, what is the same thing, the ground-relation, as reflection into self-identity, is equally essentially self-alienating reflection. The immediate to which the ground is related as to its essential presupposition is *condition*; real ground is therefore essentially conditioned. The determinateness which it contains is the otherness of itself.

Condition is, therefore, first, an immediate manifold something. Secondly, this something is related to another, to something that is ground, not of the first something, but in some other respect; for the first something is itself immediate and without a ground. According to that relation it is *posited*; the immediate something ought to be, as condition, not for itself but for something else. But at the same time, the fact that it is thus for another, is itself only a positedness; this fact that it is a posited is sublated in its immediacy, and a *something is indifferent to its being a condition*. Thirdly, condition is an immediate in such a manner that it constitutes the *presupposition* of the ground. In this determination it is the form relation of the ground, withdrawn into identity with itself, and is consequently the *content* of the ground. But the content as such is only the indifferent unity of the ground, as in form— without form there is no content. Further, it frees itself from this indifferent unity in that, in the *complete* ground, the ground relation becomes a relation external to its identity, whereby the content acquires immediacy. In so far, therefore, as condition is that in which the ground-relation has its self-*identity*, it constitutes the content of the ground; but because the content is indifferent to this form, it is only *implicitly* its content, something which has yet to become content and hence constitutes *material* for the ground. Posited as condition, something has the determination (in accordance with the second moment) of losing its indifferent immediacy and becoming moment of something else. Through its immediacy it is indifferent to this relation; but, in so far as it enters into this relation, it constitutes the *in-itself* of the ground and is for the latter the *unconditioned*. In order to be condition, it has in the ground its presupposition and is itself conditioned; but this determination is external to it.

2. Something is not through its condition; its condition is not its ground. Condition is the moment of unconditioned immediacy for the ground, but is not itself the movement and the positing that is negatively self-related and that makes itself into positedness. The ground-relation, therefore, stands over against condition. Something has, apart from its condition, also a ground. This is the empty movement of reflection, because reflection has the immediacy that is its presupposition, outside it. But it is the whole form and the self-subsistent mediating process; for the condition is not its ground. Since this mediating process is, as a positing, self-related, it is from this side also an immediate and *unconditioned*; true, it presupposes itself, but as a discarded or sublated positing; on the other hand, what it is according to its determination, that it is in and for itself. In so far as the ground relation is a self-subsistent relation-to-self, and it has within it the identity of reflection, it has *its own peculiar content* over against the content of the condition. The former is content of the ground and therefore essentially formed; the latter, on the other hand, is only an immediate material, whose relation to the ground is external to it while, at the same time, it no less constitutes the in-itself of the ground. It is thus a mixture of the self-subsistent content which has no relation to the content of the ground-determination, and of such content that enters into the ground-determination and, as its material, is meant to become a moment of it.

3. The two sides of the whole, *condition and ground*, are, then, on the one hand, *indifferent* and *unconditioned* in relation to each other; the one, as the unrelated, to which the relation in which it is condition is external, the other as the relation or form, for which the determinate being of the condition exists only as material, as something passive, whose form, which it possesses on its own account, is unessential. But further, the two sides are also *mediated*. Condition is the *in-itself* of the ground; so much is it an essential moment of the ground-relation, that it is the simple self-identity of the ground. But this, too, is sublated; this in-itself is only a positedness; the immediate determinate being is indifferent to the fact that it is condition. The fact, therefore, that the condition is an in-itself for the ground constitutes that side of it which makes it mediated. Similarly, the ground-relation, in its self-subsistence, also has a presupposition, and has its in-itself outside it. Thus each of the two sides is the *contradiction* of indifferent immediacy

and essential mediation, both in a single relation—or the contradiction of self subsistent existence and the determination of being
only a moment.

(b) *The Absolutely Unconditioned*

At first, each of the two relatively unconditioned sides is reflected
into the other; condition, as an immediate, into the form relation
of the ground, and the latter into the immediate determinate being
as its positedness; but each, apart from this reflected being of its
other in it, is self-subsistent and has its own peculiar content.

At first, *condition* is an immediate determinate being; its form
has the two moments, (*a*) of *positedness*, according to which it is,
as condition, material and moment of the ground, and (*b*) of the
in-itself, according to which it constitutes the essentiality of the
ground or its simple reflection into itself. Both sides of the form
are external to the immediate determinate being; for this is the
sublated ground relation. But, first, determinate being is in its
own self only this, to sublate itself in its immediacy and to fall to
the ground [*zugrunde zu gehen*]. *Being* is simply only the *becoming*
of essence; it is its essential nature to make itself into a positedness
and into an identity which, through negation of itself, is the
immediate. The form-determinations, therefore, of positedness
and of the self-identical in-itself, the form through which the
immediate determinate being is condition, are therefore not external to it; on the contrary, it is this reflection itself. Secondly, as
condition, being is now also posited as that which it essentially is,
namely, as moment, hence as moment of an other, and at the same
time, as an in-itself, likewise of an other; but *in itself* being only is
through the negation of itself, namely, through ground and
through ground's self-sublating, and therefore presupposing,
reflection; the in-itself of being is accordingly only a posited. This
in-itself of condition has two sides: one is its essentiality as essentiality of the ground, while the other is the immediacy of its
determinate being. Or rather, both are the same. Determinate
being is an immediate, but the immediacy is essentially the
mediated, namely, through the self-sublating ground. As this
immediacy that is mediated by a self-sublating process of mediation, it is at the same time the in-itself of the ground and the
unconditioned of its unconditioned side; but this in-itself is
itself in turn also no less only a moment or a positedness, for it is

mediated. Condition is accordingly the whole form of the ground
relation; it is its presupposed in-itself, but as presupposed it is
itself a positedness and its immediacy is this, to make itself into a
positedness and so to repel itself from itself, in such a manner that
it both falls to the ground and is ground, the ground making itself
into a positedness and thus also into a grounded, and these two
are one and the same thing.

Similarly, in the conditioned ground, the in-itself is not only
the reflection [*Scheinen*] of an other in it. This ground is the self-
subsistent, that is, the self-relating, reflection of the positing, and
consequently the self-identical; or, it is in its own self its in-itself
and its content. But it is also presupposing reflection; it is negatively related to itself and opposes its in-itself to itself as to an
other, and condition, according to its moment of in-itself as well
as according to its moment of immediate determinate being, is the
ground-relation's own moment; the immediate determinate being
is essentially only through its ground and is moment of itself as
a presupposing. This ground, therefore, is equally the whole itself.

What is present, therefore, is simply only *one* whole of form, but
equally only *one* whole of content. For the peculiar content of
condition is essential content only in so far as it is the self-identity
of reflection in the form, or, as this immediate determinate being
is in its own self the ground-relation. Further, this immediate
determinate being is only condition through the presupposing
reflection of the ground; it is the self-identity of the ground, or
its content, to which it opposes itself. Therefore the determinate
being is not merely formless material for the ground relation; on
the contrary, because it has in its own self this form it is a formed
matter, and since also in its identity with it it is indifferent to it,
it is content. Finally, it is the same content as that possessed by
ground, for it is content precisely as that which is self-identical in
the form relation.

The two sides of the whole, condition and ground, are therefore
one essential unity, equally as content and as form. They spontaneously pass over into one another or, since they are reflections,
they posit themselves as sublated, relate themselves to this their
negation and *reciprocally presuppose one another*. But at the same
time this is only a single reflection of both and therefore their
presupposing is also only one; or rather this reciprocal presupposing becomes a presupposing of their one identity as their sub-

sistence and substrate. This identity of their common content and unity of form is the *truly unconditioned, the fact in its own self*. As we saw above, condition is only the relatively unconditioned. It is therefore usually regarded as itself conditioned and a fresh condition is asked for, and thus the usual *infinite progress* from condition to condition is introduced. Now why does a condition prompt us to ask for a fresh condition, that is, why is a condition regarded as a conditioned? Because it is some finite determinate being or other. But this is a further determination, which is not contained in its Notion. Condition as such is conditioned, solely because it is a posited in-itself; it is therefore sublated in the absolutely unconditioned.

Now this contains within itself the two sides, condition and ground, as its moments; it is the unity into which these have withdrawn. Together they constitute its form or positedness. The unconditioned fact is condition of both, but it is absolute condition, that is, condition that is itself ground. Now as *ground*, it is the negative identity that has repelled itself into these two moments; first, into the shape of the sublated ground relation, of an immediate, self-external manifoldness, without unity, which relates itself to the ground as something *other* to it, and at the same time constitutes the ground's in-itself; secondly, into the shape of an internal, simple form, which is ground, but relates itself to the self-identical immediate as to an other and determines it as condition, that is, determines this its in-itself as its own moment. These two sides *presuppose* the totality in such a manner that it is that which posits them. Conversely, because they *presuppose* the totality, this in turn also seems to be conditioned by them, and the fact seems to arise from its condition and from its ground. But since these two sides have shown themselves to be an identity, the relation of condition and ground has vanished; they are reduced to an *illusory being*; the absolutely unconditioned in its movement of positing and presupposing is only the movement in which this *illusory being* sublates itself. It is the fact's own act to condition itself and to oppose itself as ground to its conditions; but its relation, as a relation between conditions and ground, is a reflection *into itself*, and its relation to them is its *union with itself*.

(c) *Emergence of the Fact* [*Sache*] *into Existence*
The absolutely unconditioned is the absolute ground that is

identical with its condition, the immediate fact in its truly essential nature. As *ground*, it relates itself negatively to itself, makes itself into a positedness; but this positedness is a reflection that is complete in both its aspects and a form-relation that is self-identical in them as we have seen from their Notion. This positedness is accordingly, first, the sublated ground, the fact as the reflectionless immediate—the side of conditions. This is the *totality* of the determinations of the fact—the fact itself, but cast out into the externality of being, the restored sphere of being. In condition, essence releases the unity of its reflection-into-self as an immediacy, which however from now on has the character of being a *conditioning* presupposition and of essentially constituting only one of the sides of essence. The conditions are, therefore, the whole content of the fact, because they are the unconditioned in the form of formless being. But they also have, by reason of this form, another shape besides the determinations of the content as it is in the fact as such. They appear as a multiplicity without unity, mixed with non-essentials and other circumstances that do not belong to the sphere of determinate being in so far as this constitutes the conditions of this *specific* fact. For the absolute, unrestricted fact, the *sphere of being itself* is the condition. The ground, which withdraws into itself, posits condition as the first immediacy and it relates itself to this as to its unconditioned. This immediacy as sublated reflection is *reflection* in the element of being, which thus develops itself as such into a whole; the form, as a determinateness of being, goes on to multiply itself and thus appears as a manifold content distinct from and indifferent to the determination of reflection. The unessential, which belongs to the sphere of being and which the latter, in so far as it is condition, strips off, is the determinateness of immediacy in which the unity of form is submerged. This form unity, as the relation of being, is present in it at first as *becoming*—the transition of one determinateness of being into another. But the becoming of being is further the transition to essence and the withdrawal into ground. The determinate being, therefore, that constitutes the conditions is, in truth, not determined as condition by something else and used by it as material; on the contrary, it is through its own act that it makes itself into a moment of another. Also, far from its becoming starting from itself as the true first and immediate, the truth is that its immediacy is only something presupposed, and the movement of its becoming is the act of reflection itself. Accordingly the truth of determinate being is to be condition; its immediacy *is*, solely through the reflection of the ground-relation which posits itself as sublated. Becoming is, therefore, like immediacy, only the illusory being of the unconditioned, in that this presupposes itself and therein has its form; and the immediacy of being is accordingly essentially only a *moment* of the form.

The other side of this reflective movement [*Scheinen*] of the unconditioned is the ground-relation as such, determined as form over against the immediacy of the conditions and the content. But it is the form of the absolute fact, and it possesses within itself the unity of its form with itself, or its *content*; and in the very act of determining this content to be condition it sublates the diversity of the content and reduces it to a moment, just as, conversely, as essenceless form it gives itself the immediacy of a subsistence in this self-identity. The reflection of the ground sublates the immediacy of the conditions and relates them, so making them moments in the unity of the fact; but the conditions are presupposed by the unconditioned fact itself, which thus sublates its own positing, or its positing directly converts itself equally into a becoming. The two are therefore one unity; the immanent movement of the conditions is a becoming, a withdrawal into ground to the positing of ground; but the ground as posited, that is to say, as sublated, is the immediate. The ground relates itself negatively to itself, makes itself into a positedness and grounds the conditions; but in thus determining immediate determinate being as a posited, the ground sublates it and thereby first constitutes itself ground. This reflection is accordingly the mediation of the unconditioned fact with itself through its negation. Or rather, the reflection of the unconditioned is at first a presupposing—but this sublating of itself is immediately a positing which determines; secondly, in this presupposing, reflection is immediately a sublating of what is presupposed and a determining from within itself; thus this determining is again a sublating of the positing and is in its own self a becoming. In this, the mediation as a return-to-self through negation has vanished; it is the simple, internal movement of reflection [*einfache, in sich scheinende Reflexion*] and groundless absolute becoming. The movement of the fact to become posited, on the one hand through its *conditions*, and on the other through its ground, is merely the *vanishing of the illusion of mediation*. The process by which the fact is posited is accordingly an emergence, the simple entry of the fact *into Existence*, the pure movement of the fact to itself.

When all the conditions of a fact are present, it enters into Existence. The fact *is, before it exists*; it is, first, as *essence* or as an *unconditioned*; secondly, it has *determinate being* or is determinate, and this in the twofold manner above considered, on the one hand, in its conditions, and on the other, in its ground. In the former, it has given itself the form of external groundless being because it is, as absolute reflection, negative self-relation, and it makes itself into its own presupposition. This presupposed unconditioned is therefore the groundless immediate, whose being is nothing except to be present as something groundless. When, therefore, all the conditions of the fact are present, that is when the totality of the fact is posited as a groundless immediate, this scattered multiplicity *inwardizes* [*erinnert*] itself in its own self. The whole fact must be present in its conditions, or all the conditions belong to its Existence, for *all* of them constitute the reflection; or, determinate being, because it is condition, is determined by form; consequently its determinations are determinations of reflection and the positing of one essentially involves the positing of the others. The *inwardization* of the conditions is at first the falling to the ground [*das Zugrundegehen*] of immediate determinate being and the becoming of the ground. But this makes the ground a posited ground, that is, it is just as much sublated ground and immediate being, as it is ground. When therefore all the conditions of the fact are present, they sublate themselves as immediate being and presupposition, and equally ground sublates itself. Ground emerges merely as an illusory being that immediately vanishes; accordingly, this emergence is the tautological movement of the fact to itself, and its mediation by conditions and ground is the vanishing of both. The emergence into Existence is therefore immediate in such a manner that it is mediated only by the vanishing of mediation.

The fact emerges from the ground. It is not grounded or posited by it in such a manner that ground remains as a substrate; on the contrary, the positing is the movement of the ground outwards to itself and its simple vanishing. Through its *union* with the conditions, ground receives an external immediacy and the moment of being. But it receives this not as something external, nor through an external relation; on the contrary, as ground, it makes itself into a positedness, its simple essentiality unites with itself in the positedness and is, in this sublation of itself, the vanishing of its difference from its positedness, and is thus simple essential immediacy. Ground, therefore, does not remain behind as something distinct from the grounded, but the truth of grounding is that in it ground is united with itself, so that its reflection into another is its reflection into itself. Consequently, the fact is not only the *unconditioned* but also the *groundless*, and it emerges from ground only in so far as ground has '*fallen to the ground*' and ceased to be ground: it emerges from the groundless, that is, from its own essential negativity or pure form.

This immediacy that is mediated by ground and condition and is self-identical through the sublating of mediation, is *Existence*.

Section Two: Appearance [Erscheinung]

Essence must appear

Being is the absolute abstraction; this negativity is not something external to being, which is being, and nothing but being, only as this absolute negativity. For the same reason, being only is as self-sublating being and is essence. But, conversely, essence as simple equality with itself is likewise *being*. The *doctrine of being* contains the first proposition: being is *essence*. The second proposition: *essence is being*, constitutes the content of the first section of the *doctrine of essence*. But this being into which essence makes itself is *essential being*, Existence; it is a being that has come forth from negativity and inwardness.

Thus essence *appears*. Reflection is the *showing of illusory being within essence itself*. [*Die Reflexion ist das* Scheinen *des Wesens* in ihm selbst.] Its determinations are enclosed within the unity simply and solely as posited, sublated determinations; or, reflection is essence which, in its positedness, is immediately identical with itself. But since this essence is ground, it gives itself a real determination [*bestimmt es sich real*] through its reflection, which is self-sublating or which returns into itself; further, since this determination, or the otherness, of the ground relation sublates itself in the reflection of the ground and becomes Existence, this endows the form determinations with an element of self-subsistence. Their illusory being completes itself to become *Appearance*.

The essentiality that has advanced to immediacy is, in the first instance, *Existence*, and an existent or *thing*—as an undifferentiated[1] unity of essence with its immediacy. It is true that the thing contains reflection, but its negativity is, in the first instance, extinguished in its immediacy; but because its ground is essentially reflection, its immediacy sublates itself and the thing makes itself into positedness.

Secondly, then, it is *Appearance*. Appearance is that which the thing is in itself, or its truth. But this merely posited Existence which is reflected into otherness is equally the transcending of itself in its infinitude; to the world of appearance is opposed the

---

[1] 'unterschiedne' in Lasson's edition is a misprint.

world that is reflected into itself, the *world of essence* [*an sich seiende Welt*].

But the being that appears and essential being, simply stand in relation to one another. Thus Existence is, thirdly, essential *relation*; what appears manifests what is essential, and this is in its Appearance.

The relation is the still imperfect union of reflection-into-otherness and reflection-into-self; the perfect interpenetration of both is *actuality*.

CHAPTER I

EXISTENCE

Just as the proposition of ground states that whatever is has a ground, or is something posited or mediated, so too we must formulate a proposition of Existence, and in these terms: *whatever is, exists*. The truth of being is to be, not a first immediate, but essence that has emerged into immediacy.

But when further it was also said, '*Whatever exists has a ground and is conditioned*', then equally it must also be said that it has no ground and is unconditioned. For Existence is the immediacy that has emerged from the sublating of the mediation by which ground and condition are related, and in emerging it sublates this emergence itself.

In so far as the proofs *of the existence* of God may be mentioned here, we may begin by recalling that besides immediate being and Existence (the being that proceeds from essence), there is yet a third being that proceeds from the Notion, namely, *objectivity*. Proof is, in general, *mediated cognition*. The various kinds of being demand or imply their own kind of mediation, so that the nature of proof, too, will differ in respect of each. The *ontological proof* proposes to start from the Notion; it makes the sum total of all realities its basis and then proceeds to subsume existence, too, under reality. It is therefore the mediation that is syllogism and that does not as yet come up for consideration here. We have already considered above Kant's objections to this proof and have remarked that Kant understands by Existence, the determinate being whereby something enters into the context of the totality of experience, that is, into the determination of an *otherness* and into relation to an *other*. Thus something, as existent, is mediated by an other, and existence in general is the side of its mediation. Now what Kant calls a concept, namely, something taken as only simply *self-related*, or conception as such, does not contain its mediation; in abstract self-identity, opposition is left out. The ontological proof would now have to demonstrate that the absolute concept, namely the concept of God, attains to a determinate being, to a mediation, or how simple essence mediates itself with mediation. This is effected by the stated subsumption of existence under its universal, namely, reality, which is assumed as the middle term between God in his concept, on the one hand, and existence on the other. This mediation, in so far as it has the form of a syllogism, is, as we have said, not under discussion here. But the preceding exposition has shown what is the true nature of this mediation of essence with Existence. The nature of proof itself will be considered in the doctrine of cognition. Here we have only to indicate what is relevant to the nature of mediation in general.

The proofs of the existence of God adduce a *ground* for this existence. It is not supposed to be an objective ground of God's existence; for this existence is in and for itself. Thus it is merely a *ground for cognition*. It thereby declares itself to be a ground that *vanishes* in the object which at first appears to be grounded by it. Now the ground that is derived from the contingency of the world implies the regress of the contingency into absolute essence; for the contingent is that which is in itself *groundless* and self-sublating. In this way, therefore, absolute essence does in fact proceed from the groundless; the ground sublates itself and with this there also vanishes the illusion of the relation that was given to God, to be that which is grounded in an other. This mediation is therefore true mediation. But this nature of its mediation is unknown to that ratiocinative [*beweisende*] reflection; on the one hand, it takes itself to be something merely subjective and by so doing removes its mediation from God himself, but, on the other hand, it does not for that reason recognize the mediating movement, that it is and how it is in *essence itself*. Its true relationship consists in this, that it is both of these things in one: mediation as such but, **of** course, at the same time a subjective, external, that is, self-external, mediation, which *sublates itself again within itself*. But in the above proof, existence is given the false relationship of appearing only as *mediated* or posited.

Thus, on the other side, Existence also cannot be considered merely as an *immediate*. Taken in the determination of an immediacy, the comprehension of God's existence has been declared to be unprovable and knowledge of it to be *only* an immediate consciousness, a *belief* in it. Knowing is supposed to have reached this conclusion, that it knows *nothing*, that is to say, that it *surrenders* again its *mediating* movement and the determinations that crop up in it. This is also evident from the foregoing; only we must add that reflection, in ending with the sublating of itself, does not therefore have for result *nothing* (for in that case the positive knowledge of essence as an *immediate* relation to it would be *separate* from that result and a spontaneous emergence, an act starting only from itself); on the contrary, this end itself, this *falling to the ground* of the mediation, is at the same time the *ground* from which the immediate proceeds. Language, as was remarked above, combines the meaning of this *downfall* [*Untergang*] and of ground; the essence of God, it is said, is the *abyss* [*Abgrund*] for finite reason. This it is, indeed, in so far as finite reason surrenders its finitude and sinks its mediating movement therein; but this *abyss*, the negative ground, is also the *positive* ground of the emergence of simply affirmative being [*Seienden*], of essence which is in its own self immediate; mediation is an *essential movement*. Mediation through ground sublates itself, but does not leave the ground behind as a substrate; in that case, what proceeded from the ground would be something posited, having its essence elsewhere, namely in the ground; but on the contrary, this ground, as an abyss, is the vanished mediation; and conversely, it is only the vanished mediation that is at the same time ground, and only through this negation the self-equal and immediate.

Existence, then, is not to be taken here as a *predicate* or as a *determination* of essence, the proposition of which would run: essence exists, or *has* existence; on the contrary, essence has passed over into Existence; Existence is essence's absolute emptying of itself or self-alienation, nor has it remained behind on the further side of it. The proposition should therefore run: essence is Existence; it is not distinct from its Existence. Essence has *passed over* into Existence in so far as essence as ground no longer distinguishes itself from itself as the grounded, or in so far as this ground has sublated itself. But this negation is equally essentially its position, or absolutely positive continuity with itself; Existence is the reflection *of the ground* into itself, its identity-with-self achieved in its negation, and therefore the mediation that has posited itself as identical with itself and thereby is an immediacy.

Now because Existence is essentially mediation-with-self, the *determinations* of the mediation *are present in it*, but in such a manner that they are also reflected into themselves and their subsistence is essential and immediate. As the immediacy that posits itself through sublation, existence is negative unity and a being-within-self; it therefore determines itself immediately as an *Existent* and as *thing*.

A. THE THING AND ITS PROPERTIES

Existence as *an existent* is posited in the form of the negative unity which it essentially is. But this negative unity is at first only an *immediate* determination, hence the one of *something* in general. But the existent something is distinct from the something that has simply affirmative being [*dem seienden Etwas*]. The former is essentially that immediacy which has arisen through the reflection of mediation into itself. The existent something is thus a *thing*.

The *thing* is distinct from its *Existence* just as *something* can be distinguished from its *being*. The thing and the existent are immediately one and the same. But because Existence is not the first immediacy of being but has within itself the moment of mediation, its further determination as thing and the distinguishing of both, is not a transition but really an analysis; and Existence as such contains this distinction itself in the moment of its mediation; the distinction of thing-in-itself and of *external* Existence.

(a) Thing-in-itself and Existence

1. The *thing-in-itself* is the existent as the *essential immediate* which has resulted from the sublated mediation. Thus mediation is equally essential to the thing; but this difference in this first or immediate Existence falls apart into *indifferent determinations*. The one side, namely the mediation of the thing, is its *non-reflected immediacy*, and therefore its being as such which, because it is at the same time determined as mediation, is a *determinate being* which is *other* to itself and within itself *manifold* and *external*. But it is not only determinate being; it stands in relation to the sublated mediation and is an essential immediacy; consequently it is determinate being as an unessential, as a positedness. (If the thing is distinguished from its Existence it is the possible, the thing of ordinary conception or figment of thought which, as such, is at the same time supposed not to exist. However, the determination of possibility and the opposition of the thing to its Existence come later.) But the thing-in-itself and its mediated being are both contained in Existence and both are themselves existences; the

thing-in-itself exists and is the essential Existence of the thing, but the mediated being is its unessential existence.

The *thing-in-itself* as the simple reflectedness of Existence within itself is not the ground of the unessential determinate being: it is the unmoved, indeterminate unity precisely because it has the determination of being sublated mediation and therefore of being only the *substrate* of the determinate being. For this reason reflection, too, as determinate being that mediates itself through other, falls *outside* the *thing-in-itself*. This is not supposed to contain within it any specific manifoldness; and it therefore only obtains this when *brought into relationship with external reflection*; but it remains indifferent to the latter. (The thing-in-itself has colour only in relation to the eye, smell in relation to the nose, and so on). Its diversity consists of the ways in which it is regarded by an other, specific relations which this other forms with the thing-in-itself and which are not the latter's own determinations.

2. Now this other is reflection which, determined as external, is first, *external to itself* and determinate manifoldness. Secondly, it is external to the essential existent and *relates itself* to it as to its absolute *presupposition*. But these two moments of external reflection, its own manifoldness and its relation to the thing-in-itself which is other to it, are one and the same. For this Existence is only external in so far as it relates itself to essential identity as *to an other*. Diversity, therefore, does not have an independent subsistence of its own on the further side of the thing-in-itself, but *is* only as illusory being over against it, in its necessary relation to it as reflex refracting itself on it. Diversity is therefore present as the relation of an other to the thing-in-itself; but this other is not anything subsisting on its own account but *is* only as relation to the thing-in-itself; but at the same time it *is* only as the repelling from this; it is thus the unsupported counter-thrust of itself within itself.

Now since the thing-in-itself is the essential identity of Existence, this essenceless reflection does not attach to it but collapses within itself externally to it. It falls to the ground and thus itself becomes essential identity or thing-in-itself. This can also be considered in the following manner: essenceless Existence has in the thing-in-itself its reflection-into-self; it is related to it in the first instance as to its other; but as the other over against that which is in itself, it is the sublating of its own self and the becoming of being-in-self. The thing-in-itself is therefore identical with external existence.

In the thing-in-itself this is displayed in the following manner. The thing-in-itself is *self-related*, essential Existence; it is identity-with-self only in so far as it contains within itself the negativity of reflection-into-itself; consequently that which appeared as an Existence external to it is a moment within it. It is, therefore, also a self-repelling thing-in-itself which *therefore is related to itself as to an other*. Hence there are now a *plurality* of things-in-themselves standing in the relation of external reflection to one another. This unessential Existence is their relation to one another as to others; but further, it is essential to these others themselves—or, in other words, this unessential Existence in collapsing within itself is a thing-in-itself, but an *other* than the first thing-in-itself; for the former is an immediate essentiality, the latter, however, the essentiality that has emerged from unessential Existence. But this other thing-in-itself is only an *other* in general; for as a self-identical thing it has no further determinateness over against the first; it is the reflection of unessential Existence into itself like the first. The determinateness of the various things-in-themselves over against one another falls therefore into external reflection.

3. This external reflection is now a relating of the things-in-themselves to one another, their *reciprocal mediation* as others. The things-in-themselves are thus the extremes of a syllogism whose middle term constitutes their external Existence, the Existence through which they are others for one another and distinct from one another. This their difference falls *only* in *their relation*; they send, as it were, determinations only from their surface into the relation and remain themselves, as absolutely reflected into themselves, indifferent towards the relation. Now this relationship constitutes the totality of Existence. The thing-in-itself stands in relation to a reflection external to it in which it possesses a multiplicity of determinations; this is the repelling of itself from itself into another thing-in-itself; this repelling is the counter-thrust of itself internally, since each is only an *other*, as a reflecting of itself out of the other; it has its positedness not in its own self but in the other, is determined only by the determinateness of the other; this other is equally determined only by the determinateness of the first. But the *two* things-in-themselves, since thus they do not contain the difference within themselves but each has it only in

the other, are not distinguished from one another; the thing-in-itself, since it is supposed to be related to the other extreme as to another thing-in-itself, is related to it as something that is not distinguished from it, and the external reflection, which should constitute the mediating connexion between the extremes, is only a relating of the thing-in-itself to itself, or essentially its reflection into itself; it is therefore only an implicit determinateness, or the determinateness of the thing-in-itself. The thing-in-itself, therefore, has the determinateness, not in a relation (external to it) to another thing-in-itself, and of this other to it; the determinateness is not merely a surface of the thing-in-itself but is the essential mediation of itself with itself as with an other. The two things-in-themselves which are supposed to constitute the extremes of the relation, since they are supposed not to possess in themselves any determinateness over against one another, *in fact collapse into one*; there is only *one* thing-in-itself, which in external reflection is related to itself, and it is *its own self-relation as to an other* that constitutes its determinateness.

This determinateness of the thing-in-itself is the *property of the thing*.

(b) Property

Quality is the *immediate* determinateness of something, the negative itself through which being is something. Thus the property of the thing is the negativity of reflection through which Existence in general is an existent and, as simple self-identity, a thing-in-itself. But the negativity of reflection, the sublated mediation, is essentially itself a mediation and a relation, though not to an other in general like quality as the non-reflected determinateness, but relation *to itself* as to an other; or, a *mediation* which immediately is no less *identity-with-self*. The abstract thing-in-itself is itself this relationship in which it returns into itself out of the other; it is thereby *determinate in its own self*; but its determinateness is a constitution which, as such, is itself a determination, and in its relationship to the other does *not pass over* into otherness and is *free* from *alteration*.

A thing has properties; they are, first, the determinate relations of the thing to *another* thing; property exists only as a mode of relationship between them and is therefore the external reflection and the side of the thing's positedness. But, secondly, the thing in this positedness is *in itself*; it maintains itself in the relation to the other and is, therefore, admittedly only a surface with which Existence is exposed to the becoming and alteration of being; but the property is not lost in this. A thing has the property of effecting this or that in another thing and of expressing itself in a peculiar manner in its relation to it. It demonstrates this property only under the condition that the other thing has a corresponding constitution, but at the same time the property is *peculiar* to the first thing and is its self-identical substrate [*Grundlage*]; it is for this reason that this reflected quality is called *property*. In this the thing passes over into an externality in which, however, the property is preserved. Through its properties the thing becomes cause, and cause is this, that it preserves itself as effect. Here, however, the thing is so far only the quiescent thing of many properties and is not yet determined as actual cause; it is so far only the implicit reflection of its determinations, not yet itself the reflection which posits them.

The thing-in-itself is, therefore, as we have seen not merely thing-in-itself in such a manner that its properties are the positedness of an external reflection; on the contrary, they are its own determinations through which it enters into relationships in a determinate manner; it is not a substrate devoid of determinations and lying beyond its external Existence, but is present in its properties as ground, that is, it is identity-with-self in its positedness; but it is, at the same time, *conditioned* ground, that is, its positedness is equally a self-external reflection; it is reflected into itself and is in itself only in so far as it is external. Through Existence, the thing-in-itself enters into external relationships and Existence consists in this externality; it is the immediacy of being and so the thing is subject to alteration; but Existence is also the reflected immediacy of the ground, and the thing is therefore *in itself* in its alteration. But this mention of the ground-relation is not to be taken here as meaning that the thing is determined simply as ground of its properties; thinghood itself is, as such, the ground-determination, the property is not distinct from its ground, nor does it constitute merely the positedness, but is the ground that has passed over into its externality and is therefore truly ground reflected into itself. Property itself, as such, is ground, implicitly a positedness, or, it constitutes the *form* of its *identity* with itself; its *determinateness* is the self-external reflection of the

ground; and the whole is ground that in its repelling and determining, in its external immediacy, is self-related ground. The
thing-in-itself exists, therefore, essentially, and that it does exist
means, conversely, that Existence is, as an external immediacy, at
the same time *being-in-self*.

Remark: The Thing-in-itself of Transcendental Idealism

Mention has already been made above [1] of the thing-in-itself in
connexion with the moment of determinate being, of being-in-self,
and it was remarked that the thing-in-itself as such is nothing else
but the empty abstraction from all determinateness, of which
admittedly we can *know nothing*, for the very reason that it is
supposed to be the abstraction from every determination. The
thing-in-itself being thus presupposed as the indeterminate, all
determination falls outside it into an alien reflection to which it is
indifferent. For *transcendental idealism* this external reflection is
consciousness. Since this philosophical system places every determinateness of things both as regards form and content, in consciousness, the fact that I see the leaves of a tree not as black but
as green, the sun as round and not square, and taste sugar as sweet
and not bitter, that I determine the first and second strokes of a
clock as successive and not as one beside the other, nor determine
the first as cause and the second as effect, and so on, all this is
something which, from this standpoint, falls in *me*, the subject.
This crude presentation of subjective idealism is directly contradicted by the consciousness of freedom, according to which I
know myself rather as the universal and undetermined, and
separate off from myself those manifold and necessary determinations, recognizing them as something external for me and belonging only to things. In this consciousness of its freedom the ego is
to itself that true identity reflected into itself, which the thing-in-
itself was supposed to be. I have shown elsewhere that this
transcendental idealism does not get away from the limitation of
the ego by the object, in general, from the finite world, but only
changes the *form* of the limitation, which remains for it an absolute,
merely giving it a subjective instead of an objective shape and
making into determinatenesses of the ego and into a turbulent
whirlpool of change within it (as if the ego were a thing) that
which the ordinary consciousness knows as a manifoldness and

[1] p. 120.

Q*

alteration belonging only to things external to it. At present we are considering only the thing-in-itself and the reflection which is in the first instance external to it; this reflection has not yet determined itself to consciousness, nor the thing-in-itself to ego. We have seen from the nature of the thing-in-itself and of external reflection that this same external reflection determines itself to be the thing-in-itself, or, conversely, becomes the first thing-in-itself's own determination. Now the inadequacy of the standpoint at which this philosophy stops short consists essentially in holding fast to the *abstract thing-in-itself* as an *ultimate* determination, and in opposing to the thing-in-itself reflection or the determinateness and manifoldness of the properties; whereas in fact the thing-in-itself essentially possesses this external reflection within itself and determines itself to be a thing with its *own* determinations, a thing endowed with properties, in this way demonstrating the abstraction of the thing as a pure thing-in-itself to be an untrue determination.

(c) *The Reciprocal Action of Things*

The thing-in-itself essentially *exists*; the external immediacy and determinateness belongs to its in-itself or to its reflection-into-self. By virtue of this, the thing-in-itself is a thing which has properties, and hence there are a number of things which are distinguished from one another not in respect of something alien to them but through themselves. These many different things stand in essential reciprocal action through their properties; the property is this reciprocal relation itself and apart from it the thing is nothing; the reciprocal determination, the middle term of the things-in-themselves, which, as extremes, are supposed to remain indifferent to this their relation, is itself the self-identical reflection and the thing-in-itself which these extremes are supposed to be. Thinghood is thus reduced to the form of indeterminate identity-with-self which has its essentiality only in its property. If, therefore, one is speaking of a thing or things in general without any determinate property, then their difference is merely indifferent, quantitative. What is considered as one thing can equally be made into or considered as several things; the separation or union of them is *external*. A book is a thing and each of its leaves is also a thing, and so too is each bit of its pages, and so on to infinity. The determinateness through which one thing is *this* thing only, lies solely in its properties. Through them it distinguishes itself from other things, because property is negative reflection and a distinguishing; the thing therefore contains the difference of itself from other things solely in its property. This is the difference reflected into itself, through which the thing, in its positedness, that is, in its relation to another, is at the same time indifferent to the other and to its relation to it. All that remains therefore to the thing without its properties is abstract being-in-self or in-itselfness, an unessential compass and external holding together. The true in-itself is the in-itself in its positedness: and this is property. With this, *thinghood has passed over into property*.

The thing in its relationship to property should be an implicit extreme, and property should constitute the middle term between the related things. But it is in this relation that the things encounter one another as the *self-repelling reflection* in which they are distinguished and related. This their difference and relation is *one* reflection and *one continuity* of them. Accordingly the things themselves fall only within this continuity which is property; and as extremes which would have a continuing Existence apart from this property, they vanish.

Consequently *property*, which was supposed to constitute the *relation* of the self-subsistent extremes, is the *self-subsistent itself*. The things, on the other hand, are the unessential. They are an *essential* only as the reflection that is self-differentiating and self-relating; but this is property. This, therefore, is not that which is sublated in the thing, nor is it the thing's mere moment; on the contrary, the thing is, in truth, only that unessential compass which, though a negative unity, is only like the one of something, namely an *immediate* one. Previously the thing was determined as an unessential compass in so far as it was made such by external abstraction which strips it of its property; but now this abstraction has happened through the transition of the thing-in-itself into property itself, but with inversion of the values: whereas in the former act of abstraction the abstract thing without its property was still vaguely conceived of as the essential, but the property as an external determination, here the thing as such spontaneously determines itself into an indifferent external form of the property. Hence property is now freed from the indeterminate and impotent *connexion* which is the one of the thing: it is that which constitutes the thing's *subsistence*, a *self-subsistent matter*. Since this is a simple continuity with itself it possesses form, in the first instance, only as *diversity*; consequently there are *various* self-subsistent matters of this kind and *the thing consists of them.*

B. THE CONSTITUTION OF THE THING OUT OF MATTERS

The transition of property into a matter or into a self-subsistent *stuff* is the familiar transition performed on sensible matter by chemistry when it seeks to represent the properties of colour, smell, taste and so on, as luminous matter, colouring matter, odorific matter, sour, bitter matter and so on, or merely straightway postulates others like heat matter or caloric, electrical and magnetic matter, in the conviction that it has got hold of properties in their truth. Equally current is the expression that things *consist of* various matters. One is careful not to call these matters things; although it would certainly be admitted that, e.g. a pigment is a thing; but I do not know whether e.g. luminous matter, heat matter or electrical matter and so on, are also called things. Things and their constituents are distinguished without it being exactly stated whether and to what extent the latter are also things or perhaps only half things; but they are at least existents in general.

The necessity of making the transition from properties to matters, or of postulating that properties are in truth matters, has resulted from the fact that properties are the essential and therefore the truly self-subsistent element of things. But at the same time, the reflection of property into itself constitutes only one side of the whole reflection; namely, the sublating of the difference and the continuity of the property (which was supposed to be an Existence for an other) with itself. Thinghood, as negative reflection-into-self and a distinguishing which repels itself from an other, is thereby reduced to an unessential moment; but in this process it has at the same time further determined itself. First, this negative moment has *preserved* itself; for property has become continuous with itself and a self-subsistent matter only in so far as the difference of things has *sublated* itself; the continuity of the property into otherness therefore itself contains the moment of the negative, and its self-subsistence is, as this *negative unity*, the restored *something* of thinghood; the negative self-subsistence over against the positive of matter. Secondly, through this the thing has advanced from its indeterminateness to complete determinateness. As *thing-in-itself* it is *abstract* identity, the *simply negative* Existence, or Existence *determined* as the *indeterminate*; next, the thing is determined by its properties, by which it is supposed to be distinguished from other things; but it is, in fact, through property that it is continuous with other things and consequently this incomplete difference sublates itself. Through this the thing has returned into itself and is now determined as *determinate*; it is *in itself determinate* or *this* thing.

But, thirdly, this return-into-self, though a self-related determination is at the same time unessential; the self-continuous *subsistence* constitutes the self-subsistent matter in which the difference of things, their intrinsic and explicit determinateness, is sublated and an externality. Therefore, though the thing as *this* thing is a complete determinateness, this determinateness is determinateness in the element of unessentiality.

Considered from the side of the movement of property, this results in the following manner. Property is not only an *external* determination but an *intrinsic* Existence. This unity of externality and essentiality, because it contains reflection-into-self and reflection-into-an-other, repels itself from itself, and is, on the one hand, determination as *simple*, self-identical, self-related self-subsistence in which the negative unity, the one of the thing, is sublated; on the other hand, it is this determination over against an other, but likewise as a one reflected into itself and intrinsically determinate; it is therefore the *matters* and *this thing*. These are the two moments of the externality which is identical with itself, or of the property reflected into itself. Property was that by which things were supposed to be distinguished; but now that it has freed itself from this its negative side, of inhering in an other, the thing, too, has been freed from its being determined by other things and has returned into itself from the relation to other; but it is at the same time only the *thing-in-itself that has become an other to itself*, because the manifold properties on their part have become independent and therefore *their negative relation in the one of the thing* is only a sublated relation. For this reason, the thing is a self-identical negation only *as against* the positive continuity of the matter.

The 'this' thus constitutes the complete determinateness of the thing, the determinateness being at the same time external. The thing consists of self-subsistent matters which are indifferent to their relation in the thing. This relation is therefore only an unessential combination of them and the difference of one thing from another depends on whether and in what amount a number of the particular matters are present in it. They pass *out of and beyond this* thing, continue themselves into other things, and the fact that they belong to this thing is not a limitation for them; and just as little are they a limitation for one another, because their negative relation is only the impotent 'this'. Therefore in their combination in the latter they do not sublate themselves; as self-subsistent they are impenetrable for one another, relate themselves in their determinateness only to themselves, and are a mutually indifferent manifoldness of subsistence; they are capable only of a quantitative limit. The thing as 'this' is this their merely quantitative relation, a mere collection, their *'also'*. It *consists* of some quantum or other of a matter, *also* of a quantum of another, and again of others; this connexion of having no connexion alone constitutes the thing.

<h2 style="text-align:center">C. DISSOLUTION OF THE THING</h2>

This thing, which has determined itself as the merely quantitative connexion of free matters, is the simply alterable thing. Its alteration consists in the exclusion from the collection or the addition to this 'also,' of one or more matters, or in the alteration of their quantitative relationship to one another. The coming-to-be and passing away of 'this' thing is the external dissolution of such external combination or the combination of matters to which it is indifferent whether they are combined or not. Matters circulate freely out of or into 'this' thing; the thing itself is absolute porosity without measure or form of its own.

The thing in its absolute determinateness through which it is 'this' thing, is thus the absolutely dissoluble thing. This dissolution is an external process of being determined, as also is the being of the thing; but its dissolution and the externality of its being is the essential element of this being; it is only the 'also', and consists only in this externality. But it also consists of its matters, and not only the abstract 'this' as such, but the *whole of 'this' thing* is the dissolution of itself. The thing, namely, is determined as an external collection of self-subsistent matters; these matters are not things, they do not have negative self-subsistence; but they are the properties as self-subsistents, that is, they are determinate and the determinateness is, as such, reflected into itself. The matters, therefore, are indeed simple and are only *self*-related; but *their content* is a *determinateness*; reflection-into-self is only the *form* of this content, which is not as such reflected into itself but, in accordance with its determinateness, relates *itself* to *an other*. The thing is, therefore, not merely the 'also' of the matters—their relation as mutually indifferent—but equally their *negative* relation; on account of their determinateness the matters themselves are this their negative reflection, which is the *puncticity* of the thing. One matter is not *that* which the other is, in accordance with the determinateness of their content as against one another; and one *is* not, in so far as the other is, in accordance with their self-subsistence.

The thing is, therefore, the interrelation of the matters of which it consists in such a manner that in it both the one and the other *also subsist*; and yet at the same time the one does *not* subsist in so far as the other does. In so far therefore as the one matter is in the thing, the other is thereby sublated; but the thing is at the same time the 'also', or the subsistence of the others. In the subsistence of the one matter, the other, therefore, does *not* subsist, and *also* it no less subsists in the former; and so with all these diverse matters reciprocally. Since, therefore, in the same respect as the one subsists the others also subsist, this one subsistence of them being the puncticity or negative unity of the thing, they thus simply *interpenetrate* one another; and since the thing is at the same time only the 'also' of them, and the matters are reflected into their determinateness, they are indifferent to one another and in their interpenetration *do not touch* one another. The matters are therefore essentially *porous*, so that one subsists in the *pores* or in the *non-subsistence* of the others; but these others are themselves porous; in their pores or non-subsistence the first and all the others also subsist; their *subsistence* is at the same time their *sublatedness* and the subsistence of *others*; and this subsistence of the others is equally this their sublatedness and the *subsistence of the first*, and in the same way of all the others. The thing is, therefore, the self-contradictory mediation of independent self-subsistence through its opposite, namely, through its negation, or of *one* self-subsistent matter through the *subsistence* and *non-subsistence* of an *other*. In *this thing*, Existence has reached its completion, namely, it is intrinsic being or *independent* subsistence, and *unessential* Existence *in one*; hence the truth of Existence is to have its being-in-self in unessentiality, or its subsisting in an other, and that, too, the absolute other, or that it has its *own nullity* for substrate. It is therefore *Appearance*.

Remark: The Porosity of Matters

It is one of the commonest determinations of ordinary thinking that a *thing consists of a number of independent matters*. On the one hand, the thing is considered to have *properties*, whose *subsistence* is the *thing*. But, on the other hand, these different determinations are regarded as matters whose subsistence is not the thing, but, conversely, the *thing consists* of them and is itself only their external combination and quantitative limit. Both properties and matters are the same *content-determinations*; only in the former case they are moments, that is, they are reflected into their negative unity as into a substrate distinct from them, namely, *thinghood*, and in the latter case they are self-subsistent, different determinations, each of which is reflected into its own unity-with-self. These matters are now further determined as an independent subsistence; but they are also together in a thing. This thing has the two determinations of being first, *this* thing, and secondly, the '*also*'. The 'also' is that which presents itself in external intuition as *spatial extension*; but the 'this', the negative unity, is the *puncticity* of the thing. The matters are together in the puncticity, and their 'also' or the extension is everywhere this puncticity; for the 'also' as thinghood is essentially also determined as a negative unity. Therefore where one of these matters is, the other also is, *in one and the same point*; the thing does not have its colour in one place, its odorific matter in another, its heat matter in a third, and so on, but in the point in which it is warm, it is also coloured, sour, electric, and so on. Now because these matters are not outside one another but are in one 'this', they are assumed to be *porous*, so that one exists in the interstices of the other. But that which is present in the interstices of the other matter is itself porous; conversely, therefore, in its pores the other exists; but not only this matter but the third, tenth, and so on. They are all porous and in the interstices of each all the others are present, just as each, with all the rest, is present in the pores of every other. Accordingly they are a multiplicity which interpenetrate one another in such a manner that those which penetrate are equally penetrated by the others, so that each again penetrates its own penetratedness. Each is posited as its negation, and this negation is the subsistence of another; but this subsistence is equally the negation of this other, and the subsistence of the first.

The usual excuse by which ordinary thinking evades the *contradiction* of the *independent* subsistence of a *number* of *matters* in *one* thing, or their mutual *indifference* in their *interpenetration*, bases itself on the *smallness* of the parts and of the pores. Where difference-in-itself, contradiction, and the negation of negation occur, in general, where thinking should be *in terms of the Notion*, ordinary thinking falls back onto external, *quantitative* difference; in regard to coming-to-be and passing away, it has recourse to gradualness, and in regard to being, to *smallness* in which the vanishing element is reduced to an *imperceptible* and the contradiction to a confusion, and the true relationship is perverted into an ill-defined image which saves the self-sublating aspect of the relationship by its obscurity.

But when more light is thrown on this obscurity it is revealed as the contradiction which is partly subjective, stemming from pictorial thinking, and partly objective, stemming from the object; the elements of the contradiction are completely contained in the thinking itself. For pictorial thinking, in the first place contains the contradiction of wanting to hold on to *perception* and to have before it things that have real being, and secondly, of ascribing a sensible existence to the imperceptible, to what is determined by reflection; the minute parts and pores are at the same time supposed to be a sensible existence and their positedness is spoken of as if it had the same kind of *reality* as that which belongs to colour, heat, etc. If, further, pictorial thinking considered more closely this *objective* nebulosity, the pores and the minute particles, it would recognize in it not only a matter and *also* its negation, so that *here* there would be matter and *alongside* it its negation, the pore, and alongside this, matter again, and so on, but also that in *this* thing it has, *in one and the same point*, (1) *self-subsistent* matter, and (2) its *negation* or porosity and the other *self-subsistent* matter, and that this porosity and the independent subsistence of the matters in one another as in a single point is a reciprocal negation and a penetration of the penetration. Recent expositions in physics of the expansion of steam in atmospheric air and of various gases in one another give more distinct prominence to one side of the Notion concerning the nature of the thing that has here come to view. They show, namely, that for example a certain volume takes up the same amount of steam whether it is empty of atmospheric air or filled with it; and also that the various gases diffuse themselves in one another in such a manner that each is as good as a vacuum for the other, or at least that they are not in any kind of chemical combination with one another, each remains uninterrupted by the other and *continuous with itself* and *in its interpenetration with the others keeps itself indifferent* to them. But the further moment in the Notion of the thing is that in this thing one matter is present where the other matter is, and the matter that penetrates is also penetrated in the same point; in other words, the self-subsistent is immediately the self-subsistence of an other. This is contradictory; but the thing is nothing else but this very contradiction; and that is why it is Appearance.

Corresponding in the spiritual sphere to the conception of these matters, is the conception of *forces* or *faculties* of the soul. Spirit is, in a much deeper sense this *one thing*, the negative unity in which its determinations interpenetrate one another. But when it is thought of as soul, it is quite frequently taken as a *thing*. Just as man in general is made to *consist* of soul and body, each of which has an independent being of its own, so too the soul is made to consist of so-called *soul forces*, each of which has a self-subsistence of its own, or is an immediate, separate activity with its own peculiar nature. It is imagined that the intellect acts separately in one place and the imagination by itself in another, that intellect, memory, and so on, are each cultivated separately, and for the time being the other forces are left inactive on one side until perhaps, or perhaps not, their turn comes. In placing them in the materially simple *soul thing* which as simple is *immaterial*, the faculties are not, it is true, represented as particular matters; but as *forces* they are taken as equally *indifferent* to one another as the said matters. But spirit is not that contradiction which the thing is, which dissolves itself and passes over into Appearance; on the contrary, it is already in its own self the contradiction that has returned into its absolute unity, namely, the Notion, in which the differences are no longer to be thought of as independent, but only as *particular*, moments in the subject, in the simple individuality.

CHAPTER 2

APPEARANCE

Existence is the immediacy of being to which essence has restored itself again. This immediacy is *in itself* the reflection of essence into itself. Essence, as Existence, has issued from its ground which has itself passed over into it. Existence is this *reflected* immediacy in so far as it is in its own self absolute negativity. It is now also *posited* as this in that it has determined itself as *Appearance*.

Accordingly Appearance is at first essence in its Existence; essence is immediately present in it. The fact that it is not immediate but *reflected* Existence, constitutes the moment of essence in it; or, Existence as *essential* Existence is Appearance.

Something is *only* Appearance—in the sense that Existence as such is only a posited being, not a being in and for itself. This constitutes its essentiality, to have within itself the negativity of reflection, the nature of essence. This is not an alien, external reflection to which essence belongs and which, by comparing essence with Existence, pronounces the latter to be Appearance. On the contrary, as we have seen, this essentiality of Existence which constitutes its Appearance, is the truth of Existence itself. The reflection by virtue of which it is this, is its own.

But if it is said that something is *only* Appearance, in the sense that contrasted with it *immediate Existence* is the truth, then the fact is that Appearance is the higher truth; for it is Existence as essential Appearance, whereas Existence, on the contrary, is still essenceless Appearance because it contains only the one moment of Appearance, namely, Existence as immediate reflection, not yet as its negative reflection. When *Appearance* is called *essenceless*, one thinks of the moment of its negativity as though the immediate by contrast were the positive and the true; but the fact is that this immediate does not as yet contain the essential truth. It is when Existence passes over into Appearance that it ceases to be essenceless.

Essence at first reflects an *illusory being* [*scheint*] within itself, within its simple identity; as such it is abstract reflection, the pure movement from nothing through nothing back to itself. Essence *appears*, so that it is now *real* illusory being, since the moments of illosory being have Existence. As we have seen, Appearance is the *thing* as the negative *mediation* of itself with itself; the differences it contains are *self-subsistent* matters which are the contradiction of being an immediate subsistence and at the same time only in an alien self-subsistence, of therefore having their subsistence in the negation of their own self-subsistence, and again for that very reason also only in the negation of this alien negation, or in the negation of their own negation. Illusory being is the same mediation, but its unstable moments have, in Appearance, the shape of immediate self-subsistence. On the other hand, the immediate self-subsistence which belongs to Existence is, on its part, reduced to a moment. Appearance is accordingly the unity of illusory being and Existence.

Appearance now determines itself further. It is essential Existence; the latter's essentiality is distinguished from Appearance as unessential and these two sides enter into relation with each other. It is therefore at first simple self-identity which also contains various content-determinations; and these themselves as well as their relation are what remains self-equal in the flux of Appearance; this is the *law of Appearance*.

Secondly, however, the law which is simple in its diversity passes over into opposition; the essential moment of Appearance becomes opposed to Appearance itself, the and *world of Appearance* is confronted by the *world of essence* [*die an sich seiende Welt*].

Thirdly, this opposition returns into its ground; that which is in itself is in the Appearance and conversely that which appears is determined as taken up into its in-itself; Appearance becomes *correlation* or *essential relation*.

A. THE LAW OF APPEARANCE

1. Appearance is the existent mediated by its *negation* which constitutes its *subsistence*. This its negation is, indeed, *another* self-subsistence; but this is equally essentially a sublated self-subsistence. The existent is accordingly the *return* of itself into itself through its negation and through the negation of this its negation; it has, therefore, *essential self-subsistence*; just as it is equally immediately a sheer *positedness* which has a *ground* and an *other* for its subsistence. In the first place, therefore, Appearance is

Existence along with its essentiality, positedness with its ground; but this ground is a *negation*; and the other self-subsistent, the ground of the first is likewise only a positedness. In other words, the existent is, as an Appearance, reflected into an other which it has for its ground, which other is itself only this, to be reflected into an other. The *essential* self-subsistence which belongs to it because it is a return-into-self is the return of the nothing through nothing back to itself on account of the negativity of the moments; the self-subsistence of the existent is, therefore, only the *essential illusory show [wesentliche Schein]*. The connexion of the reciprocally grounding existents consists therefore in this reciprocal negation, namely, that the subsistence of the one is not the subsistence of the other, but is its positedness, which relation of the positedness alone constitutes the subsistence of the existents. The ground is present as it is in truth, namely, to be a *first* that is only *presupposed*.

Now this constitutes the *negative* side of Appearance. But in this negative mediation is immediately contained the *positive identity* of the existent with itself. For it is not a *positedness relatively to* an *essential ground*, or *is not an illusory being in a self-subsistent*; it is a *positedness* that is related to a *positedness*, or is an *illusory being only in an illusory being*. It *relates* itself in this its negation or in its other, which is itself a sublated moment, *to itself*, and is therefore self-identical or positive essentiality. This identity of the existent is not the *immediacy* that belongs to Existence as such, the merely unessential which subsists in an other. On the contrary, it is the *essential content* of Appearance which has two sides, first, to be in the form of *positedness* or external immediacy, secondly, to be positedness as self-identical. According to the first side it is a determinate being, but one which is contingent, unessential and, in keeping with its immediacy, is subject to transition, coming-to-be and ceasing-to-be. According to the other side, it is the simple content determination exempt from this flux, the *enduring* element *of it*.

This content in general, besides being the simple element in that which is transitory, is also a *determinate, inwardly diverse* content. It is the reflection of Appearance into itself, of negative determinate being, and therefore essentially contains *determinateness*. But Appearance is the *simply affirmative* manifold variety which wantons in unessential manifoldness; its reflected content, on the other hand, is its manifoldness reduced to *simple difference*. The determinate essential content is, more precisely, not merely simply determinate, but, as the essential moment of Appearance, is complete determinateness; the *one* and its *other*. In Appearance each of these two has its subsistence in the other in such a manner that at the same time it is only in the other's non-subsistence. This contradiction sublates itself; and its reflection-into-self is the *identity* of their double-sided subsistence: *the positedness of the one is also the positedness of the other.* They constitute *one* subsistence, but at the same time as a *diverse*, mutually indifferent content. Hence in the essential side of Appearance, the *negative* aspect of the unessential content, its self-sublation, has returned into identity; it is an indifferent *subsistence*, which is not the sublatedness, but rather *the subsistence, of the other.*

This unity is the *law of Appearance.*

2. The law is therefore the positive side of the mediation of what appears. Appearance is at first Existence as *negative* self-mediation, so that the existent is mediated with itself through *its own non-subsistence*, through an other, and, again, through the *non-subsistence of this other*. In this is contained first, the mere illusory being and the vanishing of both, the unessential Appearance; secondly, also their *permanence* or *law;* for *each* of the two *exists* in this sublating of the other; and their positedness as their negativity is at the same time the *identical, positive* positedness of both.

This permanent subsistence which Appearance has in law, is therefore, conformable to its determination, *first,* opposed to the *immediacy* of being which Existence has. True, this immediacy is *in itself* reflected immediacy, namely the ground which has withdrawn into itself; but now in Appearance this simple immediacy is distinguished from the reflected immediacy which first started to separate itself in the *thing.* The existent thing in its dissolution has become this opposition; the *positive* side of its dissolution is that identity-with-self of what appears, as positedness, in its other positedness. Secondly, this reflected immediacy is itself determined as *positedness* over against the simply affirmative immediacy of Existence. This positedness [*Gesetztsein*] is now the essential and the truly positive. The German expression *Gesetz* [law] likewise contains this determination. In this positedness lies the essential *relation* of the two sides of the difference which law contains; they are a diverse content, each side being immediate with respect to the other, and they are this as the reflection of the vanishing content belonging to Appearance. As essential diversity, the different sides are simple self-related content-determinations. But equally, neither is immediate on its own, but each is essentially a *positedness*, or *is, only in so far as the other is*.

Thirdly, Appearance and law have one and the same content. Law is the *reflection* of Appearance into identity-with-self; Appearance, as the null *immediate*, thus stands opposed to that which is *reflected into itself*, and they are distinguished according to this form. But the reflection of Appearance by virtue of which this difference is, is also the essential identity of Appearance itself and of its reflection, which is, in general, the nature of reflection; it is the self-identical in the positedness and is indifferent to that difference which is the form, or positedness; a content, therefore, which *continues* itself from Appearance into law, the content of law and Appearance.

Accordingly, this content constitutes the *substrate* of Appearance; law is this substrate itself, Appearance is the same content, but contains still more, namely, the unessential content of its immediate being. The form-determination, too, by which Appearance as such is distinguished from law, is, namely, a *content* and is likewise a content distinguished from the content of the law. For Existence, as immediacy in general, is likewise a self-identity of matter and form which is indifferent to its form determinations and therefore a content; it is thinghood with its properties and matters. But it is the content whose self-subsistent immediacy is, at the same time, only as a non-subsistence. But the identity of the content with itself in this its non-subsistence is the other, essential content. This identity, the substrate of Appearance, which constitutes law is Appearance's own moment; it is the positive side of essentiality by virtue of which Existence is Appearance.

Accordingly, law is not beyond Appearance but is immediately *present* in it; the realm of laws is the *stable* image of the world of Existence or Appearance. But the fact is rather that both form a single totality, and the existent world is itself the realm of laws, which, as that which is simply identical, is also identical with itself in positedness or in the self-dissolving self-subsistence of Existence. Existence withdraws into law as into its ground; Appearance contains these two, the simple ground, and the dissolving movement of the manifested [*erscheinenden*] universe whose essentiality it is.

3. Law is therefore *essential* Appearance; it is the latter's reflection-into-self in its positedness, the *identical* content of itself and of unessential Existence. Now first, this identity of law with its Existence is at first only the *immediate*, simple identity, and law is indifferent to its Existence; Appearance has a further content other than the content of law. The former content is, indeed, unessential and is the withdrawal into the latter; but for law it is a first which is not posited by it; as content, therefore, it is *externally connected* with law. Appearance is a host of more precise determinations which belong to the 'this' or the concrete, and are not contained in law but are determined by an other.

Secondly, that which Appearance contains distinct from law, determined itself as a positive or as another *content*; but it is essentially a negative; it is form and its movement as such, which belongs to Appearance. The realm of laws is the *stable* content of Appearance; Appearance is the same content but presenting itself in restless flux and as reflection-into-other. It is law as the negative, simply alterable Existence, the *movement* of transition into the opposite, of self-sublation and withdrawal into unity. Law does not contain this side of restless form or negativity; Appearance, therefore, as against law is the totality, for it contains law, but also more, namely, the moment of self-moving form.

Thirdly, this defect is present in law in this way, that the content of law is at first only *diverse* and so indifferent to itself; therefore the identity of its sides with one another is at first only *immediate* and therefore *internal*, or not yet necessary. In law two content determinations are *essentially* connected (for instance, in the law of descent of a falling body, spatial and temporal magnitudes: spaces passed through vary as the squares of the times elapsed); they *are* connected; this relation is at first only an immediate one. It is, therefore, likewise at first only a *posited* relation, the immediate in general having obtained in Appearance the meaning of positedness. The essential unity of the two sides of the law would be their negativity, that is to say, the one would contain its other within itself; but this essential unity has not yet emerged in the law. (That is why the Notion of the space traversed by a falling body does not itself imply that time corresponds to it as a square. Because fall is a sensible movement it is the relation of time and space; but first, the determination of time—that is, time as it is commonly imagined—does not itself imply its relationship to space, and *vice versa*; it is said that time can quite well be imagined without space and space without time; thus the one comes only externally into relation with the other, which external relation is motion. Secondly, the further determination is indifferent, namely, the magnitudes in accordance with which space and time are related in motion. The law of this relationship is empirically ascertained and in so far it is only *immediate*; it still demands a *proof*, that is, a mediation for cognition, showing that the law not only *occurs* but is *necessary*; the law as such does not contain this proof and its objective necessity.) Law is, therefore, only the *positive*, and not the negative, essentiality of Appearance. In the latter, the content determinations are moments of form, as such passing over into their *other* and in themselves are equally not themselves but their other. Accordingly, though in law the positedness of one side of it is the positedness of the other, their content is indifferent to this relation: the content does not itself contain this positedness. Law, therefore, is indeed essential form, but not as yet real form which is reflected into its sides as content.

B. THE WORLD OF APPEARANCE AND THE WORLD-IN-ITSELF

1. The existent world tranquilly raises itself to a realm of laws; the null content of its manifold being has its subsistence in an *other*; its subsistence is therefore its dissolution. But in this other the world of Appearance also unites *with itself*; thus Appearance in its changing is also an enduring, and its positedness is law. Law is this simple identity of Appearance with itself and therefore its substrate, not its ground; for it is not the negative unity of Appearance but, as its simple identity, the immediate, that is abstract unity, *alongside* which therefore its other content *also* occurs. The content is *this* content, internally coherent, or has its negative reflection within itself. It is reflected into an other; this other is itself an Existence of Appearance; phenomenal things have their grounds and conditions in other phenomenal things.

But law is, in fact, also the *other of Appearance as such*, and its negative reflection as into its other. The content of Appearance which is distinct from the content of law is the existent, which has its negativity for its ground or is reflected into its non-being. But this *other* which is also an *existent*, is likewise reflected into its non-being; it is therefore *the same* and the phenomenon is therefore in fact reflected not into an other but *into itself*; it is just this reflection of positedness into itself that is law. But as a phenomenon it is essentially *reflected into its non-being*, or its identity is itself essentially no less its negativity and its other. Therefore the reflection-into-self of Appearance, namely law, is not only the identical substrate of Appearance, but the latter also has its opposite in law and law is its negative unity.

Now through this, the determination of law has been altered in law itself. At first, it is merely a diverse content and the formal reflection of positedness into itself, so that the positedness of one of its sides is the positedness of the other. But because it is also negative reflection-into-self, its sides are in their relationship not merely different but are negatively related to each other. Or, when law is considered merely on its own, the sides of its content are indifferent to each other; but equally they are sublated by their identity; the positedness of one is the positedness of the *other*, and therefore the subsistence of each is also the *non-subsistence of itself*. This positedness of one in the other is their negative unity and each is *not only the positedness of itself but also of the other*, or, each is itself this negative unity. The positive identity which they have in law as such is at first only their *inner* unity which stands in need of *proof* and *mediation*, because this negative is not as yet posited in them. But since the different sides of law are now determined as being different in their negative unity, or such that each of them contains its other within it, and at the same time, as a self-subsistent side, repels this its otherness from itself, the identity of law is therefore now also a *posited* and *real* identity.

Consequently, law likewise has obtained the moment of the negative form of its sides which was lacking, the moment, that is, which previously belonged still to Appearance. Existence has thus completely withdrawn into itself and has reflected itself into its absolute otherness in and for itself. That which was previously law is accordingly no longer only one side of the whole whose other side was Appearance as such, but is itself the whole. Existence is the essential totality of Appearance, so that it now also contains the moment of unessentiality which still belonged to Appearance, but as reflected, implicit unessentiality, that is, as *essential negativity*. As an immediate content, law is *determinate* in general, distinguished from other laws, and of these there is an indeterminable number. But since it now has within it essential negativity it no longer contains such a merely indifferent, contingent content determination; on the contrary, its content is all determinateness whatsoever, in an essential relation developing itself into totality. Thus Appearance which is reflected into itself is now a *world*, which *reveals* itself as a *world in and for itself* above the world *of Appearance*.

The realm of laws contains only the simple, changeless but varied content of the existent world. But now since it is the total reflection of this world it also contains the moment of its essenceless manifoldness. This moment of alterableness and alteration as reflected into self, as essential, is absolute negativity or pure form as such, whose moments however in the world in and for itself have the reality of self-subsistent but reflected Existence; just as, conversely, this reflected self-subsistence now has form within itself, by virtue of which its content is not a merely manifold, but an essentially self-coherent, content.

This world in and for itself is also called the *supersensuous world*; in so far as the existent world is characterized as *sensuous*, namely, as determined for intuition, for the immediate attitude of consciousness. The supersensuous world likewise has immediacy, Existence, but reflected, essential Existence. *Essence* has as yet no determinate being; but it *is*, and in a profounder sense than being; the *thing* is the beginning of reflected Existence; it is an immediacy that is not yet *posited* as essential or reflected; but it is in truth not a *simply affirmative* [*seiendes*] immediate. It is only as things of another, supersensuous world that things are posited first, as veritable Existences, and secondly as the true in contrast to what has simply affirmative being; in them it is acknowledged that there is a being distinct from immediate being, a being that is veritable Existence. On the one hand, the sensuous representation which ascribes Existence only to the immediate being of feeling and intuition is overcome in this determination; but, on the other hand, there is also in it unconscious reflection which, though having the conception of things, forces, the inner, and so on, does not know that such determinations are not sensuous or simply affirmative immediacies, but reflected Existences.

2. The world in and for itself is the totality of Existence;

outside it there is nothing. But since it is in its own self absolute negativity or form, its reflection-into-self is a *negative relation* to itself. It contains opposition and repels itself within itself into the essential world and into the world of otherness or the world of Appearance. Thus, because it is totality, it is also only *one side* of it, and in this determination constitutes a self-subsistence distinct from the world of Appearance. The world of Appearance has in the essential world its negative unity in which it falls to the ground and into which it withdraws as into its ground. Further, the essential world is also the positing ground of the world of Appearance; for, containing the absolute form in its essentiality, its identity sublates itself, makes itself into positedness and as this posited immediacy is the world of Appearance.

Further it is not merely ground as such of the world of Appearance, but its *determinate* ground. As the realm of laws, it is already a manifold *content*, namely, the essential content of the world of Appearance, and as ground with a content, the *determinate* ground of the *other* world, but only in respect of this content; for the world of Appearance still had other manifold content than the realm of laws, because the negative moment was still peculiarly its own. But since the realm of laws now likewise contains this moment, it is the totality of the content of the world of Appearance and the ground of all its manifoldness. But it is at the same time the negative of this totality and as such is the world *opposed* to it. That is to say, in the identity of both worlds, one of them is determined in respect of form as essential and the other as the same world but as posited and unessential, so that the *ground relation* has, it is true, been restored; but it is also the *ground relation of Appearance,* namely, as relation not of an identical content, nor of a merely diverse one, as is law, but as total relation, or as negative identity and *essential relation of the opposed sides of the content*. The realm of laws is not only this, that the positedness of a content is the positedness of another, but this identity is essentially, as we have seen, also a negative unity; each of the two sides of law is, in the negative unity, *in its own self its other* content; accordingly the other is not an indeterminate other in general, but is *its* other, or, it too contains the content determination of the first; and thus the two sides are opposed. Now since the realm of Laws contains within it this negative moment and opposition, and hence as totality repels itself from itself into a world in and for itself and a world of

Appearance, the identity of both is thus the *essential relation of opposition.* The ground relation as such is the opposition which, in its contradiction, has fallen to the ground; and Existence is the ground that has united *with itself.* But Existence becomes Appearance; ground is sublated in Existence; it reinstates itself as the return of Appearance into itself, but at the same time as sublated ground, namely, as ground relation of opposed determinations; but the identity of such determinations is essentially a becoming and a transition, no longer the ground relation as such.

The world in and for itself is, therefore, itself a world distinguished within itself into the totality of a manifold content; it is identical with the world of Appearance or the posited world and in so far its ground; but its identical relationship is at the same time determined as opposition, because the form of the world of Appearance is reflection into its otherness and this world has therefore veritably withdrawn into itself in the world in and for itself in such a manner that the latter is its opposite. The relation is, therefore, specifically this, that the world in and for itself is the *inversion* of the manifested world.

C. DISSOLUTION OF APPEARANCE

The world in and for itself is the *determinate* ground of the world of Appearance and is this only in so far as it is within itself the negative moment, and hence the totality of the content determinations and their alterations which corresponds to the world of Appearance but at the same time constitutes its completely opposed side. The two worlds are therefore in such a relationship that what is positive in the world of Appearance is negative in the world in and for itself, and conversely, what is negative in the former is positive in the latter. The north pole in the world of Appearance is *in and for itself* the south pole, and conversely; positive electricity is *in itself* negative, and so on. What is evil, a misfortune and so on, in manifested existence is *in and for itself* good and a piece of good fortune.

In point of fact it is just in this opposition of the two worlds that *their difference has vanished,* and what was supposed to be the world in and for itself is itself world of Appearance, while this conversely in its own self is the essential world. The world of Appearance is in the first instance determined as reflection into otherness, so that its determinations and Existences have their ground and subsistence in an other; but since this other is likewise a *reflection-into-an-other* they are related therein only to a self-sublating other, hence *to themselves*; the world of Appearance is thus *in its own self* the law which is identical with itself. Conversely, the world in and for itself is at first the self-identical content exempt from otherness and change; but this, as complete reflection of the world of Appearance into itself, or, because its diversity is difference reflected into itself and absolute, contains the negative moment and relation to itself as to otherness; it thereby becomes essenceless content, self-opposed and self-inverting. Further, this content of the world in and for itself has thereby also received the form of *immediate Existence*. For it is in the first instance ground of the world of Appearance; but since it has opposition within it, it is equally sublated ground and immediate Existence.

Thus the world of Appearance and the essential world are each in themselves the totality of self-identical reflection and reflection-into-an-other, or of being-in-and-for-self and Appearance. Both are self-subsistent wholes of Existence; the one is supposed to be only reflected Existence, the other immediate Existence; but each *continues* itself in its other and is therefore in its own self the identity of these two moments. What is present, therefore, is this totality which repels itself from itself into two totalities, one the *reflected*, the other the *immediate*, totality. Both, in the first instance, are self-subsistents, but they are self-subsistent only as totalities, and they are this in so far as each essentially contains within it the moment of the other. Accordingly the distinct self-subsistence of each, of that determined as *immediate* and that as *reflected*, is now so posited that each is only as essential relation to the other and has its self-subsistence *in this unity of both*.

We started from the law of Appearance; this is the identity of a varied content with another content, so that the positedness of the one is the positedness of the other. In law, this difference is still present, in that the identity of its sides is at first only an inner identity which these sides do not yet have within themselves. Thus first, this identity is not realized; the content of law is not as an identical, but an indifferent, varied content; and secondly, the content is thereby only *implicitly* determined such that the positedness of the one is the positedness of the other; this is not yet present in the content. Now, however, *law* is *realized*; its inner identity is also determinately present, and conversely the content of law is raised into ideality; for it is a content sublated within itself, reflected into itself, in that each side has its other within it and is therefore veritably identical with it and with itself.

Thus law is *essential relation*. The truth of the unessential world is, at first, a world in and for itself and *other to it*; but this world is a totality since it is itself and that first world. Thus both are immediate Existences and hence reflections into their otherness, and also for this same reason veritably reflected into self. 'World' expresses in general the formless totality of manifoldness; this world, both as essential and as manifested has fallen to the ground [*zugrunde gegangen*] in that the manifoldness has ceased to be a mere variety; as such it is still a totality or universe, but as *essential relation*. There have arisen two totalities of the content in the world of Appearance; at first they are determined as mutually indifferent self-subsistents and each has the form within itself, but not as against the other; but the form has also shown itself to be their relation, and the essential relation is the consummation of their unity of form.

CHAPTER 3

THE ESSENTIAL RELATION

The truth of Appearance is the *essential relation*, the content of which has immediate self-subsistence; *simply affirmative [seiende]* immediacy, and *reflected* immediacy or self-identical reflection. At the same time, it is in this self-subsistence a relative content, only and solely as reflection into its other, or as unity of the relation with its other. In this unity the self-subsistent content is a posited, sublated content; but it is just this unity which constitutes its essentiality and self-subsistence; this reflection into other is reflection into itself. The relation has sides because it is reflection into an other; thus it contains within itself its own difference, and the sides are a self-dependent subsistence, since in their mutually indifferent diversity they are disrupted within themselves, so that the subsistence of either side equally has its meaning only in relation to the other or in their negative unity.

The essential relation is therefore not as yet the true third to *essence* and *Existence*, though it already contains the determinate union of both. Essence is realized in it in such a manner that it has for its subsistence self-subsistent existents; and these have withdrawn from their indifference into their essential unity, so that they have this alone for their subsistence. The reflective determinations of positive and negative are likewise reflected into themselves only as reflected into their opposites; but they have no other determination but this their negative unity. The sides of the essential relation, on the other hand, are posited as self-subsistent totalities. It is the same opposition as that of positive and negative, but at the same time as an inverted world. The side of the essential relation is a totality which, however, as essentially an opposite, has a *beyond* of itself; it is only Appearance; its Existence is not its own, but rather that of its other. It is therefore disrupted within itself; but this its sublatedness consists in its being the unity of itself and its other, therefore a whole, and precisely for this reason it has self-subsistent Existence and is essential reflection-into-self.

This is the *Notion* of the relation. But at first the identity it contains is not yet complete; the totality which each related side is within itself is at first an inner; the side of the relation is in the first instance posited in *one* of the determinations of the negative unity; the self-subsistence belonging to each of the two sides is that which constitutes the form of the relation. Its identity is therefore only a *relation*, its self-subsistence falling outside it, namely in the sides; the reflected unity of this identity and the self-subsistent Existences, namely, *substance*, is not yet before us. Accordingly, although the Notion of the relation has shown itself to be the unity of reflected and immediate self-subsistence, this *Notion* is itself at first still *immediate*; its moments therefore are immediate in respect of each other, and their essential relation is unity, a unity which is only the true unity accordant with the Notion in so far as it realizes itself, that is, has *posited* itself as this unity through its movement.

The essential relation is therefore immediately the relation of *whole* and *parts*—the relation of reflected and immediate self-subsistence, so that both sides only are as at the same time reciprocally conditioning and presupposing each other.

In this relation as yet neither of the sides is posited as moment of the other, and therefore their identity is itself one side; in other words, their identity is not their negative unity. Secondly, therefore, the relation passes over into the relationship in which one side is moment of the other and in it as in its ground, the veritable self-subsistent element of both: the relation of *force* and its *expression*.

Thirdly, the inequality still present in this relation now sublates itself and the final relation is that of *inner* and *outer*. In this difference, which has become wholly formal, the relation itself falls to the ground and there emerges *substance* or the *actual* as the *absolute* unity of immediate and reflected Existence.

A. THE RELATION OF WHOLE AND PARTS

The essential relation contains first, the self-subsistence of immediacy, *reflected into itself*; as such it is the *simple form* whose moments, though Existences, too, are at the same time posited, moments held in the unity. This self-subsistence which is reflected into itself is at the same time reflection into its opposite, namely, *immediate* self-subsistence; and its subsistence is essentially as

R

much this identity with its opposite as it is its own self-subsistence. Secondly, with this identity the other side, too, is immediately posited: the immediate self-subsistence which, determined as the other, is within itself a manifold variety, but such that this manifoldness essentially *also* has within it the relation of the other side, the unity of the reflected self-subsistence. The first side, the whole, is the self-subsistence which constituted the world in and for itself; the second side, the parts, is the immediate Existence which was the world of Appearance. In the relationship of whole and parts the two sides are these self-subsistences but in such a manner that each has the other reflected in it and at the same time only is as this identity of both. Now because the essential relation is at first only the first, immediate relation, the negative unity and the positive self-subsistence are connected by '*also*'; both sides are indeed posited as *moments*, but *equally* as existent *self-subsistences*. Accordingly the distribution of these two posited moments is as follows. First, the whole, the reflected self-subsistence, is an existent; and the other, the immediate self-subsistence, is in it as moment—here the whole, the unity of both sides, constitutes the *substrate*, and the immediate Existence is a *positedness*. Conversely, on the other side, namely the side of the parts, the immediate, internally manifold Existence, is the self-subsistent substrate; on the other hand the reflected unity, the whole, is only an external relation.

2. This relation thus contains the self-subsistence of the sides, and equally their sublatedness, and it contains both simply in one relation. The whole is the self-subsistent, the parts are only moments of this unity; but equally they, too, are the self-subsistent and their reflected unity only a moment; and each is, in its *self-subsistence*, simply the *relative* of an other. This relation is therefore in its own self immediate contradiction, and sublates itself.

Considered more closely, the whole is the reflected unity which has an independent subsistence of its own; but this its subsistence is equally repelled from it; the whole is, as negative unity, negative relation-to-self; it is thus alienated from itself; it has its *subsistence* in its opposite, in the manifold immediacy, the parts. *The whole accordingly consists of parts*, so that it is not anything without them. It is therefore the whole relation and the self-subsistent totality; but for this very reason it is only a relative, for that which makes it a totality is rather its other, the parts; and it has its subsistence not within itself but in its other.

Thus the parts likewise are the whole relation. They are immediate, *as against* reflected, self-subsistence and do not subsist in the whole but on their own account. Further, they have this whole as their moment within themselves; it constitutes their relation, for without a whole there are no parts. But because they are the self-subsistent, this relation is only an external moment towards which they are, in and for themselves, indifferent. But at the same time the parts, as a manifold Existence, collapse within themselves, for this Existence is reflectionless being; they have their self-subsistence only in the reflected unity which is both this unity and also the existent manifoldness; that is to say, they have self-subsistence only *in the whole*, but at the same time, the whole is a self-subsistent other to the parts.

The whole and the parts therefore *condition* each other; but the relation here considered is at the same time higher than the relation of *conditioned* and *condition* to each other as it had determined itself above. Here this relation is *realized*, that is, it is *posited* that condition is the essential self-subsistence of the conditioned in such a manner that it is *presupposed* by the latter. Condition as such is only the *immediate* and is only *implicitly* presupposed. But the whole, though it is the condition of the parts, also contains this, that it, too, only is in so far as it has the parts for presupposition. Since, then, both sides of the relation are posited as conditioning each other, each is an immediate self-subsistence within itself, but its self-subsistence is equally mediated or posited by the other. The *whole relation* is, through this reciprocity, the return of the conditioning into itself, the non-relative, the *unconditioned*.

Now since each side of the relation has its self-subsistence not in itself but in its other, what is present is only a single identity of both in which both are only moments; but since each is in its own self self-subsistent, there are two self-subsistent Existences which are indifferent to each other.

In accordance with the first respect, that of the essential identity of both sides, *the whole is equal to the parts and the parts to the whole*. There is nothing in the whole which is not in the parts, and nothing in the parts which is not in the whole. The whole is not abstract unity, but unity as of a *diverse manifoldness*; but this unity, as that in which the elements of the *manifold* are related to one another, is the determinateness of each element through which it is part. The relation has, therefore, an inseparable identity and one self-subsistence only.

But further, although the whole is equal to the parts it is not equal *to them* as parts; the whole is reflected unity, but the parts constitute the determinate moment or the *otherness* of the unity and are the diverse manifold. The whole is not equal to them as this self-subsistent diversity, but to them *together*. But this their 'together' is nothing else but their unity, the whole as such. The whole is, therefore, in the parts only equal to itself, and the equality of the whole and the parts expresses only the tautology that *the whole as whole* is equal not to the parts but to *the whole*.

Conversely, the parts are equal to the whole; but because they are in themselves the moment of otherness, they are not equal to it as the unity, but in such a manner that *one* of the manifold determinations of the whole attaches to the part, or that they are equal to the *whole* as a manifold; that is to say, they are equal to it as a *divided whole*, that is, *to the parts*. Here we have the same tautology, that the *parts as parts* are equal, *not to the whole* as such, but in it *to themselves, the parts*.

In this way, the whole and the parts fall indifferently apart; each of these sides relates itself only to itself. But as thus held apart they destroy themselves. The whole which is indifferent to the parts is the *abstract identity* which is not internally differentiated; this is a whole only as *internally differentiated*, and moreover in such a manner that these manifold determinations are reflected into themselves and have immediate self-subsistence. And the identity of reflection has shown through its movement that it has this *reflection into its other* for its truth. Similarly the parts, as indifferent to the unity of the whole, are only the unrelated manifold, *that which is within itself other*, which as such is the other of itself and only sublates itself. This self-relation of each of the two sides is their self-subsistence; but this their self-subsistence which each has *for itself* is rather their self-negation. Accordingly each side has its self-subsistence not within itself but in the other; this other, which constitutes the subsistence, is its presupposed immediate which is *supposed* to be the first, and its beginning; but this first of each side is itself *not* a first, but has its beginning only in the other.

The truth of the relation consists therefore in the *mediation*;

its essence is the negative unity in which both the reflected and the simply affirmative [*seiende*] immediacy are sublated. The relation is the contradiction which withdraws into its ground, into the unity which, as returning, is reflected unity; but since this latter has equally posited itself as sublated it is negatively related to itself, sublates itself and makes itself into a simply affirmative [*seiende*] immediacy. But this its negative relation, in so far as it is a first and an immediate, is mediated only through its other and is equally posited. This other, the simply affirmative immediacy, is equally only as sublated; its self-subsistence is a first, but only in order to vanish, and it has an existence that is posited and mediated.

In this determination the relation is no longer that of *whole* and *parts*; the immediacy which belonged to its sides has passed over into positedness and mediation; each is posited, in so far as it is immediate, as self-sublating and passing over into the other, and in so far as it is itself negative relation, as at the same time being conditioned by the other as its positive; just as its immediate transition, too, is equally a mediated transition, being a sublating that is posited by the other. Thus the relation of whole and parts has passed over into the relation of *force and its expression*.

Remark: Infinite Divisibility

The antinomy of the infinite divisibility of matter was considered above [1] under the Notion of quantity. Quantity is the unity of continuity and discreteness; it contains in the *self-subsistent* one its *fusion* with other ones, and in this uninterrupted *continuing identity* with itself it equally contains the *negation of it*. The immediate relation of these moments of quantity being expressed as the essential relation of whole and parts (the one of quantity being part, but its continuity, the whole, which is composed of parts), the antinomy then consists in the contradiction which presented itself in the relation of whole and parts and has been resolved. For whole and parts are just as essentially related to each other, constituting only one identity, as they are mutually indifferent and have independent self-subsistence. The relation therefore is this antinomy, that the one moment in freeing itself from the other immediately introduces the other.

The existent, then, being determined as a whole, has parts, and the parts consititute its subsistence; the unity of the whole is only

[1] pp. 190 sqq.

a posited relation, an external *composition* which does not concern
the self-subsistent existent. Now in so far as this is a part it is not a
whole, not a composite, hence a *simple*. But the relation to a
whole is external to it and therefore does not concern it; the self-
subsistent is, therefore, not even in itself part; for it is part only
through that relation. But now since it is not part it is a whole,
for there is only this relation of whole and parts present and the
self-subsistent is one of the two. But as a whole, it is again composite; it again consists of parts, and *so on to infinity*. This infinitude
consists solely in the perennial alternation of the two determinations of the relation, in each of which the other immediately arises,
so that the positedness of each is the vanishing of itself. Matter
determined as whole consists of parts, and in these the whole
becomes an unessential relation and vanishes. But the part taken
in the same way by itself is also not part but the whole. The
antinomy of this inference when closely examined is really this:
because the whole is not the self-subsistent, therefore the part is
self-subsistent; but because the part is self-subsistent only *without
the whole*, it is self-subsistent *not* as part, but rather *as whole*. The
infinitude of the progress which arises is the inability to bring
together the two thoughts which the mediation contains, namely,
that each of the two determinations through its self-subsistence
and separation from the other passes over into non-self-subsis-
tence and into the other.

B. THE RELATION OF FORCE AND ITS EXPRESSION

Force is the negative unity into which the contradiction of whole
and parts has resolved itself; the truth of that first relation. The
whole and parts is the thoughtless relation which ordinary thinking
first happens to think of; or objectively it is a dead, mechanical
aggregate having, it is true, form determinations through which
the manifoldness of its self-subsistent matter is connected in a
unity; but this unity is external to the matter. But the relation of
force is the higher return-into-self in which the unity of the whole
which constituted the relation of the self-subsistent otherness,
ceases to be external and indifferent to this manifoldness.

  In the *essential relation* as now determined, the immediate and
the reflected self-subsistence are posited as sublated or as moments;
in the preceding relation they were independent, self-subsistent

sides or extremes. In this there is contained first, that the reflected unity and its immediate determinate being, in so far as both are first and immediate, sublate themselves within themselves and pass over into their other; the former, force, passes over into *its expression*, and what is expressed is a vanishing something which withdraws into force as into its ground; it *is*, only as borne and posited by force. Secondly, this transition is not only a becoming and vanishing, but is a negative relation-to-self; or, that which *alters its determination* is at the same time reflected into itself and preserves itself; the movement of force is not so much a *transition* [*Übergehen*] as a movement in which it *transposes* itself [*sich selbst über setzt*] and in this alteration posited by itself remains what it is. Thirdly, this *reflected*, self-related unity is itself sublated and a moment; it is mediated by its other and has it for *condition*; its negative self-relation, which is a first and begins the movement of its transition *out of itself*, has equally a presupposition by which it is *solicited*, and an other from which it begins.

(a) The Conditionedness of Force

Considered in its closer determinations force contains first, the moment of affirmative [*seienden*] immediacy; it itself is determined over against this immediacy as negative unity. This, however, in the determination of immediate being, is an *existent something*. This something, because it is negative unity as an immediate, appears as the first; force, on the other hand, as reflected unity appears as positedness and thus as belonging to the existent thing or to a matter. But this does not imply that force is the *form* of this thing and that the thing is determined by force; on the contrary, the thing as an immediate is indifferent to it. As thus determined, the thing contains no ground for having a force; force, on the other hand, as the side of positedness, essentially has the thing for its presupposition. When therefore it is asked how the thing or matter comes to *have* a force, then the force appears as externally connected with it and *impressed* on the thing by an extraneous power.

As this immediate subsistence, force is a *quiescent determinateness of the thing* in general; it does not express or manifest itself but is immediately an externality. Thus force is also designated as matter, and instead of magnetic, electrical, and other forces, magnetic, electrical, and other matters are assumed, or, instead of the famous *attractive force*, a subtle *aether* which holds everything together. These are the matters into which the inert, powerless, negative unity of the thing is resolved and which were considered above.

But force contains immediate Existence as moment, a moment which, though it is condition, passes over and sublates itself, not immediate Existence therefore as an existent thing. Further, it is not negation as determinateness but negative unity reflected into itself. Accordingly the thing in which the force was supposed to be no longer has any meaning here; rather is force itself a positing of externality which appears as Existence. Nor is it, therefore, merely a determinate matter; such self-subsistence has long since passed over into positedness and Appearance.

Secondly, force is the unity of reflected and immediate sub-sistence, or of the form-unity and external self-subsistence. It is both in one; it is the contact of sides of which one is in so far as the other is not, self-identical positive reflection and negated reflection. Force is thus the self-repelling contradiction; *it is active*, or it is the self-relating negative unity in which the reflected im-mediacy or essential inwardness [*Insichsein*] is posited as being only as sublated or as moment, and therefore, in so far as it dis-tinguishes itself from immediate Existence, as passing over into this. Force, then, as the determination of the reflected unity of the whole, is posited as becoming existent external manifoldness *from out of itself*.

But thirdly, force is at first only an activity *in principle* [*ansichseiende Tätigkeit*], an immediate activity; it is the reflected unity and equally essentially *the negation of it*; as different from this negation, but only as the identity of itself and its negation, it is essentially related to this as to an immediacy external to it, and has it for *presupposition* and *condition*.

Now this presupposition is not a thing standing over against it; this indifferent self-subsistence is sublated in force; as condition of force it is *a self-subsistent other to it*. But because it is not a thing, the self-subsistent immediacy having here determined itself as at the same time self-relating negative unity, this other self-subsistent *is itself force*. The activity of force is conditioned by itself as by the other to itself, by a force.

In this manner force is a relation in which each side is the same as the other. There are forces which stand in relation, and indeed are essentially related to each other. Further, they are at first simply different without further qualification; the unity of their relation is in the first instance only *inner* unity, unity *in itself*. The conditionedness through another force is thus *in itself* the act of force itself, or force is in so far at first an act of *presupposition*, a merely negatively *self*-relating act; this other force still lies *beyond* its *positing* activity, namely beyond the reflection which in its determining immediately *returns into itself*.

(b) The Solicitation of Force

Force is conditioned because it contains the moment of immediate Existence as something only *posited*—but because it is at the same time an immediate—as something *presupposed*, in which force negates itself. Accordingly, the externality which is present for force is *its own presupposing activity*, which at first is posited as *another force*.

Further, this *presupposing* is reciprocal. Each of the two forces contains the unity reflected into itself as sublated and is therefore a presupposing activity; it posits its own self as external; this moment of externality is *its own*; but since it is equally a unity reflected into itself it at the same time posits this its externality *not within itself*, but as another force.

But the external as such is self-sublating; further, this activity which reflects itself into itself is essentially related to this external as to its other, but equally as to that which *in itself is null* and *with which it is identical*. Since the presupposing activity is equally reflection-into-self, it is the sublating of this its negation and it posits the latter as something external to itself, or as external to *it*. Thus force, as conditioning, is reciprocally an impulse [*Anstoss*] for the other force against which it is active. Its attitude is not the passive one of being determined, which would involve the entry into it of something alien; the impulse only *solicits* it. It is in its own self the negativity of itself; the repelling of itself from itself is its own positing. Its act, therefore, consists in sublating the externality of this impulse; it makes it into a mere impulse and posits it as its own repelling of itself from itself, as *its own expression*.

Force which expresses itself is thus the same as that which was at first only a presupposing activity, that is, it makes itself external; but force, as expressing itself, is at the same time the activity

R*

which negates externality, *positing* it as its own. Now in so far as
in this consideration we start from force as negative unity of
itself and therefore as presupposing reflection, this is the same as
when, in the expression of force, we start from the soliciting
impulse. Thus force, *in its Notion*, is at first determined as self-
sublating identity, and *in its reality* one of the two forces is determined as soliciting and the other as being solicited. But the
Notion of force is simply the identity of positing and presupposing
reflection, or of reflected and immediate unity; and each of these
determinations is simply a moment, in unity, and thus is mediated
by the other. But equally there is nothing in the two reciprocally
related forces to determine which is to be the soliciting and which
the solicited force; or rather both form determinations belong in
the same manner to each. But this identity is not merely an
external identity of comparison but an essential unity of the
two.

For in the first instance one force is determined as *soliciting* and
the other as *being solicited*; these form determinations appear in
this way as immediate differences, present in principle, of both
forces. But they are essentially mediated. One of the forces is
solicited; this impulse is a determination posited in it from
outside. But force itself is the presupposing reflection; essentially it
reflects itself into itself and sublates the fact that the impulse is
external. Accordingly, the fact that it is solicited is its own act, or,
it is through its own determining that the other force is simply
other and is the soliciting force. The soliciting force is negatively
related to its other and so sublates the latter's externality, and in
doing so it has a positing action; but it has this only by virtue of
the presupposition of having another over against it; that is, it is
itself soliciting only in so far as it has in it an externality, hence in
so far as it is solicited. Or it solicits only in so far as it is solicited
to solicit. And so, conversely, the first force is solicited only in so
far as it itself solicits the other to solicit it, namely, the first force.
Each of the two therefore receives the impulse from the other;
but the impulse which it gives as active force consists in its receiving an impulse from the other; the impulse which it receives was
solicited by itself. Both the impulse given and that received, or the
active expression and the passive externality, are consequently not
an immediate but are mediated, and so each of the two forces is
itself the determinateness which the other has over against it, is

mediated by the other, and this mediating other is, again, its own determinative positing.

This process then in which an impulse is exerted upon one force by another force, the first force *passively* receiving the impulse but then again passing over from this passivity into activity, this is the return of force into itself. It expresses *itself*. The expression is reaction in the sense that it posits the externality as its own moment and thus sublates its having been solicited by another force. Both are therefore one: the expression of force through which it gives itself a determinate being-for-other by its negative activity directed onto itself, and the infinite return to itself in this externality, so that in it, it relates itself only to itself. The presupposing reflection, to which belong the conditionedness and the impulse, is therefore immediately also the reflection that returns into itself, and the activity is essentially reactive *against itself*. The positing of the impulse or of the externality is itself the sublating of it, and conversely, the sublating of the impulse is the positing of the externality.

(c) The Infinity of Force

Force is *finite* in so far as its moments still have the form of immediacy; its presupposing and its self-relating reflection are distinct in this determination: the former appears as an independently subsisting external force, and the other, in its relation to it, as passive. Force is thus conditioned in respect of form and likewise restricted with respect to content; for a form-determinateness also implies a restriction of content. But the activity of force consistes in *expressing itself*, that is, as we have seen, in sublating externality and determining it as that in which it is identical with itself. Therefore what force in truth expresses is that its relation to other is relation to itself, that its passivity consists in its very activity. The impulse by which it is solicited into activity is its own soliciting; the externality which affects it is not an immediate but is mediated by force itself; just as its own essential identity-with-self is not immediate but is mediated by its negation. In other words, what force expresses is this, that its *externality is identical* with its *inwardness*.

C. RELATION OF OUTER AND INNER

1. The relation of whole and parts is the immediate relation; in

it, therefore, the reflected and the affirmative immediacy each have a self-subsistence of their own; but since they stand in essential relation their self-subsistence is only their negative unity. Now this is posited in the expression of force; the reflected unity is essentially a becoming-other as translation of itself into externality; but the latter equally is immediately taken back into the former; the distinction between the self-subsistent forces is sublated; the expression of force is only a mediation of the reflected unity with itself. What is present is only an empty, transparent distinction, an illusory being, but this illusory being is the mediation which is the independent subsistence itself. Not only are they opposite determinations which sublate themselves within themselves, nor is their movement merely a transition; but partly the immediacy from which the beginning and the transition into otherness was made is itself only a posited immediacy, and partly, in consequence of this, each of the determinations is in its immediacy already the unity with its other, so that the transition is just as much the spontaneously posited return-into-self.

The inner is determined as the form of *reflected immediacy* or of essence over against the outer as the form of being, but the two are only one identity. This identity is first, the substantial unity of both as a substrate pregnant with content, or the *absolute fact* [*Sache*], in which the two determinations are indifferent, external moments. By virtue of this, it is a content and that totality which is the inner that equally becomes external, but in this externality is not the result of becoming or transition but is identical with itself. The outer, according to this determination, is not only *identical* with the inner in respect of content but both are only *one fact*. But this fact, as *simple self-identity*, is distinct from its *form determinations*, or, these are external to it; it is thus itself an inner that is distinct from its externality. But this externality consists in its being constituted by the two determinations themselves, namely, the inner and the outer. But the fact is itself nothing else but the unity of both. Hence both sides are again the same in respect of content. But in the fact they are present as an interpenetrating identity, as a substrate pregnant with content. But in externality they are, as forms of the fact, indifferent to this identity and thus to each other.

2. They are in this way the different form-determinations which have an identical substrate, not in themselves but in an other—

determinations of reflection which are for themselves: the inner as the form of reflection-into-self, of essentiality, but the outer as the form of immediacy reflected into an other, or of unessentiality. But the nature of the relation has shown that these determinations constitute one identity and one alone. Force in its expression is this, that the determining which presupposes and the determining which returns into itself are one and the same. In so far then as inner and outer have been considered as form-determinations, they are first only the simple form itself, and secondly, because in this form they are at the same time determined as opposite, their unity is pure, *abstract mediation* in which the one is *immediately* the other, and is the other *because* it is itself. Thus the inner is immediately *only* the outer, and it is the *determination of externality* because it is the inner; conversely, the outer is *only* an inner because it is *only* an outer. That is to say, since this form unity contains its two determinations as opposites, their identity is only this transition, and therein only the *other* of both, not their identity *pregnant with content*. Or, this holding fast to form is in general the side of *determinateness*. What is posited in accordance with this is not the real totality of the whole, but the totality or the fact itself only in the *determinateness* of form; since this unity is the mere conjunction of opposite determinations, then, when one of them is taken first—and it does not matter which—we must say of the substrate or fact that it is *for that reason* equally essentially in the other determinateness, but also *only* in the other, just as we said before that it is *only* in the first.

Thus something which in the first instance is *only* an inner, is for that very reason *only* an outer. Or conversely, something which is *only* an outer is just for that reason *only* an inner. Or, if the inner is determined as *essence* but the outer as *being*, then a fact, in so far as it is only in its *essence*, is for that very reason only an immediate *being*; or a fact which only *is* is precisely for that reason as yet only in its *essence*. Outer and inner are determinateness posited in such wise that each of these two determinations not only presupposes the other and passes over into it as into its truth, but, in so far as it is this truth of the other, remains *posited as determinateness* and points to the totality of both. The *inner* is therefore the consummation of *essence* with respect to form. For essence, when it is determined as inner, implies that it is defective and is, only as relation to its other, the outer; but this, equally, is not merely being or even Existence, but relates itself to essence or the inner. But what is here present is not only the relation of the two to each other but the determinate relation of the absolute form in which each is immediately its opposite, and their common relation *to their third* or rather *to their unity*. But their mediation still lacks this identical substrate that contains them both; hence their relation is the immediate conversion of the one into the other, and this negative unity which links them together is the simple point devoid of any content.

Remark: Immediate Identity of Inner and Outer

The movement of essence is in general the becoming of the Notion. In the relation of inner and outer, the essential moment of this emerges, namely, that its determinations are posited as being in negative unity in such a manner that each immediately is not only its other but also the totality of the whole. But in the Notion as such this totality is the *universal*—a substrate which is not yet present in the relation of inner and outer. In the negative identity of inner and outer which is the *immediate conversion* of one of these determinations into the other, there is also lacking that substrate which above was called the *fact*.

It is very important to notice that the unmediated *identity of form* is posited here without the movement of the fact itself, a movement pregnant with content. It occurs in the fact as this is in its *beginning*. Thus *pure being* is immediately *nothing*. In general, everything real is, in its beginning, such a merely immediate identity; for in its beginning it has not yet opposed and developed its moments; on the one hand it has not yet *inwardized* [*erinnert*] itself out of externality, and on the other hand, it has not yet *externalized* [*entäussert*] and brought forth itself out of inwardness by its activity. It is therefore only the inner as *determinateness* against the outer, and only the outer as *determinateness* against the inner. Hence it is partly *only* an immediate being; partly, in so far as it is equally the negativity which is to be the activity of the development, it is as such essentially *only* as yet an inner. This makes itself apparent in all natural, scientific and spiritual development generally and it is essential to recognize that because something is at first only *inner* or also is in its *Notion*, the first stage is for that very reason only its immediate, passive existence. Thus—to take at once the nearest example—the essential relation here considered is only *implicitly* [*an sich*] the relation, only its Notion, or is at first only *internal*, before it has moved through the mediation of the relation of *force* and has realized itself. But for this reason it is *only* the *outer*, immediate relation, the relation of *whole* and *parts*, in which the sides have a mutually indifferent subsistence. Their identity is not as yet within themselves; it is only *internal* and the sides theerfore fall apart, have an immediate, external subsistence. Thus the sphere of being as such is as yet still the completely *inner* and is therefore the sphere of simply affirmative [*seienden*] immediacy or externality. Essence is at first only the inner, and it, too, is for this reason taken as a wholly *external*, unsystematized, common element; one speaks of public instruction, the press [*Schulwesen, Zeitungswesen*], and understands thereby something common formed by an external aggregation of existing objects lacking any essential connexion or organization; or to take concrete objects, the seed of the plant, or the child, is at first only *inner* plant, *internal* man. But this is why the plant or the man as germ is an immediate, and outer, which has not as yet given itself the negative reference to itself, is something *passive*, a *prey to otherness*. Thus God, too, in his *immediate* Notion is not spirit; spirit is not the immediate, that which is opposed to mediation, but on the contrary is the essence that eternally posits its immediacy and eternally returns out of it into itself. *Immediately*, therefore, God is *only* nature. Or, nature is *only* the inner God, not God actual as spirit, and therefore not truly God. Or, in our thinking, our *first* thinking, God is only pure being, or even essence, the abstract absolute, but not God as absolute spirit, which alone is the true nature of God.

3. The *first* of the identities of inner and outer we have considered is the substrate which is indifferent to the difference of these determinations as to a form external to it, or, the identity as content. The second is the unmediated identity of their difference, the immediate conversion of each into its opposite, or the identity as pure form. But these two identities are only *the sides of one totality*; or, the totality itself is only the conversion of one into the other. The totality as substrate and content is this immediacy, which is reflected into itself, only through the presupposing reflection of form which sublates their difference and posits itself as indifferent identity, as a reflected unity, over against it. Or, the content is the form itself in so far as this determines itself as

difference, making itself into one of its sides as externality, but into the other as an immediacy that is reflected into itself, or into inner.

Conversely, it follows from this that each of the differences of form, the inner and outer, is posited within itself as the totality of itself and its other; the inner, as simple identity reflected into itself, is the immediate and accordingly is as much being and externality as essence; and the outer, as manifold, determinate being is only an outer, that is, is posited as unessential and as withdrawn into its ground, hence as an inner. This transition of each into the other is their immediate identity as substrate; but it is also their mediated identity; for it is precisely through its other that each is what it is in itself, the totality of the relation. Or, conversely, the determinateness of each side, because it is in itself the totality, is mediated with the other determinateness; thus the totality mediates itself with itself through the form or determinateness, and the determinateness is mediated with itself through its simple identity.

What something is, therefore, it is wholly in its externality; its externality is its totality and equally is its unity reflected into itself. Its Appearance is not only reflection-into-an-other but reflection-into-self, and its externality is, therefore, the expression or utterance [*Äusserung*] of what it is in itself; and since its content and form are thus utterly identical, it is, in and for itself, nothing but this, *to express* or *manifest itself*. It is the manifesting of its essence in such a manner that this essence consists simply and solely in being that which manifests itself.

The essential relation, in this identity of Appearance with the inner or with essence, has determined itself into *actuality*.

Section Three: Actuality

Actuality is the *unity of essence and Existence*; in it, *formless* essence and *unstable* Appearance, or mere subsistence devoid of all determination and unstable manifoldness, have their truth. Existence is, indeed, the immediacy which has proceeded from ground, but form is not as yet posited in it. In determining and forming itself it is Appearance; and when this subsistence which is determined only as reflection-into-an-other is developed further into reflection-into-self, it becomes *two worlds, two totalities* of the content, one of which is determined as *reflected into itself*, the other as *reflected into an other*. But the essential relation exhibits their *form relation*, the consummation of which is the *relation of inner and outer* in which the content of both is only one *identical substrate* and equally only *one identity of form*. By virtue of the fact that this identity is now also identity of form, the form determination of their difference is sublated, and it is *posited* that they are *one* absolute totality.

This unity of inner and outer is *absolute actuality*. But this actuality is, in the first instance, the *absolute* as such—in so far as it is posited as a unity in which form has sublated itself and made itself into the *empty or outer difference* of an outer and inner. *Reflection* is *external* in its relation to this absolute, which it merely contemplates rather than is the absolute's own movement. But since it is essentially this movement, it is so as the negative return of the absolute into itself.

Secondly, we have *actuality* proper. *Actuality, possibility* and *necessity* constitute the *formal moments* of the absolute, or its reflection.

Thirdly, the unity of the absolute and its reflection is the *absolute relation*, or rather the absolute as relation to itself—*substance*.

CHAPTER I

THE ABSOLUTE

The simple substantial identity of the absolute is indeterminate, or rather in it every determinateness of *essence* and *Existence*, or of *being* in general, as well as of *reflection*, has dissolved itself. Accordingly, the process of *determining what the absolute is* has a negative outcome, and the absolute itself appears only as the negation of all predicates and as the void. But since equally it must be pronounced to be the position of all predicates, it appears as the most formal contradiction. In so far as both the negating and the positing belong to external reflection, this is a formal and un-systematic dialectic which has no difficulty in picking up here and there a variety of determinations, and on the one hand demon-strates with equal ease their finitude and mere relativity as, on the other hand, since it thinks vaguely of the absolute as the totality of determinations, declares these to be immanent in it; at the same time it is unable to raise either the positions or the negations to a genuine unity. But we have to exhibit what the absolute is; but this 'exhibiting' can be neither a determining nor an external reflection from which determinations of the absolute would result; on the contrary, it is the *exposition*, and in fact the *self*-exposition, of the absolute and only a *display of what it is*.

A. THE EXPOSITION OF THE ABSOLUTE

The absolute is not merely being, nor even *essence*. The former is the first, unreflected immediacy, the latter is reflected immediacy; further, each is a totality within itself but a determinate totality. In essence, being emerges as Existence; and the connexion between being and essence has progressed to the relation of inner and outer. The inner is essence, but as *totality*, which essentially has the determination of *connexion with being* and immediately to be *being*. The outer is being, but with the essential determination of being *connected with reflection*, and equally to be immediately a relationless identity with essence. The absolute itself is the absolute unity of both; it is that which constitutes in general the *ground* of the essential relation which, as relation, merely has not yet withdrawn into this its identity and whose ground is not yet *posited*.

From this it follows that the determination of the absolute is to be the *absolute form*, but at the same time not as the identity whose moments are only simple determinatenesses, but as the identity each of whose moments is within itself the *totality* and hence, as indifferent to the form, is the complete *content* of the whole. But conversely, the absolute is the absolute content in such a manner that the content, which as such is an indifferent manifoldness, has within it the negative form relation by virtue of which its manifoldness is only *one* substantial identity.

The identity of the absolute is thus the absolute identity, since each of its parts is itself the whole, or each determinateness is the totality, that is, determinateness as such has become an utterly transparent illusory being, a difference which has *vanished in its positedness*. Essence, Existence, the world-in-itself, whole, parts, force—these reflected determinations appear to ordinary thinking as a true being which is valid in and for itself; but the absolute as against them is the ground in which they have been engulfed. Now because in the absolute, the form is only simple self-identity, the absolute does not *determine* itself; for determination is a form difference which, in the first instance, counts as such. But because at the same time it contains all difference and form-determination whatever, or because it is itself the absolute form and reflection, the *difference of the content* must also appear in it. But the absolute itself is *absolute identity*; this is its *determination*, for in it all manifoldness of the world-in-itself and the world of Appearance, or of inner and outer totality, is sublated. In the absolute itself is no *becoming*, for it is not being; not is it a self-*reflecting* determining, for it is not essence which determines itself only inwardly; nor is it an *uttering* or *expressing of itself* [*sich äussern*], for it is the identity of inner and outer. But the movement of reflection thus stands *over against* the absolute identity of the absolute. In this identity it is sublated and thus is only the inner of it; but as inner, it is *external* to it. At first, therefore, this movement consists only in sublating its act in the absolute. It is the beyond of the manifold differences and determinations and their movement, a beyond which *lies at the back of the absolute*; consequently, though it accepts them, it also destroys them; it is thus the *negative exposition* of the absolute previously mentioned. In its true presentation this exposition is the preceding whole of the logical movement of the sphere of *being and essence*, the content of which has not been raked together from outside as something given and contingent, or submerged in the abyss of the absolute by a reflection alien to that content; on the contrary, it has determined itself internally through its inner necessity, and as being's own *becoming* and as the *reflection* of essence, has withdrawn into the absolute as into its ground.

But at the same time this exposition has itself a *positive* side; for in so far as in it the finite falls to the ground, it demonstrates that its nature is to be connected with the absolute, or to contain the absolute within itself. But this side is not so much the positive exposition of the absolute itself as rather the exposition of the *determinations*, namely, that these have the absolute for their abyss, but also for their *ground*, in other words, that which gives a subsistence to them, to the illusory being, is the *absolute* itself. The illusory being is not *nothing*, but is a reflection, a *relation* to the absolute; or, it *is* illusory being in so far as *in it the absolute is reflected*. This positive exposition thus arrests the finite before it vanishes and contemplates it as an expression and image of the absolute. But the transparency of the finite, which only lets the absolute be glimpsed through it, ends by completely vanishing; for there is nothing in the finite which could preserve for it a distinction against the absolute; it is a medium which is absorbed by that which is reflected through it.

This positive exposition of the absolute is therefore itself only an illusory activity, a reflective movement [*ein Scheinen*]; for what is truly positive in the exposition and the expounded content, is the absolute itself. Any further determinations that may occur, the form into which the absolute reflects itself, is a nullity that the exposition picks up *from outside* and from which it gains a *beginning* for its activity. Such a determination has in the absolute, not its beginning, but only *its end*. Consequently, this expository process though it is an absolute act through its *relation* to the absolute into which it *withdraws*, is not so as regards its *starting point* which is a determination external to the absolute.

But the exposition of the absolute is, in fact, its *own* act, which *begins from itself* and *arrives at itself*. The absolute, merely as absolute identity, is *determinate*, namely, as the identical; it is *posited as such* by reflection as against opposition and manifoldness; or it is only the *negative* of reflection and the process of determining as such. Therefore not only is this expounding of the absolute something imperfect, but so also is this *absolute* itself which is only *arrived at.* Or, the absolute that is only an *absolute identity*, is only the *absolute of an external reflection.* It is therefore not the absolute absolute but the absolute in a determinateness, or it is *attribute.*

But the absolute is not merely attribute because it is the *subject matter* of an external reflection and therefore something determined by it. Or, reflection is not only *external* to it; but because it is *external* to it, it is *immediately internal* to it. The absolute is the absolute only because it is not abstract identity, but the identity of being and essence, or the identity of inner and outer; it is therefore itself the absolute form which makes it reflect itself into itself [*es in sich scheinen macht*] and determines it into attribute.

B. THE ABSOLUTE ATTRIBUTE

The expression which has been used, the *absolute absolute*, denotes the absolute that in *its form* has *returned* into itself, or whose form is identical with its content. The attribute is the merely *relative absolute*, a connexion which signifies simply the absolute in a *form determination.* For at first, before its completed exposition, the form is *only internal*, or what is the same thing *only external*, in general, at first *determinate* form or negation as such. But because form is at the same time form of the absolute, the attribute is the whole content of the absolute; it is the totality which previously appeared as a world, or as one of the *sides* of the *essential relation*, each of which is itself the whole. But the two worlds, the world of Appearance and the world-in-and-for-itself, were supposed to be *opposed* to each other in their essence. True, one side of the relation was equal to the other, the whole was equal to the parts, the expression of force the same content as force itself, and the outer altogether the same as the inner. But at the same time, each of these two sides was supposed to have as well an *immediate* subsistence of its own, one as simply affirmative, the other as reflected immediacy. In the absolute, on the other hand, these distinguished immediacies are reduced to an illusory being, and the *totality* which the attribute is is *posited as its true and sole subsistence*; but the *determination* in which it is is posited as *unessential* subsistence.

The absolute is attribute because as simple absolute identity it is in the determination of identity; now to the determination as such other determinations can be linked, for example, that there are also *several* attributes. But because absolute identity has only this meaning, not merely that all determinations are sublated but that it is also the reflection that has sublated itself, therefore all determinations are *posited* in this identity *as sublated*. Or the totality is posited as absolute, or the attribute has the absolute for its content and subsistence; its form determination, by virtue of which it is attribute, is therefore also posited, immediately as mere illusory being—the negative as a negative. The positive illusory being which the exposition gives itself through the attribute, in that it does not take the finite in its limitation to be something existing in and for itself but dissolves its subsistence in the absolute and extends it into attribute, sublates the very fact that it is attribute; the exposition submerges both the attribute and its distinguishing act in the *simple absolute*.

But since reflection thus returns from its distinguishing only to the *identity* of the absolute, it has not at the same time emerged from its externality and reached the veritable absolute. It has only reached determinate, abstract identity, that is, that identity which is in the *determinateness* of identity. Or, since it is as *inner* form that reflection determines the absolute into attribute, this determining is something still distinct from the externality; the inner determination does not penetrate the absolute; its utterance or expression is, as something merely posited, to vanish in the absolute.

Form, therefore, whether taken as outer or inner, whereby the absolute might be attribute, is at the same time posited as being something intrinsically null, an external illusory being, or a mere way and manner.

C. THE MODE OF THE ABSOLUTE

The attribute is first, the absolute as in simple *identity* with itself. Secondly, it is *negation*, and this *as* negation is formal reflection-into-self. These two sides constitute, in the first instance, the two *extremes* of the attribute, the *mean* of which is the attribute itself, since it is both the absolute and the determinateness. The second of these extremes is the negative as negative, the reflection which is *external* to the absolute. Or, in so far as it is taken as the inner of the absolute and it is its *own* determination to posit itself as mode, then it is the self-externality of the absolute, the loss of itself in the mutability and contingency of being, the accomplished transition of itself into opposites *without the return into itself*; the multiplicity of form and content determinations lacking the character of totality.

But mode, the *externality* of the absolute, is not merely this, but externality *posited* as externality, a mere way and manner, and hence illusory being as illusory being, or *the reflection of the form into itself*—hence the *identity-with-self which the absolute is.* Therefore it is in the mode that the absolute is in fact first posited as absolute identity; it is what it *is*, namely identity-with-self, only as self-related negativity, as a *reflective movement [Scheinen]* that is posited as *reflective movement.*

In so far then as the *exposition* of the absolute begins from its absolute identity, and passes over to attribute and from that on to mode, it has in its course completely run through all its moments. But first, in doing so its relationship to these determinations is not merely negative, but this *its act* is *the reflective movement itself,* and it is only as this that the absolute is truly *absolute identity.* Secondly, in this activity the exposition is not dealing merely with something external, nor is mode merely the uttermost externality, but because it is illusory being as illusory being it is the return-into-self, the self-dissolving reflection and it is as this that the absolute is absolute being. Thirdly, the expounding reflection seems to begin from its own determinations and from something external, and to take up the modes and also the determinations of the attribute as simply *found* outside the absolute; and its act seems to consist in merely tracing these back into an indifferent identity. But in fact it has in the absolute itself the determinateness from which it begins. For the absolute as *first* indifferent identity is itself only the *determinate absolute* or attribute, because it is the unmoved, still unreflected absolute. This *determinateness,* because it is determinateness, belongs to the reflective movement; through this alone is it determined as the *first identity,* and equally through this alone does it have absolute form and is not that which merely *is* equal to itself, but is that which *posits* itself as equal to itself.

Accordingly the true meaning of mode is that it is the absolute's own reflective movement, a *determining*; but a determining which would make it not an *other* but only that which it already *is*, the transparent externality which is the *manifestation* of itself, a movement *out of* itself, but such that this *being-outwards* is equally inwardness itself and therefore equally a positing that is not merely positedness but absolute being.

When therefore a *content* of the exposition is asked for, *what* then does the absolute manifest? the answer must be that the distinction between form and content is simply dissolved in the absolute. Or the content of the absolute is just this, *to manifest itself*. The absolute is the absolute form which, as the diremption of itself is utterly identical with itself, the negative *as* negative, or that unites with itself, and only thus is it the absolute identity-with-self which equally is *indifferent to its differences*, or is absolute *content*. The content, therefore, is only this exposition itself.

As this movement of exposition, a movement which carries itself along with it, as a way and manner which is its absolute identity-with-self, the absolute is manifestation not of an inner, nor over against an other, but it *is* only as the absolute manifestation of itself for itself. As such it is *actuality*.

Remark: The Philosophy of Spinoza and Leibniz
Corresponding to the Notion of the absolute and to the relation of reflection to it, as expounded here, is the notion of substance in Spinozism. Spinozism is a defective philosophy because in it reflection and its manifold determining is an *external thinking*. The substance of this system is *one* substance, one indivisible totality; there is no determinateness that is not contained and dissolved in this absolute; and it is sufficiently important that in this necessary notion, everything which to natural picture thinking or to the understanding with its fixed distinctions, appears and is vaguely present as something self-subsistent, is completely reduced to a mere *positedness*. *Determinateness is negation*—is the absolute principle of Spinoza's philosophy; this true and simple insight establishes the absolute unity of substance. But Spinoza stops short at *negation* as *determinateness* or quality; he does not advance to a cognition of negation as absolute, that is, *self-negating, negation*; thus *his substance does not itself contain the absolute form*, and cognition of it is not an immanent cognition. True, substance is the absolute unity of *thought* and being or extension; therefore it

contains thought itself, but only in its *unity* with extension, that is, not as *separating* itself from extension, hence in general not as a determinative and formative activity, nor as a movement which returns into and begins from itself. Two consequences follow from this: one is that substance lacks the principle of *personality*— a defect which has been the main cause of hostility to Spinoza's system; the other is that cognition is external reflection which does not comprehend and derive from substance that which appears as finite, the determinateness of the attribute and the mode, and generally itself as well, but is active as an external understanding, taking up the determinations as *given* and *tracing them back* to the absolute but not taking its *beginnings* from the latter.

The notions of substance given by Spinoza are the notions of 'cause of itself', and that substance is that whose essence includes existence—that the notion of the absolute does not require the notion of an other by which it must be formed. These notions, profound and correct as they are, are *definitions*, which are *immediately* assumed at the outset of the science. Mathematics and other subordinate sciences must begin with something *presupposed* which constitutes its element and positive foundation. But the absolute cannot be a first, an immediate; on the contrary, the absolute is essentially *its result*.

Spinoza's definition of the absolute is followed by his definition of the attribute, and this is determined as the manner in which intellect comprehends the essence of substance. Apart from the fact that intellect, in accordance with its nature, is postulated as posterior to attribute—for Spinoza defines it as mode—attribute, determination as determination of the absolute, is thus made *dependent on an other*, namely, intellect, which appears as external and immediate over against substance.

Spinoza further determines attribute as *infinite*, and infinite, too, in the sense of an *infinite plurality*. However in what follows only *two* appear, thought and extension, and it is not shown by what necessity the infinite plurality reduces itself to opposition, that, namely, of thought and extension. These two attributes are therefore adopted *empirically*. Thought and being represent the absolute in a determination; the absolute itself is their absolute unity and they themselves are only unessential forms; the order of things is the same as that of figurate conceptions or thoughts, and the one absolute is contemplated only by external reflection, by a mode, under these two determinations, once as a totality of conceptions, and again as a totality of things and their mutations. Just as it is this external reflection which makes that distinction, so too does it lead the difference back into absolute identity and therein submerges it. But this entire movement proceeds outside the absolute. True, the absolute is itself also *thought*, and so far this movement is only in the absolute; but as remarked, it is in the absolute only as unity with extension, and therefore not as this movement which is essentially also the moment of opposition. Spinoza makes the sublime demand of thought that it consider everything under the form of eternity, *sub specie aeterni*, that is, as it is in the absolute. But in the said absolute, which is only un- moved identity, the attribute, like the mode, *is* only as *vanishing*, not as *becoming*, so that here, too, the vanishing takes its positive beginning only from without.

The Third, the mode, is with Spinoza *affection* of substance, specific determinateness, and this is *in an other* and is apprehended *through this other*. The attributes have, strictly speaking, only indeterminate difference for their determination; each is *supposed* to express the totality of substance and to be understood from itself alone; but in so far as it is the absolute as determinate, it contains otherness and cannot be understood *from itself alone*. It is in the mode, therefore, that the determination of the attribute is first really posited. Further, this mode remains mere mode; on the one hand it is something immediately *given*, and on the other, its nullity is not cognized as reflection-into-self. Consequently, the Spinozistic exposition of the absolute is *complete* in so far as it starts from the absolute, then follows with the attribute, and ends with the mode; but these three are only enumerated *one after the other*, without any inner sequence of development, and the third is not negation *as* negation, not the negatively self-related negation which would be *in its own self* the return into the first identity, so that this identity would then be veritable identity. Hence the necessity of the advance of the absolute to unessentiality is lacking and also the dissolution of the unessentiality in and for itself in the identity; or, there is lacking the becoming both of identity and of its determinations.

In a similar manner, in the oriental conception of *emanation* the absolute is the light which illumines itself. Only it not only illumines itself but also *emanates*. Its emanations are *distancings*

[*Entfernungen*] from its undimmed clarity; the successive pro-ductions are less perfect than the preceding ones from which they arise. The process of emanation is taken only as a *happening*, the becoming only as a progressive loss. Thus being increasingly obscures itself and night, the negative, is the final term of the series, which does not first return into the primal light.

The lack of reflection-into-self, from which both the Spinozistic exposition of the absolute and the emanation theory suffer, is made good in the notion of the Leibnizian monad. The one-sidedness of a philosophical principle is usually countered by its opposite one-sidedness and totality, as in all of them, is usually present as a *dispersed completeness*—The monad is only one, a negative re-flected into itself; it is the totality of the content of the world. In it, the varied multiplicity has not only vanished but is in a negative manner *preserved*; (Spinoza's substance is the unity of all content; but this manifold content of the world *is* not as such in it, but in the reflection which is external to it). The monad is there-fore essentially *ideative*; but although it is finite its nature is not *passive*, the mutations and determinations in it being manifesta-tions within it of itself. It is an *entelechy*, and the manifestation is its own act. The monad is thereby also *determinate, distinguished from others*; the determinateness falls in the particular content and the way and manner of the manifestation. Consequently, the monad is *in itself* or according to its substance, the totality, *but it is not so in its manifestation*. This *limitation* of the monad necessarily falls, not in the *self-positing* or *ideating* monad, but in its in-itself [*Ansichsein*]; or it is absolute limit, a *predestination* which is posited by another being than itself. Further, since limited entities exist only as related to other limited entities, yet the monad is at the same time a self-enclosed absolute, the *harmony* of these limitations, that is, the relation of the monads to one another, falls outside them and is likewise pre-established by another being or *in itself*.

Clearly, by the principle of reflection-into-self which constitutes the fundamental determination of the monad, otherness and external influence in general are no doubt removed and the alterations of the monad are its own positing; but on the other side, passivity in relation to otherness has merely been trans-formed into an absolute limitation, into a limitation of the *being-in-self* or the *in-itself*. Leibniz ascribes to the monads a certain internal completeness, a *kind* of self-subsistence; they are *created* beings. When their limitation is considered more closely, it is evident from this account of the monads that the manifestation of themselves which belongs to them is the *totality of form*. It is an extremely important concept that the alterations of the monads are conceived of as actions in which passivity plays no part, as *manifestations* of themselves, and that the principle of reflection-into-self or of *individuation* stands out as essential. Further, it is necessary to let finitude consist in this, that the content or *substance is distinct from the form*, and also that the former is limited but the latter infinite. But now we should have to find in the concept of the *absolute monad* not only that absolute unity of form and content, but also the nature of reflection as the self-relating negativity which repels itself from itself whereby it posits and creates. True, in Leibniz's system, the further point is likewise to be found that God is the source of existence and of the essence of the monads, that is to say, that those absolute limitations in the being-in-self or the in-itself of the monads are not limitations in and for them-selves, but vanish in the absolute. But in these determinations are to be seen only the usual conceptions which are not philosophically developed, nor raised into speculative Notions. Thus the principle of individuation does not receive its profounder realization; the concepts concerning the distinction between the various finite monads and their relation to their absolute do not originate out of this being itself, or not in an absolute manner, but are the product of ratiocinative, dogmatic reflection and therefore have not achieved an inner coherence.

CHAPTER 2

ACTUALITY

The absolute is the unity of inner and outer as *initial, implicit* unity. The *exposition* appeared as *external* reflection which, on its side, has the immediate before it as something already given, but is at the same time the movement and relation of this to the absolute, and as such movement leads it back into the absolute and determines it as a mere 'way and manner'. But this 'way and manner' is the determination of the absolute itself, namely, its *initial identity* or *its merely implicit unity*. And through this reflection, too, not only is that initial in-itself posited as essenceless determination but, since the reflection is negative self-relation, it is through this alone that the in-itself becomes this mode. This reflection, as sublating itself in its determinations and in general as the self-returning movement, is first truly absolute identity and at the same time is the determining of the absolute or its modality. The mode is therefore the externality of the absolute, but equally only as the reflection of the absolute into itself; or it is the absolute's *own manifestation*, so that this manifestation is its reflection-into-self and therefore its being-in-and-for-itself.

The absolute as such manifestation, the absolute which is nothing else and has no content save that of being self-manifestation, is *absolute form. Actuality* is to be taken as this reflected absoluteness. *Being* is not yet actual: it is the first immediacy; its reflection is therefore a becoming and *transition into an other*; or its immediacy is not being-in-and-for-self. Actuality also stands higher than Existence. True, Existence is the immediacy that has proceeded from ground and conditions, or from essence and its reflection. It is therefore *in itself* what actuality is, *real reflection*, but is it not yet the *posited* unity of reflection and immediacy. Existence therefore passes over into *Appearance* in that it develops the reflection which it contains. It is the ground that has fallen to the ground; its determination is the restoration of the ground; thus it becomes essential relation and its final reflection is the positing of its immediacy as reflection-into-self, and conversely; now this unity in which Existence or immediacy, and the in-itself, the ground or the reflected are simply moments, is *actuality*. The actual is therefore *manifestation*; it is not drawn into the sphere of *alteration* by its externality, nor is it the *reflecting* of itself in *an other*, but it manifests itself; that is, in its externality it is *itself* and is *itself* in that alone, namely only as a self-distinguishing and self-determining movement.

Now in actuality as this absolute form, the moments are only as sublated or formal, not yet realized; their difference thus belongs at first to external reflection and is not determined as content.

Actuality as itself the *immediate* form-unity of inner and outer is thus in the determination of *immediacy* over against the determination of reflection-into-self; or it is an *actuality as against a possibility*. Their *relation* to each other is the *third* term, the actual determined equally as a being reflected into itself, and this at the same time as a being existing immediately. This third term is *necessity*.

But first of all, since the actual and the possible are *formal differences*, their relation is likewise merely *formal* and consists only in the fact that the one like the other is a *positedness*, or in *contingency*.

Now since in contingency, the actual as well as the possible is *positedness*, they have received determination in themselves; the actual thereby becomes, secondly, *real actuality* and with it equally emerges *real possibility* and *relative necessity*.

Thirdly, the reflection of relative necessity into itself yields *absolute necessity*, which is absolute *possibility* and *actuality*.

A. CONTINGENCY, OR FORMAL ACTUALITY, POSSIBILITY, AND NECESSITY

1. Actuality is formal in so far as, being primary actuality, it is only *immediate, unreflected* actuality, and hence is only in this form-determination but not as the totality of form. As such it is nothing more than a *being* or *Existence* in general. But because it is *essentially* not a mere immediate Existence but exists as form-unity of being-within-self or inwardness and outwardness, it immediately contains the *in-itself* or *possibility*. *What is actual is possible*.

2. This possibility is actuality reflected into itself. But even this first *reflectedness* is likewise *formal* and therefore in general

only the *determination of identity-with-self* or of the in-itself generally.

But because the determination is here the *totality* of form, this in-itself is determined as *sublated* or as essentially only in relation to actuality, as the negative of actuality, *posited* as negative. Possibility therefore contains two moments: first, the *positive* moment that it is a reflectedness-into-self; but since it is reduced in the absolute form to a moment, the reflectedness-into-self no longer counts as *essence*, but has, *secondly*, the *negative* meaning that possibility lacks something, that it points to an other, to actuality in which it completes itself.

According to the first, the merely positive side, therefore, possibility is the mere form determination of *identity-with-self* or the form of essentiality. As such it is the relationless, indeterminate receptacle for everything whatever. In the sense of this formal possibility *everything is possible that is not self-contradictory*; hence the realm of possibility is a boundless multiplicity. But each of these manifold entities is *determinate within itself* and *as against another* and contains negation; in general, indifferent *diversity* passes over into *opposition*; but opposition is contradiction. Therefore *everything* is just as much something contradictory and therefore *impossible*.

This merely formal predication of something—*it is possible*—is therefore equally as superficial and empty as the law of contradiction and any content that is admitted into it. *A is possible* means only that *A is A*. In so far as nothing is done to develop the content, this has the form of *simplicity*; not until it is resolved into its determinations does *difference* emerge in it. So long as one sticks to this simple form, the content remains something identical with itself and therefore something *possible*. But to say this is equally to say *nothing*, just as in the formal law of identity.

The possible, however, contains more than the bare law of identity. The possible is the *reflected reflectedness-into-self*, or the identical simply as *moment* of the totality, and hence is also determined as being not *in itself*; it has therefore the second determination of being *only* a possible and the *ought-to-be* of the totality of form. Possibility without this ought-to-be is *essentiality* as such; but the absolute form contains this, that essence itself is only a moment, and without being lacks its truth. Possibility is this mere essentiality so *posited* that it is only a moment and is inadequate to the absolute form. It is the in-itself determined as only a *posited*, or equally as *not being in itself*. Possibility is therefore in its own self contradiction, or it is *impossibility*.

This is expressed first of all in this way, that possibility as *form determination posited as sublated* possesses a *content* in general. This, as possible, is an in-itself, which is at the same time a sublated in-itself or an *otherness*. Because, therefore, it is only a possible content, *another* and its opposite is equally *possible*. A is A; equally, $-A$ is $-A$. These two statements each express the possibility of its content determination. But as these identical statements they are mutually indifferent; it is *not posited* in the one that the other too is added to it. Possibility is the comparing relation of both; in its determination as a reflection of the totality, possibility implies that the opposite too is possible. It is therefore the relating *ground*, that because $A = A$, *therefore* also $-A = -A$; in the possible A the possible not $-A$ is also contained and it is this very relation which determines both as possible.

But this relation, in which the one possible also contains its other, is the contradiction that sublates itself. Now, according to its determination it is the reflected, and as we have seen, the self-sublating reflected; it is therefore also the immediate and thus becomes *actuality*.

3. This actuality is not the primary but the reflected actuality, *posited as unity* of itself and possibility. The actual as such is possible; it is in immediate positive identity with possibility; but this has determined itself as *only* possibility; thus the actual too, is determined as *only a possible*. And immediately because possibility is *immediately* contained in actuality, it is contained in actuality as sublated, as *only* possibility. Conversely, actuality which is in unity with possibility is only sublated immediacy; or because formal actuality is only *immediate*, primary actuality, it is only a moment, only sublated actuality, or only *possibility*.

Here at the same time is more precisely expressed, how far possibility is actuality. For possibility is not yet *all* actuality; no question has yet arisen of real and absolute actuality; it is at first only that possibility which first presented itself, namely, formal possibility which has determined itself as being *only* possibility, and is thus formal actuality which is only *being* or *Existence* in general. Everything possible has therefore in general a *being* or an *Existence*.

This unity of possibility and actuality is *contingency*. The contingent is an actual that at the same time is determined as merely possible, whose other or opposite equally is. This actuality is therefore mere being or Existence, but posited in its truth as having the value of a positedness or of possibility. Conversely, possibility as *reflection-into-self* or the *in-itself* is posited as positedness; what is possible is an actual in this sense of actuality; it has only as much worth as contingent actuality; it is itself a contingent.

The contingent therefore presents two sides. First, in so far as it has possibility *immediately* in it—or what is the same thing, in so far as possibility is sublated in it—it is neither *positedness* nor is it mediated, but is *immediate* actuality; it has *no ground*. Because this immediate actuality also belongs to the possible, the latter no less than the actual is determined as contingent and likewise as *groundless*.

But secondly, the contingent is the actual as a merely possible or as a *positedness*; thus the possible, too, as the formal in-itself is only a positedness. Hence neither is in and for itself but has its true reflection-into-self in an other, *or it has a ground*.

The contingent, then, has no ground because it is contingent; and, equally, it has a ground because it is contingent.

It is the *posited*, unmediated *conversion* of inner and outer, or of reflectedness-into-self and being, into each other—*posited*, because possibility and actuality each has this determination within it and because they are moments of the absolute form. Thus actuality in its *immediate* unity with possibility is only Existence and is determined as something groundless that is *only a posited* or *only* a possible; or, as reflected and determinate *over against* possibility, it is separated from possibility, from reflectedness-into-self, and so equally immediately also *only* a possible. Similarly, possibility as a *simple* in-itself is an immediate, *only* a simple affirmative being, or *opposed* to actuality, it is equally an in-itself that lacks actuality, *only* a possible; but for that very reason it is again only an Existence as such that is not reflected into itself.

This *absolute unrest* of the *becoming* of these two determinations is *contingency*. But just because each immediately turns into its opposite, equally in this other it simply *unites with itself*, and this identity of both, of one in the other, is *necessity*.

The necessary is an *actual*; as such it is something immediate,

s

groundless; but equally it has its actuality *through an other* or in its ground, but at the same time is the positedness of this ground and the reflection of it into itself; the possibility of the necessary is a sublated possibility. The contingent, therefore, is necessary because the actual is determined as a possible, hence its immediacy is sublated and repelled into the *ground* or the *in-itself*, and the *grounded*, and also because this its *possibility*, the *ground-relation*, is simply sublated and posited as being. The necessary *is*, and this that simply is, is *itself the necessary*. At the same time it is *in itself*; this reflection-into-self is an *other* than that immediacy of being, and the necessity of what simply is [*des Seienden*] is *an other*. Thus what simply is, is not itself the necessary; but this in-itself is itself only a positedness; it is sublated and itself immediate. Thus actuality in that which is distinguished from it, namely possibility, is identical with itself. As this identity it is necessity.

B. RELATIVE NECESSITY, OR REAL ACTUALITY, POSSIBILITY, AND NECESSITY

1. The necessity which has resulted is *formal* because its moments are formal; that is, they are simple determinations which are a totality only as an immediate unity or as an immediate conversion of the one into the other and thus do not have the form [*Gestalt*] of self-subsistence. Hence in this formal necessity the unity is at first simple and indifferent to its differences. As *immediate* unity of the form-determinations this necessity is *actuality*; but one which has a *content*, because its unity is now *determined as indifferent* to the *distinction* between the form determinations, namely between itself and possibility. This content as an indifferent identity also contains the form as indifferent, that is, as merely *diverse* determinations, and is a *manifold* content in general. This actuality is *real actuality*.

Real actuality *as such* is in the first instance the thing of many properties, the existent world; but it is not the Existence that resolves itself into Appearance, but, as actuality, it is at the same time the in-itself and reflection-into-self; it preserves itself in the manifoldness of mere Existence; its externality is an inner relationship *to itself* alone. What is actual *can act*; something manifests its actuality through what which it produces. Its relationship to another something is the manifestation *of itself*: neither a transition—the relation between something and an other in the sphere of being—nor an appearing—where the thing is only in relation to others and, though a self-subsistent, has its reflection-into-self, its determinate essentiality, in another self-subsistent.

Now real actuality likewise has possibility immediately present within it. It contains the moment of the in-itself; but, as first of all only *immediate* unity, it is in *one* of the determinations of the form, and is thus distinguished as a simply affirmative being from the in-itself or possibility.

2. This possibility as the in-itself of *real* actuality is itself *real possibility*, and first of all, the in-itself as *pregnant with content*. Formal possibility is reflection-into-self only as abstract identity, which merely means that something is not internally self-contradictory. But if one brings into account the determinations, circumstances and conditions of something in order to ascertain its possibility, one is no longer at the stage of formal possibility, but is considering its real possibility.

This real possibility is itself an *immediate Existence*, but no longer because possibility as such, as a formal moment, is immediately its opposite, a non-reflected actuality; but, because it is *real* possibility, it straightway contains this determination within itself. The real possibility of something is therefore the existing multiplicity of circumstances which are connected with it.

This existing multiplicity is, therefore, both possibility and actuality, yet their identity is, at first, only the *content*, which is indifferent to these form-determinations; they therefore constitute the form, *determined* as against their identity. Or, *immediate*, real actuality, because it is immediate, is determined as against its possibility; as this determinate and therefore reflected possibility, it is *real possibility*. Now this is the posited *whole* of form, it is true, but of the form in its determinateness, namely, of actuality as formal or immediate, and equally of possibility as an abstract in-itself. This actuality which constitutes the possibility of something is therefore not *its own possibility*, but the in-itself of *another* actual; it is itself the actuality which ought to be sublated, possibility as possibility only. Thus real possibility constitutes the *totality of conditions*, a dispersed actuality which is not reflected into itself but is determined as being the in-itself, but the in-itself of an other, and as meant to return back into itself.

What is really possible is, according to its *in-itself*, something formally identical which, having a *simple* content-determination, is not self-contradictory; but, as self-identical, it must also not be self-contradictory in its developed and distinct circumstances and in everything with which it stands connected. But secondly, because it is manifold within itself and has manifold connexions with an other, and because variety in its own self passes over into opposition, it is contradictory. If a possibility is in question and its contradiction is to be demonstrated, one need only fasten on to the multiplicity which it contains as content or as its conditioned Existence, and from this its contradiction is easily discovered. But this is not a contradiction arising from comparison; on the contrary, manifold Existence is in its own self this, to sublate itself and to fall to the ground, and for this reason essentially contains within itself the determination of being *merely a possible*. When all the conditions of something are completely present, it enters into actuality; the completeness of the conditions is the totality as in the content, and *the something itself* is this content determined as being equally actual as possible. In the sphere of conditioned ground, the conditions have *outside them* the form— that is, the ground or the reflection which is for itself—which connects them into moments of the something in question and which produces Existence *in them*. Here, on the other hand, immediate actuality is not determined by a presupposing reflection to be condition, but it is posited that this actuality itself is possibility.

Now in self-sublating real possibility, what is sublated is a duality, for it is itself the duality of actuality and possibility. 1. Actuality is formal, or is an Existence which appeared as self-subsistent and immediate, and through its sublating becomes reflected being, the moment of an other, and thus becomes possessed of an *in-itself*. 2. This Existence was also determined as *possibility* or as an *in-itself*, but of an other. Therefore, when real possibility sublates itself, this in-itself is also sublated and passes over into actuality. Thus this movement of self-sublating real possibility produces the same moments which are already in being, but now each grows only out of the other; consequently, in this negation it also is not a *transition*, but a going-together-with-itself. Under formal possibility, because something was possible, then—not *itself*—but its *other* was also possible. Real possibility no longer has over against it *such an other*, for it is real in so far as it is itself also actuality. Consequently, when its *immediate Existence*, the circle of conditions, sublates itself, it makes itself into that *in-itself* which it already is, namely the *in-itself* of an other. And since, conversely, its moment of in-itself is thereby at the same time sublated, it becomes actuality, that is, that moment which it likewise already is. Thus what vanishes is this, that actuality was determined as the possibility or in-itself of an other, and conversely, possibility as an actuality which is *not that* whose possibility it is.

3. The *negation* of real possibility is thus its *identity*-with self; in that in its sublating it is thus within itself the recoil of this sublating, it is *real necessity*.

What is necessary *cannot be otherwise*; but what is simply *possible* can; for possibility is the in-itself that is only positedness and therefore essentially otherness. Formal possibility is this identity as transition into a sheer other; but real possibility, because it contains the other moment, actuality, is already itself necessity. Therefore what is really possible can no longer be otherwise; under the particular conditions and circumstances something else cannot follow. Real possibility and necessity are therefore only *seemingly* different; this is an identity which does not have to *become* but is already *presupposed* and lies at their base. Real necessity is therefore a relation pregnant with content; for the content is that implicit identity that is indifferent to the differences of form.

But this necessity is at the same time *relative*. For it has a *presupposition* from which it begins, it has its *starting point* in the *contingent*. For the real actual as such is the *determinate* actual, and has first of all its *determinateness* as *immediate* being in the fact that it is a multiplicity of existing circumstances; but this immediate being as determinateness is also the *negative* of itself, is an in-itself or possibility, and thus it is real possibility. As this unity of the two moments it is the totality of form, but the totality which is *still external to itself*; it is unity of possibility and actuality in such a manner that (1) manifold Existence is *immediately* or *positively* possibility—a possible, a self-identical in general, because it is an actual; (2) in so far as this possibility of Existence is posited, it is determined as *only* possibility, as immediate conversion of actuality into its opposte—or as *contingency*. Consequently this possibility which immediate actuality possesses in so far as it is condition, is only the in-itself as the possibility of an *other*. By virtue of the fact that, as was shown, this otherness sublates itself and this positedness is itself posited, real possibility does, it is true, become necessity; but the latter thus begins from that unity of the possible and the actual which is not yet reflected into itself—this *presupposing* and the *self-returning movement* are still separate—or necessity has not yet *spontaneously determined itself into contingency*.

The relativity of real necessity exhibits itself in the *content* in such a manner that it is at first only the identity which is indifferent to form, therefore is distinct from it and a *determinate content* in general. The really necessary is therefore any limited actuality which, on account of this limitation, is also only a *contingent* in some other respect.

Thus in point of fact real necessity is *in itself* also contingency. This is manifest at first in this manner: though the really necessary is a necessary *as regards form*, as regards content it is limited, and through this has its contingency. But contingency is also contained in the form of real necessity; for, as we have seen, real possibility is only *in itself* or *in principle* the necessary, but it is posited as the *otherness* of actuality and possibility towards each other. Real necessity therefore contains contingency; it is the return-into-self from that restless *otherness* of actuality and possibility towards each other, but not from itself to itself.

Here, therefore, the unity of necessity and contingency is present *in itself* or *in principle*; this unity is to be called *absolute actuality*.

C. ABSOLUTE NECESSITY

Real necessity is *determinate* necessity; formal necessity does not as yet possess any content and determinateness. The *determinateness* of necessity consists in its containing its negation, contingency, within itself. This is what it has shown itself to be.

But this determinateness *in its first simplicity* is actuality; *determinate* necessity is therefore immediately *actual necessity*. This actuality, *which is itself as such necessary*, for it contains necessity as its *in-itself*, is *absolute actuality*—actuality which can no longer be otherwise, for its *in-itself* is not possibility but necessity itself.

But because this *actuality* is posited as being *absolute*, that is, as being *itself the unity of itself and possibility*, it is only an *empty* determination, or, it is *contingency*. This *emptiness* of its determination makes it a *mere possibility*, something which can equally be *otherwise* and can be determined as a possible. But this possibility is itself *absolute*; for it is precisely the possibility of being determined equally as possibility or as actuality. Since it is this indifference twoards itself it is posited as an *empty, contingent* determination.

Thus real necessity not only *implicitly* contains contingency, but contingency also *becomes* in it; but this *becoming*, as externality, is itself only the in-itself of such necessity because it is only an *immediate determinedness*. But the becoming is not only this, it is also necessity's *own becoming*—or the *presupposition* which necessity had is its own positing. For, as real necessity, it is the sublatedness of actuality in possibility, and conversely; because it is the *simple conversion* of one of these moments into the other, it is also their *positive unity*, since each, as we saw, unites *only with itself* in the other. But as such it is *actuality*; an actuality, however, which only is as this simple coincidence of the form with itself. Its negative positing of those moments is thereby itself the *presupposing* or positing *of itself as sublated*, or of *immediacy*.

But it is in this very act that this actuality is determined as a negative; it is a union with itself out of the actuality which was real possibility; thus this new actuality develops only out of its in-itself, out of the *negation of itself*. It is thus at the same time immediately determined as *possibility*, as *mediated* by its negation. But this possibility is, therefore, immediately nothing but this *mediating*, in which the in-itself, namely, the possibility itself and immediacy, both in the same manner, are *positedness*. It is thus the necessity which is equally the sublating of this positedness or the positing of *immediacy* and the *in-itself*, and in this same act is a *determining* of this sublating as *positedness*. It is therefore necessity itself which determines itself as contingency—in its being repels itself from itself and in this very repulsion has only returned into itself, and in this return, as its being, has repelled itself from itself.

Thus form in its realization has penetrated all its differences and made itself transparent and is, as *absolute necessity*, only this simple *self-identity of being in its negation*, or in *essence*. The distinction of *content* and form itself has also vanished; for that unity of possibility in actuality, and conversely, is the *form* which in its determinateness or in positedness is indifferent towards itself, is the *fact filled with content*, in which the form of necessity ran its external course. But as such, it is this *reflected* identity of the two determinations as *indifferent* towards it, and hence the form-determination of the *in-itself* as against the *positedness*, and this possibility constitutes the limitedness of the content real necessity had. But the resolution of this difference is absolute necessity whose content is this difference which in this necessity penetrates itself.

Absolute necessity is, therefore, the truth into which actuality and possibility as such, and formal and real necessity withdraw. It is, as we have found, that being which in its negation, in essence, is self-related and is being. It is as much simple immediacy or *pure being* as simple reflection-into-self or *pure essence*; it is this, that these two are one and the same. That which is simply necessary only *is* because it *is*; it has neither condition nor ground. But equally it is pure *essence*; its being is simple reflection-into-self; it is, *because* it is. As reflection, it has a ground and condition, but it has only itself for ground and condition. It is the in-itself, but its in-itself is its immediacy, its possibility is its actuality. *It is, therefore, because it is*; as the *union* of being with itself it is essence; but because this simple is equally *immediate* simplicity, it is *being*.

Absolute necessity is thus the *reflection or form of the absolute*: the unity of being and essence, simple immediacy that is absolute negativity. Consequently, on the one hand, its differences do not have the shape of the determinations of reflection, but of *a simply affirmative [seiende] multiplicity*, a differentiated actuality which has the shape of others, self-subsistent relatively to one another. On the other hand, since its relation is absolute identity, it is the *absolute conversion* of its actuality into its possibility and of its possibility into actuality. Absolute necessity is therefore *blind*. On the one hand, the different sides, which are determined as actuality and possibility have the shape of *reflection-into-self* as *being*; both are, therefore, *free actualities*, neither of which is reflected in the other, nor will let any trace of its relation to the other show in it; grounded in itself, each is the necessary in its own self. Necessity as *essence* is concealed in this *being*; contact between these actualities appears therefore as an empty externality; the actuality of the one in the other is *only* possibility, contingency. For being is posited as absolutely necessary, as self-mediation, which is absolute negation of mediation by an other, or as being which is identical only with being; an *other* that has actuality in *being*, is therefore determined simply as something *merely possible*, as empty positedness.

But this *contingency* is rather absolute necessity; it is the *essence* of those free, inherently necessary actualities. This essence is *light-shy*, because there is in these actualities no *reflective movement*, no reflex, because they are grounded purely in themselves alone, are shaped for themselves, and manifest themselves only to *themselves*, because they are only *being*. But their *essence* will break forth in them and reveal what *it* is and what *they* are. The *simplicity* of their being and their self-support is absolute negativity; it is the *freedom* of their reflectionless [*scheinlos*] immediacy. This negative breaks forth in them because being, through this its essence, is self-contradiction, and that, too, against this being in the form of being, therefore as the *negation* of those actualities, which is *absolutely different* from their being, as their *nothing*, as an equally *free otherness* over against them as is their being. Yet it could not but be recognized in them. In their self-based shape they are indifferent towards form, are a *content*, hence *distinct* actualities and a *determinate* content. This content is the mark impressed upon them by necessity—which in its *determination* is absolute return-into-self—when it let them go free as absolutely actual; to this mark necessity appeals as witness to its claim, and, smitten by it, the actualities perish. This manifestation of that which the *determinateness* is in truth—negative self-relation—is a *blind* destruction in otherness; the *illusory showing* or *reflection* which breaks forth is, in that which *simply affirmatively is*, a *becoming* or *transition* of being into nothing. But conversely, being is equally *essence*; and *becoming* is *reflection* or an *illusory showing*. Thus the outwardness is its inwardness, their relation is absolute identity; and the *transition* of the actual into the possible, of being into nothing, is a *union-with-self*; contingency is absolute necessity, it is itself the presupposing of that first, absolute actuality.

This *identity of being with itself* in its negation is now *substance*. It is this unity as *in its negation*, or as *in contingency*; as such it is *substance* as *relation to itself*. The *blind* transition of necessity is rather the absolute's *own exposition*, the movement of the absolute within itself which, in its alienation, rather reveals itself.

s*

CHAPTER 3

THE ABSOLUTE RELATION

Absolute necessity is not so much the necessary, still less *a* necessary, but *necessity*—being, simply and solely as reflection. It is relation because it is a distinguishing whose moments are themselves its whole totality, and therefore absolutely *subsist*, but in such a manner that there is only *one* subsistence and the difference is only the *illusory being*, the *reflective movement*, of the expository process, and this illusory being is the absolute itself. Essence as such is reflection or an illusory showing; but essence as absolute relation is *illusory being posited as illusory being* which, as this self-relating, is *absolute actuality*. The absolute, which at first was expounded *by external* reflection, now, as absolute form or as necessity, expounds itself; this exposition of itself is its own positing of itself and it *is* only this self-positing. Just as the *light* of nature is neither *something* nor a *thing*, but its being is only its showing or shining [*Scheinen*], so manifestation is self-identical absolute actuality.

The sides of the absolute relation are therefore not *attributes*. In the attribute the absolute shows only in one of its moments, a moment *presupposed* and picked up by *external reflection*. But the *expositor* of the absolute is *absolute necessity* which is identical with itself as self-determining. Since it is an illusory showing that is posited as illusory being, the sides of this relation are *totalities* because they are in the determination of illusory being; for as illusory being, the differences are themselves and their opposite, or they are the whole; conversely, they are illusory being in this manner because they are totalities. Thus this distinguishing or illusory showing of the absolute is only the identical positing of itself.

This relation in its immediate Notion is the relation of *substance* and *accidents*, the immediate vanishing and becoming of the absolute illusory being within itself. When substance determines itself to *being-for-self* over against an *other*, or the absolute relation determines itself as real, then we have the *relation of causality*. Lastly, when this as self-relating passes over into *reciprocity*, the absolute relation is also *posited* in accordance with the determinations it contains; this *posited unity* of itself in its *determinations* which are *posited* as *themselves the whole*, but equally as determinations, is then *the Notion*.

A. THE RELATION OF SUBSTANTIALITY

Absolute necessity is absolute relation because it is not *being* as such, but *being* that is *because* it is, being as absolute self-mediation. This being is *substance*; as the final unity of essence and being it is the being in *all* being; it is neither the unreflected immediate, nor an abstract being standing behind Existence and Appearance, but it is immediate actuality itself and this as absolute reflectedness-into-self, as a *subsisting* in and for itself. Substance as this unity of being and reflection is essentially the *reflective movement* [*Scheinen*] and *positedness* of itself. The reflective movement is the reflective movement that is *self-related*, and it is thus that it *is*; this being is substance as such. Conversely, this being is only the *positedness* that is identical with itself, and as such it is *totality* in the form of *illusory being, accidentality*.

This reflective movement is identity as identity of form—the unity of possibility and actuality. It is first of all *becoming*, contingency as the sphere of coming-to-be and ceasing-to-be; for in accordance with the determination of *immediacy*, the relation of possibility and actuality is an *immediate conversion* of them (as in the determination of *being*) into each other, of each into that which is merely *other* to *it*. But because being is an illusory being, their relation is also one of identical reflection, of a reflection which is an illusory showing of each in the other. The movement of accidentality therefore exhibits in each of its moments the illusory showing in one another of the *categories* of being and of the *reflective determinations* of essence. The immediate *something* has a *content*; its immediacy is at the same time a reflected indifference towards form. This content is determinate, and since this determinateness is one of being, the something *passes over* into an other. But quality is also a determinateness of reflection; as such it is an indifferent *difference*. But this energizes itself into *opposition* and withdraws into the ground, which is *nothing*, but also a *reflection-into-self*. This sublates itself; but it is itself a reflected in-itself, as such is possibility, and this in-itself is, in its transition which is equally a reflection-into-self, the *necessary actual*.

This movement of accidentality is the *actuosity* [*Aktuosität*] of substance as a tranquil coming forth of itself. It is not active *against* something, but only against itself as a simple unresisting element. The sublating of *something presupposed* is the vanishing illusory being; only in the act of *sublating* the immediate does this immediate itself become, or is this reflective movement; it is the beginning from itself which first is the positing of this self from which the beginning is made.

Substance, as this identity of the reflective movement, is the totality of the whole and embraces accidentality within it, and accidentality is the whole substance itself. The differentiation of itself into the *simple identity of being* and the *flux of accidents* in it, is a form of its illusory being. The former is the formless substance of ordinary thinking for which illusory being has not determined itself as illusory being, but which clings to such an indeterminate identity as an absolute, an identity which has no truth and is only the determinateness of *immediate* actuality or equally of the *in-itself* or possibility—form determinations which fall into accidentality.

The other determination, the *flux of accidents*, is the absolute *form-unity* of accidentality, substance as *absolute power*. The ceasing-to-be of the accident is the withdrawal of itself as actuality into itself, as into its in-itself or its possibility; but this its in-itself is itself only a positedness, and therefore it is also an actuality, and because these form determinations are equally content determinations, this possible is a differently determined actual also in respect of content. Substance manifests itself through actuality with its content into which it translates the possible, as *creative* power, and through the possibility to which it reduces the actual, as *destructive* power. But the two are identical, the creation is destructive and the destruction is creative; for the negative and the positive, possibility and actuality, are absolutely united in substantial necessity.

The accidents as such—and there is a plurality of them since plurality is one of the determinations of being—have no power over one another. They are the simply affirmative something, or the something that is for itself, existing things of manifold properties, or wholes consisting of parts, self-subsistent parts, forces, which require solicitation from one another and have one another for condition. In so far as such an accidental seems to exercise power over another, it is the power of substance which embraces both within itself; as negativity it posits an unequal value, determining the one as a ceasing-to-be and the other with a different content as a coming-to-be, or the former as passing over into its possibility, the latter into actuality—ever sundering itself into the differences of form and content, and ever purging itself of this one-sidedness, yet in this very purging it has fallen back into determination and disunity. One accident, then, expels another only because its own *subsisting* is this totality of form and content itself in which it and its other equally perish.

On account of this *immediate identity* and presence of substance in the accidents, no *real* difference is as yet present. In this *first* determination substance is not yet manifested according to its whole Notion. When substance, as self-identical *being-in-and-for-self*, is distinguished from itself as totality of *accidents*, that which *mediates* is substance as *power*. This is *necessity*, the positive *persistence* of the accidents in their negativity and their mere *positedness* in their subsistence; this *middle term* is thus unity of substantiality and accidentality themselves and its *extremes* have no subsistence of their own. Substantiality is, therefore, merely the relation as immediately vanishing, it relates itself to itself not *as a negative*, and, as the immediate unity of power with itself, is in the *form* only of *its identity*, not of its *negative essence*; only one of the moments, namely, the negative or the difference, vanishes altogether, the other, the moment of identity, does not. This can also be considered in the following manner. Illusory being or accidentality is *in itself* indeed substance through power, but it is not thus *posited* as this self-identical illusory being; thus substance has only accidentality for its shape or positedness, not itself, it is not substance *as* substance. The relation of substantiality is, therefore, in the first instance, only this, that substance *manifests* itself as *formal power*, the differences of which are not substantial; it is, in fact, only as the *inner* of the accidents, and these are only *in the substance*. In other words, this relation is only totality in the form of illusory being as a *becoming*; but it is equally reflection; accidentality which *in itself* is substance is for this very reason also posited as such; thus it is *determined* as self-relating negativity towards itself—determined as self-relating simple self-*identity*; and it is *substance that exists for itself and has power*. Thus the relation of substantiality *passes over* into the *relation of causality*.

B. THE RELATION OF CAUSALITY

Substance is power, and power that is *reflected into itself* and not merely transitory, but that posits *determinations* and *distinguishes them from itself*. As self-relating in its determining, it is *itself* that which it posits as a negative or makes it into a *positedness*. Thus this is in general sublated substantiality, that which is merely posited, or *effect*; but substance which is for itself is *cause*.

This relation of causality is, in the first instance, merely this *relation* of *cause* and *effect*; as such it is the *formal* relation of causality.

(a) Formal Causality

1. Cause is *primary* in relation to effect. As power, substance *is an illusory showing*, or *has* accidentality. But as power, it is equally reflection-into-self in its illusory being; thus it *expounds* its movement of transition *and this illusory showing* or *reflective movement is determined as illusory being*, or the accident is *posited* as this, that it is only something *posited*. But substance in its determining does not begin from accidentality as if this were already an *other to start with* and only now were posited as determinateness, but the two are *one* actuosity [*Aktuosität*]. Substance as power *determines itself*; but this determining is immediately itself the sublating of the determining, and the return. *It determines itself—it*, the determinant, is thus the *immediate* and that which is itself already determinate; in determining *itself*, it therefore posits this already determinate as *determined* and thus has sublated the positedness and has returned into itself. Conversely, this return, because it is the *negative* relation of substance to itself, is itself a *determining* or repelling of itself from itself; it is through this return that the determinate *becomes*, the determinate from which substance seems to begin and which it now seems to posit as a determinate already given. The absolute actuosity is thus *cause*—the power of substance in *its truth* as manifestation, which immediately also *expounds* or *explicates* that which is *in itself*, that is, the accident (which is a positedness), in the becoming of the latter, *posits* it as *positedness—as effect*. This is therefore first, the same thing as the accidentality of the relation of substantiality, namely, substance as *positedness*; but secondly, accident as such substantially *is* only through its vanishing, as something transitory; but as effect, it is

positedness as self-identical; the cause is manifested in the effect as whole substance, namely, as reflected into itself in the positedness itself as such.

2. Over against this *positedness* reflected into itself, the determinate as determinate, stands substance as the *non-posited* original. Because substance as absolute power is the return into itself, yet this return is itself a *determining*, it is no longer merely the *in-itself* of its accident but is also *posited* as this in-itself. It is therefore as cause that substance first has actuality. But this actuality in which its *in-itself*, its determinateness in the relation of substantiality, is now posited *as determinateness*, is effect; consequently the actuality which substance has as cause, it has *only in its effect*. This is the *necessity* which is cause. It is *actual* substance because substance as power determines itself, but is at the same time cause, because it explicates this determinateness or posits it as positedness; thus it posits its actuality as positedness or as effect. This is the other of cause, positedness over against the original and *mediated* by it. But cause, as necessity, equally sublates this its mediation and as the originally self-relating activity in the *determining* of itself is, *as against* the mediated, the return into itself; for the positedness is determined *as* positedness and hence is self-identical; the cause is therefore truly actual and self-identical only in its effect. The effect is therefore *necessary* just because it is the manifestation of the cause or is this necessity which is cause. Only as this necessity is cause self-moving, beginning from itself without solicitation from an other, and the *self-subsistent source of production from out of itself*; it must *act*; its originativeness is this, that its reflection-into-self is a positing that determines, and conversely, both are one unity.

Consequently, effect contains nothing whatever that cause does not contain. Conversely, cause contains nothing which is not in its effect. Cause is cause only in so far as it produces an effect, and cause is nothing but this determination, to have an effect, and effect is nothing but this, to have a cause. Cause as such implies its effect, and effect implies cause; in so far as cause has not yet acted, or if it has ceased to act, then it is not cause, and effect in so far as its cause has vanished, is no longer effect but an indifferent actuality.

3. Now in this *identity* of cause and effect, the form through which they are distinguished as implicit determinations and as

positedness is sublated. Cause is *extinguished* in its effect; and with it the effect, too, is extinguished, for it is only the determinateness of the cause. Hence this causality which is extinguished in the effect is an *immediacy* which is indifferent to the relation of cause and effect, which attaches to it externally.

(*b*) *The Determinate Relation of Causality*

1. The *self-identity* of cause in its effect is the sublating of its power and negativity, and is therefore the unity which is indifferent to the differences of form, that is, *content*. Consequently content is only *implicitly* related to form, here, to causality. They are thus posited as [merely] diverse, and form as against content is itself only an immediately actual, a *contingent*, causality.

Further, the content as thus determinate is a content diverse in its own self; and cause is determinate in respect of its content and so, therefore, equally is effect. Content, since reflectedness here is also immediate actuality, is to this extent *actual*, but *finite*, substance.

This now is the relation of causality in its *reality and finitude*. As formal, it is the infinite relation of absolute power whose content is pure manifestation or necessity. As finite causality, on the other hand, it has a *given* content and exhausts itself in an external difference in this identical content which in its determinations is one and the same substance.

Through this identity of content, this causality is an *analytic* proposition. It is the *same fact* which presents itself once as cause and again as effect, there as something subsisting on its own account and here as positedness or determination in an other. Since these determinations of form are an *external* reflection, it is, *in point of fact*, the tautological consideration of a *subjective* understanding to determine a phenomenon as effect and from this to ascend to its cause in order to comprehend and explain it; it is merely a repetition of one and the same content; there is nothing else in the cause but what is in the effect. Rain, for example, is the cause of wetness which is its effect; the rain wets—this is an analytic proposition; the same water which is rain is wetness; as rain, this water is only in the form of a fact by itself; as wetness or moisture, on the other hand, it is adjectival, something posited, that is no longer supposed to have its subsistence in its own self; and the one determination like the other, is external to it. Thus the cause of *this colour* is a colouring agent, a *pigment*, which is one and the same actuality, once in the form of an agent external to it, that is, externally connected with an agent different from it, and again in the determination, equally external to it, of an effect. The cause of an *act* is the inner disposition in an active subject, and this is the same content and worth as the outer existence which it acquires through the deed. If the *motion* of a body is considered as effect, then its cause is a *propulsive* force; but it is the same quantum of motion that is present before and after the impulse, the same existence which the propelling body contained and communicated to the propelled body; and the quantum it communicates is the same as that which it loses itself.

The cause, for example the painter or the propulsive body, has of course a further content, besides the colours and the form which combines them into a painting, in the case of the former, and besides the motion of specific strength and direction, in the case of the latter. Only this further content is a contingent accessory which does not concern the cause; what other qualities the painter possesses, apart from his being the painter of this picture, this does not enter into this painting; only those of his properties represented in the *effect* are present in him *as cause*; he is not cause as regards the rest of his properties. And so, whether the propulsive body is stone or wood, green, yellow, and so on, this does not enter into the impulse it communicates; in this respect it is not cause.

With respect to this *tautology* of the relation of causality, it is to be remarked that it does not seem to be contained therein if the *remote*, and not the proximate, cause of an effect is adduced. The change of form suffered by the basic fact in this passage through a number of intermediate terms conceals the identity which it retains in that passage. In this multiplication of causes which have entered between that fact and the ultimate effect, the former is at the same time connected with other things and circumstances, so that the complete effect is contained, not in that first term which was pronounced to be the cause, but only in these several causes *together*. If, for example, a man developed his talent in circumstances arising from the loss of his father who was hit by a bullet in battle, then this shot (or still further back, the war or a cause of the war, and so on to infinity) could be assigned as the cause of the man's skill. But it is clear that the shot, for example, is not by itself this cause, but only the combination of it with other effective determinations. Or rather, it is not cause at all but only a single *moment* which belonged to the *circumstances of the possibility*.

Further and above all, we must note the *inadmissible application* of the relation of causality to relations of *physico-organic* and *spiritual life*. Here, what is called cause certainly reveals itself as having a different content from the effect; but the reason is that that which acts on a living being is independently determined, changed and transmuted by it, because the living thing does not let the cause come to its effect, that is, it sublates it as cause. Thus it is inadmissible to say that food is the *cause* of blood, or certain dishes or chill and damp are the *causes* of fever, and so on; it is equally inadmissible to assign the ionic climate as the *cause* of Homer's works, or Caesar's ambition as the *cause* of the downfall of the republican constitution of Rome. In history generally, spiritual masses and individuals are in play and reciprocal determination with one another; but it is rather the nature of spirit, in a much higher sense than it is the character of the living thing in general, not to receive into itself another *original* entity, or not to let a cause continue itself into it but to break it off and to transmute it. However, these relationships belong to the *Idea* where they will first come up for consideration. Here, we may further remark that in so far as the relation of cause and effect is admitted, although improperly, the effect cannot be *greater* than the cause; for the effect is nothing more than the manifestation of the cause. It has become a common jest in history to let great effects arise from small causes and to cite as the primary cause of a comprehensive and profound event an *anecdote*. Such a so-called cause is to be regarded as nothing more than an *occasion*, an *external stimulus*, of which the *inner spirit* of the event had no need, or could have used a countless host of other such in order to begin from them in the sphere of Appearance, to disengage itself and give itself manifestation. The reverse rather is true, namely, that such a petty and contingent circumstance is the occasion of the event *only* because the latter has determined it to be such. Consequently, though this arabesque painting of history which makes a huge shape spring from a slender stalk is ingenious, it is an extremely superficial treatment. It is true that in this process of a great event arising out of a small circumstance we have an instance of the conversion which spirit imposes on the external; but for this very reason, this external is not *cause in the process*, in other words, this conversion itself sublates the relationship of causality.

2. But this *determinateness* of the relationship of causality, that content and form are distinct and indifferent, extends further. The form determination is also content determination; cause and effect, the two sides of the relation, are, therefore, also *another content*. Or the content, because it is only as content of a form, has the difference of form in its own self and is essentially different. But this its form is the relationship of causality, which is a content identical in cause and effect, and consequently the different content is externally connected, on the one hand with the cause, and on the other hand with the effect; hence the content itself does *not enter into the action* and *into the relation*.

This external content is therefore devoid of any relationship, *an immediate existence*; or because it is, as content, the *implicit* identity of cause and effect, it too is an *immediate, simply affirmative identity*. This is, therefore, anything at all which has manifold determinations of its existence, *among them* also this, that in *some respect or other* it is cause or else effect. In it, the form determinations have their *substrate*, that is, their essential subsistence, and each has a particular subsistence—for their identity is their subsistence; but at the same time it is their immediate subsistence, not their subsistence as form unity or as relation.

But this thing is not only substrate but also substance, for it is identical subsistence only *as subsistence of the relation*. Further, it is *finite* substance, for it is determined as immediate *over against* its causality. But at the same time, it has causality because it is equally only the identical as this relationship. Now, as cause, this substrate is negative relation to *self*. But it itself to which it relates itself is first, a positedness, because it is determined as an *immediately* actual; this positedness, as content, is any determination whatever. Secondly, *causality* is external to it; and therefore causality itself constitutes its *positedness*. Now since it is causal substance, its causality consists in relating itself negatively to itself, therefore to its positedness and external causality. The action of this substance therefore begins from an externality, liberates itself from this external determination; and its return into itself is the preservation of its immediate existence and the sublating of its posited existence, hence of its causality as such.

Thus a stone which moves is cause; its movement is a determination which it has, but besides which it also contains many other determinations of colour, shape, and so on, which do not enter into its causality. Its immediate existence is separate from its form relation, namely, causality, and is, therefore, an *external-ity*; the stone's movement and the causality attaching to the stone in its movement are present in the stone only as a *positedness*. But the causality also belongs to the stone itself; this stems from the fact that its substantial subsistence is its identical relation to itself, but that this is now determined as positedness and is therefore at the same time a *negative relation-to-self*. Its causality, which is directed against itself as positedness or as an externality, consists therefore in sublating this and by *removing* it to return into itself, hence to that extent to be *not* self-identical in its *positedness*, but only to restore *its abstract originativeness*. Or, rain is the cause of wetness, which is the same water as the rain. This water has the determination of being rain and cause as a result of this determination being posited in it by an other; some other force, or whatever it may be, has lifted it into the air and gathered it together into a mass, the weight of which makes it fall. Its removal to a distance from the earth is a determination alien to its original self-identity, to its heaviness; its causality consists in removing this determination and restoring that identity, but also, therefore, in sublating its causality.

The second determinateness of causality now under consideration concerns *form*; this relationship is *causality as external to itself*, as the *originativeness* which is equally in its own self *positedness* or *effect*. This union of opposed determinations as *in a simply affirmative* substrate constitutes the *infinite regress* from cause to cause. The effect is the starting point; as such it has a cause, this in turn has a cause, and so on. Why has the cause a fresh cause? that is to say, why is the same side which was previously determined as *cause* now determined as *effect*, with a consequent demand for a fresh cause? For this reason, that the cause is a finite, a determinate in general; determined as *one* moment of form over against the effect, it has its determinateness or negation outside it; but for this very reason it is itself *finite*, has *its determinateness within it* and this is *positedness* or *effect*. This its identity is also posited, but it is a *third term*, the immediate substrate; causality is therefore external to itself, because here its *originativeness* is an *immediacy*. The form difference is, therefore, a primary *determinateness*, not yet determinateness *posited as* determinateness, it is a *simply affirmative otherness*. Finite reflection, on the one hand, stops short at this immediate, removes the form unity from it and makes it in one respect cause and in another respect effect; on the other hand, it transfers the form unity into the *infinite*, and through the endless progress expresses its impotence to attain and hold fast this unity.

The case is directly the same with the *effect*, or rather the infinite progress from effect to effect is entirely the same as the regress from cause to cause. In this, the cause became effect, which in turn has another cause; similarly and conversely, the effect becomes cause, which in turn has another effect. The determinate cause we are considering begins from an externality, and in its effect does not return into itself *as cause* but, on the contrary, loses its causality therein. But conversely, the effect arrives at a substrate which is substance, an originally self-related subsistence; in this substrate, therefore, this positedness *becomes positedness*, that is to say, this substance, when an effect is posited in it, *behaves as cause*. But the first effect, the positedness, which arrives at substance *externally*, is *other* than the second which is *produced by the substance*; for this second effect is determined as its reflection-into-self, but the first as an *externality* in substance. But because causality here is self-external causality, equally it, too, does not return into itself in its effect, but therein becomes *external* to itself: *its* effect again becomes a positedness in a substrate—as in *another substance*, which, however, equally makes it into a positedness, or manifests itself as cause, again repels its effect from itself, and so on, to the spurious infinity.

3. We have now to see what has developed through the movement of the determinate causal relation. Formal causality is extinguished in the effect; this *produces* the *identity* of these two moments, but only as *implicitly* the unity of cause and effect, a unity to which the form relation is external. As result, this identical is also *immediate*, in accordance with the two determinations of immediacy, first, as *in-itself*, a *content*, in which causality runs its course externally; secondly, as an *existent* substrate in which cause and effect *inhere* as distinct determinations of form. In this, they are *implicitly* one, but on account of this in-itself or externality of form, each is external to itself, and consequently in its *unity* with the other is also determined as *other* against it. Therefore, though

the cause has an effect *and is at the same time itself effect*, and the effect not only has a cause but *is also itself cause*, yet the effect which the cause *has*, and the effect *which the cause is*, are different, as are also the cause which the effect *has*, and the cause *which the effect is*.

But now the outcome of the movement of the determinate causal relation is this, that the cause is *not merely extinguished* in the effect and with it the effect, too, as in formal causality, but that the cause *in being extinguished becomes* again in the effect, that the effect *vanishes* in the cause, but equally *becomes* again in it. Each of these determinations *sublates itself in its positing*, and *posits itself in its sublating*; what is present here is not an *external transition* of causality from one substrate to another; on the contrary, this *becoming-other* of causality is at the same time its *own positing*. Causality therefore *presupposes* its own self or *conditions itself.* The identity, the substrate, which was previously only *in itself* or *implicit*, is therefore, now *determined* as *presupposition* or *posited over against* the *active* causality, and the *reflection* which was previously only *external* to the identity, now stands in a *relationship* to it.

(c) Action and Reaction

Causality is a *presupposing* act. Cause is *conditioned*; it is negative self-relation as a presupposed, external other, an other which *in itself*, but only *in itself*, is causality itself. It is, as we have found, the *substantial identity* into which formal causality passes over, which has now determined itself *over against the latter* as its negative. Or it is the same thing as the substance of the causal relation, but substance that is confronted by the power of accidentality as itself *substantial activity*. It is *passive* substance. Passive is that which is immediate or in itself, but is not also *for itself*; pure being or essence which is only in this determinateness of *abstract self-identity*. *Active* substance, as negatively self-related substance, stands over against passive substance. It is cause, in so far as in determinate causality it has restored itself through the negation of itself out of the effect, a reflected being which in its otherness or as an immediate behaves essentially as a *positing* activity and mediates itself with itself through its negation. Here, therefore, causality no longer has a substrate in which it *inheres*, and is not a form determination over against this identity, but is itself

substance; in other words, what is originative is causality alone
The *substrate* is the passive substance which has presupposed itself.

Now this cause *acts*; for it is the negative power *over itself*; at
the same time, it is its own *presupposition*; thus it acts on itself as
on an *other*, on the *passive* substance. Accordingly, first, it sublates
the otherness of this substance and in it returns into itself;
secondly, it *determines* this substance, positing this sublating of its
otherness or the return into itself as a *determinateness*. This
positedness, because it is at the same time its return-into-self, is
first of all *its effect*. But conversely, because as presupposing it
determines itself as its other, it posits the effect in the *other*, in the
passive substance. Or because the passive substance itself is
double, namely, a self-subsistent *other* and also something *presupposed* and in itself already *identical* with the active cause, the
action of this, too, is double; it is two actions in one: the sublating
of its *determinedness*, namely, of its condition, or the sublating of
the self-subsistence of the passive substance; and by thus sublating
its identity with the passive substance, it *presupposes* itself or
posits itself as *other*. Through the latter moment, the passive
substance is *preserved*; that first sublating of it also appears in
relation to the substance in such a manner that only *some determinations* in it are sublated and the identity of the passive substance
with the active substance in the effect takes place externally in it.

To this extent it suffers *violence*. Violence is the *manifestation
of power*, or power as *external*. But power is external only in so far as
causal substance in its action, that is, in the positing of itself, is at
the same time presupposing, that is, it posits itself as sublated.
Conversely, the act of violence is equally an act of power. It is
only on an other presupposed by itself on which the violent cause
acts, its effect thereon is a negative relation *to itself*, or the manifestation *of itself*. The passive is the self-subsistent that is only
something *posited*, something that is broken within itself; an
actuality which is condition, and condition, too, which is now in
its truth, that is, an actuality that is only a possibility, or, conversely, an in-itself that is only the *determinateness of the in-itself*,
is only passive. Therefore not only is it possible to do violence to
that which suffers it, but also violence *must* be done to it; that
which acts violently on the other can do so only because it is the
power over it, the power in which it *manifests* both itself and the
other. Through violence, passive substance is only *posited* as what

it is in truth, namely, to be only something *posited*, just because it is the simple positive, or immediate substance; what it is *before-hand* as condition, is the illusory immediacy which active causality strips off from it.

Passive substance therefore only receives its due through the action on it of another power. What it *loses* is that *immediacy*, the substantiality which is *alien to it*. What it, as something alien, *receives*, namely, to be determined as a *positedness*, is its own determination. But now in being posited in its positedness, or in *its own* determination, the outcome is not that it is sublated, but rather that it only *unites with its own self* and therefore *in being determined* is, in fact, *originative*. On the one hand, therefore, the passive substance is *preserved* or *posited* by the active substance, namely, in so far as the latter makes itself into a sublated substance; but, on the other hand, it is the *act of the passive substance itself* to unite with itself and thus to make itself into the originative and into *cause*. Its *being posited* by an other, and its own *becoming* are one and the same thing.

Now since passive substance is itself converted into cause, the outcome is first, that in it the effect is sublated; in this consists its *reaction* in general. Passive substance is *in itself* positedness, as passive substance; also the positedness has been *posited* in it by the other substance, in so far as it received the *effect* of the latter within it. Its reaction, therefore, equally contains the twofold result: first, that what it is *in itself* is *posited*, and secondly, that what it is *posited* as displays itself as its *in-itself*; it is *in itself positedness*, and consequently receives within it an effect through the other substance; but this positedness is, conversely, the passive substance's *own* in-itself; this is thus its *own* effect, it itself displays itself as cause.

Secondly, the reaction is *against the first active cause*. The effect which the previously passive susbtance sublates within itself is, in fact, precisely this effect of the first cause. But the cause has its substantial actuality only in its effect; when this is sublated, its causal substantiality is sublated. This happens first *in itself through itself*, in that it converts itself into effect; in this identity its negative determination vanishes and it becomes a passive substance; secondly, it happens *through the previously passive*, but now reactive, substance, which sublates its effect. In *determinate causality*, it is true that the substance which is acted upon also in turn becomes cause, thus acting *against* the positing in it of an *effect*. But it did not react *against that cause*, but posited its effect again in *another* substance, giving rise to the progress to infinity of effects; because here the cause is at first only *implicitly* identical with itself in its effect, and therefore, on the one hand, vanishes in an *immediate* identity in its *rest*, and, on the other hand, resuscitates itself in *another* substance. In conditioned causality, on the contrary, the cause is *self-related* in the effect, because it is its other as condition, as something *presupposed*, and its action is thereby just as much a *becoming* as a positing and *sublating of the other*.

Further, in all this it behaves as a passive substance; but, as we saw, it *comes into being* as a causal substance as a result of its being acted upon. That first cause, which first acts and receives its effect back into itself as reaction, thus reappears as cause, whereby the action, which in finite causality runs on into the spuriously infinite progress, is *bent round* and becomes an action that returns into itself, an infinite *reciprocal action*.

C. RECIPROCITY

In finite causality it is substances that are actively related to each other. *Mechanism* consists in this *externality* of causality, where the *reflection* of the cause *into itself* in its effect is at the same time a repelling *being*, or where, in the *self-identity* which the causal substance has in its effect, the cause equally remains something immediately *external* to it, and the effect has *passed over* into *another substance*. Now in reciprocity this mechanism is sublated; for it contains first the *vanishing* of that original *persistence* of the *immediate* substantiality, and secondly the *coming-to-be* of the *cause*, and hence *originativeness* as *self-mediating* through its *negation*.

At first, reciprocity displays itself as a reciprocal causality of *presupposed*, self-*conditioning substances*; each is alike active and passive *substance* in relation to the other. Since the two, then, are both passive and active, any distinction between them has already been sublated; the difference is only a completely transparent semblance; they are substances only inasmuch as they are the identity of the active and the passive. Reciprocity itself is therefore still only an empty mode of representing this; all that is still required is merely an external bringing together of what is already both *in itself* and *posited*. First of all, it is no longer *substrates* but substances that stand in relation to each other; in the movement of conditioned causality, the still remaining *presupposed immediacy* has been sublated, and the *conditioning* factor of the causal activity is still only the passivity of *being acted upon*, or the passivity *of the cause itself*. But further, this 'being acted upon' does not originate in *another* causal substance, but simply from a causality which is conditioned by being acted upon, or is a *mediated* causality. Consequently, this initially *external* moment which attaches to cause and constitutes the side of its passivity, is mediated *by itself*, is produced by its own activity, and is thus the *passivity posited by its own activity*. Causality is conditioned and conditioning; the *conditioning* side is *passive*, but the *conditioned* side equally is *passive*. This conditioning or passivity is the *negation* of cause by the cause itself, in that it essentially converts itself into *effect* and precisely through this is cause. *Reciprocity* is, therefore, only causality itself; cause not only *has* an effect, but in the effect it stands, *as cause*, in relation to itself.

Causality has hereby returned to *its absolute Notion*, and at the same time has attained to the *Notion* itself. At first, it is real necessity; absolute *identity* with itself, so that the difference of necessity and the related determinations in it are substances, *free actualities*, over against one another. Necessity is, in this way, *inner identity*; causality is the manifestation of this, in which its illusory show of *substantial otherness* has sublated itself and necessity is raised to *freedom*. In reciprocity, originative causality displays itself as an *arising* from its negation, from passivity, and as *a passing away* into the same, as a *becoming*; but in such a manner that at the same time this becoming is equally only *illusory*; the transition into an other is a reflection into itself; the *negation*, which is ground of the cause, is its *positive union* with itself.

In reciprocity, therefore, necessity and causality have vanished; they contain both, *immediate identity* as *connexion* and *relation*, and the *absolute substantiality* of the *different sides*, hence the absolute *contingency* of them; the original *unity* of substantial *difference*, and therefore absolute contradiction. Necessity is being, *because* it is—the unity of being with itself that has itself for *ground*; but conversely, because it has a ground it is not being, it is an altogether *illusory* being, *relation* or *mediation*. Causality is this *posited* transition of originative being, of *cause*, into illusory being or mere *positedness*, and conversely, of positedness into originativeness; but the *identity itself* of being and illusory being is still an *inner* necessity. This *inwardness* or this in-itself, sublates the movement of causality, with the result that the substantiality of the sides standing in relation is lost, and necessity unveils itself. Necessity does not become *freedom* by vanishing, but only because its still *inner* identity is *manifested*, a manifestation which is the identical movement of the different sides within themselves, the reflection of the illusory being *as* illusory being into itself. Conversely, at the same time, contingency becomes freedom, for the sides of necessity, which have the shape of independent, free actualities not reflecting themselves in one another, are now *posited as an identity*, so that these totalities of reflection-into-self in their difference are now also *reflected as identical*, or are posited as only one and the same reflection.

Absolute substance, which as absolute form distinguishes itself from itself, therefore no longer repels itself as necessity from itself, nor, as contingency, does it fall asunder into indifferent, self-external substances; on the contrary, it *differentiates* itself, on the one hand, into the totality—heretofore passive substance— which is originative as reflection out of the determinateness into itself, as a simple whole, which contains within itself its *positedness* and is *posited as self-identical therein*—the *universal*; on the other hand, it differentiates itself into the totality—heretofore causal substance—into the reflection equally out of the determinateness into itself to a negative determinateness which, as thus the *self-identical determinateness* is likewise posited as the whole, but as *self-identical negativity*—the *individual*. But because the universal is self-identical only in that it contains the *determinateness* within itself as *sublated*, and therefore the negative as negative, it is immediately the *same negativity* which *individuality* is; and individuality, because it is equally the determinate determinate, the negative as negative, is immediately the *same identity* which *universality* is. This their *simple* identity is *particularity*, which contains in immediate unity the moment of *determinateness* of the individual and the moment of *reflection-into-self* of the universal. These three totalities are, therefore, one and the same reflection, which, as *negative self-relation*, differentiates itself into these two, but into a *perfectly transparent difference*, namely, into a *determinate simplicity* or *simple determinateness* which is their one and the same identity. This is the *Notion*, the realm of *subjectivity* or of *freedom*.

VOLUME TWO

SUBJECTIVE LOGIC
or
THE DOCTRINE
OF THE NOTION

FOREWORD

This part of the logic which contains the *Doctrine of the Notion* and constitutes the third part of the whole, is also issued under the particular title *System of Subjective Logic,* for the convenience of those friends of this science who are accustomed to take a greater interest in the matters here treated and included in the scope of logic commonly so called, than in the further logical topics treated in the first two parts. For these earlier parts I could claim the indulgence of fair-minded critics on account of the scant preliminary studies in this field which could have afforded me a support, material, and a guiding thread. In the case of the present part, I may claim their indulgence rather for the opposite reason; for the logic of the *Notion,* a completely ready-made and solidified, one may say, ossified material is already to hand, and the problem is to render this material fluid and to re-kindle the spontaneity of the Notion in such dead matter. If the building of a new city in a waste land is attended with difficulties, yet there is no shortage of materials; but the abundance of materials presents all the more obstacles of another kind when the task is to remodel an ancient city, solidly built, and maintained in continuous possession and occupation. Among other things one must resolve to make no use at all of much material that has hitherto been highly esteemed.

But above all, the grandeur of the subject matter may be advanced as an excuse for the imperfect execution. For what subject matter can cognition have that is more sublime than *truth* itself! Yet the doubt whether it is not just this subject matter that requires an excuse may occur to us if we recall the sense in which Pilate put the question, *What is truth?* In the words of the poet: 'With the courtier's mien that purblind yet smiling condemns the cause of the earnest soul.'[1] Pilate's question bears the meaning—which may be regarded as an element in good manners —together with a reminder of it, that the aim of attaining truth is, as everyone knows, something given up and long since set aside, and that the unattainableness of truth is recognized even among professional philosophers and logicians. But if the question that *religion* raises as to the value of things, insights, and actions—a question which in its import has a like meaning—is once more

[1] Klopstock: *Der Messias,* seventh canto.

vindicating its claims in our days, then philosophy must surely hope that it will no longer be thought so strange if it, too, in its immediate domain once more asserts its true aim, and, after having lapsed into the manner and method of other sciences and their renunciation of the claim to truth, strives to rise again to that aim. In respect of this attempt, it is not, strictly speaking, permissible to offer any apology; but in respect of the execution, I may plead in excuse that my official duties and other personal circumstances allowed me but scattered hours of labour at a science that demands and deserves undistracted and undivided exertion.

Nuremberg, *July* 21, 1816

THE NOTION IN GENERAL

What the *nature of the Notion* is, can no more be stated offhand than can the Notion of any other object. It might perhaps seem that, in order to state the Notion of an object, the logical element were presupposed and that therefore this could not in turn have something else for its presupposition, nor be deduced; just as in geometry logical propositions as applied to magnitude and employed in that science, are premised in the form of *axioms*, determinations of cognition that *have not been and cannot be deduced*. Now although it is true that the Notion is to be regarded, not merely as a subjective presupposition but as the *absolute foundation*, yet it can be so only in so far as it has *made* itself the foundation. Abstract immediacy is no doubt a *first*; yet in so far as it is abstract it is, on the contrary mediated, and therefore if it is to be grasped in its truth its foundation must first be sought. Hence this foundation, though indeed an immediate, must have made itself immediate through the sublation of mediation.

From this aspect the *Notion* is to be regarded in the first instance simply as the third to *being* and *essence*, to the *immediate* and to *reflection*. Being and essence are so far the moments of its *becoming*; but it is their *foundation* and *truth* as the identity in which they are submerged and contained. They are contained in it because it is their *result*, but no longer as *being* and *essence*. That determination they possess only in so far as they have not withdrawn into this their unity.

Objective logic therefore, which treats of *being* and *essence* constitutes properly the *genetic exposition of the Notion*. More precisely, *substance* is already *real essence*, or *essence* in so far as it is united with *being* and has entered into actuality. Consequently, the Notion has substance for its immediate presupposition; what is *implicit* in substance is *manifested* in the Notion. Thus the *dialectical movement* of *substance* through causality and reciprocity is the immediate *genesis* of the *Notion*, the exposition of the process of its becoming. But the significance of its *becoming*, as of every becoming, is that it is the reflection of the transient into its *ground* and that the at first apparent *other* into which the former has passed constitutes its *truth*. Accordingly the Notion is the *truth* of substance; and since substance has *necessity* for its

T

specific mode of relationship, freedom reveals itself as the *truth of necessity* and as *the mode of relationship proper to the Notion*.

The progressive determination of substance necessitated by its own nature, is the *positing* of what is *in and for itself*. Now the Notion is that absolute unity of being and reflection in which being is *in and for itself* only in so far as it is no less *reflection* or *positedness*, and *positedness* is no less being that is *in and for itself*. This abstract result is elucidated by the exposition of its concrete genesis; that exposition contains the nature of the Notion whose treatment it must have preceded. The chief moments of this exposition (which has been given in detail in the Second Book of the Objective Logic) can therefore only be briefly summarized here.

Substance is the *absolute*, the actuality that is in and for itself—*in itself* as the simple identity of possibility and actuality, absolute essence containing all actuality and possibility *within itself*; and *for itself*, being this identity as absolute *power* or purely self-related *negativity*. The movement of substantiality posited by these moments consists in the following stages:

1. Substance, as absolute power or self-related negativity, differentiates itself into a relationship in which what were at first only simple moments are substances and original presuppositions. Their specific relationship is that of a *passive* substance, of the original immediacy of the simple *inwardness* or *in-itself* which, powerless to posit itself, is only an original *positedness*—and of an *active* substance, the *self-related* negativity which as such has posited itself in the form of an other and relates itself *to this* other. This other is simply the passive substance which the active substance through its own originative power has *presupposed* for itself as condition. This presupposing is to be understood in the sense that the movement of substance itself is, in the first instance, under the form of one of the moments of its Notion, the *in-itself*, and the determinateness of one of the *substances* standing in relationship is also the determinateness of this *relationship* itself.

2. The other moment is *being-for-self*, which means that the power posits *itself* as *self-related* negativity, thereby sublating again what was *presupposed*. The active substance is the cause; it *acts*, that is, it now *posits*, whereas previously it only *presupposed*; so that (*a*) to the power is now added the *illusory show* [*Schein*] of power, to the positedness the *illusory show* of positedness. What in

the presupposition was *original*, becomes in causality, *through the relation to an other*, what it is in itself; the cause produces an effect, and that, too, in another substance; it is now power in relation to an other and thus *appears* as a cause, but *is* a cause only in virtue of this *appearing*. (b) The effect enters the passive substance, whereby it now also appears as a *positedness*, but *is* a passive substance only as such positedness.

3. But there is still more present in this than only this *appearance*, namely: (a) the cause acts on the passive substance and *alters* its determination; but this is positedness, there is nothing else in it to alter; the other determination, however, that it receives is causality; the passive substance therefore becomes cause, power and activity: (b) the effect is *posited* in it by the cause; but that which is posited by the cause is the cause itself which, in acting, is identical with itself; it is this that puts itself in the place of the passive substance. Similarly, with regard to the active substance, (a) the action is the translation of the cause into the effect, into the other of the cause, into positedness, and (b) the cause reveals itself in the effect as what it is; the effect is identical with the cause, is not an other; thus the cause in acting reveals the posited being as that which the cause essentially is. Each side, therefore, in both its identical and negative relation to the other becomes the *opposite* of itself, so that the other, and therefore also each, remains *identical with itself*. But the identical and the negative relations are both one and the same; substance is self-identical only in its opposite and this constitutes the absolute identity of the substances posited as a duality. Active substance, through the act of positing itself as the opposite of itself, an act which is at the same time the sublating of its *presupposed otherness*, of passive substance, is manifested as cause or originative substantiality. Conversely, through being acted on, posited being is manifested *as* posited, the negative *as* negative, and therefore passive substance as *self-related* negativity, the cause meeting in this other simply and solely with its own self. Through this positing, then, the *presupposed* or *implicit* originativeness becomes *explicit* or *for itself*; yet this being that is in and for itself is such only in so far as this positing is equally a *sublating* of what was presupposed; in other words, absolute substance has returned to itself and so become absolute, only *out of* and *in* its *positedness*. Hence this reciprocity is the appearance that again sublates itself, the revelation that the

illusory being of causality in which the cause appears *as* cause, *is illusory being*. This infinite reflection-into-self, namely, that being is in and for itself only in so far as it is posited, is the *consummation of substance*. But this consummation is no longer *substance* itself but something higher, the *Notion*, the *subject*. The transition of the relation of substantiality takes place through its own immanent necessity and is nothing more than the manifestation of itself, that the Notion is its truth, and that freedom is the truth of necessity.

I have already mentioned in the Second Book of the Objective Logic[1] that the philosophy which adopts the standpoint of *substance* and stops there is the system of Spinoza. I also indicated there the defect of that system alike as to form and to matter. But the *refutation* of the system is another matter. With respect to the refutation of a philosophical system I have elsewhere also made the general observation that one must get rid of the erroneous idea of regarding the system as out and out *false*, as if the *true* system by contrast were only *opposed* to the false. The context itself in which Spinoza's system here finds mention provides the true standpoint of the system and the question whether it is true or false. The relation of substance resulted from the nature of essence; this relation and its exposition as a developed totality in a system is, therefore, a *necessary standpoint* assumed by the absolute. Such a standpoint, therefore, is not to be regarded as an opinion, a subjective, arbitrary way of thinking of an individual, as an aberration of speculation; on the contrary, speculative thinking in the course of its progress finds itself necessarily occupying that standpoint and to that extent the system is perfectly true; but *it is not the highest standpoint*. Yet this does not mean that the system can be regarded as *false*, as requiring and being capable of refutation; on the contrary, the only thing about it to be considered false is its claim to be the highest standpoint. Consequently, the *true* system cannot have the relation to it of being merely *opposed* to it; for if this were so, the system, as this opposite, would itself be one-sided. On the contrary, the true system as the higher, must contain the subordinate system within itself.

Further, the refutation must not come from outside, that is, it must not proceed from assumptions lying outside the system in question and inconsistent with it. The system need only refuse

[1] p. 536, Remark.

to recognize those assumptions; the *defect* is a defect only for him who starts from the requirements and demands based on those assumptions. Thus it has been said that for anyone who does not presuppose as an established fact the freedom and self-subsistence of the self-conscious subject there cannot be any refutation of Spinozism. Besides, a standpoint so lofty and so intrinsically *rich* as the relation of substance, far from ignoring those assumptions even contains them: one of the attributes of Spinoza's substance is *thinking*. On the contrary, Spinozism knows how to resolve and assimilate the determinations in which these assumptions conflict with it, so that they appear *in the system*, but in the modifications appropriate to it. The nerve, therefore, of the external refutation consists solely in clinging stubbornly to the antitheses of these assumptions, for example, to the absolute self-subsistence of the thinking individual as against the form of thought posited in absolute substance as identical with extension. The genuine refutation must penetrate the opponent's stronghold and meet him on his own ground; no advantage is gained by attacking him somewhere else and defeating him where he is not. The only possible refutation of Spinozism must therefore consist, in the first place, in recognizing its standpoint as essential and necessary and then going on to raise that standpoint to the higher one through its own immanent dialectic. The relationship of substance considered simply and solely in its own intrinsic nature leads on to its opposite, to the Notion. The exposition of substance (contained in the last book) which leads on to the Notion is, therefore, the sole and genuine refutation of Spinozism. It is the *unveiling* of substance, and this is the *genesis of the Notion*, the chief moments of which have been brought together above. The *unity* of substance is its relation of *necessity*; but this unity is only an *inner* necessity; in positing itself through the moment of absolute negativity it becomes a *manifested* or *posited identity*, and thereby the *freedom* which is the identity of the Notion. The Notion, the totality resulting from the reciprocal relation, is the unity of the *two substances* standing in that relation; but in this unity they are now free, for they no longer possess their identity as something blind, that is to say, as something merely *inner*; on the contrary, the substances now have essentially the status of an *illusory being*, of being moments of reflection, whereby each is no less immediately united with its other or its positedness and each contains its positedness *within itself*, and consequently in its other is posited as simply and solely identical with itself.

With the Notion, therefore, we have entered the realm of *freedom*. Freedom belongs to the Notion because that identity which, as absolutely determined, constitutes the necessity of substance, is now also sublated or is a positedness, and this positedness as self-related is simply that identity. The mutual opacity of the substances standing in the causal relationship has vanished and become a self-transparent clarity, for the originality of their self-subsistence has passed into a positedness; the *original* substance is original in that it is only *the cause of itself*, and this is *substance raised to the freedom of the Notion*.

This at once provides us with a more precise determination of the Notion. Because being that is in and for itself is immediately a *positedness*, the Notion in its simple self-relation is an absolute *determinateness* which, however, as purely self-related is no less immediately a simple identity. But this self-relation of the determinateness as the union of itself with itself is equally the negation of the determinateness, and the Notion as this equality with itself is the *universal*. But this identity has equally the determination of negativity; it is the negation or determinateness which is self-related; thus the Notion is the *individual*. Each of them, the universal and the individual, is the totality, each contains within itself the determination of the other and therefore these totalities are *one* and one only, just as this unity is the differentiation of itself into the free *illusion* of this duality—of a duality which, in the difference of the individual and the universal, appears as a complete opposition, yet an opposition which is so entirely *illusory* that in thinking and enunciating the one, the other also is immediately thought and enunciated.

The foregoing is to be regarded as the *Notion of the Notion*. It may seem to differ from what is elsewhere understood by 'notion' and in that case we might be asked to indicate how that which we have here found to be the Notion is contained in other conceptions or explanations. On the one hand, however, there can be no question of a confirmation based on the *authority* of the ordinary understanding of the term; in the science of the Notion its content and character can be guaranteed solely by the *immanent deduction* which contains its genesis and which already lies behind us. On the other hand, the Notion as here deduced must, of course, be recognizable in principle in what is elsewhere presented as the concept of the Notion. But it is not so easy to discover what others have said about the nature of the Notion. For in the main they do not concern themselves at all with the question, presupposing that everyone who uses the word automatically knows what it means. Latterly one could have felt all the more relieved from any need to trouble about the Notion since, just as it was the fashion for a while to say everything bad about the imagination, and then the memory, so in philosophy it became the habit some time ago, a habit which in some measure still exists, to heap every kind of slander on the Notion, on what is supreme in thought, while the incomprehensible and non-comprehension are, on the contrary, regarded as the pinnacle of science and morality.

I will confine myself here to a remark which may help one to grasp the notions here developed and may make it easier to find one's bearings in them. The Notion, when it has developed into a *concrete existence* that is itself free, is none other than the *I* or pure self-consciousness. True, I *have* notions, that is to say, determinate notions; but the *I* is the pure Notion itself which, as Notion, has come into *existence*. When, therefore, reference is made to the fundamental determinations which constitute the nature of the *I*, we may presuppose that the reference is to something familiar, that is, a commonplace of our ordinary thinking. But the *I* is, *first*, this pure self-related unity, and it is so not immediately but only as making abstraction from all determinateness and content and withdrawing into the freedom of unrestricted equality with itself. As such it is *universality*; a unity that is unity with itself only through its *negative* attitude, which appears as a process of abstraction, and that consequently contains all determinedness dissolved in it. *Secondly*, the *I* as self-related negativity is no less immediately *individuality* or is *absolutely determined*, opposing itself to all that is other and excluding it—*individual personality*. This absolute *universality* which is also immediately an absolute *individualization*, and an absolutely determined being, which is a pure positedness and is this *absolutely determined* being only through its unity with the *positedness*, this constitutes the nature of the *I* as well as of the Notion; neither the one nor the other can be truly comprehended unless the two indicated moments are grasped at the same time both in their abstraction and also in their perfect unity.

When one speaks in the ordinary way of the *understanding possessed by the I*, one understands thereby a *faculty* or *property* which stands in the same relation to the *I* as the property of a thing does to the *thing* itself, that is, to an indeterminate substrate that is not the genuine ground and the determinant of its property. According to this conception I *possess* notions and *the* Notion, just as I also possess a coat, complexion, and other external properties. Now Kant went beyond this external relation of the understanding, as the faculty of notions and of the Notion itself, to the *I*. It is one of the profoundest and truest insights to be found in the *Critique of Pure Reason* that the *unity* which constitutes the nature of the *Notion* is recognized as the *original synthetic* unity of *apperception*, as unity of the *I think*, or of self-consciousness. This proposition constitutes the so-called *transcendental* deduction of the categories; but this has always been regarded as one of the most difficult parts of the Kantian philosophy, doubtless for no other reason than that it demands that we should go beyond the mere *representation* of the relation in which the *I* stands to the *understanding*, or notions stand to a thing and its properties and accidents, and advance to the *thought* of that relation. *An object*, says Kant,[1] is that in the *notion* of which the *manifold* of a given intuition is *unified*. But all unifying of representations demands a *unity of consciousness* in the synthesis of them. Consequently it is this *unity of consciousness* which alone constitutes the connection of the representations with the object and therewith their *objective validity* and on which rests even the *possibility of the understanding*. Kant distinguishes this unity from the *subjective unity* of consciousness, the unity of representation whereby I am conscious of a manifold as either *simultaneous* or *successive*, this being dependent on empirical conditions. On the other hand, the principles of the *objective* determination of notions are, he says, to be derived solely from the principle of the *transcendental unity of apperception*. Through the categories which are these objective determinations, the manifold of given representations is so determined as to be brought into the *unity of consciousness*. According to this exposition, the unity of the notion is that whereby something is not a mere *mode of feeling*, an *intuition*, or even a mere *representation*, but is an *object*, and this objective unity is the unity of the ego with itself. In point of fact, the *com-*

[1] *Critique of Pure Reason*, 2nd edition, p 137.

prehension of an object consists in nothing else than that the ego makes it *its own*, pervades it and brings it into *its own form*, that is, into the *universality* that is immediately a *determinateness*, or a determinateness that is immediately universality. As intuited or even in ordinary conception, the object is still something *external* and *alien*. When it is comprehended, the being-in-and-for-self which it possesses in intuition and pictorial thought is transformed into a *positedness*; the *I* in *thinking* it pervades it. But it is *only* as it is in thought that the object is truly *in and for itself*; in intuition or ordinary conception it is only an *Appearance*. Thought sublates the *immediacy* with which the object at first confronts us and thus converts the object into a positedness; but this its *positedness* is *its being-in-and-for-self*, or its *objectivity*. The object therefore has its objectivity in the *Notion* and this is the *unity of self-consciousness* into which it has been received; consequently its objectivity, or the Notion, is itself none other than the nature of self-consciousness, has no other moments or determinations than the *I* itself.

Thus we are justified by a cardinal principle of the Kantian philosophy in referring to the nature of the *I* in order to learn what the *Notion* is. But conversely, it is necessary for this purpose to have grasped the *Notion* of the *I* as stated above. If we cling to the mere *representation* of the *I* as it floats before our ordinary consciousness, then the *I* is only the simple *thing*, also called *soul*, in which the Notion *inheres* as a possession or property. This representation which makes no attempt to comprehend either the *I* or the Notion cannot serve to facilitate or bring nearer the comprehension of the Notion.

The Kantian exposition cited above contains two other features which concern the Notion and necessitate some further observations. In the first place, the stage of the understanding is supposed to be preceded by the stages of *feeling* and *intuition*, and it is an essential proposition of the Kantian transcendental philosophy that *without intuitions notions* are *empty* and are valid solely as *relations* of the *manifold* given by intuition. Secondly, the Notion has been declared to be the *objective* element of knowledge, and as such, the *truth*. But on the other hand, the Notion is taken as something *merely subjective* from which we cannot *extract reality*, by which is to be understood objectivity, since reality is contrasted with subjectivity; and, in general, the Notion and the logical

T*

element are declared to be something merely *formal* which, since it abstracts from the content, does not contain truth.

Now, in the first place, as regards the relation of the understanding or the Notion to the stages *presupposed* by it, the *form* of these stages is determined by the particular science under consideration. In our science, that of pure *logic*, these stages are *being* and *essence*. In *psychology* the antecedent stages are *feeling* and *intuition*, and then *ideation* generally. In the *phenomenology* of spirit, which is the doctrine of consciousness, the ascent to the understanding is through the stages of *sensuous consciousness* and then *perception*. Kant presupposes only feeling and intuition. How incomplete to begin with this scale of stages is is revealed by the fact that he himself adds as an *appendix* to the transcendental logic or doctrine of the understanding a *treatise on the concepts of reflection*—a sphere lying between *intuition* and the *understanding* or *being* and the *Notion*.

About these stages themselves it must be remarked, first of all, that the forms of intuition, ideation and the like belong to the *self-conscious* spirit which, as such, does not fall to be considered in the science of logic. It is true that the pure determinations of being, essence and the Notion constitute the ground plan and the inner simple framework of the forms of the spirit; spirit as *intuiting* and also as *sensuous consciousness* is in the form of immediate being; and, similarly, spirit as *ideating* and as *perceiving* has risen from being to the stage of essence or reflection. But these concrete forms as little concern the science of logic as do the concrete forms assumed by the logical categories in nature, which would be *space and time*, then space and time self-filled with a content as *inorganic nature*, and lastly, *organic nature*. Similarly here, too, the Notion is to be regarded not as the act of the self-conscious understanding, not as the *subjective understanding*, but as the Notion in its own absolute character which constitutes a *stage of nature* as well as of *spirit*. Life, or organic nature, is the stage of nature at which the Notion emerges, but as blind, as unaware of itself and unthinking; the Notion that is self-conscious and thinks pertains solely to spirit. But the logical form of the Notion is independent of its non-spiritual, and also of its spiritual, shapes. The necessary premonition on this point has already been given in the Introduction. It is a point that must not wait to be established within *logic* itself but must be cleared up *before* that science is begun.

Now whatever may be the forms of the stages which precede the Notion, we come secondly to the *relation* in which the *Notion is thought to these forms*. The conception of this relation both in ordinary psychology and in the Kantian transcendental philosophy is that the empirical *material*, the manifold of intuition and representation, first *exists on its own account*, and that then the understanding *approaches* it, brings *unity* into it and by abstraction raises it to the form of *universality*. The understanding is in this way an intrinsically empty *form* which, on the one hand, obtains a reality through the said *given* content and, on the other hand, *abstracts* from that content, that is to say, *lets it drop* as something useless, but useless only for the Notion. In both these actions the Notion is not the independent factor, not the essential and true element of the prior given material; on the contrary, it is the material that is regarded as the absolute reality, which cannot be extracted from the Notion.

Now it must certainly be admitted that the Notion *as such* is not yet complete, but must rise to the *Idea* which alone is the unity of the Notion and reality; and this must be shown in the sequel to be the *spontaneous outcome of the nature of the Notion itself*. For the reality which the Notion gives itself must not be received by it as something external but must, in accordance with the requirement of the science, be derived from the Notion itself. But the truth is that it is not the material given by intuition and representation that ought to be vindicated as the *real* in contrast to the Notion. People often say, 'It is only a notion,' contrasting the notion not only with the Idea but with sensuous, spatial and temporal, palpable reality as something more excellent than the Notion; and then the *abstract* is held to be of less account than the concrete because it lacks so much of this kind of material. In this view, to abstract means to select from the concrete object for *our subjective purposes this or that mark* without thereby detracting from the worth and status of the many other properties and features left out of account; on the contrary, these as *real* retain their validity completely unimpaired, only they are left yonder, on the other side; thus it is only the *inability* of the understanding to assimilate such wealth that compels it to content itself with the impoverished abstraction. Now to regard the given material of intuition and the manifold of representation as the *real* in contrast to what is *thought*, to the Notion, is a view, the abandonment of which is not only a condition of philosophizing but is already presupposed by religion; for how can there be any need for religion, how can religion have any meaning, if the fleeting and superficial phenomena of the world of sensuous particulars are still regarded as the truth? But philosophy gives a *reasoned* insight into the true state of the case with regard to the reality of sensuous being; it assumes the stages of feeling and intuition as precedent to the understanding in so far as they are conditions of its genesis, but only in the sense that it is conditioned by their *reality*. Abstract thinking, therefore, is not to be regarded as a mere setting aside of the sensuous material, the reality of which is not thereby impaired; rather is it the sublating and reduction of that material as mere *phenomenal appearance* to the *essential*, which is manifested only in the *Notion*. Of course, if what is taken up into the Notion from the concrete phenomenon is to serve only as a *mark* or *sign*, it certainly may be any mere random sensuous particular determination of the object, selected from the others on the basis of any random external interest and of a similar kind and nature as the rest.

A capital misunderstanding which prevails on this point is that the *natural* principle or the *beginning* which forms the starting point in the *natural* evolution or in the *history* of the developing individual, is regarded as the *truth*, and the *first* in the *Notion*. Now in the order of nature, intuition or being are undoubtedly first, or are the condition for the Notion, but they are not on that account the absolutely unconditioned; on the contrary, their reality is sublated in the Notion and with it, too, the illusory show they possessed of being the conditioning reality. When it is a question, not of *truth* but merely of *history*, as in pictorial and phenomenal thinking, we need not of course go beyond merely narrating that we start with feelings and intuitions and that from the manifold of these the understanding extracts a universality or an abstraction and naturally requires for this purpose the said substrate of feelings and intuitions which, in this process of abstraction, remains for representation in the same complete reality with which it first presented itself. But philosophy is not meant to be a narration of happenings but a cognition of what is *true* in them, and further, on the basis of this cognition, to *comprehend* that which, in the narrative, appears as a mere happening.

If the superficial conception of what the Notion is, leaves all manifoldness *outside* the Notion and attributes to the latter only the form of abstract universality or the empty identity of reflection, we can at once appeal to the fact that quite apart from the view here propounded, the statement or definition of a notion expressly includes not only the genus, which itself is, properly speaking, more than a purely abstract universality, but also the *specific determinateness*. If one would but reflect attentively on the meaning of this fact, one would see that *differentiation* must be regarded as an equally essential moment of the Notion. Kant has introduced this consideration by the extremely important thought that there are synthetic judgements *a priori*. This original synthesis of apperception is one of the most profound principles for speculative development; it contains the beginning of a true apprehension of the nature of the Notion and is completely opposed to that empty identity or abstract universality which is not within itself a synthesis. The further development, however, does not fulfil the promise of the beginning. The very expression *synthesis* easily recalls the conception of an *external* unity and a *mere combination* of entities that are *intrinsically separate*. Then, again, the Kantian philosophy has not got beyond the psychological reflex of the Notion and has reverted once more to the assertion that the Notion is permanently conditioned by a manifold of intuition. It has declared intellectual cognition and experience to be a *phenomenal* content, not because the categories themselves are only finite but, on the ground of a psychological idealism, because they are *merely* determinations originating in self-consciousness. It is in keeping with this standpoint, too, that the Notion without the manifold of intuition is again declared to be *empty* and *devoid of content* despite the fact that it is a synthesis *a priori*; as such, it surely does contain determinateness and difference within itself. Moreover, since the determinateness is that of the Notion and therefore *absolute determinateness*, *individuality*, the Notion is the ground and source of all finite determinateness and manifoldness.

The merely formal position that the Notion holds as understanding is fully confirmed in the Kantian exposition of what reason is. In reason, the highest stage of thought, one ought to have expected the Notion to lose the conditionedness in which it still appears at the stage of understanding and to attain to perfect truth. But this expectation is disappointed. For Kant defines the relation of reason to the categories as merely *dialectical* and, indeed, takes the result of this dialectic to be the *infinite nothing*—

just that and nothing more. Consequently, the infinite unity of reason, too, is still deprived of the synthesis, and with it the beginning referred to above of a speculative, truly infinite Notion; reason becomes the familiar, wholly formal, merely regulative *unity of the systematic employment of the understanding*. It is declared to be an abuse when logic, which is supposed to be merely a *canon of judgment*, is regarded as an *organon* for the production of *objective* insights. The notions of reason in which we could not but have an intimation of a higher power and a profounder significance, no longer possess a *constitutive* character as do the categories, they are *mere* Ideas; certainly, we are *quite at liberty* to use them, but by these intelligible entities in which all *truth* should be completely revealed, we are to understand nothing more than *hypotheses*, and to ascribe absolute truth to them would be the height of caprice and foolhardiness, for they—*do not occur in any experience*. Would one ever have thought that philosophy would deny truth to intelligible entities because they lack the spatial and temporal material of the sensuous world?

Directly connected with this is the question of the point of view from which the Notion and the character of logic generally are to be considered, a question on which the Kantian philosophy holds the same view as is commonly taken: that is to say, in what *relation* do the *Notion* and the *science of the Notion* stand to *truth* itself. We have already quoted from the Kantian deduction of the categories that according to it the object, as that in which the manifold of intuition is *unified*, is this unity solely *through the unity of self-consciousness*. Here, therefore, the *objectivity of thought* is specifically enunciated, an identity of Notion and thing, which is *truth*. In the same way, it is also commonly admitted that when thinking appropriates a given object, this thereby suffers an alteration and is changed from something sensuous to something thought; and yet that not only is the essential nature of the object not affected by this alteration but that it is only in its Notion that it is in its *truth*, whereas in the immediacy in which it is given it is only *appearance* and a *contingency*; that the cognition that truly comprehends the object is the cognition of it as it is *in and for itself*, and that the Notion is its very objectivity. But, on the other hand, it is equally maintained that we *cannot after all, know things as they truly are in themselves* and that *truth is inaccessible to the cognitive powers of reason*; that the aforesaid truth which consists in the unity of the object and the Notion is, after all, only Appearance, and this time, again on the ground that the content is only the manifold of intuition. On this point we have already remarked that, on the contrary, it is precisely in the Notion that this manifoldness, in so far as it pertains to intuition in contrast to the Notion, is sublated and that through the Notion the object is reduced to its non-contingent essential nature. The latter enters into the sphere of Appearance and for that very reason the Appearance is not devoid of essential being, but is a manifestation of essence. But the completely liberated manifestation of essence is the Notion. These propositions of which we here remind the reader are not dogmatic assertions, for the reason that they are results that have issued from the entire immanent development of *essence*. The present standpoint to which this development has led is that the form of the *absolute* which is higher than being and essence is the *Notion*. Regarded from this aspect, the Notion has *subjugated* being and essence, which from other starting points include also feeling and intuition and representation, and which appeared as its antecedent conditions, and has proved itself to be their *unconditioned ground*. There now remains the *second* aspect, to the treatment of which this Third Book of the Logic is devoted, namely the exposition of how the Notion builds up in and from itself the reality that has vanished in it. It has therefore been freely admitted that the cognition that stops short at the Notion purely as such, is still incomplete and has only as yet arrived at *abstract truth*. But its incompleteness does not lie in its lack of that presumptive reality given in feeling and intuition but rather in the fact that the Notion has not yet given itself a reality of its *own*, a reality produced from its own resources. The demonstrated absoluteness of the Notion relatively to the material of experience and, more exactly, to the categories and concepts of reflection, consists in this, that this material as it appears *apart from* and *prior* to the Notion has no *truth*; this it has solely in its ideality or its identity with the Notion. The *derivation* of the *real* from it if we want to call it derivation, consists in the first place essentially in this, that the Notion in its formal abstraction reveals itself as incomplete and through its own immanent dialectic passes over into reality; but it does not fall back again onto a ready-made reality confronting it and take refuge in something which has shown itself to be the unessential element of Appearance because, having looked around for something better, it has failed to find it; on the contrary, it produces the reality from its own resources. It will always stand out as a marvel how the Kantian philosophy recognized the relation of thought to sensuous reality, beyond which it did not advance, as only a relative relation of mere Appearance, and perfectly well recognized and enunciated a higher unity of both in the Idea in general and, for example, in the Idea of an intuitive understanding, and yet stopped short at this relative relation and the assertion that the Notion is and remains utterly separate from reality—thus asserting as *truth* what it declared to be finite cognition, and denouncing as an unjustified extravagance and a figment of thought what it recognized as *truth* and of which it established the specific notion.

Since it is primarily logic and not science generally with whose relation to truth we are here concerned, it must further be conceded that logic as the *formal science* cannot and should not contain that reality which is the content of the further parts of philosophy, namely, the philosophical sciences of nature and of spirit. These concrete sciences do, of course, present themselves in a more real form of the Idea than logic does; but this is not by turning back again to the reality abandoned by the consciousness which has risen above its mode as Appearance to the level of science, nor by reverting to the use of forms such as the categories and concepts of reflection, whose finitude and untruth have been demonstrated in the logic. On the contrary, logic exhibits the elevation of the *Idea* to that level from which it becomes the creator of nature and passes over to the form of a concrete *immediacy* whose Notion, however, breaks up this shape again in order to realize itself as *concrete spirit*. As contrasted with these concrete sciences (although these have and retain as their inner formative principle that same logical element, or the Notion, which had served is their archetype), logic is of course a formal science; but it is the science of the *absolute form* which is within itself a totality and contains the *pure Idea of truth itself*. This absolute form has in its own self its content or reality; the Notion, not being a trivial, empty identity, possesses in its moment of negativity or of absolute determining, the differentiated determinations; the content is simply and solely these determinations of the absolute form and nothing else—a content posited by the absolute form itself and consequently also adequate to it. For this reason, this form is of quite another nature than logical form is ordinarily taken to be. It is already *on its own account truth*, since this content is adequate to its form, or the reality to its Notion; and it is the *pure truth* because the determinations of the content do not yet have the form of an absolute otherness or of absolute immediacy. When Kant, in connection with logic [1] comes to discuss the old and famous question: *what is truth?* he first of all *presents* to the reader as a triviality the explanation of the term as the agreement of cognition with its object—a definition of great, indeed of supreme, value. If we remember this definition in connection with the fundamental assertion of transcendental idealism, that reason as cognitive is incapable of apprehending *things-in-themselves*, that *reality* lies *absolutely* outside the *Notion*, then it is at once evident that a *reason* such as this which is unable to put itself in agreement with its object, the things-in-themselves, and *things-in-themselves* that are not in agreement with the Notion of reason, the Notion that is not in agreement with reality, and a reality that does not agree with the Notion, are *untrue conceptions*. If Kant had considered the Idea of an *intuitive understanding* in the light of the above definition of truth, he would have treated that Idea which expresses the required agreement, not as a figment of thought but rather as the truth.

'What we require to know' Kant goes on to say, 'is a universal and sure criterion of any cognition whatever; it would be such a criterion as would be valid for all cognitions *without distinction of their objects*; but since with such a criterion abstraction would be made from *all content* of the cognition (*relation to its object*) and truth concerns precisely this content, it would be quite *impossible* and *absurd* to ask for a mark of the *truth of this content* of cognitions.' Here, the usual conception of the formal function of logic is expressed very definitely and the argument adduced has a very convincing air. But first of all it is to be observed that it usually happens with such formal ratiocination that it forgets in its discourse the very point on which it has based its argument and of which it is speaking. It is alleged that it would be absurd to ask for the criterion of the *truth of the content* of cognition; but according to the definition it is not the *content* that constitutes the truth, but the agreement of the content with the Notion. A content such as is here spoken of, *without the Notion*, is something notionless, and

[1] *Critique of Pure Reason*, p. 83.

hence without essential being; certainly we cannot ask for the criterion of the truth of such a content, but for the very opposite reason; not, that is, because the content, as something notionless, is not the required agreement, but simply because it cannot be anything more than a mere truthless opinion. Let us leave on one side the content which causes the confusion here—the confusion into which formalism falls whenever it sets out to explain something and which makes it say the opposite of what it intends—and let us stop at the abstract view that logic is only formal and, in fact, abstracts from all content; we then have a one-sided cognition which is not to contain any object, an empty, blank form which therefore is no more an *agreement*—for an agreement essentially requires *two* terms—than it is truth. In the *a priori* synthesis of the Notion, Kant possessed a higher principle in which a duality in a unity could be cognised, a cognition, therefore, of what is required for truth; but the material of sense, the manifold of intuition, was too strong for him and he was unable to get away from it to a consideration of the Notion and the categories *in and for themselves* and to a speculative method of philosophising.

Logic being the science of the absolute form, this formal science, in order to be *true*, must possess in its own self a *content* adequate to its form; and all the more, since the formal element of logic is the pure form, and therefore the truth of logic must be the *pure truth* itself. Consequently this formal science must be regarded as possessing richer determinations and a richer content and as being infinitely more potent in its influence on the concrete than is usually supposed. The laws of logic by themselves (not counting the heterogeneous accretions of applied logic and the rest of the psychological and anthropological material) are commonly restricted, apart from the law of contradiction, to some meagre propositions concerning the conversion of judgements and the forms of syllogisms. Even here the forms which come up for treatment as well as their further modifications are only, as it were, historically taken up; they are not subjected to criticism to determine whether they are in and for themselves *true*. Thus, for example, the form of the positive judgement is accepted as something perfectly correct in itself, the question whether such a judgement is true depending solely on the content. Whether this form is *in its own self* a form of truth, whether the proposition it enunciates, the *individual* is a *universal*, is not inherently dialectical, is a question that no one thinks of investigating. It is straightway assumed that this judgement is, on its own account, capable of containing truth and that the proposition enunciated by any positive judgement is true, although it is directly evident that it lacks what is required by the definition of truth, namely, the agreement of the Notion and its object; if the predicate, which here is the universal, is taken as the Notion, and the subject, which is the individual, is taken as the object, then the one does not agree with the other. But if the *abstract* universal which is the predicate falls short of constituting a Notion, for a Notion certainly implies something more, and if, too, a subject of this kind is not yet much more than a grammatical one, how should the judgement possibly contain truth seeing that either its Notion and object do not agree, or it lacks both Notion and object? On the contrary, then, what is *impossible* and *absurd* is to attempt to grasp the truth in such forms as the positive judgement and the judgement generally. Just as the Kantian philosophy did not consider the categories in and for themselves but declared them to be finite determinations incapable of containing truth, on the wrong ground that they are subjective forms of self-consciousness, still less did that philosophy subject to criticism the forms of the Notion which are the content of ordinary logic; on the contrary, it has adopted a portion of them, namely, the functions of judgement, for the determination of the categories and accepted them as valid presuppositions. Even if we are to see in logical forms nothing more than formal functions of thought, they would for that very reason be worthy of investigation to ascertain how far, on their own account, they correspond to the *truth*. A logic that does not perform this task can at most claim the value of a descriptive natural history of the phenomena of thinking just as they occur. It is an infinite merit of Aristotle, one that must fill us with the highest admiration for the powers of that genius, that he was the first to undertake this description. It is necessary however to go further and to ascertain both the systematic connection of these forms and their value.

DIVISION

The foregoing consideration of the Notion shows it to be the unity of *being* and *essence*. Essence is the *first negation* of being, which has thereby become *illusory being*; the Notion is the *second negation* or the negation of this negation, and is therefore *being* once more, but being that has been restored as the infinite mediation and negativity of being within itself. Consequently, *being* and *essence* in the Notion no longer have the same determination that they had as *being* and *essence*, nor are they merely in a unity such that each has an *illusory being* in the other. Therefore the Notion does not differentiate itself into these determinations. It is the truth of the relationship of substance in which being and essence achieve the fulfilment of their self-subsistence and their determination through each other. The truth of substantiality proved to be the *substantial identity* which is no less a *positedness* and only as such is *substantial identity*. The positedness is a *determinate being* and *differentiation*; consequently, in the Notion, being-in-and-for-itself has attained a true and adequate reality, for the positedness is itself being-in-and-for-itself. This positedness constitutes the difference of the Notion within itself; because the positedness is immediately being-in-and-for-itself, the *different moments* of the Notion are themselves the *whole Notion, universal in their determinateness and identical with their negation.*

This, now, is the very Notion of the Notion. But it is *as yet only* its Notion; or, this Notion is itself *only* the Notion. Because it is equally being-in-and-for-self and also a positedness, or the absolute substance that manifests the *necessity* of distinct substances as an *identity*, this identity must itself posit what it is. The moments of the movement of the relationship of substantiality through which the Notion *has come to be* and the reality thereby exhibited are still only in transition into the Notion; this reality does not yet possess the determination of being the Notion's *own, self-evolved* determination; it fell in the sphere of necessity; but the Notion's own determination can only be the result of its *free* determining, a determinate being in which the Notion is identical with itself, its moments also being Notions and *posited* by the Notion itself.

At first, therefore, the Notion is only *in itself* or *implicitly* the truth; because it is *only* something *inner*, it is equally *only outer*.

It is at first simply an *immediate* and in this guise its moments have the form of immediate, *fixed determinations*. It appears as the *determinate Notion*, as the sphere of the mere *understanding*. Because this form of immediacy is still inadequate to the nature of the Notion, for this is *free*, being in relation only with itself, it is an *external* form in which the Notion cannot count as a being-in-and-for-self, but only as something *posited* or *subjective*. The Notion in the guise of immediacy constitutes the point of view for which the Notion is a subjective thinking, a reflection *external* to the subject matter. This stage, therefore, constitutes *subjectivity*, or the *formal Notion*. Its externality is manifested in the *fixed being* of its *determinations* each of which appears independently as an *isolated, qualitative* something which is only externally related to its other. But the *identity* of the Notion, which is precisely their *inner* or *subjective* essence, sets them dialectically in movement, with the result that their separatedness vanishes and with it the separation of the Notion from the object, and there emerges as their truth the *totality* which is the *objective Notion*.

Secondly, the Notion in its *objectivity* is the *subject matter in and for itself*. Through its necessary, progressive determination the *formal* Notion makes *itself* its subject matter and in this way is rid of the relation of subjectivity and externality to the object. Or, conversely, objectivity is the *real Notion* that *has emerged from its inwardness* and passed over into determinate being. In this identity with the object, the Notion thus has a *free* determinate being of *its own*. But this freedom is still only an *immediate*, not yet a *negative*, freedom. As one with the object, the Notion is *submerged* in it; its distinct moments are objective existences in which it is itself again only the *inner*. As the soul [*Seele*] of objective reality it must *give itself* the form of *subjectivity* which, as formal Notion, belonged to it immediately; thus, *in the form* of the free Notion, a form which in objectivity it still lacked, it opposes itself to that objectivity and in so doing makes the identity with it which, as *objective* Notion it possesses *in and for itself*, also a *posited* identity.

In this consummation in which it has the form of freedom even in its objectivity, the *adequate Notion* is the *Idea*. *Reason*, which is the sphere of the Idea, is the *self-revealed truth* in which the Notion possesses the realization that is wholly adequate to it, and is free, inasmuch as it cognizes this its objective world in its subjectivity and its subjectivity in its objective world.

Section One: Subjectivity

The Notion is, in the first instance, *formal*, the Notion in its *beginning* or the *immediate Notion*. In the immediate unity, its difference or positedness is itself *at first* simple and only an *illusory being* [*Schein*], so that the moments of the difference are immediately the totality of the Notion and are simply the *Notion as such*.

Secondly, however, because it is absolute negativity, it sunders itself and posits itself as the *negative* or as the *other* of itself; and further, because as yet it is only the *immediate* Notion, this positing or differentiation is characterized by the fact that the moments become *indifferent to one another* and each becomes for itself; in this *partition*, its unity is still only an external *connexion*. As such *connexion* of its moments, which are posited as *self-subsistent* and *indifferent*, it is *judgement*.

Thirdly, though the judgement does contain the unity of the Notion that has vanished into its self-subsistent moments, yet this unity is not *posited*. It becomes so through the dialectical movement of the judgement, through which it has become the *syllogism*, the Notion posited in its completeness; for in the syllogism there is posited not only the moments of the Notion as *self-subsistent* extremes, but also their *mediating unity*.

But since this *unity* itself as the unifying *middle*, and the *moments* as *self-subsistent* extremes, are in the first instance *immediately* opposed to one another, this contradictory relationship that occurs in the *formal syllogism* sublates itself, and the *completeness* of the Notion passes over into the unity of the *totality*, the *subjectivity* of the Notion into its *objectivity*.

CHAPTER I

THE NOTION

Understanding is the term usually employed to express the faculty of notions; as so used, it is distinguished from the *faculty of judgement* and the faculty of syllogisms, of the formal *reason.* But it is with *reason* that it is especially contrasted; in that case, however, it does not signify the faculty of the notion in general, but of *determinate* notions, and the idea prevails that the notion is *only* a *determinate* notion. When the understanding in this signification is distinguished from the formal faculty of judgement and from the formal reason, it is to be taken as the faculty of the *single* determinate notion. For the judgement and the syllogism or reason are, as formal, only a *product of the understanding* since they stand under the form of the abstract determinateness of the Notion. Here, however, the Notion emphatically does not rank as something merely abstractly determinate; consequently, the understanding is to be distinguished from reason only in the sense that the former is merely the faculty of the notion in general.

This universal Notion, which we have now to consider here, contains the three moments: *universality*, *particularity* and *individuality*. The difference and the determinations which the Notion gives itself in its distinguishing, constitute the side which was previously called *positedness*. As this is identical in the Notion with being-in-and-for-self, each of these moments is no less the *whole* Notion than it is a *determinate* Notion and *a determination* of the Notion.

In the first instance, it is the *pure Notion* or the determination of *universality*. But the pure or universal Notion is also only a *determinate* or *particular* Notion, which takes its place alongside other Notions. Because the Notion is a totality, and therefore in its universality or pure identical self-relation is essentially a determining and a distinguishing, it therefore contains within itself the standard by which this form of its self-identity, in pervading and embracing all the moments, no less immediately determines itself to be only the *universal* over against the distinguishedness of the moments.

Secondly, the Notion is thereby posited as this *particular* or *determinate* Notion, distinct from others.

Thirdly, *individuality* is the Notion reflecting itself out of the difference into absolute negativity. This is, at the same time, the moment in which it has passed out of its identity into its *otherness*, and becomes the *judgement*.

A. THE UNIVERSAL NOTION

The pure Notion is the absolutely infinite, unconditioned and free. It is here, at the outset of the discussion which has the Notion for its *content*, that we must look back once more at its genesis. *Essence* is the *outcome* of *being*, and the Notion the *outcome* of essence, therefore also of being. But this becoming has the significance of a self-*repulsion*, so that it is rather the *outcome* which is the *unconditioned* and *original*. *Being*, in its transition into essence, has become an *illusory being* or a *positedness*, and *becoming* or transition into an *other* has become a positing; and conversely, the *positing* or reflection of essence has sublated itself and has restored itself as a being that is *not posited*, that is *original*. The Notion is the interfusion of these moments, namely, qualitative and original being is such only as a positing, only as a return-into-self, and this pure reflection-into-self is a sheer *becoming-other* or *determinateness* which, consequently, is no less an infinite, self-relating *determinateness*.

Thus the Notion is, in the first instance, the *absolute self-identity* that is such only as the negation of negation or as the infinite unity of the negativity with itself. This *pure relation* of the Notion to itself, which is this relation by positing itself through the negativity, is the *universality* of the Notion.

As *universality* is the utterly *simple* determination, it does not seem capable of any explanation; for an explanation must concern itself with definitions and distinctions and must apply predicates to its object, and to do this to what is simple, would alter rather than explain it. But the simplicity which constitutes the very nature of the universal is such that, through absolute negativity, it contains *within itself* difference and determinateness in the highest degree. *Being* is simple as *immediate* being; for that reason it is only something *meant* or *intended* and we cannot say of it what it is; therefore, it is one with its other, with *non-being*. Its

Notion is just this, to be a simplicity that immediately vanishes in its opposite; it is *becoming*. The *universal*, on the contrary, is that *simplicity* which, because it is the Notion, no less possesses *within itself* the *richest content*.

First, therefore, it is the simple relation to itself; it is only *within itself*. Secondly, however, this identity is *within itself* absolute *mediation*, but it is not something *mediated*. The universal that is *mediated*, namely, the *abstract* universal that is opposed to the particular and the individual, this will be discussed later when we are dealing with the specific notion. Yet even the *abstract* universal involves this, that in order to obtain it we are required to *leave out* other determinations of the concrete. These determinations, simply as such, are *negations*; equally, too, the *omitting* of them is a *negating*. So that even with the abstraction, we have the negation of the negation. But this double negation is conceived of as though it were *external* to the abstraction, as though not only were the other omitted properties of the concrete distinct from the one retained, which is the content of the abstract universal, but also as though this operation of omitting the other properties and retaining the one were a process outside the properties themselves. To such an *externality* in face of that movement, the universal has not yet determined itself; it is still within itself that absolute mediation which is, precisely, the negation of the negation or absolute negativity.

By virtue of this original unity it follows, in the first place, that the first negative, or the *determination*, is not a limitation for the universal which, on the contrary, *maintains itself therein* and is positively identical with itself. The categories of being were, as Notions, essentially these identities of the determinations with themselves in their limitation or otherness; but this identity was only *in itself* the Notion; it was not yet manifested. Consequently, the qualitative determination as such was lost in its other and had for its truth a determination *distinct* from itself. The universal, on the contrary, even when it posits itself in a determination, *remains* therein what it is. It is the soul [*Seele*] of the concrete which it indwells, unimpeded and equal to itself in the manifoldness and diversity of the concrete. It is not dragged into the process of becoming, but *continues* itself through that process undisturbed and possesses the power of unalterable, undying self-preservation.

But even so, it does not merely *show*, or have an *illusory being*, in its other, like the determination of reflection; this, as a *correlate*, is not merely self-related but is a *positive relating* of itself to its other in which it *manifests itself*; but, in the first instance, it only *shows* in it, and this illusory being of each in the other, or their reciprocal determining, along with their self-dependence, has the form of an external act. The *universal*, on the contrary, is posited as the *essential being* of its determination, as the latter's *own positive nature*. For the determination that constitutes its negative is, in the Notion, simply and solely a *positedness*; in other words, it is, at the same time, essentially only the negative of the negative, and is only as this identity of the negative with itself, which is the universal. Thus the universal is also the *substance* of its determinations; but in such wise that what was a *contingency* for substance, is the Notion's own self-*mediation*, its own *immanent reflection*. But this mediation which, in the first instance, raises contingency to *necessity*, is the *manifested* relation; the Notion is not the abyss of formless substance, or necessity as the *inner* identity of things or states distinct from, and limiting, one another; on the contrary, as absolute negativity, it is the shaper and creator, and because the determination is not a limitation but is just as much utterly sublated, or posited, the illusory being is now manifestation, the manifestation *of the identical*.

The universal is therefore *free* power; it is itself and takes its other within its embrace, but without *doing violence* to it; on the contrary, the universal is, in its other, in peaceful communion with itself. We have called it free power, but it could also be called *free love* and *boundless blessedness*, for it bears itself towards its other as towards *its own self*; in it, it has returned to itself.

We have just mentioned *determinateness*, although the Notion, being as yet only the universal and only self-*identical*, has not yet advanced to that stage. However, we cannot speak of the universal apart from determinateness which to be more precise is particularity and individuality, for the universal, in its absolute negativity, contains determinateness in and for itself. The determinateness, therefore, is not introduced from outside when we speak of it in connexion with the universal. As negativity in general or in accordance with the *first, immediate* negation, the universal contains determinateness generally as *particularity*; as the *second* negation, that is, as negation of the negation, it is *absolute determinateness* or *individuality* and *concreteness*. The universal is thus the totality of the Notion; it is a concrete, and far from being empty, it has through its Notion a *content*, and a content in which it not only maintains itself but one which is its own and immanent in it. We can, indeed, abstract from the content: but in that case we do not obtain the universal of the Notion but only the *abstract* universal, which is an isolated, imperfect moment of the Notion and has no truth.

More precisely, the universal shows itself as this totality as follows. In so far as it contains determinateness, it is not merely the *first* negation, but also the reflection of this negation into itself. Taken expressly with this first negation, it is a *particular*, and it is as such that we are soon to consider it; but in this determinateness it is essentially still a universal; this side we have here still to consider. For determinateness, being in the Notion, is the total reflection, the *twofold illusory being* which on the one hand has an illusory reference *outwards*, the reflection-into-other, and on the other hand has an illusory reference *inwards*, the reflection-into-self. The former reflection involves distinction from an *other*; from this standpoint, the universal possesses a *particularity* which has its resolution in a higher universal. Now even though it is merely a relative universal, it does not lose its character of universal; it preserves itself in its determinateness, not merely as though in its connexion with the determinateness it remained indifferent to it—for then it would be merely *compounded* with it— but so that it is what we have just called the *illusory reference inwards*. The determinateness, as determinate *Notion*, is *bent back into itself* out of the externality; it is the Notion's own immanent *character*, which is an essential character by virtue of the fact that, in being taken up into the universality and pervaded by it, it equally pervades the universality, being of like compass and identical with it; it is the character that belongs to the *genus* as the determinateness that is not separated from the universal. Accordingly, the *limitation* is not outward-going but *positive*, for the Notion, through its universality, stands in free relation to itself. Thus even the determinate Notion remains within itself infinitely free Notion.

But in regard to the other side, in which the genus is limited by its specific character, it has been observed that this, as a lower genus, has its resolution in a higher universal. The latter, in its turn, can also be grasped as genus but as a more abstract one; but it always pertains only to that side of the determinate Notion which has a reference outwards. The truly higher universal is that in which this outward-going side is taken back into the universal, the second negation, in which the determinateness is present simply *as* posited or *as* illusory being. Life, ego, spirit, absolute Notion, are not universals merely in the sense of higher genera, but are concretes whose determinatenesses, too, are not species or lower genera but genera which, in their reality, are absolutely self-contained and self-fulfilled. In so far as life, ego, finite spirit are, as they certainly are, also only determinate Notions, their absolute resolution is in that universal which as truly absolute Notion is to be grasped as the Idea of infinite spirit, whose *posited* being is infinite, transparent reality wherein it contemplates its *creation*, and in this creation its own self.

The true, infinite universal which, in itself, is as much particularity as individuality, we have next to consider as *particularity*. It *determines* itself freely; the process by which it makes itself finite is not a transition, for this occurs only in the sphere of being; *it is creative power* as the absolute negativity which relates itself to its own self. As such, it differentiates itself internally, and this is a *determining*, because the differentiation is one with the universality. Accordingly, the universal is a process in which it posits the differences themselves as universal and self-related. They thereby become *fixed*, isolated differences. The isolated *subsistence* of the finite which earlier was determined as its being-for-self, and also as thinghood, as substance, is, in its truth universality, the form which which the infinite Notion clothes its differences—a form that is, in fact, one of its own differences. Herein consists the *creative power* of the Notion, a power which is to be comprehended only in this, the Notion's innermost core.

B. THE PARTICULAR NOTION

Determinateness as such belongs to being and the qualitative sphere; as determinateness of the Notion it is particularity. It is not a *limit*, as though it were related to an other *beyond* it; on the contrary, as we have just seen, it is the native, immanent moment of the universal; in particularity, therefore, the universal is not in the presence of an other, but simply of itself.

The particular contains universality, which constitutes its

substance; the genus is *unaltered* in its species, and the species are not different from the universal but only *from one another*. The particular has one and the same universality as the *other* particulars to which it is related. At the same time, by virtue of the identity of the particulars with the universal, their diversity is, *as such*, universal; it is *totality*. The particular, therefore, not only *contains* the universal but *through its determinateness* also exhibits it; consequently, the universal constitutes a *sphere* that must exhaust the particular. This totality appears, in so far as the determinateness of the particular is taken as mere *diversity*, as *completeness*. In this respect, species are complete simply because *there are* no more of them. There is no inner standard or *principle* that could apply to them, simply because *diversity* is the difference without unity in which the universality, which in its own self is absolute unity, is a merely external reflection and an unrestricted, contingent completeness. But diversity passes over into *opposition*, into an *immanent relation* of the diverse moments. Particularity, however, because it is universality, is this immanent relation, not through a transition, but in and for itself; it is in its own self totality and *simple* determinateness, essentially a *principle*. It has no *other* determinateness than that posited by the universal itself and resulting from the universal in the following manner.

The particular is the universal itself, but it is its difference or relation to an other, its *illusory reference outwards* [*sein Scheinen nach aussen*]; but there is no other present from which the particular could be distinguished, except the universal itself. The universal determines *itself*, and so is itself the particular; the determinateness is *its* difference; it is distinguished only from its own self. Therefore its species are only (*a*) the universal itself, and (*b*) the particular. The universal as the Notion is itself and its opposite, and this again is the universal itself as its posited determinateness; it embraces its opposite and in it is in union with itself. Thus it is the totality and principle of its diversity, which is determined wholly and solely by the universal itself.

Therefore there is no other true logical classification than this, that the Notion sets itself on one side as *immediate* indeterminate universality; this very indeterminateness constitutes its determinateness or makes it a particular. *Each* of them is the particular and is therefore *co-ordinate* with the other. Each of them as a particular is also *determinate as against* the universal, and in so far can be said to be *subordinate* to it. But even this universal, *as against* which the particular is determined, is for that reason itself *merely one* of the opposed sides. For if we speak of *two opposed sides*, we must supplement this by saying that it is not merely *together* that they constitute the particular—as if they were *alike* in being particulars only for external reflection—but rather that their determinateness *over against one another* is at the same time essentially only *one* determinateness, the negativity, which in the universal is *simple*.

Difference, as it shows itself here, is in its Notion and therefore in its truth. All previous difference has this unity in principle (*im Begriffe*). As immediate difference in the sphere of being, it is *limit* of an *other*; in reflection it is relative and posited as essentially relating itself to its other; here therefore the unity of the Notion begins to be *posited*, but at first it is only *illusory being* in an other. The true meaning and resolution of these determinations is just this, that they attain to their Notion, their truth; being, determinate being, something, or whole and parts, etc. substance and accidents, cause and effect, are by themselves [merely] thought-determinations; but they are grasped as determinate *Notions* when each is cognized in unity with its other or opposite determination. Whole and parts, cause and effect, for example, are not as yet different terms determined as *particulars* relatively to each other, because although *in themselves* they constitute *one* Notion, their *unity* has not yet reached the form of *universality*; thus the *difference*, too, which is in these relationships, has not as yet the form of being *one* determinateness. Cause and effect, for example, are not two different Notions, but only *one determinate* Notion, and causality, like every Notion, is a *simple* Notion.

With respect to completeness, we have seen that the determinate side of particularity is *complete* in the difference of the *universal* and the *particular*, and that these two alone constitute the particular species. In *nature*, of course, there are to be found more than two species in a genus, just as between these many species there cannot exist the relationship we have just indicated. This is the impotence of nature, that it cannot adhere to and exhibit the strictness of the Notion and runs wild in this blind irrational [*begrifflos*] multiplicity. We can *wonder* at nature's manifold genera and species and the endless diversity of her formations, for *wonderment* is *unreasoning* and its object the irrational. Nature, because it is the self-externality of the Notion, is free to indulge itself in this variety, just as spirit, too, even though it possesses the Notion in the shape of the Notion, engages in pictorial thinking and runs riot in its endless variety. The manifold natural genera or species must not be esteemed as anything more than the capricious fancies of spirit in its representations. Both indeed show traces and inklings of the Notion on all sides, but do not present a faithful copy of it because they are the side of its free self-externality. The Notion is absolute power just because it can freely abandon its difference to the shape of self-subsistent diversity, outer necessity, contingency, caprice, opinion, which however must not be taken for more than the abstract aspect of *nothingness*.

We have seen that the *determinateness* of the particular is *simple* as *principle*, but it is also simple as moment of the totality, as a determinateness opposed to the *other* determinateness. The Notion, in determining or differentiating itself, is *negatively* directed against its unity and gives itself the form of one of its ideal moments, that of *being*; as a *determinate* Notion, it has a *determinate* being in general. This being, however, no longer has the meaning of mere *immediacy*, but of universality, of an immediacy that is identical with itself through absolute mediation, an immediacy that equally contains within itself the other moment, namely, essential being or reflection. This universality with which the determinate moment is clothed is *abstract* universality. The particular has universality within it as its essential being; but in so far as the determinateness of the difference is posited and thereby has being, universality is a *form* assumed by the difference, and the determinateness as such is the *content*. The universality becomes form in so far as the difference is present as the essential moment, just as, on the contrary, in the pure universal it is present only as absolute negativity and *not as* difference *posited* as such.

Now determinateness, it is true, is the *abstract*, as against the *other*, determinateness; but this other is only universality itself which is, therefore, also *abstract*, and the determinateness of the Notion, or particularity, is again nothing more than a determinate universality. In this, the Notion is *outside itself*; since it is the *Notion* that is here outside itself, the abstract universal contains all the moments of the Notion. It is (*a*) universality, (*b*) determinateness, (*c*) the *simple* unity of both; but this unity is *immediate*, and therefore particularity is not present as totality. *In itself* it is also this *totality* and *mediation*; it is essentially an *exclusive* relation to an *other*, or sublation of the negation, namely, of the *other* determinateness—an *other*, however, that exists only in imagination, for it vanishes immediately and shows itself to be the same as its supposed *other*. Therefore, what makes this universality abstract is that the mediation is only a *condition* or is not *posited in the universality* itself. Because it is not *posited*, the unity of the *abstract* universality has the form of immediacy, and the content has the form of indifference to its universality, for the content is not present as the totality which is the universality of absolute negativity. Hence the abstract universal is, indeed, the Notion, yet it is without the Notion; it is the Notion that is not posited as such.

When people talk of the *determinate Notion*, what is usually meant is merely such an *abstract universal*. Even by *notion* as such, what is generally understood is only this notion that is no Notion, and the understanding denotes the faculty of such notions. *Demonstration* appertains to this understanding in so far as it *progresses* by *notions*, that is to say, merely by *determinations*. Such a progression by notions, therefore, does not get beyond finitude and necessity; for it, the highest is the negative infinite, the abstraction of the supreme being [*des höchsten Wesen*], which is itself the determinateness of *indeterminateness*. Absolute substance, too, though it is not this empty abstraction—from the point of view of its content it is rather the totality—is nevertheless abstract because it lacks the absolute form; its inmost truth is not constituted by the Notion; true, it is the identity of universality and particularity, or of thought and asunderness, yet this identity is not the *determinateness* of the Notion; on the contrary, *outside* substance there is an understanding—and just because it is outside it, a contingent understanding—in which and for which substance is present in various attributes and modes.

Moreover, abstraction is not *empty* as it is usually said to be; it is the *determinate* Notion and has some determinateness or other for its content. Even the supreme being, the pure abstraction, has, as already remarked, the determinateness of indeterminateness; but indeterminateness is a determinateness, because it is supposed to stand *opposed* to the determinate. But the enunciation of what it is, itself sublates what it is supposed to be; it is enunciated as one with determinateness, and in this way, out of the abstraction is established its truth and the Notion. But every determinate Notion

U

is, of course, *empty* in so far as it does not contain the totality, but only a one-sided determinateness. Even when it has some other concrete content, for example man, the state, animal, etc., it still remains an empty Notion, since its determinateness is not the *principle* of its differences; a principle contains the beginning and the essential nature of its development and realization; any other determinateness of the notion, however, is sterile. To reproach the Notion generally with being empty, is to misjudge that absolute determinateness of the Notion which is the difference of the Notion and the only true content in the element of the Notion.

Connected with the above is the reason why latterly the understanding has been so lightly esteemed and ranked as inferior to reason; it is the *fixity* which it imparts to determinatenesses and consequently to finite determinations. This fixity consists in the form of abstract universality which we have just considered; through it they become *unalterable*. For qualitative determinateness and also the determinations of reflection are essentially *limited*, and through their limitation have a relation to their *other*; hence the *necessity* of transition and passing away. But the universality which they possess in the understanding gives them the form of reflection-into-self by which they are freed from the relation-to-other and have become *imperishable*. Now though in the pure Notion this eternity belongs to its nature, yet its abstract determinations are eternal essentialities only in respect of *their form*; but their content is at variance with this form; therefore they are not truth, or imperishable. Their content is at variance with the form because it is not the determinateness itself as universal, that is, is not totality of the Notion's difference, or is not itself the whole form; but the form of the limited understanding is itself the imperfect form, namely, *abstract* universality. But further, we must recognize the infinite force of the understanding in splitting the concrete into abstract determinatenesses and plumbing the depth of the difference, the force that at the same time is alone the power that effects their transition. The concrete of *intuition* is a *totality*, but a sensuous one—a real material which has an indifferent, *sundered* existence in space and time; but surely this absence of unity in the manifold, where it is the content of intuition, ought not to be counted to it for merit and superiority over intellectual existence. The mutability that it exhibits in intuition already points to the universal; yet all that it brings to view is merely *another*, equally mutable, material; therefore, only the same thing again, not the universal which should appear and take its place. But least of all in sciences such as geometry and arithmetic, should we count it as a merit that their material involves an *intuitive* element, or imagine that their propositions are established on it. On the contrary, it is on account of that element that the material of such sciences is of an inferior nature; the intuition of figures or numbers does not procure a *scientific* knowledge of them; only *thinking* about them can do this. But if by intuition we are to understand not merely the element of sense but the *objective totality*, then it is an *intellectual* intuition; that is to say, intuition has for its object not the external side of existence, but what existence holds of imperishable reality and truth—reality, only in so far as it is essentially in the Notion and *determined* by it, the Idea, whose more precise nature has to reveal itself at a later stage. The advantage which intuition as such is supposed to have over the Notion is external reality, the Notionless element, which first receives a value through the Notion.

Since, therefore, understanding exhibits the infinite force which determines the universal, or conversely, imparts through the form of universality a fixity and subsistence to the determinateness that is in and for itself transitory, then it is not the fault of the understanding if no progress is made beyond this point. It is a subjective *impotence of reason* which adopts these determinatenesses in their fixity, and which is unable to bring them back to their unity through the dialectical force opposed to this abstract universality, in other words, through their own peculiar nature or through their Notion. The understanding does indeed give them, so to speak, a rigidity of *being* such as they do not possess in the qualitative sphere and in the sphere of reflection; but at the same time it *spiritually impregnates* them and so sharpens them, that just at this extreme point alone they acquire the capability to dissolve themselves and to pass over into their opposite. The highest maturity, the highest stage, which anything can attain is that in which its downfall begins. The fixity of the determinateness into which the understanding seems to run, the form of the imperishable, is that of self-relating universality. But this belongs properly to the Notion; and consequently in this universality is to be found expressed, and infinitely close at hand, the *dissolution* of the finite. This universality directly refutes [*arguiert*] the determinateness of

the finite and *expresses* its incongruity with the universality. Or
rather we can say that the adequacy of the finite is already to
hand; the abstract determinate is posited as one with the universality, and for that very reason is posited as not for itself—for
then it would be only a determinate—but only as unity of itself
and the universal, that is, as Notion.

Therefore the usual practice of separating understanding and
reason is, from every point of view, to be rejected. When the
Notion is regarded as irrational, this should be interpreted rather
as an incapacity of reason to recognize itself in the Notion. The
determinate and abstract Notion is the *condition*, or rather an
essential moment of reason; it is form spiritually impregnated, in
which the finite, through the universality in which it relates itself
to itself, spontaneously catches fire, posits itself as dialectical and
thereby is the *beginning* of the manifestation of reason.

In the foregoing, the determinate Notion has been presented
in its truth, and therefore it only remains to indicate what it is as
already posited therein. Difference, which is an essential moment
of the Notion though not yet posited as such in the pure
universal, receives its due in the determinate Notion. Determinateness in the form of universality is linked with the universal to
form a simple determination; this determinate universal is the
self-related determinateness; it is the determinate determinateness
or absolute negativity posited *for itself*. But the self-related determinateness is *individuality*. Just as universality is immediately in
and for itself already particularity, so too particularity is immediately in and for itself also *individuality*; this individuality is, in
the first instance, to be regarded as the third moment of the
Notion, in so far as we hold on to its *opposition* to the two other
moments, but it is also to be considered as the absolute return of
the Notion into itself, and at the same time as the posited loss of
itself.

Remark. *Universality, particularity*, and *individuality* are, according
to the foregoing exposition, the *three* determinate Notions, that is,
if one insists on *counting* them. We have already shown that number
is an unsuitable form in which to hold Notional determinations;
but for the determinations of the Notion itself it is unsuitable in
the highest degree; number, since it has the unit [*das Eins*] for its
principle, converts them as *counted* into completely isolated and

mutually indifferent determinations. We have seen from the foregoing that the truth is that the different determinate Notions, far from falling apart into number, are simply only *one* and the same Notion.

In the customary treatment of logic hitherto, various *classifications* and *species* of notions occur. We are at once struck by the inconsequential way in which the species of notions are introduced: *there are*, in respect of quantity, quality, etc., the following notions. *There are*, expresses no other justification than that we *find* such species *already to hand* and they present themselves *empirically*. In this way, we obtain an *empirical logic*—an odd science this, an *irrational* cognition of the *rational*. In proceeding thus, logic sets a very bad example of obedience to its own precepts; it permits itself for its own purpose to do the opposite of what it prescribes as a rule, namely that notions should be deduced, and scientific propositions (therefore also the proposition: there are such and such species of notions) should be proved. In this matter, the Kantian philosophy commits a further inconsequence: it *borrows* the categories, as so-called root notions, for the *transcendental logic*, from the subjective logic in which they were adopted empirically. Since it admits the latter fact, it is hard to see why transcendental logic resolves to borrow from such a science instead of directly resorting to experience.

To cite some details of this, notions are mainly classified according to their *clearness*, into *clear* and *obscure, distinct* and *indistinct, adequate* and *inadequate*. To these we can also add *complete, profuse,* [*überfliessend*] notions and suchlike superfluities. As regards the classification by *clearness*, it is readily seen that this standpoint and its related distinctions are taken from *psychological*, not from *logical*, determinations. The so-called *clear* notion is supposed to suffice for distinguishing one object from another; but this is not yet a notion, it is nothing more than a *subjective representation*. What an *obscure* notion is must be left to itself, for otherwise it would not be an obscure but a distinct notion. The *distinct* notion is supposed to be one whose *marks* can be indicated. As such it is, strictly speaking, the *determinate* notion. The *mark*, if it is taken in its correct meaning, is none other than the *determinateness* or the simple *content* of the notion, in so far as it is distinguished from the form of universality. But the *mark*, in the first instance, does not have quite this preciser meaning but is in general merely a determination whereby a *third* something takes note of an object, or the notion; it can therefore be a very contingent circumstance. In general it expresses not so much the immanence and essential nature of the determination as its relation to an understanding *external* to it. If this is really an understanding, it has the notion before it and distinguishes this only and solely by *what is in the notion*. But if the mark is supposed to be distinct from the notion, then it is a *sign* or some other determination which belongs to the *representation* of the thing, not to its notion. What the *indistinct* notion may be, can be passed over as superfluous.

But the *adequate* notion is something higher; what it really implies is the agreement of the Notion with reality, which is not the Notion as such but the *Idea*.

If the *mark* of the distinct notion were really supposed to be the determination of the notion itself, logic would find itself in difficulty over the *simple* notions which, according to another classification, are opposed to *compound*. For if a true, that is an immanent, mark of the simple notion were to be indicated, we should not be regarding it as simple; but in so far as no mark was given, it would not be a distinct notion. But here, now, the *clear* notion helps out. Unity, reality, and suchlike determinations are supposed to be *simple* notions, probably only because logicians were unable to discover their specific nature and contented themselves with having merely a *clear* notion of them, that is, no notion at all. *Definition*, that is, the statement of the notion, in general demands the statement of the genus and the specific difference. Therefore it presents the notion, not as something simple, but in *two* countable *components*. Yet surely no one will for that reason suppose such notion to be a *compound*. The simple notion seems to suggest *abstract simplicity*, a unity which does not contain within itself difference and determinateness and which therefore, too, is not the unity that belongs to the Notion. In so far as an object is present in ordinary thinking, especially in memory, or even as an abstract thought determination, it can be quite simple. Even the object that is richest in content, such as, for example, spirit, nature, the world, even God, when uncomprehendingly taken up into the simple representation of the equally simple expression: spirit, nature, the world, God, is doubtless something simple at which consciousness can stop short without going on to pick out its peculiar determination or its mark. But the objects of consciousness should not remain simple, should not remain such representations or abstract thought determinations; on the contrary, they should be *comprehended*, that is to say, their simplicity should be determined with their inner difference. The *compound* notion, however, is a contradiction in terms. We can, of course, have a notion of something composite; but a compound notion would be something worse than *materialism*, which assumes only the *substance* of the *soul* to be composite, yet none the less takes *thought* to be *simple*. Uneducated reflection first stumbles on the idea of composition, because it is the completely *external* relation, the worst form in which anything can be considered; even the lowest natures must be an *inner* unity. That the form of the untruest existence should be assigned, above all, to the ego, to the Notion, that is something we should not have expected and that can only be described as inept and barbarous.

Further, notions are divided mainly into *contrary* and *contradictory*. If, in our treatment of the notion, we are supposed to state what *determinate* notions there are, then we must adduce all possible determinations—for *all* determinations are notions, consequently determinate notions—and all the categories of *being* as well as all determinations of *essence*, would have to be adduced under the species of notions. Just as in the text-books of logic—to a greater or lesser degree, according to the whim of the author—it is related that there are *affirmative, negative, identical, conditional, necessary* notions, and so on. As the *nature of the Notion itself* has progressed beyond all such determinations and therefore these, if adduced in connexion with the *Notion*, occur out of their proper place, they only admit of superficial definitions and appear at this stage devoid of all interest. At the basis of *contrary* and *contradictory* notions—a distinction to which particular attention is paid here—lies the reflective determination of *diversity* and *opposition*. They are regarded as two particular *species*, that is, each as firmly fixed on its own account and indifferent to the other, without any thought of the dialectic and the inner nullity of these differences—as though what is *contrary* must not equally be determined as *contradictory*. The nature and the essential transition of the forms of reflection which they express have been considered in their proper place. In the Notion, identity has developed into universality, difference into particularity, opposition, which withdraws into the ground, into individuality. In these forms, those categories of reflection are present as they are in their Notion. The universal has proved itself to be not only the identical, but at the same time the different or *contrary* as against the particular and individual, and in addition, also to be opposed to them or *contradictory*; in this opposition, however, it is identical with them and is their true ground in which they are sublated. The same holds good of particularity and individuality which are likewise the totality of the determinations of reflection.

A further classification of notions is into *subordinate* and *co-ordinate*—a distinction which approaches more closely to the determination of the Notion, namely, the relationship of universality and particularity, where these terms, too, have been mentioned in passing. Only it is customary to regard them likewise as completely rigid relationships and from this point of view to put forward a number of sterile propositions about them. The most prolix discussion on this point concerns again the relation of contrariety and contradiction to subordination and co-ordination. Since *the judgement is the relation of determinate Notions*, it is only at that stage that the true relationship will come to view. That fashion of *comparing* these determinations without a thought for their dialectic or for the progressive alteration of their determination, or rather for the conjunction of opposed determinations present in them, makes the whole consideration of what is *concordant* or not concordant in them—as though the concord or discord were something *separate* and *permanent*—into something merely sterile and meaningless.

The great *Euler*, who displayed an infinitely fertile and acute mind in seizing and combining the deeper relations of algebraic magnitudes, the dry, prosaic Lambert in particular, and others, have attempted to construct a *notation* for this class of relation between determinations of the Notion by lines, figures and the like, the general intention being to *elevate*, or rather in fact *to degrade*, the logical modes of relation to a *calculus*. The utter futility of even attempting a notation is at once apparent when one compares the nature of the sign and what it is supposed to signify. The determinations of the Notion, universality, particularity and individuality, are certainly *diverse*, as are lines, or the letters of algebra; further, they are also *opposed*, and to this extent would also admit of the signs *plus* and *minus*. But they themselves, and above all their relations—even if one stops at *subsumption* and *inherence*—are in their essential nature entirely different from letters and lines and their relationships, the equality or difference of magnitude, the *plus* and *minus*, or a superimposition of lines, or their joining to form angles and the dispositions of spaces enclosed by them. It is characteristic of such objects that, in contrast to determinations of the Notion, they are mutually *external*, and have a *fixed* character. Now when Notions are so taken that they correspond to such signs, they cease to be Notions. Their determinations are not inert entities like numbers and lines whose relation does not itself belong to them; they are living movements; the distinguished determinateness of the one side is immediately internal to the other side too. What would be a complete contradiction in the case of numbers and lines is essential to the nature of the Notion. Higher mathematics, which also goes on to the infinite and allows itself contradictions, can no longer employ its usual signs for representing such determinations. To denote the conception—which is still very far from being a Notion —of the *infinite approximation* of two ordinates, or in equating a curve with an infinite number of infinitesimal straight lines, all it does is to draw two straight lines *apart from each other* and to make the straight lines approach the curve but remain *distinct* from it; for the infinite, which is here the point of interest, it refers us to *pictorial thinking*.

What has misled logicians into this attempt is primarily the *quantitative* relationship in which *universality, particularity* and *individuality* are supposed to stand to one another; the universal means, *more extensive* than the particular and the individual, and the particular means, *more extensive* than the individual. The Notion is the most concrete and richest determination because it is the ground and the *totality* of the preceding determinations, of the categories of being and of the determinations of reflection; these, therefore, are certainly also present in it. But its nature is completely misunderstood when they are retained in it in their former abstraction, when the *wider extent* of the universal is taken to mean that it is something *more* or a greater *quantum* than the particular and the individual. As absolute ground, it is the *possibility* of *quantity*, but equally so of *quality*, that is, its determinations are just as much qualitatively distinct; therefore they are taken in direct opposition to their truth when they are posited

U*

under the form of quantity alone. Thus, too, the determination of reflection is a *correlate* in which its opposite has an illusory being [*scheint*]; it is not in an external relationship like a quantum. But the Notion is more than all this; its determinations are determinate *Notions*, are themselves essentially the *totality* of all determinations. It is therefore quite inappropriate for the purpose of grasping such an inner totality, to seek to apply numerical and spatial relationships in which all determinations fall asunder; on the contrary, they are the last and worst medium which could be employed. Natural relationships such as magnetism, or colour relations, would be infinitely higher and truer symbols for the purpose. Since man has in language a means of designation peculiar to Reason, it is an idle fancy to search for a less perfect mode of representation to plague oneself with. It is essentially only spirit that can comprehend the Notion as Notion; for this is not merely the property of spirit but spirit's pure self. It is futile to seek to fix it by spatial figures and algebraic signs for the purpose of the *outer eye* and an *uncomprehending, mechanical mode of treatment* such as a *calculus*. In fact, anything else which might be supposed to serve as a symbol can at most, like symbols for the nature of God, evoke intimations and echoes of the Notion; if, however, one should seriously propose to employ them for expressing and cognizing the Notion, then the *external nature* of all symbols is inadequate to the task; the truth about the relationship is rather the converse, namely, that what in symbols is an echo of a higher determination, is only truly known through the Notion and can be approximated to the Notion only by *separating off* the sensuous, unessential part that was meant to express it.

C. THE INDIVIDUAL

Individuality, as we have seen, is already posited by particularity; this is *determinate universality* and therefore self-related determinateness, the determinate determinate.

1. In the first instance, therefore, individuality appears as the *reflection* of the Notion out of its determinateness *into itself*. It is the self-*mediation* of the Notion in so far as its *otherness* has made itself into an *other* again, whereby the Notion has reinstated itself as self-identical, but in the determination of *absolute negativity*. The negative in the universal whereby this is a *particular*, was

defined above as a twofold illusory being; in so far as the negative
is an illusory being *within* the universal, the particular remains a
universal; through the reference of the illusory being outwards it
is a *determinate*; the return of this side into the universal is twofold:
either through *abstraction* which lets drop the particular and rises
to the *higher* and the *highest genus, or else* through the *individuality*
to which the universal in the determinateness itself descends.
Here is where the false path branches off and abstraction strays
from the highway of the Notion and forsakes the truth. Its higher
and highest universal to which it raises itself is only the surface,
which becomes ever more destitute of content; the individuality it
despises is the profundity in which the Notion seizes itself and is
posited as Notion.

Universality and *particularity* appeared, on the one hand, as
moments of the *becoming* of individuality. But it has already been
shown that they are in themselves the total Notion, and consequently in *individuality* do not pass over into an *other*, but that in
individuality there is only posited what they are in and for themselves. The *universal is for itself* because it is in its own self
absolute mediation, self-reference only as absolute negativity. It is
an *abstract* universal in so far as this sublating is an *external* act
and so a *dropping* of the determinateness. This negativity, therefore,
certainly attaches to the abstract universal, but remains *outside* as
a mere *condition* of it; it is the abstractive activity itself, which holds
its universal *away* and *opposite* it and which therefore does not have
individuality within itself, and remains destitute of the Notion.
Life, spirit, God—the pure Notion itself, are beyond the grasp of
abstraction, because it deprives its products of singularity, of the
principle of individuality and personality, and so arrives at nothing
else but universalities devoid of life, spirit, colour and filling.

Yet the unity of the Notion is so indissoluble that even these
products of abstraction, though they are supposed to drop individuality are, on the contrary, *individuals* themselves. Abstraction
raises the concrete into universality in which, however, the
universal is grasped only as a determinate universality; and this is
precisely the individuality that has shown itself to be self-related
determinateness. Abstraction, therefore, is a *sundering* of the
concrete and an *isolating* of its determinations; through it only
single properties and moments are seized; for its product must
contain what it is itself. But the difference between this individu-

ality of its products and the Notion's individuality is that in the former the individual as *content* and the universal as *form*, are distinct from one another—just because the former is not present as absolute form, as the Notion itself, or the latter is not present as the totality of form. However, this more detailed consideration shows that the abstract product itself is a unity of the individual content and the abstract universality, and is therefore a *concrete* and the opposite of what it aims to be.

For the same reason the *particular*, because it is only the determinate universal, is also an individual, and conversely the individual, because it is the determinate universal, is just as much a particular. If we stick to this abstract determinateness, then the Notion has the three particular determinations, the universal, the particular, and the individual; whereas previously we had given only the universal and the particular as the species of the particular. Since individuality is the return of the Notion, as negative, into itself, this very return from the abstraction which, strictly speaking, is sublated in the return, can be placed *along with* the others as an indifferent moment and counted with them.

If individuality is reckoned as one of the *particular* determinations of the Notion, then particularity is the *totality* which embraces them all; precisely in being this totality it is the concretion of them or individuality itself. But it is also the concrete in accordance with its aspect, noted above, of *determinate universality*; as such it is the *immediate* unity in which none of these moments is posited as distinct or as the determinant, and in this form it will constitute the *middle term of the formal syllogism*.

It is self-evident that each determination made in the preceding exposition of the Notion has immediately dissolved itself and lost itself in its other. Each distinction is confounded in the very attempt to isolate and fix it. Only *mere representational thinking*, for which abstraction has isolated them, is capable of holding the universal, particular and individual rigidly apart; in this way they can be counted, and for a further distinction such thinking holds to the *completely external* one of *being*, namely, *quantity*, which is nowhere less appropriate than here. In individuality, the true relationship mentioned above, the *inseparability* of the Notion's determinations is *posited*; for as negation of the negation it contains their opposition and at the same time contains it in its ground or unity, the effected coincidence of each with its other. As this reflection is in its very own nature universality, it is essentially the negativity of the Notion's determinations, but not merely as if it were a third something distinct from them; on the contrary, it is now posited that *posited being [Gesetztsein]* is *being-in-and-for-itself*; that is, that each of the determinations pertaining to the difference is itself the *totality*. The return of the determinate Notion into itself means that it has the determination of being, *in its determinateness*, the *whole Notion*.

2. But individuality is not only the return of the Notion into itself, but immediately its loss. Through individuality, where the Notion is *internal to itself*, it becomes *external to itself* and enters into actuality. *Abstraction* which, as the *soul* of individuality is the relation of the negative to the negative, is as we have shown not something external to the universal and the particular but immanent in them, and through it they are a concrete, a content, an individual. But as this negativity, individuality is the determinate determinateness, is *differentiation* as such; through this reflection of the difference into itself, the difference becomes fixed; it is only through individuality that the determining of the particular is effected, for *individuality* is that abstraction which, simply as individuality, is now *posited abstraction*.

The individual, therefore, as self-related negativity is the immediate identity of the negative with itself; it is *a being-for-self*. Or it is the abstraction that determines the Notion according to its ideal moment of *being* as an *immediate*. In this way, the individual is a qualitative *one* or a *this*. With this quality it is first, repulsion of itself from *itself*, whereby the many *other* ones are presupposed; *secondly*, it is now a negative relation towards these presupposed *others*, and the individual is in so far *exclusive*. Universality, when related to these individuals as indifferent ones—and related to them it must be because it is a moment of the Notion of individuality—is merely their *common element*. When one understands by the universal, what is *common* to several individuals, one is starting from the *indifferent* subsistence of these individuals and confounding the immediacy of *being* with the determination of the Notion. The lowest conception one can have of the universal in its connexion with the individual is this external relation of it as merely a *common element*.

The individual, which in the sphere of reflection exists as a *this*, does not have the exclusive relation to another one which belongs to qualitative being-for-self. *This*, as the one reflected into itself, is for itself and without repulsion; or repulsion in this reflection is one with abstraction and is the reflecting *mediation* which attaches to the this in such wise that the this is a *posited* immediacy *pointed out* by someone external to it. The *this is*; it is *immediate*; but it is only this in so far as it is *pointed out*. The 'pointing out' is the reflecting movement which collects itself inwardly and posits immediacy, but as a self-external immediacy. Now the individual is certainly a this, as the immediate restored out of mediation; but it does not have the mediation outside it—it is itself a repelling separation, *posited abstraction*, yet in its very act of separating, it is a positive relation.

This act of abstraction by the individual, being the reflection of the difference into itself, is first a positing of the differentiated moments as *self-subsistent* and reflected-into-self. They immediately *are*; but further, this sundering is reflection as such, the *illusory being of the one in the other*; thus they stand in essential relation. Further, the individuals are not merely *inertly* present in relation to one another; such plurality belongs to being; the *individuality*, in positing itself as determinate, posits itself not in an external difference but in the difference of the Notion. It therefore excludes the *universal* from itself; yet since this is a moment of individuality, the universal is equally essentially related to it.

The Notion, as this relation of its *self-subsistent* determinations, has lost itself; for as such it is no longer their *posited unity*, and they are no longer present as *moments*, as the *illusory being*, of the Notion, but as subsistent in and for themselves. As individuality, the Notion in its determinateness returns into itself, and therewith the determinate moment has itself become a totality. Its return into itself is therefore the absolute, original *partition of itself*, or, in other words, it is posited as *judgement*.

CHAPTER 2

THE JUDGEMENT

The judgement is the *determinateness* of the Notion *posited* in the *Notion* itself. The Notion's determinations, or what we have seen to be the same thing, the determinate Notions, have already been considered on their own; but this consideration was more a subjective reflection or subjective abstraction. But the Notion is itself this abstractive process, the opposing of its determinations is its own determining activity. The judgement is this positing of the determinate Notions by the Notion itself. Judging is thus *another* function than comprehension, or rather it is *the other* function of the Notion as the *determining* of the Notion by itself, and the further progress of the judgement into the diversity of judgements is the progressive determination of the Notion. What kinds of determinate Notions *there are*, and how these determinations of the Notion are arrived at, has to reveal itself in the judgement.

The judgement can therefore be called the proximate *realization* of the Notion, inasmuch as reality denotes in general entry into *existence* as a *determinate being*. More precisely, the nature of this realization has presented itself in such a manner that, on the one hand, the moments of the Notion through its reflection-into-self or its individuality are self-subsistent totalities, while on the other hand the unity of the Notion is *their relation*. The determinations reflected into themselves are *determinate totalities*, no less essentially in their indifferent and disconnected subsistence as through their reciprocal mediation with one another. The determining itself is only totality in that it contains these totalities and their connexion. This totality is the judgement. It contains, therefore, first, the two self-subsistents which are called subject and predicate. What each is cannot yet really be said; they are still indeterminate, for it is only through the judgement that they are to be determined. The judgement, being the Notion as determinate, the only distinction present is the general one that the judgement contains the *determinate* Notion over against the still *indeterminate* Notion. The subject can therefore, in the first instance, be taken in relation to the predicate as the individual over against the universal, or even as the particular over against the universal, or as the individual over against the particular; so far, they confront each other only in general, as the more determinate and the more universal.

It is therefore appropriate and necessary to have these *names*, subject and predicate for the determinations of the judgement; as names, they are something indeterminate that still awaits its determination, and are, therefore, no more than names. It is partly for this reason that the Notion determinations themselves could not be used for the two sides of the judgement; but a stronger reason is because the nature of the Notion determination is emphatically to be, not something abstract and fixed, but to have and to posit its opposite within it; since the sides of the judgement are themselves Notions and therefore the totality of its determinations, each side must run through all these determinations and exhibit them within itself, whether in abstract or concrete form. Now in order to fix the sides of the judgement in a general way when their determination is altered, those names are most serviceable which remain the same throughout the alteration. The name however stands over against the matter in hand or the Notion; this distinction presents itself in the judgement as such; now the subject is in general the determinate, and is therefore more that which *immediately is*, whereas the predicate expresses the *universal*, the essential nature [*Wesen*] or the Notion; therefore the subject as such is, in the first instance, only a kind of *name*; for *what it is* is first enunciated by the predicate which contains *being* in the sense of the Notion. In the question: what *is* this? or: what kind of a plant *is* this? *what* is often understood by the *being* enquired after, is merely the *name*, and when this is learned one is satisfied and now knows what the thing *is*. This is being in the sense of the subject. But the *Notion*, or at least the essence and the universal in general, is first given by the predicate, and it is this that is asked for in the sense of the judgement. Consequently, God, spirit, nature, or whatever it may be, is as the subject of a judgement at first only the name; what such a subject *is* as regards its Notion is first enunciated in the predicate. When enquiry is made as to the kind of predicate belonging to such subject, the act of judgement necessarily implies an underlying Notion. But this Notion is first enunciated by the predicate itself.

Properly speaking, therefore, it is the mere *general idea* [*Vorstellung*] that constitutes the presupposed meaning of the subject and that leads to the naming of it; and in doing this it is contingent and a historical fact, what is, or is not, to be understood by a name. So many disputes about whether a predicate does or does not belong to a certain subject are therefore nothing more than verbal disputes, because they start from the form above mentioned; what lies at the base (*subjectum*, ὑποκείμενον) is so far nothing more than the name.

We have now to examine, secondly, how the *relation* of subject and predicate in the judgement is determined and how subject and predicate themselves are at first determined through this very relation. The judgement has in general for its sides totalities which to begin with are essentially self-subsistent. The unity of the Notion is, therefore, at first only a *relation* of self-subsistents; not as yet the *concrete* and *pregnant* unity that has returned into itself from this reality, but only a unity *outside* which the self-subsistent sides persist as *extremes that are not sublated in it*. Now consideration of the judgement can begin from the original unity of the Notion, or from the self-subsistence of the extremes. The judgement is the self-diremption of the Notion; *this unity* is, therefore, the ground from which the consideration of the judgement in accordance with its true *objectivity* begins. It is thus the *original division* [*Teilung*] of what is originally one; thus the word *Urteil* refers to what judgement is in and for itself. But regarded from the side of externality, the Notion is present in the judgement as *Appearance*, since its moments therein attain self-subsistence, and it is on this *external* side that ordinary thinking tends to fasten.

From this *subjective* standpoint, then, subject and predicate are considered to be complete, each on its own account, apart from the other: the subject as an object that would exist even if it did not possess this predicate; the predicate as a universal determination that would exist even if it did not belong to this subject. From this standpoint, the act of judgement involves the reflection, whether this or that predicate which is in someone's *head* can and should be *attached* to the *object* which exists on its own account *outside*; the very act of judging consists in this, that only through it is a predicate *combined* with a subject, so that, if this combination did not take place, each on its own would still remain what it is, the latter an existent object, the former an idea in someone's head. The predicate which is attached to the subject should, however, also *belong* to it, that is, be in and for itself identical with it. Through this significance of *attachment*, the *subjective* meaning of judgement and the indifferent, outer subsistence of subject and predicate are sublated again: this action *is* good; the *copula* indicates that the predicate belongs to the *being* of the subject and is not merely externally combined with it. In the *grammatical* sense, that subjective relationship in which one starts from the indifferent externality of the subject and predicate has its complete validity; for it is *words* that are here externally combined. We may take this opportunity of remarking, too, that though a *proposition* has a subject and predicate in the grammatical sense, this does not make it a *judgement*. The latter requires that the predicate be related to the subject as one Notion determination to another, and therefore as a universal to a particular or individual. If a statement about a particular subject only enunciates something individual, then this is a mere proposition, For example, 'Aristotle died at the age of 73, in the fourth year of the 115th Olympiad,' is a mere proposition, not a judgement. It would partake of the nature of a judgement only if doubt had been thrown on one of the circumstances, the date of the death, or the age of that philosopher, and the given figures had been asserted on the strength of some reason or other. In that case, these figures would be taken as something universal, as time that still subsists apart from this particular content of the death of Aristotle, whether as time filled with some other content, or even as empty time. Similarly, the news that my friend N. has died is a proposition; and it would be a judgement only if there were a question whether he was really dead or only in a state of catalepsy.

In the usual way of defining the judgement we may indeed accept the indeterminate expression *connexion* for the external *copula*, as also that the connected terms are at least *supposed* to be notions. But in other respects this definition is superficial in the extreme: not only, for example, that in the disjunctive judgement more than *two* so-called notions are connected, but rather that the definition is far better than its subject matter; for it is not notions at all that are meant, hardly determinations of the Notion, but really only determinations of representational thought; it was remarked in connexion with the Notion in general and the determinate Notion, that what is usually so named by no means deserves the name of Notion; where then should Notions come from in the case of the judgement? Above all, in this definition the essential feature of the judgement, namely, the difference of its determinations, is passed over; still less does it take into account the relationship of the judgement to the Notion.

As regards the further determination of the subject and predicate, we have remarked that it is really in the judgement first that they have to receive their determination. Since the judgement is the posited determinateness of the Notion, this determinateness possesses the said differences *immediately* and *abstractly* as *individuality* and *universality*. But in so far as the judgement is in general the *determinate being* or *otherness* of the Notion which has not yet restored itself to the unity whereby it is *as Notion*, there emerges also the determinateness which is notionless, the opposition of *being* and *reflection* or the *in-itself*. But since the Notion constitutes the essential *ground* of the judgement, these determinations are at least indifferent to the extent that when one belongs to the subject and the other to the predicate, the converse relationship equally holds good. The *subject* as the *individual* appears, in the first instance, as that which *simply is* or *is for itself* in accordance with the specific determinateness of the individual—as an actual object, even though it be only an object in representational thought—as for example bravery, right, agreement, etc.—on which judgement is being made. The *predicate*, on the other hand, as the *universal*, appears as this *reflection* on the object, or rather as the object's reflection into itself, which goes beyond that immediacy and sublates the determinatenesses in their form of mere being; that is, it is the *object's in-itself*. In this way, one starts from the individual as the first, the immediate, and it is *raised* by the judgement into *universality*, just as, conversely, the universal that is only *in itself* descends in the individual into determinate being or becomes a being that is *for itself*.

This signification of the judgement is to be taken as its *objective* meaning, and at the same time as the *truth* of the earlier forms of the transition. In the sphere of being, the object *becomes* and *others itself* [*verändert sich*], the finite *perishes* or *goes under* [*geht unter*] in the infinite; in the sphere of Existence, the object *issues from* its *ground* into Appearance and *falls to the ground* [*geht zugrunde*], the accident *manifests* the *wealth* of substance as well as its *power*; in being, there is *transition* into an *other*, in essence, reflected being in an *other* by which the *necessary* relation is revealed. This movement of transition and reflection [*Scheinen*] has now passed over into the *original partition* [*Teilen*] of the *Notion* which, while bringing back the individual to the *in-itself* of its universality, equally determines the universal as something *actual*. These two acts are one and the same process in which individuality is posited in its reflection-into-self, and the universal as determinate.

But now this objective signification equally implies that the said differences, in reappearing in the determinateness of the Notion, are at the same time posited only as *Appearances*, that is, that they are not anything fixed, but apply just as much to the one Notion determination as to the other. The subject is, therefore, just as much to be taken as the *in-itself*, and the predicate, on the other hand, as *determinate being*. The *subject without predicate* is what the *thing without qualities*, the *thing-in-itself* is in the sphere of Appearance—an empty, indeterminate ground; as such, it is the Notion enclosed within itself, which only receives a differentiation and determinateness in the predicate; the predicate therefore constitutes the side of the *determinate being* of the subject. Through this determinate universality the subject stands in relation to an externality, is open to the influence of other things and thereby becomes actively opposed to them. *What is there* comes forth from its *being-within-self* and enters into the *universal* element of connexion and relationship, into the negative connexions and the interplay of actuality, which is a *continuation* of the individual into other individuals and therefore universality.

The identity just demonstrated, namely, that the determination of the subject equally applies to the predicate and vice versa, is not, however, something only *for us*; it is not merely *in itself*, but is also posited in the judgement; for the judgement is the connexion of the two; the copula expresses that *the subject is the predicate*. The subject is the specific determinateness, and the predicate is this *posited* determinateness of the subject; the subject is determined only in its predicate, or, only in the predicate is it a subject; in the predicate it has returned into itself and is therein the universal. Now in so far as the subject is the self-subsistent, this identity has the relationship that the predicate does not possess a self-subsistence of its own, but has its subsistence only in the subject; it *inheres* in the subject. Since the predicate is thus distinct from the subject, it is only an *isolated* determinateness of the latter, only *one* of its properties; while the subject itself is the *concrete*, the totality of manifold determinatenesses, just as the predicate contains *one*; it is the universal. But on the other hand the predicate, too, is a self-subsistent universality and the subject, conversely, only a determination of it. Looked at this way, the predicate *subsumes* the subject; individuality and particularity are not for themselves, but have their essence and substance in the universal. The predicate expresses the subject in its Notion; the individual and the particular are contingent determinations in the subject; it is their absolute possibility. When in the case of *subsumption* one thinks of an external connexion of subject and predicate and the subject is conceived of as a self-subsistent something, the subsumption refers to the subjective act of judgement above-mentioned in which one starts from the self-subsistence of both subject and predicate. From this standpoint subsumption is only the *application* of the universal to a particular or an individual, which is placed *under* the universal in accordance with a vague idea that it is of inferior quality.

When the identity of subject and predicate are so taken that *at one time* one Notion determination applies to the former and the other to the latter, and *at another time* the converse equally holds good, then the identity is as yet still only an *implicit* one; on account of the self-subsistent diversity of the two sides of the judgement, their *posited* unity also has these two sides, in the first instance as different. But *differenceless identity* really constitutes the *true* relation of the subject to the predicate. The Notion determination is itself essentially *relation* for it is a *universal*; therefore the same determinations possessed by the subject and predicate are also possessed by their relation itself. The relation is universal, for it is the positive identity of the two, of subject and predicate; but it is also *determinate*, for the determinateness of the predicate is that of the subject; further, it is also *individual*, for in it the self-subsistent extremes are sublated as in their negative unity. However, in the judgement this identity is not as yet posited; the copula is present as the still indeterminate relation of *being* as such: A is B; for in the judgement, the self-subsistence of the Notion determinatenesses or the extremes, is the *reality* which the Notion has within it. If the *is* of the copula were already *posited* as the above determinate and pregnant *unity* of subject and predicate, as their *Notion*, it would already be *the syllogism*.

To restore this *identity* of the Notion, or rather to *posit* it, is the goal of the *movement* of the judgement. What is already *present* in the judgement is, on the one hand, the self-subsistence of subject and predicate, but also their mutually opposed determinateness, and on the other hand their none the less *abstract* relation. What the judgement enunciates to start with is that *the subject is the predicate*; but since the predicate is supposed *not* to be what the subject is, we are faced with a *contradiction* which must *resolve* itself, *pass over* into a result. Or rather, since subject and predicate are *in and for themselves* the totality of the Notion, and the judgement is the reality of the Notion, its forward movement is only a *development*; there is already present in it what comes forth from it, so that *proof* is merely an *exposition*, a reflection as a *positing* of that which is already *present* in the extremes of the judgement; but even this positing itself is already present; it is the *relation* of the extremes.

The judgement *in its immediacy* is in the first instance the judgement of *existence*; its subject is immediately an *abstract individual* which *simply is*, and the predicate is an *immediate determinateness* or property of the subject, an abstract universal.

This qualitative character of subject and predicate being sublated, the determination of the one is *reflected*, to begin with, in the other; the judgement is now, secondly, the judgement of *reflection*.

But this more external conjunction passes over into the *essential identity* of a substantial, *necessary connexion*; as such it is, thirdly, the judgement of *necessity*.

Fourthly, since in this essential identity the difference of subject and predicate has become a *form*, the judgement becomes *subjective*; it contains the opposition of the *Notion* and its *reality* and the *equation* of the two; it is the *judgement of the Notion*.

This emergence of the Notion establishes the *transition of the judgement into the syllogism*.

A. THE JUDGEMENT OF EXISTENCE

In the subjective judgement we want to see *one and the same* object *double*, first in its individual actuality, and then in its essential identity or in its Notion: the individual raised into its universality, or, what is the same thing, the universal individualized into its actuality. In this way the judgement is *truth*: for it is the agreement of the Notion and reality. But this is not the nature of the judgement *at first*; for *at first* it is immediate, since as yet no reflection and movement of the determinations has appeared in it. This *immediacy* makes the first judgement a *judgement of existence*; it can also be called the *qualitative* judgement, but only in so far as *quality* does not apply only to the determinateness of *being* but also includes the abstract universality which, on account of its simplicity, likewise has the form of *immediacy*.

The judgement of existence is also the judgement of *inherence*; because it is in the form of immediacy, and because the subject as distinguished from the predicate is the immediate, and consequently the primary and essential feature in a judgement of this kind, the predicate has the form of a non-self-subsistent determination that has its foundation in the subject.

(a) The Positive Judgement

1. The subject and predicate as we have remarked, are in the first instance names, which only receive their actual determination through the course of the judgement. However, as sides of the judgement, which is the *posited* determinate Notion, they have the determination of *moments* of the Notion, but by virtue of their immediacy, the determination is still quite *simple*: for it is not enriched by mediation, and also, in accordance with the abstract opposition, it is determined as *abstract individuality* and *universality*. The predicate, to speak of this first, is the *abstract* universal; since this abstract is conditioned by the mediation in which the individual or particular is sublated, this mediation is so far only *presupposition*. In the sphere of the Notion there can be no other *immediacy* than one in which mediation is *essentially* and *explicitly* a moment and which has come to be only through the sublating of that mediation, that is, the immediacy of the *universal*. Thus even *qualitative being*, too, is *in its Notion* a universal; but as *being*, the immediacy is not yet so *posited*; it is only as *universality* that it is the Notion determination in which is *posited* the fact that negativity essentially belongs to it. This relation is given in the judgement in which it is the predicate of a subject. Similarly, the subject is an *abstract* individual, or the *immediate* that is supposed

to be *as such*, and therefore the individual as a *something* in general. Thus the subject constitutes the abstract side of the judgement according to which the Notion has in it passed over into *externality*. As the two Notion determinations are determined, so also is their relation, the *is* or *copula*; it too can only have the significance of an immediate, abstract *being*. On account of the relation which as yet contains no mediation or negation, this judgement is called the *positive*.

2. The immediate pure enunciation of the positive judgement is, therefore, the proposition: *the individual is universal*.

This enunciation must not be put in the form: *A* is *B*; for *A* and *B* are entirely formless and consequently meaningless names; the judgement as such, however, and therefore even the judgement of existence, has Notion determinations for its extremes. *A is B* can represent any mere *proposition* just as well as a *judgement*. But in every judgement, even in those with a more richly determined form, there is asserted the proposition having this specific content: *the individual is universal*; inasmuch, namely, as every judgement is also in general an abstract judgement. With the negative judgement, how far it likewise comes under this expression, we shall deal presently. If no heed is given to the fact that in every judgement—at least, to begin with, every positive judgement, the assertion is made that the individual is a universal, this is partly because the *determinate form* whereby subject and predicate are distinguished is overlooked—the judgement being supposed to be nothing but the relation of *two* notions—and partly, probably, because the rest of the *content* of the judgement, *Gaius is learned*, or *the rose is red*, floats before the mind which is busy with the representation of *Gaius*, etc., and does not reflect on the form—although such content at least as the *logical Gaius* who has usually to be dragged in as an example, is a much less interesting content and, indeed, is expressly chosen as uninteresting in order not to divert attention from the form to itself.

In its objective signification, the proposition that the *individual is universal* connotes, as we previously had occasion to remark, on the one hand the perishableness of individual things, and on the other hand their positive subsistence in the Notion as such. The Notion itself is imperishable, but that which comes forth from it in its partition is subject to alteration and to return into its *universal* nature. But conversely, the universal gives itself a *determinate being.* Just as essence issues into a *reflected being* [*Schein*] in its determinations, ground into the *manifestation* of Existence, and substance into the revelation of itself, into its accidents, so the universal *resolves* itself into the individual; and the judgement is this *explication* of the universal, the *development* of the negativity which it already is in itself. The latter fact is enunciated by the converse proposition, the *universal is individual*, which is equally enunciated in the positive judgement. The subject, which in the first instance is the *immediate individual*, is related in the judgement itself to its *other*, namely, the universal; consequently it is posited as the *concrete*; in the sphere of being as a something *of many qualities*, or as the concrete of reflection, *a thing of manifold properties*, an *actuality of manifold possibilities*, a *substance* of such and such *accidents*. Since these manifold determinations here belong to the subject, the something or the thing, etc., is reflected into itself in its qualities, properties or accidents; or it *continues* itself through them, maintaining itself in them and equally them in itself. The positedness or determinateness belongs to the being-in-and-for-self. The subject is, therefore, in its own self the *universal*. The predicate, on the other hand, as this *universality* which is not real or concrete but *abstract*, is, in contrast to the subject, the *determinateness* and contains only *one moment* of the subject's totality to the exclusion of the others. By virtue of this negativity which, as an extreme of the judgement, is at the same time self-related, the predicate is an *abstract individual*. For example, in the proposition: *the rose is fragrant*, the predicate enunciates only *one* of the *many* properties of the rose; it singles out this particular one which, in the subject, is a concrescence with the others; just as in the dissolution of the thing, the manifold properties which inhere in it, in acquiring self-subsistence as *matters*, become *individualized*. From this side, then, the proposition of the judgement runs thus: *the universal is individual*.

In bringing together this *reciprocal determination* of subject and predicate in the judgement, we get a twofold result. *First* that immediately the subject is, indeed, something that *simply is*, an individual, while the predicate is the universal. But because the judgement is the *relation* of the two, and the subject is determined by the predicate as a universal, the subject is the universal. *Secondly*, the predicate is determined in the subject; for it is not a determination *in general*, but *of the subject*; in the proposition: *the rose is fragrant*, this fragrance is not any indeterminate fragrance, but that of the rose; the predicate is therefore *an individual*. Now since subject and predicate stand in the relationship of the judgement, they have to remain mutually opposed as determinations of the Notion; just as in the *reciprocity* of causality, before it attains its truth, the two sides have to retain their self-subsistence and mutual opposition in face of the sameness of their determination. When, therefore, the subject is determined as a universal, we must not take the predicate also in its determination of universality—else we should not have a judgement—but only in its determination of individuality; similarly, when the subject is determined as an individual, the predicate is to be taken as a universal. Reflection on the above mere identity yields the two identical propositions:

The individual is individual,
The universal is universal,

in which the sides of the judgement would have fallen completely asunder and only their self-relation would be expressed, while their relation to one another would be dissolved and the judgement consequently sublated. Of the two original propositions, one, *the universal is individual*, enunciates the judgement in respect of its *content*, which in the predicate is a singled out determination, while in the subject it is the totality of them; the other, *the individual is universal*, enunciates the *form* which is stated immediately by the proposition itself. In the immediate positive judgement the extremes are still simple: form and content are, therefore, still united. In other words, it does not consist of two propositions; the twofold relation which we found in it directly constitutes the *one* positive judgement. For its extremes appear as (*a*) self-subsistent, abstract sides of the judgement, and (*b*) each side is determined by the other, by virtue of the copula connecting them. But for that very reason, the difference of form and content is *implicit* in it, as we have seen; to wit, what is implied in the first proposition: *the individual is universal*, pertains to the form, because it expresses the *immediate determinateness* of the judgement. On the other hand, the relationship expressed by the other proposition: *the universal is individual*, that is to say, that the subject is determined as universal, but the predicate as particular or individual concerns the *content*; for the sides of the judgement arise only through the reflection-into-self whereby the immediate determinatenesses are sublated, with the result that the form converts itself into an identity that has withdrawn into itself and persists in opposition to the distinction of form: that is, it converts itself into content.

3. Now if the two propositions, the one of form and the other of content:

Subject   *Predicate*

The individual is universal

The universal is individual,

were, because they are contained in the *one* positive judgement, to be united, so that both subject and predicate alike were determined as unity of individuality and universality, then both subject and predicate would be the *particular*; and this must be recognized as *implictly* their inner determination. Only, on the one hand, this combination would only have been effected by an external reflection, and, on the other hand, the resultant proposition, *the particular is the particular*, would no longer be a judgement, but an empty identical proposition like those already derived from the positive judgement, namely, *the individual is individual*, and *the universal is universal*. Individuality and universality cannot yet be united into particularity, because in the positive judgement they are still posited as *immediate*. In other words, the judgement must still be distinguished in respect of its form and content, just because subject and predicate are still distinguished as immediacy and something mediated, or because the judgement, according to its relation, is both self-subsistence of the related sides and also their reciprocal determination or mediation.

First, then, the judgement considered in respect of its *form* asserts that *the individual is universal*. But the truth is that such an *immediate* individual is *not* universal; its predicate is of wider scope and therefore does not correspond to it. The subject is an *immediate* being-for-self and therefore the *opposite* of that abstraction, of that universality posited through mediation, which was supposed to be predicated of it.

Secondly, when the judgement is considered in respect of its *content*, or as the proposition, *the universal is individual*, the subject is a universal of qualities, a concrete that is infinitely determined;

and since its determinatenesses are as yet only qualities, properties or accidents, its totality is the *spuriously infinite plurality*
of them. Such a subject therefore is, on the contrary, *not a single*
property such as its predicate enunciates. Both propositions,
therefore, must be *denied* and the positive judgement must be
posited rather as *negative*.

(b) The Negative Judgement

1. We have already referred above to the prevalent idea that it
depends merely on the content of the judgement whether it be
true or not, since logical truth concerns only the form and demands
only that the said content shall not contradict itself. The form of
the judgement is taken to be nothing more than the relation of
two notions. But we have seen that these two notions do not have
merely the relationless character of a *sum*, but are related to one
another as *individual* and *universal*. These determinations constitute
the truly logical *content*, and, be it noted, constitute in this abstraction the content of the positive judgement; all *other content*
that appears in a judgement (the *sun* is *round*, *Cicero was a great
orator in Rome*, it is *day now*, etc.) does not concern the judgement
as such; the judgement merely enunciates that the *subject* is
predicate, or, more definitely, since these are only names, that
the individual is universal and vice versa. By virtue of this *purely
logical content*, the positive judgement is *not true*, but has its truth
in the negative judgement. All that is demanded of the content
is that it shall not contradict itself in the judgement; but as has
been shown it does contradict itself in the above judgement. It is,
however, a matter of complete indifference if the above logical
content is also called form, and by content is understood merely
the remaining empirical filling; in that case, the form does not
imply merely an empty identity, the determinate content lying
outside it. The positive judgement has, then, through its *form* as
positive judgement no truth; whoever gives the name of *truth*
to the *correctness* of an *intuition* or *perception*, or to the agreement
of the *picture-thought* with the object, at any rate has no expression
left for that which is the subject matter and aim of philosophy. We
should at least have to call the latter the truth of reason; and it will
surely be granted that judgements such as: Cicero was a great
orator, and: it is day now, and so on, are not truths of reason. But
they are not such not because they have, as it were contingently,

an empirical content, but because they are merely positive judgements that can have and are supposed to have no other content than an immediate individual and an abstract determination.

The positive judgement has its proximate truth in the negative: the *individual is not* abstractly *universal—but on the contrary*, the predicate of the individual, because it is such a predicate or—taking it by itself apart from its relation to the subject—because it is an *abstract* universal, is itself determinate; the *individual* is, therefore, *in the first instance* a *particular*. Further, in accordance with the other proposition contained in the positive judgement, the negative judgement asserts that the *universal* is not abstractly *individual, but on the contrary*, this predicate, just because it is a predicate, or because it stands in relation to a universal subject, is something wider than a mere individuality, and the *universal* is therefore likewise *in the first instance* a *particular*. Since this universal, as subject, is itself in the judgement determination of individuality, the two propositions reduce to one: *the individual is a particular*.

We may remark (*a*) that here the predicate proves to be in the determination of *particularity* of which we have already made mention; but here it is not posited by external reflection, but has arisen by means of the negative relation exhibited by the judgement. (*b*) This determination here results only for the predicate. In the *immediate* judgement, the judgement of existence, the subject is the underlying basis; the *determination* seems therefore *to run its course* at first in the *predicate*. But as a matter of fact this first negation cannot as yet be a determination, or strictly speaking a *positing of the individual*, for the individual is the *second* negation, the negative of the negative.

The individual is a particular, is the *positive* expression of the negative judgement. This expression is not itself a positive judgement, for the latter, by reason of its immediacy, has only abstractions for its extremes, while the particular, precisely through the positing of the relation of the judgement presents itself as the first *mediated* determination. But this determination is not to be taken only as moment of the extreme, but also—as it really is in the first instance—as *determination* of the *relation*; in other words, the judgement is to be regarded also as *negative*.

This transition is based on the relationship of the extremes and their connexion generally in the judgement. The positive judgement is the relation of the *immediately* individual and universal, therefore the relation of things, one of which at the same time is *not* what the other is; the relation is, therefore, no less essentially *separation* or *negative*; that is why the positive judgement had to be posited as negative. It was, therefore, unnecessary for logicians to make such a fuss over the *not* of the negative judgement being attached to the *copula*. In the judgement, what is *determination* of the extreme is no less a *determinate relation*. The judgement's determination, or the extreme, is not the purely qualitative determination of *immediate* being which is supposed to confront only an *other outside it*. Nor is it determination of reflection, which, in accordance with its general form, has a positive and negative bearing, each being posited as exclusive, and only *implicitly* identical with the other. The judgement's determination, as determination of the Notion, is in its own self a universal, posited as *continuing* itself into its other determinations. Conversely, the *relation* of the judgement is the same determination as that possessed by the extremes; for it is just this universality and continuation of them into one another; in so far as these are distinguished, the relation also has negativity in it.

The above-stated transition from the form of the *relation* to the form of the *determination* has for its *immediate consequence* that the *not* of the *copula* must no less be attached to the predicate and the predicate determined as the *not-universal*. But by an equally immediate consequence the not-universal is the *particular*. If we stick to the *negative* in the completely abstract determination of immediate *not-being*, then the predicate is only the *completely indeterminate* not-universal. This determination is commonly treated in logic in connexion with *contradictory* notions and it is inculcated as a matter of importance that in the *negative* of a notion one is to stick to the negative only and it is to be regarded as the merely *indeterminate* extent of the *other* of the positive notion. Thus the mere *not-white* would be just as much red, yellow, blue, etc., as black. But *white* as such is a *notionless* determination of intuition; the *not* of white is then equally notionless *not-being*, an abstraction that has been considered at the very beginning of the logic, where we learned that its proximate truth is *becoming*. To employ as examples, when treating of the terms of the judgement, such notionless contents drawn from intuition and pictorial thinking, and to take determinations of *being* and *reflection* for terms of the judgement, is the same *uncritical* procedure as the Kantian application of the notions of the understanding to the infinite Idea of reason or the so-called *thing-in-itself*; the *Notion*, which also includes the *judgement* that proceeds from it, is the veritable *thing-in-itself* or the *rational*; those other determinations, however, are proper to *being* or *essence* and have not yet been developed into forms which exhibit them as they are in their truth, in the *Notion*. If we stop at white and red as *sensuous* images, we are giving, as is commonly done, the name of Notion to what is only a determination of pictorial thinking; in that case the not-white and not-red are of course not positive predicates, just as also the not-triangular is something completely indeterminate, for a determination based on number and quantum is essentially *indifferent* and *notionless*. But this kind of sensuous content, like *not-being* itself, must be *conceptually grasped* and must lose that indifference and abstract immediacy which it has in blind, static, pictorial thinking. Already in determinate being, the meaningless *nothing* becomes the *limit*, through which *something* does, after all, *relate* to an *other* outside it. But in reflection, it is the *negative* that *essentially relates* to a *positive* and hence is *determinate*; a negative is already no longer that *indeterminate not-being*; it is posited as existing only in so far as the positive is its counterpart, the third member of the triad being their *ground*; the negative is thus confined within an enclosed sphere in which, what the one is *not*, is something *determinate*. But more than this, in the absolutely fluid continuity of the Notion and its determinations the *not* is immediately a positive, and the *negation* is not merely a determinateness but is taken up into the universality and posited as identical with it. The not-universal is therefore immediately the *particular*.

2. Since the negation affects the relation of the judgement, and we are dealing with the *negative judgement* still as such, it is *in the first place still a judgement*; consequently we have here the relationship of subject and predicate, or of individuality and universality, and their relation, *the form of the judgement*. The subject as the immediate which forms the basis remains unaffected by the negation; it therefore retains its determination of having a predicate, or its relation to the universality. What is negated, therefore, is not the universality as such in the predicate, but the abstraction or determinateness of the latter which appeared as *content* in contrast to that universality. Thus the negative judge-

ment is not total negation; the universal sphere which contains the predicate still subsists, and therefore the relation of the subject to the predicate is essentially still *positive*; the still remaining *determination* of the predicate is just as much a *relation*. If, for example, it is said that the rose is *not* red, it is only the *determinateness* of the predicate that is negated and separated from the universality which likewise belongs to it; the universal sphere, *colour*, is preserved; in saying that the rose is not red, it is assumed that it *has* a colour, but a different one. In respect of this universal sphere the judgement is still positive.

The individual is a *particular*—this positive form of the negative judgement enunciates immediately that the particular contains universality. But in addition it also expresses that the predicate is not merely a universal but also a determinate universal. The negative form implies the same; for though for example the rose is not red, it must not merely retain the universal sphere of colour for predicate but must also have *some other specific colour*; thus it is only the *single* determinateness of red that is negated; and not only is the universal sphere left but determinateness, too, is preserved, though converted into an *indeterminate* or general determinateness, that is, into particularity.

3. The *particularity* which we have found to be the positive determination of the negative judgement is the mediating term between individuality and universality; thus the negative judgement is now, in general, the mediating term leading to the third step, to the *reflection of the judgement of existence into itself*. It is, in its objective significance, merely the moment of alteration of the accidents—or, in the sphere of existence, of the isolated properties of the concrete. Through this alteration the complete determinateness of the predicate, or the *concrete*, emerges as posited.

The individual is particular, according to the positive enunciation of the negative judgement. But the individual is also *not* a particular, for particularity is of wider extent than individuality; it is therefore a predicate that does not correspond to the subject, and in which, therefore, it does not yet possess its truth. *The individual is only an individual*, the negativity that relates not to an *other* whether positive or negative, but only to itself. The rose is not a thing of *some* colour or *other*, but has only the specific colour that is rose-colour. The individual is not an undetermined determinate, but the determined determinate.

Starting from this positive form of the negative judgement, this negation of it appears again as only a *first* negation. But it is not so. On the contrary, the negative judgement is already in and for itself the second negation or the negation of the negation, and what it is in and for itself must be posited. That is to say, it *negates* the *determinateness* of the predicate of the positive judgement, the predicate's *abstract* universality, or, regarded as content, the single quality which the predicate contains of the subject. But the negation of the determinateness is already the second negation, and therefore the infinite return of individuality into itself. With this, therefore, the *restoration* of the concrete totality has been achieved, or rather, the subject is now for the first time *posited* as an individual, for through negation and the sublating of the negation it is mediated with itself. The predicate, too, on its side, has herewith passed over from the first universality to absolute determinateness and has equated itself with the subject. Thus the judgement runs: the individual is individual. From the other side, inasmuch as the subject was equally to be taken as *universal*, and as the predicate (which in contrast to that determination of the subject is the individual) *widened* itself in the negative judgement into *particularity*, and as now, further, the negation of this *determinateness* is no less the *purification* of the universality contained in the predicate, this judgement also runs: the universal is the universal.

In these two judgements, which we had previously reached by external reflection, the predicate is already expressed in its positivity. But first, the negation of the negative judgement must itself appear in the form of a negative judgement. We saw that in it there still remained a *positive relation* of the subject to the predicate, and the *universal sphere* of the latter. From this side, therefore, the negative contained a universality more purged of limitation than the positive judgement, and for that reason must be all the more negated of the subject as an individual. In this manner, the *whole extent* of the predicate is negated and there is no longer any positive relation between it and the subject. This is the *infinite judgement*.

(c) The Infinite Judgement
The negative judgement is as little a true judgement as the positive. But the infinite judgement which is supposed to be its truth is,

x

according to its negative expression, *negatively infinite*, a judgement in which even the form of judgement is set aside. But this is a *nonsensical judgement*. It is supposed to be a *judgement*, and consequently to contain a relation of subject and predicate; yet *at the same time* such a relation is supposed *not* to be in it. Though the name of the infinite judgement usually appears in the ordinary logics, it is not altogether clear what its nature really is. Examples of negatively infinite judgements are easily obtained: determinations are negatively connected as subject and predicate, one of which not only does not include the determinateness of the other but does not even contain its universal sphere; thus for example spirit is not red, yellow, etc., is not acid, not alkaline, etc., the rose is not an elephant, the understanding is not a table, and the like. These judgements are *correct* or *true*, as the expression goes, but in spite of such truth they are nonsensical and absurd. Or rather, they are *not judgements at all*. A more realistic example of the infinite judgement is the *evil* action. In *civil litigation*, something is negated only as the property of the other party, it being conceded that it should be theirs if they had the right to it; and it is only the title of right that is in dispute; the universal sphere of right is therefore recognized and maintained in that negative judgement. But *crime* is the *infinite judgement* which negates not merely the particular right, but the universal sphere as well, negates *right as right*. This infinite judgement does indeed possess *correctness*, since it is an actual deed, but it is nonsensical because it is related purely negatively to morality which constitutes its universal sphere.

The *positive* moment of the infinite judgement, of the negation of the negation, is the *reflection of individuality* into itself, whereby it is posited for the first time as a *determinate determinateness*. According to that reflection, the expression of the judgement was: *the individual is individual*. In the judgement of existence, the subject appears as an *immediate* individual and consequently rather as a mere *something* in general. It is through the mediation of the negative and infinite judgements that it is for the first time *posited* as an individual.

The individual is hereby *posited* as continuing itself *into its predicate*, which is identical with it; consequently, too, the universality no longer appears as *immediate* but as a *comprehension* of distinct terms. The positively infinite judgement equally runs:

the universal is universal, and as such is equally posited as the return into itself.

Now through this reflection of the terms of the judgement into themselves the judgement has sublated itself; in the negatively infinite judgement the difference is, so to speak, *too great* for it to remain a judgement; the subject and predicate have no positive relation whatever to each other; in the positively infinite judgement, on the contrary, only identity is present and owing to the complete lack of difference it is no longer a judgement.

More precisely, it is the *judgement of existence* that has sublated itself; hereby there is *posited* what the *copula* of the judgement contains, namely, that the qualitative extremes are sublated in this their identity. Since however this unity is the Notion, it is immediately sundered again into its extremes and appears as a judgement, whose terms however are no longer immediate but reflected into themselves. The *judgement of existence* has passed over into the *judgement of reflection.*

B. THE JUDGEMENT OF REFLECTION

In the judgement that has now arisen, the subject is an individual as such; and similarly the universal is no longer an *abstract* universality or a *single property*, but is posited as a universal that has gathered itself together into a unity through the relation of distinct terms; or, regarding it from the point of view of the content of various determinations in general, as the *taking together* of various properties and existences. If examples are to be given of predicates of judgements of reflection, they must be of another kind than for judgements of existence. It is in the judgement of reflection that we first have, strictly speaking, a *determinate content*, that is, a content as such; for the content is the form determination which is reflected into identity as distinct from the form in so far as this is a distinct determinateness—as it still is in the judgement. In the judgement of existence the content is merely an immediate, or abstract, indeterminate content. The following may therefore serve as examples of judgements of reflection: man is *mortal*, things are *perishable*, this thing is *useful*, *harmful*; *hardness*, *elasticity* of bodies, *happiness*, etc. are predicates of this peculiar kind. They express an essential determination, but one which is in a *relationship* or is a *unifying* universality.

This *universality*, which will further determine itself in the movement of the judgement of reflection, is still distinct from the *universality of the Notion* as such; true, it is no longer the abstract universality of the qualitative judgement, but it still possesses a relation to the immediate from which it proceeds and has the latter as the basis of its negativity. The Notion determines the existent, in the first instance, to *determinations of relation*, to self-continuities in the diverse multiplicity of concrete existence—yet in such a manner that the genuine universal, though it is the inner essence of that multiplicity, is still *in the sphere of Appearance*, and this *relative* nature—or even the *mark*—of this multiplicity is still not the moment of being-in-and-for-self of the latter.

It may suggest itself to define the judgement of reflection as a judgement of *quantity*, just as the judgement of existence was also defined as *qualitative* judgement. But just as *immediacy* in the latter was not merely an immediacy which *simply is*, but one which was essentially also mediated and *abstract*, so here, too, that sublated immediacy is not merely sublated quality, and therefore not merely *quantity*; on the contrary, just as quality is the most external immediacy, so is quantity, in the same way, the *most external determination* belonging to mediation.

Further, as regards the *determination* as it appears in its movement in the judgement of reflection, it should be remarked that in the judgement of existence the *movement* of the determination showed itself in the *predicate*, because this judgement was in the determination of immediacy and the subject consequently appeared as the basis. For a similar reason, in the judgement of reflection, the onward movement of determining runs its course *in the subject*, because this judgement has for its determination the *reflected in-itself*. Here therefore the essential element is the *universal* or the predicate; hence it constitutes the *basis* by which, and in accordance with which, the subject is to be measured and determined. However, the predicate also receives a further determination through the further development of the form of the subject; but this occurs *indirectly*, whereas the development of the subject is, for the reason stated, a *direct* advance.

As regards the objective signification of the judgement, the individual, through its universality, enters into existence, but in an essential determination of relationship, in an essentiality which maintains itself throughout the multiplicity of the world of Appearance; the subject is *supposed* to be determinate in and for itself; this determinateness it possesses in its predicate. The individual, on the other hand, is reflected into this its predicate which is its universal essence; the subject is in so far a concrete existence in the world of Appearance. The predicate in this judgement no longer *inheres* in the subject; it is rather the *implicit being* under which this individual is *subsumed* as an accidental. If the judgements of existence may also be defined as *judgements* of *inherence*, judgements of reflection are, on the contrary, *judgements of subsumption*.

(a) The Singular Judgement

Now the immediate judgement of reflection is again, *the individual is universal*—but with subject and predicate in the stated signification; it can therefore be more precisely expressed as *this is an essential universal*.

But a 'this' is *not* an essential universal. This judgement which, as regards its general form, is simply *positive*, must be taken negatively. But since the judgement of reflection is not merely a positive one, the negation does not directly affect the predicate, which does not inhere but is the *in itself*. It is the subject rather that is alterable and awaits determination. Here, therefore, the negative judgement must be understood as asserting *not a 'this'* is a universal of reflection—an *in-itself* of this kind has a more universal existence than merely in a 'this'. Accordingly, the singular judgement has its proximate truth in the *particular* judgement.

(b) The Particular Judgement

The non-individuality of the subject, which must be posited instead of its individuality in the first judgement of reflection, is *particularity*. But individuality is determined in the judgement of reflection as *essential individuality*; particularity cannot therefore be a *simple, abstract* determination, in which the individual would be sublated and the concrete existent destroyed, but must be merely an extension of the individual in external reflection. The subject is, therefore, *these* or a *particular number* of *individuals*.

This judgement, that *some individuals are a universal of reflection*, appears at first as a positive judgement, but it is negative as well; for *some* contains universality. In this respect it may be regarded as *comprehensive*; but in so far as it is particularity, it is no less inadequate to that universality. The *negative* determination which the subject has received through the transition of the singular judgement is, as we have shown above, also a determination of the relation, of the *copula*. The judgement: *some* men are happy, involves *the immediate consequence* that *some* men are *not* happy. If *some* things are useful, then for this very reason *some* things are *not* useful. The positive and negative judgements no longer fall apart, but the particular judgement immediately contains both at the same time, just because it is a judgement of reflection. But the particular judgement is, for this reason, *indeterminate*.

If, in the example of such a judgement, we examine further the subject, *some men, animals,* etc., we find that it contains besides the particular form-determination *some,* the content-determination *man,* etc. The subject of the singular judgement could be expressed by *this man,* a single individual, which really pertains to an external pointing; it might therefore be better expressed, say, by *Gaius.* But the subject of the particular judgement can no longer be, *some Gaii*; for Gaius is supposed to be an individual as such. To the *some* is therefore added a more universal *content,* say, *men, animals,* etc. This is not merely an empirical content, but one determined by the form of the judgement; that is to say, it is a *universal,* because *some* contains universality and this must at the same time be separated from the individuals, since reflected individuality forms the basis. More precisely, this universality is also the *universal nature* or *genus* man, animal—that universality which is the result of the judgement of reflection, *anticipated*; just as the positive judgement, in having the *individual* for subject, anticipated the determination which is the result of the judgement of existence. Thus the subject that contains the individuals, their relation to particularity and the universal nature, is already posited as the totality of the determinations of the Notion. But this is really an external reflection. What is, in the first instance, already posited in the subject by its form, in respect of the mutual *relation* of these determinations, is the *extension* of the '*this*' to particularity; but this generalization is not adequate to the 'this'; '*this*' is something completely determined, but '*some*' is indeterminate. The extension must be appropriate to the '*this*' and therefore, in conformity with it, be *completely determined*; such an extension is totality, or, in the first instance, *universality*.

This universality has the 'this' as its basis, for the individual here is the individual reflected into itself; its further determinations, therefore, run their course in it *externally*; and just as particularity for this reason determined itself as *some*, so the universality which the subject has attained is *allness*, and the particular judgement has passed over into the *universal*.

(c) The Universal Judgement

Universality, as it appears in the subject of the universal judgement, is the external universality of reflection, *allness;* '*all*' means all *individuals*, and in it the *individual* remains unchanged. This universality is, therefore, only a *taking together* of independently existing individuals; it is the *community* of a property which only belongs to them in *comparison*. It is this community that is usually the first thing that occurs to subjective, unphilosophical thinking when universality is mentioned. It is given as the obvious reason why a determination is to be regarded as universal that *it belongs to a number of things*. It is mainly this concept of universality, too, that *analysis* has in mind when, for example, it takes the development of a function in a *polynomial* to be *more universal* than its development in a *binomial*, because the *polynomial* presents *more individual terms* than the *binomial*. The demand that the function should be presented in its universality requires, strictly speaking, a *pantonomial*, the exhausted infinity; but here the limitation of this demand becomes apparent, and the representation of the *infinite* number of terms has to content itself with its *ought*, and therefore also with a *polynomial*. But in fact the binomial is already the pantonomial in those cases where the *method* or *rule* affects only the dependence of one term on another, and the dependence of several terms on their predecessors does not particularize itself, but one and the same function remains the base. The *method* or *rule* is to be regarded as the genuine *universal;* in the progress of the development or in the development of a polynomial the rule is merely *repeated*; so that it gains nothing in universality through the increased number of the terms. We have already in an earlier chapter spoken of the spurious infinity and its illusory nature; the universality of the Notion is the *reached beyond*; the spurious infinity remains afflicted with the beyond as an unattainable goal, for it remains the mere *progress* to infinity. When universality is pictured merely as *allness*, a universality which is supposed to be exhausted in the individuals as individuals, then this is a relapse into that spurious infinity; or else mere *plurality* is taken for allness. Plurality, however, no matter how great, remains unalterably mere plurality, and is not allness. But there is, here, a vague awareness of the true universality of the *Notion*; it is the Notion that forces its way beyond the stubborn individuality to which unphilosophical thinking clings and beyond the externality of its reflection, substituting allness *as totality*, or rather that being which is categorically in and for itself.

This is apparent, too, in allness which is in general the *empirical* universality. Inasmuch as the individual as an immediate is presupposed and therefore *already given* and externally *adopted*, the reflection which gathers it into allness is equally external. But because the individual as 'this', is absolutely indifferent to this reflection, the universality and an individual of this kind cannot combine to form a unity. For this reason, this empirical allness remains a *task*, something which *ought to be done* and which cannot therefore be represented as *being*. Now an empirically universal proposition—for nevertheless such are advanced—rests on the tacit agreement that if only no contrary *instance* can be adduced, the *plurality* of cases shall count as *allness*; or, that *subjective* allness, namely, those cases which *have come to our knowledge*, may be taken for an *objective* allness.

Now a closer examination of the *universal judgement* now before us, reveals that the subject, which, as previously remarked, contains the true universality as *presupposed*, now also contains it as *posited* in it. *All men* expresses first, the *genus* man, secondly this genus as sundered into individuals, but so that the individuals are at the same time extended to the universality of the genus; conversely, the universality through this connexion with individuality is just as completely determined as the individuality; thus the *posited* universality has been equated with the *presupposed*.

Strictly speaking, however, we should not anticipate what is *presupposed*, but should consider the result in the form determination on its own. Individuality, through this extension of itself to allness, is *posited* as negativity, which is identical self-relation. It has not therefore remained that first individuality, that for example of Gaius, but is the determination that is identical with universality, or is the absolutely determined being of the universal. That *first* individuality of the individual judgement was not the *immediate* one of the positive judgement, but came into being through the dialectical movement of the judgement of existence as such; it was already determined as the *negative identity* of the terms of that judgement. This is the true presupposition in the judgement of reflection; in contrast to the *positing* which runs its course in that judgement, that *first* determinateness of individuality was the latter's *in-itself*; thus, what individuality is *in itself*, is now, through the movement of the judgement of reflection, *posited*, namely, individuality as identical self-relation of the determinate. Therefore this *reflection*, which extends individuality to allness, is not external to it; on the contrary, this reflection merely makes *explicit* what it already is *in itself*. Hence the result is in truth *objective universality*. The subject has thus stripped off the form determination of the judgement of reflection which passed from *this* through *some* to *allness*; instead of *all men* we have now to say *man*.

The universality which has hereby come into being is the *genus* —the universality which is in its own self a concrete. The genus does not *inhere* in the subject; it is not a *single* property, or a property at all, of the subject; it contains all the single determinatenesses dissolved in its substantial solidity. In virtue of the fact that it is posited as this negative identity with itself, it is essentially a subject, but it is no longer *subsumed* in its predicate. In consequence, the nature of the judgement of reflection is altogether changed.

That judgement was essentially a judgement of *subsumption*. The predicate was determined, in contrast to its subject, as the *implicit* universal; according to its content, it could be taken as an essential determination of relation, or also as a mark—a determination which makes the subject merely an essential *Appearance*. But when the predicate is determined to *objective universality*, it ceases to be subsumed under such a determination of relation, or comprehensive reflection; on the contrary, such a predicate in contrast to this universality is a particular. The relationship of subject and predicate has therefore become inverted and hence the judgement has, first of all, sublated itself.

This sublation of the judgement coincides with the advance in the *determination of the copula*, which we have still to consider; the sublation of the terms of the judgement is the same thing as their

x*

transition into the copula. In other words, the subject, in raising itself to universality has, in this determination become equated with the predicate, which as reflected universality also contains particularity within itself; subject and predicate are therefore identical, that is they have coalesced into the copula. This identity is the genus or absolute nature of a thing. In so far, therefore, as this identity again sunders itself into a judgement it is the *inner nature* through which subject and predicate are related to one another—a relation of *necessity* in which these terms of the judgement are only unessential differences. *What belongs to all the individuals of a genus belongs to the genus by its nature*, is an immediate consequence and the expression of what we have seen, that the subject, for example *all men*, strips off its form determination, and *man* is to take its place. This intrinsic and explicit connection constitutes the basis of a new judgement, the *judgement of necessity*.

C. THE JUDGEMENT OF NECESSITY

The determination to which universality has advanced is, as we have seen, the *universality which is in and for itself* or *objective*, to which in the sphere of essence *substantiality* corresponds. It is distinguished from the latter in that it belongs to the Notion and is therefore not merely the *inner* but also the *posited* necessity of its determinations; or, in other words, the *difference* is immanent in it, whereas substance has its difference only in its accidents, but not as principle within itself.

Now in the judgement, this objective universality is *posited*; first, therefore, with this its essential determinateness as immanent in it, secondly, with its determinateness distinguished from it as *particularity*, of which this universality constitutes the substantial basis. In this way it is determined as *genus* and *species*.

(a) The Categorical Judgement

The *genus* essentially sunders itself, or repels itself into *species*; it is genus only in so far as it comprehends species under itself; the species is species only in so far as on the one hand it exists in the individuals, and on the other hand is in the genus a higher universality. Now the *categorical judgement* has such a universality for its predicate, a predicate in which the subject possesses its *immanent* nature. But the categorical judgement is itself the first or

immediate judgement of necessity; accordingly the determinateness of the sbuject whereby it is a particular or individual over
against the genus or species, so far belongs to the immediacy of
external existence. But objective universality, too, has here as yet
only its *immediate* particularization; hence it is on the one hand
itself a determinate universality in contrast to which there are
higher genera; on the other hand, it is not exactly the *proximate*
genus, that is, its determinateness is not exactly the principle of
the specific particularity of the subject. But what is *necessary* in it
is the *substantial identity* of the subject and predicate, contrasted
with which that property of the subject which distinguishes it from
the predicate is only an unessential positedness, or even merely a
name; the subject is reflected in its predicate into its being-in-and-
for-self. A predicate of this kind should not be classed with the
predicates of the preceding judgements; to throw, for example,
the judgements

> The rose is red,
> The rose is a plant,
> or This ring is yellow,
> It is gold,

into the one class, and to regard such an external property as the
colour of a flower as a predicate on the same level as its vegetable
nature, is to overlook a difference which must strike the meanest
intelligence. The categorical judgement must therefore be
definitely distinguished from the positive and negative judgements;
in the latter, what is predicated of the subject is a *single contingent*
content; in the former, the content is the totality of the form
reflected into itself. Here therefore the *copula* has the meaning of
necessity, whereas in the others it merely signifies abstract,
immediate *being*.

The *determinateness* of the subject, which makes it a *particular*
in contrast to the predicate, is in the first instance something
contingent; subject and predicate are not *necessarily* related by the
form or determinateness; the necessity is, therefore, still an
inner necessity. But the subject is subject only as a *particular*, and
in so far as it possesses objective universality it must possess it
essentially in accordance with that primarily immediate determinateness. The objective universal in *determining* itself, that is in
positing itself in the judgement, is essentially in an identical

relation with this expelled *determinateness* as such, that is, it is essential that the determinateness is not posited as a mere contingency. It is only through this *necessity* of its immediate being that the categorical judgement conforms to its objective universality and in this way it has passed over into the *hypothetical judgement*.

(b) The Hypothetical Judgement

If A is, then B is; or, the being of A is not its own being, but the being of another, of B. What is posited in this judgement is the *necessary connexion* of immediate determinatenesses, a connexion which is not yet posited in the categorical judgement. There are here *two* immediate Existences or external contingencies, of which in the categorical judgement there is at first only one, the subject; but since one is external to the other, this other is also external to the first. In accordance with this immediacy, the *content* of the two sides is still mutually indifferent; hence this judgement is in the first instance a proposition of empty form. Now in the first place the immediacy is indeed as such a self-subsistent, concrete *being*; but secondly, the relation of this being is the essential point; therefore this being is just as much a mere *possibility*; the hypothetical judgement involves, not *that A is* or *that B is*, but only that *if* one is, *then* the other is; only the connexion of the extremes is posited as being, not the extremes themselves. On the contrary, in this necessity each extreme is posited as equally the *being of an other*. The principle of identity affirms that *A* is only *A*, not *B*; and that *B* is only *B*, not *A*; in the hypothetical judgement, on the contrary, the being of finite things is posited by the Notion in accordance with their formal truth, namely that the finite is its own being, but equally is not its *own* being, but that of an other. In the sphere of being, the finite *alters* and becomes an other; in the sphere of essence it is *Appearance*, and being is posited as consisting in the *reflection* of an other in it, and *necessity* is the inner relation, not yet posited as such. But the Notion is the *positing* of this identity so that what is, is not an abstract self-identity but a *concrete* identity and is immediately in its own self the being of an other.

By employing reflective relationships, the hypothetical judgement can be more precisely characterized as a relationship of *ground* and *consequent*, *condition* and *conditioned*, *causality*, etc.

Just as in the categorical judgement substantiality appeared in the form of its Notion, so, too, does the nexus of causality in the hypothetical judgement. This and the other relationships all come under the hypothetical judgement; but here they are no longer relationships of *self-subsistent sides*, but these sides are essentially only moments of one and the same identity. However, in the hypothetical judgement they are not yet opposed as Notion determinations, as individual or particular to universal, but at first only as *moments in general*. Thus the hypothetical judgement has rather the shape of a proposition; just as the particular judgement has an indeterminate content, so the hypothetical is indeterminate in form, since its content is not determined as a relationship of subject to predicate. Yet since the being is the being of an other, for that very reason it is *in itself* a *unity of itself* and *its other*, and consequently *universality*; at the same time it is, strictly speaking, only a *particular*, for it is a determinate and in its determinateness is not purely self-related. But it is not the *simple*, abstract particularity that is posited; on the contrary, through the *immediacy* which the *determinatenesses possess*, the moments of the particularity are distinguished; at the same time, through the unity of the moments which constitutes their relation, the particularity is also their totality. What therefore is truly posited in this judgement is universality as the concrete identity of the Notion, whose determinations have no subsistence of their own but are only particularities posited in that identity. As such, it is the *disjunctive judgement*.

(c) *The Disjunctive Judgement*

In the categorical judgement, the Notion is objective universality and an external individuality. In the hypothetical judgement, the Notion in its negative identity emerges in this externality. Through this identity, its moments receive the same determinateness, now posited in the disjunctive judgement, that they possess immediately in the hypothetical judgement. Hence the disjunctive judgement is objective universality posited at the same time in union with the form. It therefore contains first concrete universality or the genus in *simple* form as the subject, and secondly the *same* universality but as totality of its distinct determinations. A is either B or C. This is the *necessity of the Notion*, in which first the identity of the two extremes is one and the same extent, content and universality;

secondly they are distinguished according to the form of the Notion-determinations, but in such a manner that, by reason of that identity, this distinction is a *mere form*. Thirdly, the identical objective universality appears for that reason as the determination that is reflected into itself in contrast to the unessential form, that is, as the *content*, but a content which possesses within itself the determinateness of form, once as the simple determinateness of the *genus*, and again, this same determinateness developed into its difference—in which way it is the particularity of the *species* and their *totality*, the universality of the genus. The particularity in its development constitutes the *predicate*, for it is the *more universal* in so far as it embraces the entire universal sphere of the subject, and this too in its detailed particularization.

A closer examination of this particularization shows first of all that the genus constitutes the substantial universality of the species; the subject is therefore *both B and C*; this *both-and* denotes the *positive* identity of the particular with the universal; this objective universal completely maintains itself in its particularity. Secondly, the species *mutually exclude one another; A* is *either B or C*; for they are the *specific difference* of the universal sphere. This *either-or* is their *negative* relation. Yet in this they are just as identical as in their positive relation; the genus is their *unity* as *determinate* particulars. If the genus were an abstract universality as in the judgements of existence, the species would also have to be taken as only *diverse* and mutually indifferent; but it is not that external universality which results merely from *comparison* and *omission* but is the immanent and concrete universality of the species. An empirical disjunctive judgement lacks necessity; *A* is either *B* or *C* or *D*, etc., because the species *B*, *C* and *D*, etc., have *already been given*; strictly speaking, this cannot give us an *either-or*, for species of this kind constitute, as it were, a merely subjective completeness; true, *one* species excludes the *other*; but *either-or* excludes *every further* species and shuts off within itself a total sphere. This totality has its *necessity* in the negative unity of the objective universal, which dissolves individuality within itself and possesses it as a simple *principle* of difference immanent in it by which the species are *determined* and *related*. Empirical species, on the contrary, have their differences in some contingency or other which is an external principle and therefore not *their* principle, and consequently also not the immanent determinateness of the genus; for this reason they are also not related to one another according to their determinateness. But it is through the *relation* of their determinateness that the species constitute the universality of the predicate. It is here really that the so-called *contrary* and *contradictory* notions should first find their place; for in the disjunctive judgement is posited the essential difference of the Notion; but in it they at the same time also possess their truth, namely, that the contrary and contradictory themselves are each distinguished as contrary and contradictory. Species are contrary in so far as they are merely *diverse*, that is to say in so far as they possess through the genus as their objective nature an existence that is in and for itself; they are *contradictory* in so far as they exclude one another. But each of these determinations by itself is one-sided and lacks truth; in the *either-or* of the disjunctive judgement their unity is posited as their truth, in accordance with which the species' self-subsistent existence as *concrete universality* is itself also the *principle* of the negative unity whereby they mutually exclude one another.

By the just demonstrated identity of subject and predicate in accordance with the negative unity, the genus in the disjunctive judgement is determined as the *proximate* genus. This expression indicates in the first place, a mere quantitative difference of *more* or *less*—determinations possessed by a universal in relation to a particularity coming under it. From this point of view, it remains contingent what is properly the proximate genus. In so far, however, as the genus is taken as a universal formed merely by the omission of determinations, it cannot really form a disjunctive judgement; for it is contingent whether it has retained the determinateness which constitutes the principle of the *either-or*; the genus would not be exhibited at all in the species according to its *determinateness*, and the species could only possess a contingent completeness. In the categorical judgement, the genus is at first only in this abstract form over against the subject, and therefore not necessarily the proximate genus to it and is so far external. But when the genus is a concrete, essentially *determinate* universality, then it is, as a simple determinateness, the unity of the *moments of the Notion*, which in this simplicity are only sublated, but have their real difference in the species. Accordingly, a genus is the *proximate* genus of a species in so far as the latter has its specific difference in the essential determinateness of the genus, and the species as a whole are differentiated by a principle that lies in the nature of the genus.

The aspect just considered constitutes the identity of subject and predicate from the aspect of their *determinedness* in general, an aspect which has been posited by the hypothetical judgement, whose necessity is an identity of immediate and diverse things and therefore essentially a negative unity. It is this negative unity in general that separates subject and predicate, but now it is itself posited as differentiated—in the subject as a *simple* determinateness, in the predicate as *totality*. This separation of subject and predicate is the *difference of the Notion*; and thus the *totality* of the *species* in the predicate cannot be *any other difference*. The *reciprocal determination* of the *disjunctive* terms is therefore given by this. It reduces to the difference of the Notion, for it is this alone that disjoins itself and in its determination reveals its negative unity. However, the species is considered here only in respect of its simple Notion determinateness, not in respect of the *shape* in which it has come forth from the Idea into a further self-subsistent *reality*; this latter is indeed *dropped* in the simple principle of the genus; but the *essential* distinction must be a moment of the Notion. In the judgement here considered, it is really the Notion's *own* progressive determination that now *posits* its disjunction; the same thing that we found, when considering the Notion, to be its essential and explicit determination, its differentiation into determinate Notions. Now because the Notion is the universal, both the positive and the negative totality of the particulars, it is *itself* for that very reason also immediately *one of its disjunctive members*; the *other*, however, is this universality resolved into *its particularity*, or the determinateness of the Notion *as determinateness*, that determinateness in which the universality exhibits itself as totality. If the disjunction of a genus into species has not yet attained this form, this is a proof that it has not risen to the determinateness of the Notion and has not proceeded from the Notion. *Colour* is either violet, indigo, blue, green, yellow, orange or red; even the empirical confusion and impurity of such a disjunction is at once apparent; just from this aspect alone it must be termed barbarous. When colour has been grasped as the *concrete unity* of light and dark, then this *genus* contains within it the *determinateness* which constitutes the *principle* of its particularization into species. But of these species, one must be the utterly simple colour which contains the opposition in equipose and confined and negated in the colour's intensity; over against this there must be presented the opposition of the relationship between light and dark, to which must be added, since a natural phenomenon is involved, the indifferent neutrality of the opposition. When mixtures such as violet and orange, and differences of degree, such as blue and light blue, are taken for species, this can only result from a completely thoughtless procedure that shows too little reflection even for empiricism. But this is not the place to discuss what further distinct and more precisely determined forms disjunction may have, according as they occur in the element of Nature or of spirit.

In the first instance, the disjunctive judgement has the members of the disjunction in its predicate; but it is itself no less disjoined; its subject and predicate are the members of the disjunction. They are the moments of the Notion, posited in their determinateness but at the same time as identical; *identical* (*a*) in the objective universality which, in the subject is the simple *genus*, and in the predicate is the universal sphere and the totality of the moments of the Notion, and (*b*) in the *negative* unity, in the developed connexion of necessity, in accordance with which the *simple determinateness* in the subject is sundered into the *difference of the species*, and in this very difference is their essential relation and self-identity.

This unity, the copula of this judgement into which the extremes have coalesced through their identity, is therefore the Notion itself, and the Notion, too, *as posited*; the mere judgement of necessity has thereby risen into the *judgement of the Notion*.

D. THE JUDGEMENT OF THE NOTION

The ability to form *judgements of existence* such as 'the rose is red', 'snow is white', and so forth, will hardly count as evidence of great powers of judgement. The *judgements of reflection* are rather *propositions*; in the judgement of necessity the object appears, it is true, in its objective universality, but it is only in the judgement now to be considered that *its relation to the Notion is found*. In this judgement the Notion is laid down as the basis, and since it is in relation to the object, it is an *ought-to-be* to which the reality may or may not be adequate. Therefore it is only a judgement of this kind that contains a true appreciation; the predicates *good*, *bad*, *true*, *beautiful*, *correct*, etc. express that the thing is *measured* against its universal *Notion* as the simply presupposed *ought-to-be* and is, or is not, in *agreement* with it.

The judgement of the Notion has been called the judgement of *modality* and it has been regarded as containing that form of the relationship between subject and predicate which is found in an external understanding, and to be concerned with the value of the copula only *in relation to thinking*. According to this view, the *problematical* judgement is one where the affirmation or denial is taken as *optional* or *possible*; the *assertoric*, where it is taken as *true*, that is as *actual*; and the *apodeictic*, where it is taken as *necessary*. It is easy to see why it is so natural in the case of this judgement to step out of the sphere of judgement itself and to regard its determination as something merely *subjective*. For here it is the Notion, or the subjective, that reappears in the judgement and stands in relationship to an external actuality. But this subjectivity is not to be confused with *external reflection*, which of course is also something subjective, but in a different sense from the Notion itself; on the contrary, the Notion that re-emerges from the disjunctive judgement is the opposite of a mere *contingent mode*. The earlier judgements are in this sense merely subjective, for they are based on an abstraction and one-sidedness in which the Notion is lost. The judgement of the Notion, on the contrary, is objective and the truth as against those earlier judgements, just because it has for its basis the Notion, not the Notion in external reflection or in *relation to* a subjective, that is contingent, *thinking*, but the Notion in its determinateness as Notion.

In the disjunctive judgement the Notion was posited as identity of the universal nature with its particularization; consequently the relation of the judgement was cancelled. This *concretion* of universality and particularization is, at first, a simple result; it has now to develop itself further into totality, since the moments which it contains are at first swallowed up in it and as yet do not confront one another in determinate self-subsistence. The defect of the result may also be more definitely expressed by saying that in the disjunctive judgement, although objective *universality* has completed itself *in its particularization*, yet the negative unity of the latter merely returns *into the former* and has not yet determined itself to the third moment, that of *individuality*. Yet in so far as the result itself is *negative unity*, it is indeed already this *individuality*; but as such it is only this *one* determinateness, which has now to *posit* its negativity, sunder itself into the *extremes* and in this way finally develop *into the syllogism*.

The proximate diremption of this unity is the judgement in which it is posited first as subject, as an *immediate individual*, and then as predicate, as the determinate relation of its moments.

(a) *The Assertoric Judgement*

The judgement of the Notion is at first *immediate*; as such it is the *assertoric* judgement. The subject is a concrete individual in general, and the predicate expresses this same as the *relation* of its *actuality*, determinateness, or *constitution* to its *Notion*. (This house is *bad*, this action is *good*.) More precisely, therefore, it involves (*a*) that the subject *ought* to be something; its *universal nature* has posited itself as the self-subsistent Notion; and (*b*) *particularity* which, not only on account of its immediacy but also on account of its express differentiation from its self-subsistent universal nature, appears as an *external existence* with such and such a *constitution*; this, on its side, because of the Notion's self-subsistence, is also indifferent to the universal and may or may not conform to it. This constitution is the *individuality*, which lies beyond the necessary *determination* of the universal in the disjunctive judgement, a determination which only appears as the particularization of the *species* and as the negative *principle* of the genus. Thus the concrete universality which has emerged from the disjunctive judgement is sundered in the assertoric judgement into the form of *extremes*, to which the Notion itself as the posited unity that relates them is still lacking.

For this reason the judgement is so far merely *assertoric*; the verification is a subjective *assurance*. The fact that something is good or bad, correct, suitable or not, is connected with an external third factor. But the fact that the connexion is *externally posited* means that it is, at first, only *implicit* or *internal*. When therefore something is good or bad, etc. no one will suppose that it is, say, good only in *subjective consciousness* but perhaps bad in itself, or that good and bad, correct, suitable, etc., are not predicates of the objects themselves. The merely subjective element in the assertion of this judgement consists therefore in the fact that the *implicit* connexion of subject and predicate is not yet *posited*, or, what is the same thing, that it is only *external*; the copula is still an immediate, *abstract being*.

Accordingly, the assurance of the assertoric judgement is confronted with equal right by its contradictory. When one is assured that 'this action is good', then the opposite assurance that 'this action is bad', is equally justified. Or, considering the judgement *in itself*, because the subject of the judgement is an *immediate individual*, in this abstraction it does not as yet possess posited *within it* the *determinateness* that should contain its relation to the universal Notion; thus the subject is still something contingent which may or may not conform to the Notion. The judgement is therefore essentially *problematic*.

(b) The Problematic Judgement

The *problematic* judgement is the assertoric in so far as the latter must be taken both positively and negatively. From this qualitative side, the *particular* judgement is likewise a problematic one, for it is equally valid positively and negatively; similarly, in the *hypothetical* judgement, the being of the subject and predicate is problematic; also, it is posited by the particular and hypothetical judgements that the individual and the categorical judgements are as yet merely subjective. But in the problematic judgement as such this positing is more immanent than in the judgements just mentioned, because in it the *content of the predicate* is *the relation of the subject to the Notion*, and here, therefore, the *determination of the immediate as something contingent* is itself given.

At first, it appears only problematic whether the predicate is to be coupled with a certain subject or not, and so far the indeterminateness falls in the copula. From this, no determination can emerge for the *predicate*, for this is already the objective, concrete universality. The problematic element, therefore, concerns the immediacy of the *subject* which is hereby determined as a *contingency*. But further, we must not for that reason abstract from the individuality of the subject; if this latter were purged of its individuality altogether, it would be merely a universal; the predicate contains just this, that the Notion of the subject is to be posited in relation to its individuality. We cannot say: *the house* or *a house* is good, but: *according to its constitution*. The problematic element in the subject itself constitutes its *moment of contingency*, the *subjectivity* of the *thing* over against its objective nature or its Notion, its merely *contingent mode* or its *constitution*.

Hence the *subject* itself is differentiated into its universality or objective nature, what it *ought* to be, and the particular constitution of its existence. Thus it contains the *ground* of its *being* or *not being* what it *ought to be*. In this way, it is equated with the predicate. The *negativity* of the problematic element, in so far as it is directed against the immediacy of the *subject*, accordingly means only this original partition of the subject which is already *in itself* the unity of the universal and particular, *into these its moments*—a partition which is the judgement itself.

It may further be remarked that each of the *two* sides of the subject, its Notion and its constitution, could be called its *subjectivity*. The *Notion* is the universal essence of a thing or a fact [*Sache*] withdrawn into itself, its negative unity with itself; this constitutes its subjectivity. But a thing is also essentially *contingent* and has an *external constitution*; this may equally be called the mere subjectivity of the thing in contrast to the other side, its objectivity. The thing itself is just this, that its Notion, as the negative of itself, negates its universality and projects itself into the externality of individuality. The *subject* of the judgement is here posited as this duality; those opposite significations of subjectivity are, in accordance with their truth, brought into a unity. The signification of the subjective element has itself become problematic by reason of its *having lost* the immediate *determinateness* which it possessed in the immediate judgement, and its determinate *opposition* to the *predicate*. This opposite signification of subjective which occurs even in the ratiocination of ordinary reflection might of itself at least draw attention to the fact that subjectivity in *one* of these significations *alone*, has no truth. The twofold signification is the manifestation of this truth that each by itself is one-sided.

When the problematic element is thus posited as the problematic element of the *thing*, as the thing with its *constitution*, then the judgement itself is no longer problematic, but *apodeictic*.

(c) *The Apodeictic Judgement*

The subject of the apodeictic judgement (the house constituted so and so is *good*, the action constituted so and so is *right*) has within it, first, the universal, what it *ought to be*, and secondly, its *constitution*; this latter contains the *ground* why a predicate of the Notion judgement applies or does not apply to the *whole subject*, that is, whether the subject corresponds to its Notion or not. This judgement, then, is *truly* objective; or it is the *truth of the judgement* in general. Subject and predicate correspond to each other and have the same content, and this *content* is itself the posited *concrete universality*; it contains, namely, the two moments, the objective universal or the *genus*, and the *individualized* universal. Here, therefore, we have the universal which is *itself* and continues itself through *its opposite* and is a universal only as *unity* with this opposite. A universal of this kind, such as the predicate *good*, *suitable, correct*, etc., is based on an *ought-to-be* and at the same time contains the *correspondence* of *existence* to that ought-to-be; it is not this ought-to-be or the genus by itself, but this *correspondence* that is the *universality* which constitutes the predicate of the apodeictic judgement.

The *subject* likewise contains these two moments in *immediate* unity as the *fact [Sache]*. But it is the truth of the fact that it is internally *split* into *what it ought-to-be* and *what it is*; this is the *absolute judgement on all actuality*. It is because this original partition, which is the omnipotence of the Notion, is just as much a return into its unity and an absolute relation of the *ought-to-be* and *being* to each other that makes what is actual into *a fact*; its inner relation, this concrete identity, constitutes the *soul* of the fact.

The transition from the immediate simplicity of the fact to the *correspondence* which is the determinate relation of its ought-to-be and its being—or the copula—is now seen, on closer examination, to lie in the particular *determinateness* of the fact. The genus is the universal *in and for itself*, which as such appears as the unrelated; while the determinateness is that which in that universal is reflected *into itself*, yet at the same time is reflected *into an other*. The judgement therefore has its *ground* in the constitution of the subject and thereby is *apodeictic*. Hence we now have before us the *determinate* and *fulfilled* [*erfüllte*] copula, which formerly consisted in the abstract '*is*', but has now further developed itself into *ground* in general. It appears at first as an immediate *determinateness* in the subject, but it is no less the *relation* to the predicate which has no other *content* than this very *correspondence*, or the relation of the subject to the universality.

Thus the form of the judgement has perished; first because subject and predicate are *in themselves* the same content; secondly because the subject through its determinateness points beyond itself and relates itself to the predicate; but also, thirdly, *this relating* has passed over into the predicate, alone constitutes its content, and is thus the *posited* relation, or the judgement itself. Thus the concrete identity of the Notion which was the *result* of the disjunctive judgement and which constitutes the *inner* basis of the Notion judgement—which identity was at first posited only in the predicate—is now restored *in the whole*.

If we examine the positive element of this result which effects the transition of the judgement into another form, we find, as we have seen, that subject and predicate in the apodeictic judgement are each the whole Notion. The *unity* of the Notion as the *deter-minateness* constituting the copula that relates them, is at the same time *distinct* from them. At first, it stands only on the other side of the subject as the latter's *immediate constitution*. But since it is essentially that which *relates* subject and predicate, it is not merely such immediate constitution but the *universal* that *perme-ates* both subject and predicate. While subject and predicate have the same *content*, the *form relation*, on the other hand, is posited through this determinatenes, *determinateness as a universal* or *particularity*. Thus it contains within itself the two form deter-minations of the extremes and is the *determinate* relation of subject and predicate; it is the *fulfilled copula* of the judgement, the *copula pregnant with content*, the unity of the Notion that has re-emerged from the *judgement* in which it was lost in the extremes. Through this *impregnation of the copula* the judgement has become the *syllogism*.

CHAPTER 3

THE SYLLOGISM

We have found the *syllogism* to be the restoration of the *Notion* in the *judgement*, and consequently the unity and truth of both. The Notion as such holds its moments sublated in *unity*; in the judgement this unity is internal or, what is the same thing, external; and the moments, although related, are posited as *self-subsistent extremes*. In the *syllogism* the Notion determinations are like the extremes of the judgement, and at the same time their determinate *unity* is posited.

Thus the syllogism is the completely posited Notion; it is therefore the *rational*. The understanding is regarded as the faculty of the *determinate* Notion which is held fast *in isolation* by abstraction and the form of universality. But in reason the *determinate* Notions are posited in their *totality* and *unity*. Therefore, not only is the syllogism rational, but *everything rational is a syllogism*. The syllogistic process has for a long time been ascribed to reason; yet on the other hand reason in and for itself, rational principles and laws, are spoken of in such a way that it is not clear what is the connexion between the former reason which syllogizes and the latter reason which is the source of laws and other eternal truths and absolute thoughts. If the former is supposed to be merely formal reason, while the latter is supposed to be creative of content, then according to this distinction it is precisely the *form* of reason, the syllogism, that must not be lacking in the latter. Nevertheless, to such a degree are the two commonly held apart, and not mentioned together, that it seems as though the reason of absolute thoughts was ashamed of the reason of the syllogism and as though it was only in deference to tradition that the syllogism was also adduced as an activity of reason. Yet it is obvious, as we have just remarked, that the logical reason, if it is regarded as *formal* reason, must essentially be recognizable also in the reason that is concerned with a content; the fact is that no content can be rational except through the rational form. In this matter we cannot look for any help in the common chatter about reason; for this refrains from stating what is to be understood by *reason*; this supposedly rational cognition is mostly so busy with its objects that it forgets to cognize reason itself and only distinguishes and characterizes it by the objects that it possesses. If reason is supposed to be the cognition that knows about God, freedom, right and duty, the infinite, unconditioned, supersensuous, or even gives only ideas and feelings of these objects, then for one thing these latter are only negative objects, and for another thing the first question still remains, what it is in all these objects that makes them rational. It is this, that the infinitude of these objects is not the empty abstraction from the finite, not the universality that lacks content and determinateness, but the universality that is fulfilled or realized, the Notion that is *determinate* and possesses its determinateness in this true way, namely, that it differentiates itself within itself and is the unity of these fixed and determinate differences. It is only thus that reason *rises* above the finite, conditioned, sensuous, call it what you will, and in this negativity is essentially *pregnant with content*, for it is the unity of determinate extremes; as such, however, the *rational* is nothing but the *syllogism*.

Now the syllogism, like the judgement, is in the first instance *immediate*; hence its determinations (*termini*) are *simple, abstract* determinatenesses; in this form it is the *syllogism of the understanding*. If we stop short at this form of the syllogism, then the rationality in it, although undoubtedly present and posited, is not apparent. The essential feature of the syllogism is the *unity* of the extremes, the *middle term* which unites them, and the *ground* which supports them. Abstraction, in holding rigidly to the *self-subsistence* of the extremes, opposes this *unity* to them as a determinateness which likewise is fixed and *self-subsistent*, and in this way apprehends it rather as *non-unity* than as unity. The expression *middle term* (*medius terminus*) is taken from spatial representation and contributes its share to the stopping short at the *mutual externality* of the terms. Now if the syllogism consists in the *unity of the extremes* being *posited* in it, and if, all the same, this unity is simply taken on the one hand as a particular on its own, and on the other hand as a merely external relation, and *non-unity* is made the essential relationship of the syllogism, then the reason which constitutes the syllogism contributes nothing to rationality.

First, the *syllogism of existence* in which the terms are thus immediately and abstractly determined, demonstrates in itself (since, like the judgement, it is their *relation*) that they are not in fact such abstract terms, but that each contains the *relation to the other* and that the middle term is not only particularity as opposed to the determinations of the extremes but contains these terms *posited* in it.

Through this its dialectic it is converted into the *syllogism of reflection*, into the second syllogism. The terms of this are such that each essentially *shows in*, or is *reflected into, the other*; in other words they are posited as *mediated*, which they are supposed to be in accordance with the nature of the syllogism in general.

Thirdly, in that this *reflecting* or mediatedness of the extremes is reflected into itself, the syllogism is determined as the *syllogism of necessity*, in which the mediating element is the objective nature of the thing. As this syllogism determines the extremes of the Notion equally as totalities, the *syllogism* has attained to the correspondence of its Notion or the middle term, and its existence or the differences of the extremes; that is, it has attained to its truth and in so doing has passed out of subjectivity into *objectivity*.

A. THE SYLLOGISM OF EXISTENCE

1. The syllogism in its *immediate* form has for its moments the determinations of the Notion as *immediate*. Hence they are the abstract determinatenesses of form, which are not yet developed by mediation into *concretion*, but are only *single* determinatenesses. The first syllogism is, therefore, strictly the *formal* syllogism. The *formalism* of the syllogizing process consists in stopping short at the determination of this first syllogism. The Notion, differentiated into its *abstract* moments, has *individuality* and *universality* for its extremes, and appears itself as the *particularity* standing between them. On account of their immediacy they are merely self-related determinatenesses, and one and all a *single content*. Particularity constitutes the middle term in the first instance since it unites *immediately* within itself the two moments of individuality and universality. On account of its determinateness it is on the one hand subsumed under the universal, while on the other hand the individual, as against which it possesses universality, is subsumed under it. But this *concretion* is in the first instance merely a *duality of aspect*; on account of the immediacy in which the middle term presents itself in the immediate syllogism. it appears as a *simple* determinateness, and the *mediation* which it constitutes is not

yet posited. Now the dialectical movement of the syllogism of existence consists in the positing in its moments of the mediation that alone constitutes the syllogism.

(a) First Figure of the Syllogism

I–P–U is the general schema of the determinate syllogism. Individuality unites with universality through particularity; the individual is not universal immediately, but through the medium of particularity; and conversely the universal similarly is not immediately individual but descends to individuality through particularity. These determinations confront each other as *extremes* and are united in a *different* third term. Each is determinateness; in this they are *identical*; this their general determinateness is *particularity*. But they are no less *extremes* against this particularity than against each other, because each is present in its *immediate* determinateness.

The general significance of this syllogism is that the individual, which as such is infinite self-relation and therefore would be merely *inward*, emerges by means of particularity into *existence* as into universality, in which it no longer belongs merely to itself but stands in an *external relationship*; conversely the individual, in separating itself into its determinateness as a particularity, is in this separation a concrete individual and, as the relation of the determinateness to itself, a *universal*, self-related individual, and consequently is also truly an individual; in the extreme of universality it has withdrawn from externality *into itself*. In the first syllogism, the syllogism's objective significance is only *superficially* present, since in it the determinations are not yet posited as the unity which constitutes the essence of the syllogism. It is still subjective in so far as the abstract significance possessed by its terms is not thus isolated in and for itself but only in subjective consciousness. Moreover, the relationship of individuality, particularity and universality is as we have seen the *necessary and essential form-relationship* of the determinations of the syllogism; the defect consists not in this determinateness of the form, but in the fact that *under this form* each single determination is not at the same time *richer*. Aristotle has confined himself rather to the mere relationship of *inherence*, in stating the nature of the syllogism as follows: *When three terms are related to one another in such a manner that one extreme is in the whole of the middle term and this middle term is in the whole of the other extreme, then these two extremes are necessarily united in a conclusion.* What is expressed here is more the mere repetition of the *like relationship* of inherence between one extreme to the middle term, and again between the middle term and the other extreme, than the determinateness of the three terms to one another. Now since the syllogism rests on the stated relative determinateness of the terms, it is immediately evident that other relationships of the terms which are given by the other figures can only have validity as syllogisms of the understanding [*Verstandesschlüsse*] in so far as they can be *reduced* to that original relationship; they are not *different species* of figures which stand *alongside* the *first*; on the contrary, on the one hand, in so far as they purport to be correct syllogisms, they rest solely on the essential form of the syllogism in general, which is the first figure; on the other hand, in so far as they deviate from it they are transformations into which that first abstract form necessarily passes, thereby further determining itself and advancing to totality. We shall presently see what this process is.

I–P–U is thus the general schema of the syllogism in its determinateness. The individual is subsumed under the particular, and the latter under the universal; therefore the individual too is subsumed under the universal. Or the particular inheres in the individual and the universal in the particular; *therefore* the universal also inheres in the individual. From one aspect, namely, in relation to the universal, the particular is subject; in relation to the individual it is predicate; or, in relation to the former it is an individual, in relation to the latter it is a universal. Because the two determinatenesses are united in it, the extremes are linked together by this their unity. The *therefore* appears as the conclusion that has taken place in the *subject*, a conclusion deduced from *subjective* insight into the relationship between the two *immediate* premises. As subjective reflection enunciates the two relations of the middle term to the extremes as particular and indeed immediate *judgements* or *propositions*, the conclusion as the *mediated* relation is also, of course, a particular *proposition*, and the *consequently* or *therefore* is the expression of the fact that it is the mediated one. But this *therefore* is not to be regarded as an external determination in this proposition, as if it had its ground and seat only in subjective reflection; on the contrary, it is grounded in the nature of the extremes themselves whose *relation* again is expressed as a *mere judgement* or *proposition* only for the purpose of, and by means of, abstractive reflection, but whose *true relation* is posited as the middle term. That *therefore I is U* is a *judgement*, is a merely subjective circumstance; the very meaning of the syllogism is that this is not merely a *judgement*, that is, not a relation effected by the *mere copula* or the empty *is*, but one effected by the determinate middle term which is pregnant with content.

Consequently, to regard the syllogism merely as consisting *of three judgements*, is a formal view that ignores the relationship of the terms on which hinges the sole interest of the syllogism. It is altogether a merely subjective reflection that splits the relation of the terms into separate premisses and a conclusion distinct from them:

> All men are mortal,
> Gaius is a man,
> Therefore he is mortal.

At the approach of this kind of syllogism we are at once seized with a feeling of boredom; this stems from that unprofitable form which by means of the separate propositions presents a semblance of difference that immediately dissolves in the fact itself. It is mainly this subjective shape that gives the syllogistic process the appearance of a subjective *makeshift*, to which reason or understanding resorts when it cannot cognize *immediately*. The nature of things, the rational element, certainly does not set to work by first framing for itself a major premiss, the relation of a particularity to a subsistent universal, and then secondly, picking up a separate relation of an individuality to the particular, out of which thirdly and lastly a new proposition comes to light. This syllogistic process that advances by means of separate propositions is nothing but a subjective form; the nature of the fact is that the differentiated Notion determinations of the fact are united in the essential unity. This rationality is not a makeshift; on the contrary, in contrast to the *immediacy* of relation that still obtains in the *judgement*, it is the *objective* element; and the former immediacy of cognition is rather the merely subjective element, whereas the syllogism is the truth of the judgement. Everything is a *syllogism*, a universal that through particularity is united with individuality; but it is certainly not a whole consisting of *three propositions*.

2. In the *immediate* syllogism of the understanding the terms have the form of *immediate determinations*; it is now to be considered from this aspect according to which they are a *content*. It may thus be regarded as the *qualitative* syllogism, just as the judgement of existence has the same aspect of qualitative determination. Accordingly the terms of this syllogism, like the terms of that judgement, are *individual* determinatenesses, the determinateness through its self-relation being posited as indifferent to the *form* and hence as content. The *individual* is any immediate concrete object; *particularity* a single one of its determinatenesses, properties or relationships; *universality* again a still more abstract, more individual determinateness in the particular. Since the subject as *immediately* determined is not yet posited in its Notion, its concretion is not reduced to the essential Notion determinations; its self-related determinateness is, therefore, an indeterminate, infinite *multiplicity*. In this immediacy the individual possesses an infinite number of determinatenesses which belong to its particularity, each of which therefore may constitute a middle term for it in a syllogism. But through *any other* middle term it is united *with another universal*; through each of its properties it stands in a different connexion and context of existence. Further, the middle term is also a concrete in comparison with the universal; it contains several predicates itself, and the individual in turn can be united through the same middle term with several universals. In general, therefore, it is *completely contingent* and *arbitrary* which of the many properties is adopted for the purpose of connecting it with a predicate; other middle terms are transitions to other predicates, and even the same middle term may by itself be a transition to various predicates, for as a particular against the universal it contains several determinations.

But not only is an indefinite number of syllogisms equally possible for one subject and not only is any single syllogism *contingent* in respect of its content, but these syllogisms that concern the same subject must also pass over into *contradiction*. For difference in general, which in the first instance is an indifferent *diversity*, is no less essentially *opposition*. The concrete is no longer something belonging merely to the sphere of Appearance, but is concrete through the unity in the Notion of the opposites that have become determined as moments of the Notion. Now when, in accordance with the qualitative nature of the terms in the formal syllogism, the concrete is grasped in respect of a single one of the determinations belonging to it, the syllogism assigns to it the predicate corresponding to this middle term; but as from another side the opposite determinateness is inferred, this shows the former conclusion to be false, although its premisses by themselves and equally its inference are quite correct. If from the middle term, that a wall has been painted blue, it is inferred that therefore the wall is blue, this is a correct inference; yet in spite of this syllogism the wall can be green if it has also been painted over yellow, from which latter circumstance taken by itself it would follow that it was yellow. If from the middle term of sense-nature it is inferred that man is neither good nor evil, because neither the one nor the other can be predicated of sense, the syllogism is correct but the conclusion is false; because as man is a concrete being, the middle term of spirituality is equally valid. From the middle term of the gravitation of the planets, satellites and comets towards the sun, it correctly follows that these bodies fall into the sun; but they do not fall into it, because each is no less its own centre of gravity, or, as it is said, they are impelled by centrifugal force. Similarly, from the middle term of sociality we can deduce the community of goods among citizens, but from the middle term of individuality, if it is pursued with equal abstractness, there follows the dissolution of the state, as has happened for example in the Holy Roman Empire from holding to the latter middle term. It is justly held that there is nothing so inadequate as a formal syllogism of this kind, since it is a matter of chance or caprice which middle term is employed. No matter how elegantly a deduction of this kind has run its course through syllogisms, however fully its correctness may be conceded it still leads to nothing of the slightest consequence, for the fact always remains that there are still other middle terms from which the exact opposite can be deduced with equal correctness. The Kantian *antinomies* of reason amount to nothing more than that from a notion first one of its determinations is laid down as basis, and then with equal necessity, the other. In these cases this inadequacy and contingency of a syllogism must not merely be shifted on to the content, as though these defects were independent of the form and the latter alone were the concern of logic. On the contrary, it lies in the form of the formal syllogism that the content is such a one-sided quality; it is determined to this one-sidedness by the said *abstract* form. It is, namely, one single quality of the many qualities or determinations of a concrete object or Notion because *according to the form* it is not supposed to be anything more than such an immediate, single determinateness. The extreme of individuality, as *abstract individuality*, is the *immediate* concrete, consequently the infinite or indeterminable manifold; the middle term is the equally *abstract particularity*, consequently a single one of these manifold qualities, and similarly the other extreme is the *abstract universal*. Therefore it is essentially on account of its form that the formal syllogism is wholly contingent as regards its content; and contingent, not in the sense that it is contingent for the syllogism whether *this* or *another* object be submitted to it— logic abstracts from this content—but in so far as a subject forms the basis it is contingent what kind of content determinations the syllogism shall infer from it.

3. The determinations of the syllogism are determinations of content in so far as they are immediate, abstract, and reflected into themselves. But their essential nature, on the contrary, is that they are not such mutually indifferent, intro-reflected determinations, but *determinations* of *form*; as such they are essentially *relations*. These relations are first, those of the extremes to the middle term—relations that are *immediate*, the *propositiones praemissae*, and, to name them, the *propositio major*, the relation of the particular to the universal, and the *propositio minor*, the relation of the individual to the particular. Secondly we have the relation of the extremes to one another, which is the *mediated* relation, *conclusio*. The *immediate* relations, the premises, are propositions or judgements in general, and *contradict the nature of the syllogism* according to which the different Notion determinations are not related immediately, but their unity should also be posited; the truth of the judgement is the syllogism. All the less can the premises remain immediate relations, since their content consists of immediately *distinguished* determinations and they are therefore not immediately identical in and for themselves—unless they are pure, identical propositions, that is empty tautologies that lead to nothing.

Accordingly, it is commonly demanded of the premises that they shall be *proved*, that is, that *they likewise shall be presented as conclusions*. Consequently, the two premises yield two further syllogisms. But these *two* new syllogisms in turn yield between them *four* premises which demand *four* new syllogisms; these have *eight* premises whose *eight* syllogisms in turn yield for their *sixteen* premises *sixteen* syllogisms, and *so on* in a geometrical progression to *infinity*.

Thus there here comes to view again the *progress to infinity* which appeared before in the lowlier *sphere of being*, but which was no longer to be expected in the domain of the Notion, of the absolute reflection-into-self out of the finite, in the region of free infinitude and truth. It was shown in the sphere of being that whenever we find the spurious infinite that runs away into a progression, we are faced with the contradiction of a *qualitative being* and an *impotent ought-to-be* that goes out and away beyond it; the progression itself is the repetition of the demand for unity in opposition to the qualitative, and of the persistent relapse into the limitation which is inadequate to that demand. Now in the formal syllogism the *immediate* relation or the qualitative judgement is the basis, and the *mediation* of the syllogism that which is posited as the higher truth over against it. The unending process of proving the premises does not resolve this contradiction but only perpetually renews it and is the repetition of one and the same original defect. The truth of the infinite progression consists, on the contrary, in the sublation of the progression itself and the form which is already determined by it as defective. This form is that of mediation as $I-P-U$. The two relations $I-P$ and $P-U$ are to be mediated relations; if this is effected in the same way the defective form $I-P-U$ will merely be duplicated, and so on to infinity. P has to I also the form determination of a *universal*, and to U the form determination of an *individual*, because these relations are, in general, judgements. Therefore they require mediation; but mediation in the form just mentioned only results in the re-appearance of the relationship that was to have been sublated.

The mediation must therefore be effected in another manner. For the mediation of $P-U$, we have I; accordingly the mediation must take the form $P-I-U$. To mediate $I-P$, we have U; this mediation therefore becomes the syllogism $I-U-P$.

When we examine this transition in the light of its Notion, we find in the first place that the mediation of the formal syllogism is, as has been shown, *contingent* in respect of its *content*. The

Y

immediate *individual* has in its determinatenesses an indeterminable number of middle terms, and these in turn have a similar number of determinatenesses in general; so that it depends entirely on an external *caprice* or simply on some *external circumstance* and contingent determination, with what kind of a universal the subject of the syllogism shall be united. As regards content, therefore, the mediation is not anything necessary or universal; it is not grounded in the *Notion of the fact*; on the contrary, the *ground* of the syllogism is something external to it, that is, something *immediate*; but among the Notion determinations the immediate is the *individual*.

As regards the *form*, the *mediation* likewise has for its *presupposition* the *immediacy of the relation*; therefore the mediation is itself mediated, and mediated by the *immediate*, that is, the *individual*. More precisely, through the *conclusion* of the first syllogism, the individual has become the mediating factor. The conclusion is *I–U*; the *individual* is thereby posited as a *universal*. In one premiss, the minor *I–P*, it is already present as a *particular*; hence it is that in which these two determinations are united. Or we may say that the conclusion in and for itself enunciates the individual as a universal, and that too not in an immediate manner but through mediation; consequently as a necessary relation. The *simple* particularity was the middle term; in the conclusion this particularity is *posited* in its *developed* form as the *relation of the individual and universality*. But the universal is still a qualitative determinateness, a predicate of the *individual*; the individual in being determined as a universal is *posited* as the universality of the extremes or as the middle term; by itself it is the extreme of individuality, but because it is now determined as a universal it is at the same time the unity of the two extremes.

(b) The Second Figure: P–I–U

1. The truth of the first qualitative syllogism is that something is united with a qualitative determinateness as a universal, not in and for itself but through a contingency or in an individuality. In such a quality, the *subject* of the syllogism has not returned into its Notion, but is apprehended only in its *externality*; immediacy constitutes the ground of the relation and consequently the mediation; thus the individual is in truth the middle term.

But further, the syllogistic relation is the sublation of the immediacy; the conclusion is not an immediate relation but relation by means of a third term; it contains therefore a *negative* unity; consequently the mediation is now determined as possessing within itself a *negative* moment.

In this second syllogism the premisses are: *P–I* and *I–U*; only the first of these premisses is still immediate; the second, *I–U*, is already mediated, namely by the first syllogism. The second syllogism therefore presupposes the first, just as conversely the first presupposes the second. Here the two extremes are distinguished as particular and universal; thus the latter still keeps its *place*; it is predicate. But the particular has changed places; it is subject, or posited in the *determination of the extreme of individuality*, just as the *individual* is posited in the *determination of middle term*, or of particularity. Both are therefore no longer the abstract immediacies that they were in the first syllogism. However, they are not yet posited as concretes; in standing in the *place* of the other, each is posited in its own determination and at the same time, though only *externally*, in the determination of the *other*.

The *specific* and *objective meaning* of this syllogism is that the universal is not *in and for itself* a determinate particular—for on the contrary it is the totality of its particulars—but is *one* such of its species *through the medium of individuality*; the rest of its species are excluded from it by the immediate externality. On the other hand the particular likewise is not immediately and in and for itself the universal, but the negative unity strips it of its determinateness and thereby raises it into universality. The individuality stands in a *negative* relationship to the particular in so far as it is supposed to be its predicate; it is *not* predicate of the particular.

2. But in the first instance the terms are still immediate determinatenesses; they have not of themselves developed into any objective significance; the altered *position* which two of them occupy is the form, which is as yet only external to them. Therefore they are still, as in the first syllogism, simply a mutually indifferent content—two qualities that are connected, not in and for themselves, but by means of a contingent individuality.

The syllogism of the first figure was the *immediate* syllogism or, otherwise expressed, the syllogism in its Notion as *abstract form* which has not yet realized itself in its determinations. The transition of this pure form into another figure is on the one hand the beginning of the realization of the Notion, in that the *negative* moment of mediation, and thereby a further determinateness of form, is posited in the initially immediate qualitative determinateness of the terms. But this is at the same time an *alteration* of the pure form of the syllogism; the latter no longer completely corresponds to its pure form, and the determinateness posited in its terms differs from the original form determination. Regarded merely as a subjective syllogism proceeding in an external reflection, it counts as a *species* of syllogism which ought to correspond to the genus, namely to the general schema I–P–U. But to begin with it does not correspond to this; its two premises are P–I, or I–P, and I–U; hence the middle term is in both cases subsumed or in both cases the subject, in which accordingly the two other terms inhere. It is therefore not a middle term, for this should on the one hand subsume or be predicate, and on the other hand be subsumed or be subject, or one of the terms should inhere in it while it itself inheres in the other. The true meaning of the fact that this syllogism does not correspond to the general form of the syllogism, is that the general form has passed over into this syllogism since the truth of that form consists in its being a subjective and contingent connecting of the terms. If the conclusion in the second figure (that is, without taking advantage of the restriction about to be mentioned, which converts it into something indeterminate) is correct, then it is so because it is so on its own account, not because it is the conclusion of this syllogism. But the same is the case with the conclusion of the first figure; it is this, its truth, that is posited by the second figure. In the view that holds the second figure to be merely one species, the necessary transition of the first into this second form is overlooked and the former is adhered to as the true form. Consequently, if in the second figure (which from ancient custom is quoted without further reasons as *the third*) we are likewise supposed to have a syllogism *correct* in this subjective sense, then it would have to be conformable to the first; hence, since one premiss I–U has the relationship of the subsumption of the middle term under one extreme, then it would have to be possible to give the other premiss, P–I, the opposite relation to that which it has and to subsume P under I. But such a relation would be the sublation of the determinate judgement I is P, and could only occur in an indeterminate, in a particular judgement; consequently the conclusion in this figure can only be particular. The particular judgement, however, as remarked above, is both positive and negative—

a conclusion to which for that very reason no great value can be attached. Since too the particular and universal are the extremes, and are immediate, mutually indifferent determinatenesses, their relationship is itself indifferent; either can be taken at choice as major or minor term and therefore, too, either premiss can be taken as major or minor.

3. The conclusion, being positive as well as negative, is thus a relation indifferent to these determinatenesses and hence a *universal* relation. More precisely, the mediation of the first syllogism was *in itself* a contingent one; in the second syllogism this contingency is *posited*. Hence it is the self-sublating mediation; the mediation has the determination of individuality and immediacy; what is united by this syllogism must on the contrary be *in itself* and *immediately* identical; for this middle term, *immediate individuality*, is determined in an infinitely manifold and external manner. In it, therefore, is rather posited the self-*external* mediation. But the externality of the individuality is universality; the above mediation by means of the immediate individual points beyond itself to *its other* form, and the mediation is therefore effected by the *universal*. In other words, what is to be united by the second syllogism must be conjoined *immediately*; the immediacy on which this syllogism is based cannot bring about a definite conclusion. The immediacy to which it points is the opposite to its own—the sublated first immediacy of being—therefore the *universal* that is reflected into itself, or the *implicit, abstract universal*.

From the point of view we have just considered, the transition of this syllogism was an *alteration* like transition in the sphere of being, because the qualitative element, that of immediate individuality, lies at its base. But according to the Notion, individuality unites the particular and universal in so far as it *sublates* the *determinateness* of the particular, and this presents itself as the contingency of this syllogism; the extremes are not united by their determinate relation which they have for a middle term; this term is therefore *not* their *determinate unity*, and the positive unity which still attaches to the middle term is only *abstract universality*. But with the positing of the middle term in this determination, which is its truth, we have another form of the syllogism.

(c) The Third Figure: I–U–P

1. This third syllogism no longer has any immediate premiss; the

relation $I-U$ has been mediated by the first syllogism, the relation $P-U$ by the second. Hence it presupposes the first two syllogisms; but conversely, they both presuppose it, and in general each presupposes the other two. In this figure, therefore, the determination of the syllogism is in general completed. What this reciprocal mediation precisely contains is this, that each syllogism, although by itself mediation, is none the less not in its own self the totality of the mediation but contains an immediacy whose mediation lies outside it.

The syllogism $I-U-P$, regarded in itself, is the truth of the formal syllogism; it expresses that the mediation of the formal syllogism is the abstractly universal mediation, and that the extremes are not contained in the middle term according to their essential determinateness but only according to their universality; and that therefore what was supposed to be mediated in it is precisely what is not brought into unity. Here then is made explicit in what the formalism of the syllogism consists; its terms have an immediate content which is indifferent to the form, or, what is the same thing, they are determinations of form which have not yet reflected themselves into determinations of content.

2. The middle term of this syllogism is indeed the unity of the extremes, but a unity in which abstraction is made from their determinateness; it is the *indeterminate* universal. But since this universal is at the same time distinguished as *abstract* from the extremes as *determinate*, it is itself still a *determinate* relatively to them, and the whole is a syllogism whose relation to its Notion has now to be considered. The middle term, as the universal, is the subsuming term or predicate to *both* its extremes, and does not occur once as subsumed or as subject. In so far, therefore, as it is supposed to correspond, as *a species* of syllogism, to the syllogism, it can do so only on condition that when one relation $I-U$, already possesses the proper relationship, the other relation $U-P$ also possesses it. This occurs in a judgement in which the relationship of subject and predicate is indifferent, in a *negative* judgement. In this way the syllogism becomes legitimate, but the conclusion necessarily negative.

Thus it is now also indifferent which of the two determinations of this proposition is taken as predicate and which as subject; and in the syllogism, whether it is taken as extreme of individuality or of particularity, therefore as minor or major term. Since on the common assumption it depends on this which of the premisses is to be major and which minor, this too has become a matter of indifference. This is the ground of the ordinary *fourth figure* of the syllogism, a figure unknown to Aristotle and which in any case is concerned with a wholly empty and pointless distinction. In it the immediate position of the terms is the *reverse* of their position in the first figure. Since subject and predicate of the negative conclusion in the formal treatment of the judgement do not have the definite relationship of subject and predicate, but either can take the place of the other, it is indifferent which term is taken as subject and which as predicate; therefore equally indifferent which premiss is taken as major and which as minor. This indifference, aided as it is by the determination of particularity (especially when it is observed that this can be taken in the comprehensive sense) makes this fourth figure a sheer futility.

3. The objective significance of the syllogism in which the universal is the middle term, is that the mediating element, as unity of the extremes, is *essentially a universal*. But since the universality is in the first instance only qualitative or abstract universality, it does not contain the determinateness of the extremes; their conjunction, if it is to be effected, must similarly have its ground in a mediation lying outside this syllogism and is in respect of this latter just as contingent as in the case of the preceding forms of the syllogism. But now since the universal is determined as the middle term, and the determinateness of the extremes is not contained in it, this middle term is posited as a wholly indifferent and external one.

As the immediate result of this bare abstraction, we obtain, of course, a *fourth figure* of the syllogism, namely that of the *relationless* syllogism *U–U–U*, which abstracts from the qualitative difference of the terms and consequently has for its determination their merely external unity, namely their *equality*.

(d) The Fourth Figure: U–U–U, or the Mathematical Syllogism

1. The mathematical syllogism runs: if two things or determinations are equal to a third, they are equal to each other. Here the relationship of inherence or subsumption of the terms is extinguished.

The mediating factor is a third in general, but it has absolutely no determination whatever as against its extremes. Each of the three can therefore equally well be the third, mediating term. Which one is to be used for this purpose, and which of the three relations, therefore, are to be taken as immediate and which as mediated, depends on external circumstances and other conditions, namely on which two of them are the immediately *given* terms. But this determination does not concern the syllogism itself and is completely external.

2. The mathematical syllogism ranks as an *axiom* in mathematics, as *an absolutely self-evident, primitive proposition*, that neither admits nor requires any proof, that is any mediation, and neither presupposes anything else nor can be deduced from anything else. If its prerogative of being immediately *self-evident* is looked at more closely, it will be seen that it lies in the formalism of this syllogism which abstracts from all qualitative distinction of the terms and only takes up their quantitative equality or inequality. But for this very reason it is not without presupposition or unmediated; the quantitative determination, which is the only thing in it taken into account, *is* only *through abstraction* from qualitative difference and from the determinations of the Notion. Lines, figures, posited as equal to one another, are understood only in terms of their magnitude; a triangle is affirmed to be equal to a square, but not as triangle to square, but only in regard to magnitude, etc. Similarly, the Notion and its determinations do not enter into this syllogizing; there is no *comprehending* at all [that is, in terms of the Notion] in this process; and understanding too has not even the formal, abstract determinations of the Notion before it. The self-evidence of this syllogism, therefore, rests merely on the fact that its thought content is so meagre and abstract.

3. But the *result of the syllogism of existence* is not merely this abstraction from all Notional determinateness; the *negativity* of the immediate, abstract determinations which emerged from it has yet another *positive* side, namely that the abstract determinateness has had *its other posited* in it and thereby has become *concrete*.

In the first place, the syllogisms of existence all mutually *presuppose* one another and the extremes united in the conclusion are only genuinely and in and for themselves united in so far as they are *otherwise* united by an identity that has its ground elsewhere; the middle term, as it is constituted in the syllogisms we have considered, is *supposed* to be their Notion unity, but is only a formal determinateness that is not posited as their concrete unity. But this *presupposed* element of each of those mediations is not merely a *given immediacy* in general, as in the mathematical syllogism, but is itself a mediation, namely, for each of the two other syllogisms. Therefore what we truly have before us is not mediation based on a given immediacy, but mediation based on mediation. Hence this is not the quantitative mediation that abstracts from the form of mediation, but rather the *mediation that relates itself to mediation*, or the *mediation of reflection*. The circle of reciprocal presupposing that these syllogisms unite to form with one another is the return of this act of presupposition into itself, which herein forms a totality, and thus the *other* to which each individual syllogism points is not placed through abstraction *outside* the circle but embraced *within* it.

Further, from the side of the *individual determinations of the form* it has been seen that in this entirety of the formal syllogisms each individual term has in turn taken the *place of middle term*. This was determined as *particularity*; subsequently, through the dialectical movement it determined itself as *individuality* and *universality*. Similarly, each of these determinations occupied in turn the *places of the two extremes*. *The merely negative result* is the extinction of the qualitative form determinations in the merely quantitative, mathematical syllogism. But what we truly have here is the *positive result*, that mediation is not effected through an *individual* qualitative determinateness of form, but through the *concrete identity* of the determinations. The defect and formalism of the three syllogistic figures considered above consists just in this, that an individual determinateness of this kind was supposed to constitute their middle term. Mediation has thus determined itself as the indifference of the immediate or abstract form determinations and as positive *reflection* of one into the other. The immediate syllogism of existence has thereby passed over into the *syllogism of reflection*.

Remark: The Common View of the Syllogism

In the account here given of the nature of the syllogism and its various forms, passing reference has also been made to what in the usual consideration and treatment of syllogisms constitutes the main interest, namely, how a correct conclusion may be obtained in each figure; however, in those references only the main point has been indicated, and those cases and complexities which arise

Y*

when the distinction of positive and negative judgements, together with the quantitative determination—especially particularity—is also dragged in, have been passed over. Some remarks on the ordinary view and mode of treatment of the syllogism in logic will be in place here. It is a familiar fact that this doctrine was elaborated into such finely drawn distinctions that its so-called subtleties have been the object of universal aversion and disgust. The *natural understanding* in asserting itself in every department of mental and spiritual culture against the unsubstantial forms of reflection, also turned against this artificial knowledge of the forms of reason and supposed itself able to dispense with such a science on the ground that it performed the individual operations of thought specified therein naturally and spontaneously without any special instruction. In point of fact, if a pre-condition of rational thinking were the laborious study of syllogistic formulae, mankind would in that respect be in the same sorry plight as they would be, as already remarked in the Preface in another respect, if they could not walk or digest without having studied anatomy and physiology. Granting that the study of these sciences may not be without profit for the regulation of one's diet, we must undoubtedly credit the study of the forms of reason with an even more important influence on the correctness of thinking. But without going into this aspect of the matter which concerns the education of subjective thinking and therefore, strictly speaking, pedagogics, it must be admitted that the study which has for its subject matter the modes and laws of operation of reason, must in its own self be of the greatest interest—of an interest at least not inferior to an acquaintance with the laws of nature and of her particular forms. If it is not thought a small matter to have discovered some sixty species of parrots, one hundred and thirty-seven species of veronica, etc., much less ought it to be thought a small matter to discover the forms of reason; is not a figure of the syllogism something infinitely superior to a species of parrot or veronica?

Therefore, though contempt for the knowledge of the forms of reason must be regarded as sheer barbarism, equally we must admit that the ordinary presentation of the syllogism and its particular formations is not a *rational* cognition, not an exposition of them as *forms of reason*, and that syllogistic wisdom by its own worthlessness has brought upon itself the contempt which has been its lot. Its defect consists in its simply stopping short at the *understanding's form* of the syllogism in which the Notion determinations are taken as *abstract*, formal terms. It is all the more inconsequent to cling to these determinations as abstract qualities, since in the syllogism it is their *relations* that constitute the essential feature, and inherence and subsumption already imply that the individual, because the universal inheres in it, is itself a universal, and the universal, because it subsumes the individual, is itself an individual; more exactly, the syllogism expressly posits this very *unity* as *middle term*, and its determination is precisely *mediation*, that is, the Notion determinations no longer, as in the judgement, have for basis their mutual externality, but rather their unity. It is thus the Notion of the syllogism that declares the imperfection of the formal syllogism in which the middle term is fixedly held, not as unity of the extremes but as a formal, abstract determination qualitatively distinct from them. The treatment is rendered still less meaningful by the fact that also relations or judgements in which even formal determinations become indifferent, as in negative and particular judgements, and which therefore approximate to propositions, are still regarded as perfect relationships. Now since the qualitative form *I–P–U* is generally accepted as the ultimate and absolute, the dialectical treatment of the syllogism no longer operates; the remaining syllogisms are consequently regarded not as *necessary alterations* of that first form but as *species*. In this case, it is indifferent whether the first formal syllogism itself is regarded only as a kind of species *alongside* the rest, or as *genus* and *species* at the same time; the latter occurs when the other syllogisms are reduced to the first. If this reduction is not expressly effected, yet the basis is always the same formal relationship of external subsumption expressed by the first figure.

This formal syllogism is the contradiction that the middle term which is supposed to be the determinate unity of the extremes does not appear as this unity but as a determination qualitatively distinct from those extremes whose unity it is supposed to be. Because the syllogism is this contradiction, it is in its own nature dialectical. Its dialectical movement exhibits it in each of the moments of the Notion, so that not only the above relationship of subsumption or particularity, but *equally essentially* negative unity and universality are moments in the union of the extremes. In so far as each of these by itself is equally only a one-sided moment of particularity, they are likewise imperfect middle terms, but at the same time they constitute the developed determinations of the middle term; the entire course through the three figures presents the middle term in each of these determinations, and the true result that emerges from it is that the middle is not an individual Notion determination but the totality of them all.

The defect of the formal syllogism, therefore, does not lie in the *form of the syllogism*—on the contrary, this is the form of rationality—but in the fact that the form appears only as an *abstract* and therefore notionless form. It has been shown that the abstract determination, on account of its abstract relation-to-self, can equally be regarded as content; this being so, the formal syllogism merely serves to show that a relation of a subject to a predicate follows or does not follow *only from this middle term*. Nothing is gained in having proved a proposition by a syllogism of this kind; on account of the abstract determinateness of the middle term, which is a Notionless quality, other middle terms can just as well be given from which the opposite follows; in fact, from the same middle term opposite predicates may in turn be deduced by further syllogisms. Besides being of little service, the formal syllogism is also a very simple affair; the numerous rules which have been invented are tiresome not only because they contrast so strongly with the simple nature of the fact but also because they relate to cases where the formal worth of the syllogism is furthermore diminished by the external form determination, above all, particularity (especially as for this purpose it must be taken in a comprehensive sense), and where even in respect of form nothing but completely worthless results are deduced. However, the most merited and most important aspect of the disfavour into which syllogistic doctrine has fallen is that this doctrine is such a long-drawn out, notionless occupation with a subject matter whose sole content is the *Notion* itself. The numerous syllogistic rules remind one of the procedure of arithmeticians who similarly give a host of rules about arithmetical operations, all of which rules presuppose that one has not the *Notion* of the operation. But numbers are a notionless material and the operations of arithmetic are an external combining or separating of them, a mechanical procedure—indeed, calculating machines have been invented which perform these operations; whereas it is the harshest and most glaring of contradictions when the form determinations of the syllogism, which are Notions, are treated as a notionless material.

The extreme example of this irrational treatment of the Notion determinations of the syllogism is surely Leibniz's subjection of the syllogism to the calculus of combinations and permutations[1] and has reckoned thereby how many positions of the syllogism are possible—that is, with respect to the distinctions of positive and negative, of universal, particular, indeterminate and singular judgements; 2,048 such combinations are found to be possible of which, after the exclusion of the useless figures, twenty-four useful figures remain. Leibniz makes much of the usefulness of the analysis of combinations for ascertaining not only the forms of the syllogism but also the combinations of other concepts. The operation by which this is ascertained is the same as that by which it is calculated how many combinations of letters are possible in an alphabet, how many throws are possible in a game of dice, how many kinds of play with an ombre card, etc. Here therefore we find the determinations of the syllogism put in the same class with the points of the die and the ombre card, the rational is taken as a dead and non-rational thing, and the characteristic feature of the Notion and its determinations as spiritual essences *to relate themselves* and through this relating to *sublate* their *immediate* determination, is ignored. This Leibnizian application of the calculus of combinations and permutations to the syllogism and to the combination of other notions, differed from the notorious *Art of Lully*[2] solely in being more methodical on the *arithmetical* side, but for the rest, they were both equally meaningless. Connected with this was a pet idea of Leibniz, embraced by him in his youth, and in spite of its immaturity and shallowness not relinquished by him even in later life, the idea of a *characteristica universalis* of notions—a language of symbols in which each notion would be represented as a relation proceeding from others or in its relation to others— as though in rational combinations, which is essentially dialectical, a content still retained the same determinations *that it possesses when fixed in isolation.*

Ploucquet's[3] calculus has undoubtedly got hold of the most consistent method by which the relationship of the syllogism is made capable of being subjected to a calculus. It rests upon the

[1] *Opp. Tom. II*, p. 1.
[2] Raymundus Lullus, c 1232–1315: *Ars magna s. generalis*
[3] Ploucquet, Gottfried, 1716–1790: *Principia de Substantiis et Phaenomenis, Accedit Methodus Calculandi in Logicis Ab Ipso Inventa*, 1753.

abstraction from the difference of relationship, from the difference of individuality, particularity and universality in the judgement and upon strict adherence to the *abstract identity* of subject and predicate whereby they are in a *mathematical equality*—in a relation which converts the syllogizing process into a completely meaningless and tautological formulation of propositions. In the proposition: *the rose is red*, the predicate is not to denote red in general but only the specific *red of the rose*; in the proposition: *all Christians are men*, the predicate is to denote only those men who are Christians; from this proposition and the proposition: *the Jews are not Christians*, there follows the conclusion (which did not particularly commend this syllogistic calculus to Mendelssohn) *therefore the Jews are not men* (namely, not those men that the Christians are). Ploucquet states as a consequence of his discovery: '*posse etiam rudes mechanice totam logicam doceri, uti pueri arithmeticam docentur, ita quidem, ut nulla formidine in ratiociniis suis errandi torqueri, vel fallaciis circumveniri possint, si in calculo non errant.*' This recommendation, that by means of the calculus the whole of logic can be *mechanically* brought within reach of the uneducated, is surely the worst thing that can be said of a discovery bearing on the presentation of the science of logic.

B. THE SYLLOGISM OF REFLECTION

The course of the qualitative syllogism has sublated what was *abstract* in its terms with the result that the term has posited itself as a determinateness in which the other determinateness is also *reflected*. Besides the abstract terms, the syllogism also contains their *relation*, and in the conclusion this relation is posited as mediated and necessary; therefore each determinateness is in truth posited not as an individual, separate one, but as a relation to the other, as a *concrete* determinateness.

The middle term was abstract particularity, by itself a simple determinateness, and was a middle term only externally and relatively to the self-subsistent extremes. Now it is posited as the *totality* of the terms; as such it is the *posited* unity of the extremes, but in the first instance it is the unity of reflection which embraces them within itself—an inclusion which, as the *first* sublating of immediacy and the first relating of the terms, is not yet the absolute identity of the Notion.

The extremes are the determinations of the judgement of re-flection, *individuality* proper and *universality* as a connective determination or a reflection embracing a manifold within itself. But the individual subject also contains, as we have seen in the case of the judgement of reflection, besides the bare individuality which belongs to form, determinateness as universality absolutely re-flected into itself, as presupposed, that is here still immediately assumed, *genus*.

From this determinateness of the extremes which belongs to the progressive determination of the judgement, there results the precise content of the *middle term*, which is essentially the point of interest in the syllogism since it distinguishes syllogism from judgement. It contains (1) *individuality*, but (2) individuality extended to universality as *all*, (3) universality which forms the basis and absolutely unites within itself individuality and abstract universality—that is, *the genus*. It is in this way that the syllogism of reflection is the first to possess *genuine determinateness of form*, in that the middle term is *posited* as the totality of the terms; the immediate syllogism is by contrast *indeterminate*, because the middle term is still only abstract particularity in which the mo-ments of its Notion are not yet posited. This first syllogism of reflection may be called *the syllogism of allness*.

(a) *The Syllogism of Allness*

1. The syllogism of allness is the syllogism of understanding in its perfection, but is as yet no more than that. That the middle term in it is not *abstract* particularity but is developed into its moments and is therefore concrete, is indeed an essential requirement for the Notion; but the form of *allness* so far only gathers the individual externally into universality, and conversely still preserves the individual in the universality as something possessing immediately a separate self-subsistence. The negation of the immediacy of the determinations which was the result of the syllogism of existence, is only the *first* negation, not yet the negation of the negation or absolute reflection into self. Therefore the single determinations still form the basis of the universality of reflection that embraces them within itself; in other words, allness is still not the uni-versality of the Notion but the external universality of reflection.

The syllogism of existence was contingent because its middle term, as a single determinateness of the concrete subject, admits of an indeterminable number of other such middle terms, and therefore the subject could be united in the syllogism with indeterminably different and even contradictory predicates. But since the middle term now contains *individuality* and is thereby itself concrete, it can only serve to connect the subject with a predicate which belongs to the subject as concrete. If for example from the middle term *green* it should be inferred that a picture was pleasing because green is pleasing to the eye, or that a poem or building was beautiful because it possessed *regularity*, the picture, etc., might all the same be ugly on account of other qualities from which this latter predicate could be inferred. On the other hand, since the middle term has the determination of *allness*, it contains the greenness or regularity as *a concrete*, which just for that reason is not the abstraction of something merely green or merely regular; with this *concrete* then only those predicates can be connected which conform to *the totality of the concrete* thing. In the judgement: what is green or regular is pleasing, the subject is only the abstraction of green or regularity; in the proposition: all green or regular things are pleasing, the subject is, on the contrary: all actual concrete objects that are green or regular—objects, therefore, which are taken as *concrete with all their properties* that they possess besides greenness or regularity.

2. But this very perfection of the syllogism of reflection makes it a mere delusion. The middle term has the determinateness '*all*'; to this is *immediately* attached in the major premiss the predicate that is united with the subject in the conclusion. But '*all*' are '*all individuals*'; therefore in the major premiss the individual subject already immediately possesses this predicate and *does not obtain it first through the syllogism*. Or to put it otherwise the subject obtains through the conclusion a predicate as a consequence; but the major premiss already contains this conclusion within it; *therefore the major premiss is not correct on its own account*, or is not an immediate, presupposed judgement, but *already presupposes the conclusion* whose ground it was supposed to be. In the favourite perfect syllogism:

> All men are mortal
> Now Gaius is a man
> Therefore Gaius is mortal,

the major premiss is correct only because and in so far as the *conclusion is correct*; if Gaius should chance to be not mortal, the major premiss would not be correct. The proposition which was supposed to be the conclusion must already be immediately correct on its own account, because otherwise the major premiss could not embrace all individuals; before the major premiss can pass as correct, there is the *prior* question whether the conclusion itself may not be an *instance* against it.

3. In the case of the syllogism of existence we found from the Notion of the syllogism that the premisses, as *immediate*, contradicted the conclusion, that is to say the *mediation* demanded by the Notion of the syllogism, and that the first syllogism therefore presupposed others and conversely these others presupposed it. In the syllogism of reflection, this is posited in the syllogism itself, namely, that the major premiss presupposes its conclusion, in that the former contains that connexion of the individual with a predicate which is supposed to appear only as conclusion.

What, then, we really have here may be expressed in the first instance by saying that the syllogism of reflection is only an external, empty *show of syllogizing*—hence that the essence of this syllogizing rests on subjective *individuality* and that therefore this latter constitutes the middle term and is to be posited as such— the individuality that is individuality as such and possesses universality only externally. We may also say that the precise content of the syllogism of reflection showed that the relation in which the individual stands to its predicate is *immediate*, not inferred, and that the major premiss, the connexion of a particular with a universal, or, more precisely, of a formal universal with an intrinsic universal, is mediated by the relation of individuality which is present in the former—of individuality as allness. But this is *the syllogism of induction*.

(b) The Syllogism of Induction

1. The syllogism of allness comes under the schema of the first figure, *I–P–U*; the syllogism of induction under that of the second, *U–I–P*, as it again has individuality for middle term, not *abstract* individuality but individuality as *complete*, namely, posited with its opposite determination, universality. *One extreme* is some predicate or other that is common to all these individuals; its relation to them constitutes the immediate premisses, of which

one, in the preceding syllogism was supposed to be the conclusion. The *other* extreme may be the immediate *genus* as it is
found in the middle term of the preceding syllogism or in the
subject of the universal judgement and which is exhausted in all
the individuals or species collectively of the middle term. Accordingly the syllogism has the shape:

$$
\begin{array}{c}
i \\
i \\
U\text{-}\text{-}P \\
i \\
i \\
ad \\
infinitum
\end{array}
$$

2. The second figure of the formal syllogism *U–I–P* did not
correspond to the schema, because *I* which constitutes the middle
term was not the subsuming term or predicate. In induction this
defect is eliminated; here the middle term is *all the individuals*; the
proposition: *U–I*, which contains as subject the objective universal or genus separated off to form an extreme, has a predicate
that is at least co-extensive with the subject, and consequently
for external reflection is identical with it. Lion, elephant, and so on
constitute the genus of quadruped; the difference, that the *same*
content is posited once in individuality and again in universality,
is accordingly a mere *indifferent determination of form*—an indifference which is the result of the formal syllogism posited in the
syllogism of reflection, and here is posited through the equality of
extension.

Induction, therefore, is not the syllogism of mere *perception* or
of contingent existence, like the corresponding second figure, but
the syllogism of *experience*—of the subjective taking together of
the individuals into the genus and of the conjoining of the genus
with a universal determinateness because this latter is found in all
the individuals. It has also the objective significance that the
immediate genus determines itself through the totality of individuality to a universal property, has its existence in a universal
relationship or mark. But the objective significance of this, as of
the other syllogisms, is at first only its inner Notion, and is not yet
posited here.

3. On the contrary, induction is still essentially a subjective

syllogism. The middle terms are the individuals in their immediacy; the subjective taking together of them into the genus by means of allness is an *external* reflection. On account of the persistent *immediacy* of the individuals and their consequent *externality*, the universality is only completeness, or rather remains *a problem*. In induction, therefore, the *progress* into the spurious infinite once more makes its appearance; *individuality* is supposed to be posited as *identical* with *universality*, but since the *individuals* are no less posited as *immediate*, that unity remains only a perennial *ought-to-be*; it is a unity of *likeness*; those which are supposed to be identical are, at the same time, supposed *not* to be so. It is only when the *a, b, c, d, e* are carried on to infinity that they constitute the genus and give the completed experience. The *conclusion* of induction thus remains *problematical*.

But induction, in expressing that perception in order to become experience *ought* to be carried on *to infinity*, presupposes that the genus is *in and for itself* united with its determinateness. Therefore, strictly speaking, it rather presupposes its conclusion as something immediate, just as the syllogism of allness presupposes the conclusion for one of its premises. An experience that rests on induction is accepted as valid *although* the perception is admittedly *incomplete*; but the assumption that no *contradictory instance* of that experience can arise is only possible if the experience is true *in and for itself*. Thus the syllogism by induction, though indeed based on an immediacy, is not based on that immediacy on which it is supposed to be based, on the *merely affirmative [seiende]* immediacy of *individuality*, but on the immediacy which is *in and for itself*, the *universal* immediacy. The fundamental character of induction is that it is a syllogism; if individuality is taken as the essential, but universality as only the external, determination of the middle term, then the middle term would fall asunder into two unconnected parts and we should not have a syllogism; this externality belongs rather to the extremes. It is only as *immediately identical* with *universality* that *individuality* can be the middle term; such universality is properly *objective* universality, the *genus*. This may also be looked at in this way: universality is *external but essential* in the determination of individuality that forms the basis of the middle term of induction; but such an *external* is no less immediately its opposite, the *internal*. The truth of the syllogism of induction is, therefore, a syllogism that has for its middle term an individuality that is immediately *in its own self* universality; this is the *syllogism of analogy*.

(c) The Syllogism of Analogy

1. This syllogism has for its abstract schema the third figure of the immediate syllogism *I–U–P*. But its middle term is no longer just any single quality, but universality that is the *reflection-into-self of a concrete*, and hence its *nature*; and conversely, because it is thus the universality of a concrete, it is at the same time in its own self this *concrete*. Here, then, the middle term is an individual but an individual taken in its universal nature; further, another individual forms an extreme possessing the same universal nature with the former. For example:

> The *earth* is inhabited,
> The moon is *an earth*,
> Therefore the moon is inhabited.

2. Analogy is the more superficial, the more the universal in which the two individuals are one, and according to which one individual becomes the predicate of the other, is a mere *quality*, or (quality being taken subjectively) some *mark* or other, when the identity of the two therein is taken as a mere *similarity*. Superficiality of this kind, however, to which a form of understanding or reason is reduced by being degraded to the sphere of mere *representation*, should not find a place in logic at all. Also it is improper to represent the major premiss of this syllogism as though it should run: that which resembles an object in some characteristics resembles it in others also. By so doing, the *form of the syllogism* is expressed in the shape of a content, while the empirical content, the content properly so called, is relegated to the minor premiss. In this way the whole form, for example, of the first syllogism, could be expressed as its major premiss: *That which is subsumed under some other thing in which a third inheres, has also that third inherent in it: now . . .* , and so forth. But the importance of the syllogism itself does not depend on the empirical content, and to convert its own form into the content of a major premiss is no less a matter of indifference than to take any other empirical content for that purpose. But in so far as the importance of the syllogism of analogy does not depend on the former content which

contains nothing but the form peculiar to the syllogism, then the importance of the first syllogism would not depend on it either, that is to say, would not depend on that which makes the syllogism a syllogism. The main point always is the form of the syllogism, whether it have the form itself or something else for its empirical content. Thus the syllogism of analogy is a peculiar form, and it is quite futile not to regard it as such on the ground that its form can be converted into the content or matter of a major premiss, whereas logic is not concerned with the matter. What may lead to this misunderstanding in the case of the syllogism of analogy and perhaps also in the case of the syllogism of induction, is that in them the middle term and the extremes, too, are further determined than in the merely formal syllogism, and therefore the form determination, because it is no longer simple and abstract, must appear also as a *determination of content*. But the fact that the form determines itself to content in this way is in the first place a necessary advance of the formal element and therefore essentially concerns the nature of the syllogism; and therefore, secondly, a content determination of this kind cannot be regarded in the same way as any other empirical content, nor can abstraction be made from it.

When we consider the form of the syllogism of analogy in the above expression of its major premiss, which states that if two objects agree in one or more properties, then a property which one possesses also belongs to the other, it may seem that this syllogism contains *four terms*, the *quaternio terminorum*—a circumstance which entails the difficulty of bringing analogy into the form of a formal syllogism. There are *two* individuals, *thirdly*, a property immediately assumed as common, and *fourthly* the other property which one individual immediately possesses but which the other first obtains through the syllogism. This arises from the fact that, as we have seen, in the analogical syllogism the *middle term* is posited as individuality, but immediately *also* as the true universality of the latter. In *induction*, the middle term is, apart from the two extremes, an indeterminable number of individuals; in this syllogism therefore an infinite number of terms ought to be enumerated. In the syllogism of allness the universality in the middle term is so far merely the external form determination of allness; in the syllogism of analogy, on the contrary, it is essential universality. In the above example the middle term, *the earth*, is taken as a concrete that in its truth is as much a universal nature or genus as an individual.

From this aspect, the *quaternio terminorum* would not render analogy an imperfect syllogism. Yet it does so from another aspect; for although one subject has the same universal nature as the other, it is undetermined whether the determinateness which is inferred for the second subject belongs to the first by virtue of its *nature* or by virtue of its *particularity*; whether for example the earth is inhabited as a heavenly body *in general*, or only as this *particular* heavenly body. Analogy is still a syllogism of reflection inasmuch as individuality and universality are *immediately* united in its middle term. On account of this immediacy, the *externality* of the unity of reflection is still with us; the individual is only *implicitly* the genus, it is not posited in that negativity by which its determinateness would be the determinateness proper to the genus itself. For this reason the predicate which belongs to the individual of the middle term is not already predicate of the other individual although both belong to the one genus.

3. *I–P* (the moon is inhabited) is the conclusion; but one premiss (the earth is inhabited) is likewise *I–P*; inasmuch as *I–P* is supposed to be a conclusion it involves the demand that the said premiss shall be one also. Hence this syllogism is in its own self the demand for itself to counter the immediacy which it contains, in other words it presupposes its conclusion. A syllogism of existence has its presupposition in the *other* syllogisms of existence; in the case of the syllogisms just considered the presupposition has been placed within them, because they are syllogisms of reflection. Since then the syllogism of analogy is the demand for its own mediation against the immediacy with which its mediation is burdened, it is the moment of *individuality* whose sublation it demands. Thus there remains for middle term the objective universal, the *genus*, purged of immediacy. In the syllogism of analogy the genus was a moment of the middle term only as an *immediate presupposition*; since the syllogism itself demands the sublation of the presupposed immediacy, the negation of the individuality, and consequently the universal, is no longer immediate, but *posited*. The syllogism of reflection contained only the *first* negation of immediacy; now the second has appeared, and with it the external universality of reflection is determined into universality in and for itself. Regarded from the positive side the con-

clusion shows itself to be identical with the premiss, the mediation as having coincided with its presupposition; thus there is an identity of the universality of reflection by which it has become a higher universality.

Looking over the course of the syllogisms of reflection, we see that the mediation is in general the *posited* or *concrete* unity of the form determinations of the extremes; the reflection consists in this positing of one determination in the other; thus the mediating element is *allness*. But *individuality* appears as the essential ground of allness and universality only as an external determination in it, as *completeness*. But universality is *essential* to the individual if it is to be a middle term that unites; the individual is therefore to be taken as *in itself* a universal. But the individual is not united with universality in this merely positive manner but is sublated in it and a negative moment; thus the universal is that whose essential being has become actual, the posited genus, and the individual as immediate is rather the externality of the genus, or it is an *extreme*. The syllogism of reflection taken in general comes under the schema *P–I–U*, in which the individual is still as such the essential determination of the middle term; but in that its immediacy has sublated itself, and the middle term has determined itself as the universality that is in and for itself, the syllogism has entered under the formal schema *I–U–P*, and the syllogism of reflection has passed over into the *syllogism of necessity*.

C. THE SYLLOGISM OF NECESSITY

The mediating element has now determined itself (1) as *simple* determinate universality, like the particularity in the syllogism of existence, but (2) as *objective* universality, that is to say, universality which contains the entire determinateness of the distinguished extremes like the allness of the syllogism of reflection, a *fulfilled* yet *simple* universality—the *universal nature* of the fact, the *genus*.

This syllogism is *pregnant with content*, because the *abstract* middle term of the syllogism of existence posited itself as *determinate difference* to become the middle term of the syllogism of reflection, while this difference has reflected itself into simple identity again. This syllogism is therefore the syllogism of *necessity*, for its middle term is not some alien immediate content, but the reflection-into-self of the determinateness of the extremes.

These possess in the middle term their inner identity, the determinations of whose content are the form determinations of the extremes. Consequently, that which differentiates the terms appears as an *external* and *unessential* form, and the terms themselves as moments of *a necessary* existence.

In the first instance this syllogism is immediate, and thus formal in so far as the *connexion* of the terms is the *essential nature* as *content*, and this content is present in the distinguished terms in only a *diverse form*, and the extremes by themselves are merely an *unessential* subsistence. The realization of this syllogism has so to determine it that the *extremes* also shall be posited as this *totality* which initially the middle term is, and that the *necessity* of the relation which is at first only the substantial *content*, shall be a relation of the *posited form*.

(a) The Categorical Syllogism

1. The categorical syllogism has the categorical judgement for one or both of its premises. Here, with this syllogism, as with the judgement, is associated the more specific significance that its middle term is *objective universality*. Superficially the categorical syllogism too is taken for nothing more than a mere syllogism of inherence.

The categorical syllogism in its substantial significance is the *first syllogism of necessity*, in which a subject is united with a predicate through *its substance*. But substance raised into the sphere of the Notion is the universal, posited as being in and for itself in such a manner that it has for the form or mode of its being, not accidentality, which is the relationship peculiar to substance, but the Notion-determination. Its differences are therefore the extremes of the syllogism and, precisely, universality and individuality. The former, in contrast to the *genus*, which is the precise determination of the *middle term*, is abstract universality or universal determinateness—the accidentality of substance gathered into simple determinateness which however is its essential difference, *specific difference*. But individuality is the actual, in itself the concrete unity of genus and determinateness; here, however, in the immediate syllogism it appears at first as immediate individuality, accidentally gathered into the form of a subsistence *on its own*. The relation of this extreme to the middle term constitutes a categorical judgement; but since the other extreme, too, according to the above-stated determination, expresses the specific difference of the genus or its determinate principle, this other premiss is also categorical.

2. This syllogism, as the first and therefore immediate syllogism of necessity, comes in the first instance under the schema of the first formal syllogism *I–P–U*. But as the middle term is the essential *nature* of the individual and not *just any* of its determinate-nesses or properties, and as, similarly, the extreme of universality is not just any abstract universal nor again merely a single quality, but the universal determinateness, the *specific principle of difference*, the subject is no longer contingently united through the syllogism with *any quality* through *any* middle term. Consequently, as the relations too of the extremes to the middle term have not that external immediacy which they had in the syllogism of existence, the demand for proof, which occurred in the latter and led to the infinite progress, does not arise.

Further, this syllogism does not, as does a syllogism of reflection, presuppose its conclusion for its premisses. The terms, in keeping with their substantial content, stand in a relation to one another which is *in and for itself* identical; we have here *one* essential nature pervading the three terms, a nature in which the determinations of individuality, particularity and universality are merely *formal* moments.

To this extent therefore the categorical syllogism is no longer subjective; in the above identity, objectivity begins; the middle term is the pregnant identity of its extremes which are contained therein in their self-subsistence, for their self-subsistence is the above substantial universality, the genus. The subjective element of the syllogism consists in the indifferent subsistence of the extremes relatively to the Notion or middle term.

3. But this syllogism still continues to be subjective, in that the said identity is still the substantial identity or *content*, but is still not at the same time *identity of form*. Consequently, the identity of the Notion is still an *inner* bond of union, and therefore as relation is still *necessity*; the universality of the middle term is substantial, *positive* identity, but is not equally the *negativity of its extremes*.

More precisely, the immediacy of this syllogism, which immediacy is not yet *posited* as that which it is *in itself*, is present in the following manner. What is really immediate in the syllogism is the *individual*. This is subsumed under its genus as middle term; but under the same genus come also an *indefinite number* of other individuals; it is therefore *contingent* that only *this* individual is posited as subsumed under it. But further, this contingency does not merely belong to the external reflection which finds the individual posited in the syllogism to be contingent by *comparison* with others; on the contrary, it is because the individual itself is related to the middle term as to its objective universality that it is posited as *contingent*, as a subjective actuality. On the other hand, in that the subject is an *immediate* individual, it contains determinations which are not contained in the middle term as the universal nature; therefore it also has a specific nature of its own indifferent to the middle term and possessing a content peculiar to itself. Hence, conversely, this other term also has an indifferent immediacy and an Existence distinct from the former. The same relationship also obtains between the middle term and the other extreme; for this likewise has the determination of immediacy and hence of a being that is contingent relatively to its middle term.

Accordingly, what is posited in the categorical syllogism is on the one hand extremes standing in such a relationship to the middle term that they possess *in themselves* objective universality or a self-subsistent nature, and at the same time appear as immediate terms and therefore as mutually *indifferent actualities*. But on the other hand they are equally determined as *contingent*, that is to say, their immediacy is *sublated* in their identity. But by reason of the said self-subsistence and totality of the actuality, this identity is only formal and inner; the syllogism of necessity has hereby determined itself to the *hypothetical syllogism*.

(b) The Hypothetical Syllogism

1. The hypothetical judgement contains only the necessary *relation* without the immediacy of the related terms. 'If *A* is, then *B* is'; or, the being of *A* is equally the being *of another*, of *B*; so far, it is not stated either that *A is*, or that *B is*. The hypothetical syllogism adds this *immediacy* of being:

If *A* is, then *B* is,
But *A is*,
Therefore *B* is.

The minor premiss by itself enunciates the immediate being of *A*.

But it is not only this that is added to the judgement. The syllogism contains the relation of subject and predicate, not as the abstract copula, but as the pregnant *mediating* unity. Accordingly, the being of *A* is to be taken *not as a mere immediacy*, but essentially as the *middle term of the syllogism*. This is to be examined more closely.

2. In the first place, the relation of the hypothetical judgement is *necessity* or inner *substantial identity* associated with external diversity of Existence, or mutual indifference of being in the sphere of Appearance—an identical *content* which forms the internal basis. The two sides of the judgement therefore do not appear as an immediate being but as a being held within the necessity and thus at the same time as *sublated* being or being only in the sphere of Appearance. Further, as sides of the judgement they stand to one another as *universality* and *individuality*; one of them, therefore, is the above content as *totality of conditions*, the other as *actuality*. It is, however, indifferent which side is taken as universality and which as individuality. That is to say, in so far as the conditions are still the *inner*, *abstract* side of an actuality, they are the *universal*, and it is through their being *gathered together into an individuality* that they enter into *actuality*. Conversely, the conditions are a *separated, scattered* Appearance which only in *actuality* obtains *unity* and significance and a *universally valid existence*.

The precise relation between the two sides that has here been assumed as the relation of condition and conditioned, may however also be taken as that of cause and effect, of ground and consequent—here this is indifferent; but the relation of condition corresponds more closely to the relation that obtains in the hypothetical judgement and syllogism, inasmuch as condition appears essentially as an indifferent Existence, whereas ground and cause are spontaneously transitive [*übergehend*]; also condition is a more universal determination in that it comprehends both sides of the above relations, since effect, consequent, etc., is just as much condition of the cause, ground, etc., as the latter are of the former.

Now *A* is the *mediating* being in so far as first it is an immediate being, an indifferent actuality, and secondly, in so far as it is no

less an *intrinsically contingent*, self-sublating being. What translates the conditions into the actuality of the new shape whose
conditions they are is the fact that they are not being in its abstract
immediacy, but *being in its Notion*, in the first instance, *becoming*;
but as the Notion is no longer transition they are more specifically
individuality as self-related *negative* unity. The conditions are a
scattered material that waits and demands to be used; this
negativity is the mediating element, the free unity of the Notion.
It determines itself as *activity*, since this middle term is the
contradiction of the *objective universality* or the totality of the
identical content, and the *indifferent immediacy*. This middle term
is therefore no longer merely an inner necessity, but a *necessity*
that *is*; the objective universality contains self-relation as a *simple
immediacy*, as being; in the categorical syllogism this moment is
in the first instance a determination of the extremes, but as against
the objective universality of the middle term it determines itself
as *contingency*, consequently, as something only *posited* and also
sublated, that is, as something withdrawn into the Notion or into
the middle term as unity, which middle term itself in its objectivity is now also being.

The conclusion, 'therefore *B* is', expresses the same contradiction,
that *B* is in the form of *immediate* being, but equally has its being
through an other, or is *mediated*. In respect of its form, therefore,
it is the same Notion that the middle term is, distinguished from
necessity only as the *necessary*—in the wholly superficial form of
individuality as against universality. The absolute *content* of *A*
and *B* is the same; they are only two different names for the same
underlying fact for *ordinary thinking* [*Vorstellung*] which clings to
the appearance of the diversified shape of determinate being and
distinguishes between the necessary and its necessity; but in so
far as this necessity were to be separated from *B*, *B* would not be
the necessary. Thus we have here the identity of the *mediating*
and the *mediated*.

3. The hypothetical syllogism in the first instance exhibits
necessary relation as connexion through the *form* or *negative unity*,
just as the categorical syllogism exhibits through the positive
unity, substantial *content*, objective universality. But *necessity*
collapses into the *necessary*; the *form-activity* of translating the
conditioning into the conditioned actuality is *in itself* the unity in
which the determinatenesses of the opposition, that previously

were liberated into an indifferent determinate existence, are *sublated*, and the difference of A and B is an empty name. Thus it is a unity reflected into itself—hence an *identical* content; and it is so not merely *implicitly* but it is also *posited* as such through this syllogism, in that the being of A is also not its own but B's, and *vice versa*, and in general the being of one is the being of the other, and in the conclusion the immediate being or indifferent determinateness appears specifically as mediated; the externality of the determinatenesses has therefore sublated itself and *their unity into which they have withdrawn is posited*.

The mediation of the syllogism has hereby determined itself as *individuality*, *immediacy*, and as *self-related negativity*, or as an identity that differentiates itself and gathers itself into itself out of that difference—as absolute form, and for that very reason as objective *universality*, a *content* that is identical with itself. The syllogism in this determination is the *disjunctive syllogism*.

(c) The Disjunctive Syllogism

As the hypothetical syllogism in general comes under the schema of the second figure of the formal syllogism, *U–I–P*, so the disjunctive syllogism comes under the schema of the third figure, *I–U–P*. But the middle term is the *universality* that is *pregnant with form*; it has determined itself as *totality*, as *developed* objective universality. Consequently the middle term is not only universality but also particularity and individuality. As universality it is first the substantial identity of the genus; but secondly an identity that *embraces within itself particularity*, but a particularity *co-extensive with this identity of the genus*; it is therefore the universal sphere that contains its total particularization—the genus disjoined into its species: A that is B and C and D. But particularization is differentiation and as such is just as much the *either-or* of B, C and D, the *negative* unity, the *reciprocal* exclusion of the terms. Further, this exclusion is not merely a reciprocal exclusion, or the determination merely a relative one, but it is just as essentially a *self-related* determination, the particular as *individuality* to the exclusion of the *others*.

> A is either B or C or D,
> But A is B,
> Therefore A is neither C nor D.

or again:

> A is either B or C or D,
> But A is neither C nor D,
> Therefore A is B.

A is subject not only in the two premisses but also in the conclusion. In the first premiss it is a universal, and in its predicate,
the *universal* sphere particularized into the totality of its species;
in the second premiss it appears as *determinate* or as a species; in
the conclusion it is posited as the exclusive, *individual* determinateness. Or again, it already appears in the minor premiss as exclusive individuality and is positively posited in the conclusion as
the determinate which it is.

Hence what appears in general as *mediated* is the *universality*
of A with *individuality*. But the *mediating* factor is this A, which
is the *universal* sphere of its particularizations and is determined
as an *individual*. Consequently the truth of the hypothetical
syllogism, namely the unity of the mediating and the mediated, is
posited in the disjunctive syllogism, which for this reason is equally
no longer a syllogism at all. For the middle term, which is posited
in it as the totality of the Notion, contains itself the two extremes
in their complete determinateness. The extremes, in distinction
from this middle term, appear only as a positedness which no
longer possesses any determinateness peculiar to itself as against
the middle term.

Considering this point further with more particular reference
to the hypothetical syllogism, we see that in the latter we had a
substantial identity as the *inner* bond of necessity, and a *negative
unity* distinguished therefrom—namely, the activity or form which
translated one existence into another. The disjunctive syllogism is
in general in the determination of *universality*; its middle term is
the A as *genus* and as perfectly *determinate*; through this unity,
that content which previously was inner is also *posited* and, conversely, the positedness or form is not the external, negative unity
over against an indifferent existence, but is identical with the said
substantial content. The whole form determination of the Notion
is posited in its determinate difference and at the same time in the
simple identity of the Notion.

In this way then the *formalism of the syllogistic process*, and with
it the subjectivity of the syllogism and of the Notion in general,

has sublated itself. This formal or subjective side consisted in the fact that the mediating factor of the extremes is the Notion as an *abstract* determination, and this latter is *distinct* from the extremes whose unity it is. In the consummation of the syllogism, on the other hand, where objective universality is no less posited as totality of the form determinations, the distinction of mediating and mediated has disappeared. That which is mediated is itself an essential moment of what mediates it, and each moment appears as the totality of what is mediated.

The figures of the syllogism exhibit each determinateness of the Notion *individually* as the middle term, which at the same time is the Notion as an *ought-to-be*, a demand that the mediating factor shall be the Notion's totality. But the different genera of the syllogism exhibit the stages of *impregnation* or concretion of the middle term. In the formal syllogism the middle term is only posited as totality by all the determinatenesses, though each *singly*, functioning as the mediating factor. In the syllogisms of reflection the middle term appears as the unity that gathers together *externally* the determinations of the extremes. In the syllogism of necessity it has likewise determined itself to the unity that is no less developed and total than simple, and the form of the syllogism which consisted in the difference of the middle term from its extremes has thereby sublated itself.

Thus the Notion as such has been realized; more exactly, it has obtained a reality that is *objectivity*. The *first reality* was that the *Notion*, as within itself negative unity, sunders itself, and as *judgement* posits its determinations in a determinate and in-different difference, and in the syllogism sets itself in opposition to them. In this way it is still the inwardness of this its externality, but the outcome of the course of the syllogisms is that this externality is equated with the inner unity; the various determinations return into this unity through the mediation in which at first they are united only in a third term, and thus the externality exhibits in its own self the Notion, which therefore is no longer distinguished from it as an inner unity.

However, this determination of the Notion which has been considered as *reality*, is, conversely, equally a *positedness*. For it is not only in this result that the truth of the Notion has exhibited itself as the identity of its inwardness and externality; already in the judgement the moments of the Notion remain, even in their mutual indifference, determinations that have their significance only in their relation. The syllogism is *mediation*, the complete Notion in its *positedness*. Its movement is the sublating of this mediation, in which nothing is in and for itself, but each term *is* only by means of an other. The result is therefore an *immediacy* which has issued from the *sublating of the mediation*, a *being* which is no less identical with the mediation, and which is the Notion that has restored itself out of, and in, its otherness. This *being* is therefore a *fact* [*eine Sache*] that is *in and for itself—objectivity*.

Section Two: Objectivity

In Book One of the Objective Logic, abstract *being* was exhibited as passing over into *determinate being*, but equally as withdrawing into essence. In Book Two, essence reveals itself as determining itself into *ground*, thereby entering into *Existence* and realizing itself as *substance*, but again withdrawing into the *Notion*. Of the Notion, now, we have shown to begin with that it determines itself into *objectivity*. It is self-evident that this latter transition is identical in character with what formerly appeared in *metaphysics* as the *inference* from the *notion*, namely, the *notion of God*, to *his existence*, or as the so-called *ontological proof* of the *existence of God*. It is equally well known that Descartes' sublimest thought, that God is that *whose notion includes within itself its being*, after being degreaded into the defective form of the formal syllogism, that is, into the form of the said proof, finally succumbed to the *Critique of Reason* and to the thought that *existence cannot be extracted from the notion*. Some points connected with this proof have already been elucidated. In Vol. I, pp. 86 sqq., where *being* has vanished in its immediate opposite, *non-being*, and *becoming* has shown itself as the truth of both, attention was drawn to the confusion that arises when, in the case of a particular determinate being, what is fixed on is not the *being* of that determinate being but its *determinate content*; then, comparing *this determinnte content*, for example a hundred dollars, with another *determinate content*, for example, with the context of my perception or the state of my finances, it is found that it makes a difference whether the former content is added to the latter or not—and it is imagined that what has been discussed is the difference between being and non-being, or even the difference between being and the Notion. Further, in the same Vol., p.112 and Vol. II, p.442 we elucidated a determination that occurs in the ontological proof, that of *a sum-total of all realities*. But the essential subject matter of that proof, *the connexion of the Notion and determinate being*, is the concern of our consideration of the *Notion* just concluded, and the entire course through which the Notion determines itself into *objectivity*. The Notion, as absolutely self-identical negativity, is self-determining; we have remarked that the Notion, in determining itself into *judgement* in individuality, is already positing

z

itself as something *real*, something that *is*; this still abstract reality completes itself in *objectivity*.

Now though it might seem that the transition from the Notion into objectivity is not the same thing as the transition from the Notion of God to his existence, it should be borne in mind on the one hand that the determinate *content*, God, makes no difference in the logical process, and the ontological proof is merely an application of this logical process to the said content. On the other hand however it is essential to bear in mind the remark made above that the subject only obtains determinateness and content in its predicate; until then, no matter what it may be for feeling, intuition and pictorial thinking, for rational cognition it is only a *name*; but in the predicate with its determinateness there begins, at the same time, *realization* in general. The predicates, however, must be grasped as themselves still included within the Notion, hence as something subjective, which so far has not emerged into existence; to this extent we must admit on the one hand that the *realization* of the Notion in the judgement is still not complete. On the other hand however the mere determination of an object by predicates, when that determination is not at the same time the realization and objectifying of the Notion, also remains something so subjective that it is not even the genuine cognition and *determination of the Notion* of the object—subjective in the sense of abstract reflection and uncomprehended pictorial thinking. God, as the living God, and still more as absolute spirit, is known only in his *activity*; man was early instructed to recognize God in his *works*; only from these can proceed the *determinations*, which are called his properties, and in which, too, his *being* is contained. Thus the philosophical [*begreifende*] cognition of his *activity*, that is, of himself, grasps the *Notion* of God in his *being* and his being in his Notion. *Being* merely as such, or even *determinate being*, is such a meagre and restricted determination, that the difficulty of finding it in the Notion may well be the result of not having considered what being or determinate being itself is. *Being as the wholly abstract, immediate relation to self*, is nothing else than the abstract moment of the Notion, which moment is abstract universality. This universality also effects what one demands of being, namely, to be *outside* the Notion; for though this universality is moment of the Notion, it is equally the difference, or abstract judgement, of the Notion in which it opposes itself to itself.

The Notion, even as formal, already immediately contains *being* in a *truer* and *richer* form, in that, as self-related negativity, it is *individuality*.

But of course the difficulty of finding *being* in the Notion as such and equally in the Notion of God, becomes insuperable when the being is supposed to be that which obtains *in the context of outer experience* or *in the form of sensuous perception, like the hundred dollars in my finances*, something to be grasped with the hand, not with the mind, something visible essentially to the outer, not to the inner eye; in other words, when that being which things possess as sensuous, temporal and perishable, is given the name of reality or truth. A philosophizing that in its view of being does not rise above sense, naturally stops short at merely abstract thought, too, in its view of the Notion; such thought stands opposed to being.

The custom of regarding the Notion merely as something one-sided, such as abstract thought is, will already hinder the acceptance of what was suggested above, namely, to regard the transition from the *Notion of God* to his *being*, as an *application* of the logical course of objectification of the Notion presented above. Yet if it is granted, as it commonly is, that the logical element as the formal element constitutes the form for the cognition of every determinate content, then the above relation must at least be conceded, unless in this opposition between Notion and objectivity, one stops short at the untrue Notion and an equally untrue reality, as something ultimate. But in the exposition *of the pure Notion*, it was further made clear that this is the absolute, divine Notion itself, so that in truth the relationship of our *application* would not obtain, and the logical process in question would in fact be the immediate exposition of God's self-determination to being. But on this point it is to be remarked that if the Notion is to be presented as the Notion of God, it is to be apprehended as it is when taken up into the *Idea*. This pure Notion passes through the finite forms of the judgement and syllogism because it is not yet posited as in its own nature explicitly one with objectivity but is grasped only in process of becoming it. Similarly this objectivity, too, is not yet the divine existence, is not yet the reality that is reflected in the divine Idea. Yet objectivity is just that much richer and higher than the *being or existence* of the ontological proof, as the pure Notion is richer and higher than that metaphysical void of the *sum total of all reality*. But I reserve for another occasion the more detailed elucidation of the manifold misunderstanding that has been brought by logical formalism into the ontological, as well as the other, so-called proofs of God's existence, as also the Kantian criticism of them, and by establishing their true significance, to restore the fundamental thoughts of these proofs to their worth and dignity.

As previously remarked, we have already met with several forms of immediacy, though in different determinations. In the sphere of being immediacy is being itself and determinate being; in the sphere of essence it is existence, and then actuality and substantiality; in the sphere of the Notion, besides immediacy as abstract universality, there is now objectivity. When the exactitude of philosophical distinctions of the Notion is not involved, these expressions may be used as synonymous; but the determinations mentioned have issued from the necessity of the Notion. *Being* is in general the *first* immediacy, and *determinate being* is the same *plus* the first determinateness. *Existence*, along with things, is the immediacy that issues from the *ground*—from the self-sublating mediation of the simple reflection of essence. But *actuality* and *substantiality* is the immediacy that has issued from the sublated difference of the still unessential Existence as Appearance and its essentiality. Finally, *objectivity* is the immediacy to which the Notion determines itself by the sublation of its abstraction and mediation. Philosophy has the right to select from the language of common life which is made for the world of pictorial thinking, such expressions as *seem to approximate* to the determinations of the Notion. There cannot be any question of *demonstrating* for a word selected from the language of common life that in common life, too, one associates with it the same Notion for which philosophy employs it; for common life has no Notions, but only pictorial thoughts and general ideas, and to recognize the Notion in what is else a mere general idea is philosophy itself. It must suffice therefore if pictorial thinking, in the use of its expressions that are employed for philosophical determinations, has before it some vague idea of their distinctive meaning; just as it may be the case that in these expressions one recognizes nuances of pictorial thought that are more closely related to the corresponding Notions. One will be less ready, perhaps, to admit that something can *be* without *existing*; but at least, one will hardly use '*being*' as copula of the judgement as interchangeable with the expression '*to exist*' and say, 'this article *exists* dear, suitable, etc.', 'gold *exists* a metal or metallic', instead of 'this article *is* dear, suitable, etc.', 'gold *is* a metal or metallic'.[1] And surely it is usual to distinguish between *being* and *appearing*, *appearance* and *actuality*, as well as to distinguish mere *being* from *actuality*, and still more all these expressions from *objectivity*. However, even should they be employed synonymously, philosophy will in any case be free to utilize such empty superfluity of language for its distinctions.

When treating of the apodeictic judgement—the consummation of the judgement—where the subject loses its determinateness as against the predicate, we referred to the twofold meaning of *subjectivity* originating therefrom, namely, the subjectivity of the Notion, and equally of the externality and contingency opposed to the Notion. A similar twofold meaning also appears for objectivity which stands *opposed* to the self-subsistent *Notion*, yet is also the *being that is in and for itself*. In the former sense, the object stands opposed to the $I = I$ which in subjective idealism is enunciated as the absolutely true; in that case it is the manifold world in its immediate existence with which the ego or the Notion only engages in never-ending struggle, in order, by the negation of the *intrinsic nullity* of this other, to give to the first certainty of self the *actual truth* of its equality with itself. In a less specific sense it denotes an object in general for any interest or activity of the subject.

But in the opposite sense, objectivity signifies that which is *in and for itself*, and free from limitation and opposition. Rational principles, perfect works of art, etc., are called *objective* in so far as they are free and above all contingency. Although rational, theoretical or ethical principles belong only to subjectivity, to consciousness, yet that element in the latter that is in and for itself is called objective; the cognition of truth is placed in cognizing the object as object, free from anything added by subjective reflection, and right conduct in the obedience to objective laws that are not subjective in origin and admit no caprice and no treatment that might overthrow their necessity.

At the present standpoint of our exposition objectivity signifies,

[1] In a French report where the officer in command states that he was waiting for the wind, which usually rose near the island towards morning, to steer to shore, the expression occurs: *le vent ayant été longtemps sans exister*; here the distinction has arisen merely from the other common idiom, for example, '*il a été longtemps sans m'écrire*'.

in the first instance, *the absolute being of the Notion*, that is, the Notion that has sublated the *mediation* posited in its self-determination and converted it into *immediate* relation-to-self. Consequently this immediacy is itself immediately and wholly pervaded by the Notion, just as the Notion's totality is immediately identical with its being. But since, further, the Notion has equally to restore the free being-for-self of its subjectivity, there arises a relationship between the Notion as *end* and objectivity. In this relationship the immediacy of the objectivity becomes the negative element over against the end, an element to be determined by the activity of the end; this immediacy thus acquires the other significance, that of being in and for itself null in so far as it stands opposed to the Notion.

First, then, objectivity is an immediacy whose moments, by virtue of the totality of all the moments, exist in a self-subsistent indifference as *objects outside one another*, and in their relationship possess the *subjective unity* of the Notion only as an *inner* or an *outer* unity. This is *mechanism*.

But secondly, this unity reveals itself as the immanent law of the objects themselves, and thus their relationship becomes their *peculiar* specific difference founded on their law; it becomes a relation in which their determinate self-subsistence sublates itself. This is *chemism*.

Thirdly, this essential unity of the objects is thereby posited as distinct from their self-subsistence; it is the subjective Notion, but posited as in and for itself related to objectivity, as *end*. This is *teleology*.

Since the end is the Notion that is posited as in its own self relating itself to objectivity and as sublating by its own act its defect of being subjective, the purposiveness which is at first *external* becomes, through the realization of the end, *internal* and the *Idea*.

CHAPTER I

MECHANISM

As objectivity is the totality of the Notion withdrawn into its unity, an immediate is thereby posited that is in and for itself this totality, and is also *posited* as such, although in it the negative unity of the Notion has not as yet detached itself from the immediacy of this totality; in other words, objectivity is not yet posited as *judgement*. In so far as it has the Notion immanent in it, it contains the difference of the Notion, but on account of the objective totality, the differentiated moments are *complete* and *self-subsistent objects* which consequently, even in their relation, stand to one another only as *self-subsistent* things and remain *external* to one another in every combination. This is what constitutes the character of *mechanism*, namely, that whatever relation obtains between the things combined, this relation is one *extraneous* to them that does not concern their nature at all, and even if it is accompanied by a semblance of unity it remains nothing more than *composition, mixture, aggregation* and the like. *Spiritual* mechanism also, like *material*, consists in this, that the things related in the spirit remain external to one another and to spirit itself. A *mechanical style of thinking, a mechanical memory, habit, a mechanical way of acting*, signify that the peculiar pervasion and presence of spirit is lacking in what spirit apprehends or does. Although its theoretical or practical mechanism cannot take place without its self-activity, without an impulse and consciousness, yet there is lacking in it the freedom of individuality, and because this freedom is not manifest in it such action appears as a merely external one.

A. THE MECHANICAL OBJECT

The object is, as we have seen, the *syllogism*, whose mediation has been sublated [*ausgeglichen*] and has therefore become an immediate identity. It is therefore in and for itself a universal—universality not in the sense of a community of properties, but a universality that pervades the particularity and in it is immediate individuality.

1. In the first place therefore the object does not differentiate itself into *matter* and *form*—a matter as the self-subsistent universal side of the object and a form as the particular and individual side; such an abstract difference of individuality and universality is excluded by the Notion of object; if it is regarded as matter it must be taken as in principle formed matter. Similarly, it may be defined as a thing with properties, as a whole consisting of parts, as a substance with accidents, or in terms of other relationships of reflection; but these relationships have been altogether superseded already in the Notion; the object therefore has neither properties nor accidents, for these are separable from the thing or the substance, whereas in the object the particularity is absolutely reflected into the totality. In the parts of a whole, there is indeed present that self-subsistence which belongs to the differences of the object, but these differences are themselves directly and essentially objects, totalities, that are not, like parts, determined as such in contrast to the whole.

The object is therefore in the first instance *indeterminate*, in so far as it has no determinate opposition in it; for it is the mediation that has collapsed into immediate identity. In so far as the *Notion is essentially determinate*, the object possesses determinateness as a *manifoldness* which though complete is otherwise *indeterminate*, that is, *contains no relationships*, and which constitutes a totality that at first is similarly no further determined; *sides* or *parts* that may be distinguished in it belong to an external reflection. This quite indeterminate difference therefore means only that there are a *number* of objects, each of which only contains its determinateness reflected into its universality and does not reflect itself *outwards*. Because this indeterminate determinateness is essential to the object, the latter is within itself a *plurality* of this kind, and must therefore be regarded as a *composite* or *aggregate*. It does not however consist of *atoms*, for these are not objects because they are not totalities. The Leibnizian *monad* would be more of an object since it is a total representation of the world, but confined within its *intensive subjectivity* it is supposed at least to be essentially *one* within itself. Nevertheless, the monad determined as an *exclusive one* is only a principle that *reflection assumes*. Yet the monad is an object, partly in that the ground of its manifold representations—of the developed, that is, the *posited* determinations of its merely *implicit* totality—lies *outside it*, and partly also in that it is indifferent to the monad that it constitutes an object *along with others*; it is thus in fact not *exclusive* or *determined for itself*.

2. As the object, then, in its determined being is a totality and yet on account of its indeterminateness and immediacy is not the *negative unity* of that determined being, it is *indifferent* to the *determinations* as *individual,* as determined in and for themselves, just as these latter are themselves *indifferent* to one another. These, therefore, are not comprehensible from it nor from one another; its totality is the form of general reflectedness of its manifoldness into individuality in general which is in its own self indeterminate. The determinatenesses, therefore, that it contains, do indeed belong to it, but the *form* that constitutes their difference and combines them into a unity is an external, indifferent one; whether it be a *mixture,* or again an *order,* a certain *arrangement* of parts and sides, all these are combinations that are indifferent to what is so related.

Thus the object, like any determinate being in general, has the determinateness of its totality *outside it* in *other* objects, and these in turn have theirs *outside them,* and so on to infinity. The return-into-self of this progression to infinity must indeed likewise be assumed and represented as a *totality,* a *world*; but that world is nothing but the universality that is confined within itself by indeterminate individuality, that is, a *universe.*

The object, therefore, being in its determinateness equally indifferent to it, it is the object's own nature that points it *outside and beyond itself* to other objects for its determination; but to these others, their *determinant function* is similarly a *matter of indifference.* Consequently, a principle of self-determination is nowhere to be found; *determinism*—the standpoint occupied by cognition when it takes the object, just as we have found it here, to be the truth—assigns for each determination of the object that of another object; but this other is likewise indifferent both to its being determined and to its active determining. For this reason determinism itself is also indeterminate in the sense that it involves the progression to infinity; it can halt and be satisfied at any point at will, because the object it has reached in its progress, being a formal totality, is shut up within itself and indifferent to its being determined by another. Consequently, the *explanation* of the determination of an object and the progressive determining of the object made for the

z*

purpose of the explanation, is only an *empty word*, since in the other object to which it advances there resides no self-determination.

3. Now as the determinateness of an object *lies in an other*, no determinate difference is to be found between them; the determinateness is merely *doubled*, once in one object and again in the other, something utterly *identical*, so that the explanation or comprehension is *tautological*. This tautology is an external futile see-saw; since the determinateness obtains from the objects which are indifferent to it no peculiar distinctiveness and is therefore only identical, there is before us only *one* determinateness; and its being doubled expresses just this externality and nullity of a difference. But at the same time the objects are *self-subsistent* in regard to one another; therefore in the identity above-mentioned they remain absolutely *external* to one another. Here, then, we have the manifest *contradiction* between the complete mutual *indifference* of the objects and the *identity* of their *determinateness*, or the contradiction of their complete *externality* in the *identity* of their determinateness. This contradiction is, therefore, the *negative unity* of a number of objects which, in that unity, simply repel one another: this is the *mechanical process*.

B. THE MECHANICAL PROCESS

If objects are regarded merely as self-enclosed totalities, they cannot act on one another. In this determination they are the same thing as the *monads*, which for this very reason were thought of as exercising no influence whatever on one another. But the concept of a monad is, just for this reason, a defective reflection. For first it is a *determinate* conception of the monad's merely *implicit* totality; as a *certain degree* of the development and *positedness* of its representation of the world, it is *determinate;* now while it is a self-enclosed totality, it is also indifferent to this determinateness; therefore the determinateness is not its own, but one that is *posited* by *another* object. Secondly it is an *immediate* in general, in so far as it is supposed to be merely a *mirroring entity*; its relation to itself is therefore *abstract universality*; hence it is a *determinate being open to others*. To gain the freedom of substance it is not sufficient to represent it as a totality that is *complete within itself* and has nothing to receive *from without*. On the contrary, the mechanical [*begrifflose*], merely mirrored relation to itself is precisely a *passivity* towards another. Similarly *determinateness*, whether taken as the determinateness of something that *is* or of a *mirroring* entity, that is a *degree* of the monad's own spontaneous development, is something *external*; the degree that the development reaches has its *limit* in an other. To shift the reciprocity of substances on to a *predetermined harmony* means nothing more than to convert it into a *presupposition*, that is, to withdraw it from the Notion. The need to avoid the *interaction* of substances was based on the moment of absolute *self-subsistence* and *originality* which was made a fundamental assumption. But since the *positedness*, the degree of development, does not correspond to this *in-itself*, it has for that very reason its ground in an other.

When treating of the relationship of substantiality, we showed that it passes over into the causal relationship. But here what *is*, no longer has the determination of a *substance*, but of an object; the causal relationship has been superseded in the Notion; the originality of one substance in relation to the other has shown itself to be illusory, its action to be transition into the opposed substance. This relationship therefore has no objectivity. Hence in so far as the one object is posited in the form of subjective unity as active cause, this no longer counts as an *original* determination but as something *mediated*; the active object has this its determination only by means of another object. *Mechanism*, since it belongs to the sphere of the Notion, has that posited within it which proved to be the truth of the causal relationship, namely that the cause, which is supposed to be the original and self-subsistent factor is essentially effect, positedness, as well. In mechanism therefore the causality of the object is immediately a non-originality; it is indifferent to this its determination, therefore its being cause is for it something contingent. To this extent, one might indeed say that the causality of substances is *only a subjective conception*. But this causality as thus represented is precisely *mechanism*; for mechanism is this, that causality as *identical* determinateness of different substances and hence as the extinction of their self-subsistence in this identity, is a *mere positedness*; the objects are indifferent to this unity and maintain themselves in face of it. But, no less is this their indifferent *self-subsistence* also a mere *positedness*; they are therefore capable of *mixing* and *aggregating* and of becoming, as an *aggregate*, *one object*. Through this indifference both to their transition and to their self-subsistence, substances are *objects*.

(a) The Formal Mechanical Process

The mechanical process is the positing of what is contained in the Notion of mechanism, and therefore, in the first instance, of a *contradiction*.

1. It follows from the Notion just indicated that the interaction of objects takes the form of the *positing* of the *identical* relation of the objects. This consists merely in giving to the determinateness that is determined, the form of *universality*; this is *communication*, which does not involve transition into an opposite. *Spiritual communication*, which moreover takes place in that element which is the universal in the form of universality, is explicitly an *ideal* relation in which *a determinateness continues* itself from one person into another unimpaired, and universalizes itself without any alteration whatever—as a scent freely spreads in the unresisting atmosphere. But even in communication between material objects, their determinateness *spreads*, so to speak, in a similarly ideal manner; personality is an infinitely more intense *impenetrability* [*Härte*] than objects possess. The formal totality of the object in general, which is indifferent to the determinateness and hence is not a self-determination, makes it undistinguished from the other object and thus renders the interaction primarily an unimpeded continuation of the determinateness of the one in the other.

Now in the spiritual sphere there is an infinitely manifold content that is communicable; for being taken up into intelligence it receives this *form* of universality in which it becomes communicable. But the universal that is such not merely through the form but in and for itself, is the *objective* as such, both in the spiritual and in the material sphere; as against which the individuality of outer objects as well as of persons is an unessential element that can offer it no resistance. Laws, morals, rational conceptions in general, are in the spiritual sphere such communicable entities which penetrate individuals in an unconscious manner and exert their influence on them. In the material sphere the communicable entities are motion, heat, magnetism, electricity and the like—which, even if people insist on representing them as stuffs or matters, must be characterized as *imponderable* agents—

agents lacking that element of materiality which is the foundation *of matter's individualized existence.*

2. Now if in the interaction of objects their *identical* universality is first posited, it is equally necessary to posit the other moment of the Notion, *particularity*; objects accordingly demonstrate also their *self-subsistence*, maintain themselves as mutually external and establish an *individuality* in that universality. This establishing is *reaction* in general. To begin with, reaction is not to be conceived as a *mere suspension* of the action and of the communicated determinateness; what is communicated is, as a universal, positive in the particular objects and only *particularizes itself* in their diversity. So far, then, what is communicated remains what it is; it merely *distributes* itself to the objects or is determined by their particularity. The cause gets lost in its other, the effect, the activity of the causal substance in its action; but the *active object* only becomes a *universal*; its action is primarily not a loss of its determinateness but a *particularization*, whereby the object which at first was the whole of that *individual* determinateness in it, is now a *species* of it, and through this the *determinateness* is posited for the first time as a universal. The two processes, the raising of the individual determinateness into universality in communication, and the particularization of it, or the reduction of what was solely a one to a *species*, in distribution, are one and the same.

Now *reaction* is equal to *action.* The manner in which this first appears, is that the second object *has taken up into itself* the entire universal, and so is now active against the first. Thus its reaction is the same as the action, a *reciprocal repulsion* of the *impulse.* Secondly, what is communicated is the objective element; it therefore *remains* the substantial determination of the objects along with the presupposition of their diversity; thus the universal specifies itself at the same time in them, and each object therefore does not merely give back the whole action, but has its specific share. But thirdly, reaction is a *wholly negative action* in so far as each object through the *elasticity of its self-subsistence* expels the positedness of an other in it and maintains its relation-to-self. The specific particularity of the communicated determinateness in the objects, what was before called a species, returns to *individuality,* and the object asserts its externality in face of the *communicated universality.* The action thereby passes over into *rest*. It shows itself to be a merely *superficial*, transient alteration in the self-enclosed indifferent totality of the object.

3. This return constitutes the *product* of the mechanical process. *Immediately*, the object is *presupposed* as an individual; further, it is a particular in relation to others; and again thirdly, as something indifferent to its particularity, as a universal. The *product* is that *presupposed* totality of the Notion now *posited* as a totality. It is the conclusion in which the communicated universal is united with individuality through the particularity of the object; but at the same time in rest the *mediation* is posited as a mediation that has *sublated* itself; in other words, it is posited that the product is indifferent to this determining of it, and that the determinateness it has received is an external one in it.

Accordingly the product is the same as the object that first enters into the process. But at the same time it is through this movement that it is first *determined*; *in general*, it is *only as a product* that the mechanical object is an *object*; because it is only *through the mediation of an other* in it that it is what it is. Thus in being a product it is what it is supposed to be in and for itself, a *compound* or *mixture*, a certain *order* and *arrangement* of parts, in general, something whose determinateness is not a self-determination but one that is *posited*.

On the other hand, it is no less true that the *result* of the mechanical process *does not already exist before that process*; its *end* is not in its *beginning* as in the case of the teleological end. The product is a determinateness in the object as an *externally* posited one. Therefore, as regards its *Notion*, this product is indeed the same thing as the object already is from the beginning. But in the beginning the external determinateness does not yet appear as *posited*. To this extent the result is something *quite other* than the first determinate being of the object for which it is something utterly contingent.

(*b*) *The real mechanical process*

The mechanical process passes over into *rest*. That is to say the determinateness which the object obtains through the process is only an *external* one. Equally external to it is this rest itself, since rest is the opposite determinateness to the *action* of the object, but every determinateness is indifferent to the object; rest can therefore be regarded as produced by an *external* cause, just as much as it was indifferent to the object to be active.

Now further, since the determinateness is a *posited* one and the Notion of the object has *returned to itself through mediation*, the object contains the determinateness as one that is reflected into itself. Hence in the mechanical process the objects and the process itself have a more precisely determined relationship. They are not merely diverse, but are now *specifically distinguished* as against one another. The result of the formal process which on the one hand is determinationless rest, is therefore, on the other hand, through the reflection into self of the determinateness, the *distribution of the opposition* which the object as such contains, among several objects standing in a mechanical relationship to one another. The object that on the one hand lacks all determination whatever and is neither *elastic* nor *self-subsistent* in its relationships, has on the other hand a *self-subsistence* that is *impenetrable* to other objects. Objects now also have as against one another this more specific opposition of *self-subsistent individuality* and a *universality that lacks self-subsistence*. The precise difference may be conceived as a merely *quantitative* one, as a difference of the magnitude of *mass* in the bodies, or as a difference of *intensity*, or in various other ways. But in general the difference is not to be adhered to in that abstraction; as objects, both are also *positively* self-subsistent.

Now the first moment of this real *process* is, as before, *communication*. The *weaker* can be seized and penetrated by the *stronger* only in so far as it accepts the latter and constitutes one *sphere* with it. Just as in the material sphere the weak is secured against the disproportionately strong (as a sheet hanging free in the air is not pierced by a musket ball, or a weak organic receptivity is less susceptible to strong, than to weak, stimuli), so the wholly feeble spirit is safer from the strong spirit than one that stands nearer to the strong. Imagine if you like someone quite dull-witted and ignoble, then on such a person lofty intelligence and nobility can make no impression. The only consistent defence *against* reason is to have no dealings with it at all. Where the object that is not self-subsistent cannot make contact with one that is and no communication can take place between them, the latter can also offer no *resistance*, that is, cannot specify the communicated universal for itself. If they were not in the same sphere, their relation to one another would be an infinite judgement, and no process between them would be possible.

Resistance is the precise moment of the overpowering of the one object by the other, for it is the incipient moment of the distribution of the communicated universal and of the positing of the self-related negativity, of the individuality to be established. Resistance is *overcome* where the determinateness of the object is *inadequate* to the communicated universal that has been taken up by the object and is supposed to individualize itself in it. The object's relative lack of self-subsistence manifests itself in the fact that its *individuality* lacks the *capacity* for what is *communicated* and therefore is disrupted by it, because it cannot constitute itself as *subject* in this universal, or make this latter its *predicate*. It is only in this second aspect that the *violence* [*Gewalt*] exercised on an object is something *extraneous* to it. What turns *power* [*Macht*] into *violence* is this, that though power, an objective universality, is *identical* with the *nature* of the object, its determinateness or negativity is not its own *negative reflection* into itself by which it is an individual. In so far as the negativity of the object is not reflected into itself in the power, and the power is not the object's own self-relation, it is, as against the power, only *abstract* negativity whose manifestation is extinction.

Power, as *objective universality* and as violence directed *against* the object, is what is called *fate*—a conception that falls within mechanism in so far as it is called *blind*, that is, its *objective universality* is not recognized by the subject in its specific peculiarity. To make a few observations on this point: the fate of the living being is in general the *genus*, which manifests itself through the perishableness of the living individuals, which in their *actual individuality* do not possess the genus as genus. As mere objects, merely animate natures, like all other things of a lower grade, have no fate; what befalls them is a contingency; but *in their Notion as objects* they are *external* to themselves; therefore the alien power of fate is nothing else but their *own immediate nature*, externality and contingency itself. Only self-consciousness has a fate in the proper meaning of the word, because it is *free*, and therefore in the *individuality* of its ego possesses a being that is absolutely *in and for itself* and can oppose itself to its objective universality and *estrange* itself from it. By this very separation, however, it excites against itself the mechanical relationship of a fate. In order therefore that this fate should be able to have power over it, it must have given itself some determinateness or other conflicting with the essential universality; it must have committed a *deed*. By this, it has made itself into a *particular*, and this existence as abstract universality, is at the same time the side open to the communication of its estranged essence; it is on this side that it is drawn into the process. The nation without deeds is without blame; it is wrapped in objective moral universality and dissolved in it and lacks that individuality which, while it moves the unmoved, and gives itself a determinateness outwards and an abstract universality separated from the objective universality, yet in so doing converts the subject into something estranged from its essence, into an *object*, and brings it into the relationship of *externality* towards its nature, into that of mechanism.

(c) The Product of the Mechanical Process

The product of *formal* mechanism is the object in general, an indifferent totality in which *determinateness* appears as *posited*. The object having hereby entered the process as a *determinate* thing, the extinction of the process results on the one hand in *rest*, as the original formalism of the object, the negativity of its being determined for itself. But on the other hand the sublating of the determinedness as the *positive reflection of it* into itself, is the determinateness that has withdrawn into itself or the *posited totality of the Notion*—the *true individuality* of the object. The object, determined at first in its indeterminate universality then as a *particular*, is now determined as *objectively an individual*, so that in it that mere *semblance of individuality* which is only a self-subsistence *opposing* itself to the substantial universality, has been sublated.

This reflection into self then is, as we have seen, the objective oneness of the objects, a oneness which is an individual self-subsistence—the *centre*. Secondly, the reflection of negativity is a universality that is not a fate confronting the determinateness, but a fate immanently determined and rational—a universality that *particularizes itself from within*, the difference that is at rest and is constant in the unstable particularity of objects and in their process; in other words, the *law*. This result is the truth, and therefore also the foundation, of the mechanical process.

C. ABSOLUTE MECHANISM

(a) The Centre

In the first place then the empty manifoldness of objects is gathered into objective individuality, into the simple self-determining *centre*. Secondly, in so far as the object as an immediate totality retains its indifference to determinateness, the latter is present in it also as unessential or as a *mutual externality* of many objects. The prior, the essential determinateness, on the other hand, constitutes the *real middle term* between the many mechanically interacting bodies, by which they are united *in and for themselves*, and is their objective universality. Universality exhibited itself at first in the relationship of *communication* as present only through *positing*; but as *objective* universality it is the pervading immanent essence of the objects.

In the material world it is the *central body* that is the *genus*, but it is the *individual* universality of the single objects and their mechanical process. The relationship in which the unessential single bodies stand to one another is one of mutual *thrust* and *pressure*; this kind of relationship does not hold between the central body and the objects whose essence it is, for their externality no longer constitutes their basic determination. Their identity with the central body is, therefore, rather rest, namely, the *being in their centre*; this unity is their absolute Notion. It remains, however, merely an *ought-to-be*, since the externality of the objects which is still also posited does not correspond to that unity. Their consequent *striving* towards the centre is their absolute universality, not a universality posited by *communication*; it consitutes the true *rest* that is itself *concrete* and not *posited from outside*, into which the process of the non-self-subsistent bodies must return. That is why it is an empty abstraction to assume in mechanics that a body set in motion would continue to move in a straight line to infinity if external resistance did not rob it of its motion. *Friction*, or whatever other form resistance takes, is only the manifestation of *centrality*; for it is centrality that in an absolute manner brings the body back to itself; for the thing in contact with which the moving body meets friction has the power of resistance solely through its union with the centre. In the *spiritual* sphere the centre and unity with the centre assume higher forms; but the unity of the Notion and its reality which here, to begin with, is mechanical centrality, must there too constitute the basic determination.

Thus the central body has ceased to be a mere *object*, for in the latter the determinateness is an unessential element; for the central body no longer possesses the objective totality only *implicitly* but also *explicitly*. It can therefore be regarded as an *individual*. Its determinateness is essentially different from a mere *order* or *arrangement* and *external connexion* of parts; as determinateness in and for itself it is an *immanent* form, a self-determining principle in which the objects inhere and by which they are bound together into a genuine One.

But this central individual is thus at first only a *middle term* which as yet has no true extremes; but as negative unity of the total Notion it sunders itself into such. Or in other words the previously non-self-subsistent, self-external objects are likewise by the regress of the Notion determined into individuals; the identity of the central body with itself which is still a *striving*, is infected with *externality* which, being taken up into the central body's *objective individuality*, has this latter determination communicated to it. Through this centrality of their own, these individuals placed outside that first centre, are themselves centres for the non-self-subsistent objects. These second centres and the non-self-subsistent objects are brought into unity by the above absolute middle term.

But the relative individual centres themselves also constitute the middle term of a *second syllogism*, a middle term that on the one hand is subsumed under a higher extreme, namely the objective *universality* and *power* of the absolute centre, and on the other hand subsumes under itself the non-self-subsistent objects whose superficial or formal individualization is supported by it. Again, these non-self-subsistent objects are the middle term of a *third*, the *formal syllogism*, in that they are the link between the absolute and the relative central individuality to the extent that the latter has in them its externality by virtue of which the *relation-to-self* is at the same time a *striving* towards an absolute centre. The formal objects have for their essence the identical *gravity* of their immediate central body in which they inhere as in their subject and the extreme of individuality; through the externality which they constitute, that body is subsumed under the absolute central body; they are, therefore, the formal middle term of *particularity*. But the absolute individual is the objectively universal middle term which brings into unity and holds fast the being-within-self or inwardness of the relative individual and its externality. Similarly, too, the *government*, the *individual citizens* and the *needs* or *external life* of the individuals, are three terms, each of which is the middle of the other two. The *government* is the absolute centre in which the extreme of the individuals is united with their external existence; similarly, the *individuals* are the middle term that activate that universal individual into external concrete existence and translate their moral essence into the extreme of actuality. The third syllogism is the formal syllogism, that of an illusory show, in which the individuals purport to be linked to this universal absolute individuality by their *needs* and external existence; a syllogism which, as merely subjective, passes over into the others and in them has its truth.

This totality, whose moments are themselves the complete relationships of the Notion, the *syllogisms* in which each of the three different objects runs through the determination of middle term and of extremes, constitutes *free mechanism*. In it the different objects have for their basic determination the objective universality, the *pervasive* gravity that maintains its *identity* in the *particularization*. The relations of *pressure, thrust, attraction* and the like, as also *aggregations* or *mixtures*, belong to the relationship of externality which forms the basis of the third of this group of syllogisms. *Order*, which is the merely external determinateness of objects, has passed over into the determination that is immanent and objective; this is *law*.

(b) Law

In law, the more specific difference between the *ideal reality* of objectivity and its *external reality* is made prominent. The object, as *immediate* totality of the Notion, does not yet possess externality as distinct from the *Notion* which is not yet posited for itself. The object, being withdrawn into itself through the process, there has arisen the opposition of *simple centrality* against an *externality* which is now determined *as* externality, that is, *is posited* as that which is not *in and for itself*. That identical or ideal aspect of individuality is, on account of the relation to externality, an *ought-to-be*; it is that unity of the Notion, absolutely determined and self-determining, to which that external reality does not correspond, and therefore gets no further than a *striving* towards it. But individuality is *in and for itself the concrete principle of negative unity*, and *as such* itself *totality*, a unity that sunders itself into the *specific differences of the Notion* and abides within its self-identical universality; it is thus the centre *expanded* within its pure ideality *by difference*.

This reality which corresponds to the Notion is the *ideal* reality that is distinct from the reality that was merely a *striving*; it is the difference, not as in the first instance a plurality of objects, but difference in its essential nature and taken up into pure universality. This real ideality is the *soul* of the previously developed objective totality, *the absolutely determined identity* of the system.

The objective *being-in-and-for-self* appears therefore more specifically in its totality as the negative unity of the centre, which divides itself into *subjective individuality* and *external objectivity*, maintains the former in the latter and determines it in an ideal difference. This self-determining unity that absolutely reduces external objectivity to ideality is the principle of *self-movement* the *determinateness* of this animating principle, which is the difference of the Notion itself, is *law*. Dead mechanism was the mechanical process considered above of objects that appeared immediately as self-subsistent but which for that very reason are, in truth, not self-subsistent and have their centre outside themselves; this process, which passes over into *rest*, exhibits either *contingency* and indeterminate dissimilarity or *formal uniformity*. This uniformity is indeed a *rule*, but not a *law*. Only free mechanism has a *law*, the spontaneous determination of pure individuality or *of the explicated Notion*; as difference, it is in its own self the imperishable source of self-kindling movement, and since in the ideality of its difference it relates itself to itself alone, it is *free necessity*.

(c) Transition of Mechanism

This soul, however, is still submerged in its body: the Notion of the objective totality, *determinate now* but *inner*, is free necessity—the law has not yet confronted its object; it is the *concrete* centrality as universality *immediately* expanded into its objectivity. This ideality, therefore, has not the *objects themselves* for its determinate difference; these are *self-subsistent individuals* of the totality, or also, if we look back to the formal stage, non-individual, external *objects*. Law is indeed immanent in them and constitutes their nature and power; but its difference is confined within its ideality, and the objects are not themselves differentiated into the ideal difference of the law. But it is solely in the ideal centrality and its laws that the object possesses its essential self-subsistence; it is therefore powerless to resist the judgement of the Notion and to maintain itself in abstract, indeterminate self-subsistence and aloofness. By virtue of the ideal difference immanent in it, its existence is a *determinateness posited by the Notion*. Its lack of self-subsistence is in this way no longer merely a *striving* towards the *centre*, as against which, just because its relation to it is only a striving, it still has the appearance of a self-subsistent external object; on the contrary, it is a striving towards the *object specifically opposed to it*; and similarly the centre itself has in consequence fallen asunder and its negative unity passed has over into *objectified opposition*. Centrality is, therefore, now a *relation* of these reciprocally negative objectivities in a state of mutual tension. Thus free mechanism determines itself into chemism.

CHAPTER 2

CHEMISM

Chemism constitutes in objectivity as a whole, the moment of judgement, of the difference that has become objective, and of the process. Since it already begins with determinateness and positedness and the chemical object is at the same time an objective totality, its immediate course is simple and is completely determined by its presupposition.

A. THE CHEMICAL OBJECT

The chemical object is distinguished from the mechanical by the fact that the latter is a totality indifferent to determinateness, whereas in the case of the chemical object the *determinateness*, and consequently the *relation to other* and the kind and manner of this relation, belong to its nature. This determinateness is at the same time essentially a *particularization*, that is, it is taken up into universality; thus it is a *principle—universal determinateness*, the determinateness not only of the *one individual object* but also of the *other*. In the chemical object, therefore, we now have the distinction between its Notion as the inner totality of the two determinatenesses, and the determinateness that constitutes the nature of the individual object in its *externality* and *concrete existence*. Since in this way it is *in itself* or *implicitly* the whole Notion, it has in its own self the *necessity* and the *urge* to sublate its opposed, *one sided-existence* and to give itself an existence as that *real whole* that according to its Notion it is.

With regard to the expression *chemism* for the relation of the difference of objectivity as it has presented itself, it may be further remarked that the expression must not be understood here as though this relation only exhibited itself in that form of elemental nature to which the name chemism so called is strictly applied. Even the meteorological relation must be regarded as a process whose parts have the nature more of physical than chemical elements. In the animate world, the sex relation comes under this schema and it also constitutes the *formal* basis for the spiritual relations of love, friendship, and the like.

Examined more closely the chemical object, as a *self-subsistent* totality in general, is in the first instance an object that is reflected into itself and to that extent is distinct from its reflectedness outwards—an indifferent *base*, the individual not yet specified as different; the *person*, too, is such a base related at first only to itself. But the immanent determinateness which constitutes its *difference*, is first reflected into itself in such a manner that this retraction of the relation outwards is only formal abstract universality; thus the relation outwards is the determination of its immediacy and concrete existence. From this aspect, it does not *in its own self* return into the individual totality; and the negative unity has the two moments of its opposition in two *particular objects*. Accordingly, a chemical object is not comprehensible from itself alone, and the being of one is the being of the other. But secondly, the determinateness is absolutely reflected into itself and is the concrete moment of the individual Notion of the whole, which Notion is the universal essence, the *real genus* of the particular object. The chemical object, which is thus the contradiction of its immediate positedness and its immanent individual Notion, is a *striving* to sublate the determinateness of its existence and to give concrete existence to the objective totality of the Notion. Therefore, though it also lacks self-subsistence, it spontaneously tenses itself against this deficiency and initiates the *process* by its self-determining.

B. THE CHEMICAL PROCESS

1. It begins with the presupposition that the objects in tension, tensed as they are against themselves, are in the first instance by that very fact just as much tensed against one another—a relationship that is called their *affinity*. Since each through its Notion stands in contradiction to the one-sidedness of its own existence and consequently strives to sublate it, there is immediately posited in this fact the striving to sublate the one-sidedness of the other object; and through this reciprocal adjustment and combination to posit a reality conformable to the Notion, which contains both moments.

As each of the objects is posited as self-contradictory and self-sublating in its own self, it is only by an *external compulsion* [*Gewalt*] that they are held apart from one another and from their reciprocal integration. Now the middle term whereby these extremes are concluded into a unity is first the *implicit* nature of both, the whole Notion that holds both within itself. Secondly, however, since in their concrete existence they stand confronting each other, their absolute unity is also a still formal element having an *existence distinct* from them—the element of *communication* in which they enter into external *community* with each other. Since the real difference belongs to the extremes, this middle term is only the abstract neutrality, the real possibility of those extremes; it is, as it were, the *theoretical element* of the concrete existence of chemical objects, of their process and its result. In the material world *water* fulfils the function of this medium; in the spiritual world, so far as the analogue of such a relation has a place there, the *sign* in general, and more precisely *language*, is to be regarded as fulfilling that function.

The relationship of the objects, as a mere communication in this element, is on the one hand a quiescent coming-together, but on the other hand it is no less a *negative bearing* of each to the other; for in communication the concrete Notion which is their nature is posited as a reality, with the result that the *real differences* of the objects are reduced to *its* unity. Their previous self-subsistent *determinateness* is thus sublated in the union that conforms to the Notion, which is one and the same in both, and thereby their opposition and tension are weakened, with the result that in this reciprocal integration the striving reaches its quiescent *neutrality*.

The process is in this way *extinguished*; the contradiction between the Notion and reality being resolved, the extremes of the syllogism have lost their opposition and have thus ceased to be extremes both against each other and against the middle term. The *product* is *neutral*, that is, a product in which the ingredients, which can no longer be called objects, have lost their tension and with it those properties which belonged to them as tensed, while the *capability* of their former self-subsistence and tension is preserved. For the negative unity of the neutral product proceeds from a *presupposed* difference; the *determinateness* of the chemical object is identical with its objectivity, it is original. Through the process just considered this difference is as yet only *immediately* sublated; the determinateness is, therefore, as yet not absolutely reflected into itself, and consequently the product of the process is only a formal unity.

2. Now in this product, the tension of the opposition and the negative unity, as activity of the process, are indeed extinct. But since this unity is essential to the Notion and has at the same time come into concrete existence, it is still present, though its place is *outside* the neutral object. The process does not spontaneously re-kindle itself, for it had the difference only for its *presupposition* and did not itself *posit* it. This self-subsistent negativity outside the object, the existence of the *abstract* individuality whose being-for-self has its reality in the *indifferent object*, is now tensed within itself against its abstraction, and is an inward restless activity that turns outwards to consume. It relates itself *immediately* to the object whose quiescent neutrality is the real possibility of its opposition; that object is now the *middle term* of the previously merely formal neutrality, now inwardly concrete and determinate.

The more precise immediate relation of the *extreme* of *negative unity* to the object is that the latter is determined by it and thereby disrupted. This disruption may in the first instance be regarded as the restoration of that opposition of the objects in tension with which chemism began. But this determination does not constitute the other extreme of the syllogism but belongs to the immediate relation of the differentiating principle to the middle term in which this principle gives itself its immediate reality; it is the determinateness that the middle term in the disjunctive syllogism also possesses besides being the universal nature of the object, and by virtue of which the object is both objective universality and also determinate particularity. The *other extreme* of the syllogism stands opposed to the external *self-subsistent extreme* of individuality; it is therefore the equally self-subsistent extreme of *universality*; hence the disruption suffered by the real neutrality of the middle term in this extreme is that it is split up into moments whose relationship is not that of difference, but of *indifference*. Accordingly these moments are the abstract indifferent *base* on the one side, and its *energizing* principle on the other, which latter by its separation from the base attains likewise the form of indifferent objectivity.

This disjunctive syllogism is the totality of chemism in which the same objective whole is exhibited first as self-subsistent *negative* unity, then in the middle term as *real* unity, and finally as the chemical reality resolved into its *abstract* moments. In these latter the determinateness has not reached its *reflection-into-self* in an other as in the neutral product, but has in itself returned into its abstraction, and is an *originally determinate element*.

3. These elementary objects are accordingly liberated from chemical tension; in them, the original basis of that *presupposition* with which chemism began has been *posited* through the real process. Now further, the inner *determinateness* as such of these objects is essentially the contradiction of their *simple indifferent subsistence* and themselves as *determinateness*, and is the urge outwards that sunders itself and posits tension in its object and in *another* object in order to have something with which it can enter into a relation of difference and in which it can neutralize itself and give to its simple determinateness an existent reality. Consequently, on the one hand chemism has returned into its beginning in which objects in a state of reciprocal tension seek one another and then by a formal, external middle term, unite to form a neutral product. On the other hand, chemism by this return into its *Notion* sublates itself and has passed over into a higher sphere.

C. TRANSITION OF CHEMISM

Even ordinary chemistry shows examples of chemical alterations in which a body, for example, imparts a higher oxidation to one part of its mass and thereby reduces another part to a lower degree of oxidation, in which lower degree alone it can enter into a neutral combination with another [chemically] different body brought into contact with it, a combination for which it would not have been receptive in that first immediate degree. What happens here is that the object does not relate itself to another in accordance with an immediate, one-sided determinateness, but that in accordance with the inner totality of an original *relation* it *posits* the *presupposition* which it requires for a real relation and thereby gives itself a middle term through which it unites its Notion with its reality; it is absolutely determined individuality, the concrete Notion as principle of the *disjunction* into *extremes* whose *re-union* is the activity of *the same* negative principle, which thereby returns to its first determination, but returns *objectified*.

Chemism itself is *the first negation* of *indifferent* objectivity and of the *externality* of determinateness; it is therefore still infected with the immediate self-subsistence of the object and with externality. Consequently it is not yet for itself that totality of self-determination that proceeds from it and in which rather it is sublated. The three syllogisms yielded by the foregoing exposition constitute its totality; the first has for middle term formal neutrality and for extremes the objects in tension; the second has for middle term the product of the first, real neutrality, and for extremes the sundering activity and its product, the indifferent element; while the third is the self-realizing Notion, which posits for itself the presupposition by which the process of its realization is conditioned—a syllogism that has the universal for its essence. On account, however, of the immediacy and externality attaching to chemical objectivity, *these syllogisms still fall apart*. The first process whose product is the neutrality of the objects in tension is extinguished in its product, and it is an externally applied differentiation that re-kindles it; conditioned by an immediate presupposition, it exhausts itself in it. Similarly, the separation of the [chemically] different extremes out of the neutral product, as also their decomposition into their abstract elements, must proceed from *conditions* and stimulations of activity *externally brought into play*. Also, although the two essential moments of the process, on the one side neutralization, on the other separation and reduction, are combined in one and the same process, and the *union* of the extremes by weakening of the tension between them is also a *sundering* into such extremes, yet on account of the still underlying externality they constitute *two different* sides; the extremes that are separated in that same process are different objects or materials from those that unite in it; in so far as the former emerge again from the process as [chemically] different they must turn outwards; their new neutralization is a different process from the neutralization that took place in the first process.

But these various processes, which have proved themselves necessary, are so many stages by which *externality* and *conditionedness* are sublated and from which the Notion emerges as a totality determined in and for itself and not conditioned by externality. In the first process, the mutual externality of the different extremes that constitute the whole reality, or the distinction between the *implicitly* determinate Notion and its *existent* determinateness, is sublated; in the second, the externality of the real unity, the union as merely *neutral*, is sublated; more precisely, the formal activity in the first instance sublates itself in equally formal bases or indifferent determinatenesses, whose *inner Notion* is now the indrawn absolute activity as inwardly self-realizing, that is, the activity that *posits* the determinate differences within itself and through this *mediation* constitutes itself as real unity—a mediation which is thus the Notion's *own* mediation, its self-determination, and in respect of its reflection thence into itself, an immanent *presupposing*. The third syllogism, which on the one hand is the restoration of the preceding processes, on the other hand sublates the last remaining moment of *indifferent* bases— the wholly abstract external *immediacy*, which in this way becomes the Notion's *own* moment of self-mediation. The Notion which has thus sublated all the moments of its objective existence as external, and posited them within its simple unity, is thereby completely liberated from objective externality, to which it relates itself only as to an unessential reality. This objective free Notion is end.

CHAPTER 3

TELEOLOGY

Where *purposiveness* is discerned, an *intelligence* [*Verstand*] is assumed as its author, and for the end we therefore demand the Notion's own free Existence. Teleology is especially contrasted with *mechanism*, in which the determinateness posited in the object, being external, is essentially one in which no *self-determination* is manifested. The opposition between *causae efficientes* and *causae finales*, between merely *efficient* and *final* causes, relates to this distinction; and this distinction, taken in a concrete form, is also made the criterion for deciding whether the absolute essence of the world is to be conceived as blind natural mechanism or as an intelligence that determines itself in accordance with ends. The antinomy between *fatalism*, along with *determinism* and *freedom*, is likewise concerned with the opposition of mechanism and teleology; for the free is the Notion in its Existence.

Earlier metaphysics has treated these concepts as it has treated others; it has for one thing presupposed a certain conception of the world and laboured to show that one or the other concept fitted it, while the opposite one was defective because it failed to *explain* that conception; and again, while doing this, it has not examined the concept of mechanical cause and of end, to see which possesses truth *in and for itself*. When this has been established independently, the objective world may present us with mechanical and final causes; but their existence is not the standard of *truth*: on the contrary, truth is the criterion that decides which of these existences is the true one. Just as the subjective understanding also exhibits errors in itself, so the objective world also exhibits aspects and stages of truth that by themselves are still one-sided, incomplete and only relationships in the sphere of Appearance. If mechanism and purposiveness stand opposed to one another, they cannot for that very reason be taken as *indifferent* concepts, each of which is correct on its own account, possessing as much validity as the other, the only question being where one or the other may be applied. This equal validity of both rests merely on the fact that they *are*, that is to say, that we *have* them both. But since they are opposed, the necessary preliminary question is, which of the two is the true one; and the higher and real question is, *whether their truth is not a third concept, or whether one of them is the truth of the other*. But the *relation of end* has proved to be the truth of *mechanism*—what exhibited itself as chemism is included with mechanism in so far as end is the Notion in free Existence; and to end stands opposed in general the unfreedom of the Notion, its submergence in externality; both of them, therefore, mechanism and chemism, are included under natural necessity; for in the former the Notion does not *exist* in the object, since the object as mechanical does not contain self-determination, while in chemism the Notion either has a one-sided Existence in a state of tension, or, in emerging as the unity that disjoins the neutral object into tensed extremes, is external to itself in so far as it sublates this disjunction.

The more the teleological principle was linked with the concept of an *extramundane* intelligence and to that extent was favoured by piety, the more it seemed to depart from the true investigation of nature, which aims at cognizing the properties of nature not as extraneous, but as *immanent determinatenesses* and accepts only such cognition as a valid *comprehension*. As end is the Notion itself in its Existence, it may seem strange that the cognition of objects from their Notion appears rather as an unjustified trespass into a *heterogeneous* element, whereas mechanism, for which the determinateness of an object is a determinateness posited in it externally and by another object, is held to be a *more immanent* point of view than teleology. Of course mechanism, at least the ordinary unfree mechanism, and also chemism, must be regarded as an immanent principle in so far as the *external* determinant is itself *again just such another* object, externally determined and indifferent to such determining, or, in the case of chemism, the other object is one likewise chemically determined; in general, an essential moment of the totality always lies in something outside it. These principles therefore remain confined within the same natural form of finitude; yet though they do not seek to go beyond the finite and lead only to finite causes in their explanation of phenomena, which themselves demand a further progress, at the same time they expand themselves, partly into a formal totality in the concept of force, cause, and similar determinations of reflection which are supposed to denote a *primariness*, and partly also through the abstract *universality* of a *sum total* of forces, a *whole* of reciprocal causes. Mechanism shows itself to be a striving for totality in the fact that it seeks to grasp nature *by itself* as a *whole* that for *its Notion* does not require any other—a totality that is not found in end and the extra-mundane intelligence associated with it.

Now purposiveness shows itself in the first instance as a *higher being* in general, as an *intelligence* that *externally* determines the multiplicity of objects by *a unity that exists in and for itself*, so that the indifferent determinatenesses of the objects become *essential through this relation*. In mechanism they become so through the *mere form of necessity*, their *content* being indifferent; for they are supposed to remain external, and it is only understanding as such that is supposed to find satisfaction in cognizing its own connective principle, abstract identity. In teleology, on the contrary, the content becomes important, for teleology presupposes a Notion, something *absolutely determined* and therefore self-determining, and so has made a distinction between the *relation* of the differences and their reciprocal determinedness, that is the *form*, and the *unity that is reflected into itself, a unity that is determined in and for itself* and therefore *a content*. But when the content is otherwise a *finite* and insignificant one, it contradicts what it is supposed to be; for end, according to its form, is a totality *infinite within itself*—especially when the activity that operates in accordance with ends is assumed to be an *absolute* will and intelligence. The reason why teleology has incurred so much the reproach of triviality is that the ends that it exhibited are more important or more trivial, as the case may be; and it was inevitable that the end relation of objects should so often appear trifling, since it appears to be so external and therefore contingent. Mechanism, on the contrary, leaves to the determinatenesses of objects, as regards their import, their contingent status, to which the object is indifferent, and these determinatenesses are not supposed to have, either for the objects or for the subjective intelligence, any higher validity. This principle, therefore, in its context of external necessity gives the consciousness of infinite freedom as compared with teleology, which sets up for something absolute what is trivial and even contemptible in its content, in which the more universal thought can only find itself infinitely cramped and even feel disgusted.

The formal disadvantage from which this teleology immediately suffers is that it only goes as far as *external purposiveness*. The

Notion being thus posited as something formal, then for such teleology the content is also something that for the Notion is given externally in the manifoldness of the objective world—in those very determinatenesses which are also the content of mechanism, but appearing there as something external and contingent. On account of this community of content, it is solely the *form of purposiveness* by itself that constitutes what is essential in this teleology. In this respect, without as yet attending to the difference of outer and inner purposiveness, the end-relation in general has proved itself to be in and for itself the *truth of mechanism*. Teleology possesses in general the higher principle, the Notion in its Existence, which is in and for itself the infinite and absolute—a principle of freedom that in the utter certainty of its self-determination is absolutely liberated from the *external determining* of mechanism.

One of Kant's great services to philosophy consists in the distinction he has made between relative or *external,* and *internal* purposiveness; in the latter he has opened up the Notion of life, the Idea, and by so doing has done *positively* for philosophy what the *Critique of Reason* did but imperfectly, equivocally, and only *negatively,* namely, raised it above the determinations of reflection and the relative world of metaphysics. It has been remarked that the opposition of teleology and mechanism is in the first instance the more general opposition of *freedom* and *necessity.* Kant has exhibited the opposition in this form among the *antinomies* of reason, namely, as the *third conflict of the transcendental ideas.* His exposition, which was referred to earlier, I cite quite briefly, as the gist of it is so simple as to require no detailed analysis, and the peculiar features of the Kantian antinomies have been elucidated in more detail elsewhere.

The *thesis* of the antinomy here to be considered runs thus: Causality according to natural laws is not the sole causality from which the phenomena of the world can one and all be derived. For their explanation a causality through freedom must be assumed as well.

The *antithesis* is: There is no freedom, but everything in the world happens solely according to natural laws.

As in the case of the other antinomies, the proof first sets to work apagogically, the opposite of each thesis being assumed; secondly and conversely, in order to show the contradictory nature of this

AA

assumption, its opposite, which is accordingly the proposition to be proved, is assumed and presupposed as valid. The whole roundabout method of proof could therefore be spared; the proof consists in nothing but the assertorical affirmation of the two opposed propositions.

Thus in order to prove the *thesis* we have first to assume that there is *no other causality* than that according to *natural laws*, that is, according to the necessity of mechanism in general, including chemism. This proposition we find to be self-contradictory, because we take natural law to consist just in this, that nothing happens without a cause sufficiently determined *a priori*, which cause therefore must contain an absolute spontaneity within itself; that is, the assumption opposed to the thesis is contradictory because it contradicts the thesis.

In order to prove the *antithesis*, we are to postulate that there exists a *freedom*, as a particular kind of causality, that absolutely initiates a state of things and therefore also a series of consequences of that state. But now, since such a beginning presupposes a state that has *no causal connexion* whatever with its predecessor, it contradicts *the law of causality* which alone makes unity of experience, and experience at all, possible; in other words the assumption of freedom, which is opposed to the antithesis, cannot be made because it contradicts the antithesis.

What is essentially the same antinomy recurs in the *Critique of Teleological Judgement* as the opposition between the assertion that all *production of materal things takes place according to merely mechanical laws* and the assertion that *some cases of production of material things according to such laws are not possible*. The Kantian solution of this antinomy is the same as the general solution of the others; namely that reason can prove neither the one proposition nor the other, because we cannot have *a priori* any determining principle of the possibility of things according to merely empirical natural laws; that further, therefore, both must be regarded not as *objective propositions* but as *subjective maxims*; that on the one hand *I* am always to *reflect* on all natural events according to the principle of natural mechanism alone, but that this does not prevent me, *when occasion demands it*, from *investigating* certain natural forms in accordance with *another maxim*, namely, on the principle of final causes; as though now these *two maxims*, which moreover are supposed to be necessary only for *human reason*, did not stand in the same opposition as the *propositions* in question. As was remarked before, this whole standpoint fails to examine the sole question to which philosophic interest demands an answer, namely, which of the two principles possesses truth in and for itself; but for this point of view it makes no difference whether the principles are to be regarded as *objective*, which means here, externally existing determinations of nature, or as mere *maxims* of a *subjective* cognition; rather, that is a subjective, that is, a contingent conjunction which, as the *occasion demands*, applies one or the other maxim according as it holds it to be appropriate to the given objects, but without further enquiry into the *truth* of these determinations themselves, whether these are determinations of the objects or of cognition.

However unsatisfactory, therefore, the Kantian discussion of the teleological principle is in respect of its essential point of view, nevertheless the position that Kant gives to it is worthy of note. In ascribing it to a *reflective judgement*, he makes it a connecting *middle term* between the *universal of reason* and the *individual of intuition*; further, he distinguishes this *reflective* judgement from the *determining* judgement, the latter merely *subsuming* the particular under the universal. Such a suniversal which merely *subsumes*, is an *abstraction* which only becomes *concrete* in something *else*, in the particular. End, on the contrary, is the *concrete universal*, which possesses in its own self the moment of particularity and externality and is therefore active and the urge to repel itself from itself. The Notion, as end, is of course an *objective judgement*, in which one determination, the *subject*, namely the concrete Notion, is self-determined, while the other is not merely a predicate but external objectivity. But the end relation is not for that reason a *reflective* judging that considers external objects only according to a unity, *as though* an intelligence had given this unity *for the convenience of our cognitive faculty*; on the contrary it is the absolute truth that judges *objectively* and determines external objectivity absolutely. Thus the end-relation is more than *judgement*; it is the *syllogism* of the self-subsistent free Notion that unites itself with itself through objectivity.

End has shown itself to be the *third* to mechanism and chemism; it is their truth. Since it still stands within the sphere of objectivity, or of the immediacy of the total Notion, it is still affected by externality as such and is confronted by an objective world to which it relates itself. From this side, mechanical causality, which in general is to be taken as including chemism, still makes its appearance in this *end relation* which is the *external* one, but as *subordinate to it* and as sublated in and for itself. As regards the more precise relationship, the mechanical object is, as an immediate totality, indifferent to its being determined, and on the other hand is equally indifferent to being a determinant. This external determinedness has now developed into self-determination and accordingly the Notion, which in the object was merely the *inner*, or what is the same thing, merely the *outer* Notion, is now *posited*; end is, in the first instance, just this very Notion that is external to the Notion of mechanism. Thus for chemism too, end is the self-determining principle which brings back into the unity of the Notion the external determinedness by which it is conditioned. From this can be seen the nature of the subordination of the two previous forms of the objective process; the other, which in them lies in the infinite progress, is the Notion posited at first as external to them, which is end; not only is the Notion their substance, but externality, too, is for them an essential moment constituting their determinateness. Thus mechanical or chemical technique, through its character of being externally determined, offers itself spontaneously to the end relation, which we have now to consider more closely.

A. THE SUBJECTIVE END

In the *centrality* of the objective sphere, which is an indifference to determinateness, the *subjective* Notion has first rediscovered and posited the *negative point of unity*; but in chemism it has posited the *objectivity* of the *Notion determinations* by which it is first posited as *concrete objective Notion*. Its determinateness or simple difference now possesses within itself the *determinateness of externality*, and its simple unity is consequently the unity that repels itself from itself and in so doing maintains itself. End therefore is the subjective Notion as an essential effort and urge to posit itself externally. In this process it is exempt from transition. It is neither a force expressing itself nor a substance and cause manifesting itself in accidents and effects. Force that has not expressed itself is only an abstract inner; that is, it is only in its expression, to which it must be solicited, that it has a determinate being.

Similarly with cause and substance; since they have actuality only in the accidents and the effect, their activity is transition, against which they do not maintain themselves in freedom. End may indeed also be defined as force and cause, but these expressions fulfil only an incomplete side of its significance; if they are to be predicated of it as it truly is, they can be predicated only in a way that sublates their Notion: as a force that solicits itself to expression, as a cause that is cause of itself, or whose effect is immediately cause.

When purposiveness is ascribed to an *intelligence*, as was mentioned above, then in doing so regard is had to the *specific element of the content*. But in general end is to be taken as the *rational in its concrete existence*. It manifests *rationality* because it is the concrete Notion, which holds the *objective difference within its absolute unity*. It is therefore essentially in its own self *syllogism*. It is the self-equal universal and this, as containing self-repellent negativity, is in the first instance universal, and therefore as yet *indeterminate, activity*; but because this is negative relation-to-self it *determines* itself immediately, giving itself the moment of *particularity*, which, as likewise the *totality of the form reflected into itself*, is *content as against the posited* differences of the form. Equally immediately this negativity, through its relation-to-self, is absolute reflection of the form into itself and *individuality*. On the one hand this reflection is the *inner universality* of the *subject*, while on the other it is a *reflection outwards*; and to this extent end is still a subjective end and its activity is directed against external objectivity.

For end is the Notion that has come to itself in objectivity; the determinateness it has given itself in that sphere is that of *objective indifference* to and *externality* of its determinedness; its self-repellent negativity is, therefore, one whose moments, being determinations only of the Notion itself, also have the form of objective indifference to one another. Even in the formal *judgement*, *subject* and *predicate* are determined as self-subsistent in their relationship; but their self-subsistence is so far only abstract universality. It has now attained the determination of *objectivity*; but as moment of the Notion, this complete difference is enclosed within the simple unity of the Notion. Now in so far as end is this total *reflection* of objectivity *into itself* and is so *immediately*, in the first place, the self-determination or particularity as *simple* reflection into self is distinct from the *concrete* form, and is a *determinate content*. From this side end is *finite*, although in respect of its form it is infinite subjectivity. Secondly, because its determinateness has the form of objective indifference, it has the shape of a *presupposition*, and from this side its finitude consists in its being confronted by an *objective*, mechanical and chemical *world* to which its activity relates itself as to something *already there*; its self-determining activity is thus, in its identity, immediately *external to itself* and as much reflection outwards as reflection-into-self. To this extent end still has a genuinely *extramundane* existence —to the extent, namely, that it is confronted by this objectivity, just as the latter on the other hand confronts it as a mechanical and chemical whole not yet determined and pervaded by the end.

Accordingly, the movement of end can now be expressed as having for its aim to sublate its *presupposition*, that is the immediacy of the object, and to *posit* the object as determined by the Notion. This negative attitude towards the object is just as much a negative attitude towards itself, a sublating of the subjectivity of the end. Positively, it is the realization of the end, namely, the union of objective being with it, so that this being, which, as a moment of the end is immediately the determinateness identical with it, shall appear as *external* determinateness, and conversely the objective as *presupposition* shall instead be *posited* as determined by the Notion. End is in its own self the urge to realize itself; the determinateness of the moments of the Notion is externality; but their *simplicity* in the unity of the Notion is inadequate to the nature of this unity, and the Notion therefore repels itself from itself. This repulsion is in general the *resolution* [*Entschluss*] of the relation of the negative unity to itself, whereby it is *exclusive* individuality; but by this *exclusion* [*Ausschliessen*] it *resolves* itself [*sich entschliesst*] or *opens up* itself [*schliesst sich auf*], because this exclusion is a *self-determining*, a positing of *its own self*. On the one hand subjectivity in determining itself makes itself into particularity, gives itself a content which, enclosed within the unity of the Notion, is still an inner one; but this *positing*, the simple reflection-into-self, is immediately, as we have seen, also a *presupposing*; and in the same moment in which the subject of the end determines *itself*, it is related to an indifferent, external objectivity which is to be equated by it with the said inner determinateness, that is to say, is to be posited as something *determined by the Notion*, and in the first instance as *means*.

B. THE MEANS

The first immediate positing in end is at one and the same time the positing of an *internality*, that is, of something determined as *posited*, and the presupposing of an objective world which is indifferent to the determination of end. But the subjectivity of end is *absolute negative unity*: its second determining is, therefore, the sublating of this presupposition altogether; this sublating is the *return-into-self* in so far as by it is sublated that moment of the *first negative*, the positing of the negative as against the subject, the external object. But as against the presupposition or the immediacy of the determining, as against the objective world, it is as yet only the *first* negation, itself immediate and therefore external. This positing is therefore not yet the realized end itself, but only the *initial* step towards it. The object thus determined is so far only the *means*.

The end unites itself through a means with objectivity, and in objectivity with itself. The means is the middle term of the syllogism. The end, because it is finite, requires a means for its realization—a means, that is a middle term, that at the same time has the shape of an *external* existence indifferent to the end itself and its realization. The absolute Notion possesses mediation within itself in such a manner that its first positing is not a presupposing whose object would have indifferent externality for its fundamental determination; on the contrary, the world as a creation has only the form of such externality, but its fundamental determination is really constituted by its negativity and positedness. The finitude of end consists accordingly in this, that its determining is altogether external to itself, and so its first determining, as we have seen, divides itself into a positing and a presupposing; therefore the *negation* of this determining, too, is so far only in one aspect already a reflection-into-self; in the other, it is in fact merely a *first* negation; in other words the very reflection-into-self is also external to itself and a reflection outwards.

The means is therefore the *formal* middle term of a *formal* syllogism; it is *external* as against the *extreme* of the subjective end, and therefore also to the extreme of the objective end; just as particularity in the formal syllogism is an indifferent *medius terminus* that can be replaced by others. Further, just as this particularity is middle term only by being determinateness in relation to one extreme and a universal in relation to the other, and therefore owes its mediating determination to its relation to other terms, so the means, too, is only the mediating middle term, first because it is an immediate object, secondly because it is a means by virtue of the relation it possesses *externally* to the extreme of the end—a relation that is for it a form to which it is indifferent.

Notion and objectivity are therefore only externally combined in the means, which is accordingly a merely *mechanical object.* The relation of the object to the end is a premiss, or the immediate relation which with regard to the end has been shown to be *reflection into itself,* the means, is an inhering predicate; its objectivity is subsumed under the determination of end which on account of its concretion is universality. By virtue of this determination of end present in the means, the latter is now also subsumptive in relation to the other extreme of the initially still indeterminate objectivity. Conversely, in contrast to the subjective end, the means, as *immediate objectivity,* has a *universality of existence* that the subjective individuality of the end still lacks. The end being thus in the first instance only an external determinateness in the means, it is itself, as a negative unity, outside it; just as the means is a mechanical object that possesses the end only as a determinateness, not as simple concretion of the totality. As the unifying element, however, the middle term must itself be the totality of the end. It has been seen that the determination of end in the means is at the same time reflection-into-self; it is in so far *formal* self-relation, since the *determinateness,* as *real indifference,* is posited as the *objectivity* of the means. But for this very reason, this, in one respect, pure subjectivity, is at the same time also *activity.* In the subjective end the negative relation-to-self is still identical with determinateness as such, with content and externality. But in the incipient objectification of the end, in the becoming-other of the simple Notion, these moments separate themselves, or conversely, it is in such separation that this becoming-other or externality consists.

Consequently, this whole middle term is itself the totality of the syllogism, in which the abstract activity and the external means constitute the extremes, and their middle term is constituted by that determinateness of the object by the end, which makes it a means. But further, *universality* is the *relation* of the activity of the end and the means. The means is an object, *in itself* the totality of the Notion; it has no power of resistance against the end, as it has in the first instance against another immediate object. To the end, therefore, which is the posited Notion, it is absolutely penetrable, and receptive of this communication, because it is *in itself* identical with the end. But now it is also *posited* as penetrable by the Notion, for in centrality it is an object striving towards the negative unity; similarly in chemism, it is as a neutral and also as a *different* object, no longer self-subsistent. Its lack of self-subsistence consists precisely in its being only *in itself* the totality of the Notion; but the latter is a being-for-self. Consequently the object has the character of being powerless against the end and of serving it; the end is the object's subjectivity or soul, that has in the object its external side.

The object, being in this manner *immediately* subjected to the end, is not an extreme of the syllogism; but this relation constitutes one of its premises. But the means has also a side from which it still has self-subsistence as against the end. The objectivity that is connected with the end in the means is still external to it, because it is only immediately so connected; and therefore the *presupposition* still persists. The activity of the end through the means is for that reason still directed against this presupposition, and the end is activity and no longer merely an urge and a striving, precisely because the moment of objectivity is posited in the means in its determinateness as something external, and the simple unity of the Notion now has this objectivity *as such* in itself.

C. THE REALIZED END

1. The end in its relation to the means is already reflected into itself, but its *objective* return into itself is not yet posited. The activity of the end through its means is still directed against objectivity as an original presupposition; the nature of this activity is precisely this, to be indifferent to the determinateness. Were the activity again to consist in merely determining the immediate objectivity, the product would again be merely a means, and so on to infinity; the outcome would be only a means suitable to the end, but not the objectivity of the end itself. Therefore the end

AA*

which is active in its means, in determining the immediate object must not do so *as a determinant external to it*, and consequently the object must spontaneously conform to the unity of the Notion; in other words, the former external activity of the end through its means must determine itself as *mediation* and sublate its own self.

The relation of the activity of the end through the means to the external object is in the first instance the *second premiss* of the syllogism—an *immediate* relation of the middle term to the other extreme. It is *immediate* because the middle term has an external object in it and the other extreme is another such object. The means is effective and potent against the latter because its own object is connected with the self-determining activity, while for the other object the immediate determinateness that it possesses is an indifferent one. Their process in this relation is none other than the mechanical or chemical one; in this objective externality the previous relationships emerge but under the dominance of the end. These processes, however, as they themselves showed, spontaneously return into the end. If, therefore, in the first instance, the relation of the means to the external object it has to work upon is an immediate one, it has already at an earlier stage exhibited itself as a syllogism, the end having proved itself to be their true middle term and unity. As, therefore, the means is the object that stands on the side of the end and has within it the activity of the end, the mechanism that is found here is at the same time the return of objectivity into itself, into the Notion, which however is already presupposed as the end; the negative attitude of purposive activity towards the object is thus not an *external* attitude, but the alteration and transition of objectivity in its own self into the end.

That the end relates itself immediately to an object and makes it a means, as also that through this means it determines another object, may be regarded as *violence [Gewalt]* in so far as the end appears to be of quite another nature than the object, and the two objects similarly are mutually independent totalities. But that the end posits itself in a *mediate* relation with the object and *interposes* another object *between* itself and it, may be regarded as the *cunning* of reason. The finitude of rationality has, as remarked, this side, that the end enters into relationship with the presupposition, that is, with the externality of the object. In the *immediate relation* to the object, it would itself enter into the sphere of mechanism or chemism and thereby be subject to contingency and the loss of its determination as the Notion that is in and for itself. But as it is, it puts forward an object as means, allows it to wear itself out in its stead, exposes it to attrition and shields itself behind it from mechanical violence.

Further, since the end is finite it has a finite content; accordingly it is not an absolute, nor simply something that in its own nature is *rational*. But the *means* is the external middle term of the syllogism which is the realization of the end; in the means, therefore, the rationality in it manifests itself as such by maintaining itself in *this external other*, and precisely *through* this externality. To this extent the *means* is *superior* to the *finite* ends of *external* purposiveness: the *plough* is more honourable than are immediately the enjoyments procured by it and which are ends. The *tool* lasts, while the immediate enjoyments pass away and are forgotten. In his tools man possesses power over external nature, even though in respect of his ends he is, on the contrary, subject to it.

But the end does not merely keep outside the mechanical process; rather it maintains itself in it and is its determination. The end, as the Notion that freely exists in face of the object and its process and is a self-determining activity, is no less the absolute truth of mechanism, and therefore in mechanism it is only meeting with itself. The power of the end over the object is this explicit identity and its activity is the manifestation of it. The end as *content* is the *determinateness* that exists in and for itself, which appears in the object as indifferent and external; but the activity of the end is, on the one hand, the *truth* of the process and as negative unity the *sublating of the illusory show of externality*. From the *abstract* point of view, it is the indifferent determinateness of the object that equally externally is replaced by another; but the simple *abstraction* of the determinateness is in its *truth* the totality of the negative, the concrete Notion that posits externality within itself.

The *content* of the end is its negativity as *simple particularity reflected into itself*, distinguished from its totality as *form*. On account of this *simplicity* whose determinateness is in and for itself the totality of the Notion, the content appears as the *permanently identical* element in the realization of the end. The teleological process is the *translation* of the Notion that has a distinct concrete existence as Notion into objectivity; this translation into a presupposed other is seen to be the meeting of the Notion *with itself through itself*. Now the content of the end is this identity that has a concrete existence in the form of the identical. In every transition the Notion maintains itself; for example, when cause becomes effect it is only the cause meeting with itself in the effect; but in the teleological transition it is the Notion that as such already has a concrete existence *as cause*, as the absolute concrete unity that is *free* in the face of objectivity and its external determinability. The externality into which the end translates itself is itself, as we have seen, already posited as moment of the Notion, as form of its immanent differentiation. The end possesses, therefore, in externality *its own moment*; and the content, as content of the concrete unity, is its *simple form*, which not merely remains *implicitly* self-identical in the distinct moments of the end—as subjective end, as means and mediating activity, and as objective end—but also has a concrete existence as the abiding self-identical.

It can therefore be said of the teleological activity that in it the end is the beginning, the consequent the ground, the effect the cause, that it is a becoming of what has become, that in it only what already exists comes into existence, and so forth; which means that in general all the determinations of relationship belonging to the sphere of reflection or of immediate being have lost their distinctions, and what was enunciated as an *other*, such as end, consequent, effect, etc., no longer has in the end relation the determination of an other, but on the contrary is posited as identical with the simple Notion.

2. Now examining more closely the product of the teleological activity, we see that it contains the end only externally, in so far as it is an absolute presupposition over against the subjective end; that is to say, in so far as we stop short at the point of view that the purposive activity through its means is only in a mechanical relation with the object, and instead of positing one indifferent determinateness of the latter posits *another* equally external to it. A determinateness of this kind, which an object possesses through the end, differs in general from another merely mechanical one by the fact that the former is moment of a *unity*, so that although the determinateness is indeed external to the object, yet it is not in its own self something merely external. The object that exhibits such a unity is a whole, towards which its parts, its own externality, is

indifferent; a determinate *concrete* unity which unites within itself distinct relations and determinatenesses. This unity which cannot be comprehended from the specific nature of the object, and as regards determinate content is another content than that peculiar to the object, is not *by itself* a mechanical determinateness, but it is still mechanically related to the object. Just as in this product of the purposive activity the content of the end and the content of the object are external to each other, so a like relation holds between the determinations of this activity in the other moments of the syllogism—in the unifying middle term, between the purposive activity and the object which is means, and in the subjective end, the other extreme, between the infinite form as totality of the Notion and its content. According to the *relation* by which the subjective end is united with objectivity, both premisses alike—the relation of the object determined as means to the still external object, and the relation of the subjective end to the object which is made means—are immediate relations. The syllogism therefore suffers from the defect of the formal syllogism in general, that the relations of which it consists, are not themselves conclusions or mediations, but in fact already presuppose the conclusion for whose production they are supposed to serve as means.

If we consider one of the *premisses*, the immediate relation of the subjective end to the object which thereby becomes the means, then the former cannot immediately relate itself to the latter; for the latter is no less immediate than the object of the other extreme, in which the end is to be realized *through mediation*. Since they are thus posited as *diverse*, it is necessary to interpolate between this objectivity and the subjective end a means of their relation; but this means is likewise an object already determined by the end, and between that object's objectivity and the teleological determination a new means must be interpolated, and so on to infinity. Thus there is posited the *infinite progress of mediation*. The same thing takes place in respect of the other premiss, the relation of the means to the as yet undetermined object. Since they are absolutely self-subsistent, they can only be united in a third, and so on to infinity. Or conversely, since the premisses already presuppose the *conclusion*, the conclusion, being based on these merely immediate premisses, can only be imperfect. The conclusion or the *product* of the purposive act is nothing but an object determined by an end external to it; *consequently it is the same thing as the means*. In such a product, therefore, *only a means*, not *a realized end*, has resulted, or the end has not truly attained an objectivity in it. It is therefore a matter of complete indifference whether we regard an object determined by external end as a realized end or only as a means; the determination here is relative, external to the object itself and not objective. All objects, therefore, in which an external end is realized, are equally only a means of the end. Whatever is intended to be used for realizing an end and to be taken essentially as means, is a means which, in accordance with its destiny, is to be destroyed. But the object that is supposed to contain the realized end, and to represent the objectivity of the end, is also perishable; it too fulfils its end not by a tranquil existence in which it preserves itself, but only in so far as it is worn away; for only thus does it conform to the unity of the Notion, in that its externality, that is, its objectivity, sublates itself in that unity. A house, a clock, may appear as ends in relation to the tools employed for their production; but the stones and beams, or wheels and axles, and so on, which constitute the actuality of the end fulfil that end only through the pressure that they suffer, through the chemical processes with air, light, and water to which they are exposed and that deprive man of them by their friction and so forth. Accordingly, they fulfil their destiny only by being used and worn away and they correspond to what they are supposed to be only through their negation. They are not positively united with the end, because they possess self-determination only externally and are only relative ends, or essentially nothing but means.

These ends, as we have seen, have in general a limited content; their form is the infinite self-determination of the Notion, which through that content has limited itself to an external individuality. The limited content makes these ends inadequate to the infinity of the Notion and reduces them to an untruth; such a determinateness is already through the sphere of necessity, through being, at the mercy of becoming and alteration and must pass away.

3. Thus we obtain the result that external purposiveness which has as yet only the form of teleology, really only comes to be a means, not an objective end—because the subjective end remains an external subjective determination; or, in so far as the end is active and realizes itself, though only in a means it is still connected with the object *immediately*, immersed in it; it is itself an object, and the end, one may say, does not attain to a means, because the

realization of the end is a prior requirement before that realization could be brought about through a means.

In fact, however, the result is not only an external end relation, but the truth of it, an internal end relation and an objective end. The externality of the object, self-subsistent as against the Notion, which the end presupposes for itself is *posited* in this presupposition as an unessential illusory show and is also already sublated in and for itself; the activity of the end is therefore, strictly speaking, only the representation of this illusory show and the sublating of it. As the Notion has shown us, the first object becomes by communication a means, because it is in itself totality of the Notion, and its determinateness which is none other than externality itself is posited merely *as* something external and unessential and therefore appears within the end itself as the end's own moment, not as a self-subsistent moment relatively to the end. Thus the determination of the object as a means is purely an immediate one. Accordingly, in order to make that object a means, the subjective end requires to use no violence against the object, no reinforcement against it other than the reinforcing of itself; the *resolve* [*Entschluss*], the explication [*Aufschluss*], this determination of itself, is the *merely posited* externality of the object, which appears therein as immediately subjected to the end and possesses no other determination counter to it than that of the nullity of the being-in-and-for-self.

The second sublating of objectivity by objectivity differs from the above as follows: the former sublation, as the first, is the end in objective *immediacy*, and therefore the second is not merely the sublating of a first immediacy but of both, of the objective as something merely posited, and of the immediate. In this way, the negativity returns into itself in such a manner that it is equally a restoration of the objectivity but of an objectivity identical with it, and in this it is as at the same time also a positing of the objectivity as an external objectivity determined only by the end. Through the latter circumstance this product remains as before also a means; through the former it is objectivity that is identical with the Notion, the realized end, in which the side of being a means is the reality of the end itself. In the realized end the means vanishes, for it would be the objectivity that is as yet only immediately subsumed under the end, and in the realized end objectivity is present as the return of the end into itself; further, with it there also vanishes the mediation itself as a relation of something external, on the one side, into the concrete identity of the objective end, and on the other, into the same identity as abstract identity and immediacy of existence.

Herein is also contained the mediation that was demanded for the first premiss, the immediate relation of the end to the object. The realized end is also means, and conversely the truth of the means is just this, to be itself a real end, and the first sublating of objectivity is already also the second, just as the second proved to contain the first, as well. That is to say, the Notion *determines itself*; its determinateness is external indifference, which is immediately determined in the resolution [*Entschluss*] as *sublated*, namely as *internal, subjective* indifference, and at the same time as a *presupposed object*. Its further passage out from itself which appeared, namely, as an *immediate* communication and subsumption of the presupposed object under it, is at the same time a sublating of the former determinateness of externality that was internal and *enclosed within the Notion*, that is, posited as sublated, and at the same time a sublating of the presupposition of an object; consequently, this apparently first sublating of the indifferent objectivity is already the second as well, a reflection-into-self that has passed through mediation, and the realized end.

Since the Notion here in the sphere of objectivity, where its determinateness has the form of *indifferent externality*, is in reciprocal action with itself, the exposition of its movement here becomes doubly difficult and involved, because this movement is itself double and a first is always a second also. In the Notion taken by itself, that is in its subjectivity, its difference from itself appears as an *immediate* identical totality on its own account; but since its determinateness here is indifferent externality, its identity with itself in this externality is also immediately again self-repulsion, so that what is determined as external and indifferent to the identity is the identity itself; and the identity as identity, as reflected into itself, is rather its other. Only by keeping this firmly in mind can we grasp the objective return of the Notion into itself, that is, the true objectification of the Notion—grasp that each of the single moments through which this mediation runs its course is itself the entire syllogism of those moments. Thus the original *inner* externality of the Notion through which it is self-repellent unity, the end and the striving of the end towards objectification, is the immediate positing or presupposition of an external object; the *self-determination* is also the determination of an *external object* not determined by the Notion; and conversely, the latter determination is self-determination, that is, externality sublated and *posited as internal*—or the certainty of the *unessentiality* of the external object. Of the second relation, the determination of the object as means, it has just been shown how it is within itself the mediation of the end in the object with itself. Similarly, the third relation, mechanism, which proceeds under the dominance of the end and sublates the object by the object, is on the one hand a sublating of the means, of the object already posited as sublated and is therefore a second sublating and a reflection-into-self; while on the other hand it is a first determining of the external object. The latter, as has been remarked, is the production again in the realized end only of a means; the subjectivity of the finite Notion, contemptuously rejecting the means, has attained to nothing better in its goal. But this reflection that the end is reached in the means, and that in the fulfilled end, means and mediation are preserved, is the *last result of the external end-relation*, a result in which that relation has sublated itself, and which it has exhibited as its truth. The third syllogism that was considered last is distinguished by the fact that it is, in the first place, the subjective purposive activity of the preceding syllogisms, but is also the *spontaneous* sublation of external objectivity, and therewith of externality in general, and hence is *the totality in its positedness*.

First we saw subjectivity, the Notion's *being-for-self*, pass over into its *in-itself*, *objectivity*, to be followed by the reappearance in the latter of the negativity of the Notion's being-for-self; in that negativity the Notion has determined itself in such a manner that its *particularity* is an *external objectivity*, or it has determined itself as a simple concrete unity whose externality is its self-determination. The movement of the end has now reached the stage where the moment of externality is not merely posited in the Notion, where the end is not merely an *ought-to-be* and a *striving* to realize itself, but as a concrete totality is identical with the immediate objectivity. This identity is on the one hand the simple Notion and the equally *immediate* objectivity, but on the other hand, it is just as essentially a *mediation*, and only through the latter as a self-sublating mediation is it that simple immediacy;

the Notion is therefore essentially this: to be distinct as an explicit identity from its *implicit* objectivity, and thereby to possess externality, yet in this external totality to be the totality's self-determining identity. As such, the Notion is now the *Idea*.

Section Three: The Idea

The Idea is the *adequate Notion*, that which is objectively *true*, or the *true as such*. When anything whatever possesses truth, it possesses it through its Idea, or, *something possesses truth only in so far as it is Idea*. The expression 'idea' has often been employed in philosophy as in ordinary life for 'notion', indeed, even for a mere ordinary conception: 'I have no *idea* yet of this lawsuit, building, neighbourhood', means nothing more than the ordinary conception. Kant has reclaimed the expression Idea for the *notion of reason*. Now according to Kant, the notion of reason is supposed to be the notion of the *unconditioned*, but a notion *transcendent* in regard to phenomena, that is, no *empirical use* can be made of such notion that is *adequate to it*. The notions of reason are to serve for the comprehension of perceptions, the notions of the understanding for understanding them. But in fact, if the latter really are *Notions*, then *they are Notions*—they enable one to comprehend [*begreifen*], and an *understanding* of perceptions by means of notions of the understanding will be a *comprehension* of them. But if understanding is only a determining of perceptions by such categories as for example whole and parts, force, cause, and the like, it signifies only a determining by reflection; and similarly, by understanding can be meant only the specific *representation* of a completely determined sensuous content; thus when someone, having been directed that at the end of the wood he must turn left, replies 'I *understand*', *understanding* means nothing more than the grasping of something in pictorial thought and in memory. '*Notion of reason*', too, is a somewhat clumsy expression; for the Notion is something altogether rational; and in so far as reason is distinguished from understanding and the Notion as such, it is the totality of the Notion and of objectivity. In this sense the Idea is the *rational*; it is the unconditioned, because only that has conditions which essentially relates itself to an objectivity, but an objectivity that it has not itself determined but which still confronts it in the form of indifference and externality, just as the external end still had conditions.

Reserving then the expression 'Idea' for the objective or real Notion and distinguishing it from the Notion itself and still more from mere pictorial thought, we must also reject even more vigor-

ously that estimate of the Idea according to which it is not anything actual, and true thoughts are said to be *only ideas*. If *thoughts*
are merely *subjective* and contingent, they certainly have no further
value; but in this respect they are not inferior to temporal and
contingent *actualities* which likewise have no further value than
that of contingencies and phenomena. On the other hand if,
conversely, the Idea is not to have the value of truth, because in
regard to phenomena it is *transcendent*, and no congruent object
can be assigned to it in the world of sense, this is an odd misunderstanding that would deny objective validity to the Idea
because it lacks that which constitutes Appearance, namely, the
untrue being of the objective world. In regard to practical Ideas,
Kant recognizes that 'nothing can be more harmful and unworthy
of a philosopher than the *vulgar* appeal to an *experience* that
allegedly conflicts with the Idea. This very experience would not
even exist if, for example, political institutions had been established
at the proper time in conformity with Ideas, and if *crude conceptions*, crude just because they had been drawn from experience,
had not taken the place of Ideas and so nullified every good intention.' Kant regards the Idea as a necessity and as the goal which,
as the *archetype*, it must be our endeavour to set up for a maximum
and to which we must strive to bring the condition of the actual
world ever nearer.

But having reached the result that the Idea is the unity of the
Notion and objectivity, is the true, it must not be regarded merely
as a *goal* to which we have to approximate but which itself always
remains a kind of *beyond*; on the contrary, we must recognize that
everything actual *is* only in so far as it possesses the Idea and
expresses it. It is not merely that the object, the objective and
subjective world in general, *ought to be congruous* with the Idea,
but they are themselves the congruence of Notion and reality; the
reality that does not correspond to the Notion is mere *Appearance*,
the subjective, contingent, capricious element that is not the truth.
When it is said that no object is to be found in experience that is
perfectly congruous with the *Idea*, one is opposing the Idea as a
subjective standard to the actual; but what anything actual is
supposed in truth *to be*, if its Notion is not in it and if its objectivity
does not correspond to its Notion at all, it is impossible to say;
for it would be nothing. It is true that the mechanical and chemical
object, like the non-spiritual subject and the spirit that is conscious

only of the finite, not of its essence, do not, according to their various natures, have their Notion existent in them *in its own free form*. But they can only be true at all in so far as they are the union of their Notion and reality, of their soul and their body. Wholes like the state and the church cease to exist when the unity of their Notion and their reality is dissolved; man, the living being, is dead when soul and body are parted in him; dead nature, the mechanical and chemical world—taking, that is, the dead world to mean the inorganic world, otherwise it would have no positive meaning at all—dead nature, then, if it is separated into its Notion and its reality, is nothing but the subjective abstraction of a thought form and a formless matter. *Spirit* that was not Idea, was not the unity of the Notion with its own self, or the Notion that did not have the Notion itself for its reality would be dead, spiritless spirit, a material object.

The Idea being the unity of Notion and reality, *being* has attained the significance of *truth*; therefore what now *is* is only what is Idea. Finite things are finite because they do not possess the complete reality of their Notion within themselves, but require other things to complete it—or, conversely, because they are presupposed as objects, hence possess the Notion as an external determination. The highest to which they attain on the side of this finitude is external purposiveness. That actual things are not congruous with the Idea is the side of their *finitude* and *untruth*, and in accordance with this side they are *objects*, determined in accordance with their various spheres and in the relationships of objectivity, either mechanically, chemically or by an external end. That the Idea has not completely leavened its reality, has imperfectly subdued it to the Notion, this is a possibility arising from the fact that the Idea itself has a *restricted content*, that though it is essentially the unity of Notion and reality, it is no less essentially their difference; for only the object is their immediate, that is, merely *implicit* unity. But if an object, for example the state, *did not correspond at all* to its Idea, that is, if in fact it was not the Idea of the state at all, if its reality, which is the self-conscious individuals, did not correspond at all to the Notion, its soul and its body would have parted; the former would escape into the solitary regions of thought, the latter would have broken up into the single individualities. But because the Notion of the state so essentially constitutes the nature of these individualities, it is present in them as an urge so powerful that they are impelled to translate it into reality, be it only in the form of external purposiveness, or to put up with it as it is, or else they must needs perish. The worst state, one whose reality least corresponds to the Notion, in so far as it still exists, is still Idea; the individuals still obey a dominant Notion.

However, the Idea has not merely the more general meaning of the *true being*, of the unity of *Notion* and *reality*, but the more specific one of the unity of *subjective Notion* and *objectivity*. That is to say, the Notion as such is itself already the identity of itself and *reality*; for the indefinite expression 'reality' means in general nothing else but *determinate being*, and this the Notion possesses in its particularity and individuality. Similarly too, *objectivity* is the total *Notion* that out of its determinateness has withdrawn into *identity* with itself. In the former subjectivity the determinateness or difference of the Notion is an *illusory being* [*Schein*] that is immediately sublated and has withdrawn into being-for-self or negative unity; it is an *inhering* predicate. But in this objectivity the determinateness is posited as an immediate totality, as an external whole. Now the Idea has shown itself to be the Notion liberated again into its subjectivity from the immediacy in which it is submerged in the object; to be the Notion that distinguishes itself from its objectivity, which however is no less determined by it and possesses its substantiality only in that Notion. This identity has therefore rightly been defined as the *subject-object*, for it is as well the formal or subjective Notion as it is the object as such. But this must be understood more precisely. The Notion, having truly attained its reality, is this absolute judgement whose *subject*, as self-related negative unity, distinguishes itself from its objectivity and is the latter's being-in-and-for-self, but essentially relates itself to it through itself; it is therefore its *own end* [*Selbstzweck*] and the *urge* to realize it; but for this very reason the subject does not possess objectivity in an immediate manner, for if it did it would be merely the totality of the object as such lost in objectivity; on the contrary, objectivity is the realization of the end, an objectivity *posited* by the activity of the end, an objectivity which, as *positedness*, possesses its subsistence and its form only as permeated by its subject. As objectivity, it has in it the moment of the *externality* of the Notion and is therefore in general the side of finitude, change and Appearance, a side, however, which meets with extinction in its retraction into the negative unity of the Notion; the negativity whereby its indifferent mutual externality exhibits itself as unessential and a positivity, is the Notion itself. The Idea is, therefore, in spite of this objectivity utterly *simple* and *immaterial*, for the externality exists only as determined by the Notion and as taken up into its negative unity; in so far as it exists as indifferent externality it is not merely at the mercy of mechanism in general but exists only as the transitory and untrue. Although therefore the Idea has its reality in a material externality, this is not an abstract *being* subsisting on its own account over against the Notion; on the contrary, it exists only as a *becoming* through the negativity of indifferent being, as a simple determinateness of the Notion.

This yields the following more precise definitions of the Idea. First, it is the simple truth, the identity of the Notion and objectivity as *a universal* in which the opposition and subsistence of the particular is dissolved into its self-identical negativity and is equality with itself. Secondly, it is the *relation* of the explicit subjectivity of the simple Notion and its objectivity which is *distinguished* therefrom; the former is essentially the *urge* to sublate this separation, and the latter is the indifferent positedness, the subsistence that is in and for itself null. As this relation, the Idea is the *process* of sundering itself into individuality and its inorganic nature, and again of bringing this inorganic nature under the power of the subject and returning to the first simple universality. The *identity* of the Idea with itself is one with the *process*; the thought which liberates actuality from the illusory show of purposeless mutability and transfigures it into the Idea must not represent this truth of actuality as a dead repose, as a mere *picture*, lifeless, without impulse or movement, as a genius or number, or an abstract thought; by virtue of the freedom which the Notion attains in the Idea, the Idea possesses within itself also the *most stubborn opposition*; its repose consists in the security and certainty with which it eternally creates and eternally overcomes that opposition, in it meeting with *itself*.

In the first instance, however, the Idea is once again only *immediate* or only in its *Notion*; objective reality is, it is true, conformable to the Notion, but it is not yet liberated into the Notion, and the latter does not exist explicitly *for itself as Notion*. Thus though the Notion is *soul*, it is soul in the guise of an *immediate*, that is, its determinateness does not appear *as* soul itself, it has not grasped itself as soul, it does not possess its objective reality within itself; the Notion is as a soul that is not yet *fully a soul*.

At this first stage the Idea is *Life*: the Notion that, distinguished from its objectivity, simple within itself, pervades its objectivity and, as its own end, possesses its means in the objectivity and posits the latter as its means, yet is immanent in this means and is therein the realized end that is identical with itself. This Idea, on account of its immediacy, has *individuality* for the form of its existence. But the reflection-into-self of its absolute process is the sublating of this immediate individuality; thereby the Notion which, as universality in this individuality, is the *inwardness* of the latter, converts the externality into universality, or posits its objectivity as being the same as itself.

In this second stage, the Idea is the Idea of the *true* and the *good*, as *cognition* and *volition*. In the first instance, it is finite cognition and finite volition, in which the true and the good are still distinguished and each appears as yet only as a *goal*. The Notion has, in the first instance, liberated *itself* into itself and as yet given itself only an *abstract objectivity* for its reality. But the process of this finite cognition and action converts the initially abstract universality into a totality, whereby it becomes a *complete objectivity*. Or, to consider it from the other side, finite, that is, subjective spirit, *makes* for itself the *presupposition* of an objective world, just as life *has* such a presupposition; but its activity consists in sublating this presupposition and converting it into a positedness. In this way its reality is for it the objective world, or conversely, the objective world is the ideality in which it cognizes itself.

Thirdly, spirit cognizes the Idea as its *absolute truth*, as the truth that is in and for itself; the infinite Idea in which cognition and action are equalized, and which is the *absolute knowledge of itself*.

CHAPTER I

LIFE

The Idea of Life is concerned with a subject matter so concrete, and if you will so real, that with it we may seem to have over-stepped the domain of logic as it is commonly conceived. Certainly, if logic were to contain nothing but empty, dead forms of thought, there could be no mention in it at all of such a content as the Idea of life. But if absolute truth is the subject matter of logic, and *truth* as such is essentially *in cognition*, then *cognition* at least would have to be discussed. So-called pure logic is usually followed up with an *applied* logic—a logic dealing with *concrete cognition*, not to mention the mass of *psychology* and *anthropology* that it is often deemed necessary to interpolate into logic. But the anthropological and psychological side of cognition is concerned with its *manifested aspect [Erscheinung]*, in which the Notion on its own account has not yet come to have an objectivity the same as itself, that is, to have itself for object. The part of logic that treats of this concrete side does not belong to *applied logic* as such; if it did, then every science would have to be dragged into logic, for each is an applied logic in so far as it consists in apprehending its subject matter in forms of thought and the Notion. The subjective Notion has presuppositions which present themselves in psychological, anthropological and other forms. But to logic belong only the presuppositions of the pure Notion in so far as they have the form of pure thoughts, of abstract essentialities, that is, the determinations of *being* and *essence*. Similarly, in respect of *cognition*, the Notion's apprehension of itself, logic will not deal with other shapes of its presupposition but only with that which is itself Idea; this latter, however, necessarily falls to be dealt with in logic. Now this presupposition is the *immediate* Idea; for since cognition is the Notion in so far as this is for itself but as a subjectivity is in relation to an objectivity, the Notion is related to the Idea as *presupposed* or *immediate* Idea. But the immediate Idea is *life*.

To this extent the necessity of treating of the Idea of life in logic would be based on the necessity, otherwise recognized, too, of treating here of the concrete Notion of cognition. But this Idea has come upon the scene through the Notion's own necessity; the *Idea*, that which is *true* in and for itself, is essentially the subject matter of logic; since it is at first to be considered in its immediacy, it must be apprehended and cognized in this determinateness in which it is *life*, in order that its treatment shall not be an empty affair devoid of determinate content. All that we need perhaps to remark is how far the logical view of life differs from any other scientific view of it; this is not the place, however, to concern ourselves with how life is treated in the unphilosophical sciences, but only with differentiating logical life as pure Idea from natural life which is dealt with in the *philosophy of nature*, and from life in so far as it stands in connexion with *spirit*. The former of these, as the life of nature, is life as projected into the *externality of existence* and having its *condition* in inorganic nature, and where the moments of the Idea are a multiplicity of actual formations. Life in the Idea is without such *presuppositions* which are in the form of shapes of actuality; its presupposition is the *Notion* as we have considered it, on the one hand as subjective, on the other hand as objective. In nature life appears as the highest stage, a stage that nature's externality attains by withdrawing into itself and sublating itself in subjectivity. In Logic it is simple inwardness [*Insichsein*], which in the Idea of life has attained an externality that genuinely corresponds to it; the Notion that earlier appeared on the scene as subjective Notion is the soul of life itself; it is the urge that mediates for itself its reality throughout objectivity. Nature, having reached this Idea from the starting point of its externality, transcends itself; its end does not appear as its beginning, but as its limit, in which it sublates itself. Similarly, in the Idea of life the moments of its reality do not receive the shape of external actuality but remain enclosed within the form of the Notion.

In *spirit*, however, life appears partly as opposed to it, partly as posited as at one with it, this unity being reborn as the pure offspring of spirit. For here life is to be taken generally in its proper sense as *natural life*, for what is called the *life of spirit* as spirit, is its peculiar nature that stands opposed to mere life; just as we speak, too, of the nature of *spirit*, although spirit is not a natural being and is rather the opposite of nature. Life as such, then, is for spirit partly a *means*, and as such spirit opposes it to itself; partly spirit is a living individual and life is its body; and again, this unity of spirit with its living corporeality is born from spirit

itself as an *ideal*. None of these relations to spirit concerns logical
life and life is to be considered here neither as instrument [*Mittel*]
of a spirit, nor as a moment of the ideal and of beauty. In both
cases, as *natural* life and as life standing in relation *with spirit*,
life possesses a *determinateness of its externality*, in the first case
through its presuppositions which are other formations of nature,
in the second case through the ends and the activity of spirit. The
Idea of life by itself is free from the former presupposed and conditioning objectivity as well as from relation to the latter subjectivity.

Life, considered now more closely in its Idea, is in and for itself
absolute *universality*; the objectivity that it possesses is permeated
throughout by the Notion and has the Notion alone for substance.
What is distinguished as part, or in accordance with some other
external reflection, has within itself the whole Notion; the Notion
is the *omnipresent* soul in it, which remains simple self-relation and
remains a one in the multiplicity belonging to objective being.
This multiplicity, as self-external objectivity, has an indifferent
subsistence, which in space and time, if these could already be
mentioned here, is a mutual externality of wholly diverse and self-
subsistent elements. But in life externality is at the same time
present as the *simple determinateness* of its Notion; thus the soul
is an omnipresent outpouring of itself into this multiplicity and at
the same remains absolutely the simple oneness of the concrete
Notion with itself. The thinking that clings to the determinations
of the relationships of reflection and of the formal Notion, when it
comes to consider life, this unity of its Notion in the externality of
objectivity, in the absolute multiplicity of atomistic matter, finds
all its thoughts without exception are of no avail; the omnipresence
of the simple in manifold externality is for reflection an absolute
contradiction, and as reflection must at the same time apprehend
this omnipresence from its perception of life and therefore admit
the actuality of this Idea, it is an *incomprehensible mystery* for it,
because it does not grasp the Notion, and the Notion as the substance of life. This simple life, however, is not only omnipresent;
it is absolutely the *subsistence* and *immanent substance* of its
objectivity; but as subjective substance it is the *urge*, and moreover the *specific urge*, of the *particular* difference, and no less
essentially the one and universal urge of the specialized difference
that reduces this its particularization into unity and maintains it

therein. It is only as this *negative unity* of its objectivity and particularization that life is a self-related life that is for itself, a soul. As such it is essentially an individual, which relates itself to objectivity as to an *other*, to a non-living nature. Consequently the original *judgement* of life consists in this, that it detaches itself as an individual subject from objectivity, and in constituting itself the negative unity of the Notion, makes the *presupposition* of an immediate objectivity.

Life is therefore first to be considered as a *living individual* that is for itself the subjective totality and is presupposed as indifferent to an objectivity that confronts it as indifferent.

Secondly, it is the *life process*, the process of sublating its presupposition, positing as negative the objectivity that is indifferent to it and actualizing itself as that objectivity's power and negative unity. By so doing it makes itself into the universal that is the unity of itself and its other.

Hence life is thirdly the *genus process*, the process of sublating its individualization and relating itself to its objective existence as to *itself*. Accordingly, this process is on the one hand the return to its Notion and the repetition of the first diremption, the becoming of a new individuality and the death of the first, immediate one; but on the other hand, the *Notion* of life that has *withdrawn into itself* is the becoming of the Notion that is in relationship with itself and exists universally and freely for itself—the transition into *cognition*.

A. THE LIVING INDIVIDUAL

1. The Notion of life, or universal life, is the immediate Idea, the Notion whose objectivity corresponds to it; but its objectivity corresponds to it only in so far as the Notion is the negative unity of this externality, that is to say, *posits* it as corresponding to the Notion. The infinite relation of the Notion to itself is as negativity a self-determining, the diremption of itself *into itself as subjective individuality and itself as indifferent universality*. The Idea of life in its immediacy is as yet only the creative universal soul. By reason of this immediacy, its first negative relation of the Idea within it is the self-determination of itself as *Notion*—the *implicit* positing that only becomes *explicit* or *for itself* through its return into itself—a creative *presupposing*. Through this self-determining, the *universal* life becomes a *particular*; it has thereby sundered

itself into the two extremes of the judgement, which immediately becomes a syllogism.

The determinations of the opposition are the general determinations of the *Notion*, for it is the Notion which has been sundered; but the *filling* of these determinations is the Idea. One extreme is the *unity* of the Notion and reality, which is the Idea, as the *immediate* unity that at an earlier stage appeared as *objectivity*. But here it is in a different determination. There it was the unity of Notion and reality, where the Notion has passed over into the reality in which it is merely lost; it did not stand over against the reality, or in other words, because the Notion is for the reality only an inner, it is merely a reflection *external* to it. That objectivity is therefore the immediate itself in an immediate form. Here, on the contrary, it has proceeded only from the Notion, so that its essence is positedness, and it exists as a *negative*. It is to be regarded as the *side of the universality of the Notion*, consequently as *abstract* universality, essentially only *inhering* in the subject and in the form of immediate *being* which, posited on its own account, is indifferent to the subject. Thus the totality of the Notion which attaches to the objectivity is, as it were, only *lent* to it; the last self-subsistence that objectivity possesses as against the subject is this *being* which, in its truth, is only the above moment of the Notion, the Notion that, as *presupposing*, is in the first determinateness of an *implicit* positing, which does not yet exist *as* a positing, as the unity that is reflected into itself. Self-subsistent objectivity, therefore, having proceeded from the Idea, is immediate being only as the *predicate* of the judgement of the Notion's self-determination—a being that is indeed distinct from the subject, but at the same time is essentially posited as *moment* of the Notion.

In respect of content this objectivity is the totality of the Notion; but this totality is confronted by the subjectivity or negative unity of the Notion, which constitutes the true centrality, namely the Notion's free unity with itself. This *subject* is the Idea in the form of *individuality*, as simple but negative self-identity— the *living individual*.

This is in the first place life as *soul*, as the Notion of itself that is completely determined within itself, the initiating, self-moving *principle*. The Notion in its simplicity contains determinate externality as a *simple* moment enclosed within it. But, further, this soul *in its immediacy* is immediately external and possesses an objective being of its own—a reality that is subjugated to the end, the immediate *means*, in the first instance, objectivity as *predicate* of the subject; but further, objectivity is also the *middle term* of the syllogism; the corporeality of the soul is that whereby the soul unites itself with external objectivity. The living being possesses corporeality in the first instance as reality that is immediately identical with the Notion; thus it has this corporeality in general by *nature*.

Now because this objectivity is predicate of the individual and taken up into the subjective unity, the earlier determinations of the object, the mechanical or chemical relationship does not attach to it, still less the abstract relationship of reflection, of whole and parts and the like. As externality it is indeed *capable* of such relationships, but to that extent it is not a living being; when the living thing is regarded as a whole consisting of parts, or as a thing operated on by mechanical or chemical causes, as a mechanical or chemical product, whether it be regarded merely as such product or also as determined by an external end, then the Notion is regarded as external to it and it is treated as a *dead* thing. Since the Notion is immanent in it, the *purposiveness* of the living being is to be grasped as *inner*; the Notion is in it as determinate Notion, distinct from its externality, and in its distinguishing, pervading the externality and remaining identical with itself. This objectivity of the living being is the *organism*; it is the *means and instrument* of the end, perfect in its purposiveness since the Notion constitutes its substance; but for that very reason this means and instrument is itself the realized end, in which the subjective end is thus immediately brought into unity with itself. In respect of its externality the organism is a manifold, not of *parts* but of *members*. These members, as such, (*a*) subsist only in the individuality; in so far as they are external and can be apprehended in this externality, they are separable; but when separated, they revert to the mechanical and chemical relationships of common objectivity. (*b*) Their externality is opposed to the negative unity of the living individuality; the latter is therefore the *urge* to posit the abstract moment of the Notion's determinateness as a real difference; since this difference *is immediate*, it is the *urge* of each *single, specific moment* to produce itself, and equally to raise its particularity to universality, sublate the other moments external to it and produce itself at their expense, but no less to sublate itself and make itself a means for the others.

2. This *process* of the living individuality is restricted to that individuality itself and still falls entirely within it. Above, in the syllogism of external purposiveness, we considered its first premiss, namely that the end relates itself immediately to objectivity and makes it a means, and we found that in this premiss the end does indeed remain similar to itself and has withdrawn into itself in the objectivity, but that the objectivity has not yet *in its own self* sublated itself, and therefore the end is to that extent not yet *in and for itself* in this premiss, and only becomes so in the conclusion. The process of the living being with itself is this same premiss, but in so far as the latter is also conclusion, and in so far as the immediate relation of the subject to objectivity, which objectivity thereby becomes a means and instrument, is at the same time the *negative unity* of the Notion in its own self; the end realizes itself in this its externality by being the subjective power over that externality and the process in which the externality displays its self-dissolution and its return into this the negative unity of the end. The restlessness and mutability of the external side of the living being is the manifestation in it of the Notion, which as in its own self negativity only has an objectivity in so far as the latter's indifferent subsistence reveals itself as self-sublating. The Notion therefore produces itself by its urge in such a manner that the product, the Notion being its essence, is itself the producing agent; that is to say the product is product only as the externality that equally posits itself as negative, or is product only in being the process of production.

3. Now the Idea just considered is the *Notion* of the *living subject* and *its process*; the determinations, which are in relationship with each other, are the self-related *negative unity* of the Notion and *objectivity*, which is the Notion's *means*, but in which it has *returned* into itself. But since these are moments of the Idea of life *within its Notion*, they are not the specific Notion-moments of the *living individual in its reality*. The objectivity or corporeality of this individual is a concrete totality; the above moments are the sides out of which life constitutes itself; they are therefore not the moments of this life that is already constituted by the Idea. But the living *objectivity* as such of the individual, since it is ensouled by the Notion and has the Notion for its substance, also possesses

for its essential difference the determinations of the Notion, *universality*, *particularity* and *individuality*; accordingly the *shape* [*Gestalt*], in which they are *externally* distinguished, is divided or incised (*insectum*) on the basis of that difference.

Thus it is in the first place *universality*, the purely internal vibration of vitality, or *sensibility*. The Notion of universality, as we have found it above, is simple immediacy, which however is this only by being within itself absolute negativity. This Notion of *absolute difference* with its negativity *dissolved* in *simplicity* and self-similar, is brought to view [*Anschaung*] in sensibility. It is inwardness [*Insichsein*], not as abstract simplicity but as an infinitely *determinable* receptivity, which in its *determinateness* does not become something manifold and external, but is simply reflected into itself. *Determinateness* is present in this universality as simple *principle*; the individual external determinateness, a so-called *impression*, returns from its external and manifold determination into this simplicity of *self-feeling*. Sensibility may therefore be regarded as the determinate being of the inwardly existent soul, since it receives all externality into itself, while reducing it to the perfect simplicity of self-similar universality.

The second determination of the Notion is *particularity*, the moment of the *posited* difference, the opening up of the negativity that is locked up in simple self-feeling, or is an ideal, not yet a real, determinateness in it, that is, *irritability*. On account of the abstraction of its negativity, feeling is an urge; it *determines* itself; the self-determination of the living being is its judgement or its self-limitation [*Verendlichung*], whereby it relates itself to the external as to a *presupposed* objectivity and is in reciprocal *activity* with it. Now as a *particular* living being it is on one side a *species* alongside other species of living beings; the *formal* reflection of this *indifferent diversity* into itself is the formal *genus* and its systematization; but the individual reflection is this, that the particularity, the negativity of its determinateness, as a direction outwards, is the self-related negativity of the Notion.

According to this third determination the living being is an *individual*. The precise determination of this reflection-into-self is such that in irritability, the living being is its own externality to itself, to the objectivity which it possesses immediately as its means and instrument, and which is externally determinable. The reflection-into-self sublates this immediacy—on the one side as a theoretical reflection, that is, in so far as the negativity is present as the simple moment of sensibility that was considered in the latter and which constitutes *feeling*—on the other side as real reflection, in that the unity of the Notion posits itself *in its external objectivity* as negative unity; this is *reproduction*. The first two moments, sensibility and irritability, are abstract determinations; in reproduction life is *concrete* and is vitality; in it, as in its truth, life for the first time has also feeling and the power of resistance. Reproduction is the negativity as simple moment of sensibility, and irritability is only a living power of resistance, so that the relationship to the external is reproduction and individual identity with self. Each of the individual moments is essentially the totality of all; their difference constitutes the ideal form determinateness, which is posited in reproduction as concrete totality of the whole. This whole is, therefore, on the one hand opposed as a third, namely as a *real* totality, to the former determinate totalities, while on the other hand it is their implicit essential nature, and at the same time that in which they are embraced as moments, and in which they have their subject and their subsistence.

With reproduction as the moment of individuality, the living being posits itself as an *actual* individuality, a self-related being-for-self; but at the same time it is a real *relation outwards*, the reflection of *particularity* or irritability *towards an other*, towards the *objective* world. The process of life, which is enclosed within the individual, passes over into a relation to the presupposed objectivity as such, in consequence of the fact that when the individual posits itself as a *subjective* totality, the *moment of its determinateness* as a *relation* to externality becomes a *totality* as well.

B. THE LIFE-PROCESS

The living individual, in shaping itself inwardly, tenses itself against its original act of presupposition, and opposes itself as an absolute subject to the presupposed objective world. The subject is its own end [*Selbstzweck*], the Notion, which has its means and subjective reality in the objectivity that is subjugated to it. As such, it is constituted as the Idea in and for itself and as a being that is essentially self-subsistent, in face of which the presupposed external world has the value only of something negative and lacking

BB

self-subsistence. In its self-feeling the living being has this *certainty* of the intrinsic *nullity* of the *otherness* confronting it. Its urge is the need to sublate this otherness and to give itself the truth of this certainty. The individual is, as subject, in the first instance no more than the *Notion* of the Idea of life; its subjective inward process in which it draws on its own resources, and the immediate objectivity which it posits conformably to its Notion as a natural means is mediated by the process that relates itself to the completely posited externality, to the objective totality standing *indifferently* alongside it.

This process begins with *need*, that is, with a moment that is twofold. First the living being determines itself, in so doing posits itself as denied, and thereby relates itself to an *other* to it, to the indifferent objectivity; but secondly, it is equally not lost in this loss of itself but maintains itself therein and remains the identity of the self-similar Notion; thus it is the urge to posit this *other* world *as its own*, as similar to itself, to sublate it and to objectify *itself*. By doing this, its self-determination has the form of objective externality, and as it is at the same time identical with itself it is absolute *contradiction*. The immediate shape is the Idea in its simple Notion, objectivity that is conformable to the Notion; as such, it is *good* by nature. But since its negative moment realizes itself as an objective particularity, that is, since each of the essential moments of its unity is realized as a separate totality, the Notion is *sundered* into an absolute disparity with itself; and since, all the same, it is absolute identity in this disharmony, the living being is *for itself* this disharmony and has the feeling of this contradiction, which is *pain*. *Pain* is therefore the prerogative of living natures; because they are the existent Notion, they are an actuality of infinite power such that they are within themselves the *negativity* of themselves, that this *their negativity* is *for them*, and that they maintain themselves in their otherness. It is said that contradiction is unthinkable; but the fact is that in the pain of a living being it is even an actual existence.

This diremption of the living being within itself is *feeling*, the diremption being taken up into the simple universality of the Notion, into sensibility. From pain begin the *need* and the *urge* that constitute the transition by which the individual, which is explicitly the negation of itself, becomes also explicitly its own identity—an identity that exists only as the negation of the former negation. The identity that is in the urge as such is the subjective certainty of itself, in accordance with which it relates itself to its external, indifferently existing world as to an Appearance, to an intrinsically Notionless and unessential actuality. This actuality has to await the subject, which is the immanent end, before it receives the Notion into itself. The indifference of the objective world to the determinateness, and consequently to the end, constitutes its external capability of being conformable to the subject; whatever other specifications it may possess, its mechanical determinability, the absence of the freedom of the immanent Notion, constitutes its impotence to maintain itself against the living being. In so far as the object confronts the living being in the first instance as an indifferent externality, it can act upon it mechanically; but in doing so it is not acting as on a living being; where it enters into relationship with a living being it does not act on it as a cause, but *excites* it. Because the living being is an urge, externality cannot approach or enter it except in so far as it is in its own very nature already *in the living being*; therefore the action on the subject consists merely in the latter finding the externality presented to it *conformable*. This externality may not be conformable to the subject's totality, but at least it must correspond to a particular side of it, and this possibility resides simply in the fact that the subject in its external relationship is a particular.

Now the subject, as specifically related in its need to the externality, and so itself an externality or instrument, uses *violence* on the object. Its particular character, its finitude in general, falls into the more specific manifestation of this relationship. The external element in this is the process of objectivity in general, mechanism and chemism. But this process is immediately broken off and the externality transformed into internality. The external purposiveness that is produced at first by the activity of the subject in the indifferent object is sublated by reason of the fact that the object, relatively to the Notion, is not a substance, and that therefore the Notion cannot become merely the object's external form, but must posit itself as its essence and immanent pervading determination, in conformity with the Notion's original identity.

With the seizure of the object, therefore, the mechanical process passes over into the inner process by which the individual *appropriates* the object in such a manner as to deprive it of its peculiar nature [*Beschaffenheit*], convert it into a means for itself, and give its own subjectivity to it for substance. This assimilation accordingly coincides with the individual's process of reproduction considered above; in this process the individual in the first instance draws upon itself in making its own objectivity its object; the mechanical and chemical conflict of its members with external things is an objective moment of itself. The mechanical and chemical side of the process is a beginning of the dissolution of the living being. Since life is the truth of these processes, and therefore as a living being is the concrete existence of this truth and the power dominating these processes, it takes them within its embrace, pervades them as their universality, and their product is completely determined by it. This conversion of them into the living individuality constitutes the return of this latter into itself, so that production, which as such would be transition into an other, becomes reproduction, in which the living being posits itself as self-identical *for itself*.

The immediate Idea is also the immediate, not the *explicit*, identity of the Notion and reality; through the objective process the living being gives itself its feeling of *self*; for in that process it *posits* itself as what it is in and for itself, namely, as a self-identity and the negative unity of the negative in its otherness, which is posited as indifferent to it. In this coming together of the individual and its objectivity, that at first was presupposed as indifferent to it, the individual, which on one side has constituted itself an actual unity, has none the less *sublated its particularity* and raised itself to *universality*. Its particularity consisted in the diremption by which life posited as its species the individual life and the objectivity external to it. Through the external life process it has thus posited itself as real universal life, that is, as *genus*.

C. THE GENUS

The living individual, at first disengaged from the universal Notion of life, is a presupposition that is not as yet authenticated by the living individual itself. Through its process with the simultaneously presupposed world, it has posited itself *on its own account* as the negative unity of its otherness, as the foundation of itself; as such it is the actuality of the Idea, in such a manner that now the individual brings itself forth out of *actuality*, whereas before it proceeded only from the *Notion*, and that its genesis which was an act of *presupposing*, now becomes its production.

But the further determination that it has attained by the sublation of the opposition is that of being the *genus* as identity of itself with its previously indifferent otherness. This Idea of the individual, since it is this essential identity, is essentially the particularization of itself. This its diremption, in accordance with the totality from which it proceeds, is the duplication of the individual—a presupposing of an objectivity that is identical with it, and a relationship of the living being to itself as to another living being.

This universal is the third stage, the truth of life in so far as this is still confined within its sphere. This sphere is the self-related process of the individual, where externality is its immanent moment; secondly, this externality is itself, as a living totality, an objectivity that for the individual is its own self, an objectivity in which, not as *sublated* but as *persisting*, the individual has the certainty of itself.

Now because the relationship of the genus is the identity of individual self-feeling in what is at the same time another self-subsistent individual, it is *contradiction*; thus the living being is again an *urge*. Now the genus is indeed the consummation of the Idea of life, but at first it is still within the sphere of immediacy; this universality is therefore *actual* in an *individual* shape—the Notion, whose reality has the form of immediate objectivity. Consequently, though the individual is indeed *in itself* genus, it is not *explicitly* or *for itself* the genus; what is *for* it is as yet only another living individual; the Notion distinguished from itself has for object, with which it is identical, not itself as Notion but a Notion that as a living being has at the same time external objectivity for it, a form that is therefore immediately reciprocal.

The identity with the other individual, the individual's universality, is thus as yet only *internal* or *subjective*; it therefore has the longing to posit this and to realize itself as a universal. But this *urge* of the genus can realize itself only by sublating the single individualities which are still particular relatively to one another. In the first instance, in so far as it is these latter which, *in themselves* universal, satisfy the tension of their longing and dissolve themselves into the universality of their genus, their realized identity is the negative unity of the genus that is reflected into itself out of its diremption. It is thus the individuality of life itself, *generated* no longer from its Notion, but from the *actual* Idea. In the first instance, it is itself only Notion that has yet to objectify itself, but it is *the actual Notion—the germ of a living individual.* The germ is visible evidence to *ordinary perception* of what the Notion is, and it demonstrates that the *subjective Notion* has *external actuality.* For the germ of the living being is the complete concretion of individuality, in which all its diverse aspects, properties and articulated differences are contained in their *entire determinateness,* and the initially *immaterial,* subjective totality is undeveloped, simple and non-sensuous; the germ is thus the entire living being in the inner form of the Notion.

The reflection of the genus into itself is from this side the means whereby it obtains *actuality,* the moment of negative unity and individuality being thereby posited in it—the propagation of the living species. The Idea, which as life, is still in the form of immediacy, thus falls back into actuality and this its reflection is only repetition and the infinite progress, in which it does not emerge from the finitude of its immediacy. But this return into its first Notion has also the higher side, that the Idea has not merely run through the mediation of its processes within its immediacy, but by this very act has sublated this immediacy and thereby raised itself to a higher form of its existence.

That is to say, the process of the genus, in which the single individuals sublate in one another their indifferent immediate existence and in this negative unity expire, has further for the other side of its product the *realized genus,* which has posited itself identical with the Notion. In the genus process, the separated individualities of individual life perish; the negative identity in which the genus returns into itself, while it is on the one hand the process of *generating individuality,* is on the other hand the *sublating of it,* and is thus the genus coming together with itself, the *universality* of the Idea in process of *becoming for itself.* In copulation the immediacy of the living individuality perishes; the death of this life is the procession of spirit. The Idea, which as genus is *implicit,* is now *explicit,* in that it has sublated its particularity which constituted the living species, and has thereby given itself a *reality* that is *itself simple universality.* As such it is the Idea that *relates itself to itself as Idea,* the universal that has universality for its determinateness and existence—the Idea of *cognition.*

CHAPTER 2

THE IDEA OF COGNITION

Life is the immediate Idea, or the Idea as its *Notion* not yet realized in its own self. In its *judgement*, the Idea is *cognition* in general.

The Notion is, as Notion, *for itself* in so far as it *freely* exists as abstract universality or as genus. As such, it is its pure self-identity, which inwardly differentiates itself in such a manner that the differentiated moment is not an *objectivity*, but is likewise liberated into subjectivity or the form of simple self-likeness, and hence the object of the Notion is the Notion itself. Its *reality* in general is the *form of its determinate being*, and the point of interest is the determination of this form; on this determination rests the difference between what the Notion is *in itself* or as *subjective*, and what it is when submerged in objectivity, and then in the Idea of life. In the latter it is indeed distinguished from its external reality and posited *for itself*, yet this its being-for-self it possesses only as the identity that is a relation to itself as submerged in its subjugated objectivity, or to itself as indwelling, substantial form. The elevation of the Notion above life means that its reality is the Notion form liberated into universality. Through this judgement the Idea is duplicated into the subjective Notion whose reality is the Notion itself, and into the objective Notion that is in the form of life. *Thinking*, *spirit*, *self-consciousness*, are determinations of the Idea where it has itself for object, and its determinate being, that is, the determinateness of its being, is its own difference from itself.

The *metaphysics of the spirit*, or, as it was more commonly expressed, of the *soul*, revolved round the determinations of substance, simplicity, immateriality—determinations in which the *general idea* of spirit taken from *empirical* consciousness, was laid down as subject, and it was then asked, What predicates agree with our observations? This kind of procedure could get no further than the procedure of physics, which reduces the world of phenomena to general laws and reflective determinations since it too was based on spirit merely in its *phenomenal* aspect; in fact this procedure was bound to fall short even of the scientific character of physics. Since spirit is not only infinitely richer than nature, but also, its essence is constituted by the absolute unity of opposites in the *Notion*, it exhibits in its phenomenal aspect and relation to externality contradiction in its extreme form. Consequently, it must be possible to adduce an experience in support of each of the opposed reflective determinations, or starting from experience it must be possible to arrive at opposite determinations by way of formal syllogistic reasoning. Since the predicates immediately yielded by spirit's phenomenal aspect in the first instance still belong to empirical psychology, there only remain, strictly speaking, for the metaphysical consideration, the wholly inadequate determinations of reflection. Kant, in his criticism of *rational psychology*, adheres to this metaphysics, insisting that, in so far as rational psychology purports to be a rational science, the smallest *addition* from observation to the *general idea* of self-consciousness would transform that science into an *empirical* one and mar its rational purity and its independence of all experience. Consequently, on this view, nothing is left but the simple representation, 'I', a representation devoid of any content of its own, of which we cannot even say that it is a *notion*, but a mere *consciousness* that *accompanies every notion*. Now according to the further Kantian conclusions, by this 'I', or if you like, *it* (the *thing*) that thinks, nothing further is represented than a transcendental subject of thoughts $= x$, which is cognized only through the thoughts which are its *predicates*, and of which, taken in its isolation, we can *never* have the *least conception*. In this context, the 'I' has the *inconvenience*, to use Kant's own expression, that *we must already make use of it* whenever we want to make any judgement about it; for it is not so much a *single representation* by which a particular object is distinguished, but rather a *form* of representation in general in so far as this is to be called cognition. Now the paralogism committed by rational psychology, says Kant, consists in this, that *modes* of self-consciousness in thinking are converted into *notions of the understanding* as applied to an *object*; that the '*I think*' is taken as a *thinking being*, a *thing-in-itself*; and that in this way, from the fact that I always occur in consciousness as a *subject*, and that too as a *singular* subject, *identical* in all the multiplicity of representation, and distinguishing myself from the latter as from something external to me, the unjustified inference is drawn that the 'I' is a *substance*, and further a qualitatively *simple* being, and a *one*, and something that has a *real existence independently* of the things of time and space.

I have drawn out this exposition in some detail, because it shows clearly the nature of the previous *metaphysics of the soul* and especially, too, the nature of the *criticism* by which it was made obsolete. The former aimed at determining the *abstract essence* of the soul; in doing so, it started originally from observation and converted the empirical universality of observation and the wholly *external* reflective determination attaching to the individuality of the actual, into the form of the above-mentioned *determinations of essence*. Kant in his criticism had generally in mind only the state of the metaphysics of his time, which in the main adhered to these abstract, one-sided determinations wholly devoid of dialectic; the genuinely *speculative* ideas of older philosophers on the notion of spirit he neither heeded nor examined. In his criticism then of those determinations, he followed quite simply Hume's style of scepticism; that is to say, he holds fast to the 'I' as it appears in self-consciousness, from which, however, since it is its essence—the *thing-in-itself*—that we are to cognize, everything empirical must be omitted; nothing then is left but this phenomenon of the '*I think*' that accompanies every representation—of which '*I think*' we have *not the slightest conception*. Certainly, it must be conceded that we have not the least conception of the 'I', or of anything whatever, not even of the Notion itself, so long as we do not really *think*, but stop short at the simple, fixed *general idea* [*Vorstellung*] and the *name*. It is an odd thought—if it can be called a thought at all—that I must already *make use* of the 'I' in order to judge of the 'I'; the 'I' that *makes use* of self-consciousness as a means in order to judge, this is indeed an *x* of which, as well as of the relationship of such 'making use', we cannot have the slightest conception. But surely it is ridiculous to call this nature of self-consciousness, namely, that the 'I' thinks itself, that the 'I' cannot be thought without its being the 'I' that thinks, an *inconvenience* and, as though there was a fallacy in it, a *circle*. It is this relationship through which, in immediate self-consciousness, the absolute, eternal nature of self-consciousness and the Notion itself manifests itself, and manifests itself for this reason, that self-consciousness is just the *existent* pure *Notion*, and therefore *empirically perceptible*, the absolute relation-to-self that, as a separating judgement, makes itself its own object and is solely this

BB*

process whereby it makes itself a circle. A stone does not have this *inconvenience*; when it is to be thought or judged. it does not stand in its own way. It is relieved from the burden of making use of *itself* for this task; it is something else outside it that must give itself this trouble.

These conceptions, which must be called barbarous, place the defect in the fact that in thinking of the 'I', the 'I' as *subject* cannot be omitted; but the same defect then also appears the other way round, namely in this way, that 'I' occurs *only* as *subject of self-consciousness*, or I can *use* myself only as *subject* of a judgement, and the *intuition* is lacking by which the 'I' might be *given* as an *object*; but the notion of a thing that can exist only as subject does not so far involve any objective reality at all. If external intuition, determined in space and time, is required for objectivity, and it is this that is missing here, then it is quite clear that by objectivity is meant merely sensuous reality; and to have risen above *that* is a condition of thinking and of truth. But of course, if 'I' is taken not in its Notion but as a mere, simple, general idea, in the way we pronounce 'I' in everyday consciousness, then it is the abstract determination and not the self-relation that has itself for object. In that case, it is only *one* of the extremes, a one-sided subject without its objectivity, or else it would be merely an object without subjectivity, were it not for the inconvenience alluded to, that the thinking subject cannot be eliminated from the 'I' as object. But in fact the same inconvenience occurs with the former determina-tion, with the 'I' as subject; the 'I' thinks *something*, itself or something else. This inseparability of the two forms in which it opposes itself to itself belongs to the innermost nature of its Notion and of the Notion itself; it is precisely what Kant wants to stave off in order to retain the mere *general idea*, which does not inwardly differentiate itself and therefore, of course, lacks the Notion. Now a Notionless conception of this kind may indeed oppose itself to the abstract reflective determinations or categories of the previous metaphysics: for in one-sidedness it stands on a level with them, though these are indeed on a higher level of thought; but on the other hand it appears all the more meagre and empty when com-pared with the profounder ideas of ancient philosophy on the con-ception of the soul or of thinking, as for example the genuinely speculative ideas of Aristotle. If the Kantian philosophy in-vestigated the reflective categories in question, it was even more bound to investigate the firmly held abstraction of the empty 'I', the presumed idea of the thing-in-itself, which, precisely on account of its abstraction, proves on the contrary to be something completely untrue. The experience of the inconvenience complained of is itself the empirical fact in which the untruth of that abstraction expresses itself.

Mendelssohn's proof of the persistence of the soul is the only one mentioned in the Kantian critique of rational psychology, and I cite here the Kantian refutation of it on account of the remarkable nature of the argument employed to disprove it. The proof in question is based on the *simplicity* of the soul, by virtue of which it is incapable of alteration, *of transition into an other*, in time. Qualitative simplicity is in general the form of *abstraction* considered above; as *qualitative* determinateness it was investigated in the sphere of being, and it was proved that the qualitative, as such abstractly self-related determinateness, is on the contrary for that very reason dialectical, and is merely transition into an other. But in treating of the Notion it was shown that when it is considered in relation to persistence, indestructibility, imperishableness, it is the absolutely true being and the eternal, just because it is not *abstract*, but *concrete* simplicity, is determined not as abstractly self-related, but as the unity *of itself and its other*; it cannot therefore pass into that other as though it altered itself in it for the very reason that the *other* to which it is determined is the Notion itself, so that in this transition it only comes to itself. Now the Kantian criticism opposes to the said *qualitative* determination of the unity of the Notion, the *quantitative*. Although the soul is not a manifold of juxtaposed parts and contains no *extensive* magnitude, yet we are told consciousness has *a degree*, and the soul like *every concrete existent* has an *intensive magnitude*; but this postulates the possibility of transition into nothing by a *gradual passing away*. Now what is this refutation but the application to spirit of a category *of being*, of *intensive magnitude*—a determination that has no truth in itself but on the contrary is sublated in the Notion?

Metaphysics—even the metaphysics that restricted itself to fixed concepts of the understanding and did not rise to speculative thinking, to the nature of the Notion and of the Idea—had for its aim *the cognition of truth*, and investigated its objects to ascertain whether they were *true* things or not, substances or phenomena.

The victory of the Kantian criticism over this metaphysics consists, on the contrary, in doing away with the investigation that
has *truth* for its aim, and this aim itself; it omits altogether to
raise the one question of interest, whether a particular subject,
here the *abstract 'I' of ordinary thinking* possesses truth in and for
itself. But to cling to phenomena and the mere conceptions given
in everyday consciousness is to renounce the Notion and philosophy. Anything rising above this is stigmatized in the Kantian
criticism as something high-flown to which reason is in no way
entitled. As a matter of fact, the Notion does reach beyond the
Notion-less, and the immediate justification for going beyond it is
first, the Notion itself, and secondly, from the negative side, the
untruth of phenomena and of ordinary thinking, as well as of
abstractions like things-in-themselves and the above 'I', that is
supposed not to be an object to itself.

In the content of this logical exposition it is from the *Idea of
life* that the Idea of spirit has issued, or what is the same thing,
that the Idea of spirit has proved itself to be the truth of the Idea
of life. As this result, the Idea possesses its truth in and for itself,
with which one may then also compare the empirical side or the
manifestation of spirit to see how far the latter accords with the
former. We have seen that *life* is the Idea, but at the same time it
has shown itself not to be as yet the true representation or mode
of the Idea's existence. For in life, the reality of the Idea exists as
individuality; universality or genus is the *inwardness*; the truth of
life as absolute negative unity is therefore to sublate the abstract,
or what is the same, the immediate, individuality, and as *identical*,
to be self-identical, as genus, to be self-similar. Now this Idea is
spirit. In this context we may once more remark that spirit is here
considered in the form that belongs to this Idea as logical. For it
has other shapes as well that may be mentioned here in passing;
in these it falls to be considered in the concrete sciences of spirit,
namely as *soul, consciousness and spirit as such*.

The name *soul* was formerly employed for the individual finite
spirit generally, and rational or empirical *psychology* was intended
to be synonymous with *doctrine of spirit*. The expression *soul*
evokes a mental picture of it as a *thing* like other things; one en-
quires as to its *seat*, the specific position in *space* from which its
forces operate; still more, as to how this thing can be *imperishable*,
how it can be subject to *temporal* conditions and yet be exempt

from alteration therein. The system of *monads* exalts matter to the psychical [*Seelenhaftigkeit*]; in this conception the soul is an atom like the atoms of matter in general; the atom that rises as steam from the coffee cup is capable in favourable circumstances of developing into a soul; it is only the *greater* obscurity of its ideation that distinguishes it from a thing of the kind that manifests as soul.

The Notion that is for itself is necessarily also in *immediate existence*; in this substantial identity with life, as submerged in its externality, it is the subject matter of *anthropology*. But even anthropology must regard as alien to it the metaphysics that makes this form of *immediacy* into a *psychical thing*, into an *atom*, like the atoms of matter. To anthropology must be left only that obscure region where spirit is subjected to what were once called *sidereal* and *terrestrial* influences, where it lives as a natural spirit in *sympathy* with Nature and becomes aware of Nature's changes in *dreams and presentiments*, and indwells the brain, the heart, the ganglia, the liver, and so forth. According to Plato, God, mindful that even the *irrational* part of the soul should partake of his bounty and share in higher things, gave to the liver the gift of prophecy above which self-conscious man is exalted. To this irrational side belong further the conditions of ordinary thinking and higher spiritual activity in so far as this activity is subjected in the individual subject to the play of a wholly contingent physical constitution, of external influences and particular circumstances.

This lowest of the concrete shapes in which spirit is sunk in the material, has its immediate superior in *consciousness*. In this form the free Notion, as *ego that is for itself*, is withdrawn from objectivity, but relates itself to it as *its other*, as an object confronting it. Here spirit is no longer present as soul; on the contrary, in the *certainty* of itself, the *immediacy* of *being* has the significance of *a negative* for it; consequently, its identity with itself in the objectivity is at the same time still only an *illusory show*, since the objectivity, too, still has the form of an *implicit* being. This stage is the subject matter of the *phenomenology of spirit*—a science which stands midway between the science of the natural spirit and spirit as such. The phenomenology of spirit considers spirit that is *for itself*, but at the same time in its *relation to its other*, an other which, as we have recalled, is determined by that relation as both *implicitly* an object and also as negated. Thus it considers spirit in its *manifestation*, as exhibiting itself in its counterpart.

But the higher truth of this form is *spirit that is for itself*; for spirit in this form, the object that for consciousness has an *implicit* being has the form of spirit's own determination, of *ordinary thinking* as such; this *spirit*, acting on the determinations as on its own, on feelings, representations, thoughts, is thus infinite within itself and in its form. The consideration of this stage belongs to the *doctrine of spirit* proper, which would embrace what is the subject matter of ordinary *empirical psychology*, but which, to be the science of spirit, must not go empirically to work, but be scientifically conceived. Spirit is at this stage *finite* spirit, in so far as the *content* of its determinateness is an immediate, given content; the science of finite spirit has to display the process in which it liberates itself from this its determinateness and goes on to grasp the truth of itself, which is infinite spirit.

On the other hand, the *Idea of spirit* as the subject matter of *logic* already stands within the pure science; it has not therefore to watch spirit progressing through its entanglement with nature, with immediate determinateness and material things, or with pictorial thinking; this is dealt with in the three sciences mentioned above. The Idea of spirit already has this progress behind it, or what is the same thing, still before it—the former when logic is taken as *the last* science, the latter when logic is taken as *the first* science, out of which the Idea first passes over into nature. In the logical Idea of spirit, therefore, the 'I' is immediately the free Notion, as it revealed itself to be in issuing from the Notion of nature as nature's truth, the free Notion that in its judgement is itself the object, *the Notion as its Idea*. But even in this shape the Idea is still not consummated.

While the Idea is indeed the free Notion that has itself for object, yet it is *immediate*, and just because it is immediate it is still the Idea in its *subjectivity*, and therefore in its finitude in general. It is the end that has to realize itself, or it is the *absolute Idea* itself still in its *manifested* aspect. What it *seeks* is the *true*, this identity of the Notion itself and reality, but as yet it is only seeking it; for it is here in its *first* stage still *subjective*. Consequently though the object that is for the Notion is here also a given object, it does not enter into the subject as an object operating on it, or as an object having a constitution of its own, or as a picture thought; on the contrary, the subject converts it into *a determination of the Notion*. It is the Notion that is active in the object, relates itself to itself therein, and by giving itself its reality in the object finds *truth*.

The Idea is therefore in the first instance one of the extremes of a syllogism, as the Notion that as end has initially its own self for subjective reality; the other extreme is the limitation of subjectivity, the objective world. The two extremes are identical in that they are the Idea; first their unity is that of the Notion, which in one is only *for itself*, in the other only *in itself*; secondly in one the reality is abstract, in the other it is present in its concrete actuality. This unity is now *posited* by cognition; and since this is the subjective Idea that, as end, proceeds from itself, the unity appears, at first, only as a *middle term*. The cognizing subject, through the determinateness of its Notion, namely abstract being-for-self, relates itself, it is true, to an outer world, but it does so in the absolute self-certainty of itself, in order to raise its own implicit reality, this formal truth, into real truth. It possesses in its Notion the *entire essentiality* of the objective world; its process consists in positing for itself the concrete content of that world as identical with the *Notion*, and conversely, in positing the latter as identical with objectivity.

Immediately, the Idea as manifested Idea is the *theoretical* Idea, *cognition* as such. For immediately the objective world has the form of *immediacy* or of *being* for the Notion that exists for itself; just as the latter, at first, is to itself only the abstract Notion of itself, confined within itself; it is therefore merely a *form*; its reality that it has within it is no more than its simple determinations of *universality* and *particularity*, while the individuality or *specific determinateness*, the content, is received by this form from outside.

A. THE IDEA OF THE TRUE

The subjective Idea is in the first instance an *urge*. For it is the contradiction of the Notion to have itself for *object* and to be its own reality, yet without the object being an other, that is, self-subsistent over against it, or without the difference of the Notion from itself possessing at the same time the essential determination of *diversity* and indifferent existence. The specific nature of this urge is therefore to sublate its own subjectivity, to make its first, abstract reality into a concrete one and to fill it with the *content* of the world presupposed by its subjectivity. From the other side, this urge is determined in the following manner: the Notion is, it is true, the absolute certainty of itself; but its *being-for-self* is confronted by its presupposition of a world having the form of *implicit* being, but a world whose indifferent *otherness* has for the self-certainty of the Notion the value merely of an *unessentiality*; it is thus the urge to sublate this otherness and to intuit in the object its identity with itself. This reflection-into-self is the sublated opposition, and the individuality which initially appears as the presupposed *implicit being* of a world is now *posited* as individuality and made actual for the subject; accordingly the reflection-into-self is the self-identity of the form restored out of the opposition—an identity that is therefore determined as indifferent to the form in its distinctiveness and is *content*.

This urge is therefore the urge to *truth* in so far as truth is in *cognition*, accordingly to *truth* in its proper sense as *theoretical* Idea. *Objective* truth is no doubt the Idea itself as the reality that corresponds to the Notion, and to this extent an object may or may not possess truth; but, on the other hand, the more precise meaning of truth is that it is truth *for* or *in* the subjective Notion, in *knowing*. It is the relation of the Notion judgement which showed itself to be the formal judgement of truth; in it, namely, the predicate is not merely the objectivity of the Notion, but the relating comparison of the Notion of the subject-matter with its actuality. This realization of the Notion is *theoretical* in so far as the Notion, as *form*, has still the determination of *subjectivity*, or has still the determination for the subject of being its own determination. Because cognition is the Idea as end, or as subjective, the negation of the world presupposed as an *implicit being* is the *first* negation; therefore also the conclusion in which the objective is posited in the subjective, has at first only this meaning, that the *implicit being* is only *posited* in the form of subjectivity, or in the Notion determination, and for this reason is not, in that form, in and for itself. Thus the conclusion only attains to a *neutral unity* or a *synthesis*, that is, to a unity of things that are originally separate and only are externally so conjoined. Since therefore in this cognition the Notion posits the object as *its own*, the Idea in the first instance only gives itself a content whose basis is *given*, and in which only the form of externality has been sublated. Accordingly, this cognition still retains its *finitude* in its realized end; in its realized end it has at the same time *not* attained its end, and *in its truth* has *not* yet arrived at *truth*. For in so far as in the result the content still has the character of a *datum*, the presupposed *implicit being* confronting the Notion is not sublated; equally therefore the unity of Notion and reality, truth, is also not contained in it. Oddly enough, it is this side of *finitude* that latterly has been clung to, and accepted as the *absolute* relation of cognition—as though the finite as such was supposed to be the absolute! At this standpoint, the object is credited with being an unknown *thing-in-itself behind* cognition, and this character of the object, and with it truth too is regarded as an absolute *beyond* for cognition. In this view of cognition, thought determinations in general, the categories, reflective determinations, as well as the formal Notion and its moments, are assigned the position of being finite determinations not in and for themselves, but finite in the sense that they are subjective in relation to this empty *thing-in-itself*; the fallacy of taking this untrue relation of cognition as the true relation has become the universal opinion of modern times.

From this determination of finite cognition it is immediately evident that it is a contradiction that sublates itself—the contradiction of a truth that at the same time is supposed not to be truth—of a cognition of what *is*, which at the same time does not cognize the thing-in-itself. In the collapse of this contradiction, its content, subjective cognition and the thing-in-itself, collapses, that is, proves itself an untruth. But cognition must, in the course of its own movement, resolve its finitude and with it its contradiction; this examination of it made by us is an external reflection; but cognition is itself the Notion, the Notion that is its own end and therefore through its realization fulfils itself, and in this very fulfilment sublates its subjectivity and the presupposed implicit being. We have therefore to consider cognition in its own self in its positive activity. Since this Idea is, as we have seen, the urge of the Notion to realize itself *for itself*, its activity consists in determining the object, and by this determining to relate itself in the object identically to itself. The object is in general something simply determinable, and in the Idea it has this essential side of not being in and for itself opposed to the Notion. Because cognition is still finite, not speculative, cognition, the presupposed objectivity has not as yet for it the shape of something that is in its own self simply and solely the Notion and that contains nothing with a particularity of its own as against the latter. But the fact that it counts as an implicit beyond, necessarily implies that its *determinability by the Notion* is a determination it possesses essentially; for *the Idea* is the Notion that exists for itself, is that which is absolutely infinite within itself, in which the object is *implicitly* sublated and the end is now solely to sublate it *explicitly*. Hence, though the object is presupposed by the Idea of cognition as possessing an *implicit being*, yet it is essentially in a relationship where the Idea, certain of itself and of the nullity of this opposition, comes to the realization of its Notion in the object.

In the syllogism whereby the subjective Idea now unites itself with objectivity, the *first premiss* is the same form of immediate seizure and relation of the Notion to the object that we saw in the relation of end. The determining activity of the Notion upon the object is an immediate *communication* of itself to the object and unresisted *pervasion* of the latter by the Notion. In this process the Notion remains in pure identity with itself; but this its immediate reflection-into-self has equally the determination of objective immediacy; that which *for the Notion* is its own determination, is equally a *being*, for it is the *first* negation of the presupposition. Therefore the posited determination ranks just as much as a presupposition that has been merely *found*, as an *apprehension* of a *datum*; in fact the activity of the Notion here consists merely in being negative towards itself, restraining itself and making itself passive towards what confronts it, in order that the latter may be able to *show* itself, not as determined by the subject, but as it is in its own self.

Accordingly in this premiss this cognition does not appear even as an *application* of logical determinations, but as an acceptance and apprehension of them just as given, and its activity appears to be restricted merely to the removal of a subjective obstacle, an external husk, from the subject-matter. This cognition is *analytic* cognition.

(a) Analytic Cognition

We sometimes find the difference between analytic and synthetic cognition stated in the form that one proceeds from the known to the unknown, the other from the unknown to the known. But if this distinction is closely examined, it will be difficult to discover in it a definite thought, much less a Notion. It may be said that cognition begins in general with ignorance, for one does not learn to know something with which one is already acquainted. Conversely, it also begins with the known; this is a tautological proposition; that with which it begins, which therefore it actually cognizes, is *ipso facto* something known; what is not as yet known and is to be known only later is still an unknown. So far, then, it must be said that cognition, once it has begun, always proceeds from the known to the unknown.

The distinguishing feature of analytic cognition is already defined in the fact that as the first premiss of the whole syllogism, analytic cognition does not as yet contain mediation; it is the immediate communication of the Notion and does not as yet contain otherness, and in it the activity empties itself of its negativity. However, this immediacy of the relation is for that reason itself a mediation, for it is the negative relation of the Notion to the object, but a relation that annuls itself, thereby making itself simple and identical. This reflection-into-self is only subjective, because in its mediation the difference is present still only in the form of the presupposed *implicit* difference, as difference *of the object* within itself. The determination, therefore, brought about by this relation, is the form of simple *identity*, of *abstract universality*. Accordingly, analytic cognition has in general this identity for its principle; and transition into an other, the connexion of different terms, is excluded from itself and from its activity.

If we look now more closely at analytic cognition, we see that it starts from a *presupposed*, and therefore individual, *concrete* subject matter; this may be an object already *complete in itself* for ordinary thought, or it may be a *problem*, that is to say, given only in its circumstances and conditions, but not yet disengaged from them and presented on its own account in simple self-subsistence. Now the analysis of this subject matter cannot consist in its being merely *resolved* into the particular *picture thoughts* which it may contain; such a resolution and the apprehension of such picture thoughts is a business that would not belong to cognition, but would merely be a matter of a closer *acquaintance*, a determination within the sphere of *picture-thinking*. Since analysis is based on the Notion, its products are essentially Notion-determinations, and that too as determinations *immediately contained* in the subject matter. We have seen from the nature of the Idea of cognition, that the activity of the subjective Notion must be regarded from one side merely as the *explication* of *what is already in the object*, because the object itself is nothing but the totality of the Notion. It is just as one-sided to represent analysis as though there were nothing in the subject matter that was not *imported* into it, as it is one-sided to suppose that the resulting determinations are merely *extracted* from it. The former view, as everyone knows, is enunciated by subjective idealism, which takes the activity of cognition in analysis to be merely a one-sided *positing*, beyond which the *thing-in-itself* remains concealed; the other view belongs to so-called realism which apprehends the subjective Notion as an empty identity that *receives* the thought determinations into itself *from outside*. Analytic cognition, the transformation of the given material into logical determinations, has shown itself to be two things in one: a *positing* that no less immediately determines itself as a *presupposing*. Consequently, by virtue of the latter, the logical element may appear as something *already complete* in the object, just as by virtue of the former it may appear as the *product* of a merely subjective activity. But the two moments are not to be separated; the logical element in its abstract form into which analysis raises it, is of course only to be found in cognition, while conversely it is something not merely *posited*, but possessing *being in itself*.

Now since analytic cognition is the transformation indicated above, it does not pass through any further *middle term*; the determination is in so far *immediate* and has just this meaning, to be peculiar to the object and in itself to belong to it, and therefore to be apprehended from it without any subjective mediation. But further, cognition is supposed also to be a *progress*, an *explication of differences*. But because, in accordance with the determination it has here, it is Notion-less and undialectical, it possesses only a *given difference*, and its progress takes place solely in the determinations of the *material*. It seems to have an *immanent* progress only in so far as the derived thought determinations can be analysed afresh, in so far as they are a concrete; the highest and ultimate point of this process of analysis is the abstract highest essence, or abstract subjective identity—and over against it, diversity. This progress is, however, nothing but the mere repetition of the one original act of analysis, namely, the fresh determination as a *concrete*, of what has already been taken up into the abstract form of the Notion; this is followed by the analysis of it, then by the determination afresh as a concrete of the abstract that emerges from it, and so forth. But the thought-determinations seem also to contain a transition within themselves. If the object is determined as a whole, then of course one advances from this to the *other* determination of *part*, from *cause* to the other determination of *effect*, and so on. But here this is no advance, since whole and part, cause and effect, are *relationships* and moreover, for this formal cognition, relationships *complete in themselves* such that in them one determination is *already found* essentially linked to the other. The subject matter that has been determined as *cause* or as *part* is *ipso facto* determined by the *whole* relationship, that is, determined already by both sides of it. Although the relationship is *in itself* something synthetic, yet for analytic cognition this connexion is as much a mere *datum* as any other connexion of its material and therefore is not relevant to its own peculiar business. Whether a connexion of this kind be otherwise determined as *a priori* or *a posteriori* is here a matter of indifference, for it is apprehended as something *found already there*, or, as it has also been described, as a *fact* of consciousness that with the determination *whole* is linked the determination *part*, and so forth. While Kant has made the profound observation that there are synthetic *a priori* principles and has recognized their root in the unity of self-consciousness and therefore in the identity of the Notion with itself, yet he adopts the *specific* connexion, the concepts of relation and the synthetic principles themselves *from formal logic* as *given*; their justification [*Deduktion*] should have been the exposition of the transition of that simple unity of self-consciousness into these its determinations and distinctions; but Kant spared himself the trouble of demonstrating this genuinely synthetic progress—the self-producing Notion.

It is a familiar fact that *arithmetic* and the more general *sciences of discrete magnitude* especially, are called *analytical science* and *analysis*. As a matter of fact, their method of cognition is immanently analytical in the highest degree and we shall briefly consider the basis of this fact. All other analytic cognition starts from a concrete material that in itself possesses a contingent manifoldness; on this material depends all distinction of content and progress to a further content. The material of arithmetic and algebra, on the other hand, is something that has already been made wholly abstract and indeterminate and purged of all peculiarity of relationship, and to which, therefore, every determination and connexion is something external. Such a material is the principle of discrete magnitude, the *one*. This relationless atom can be increased to a *plurality*, and externally determined and unified into a sum; this process of increasing and delimiting is an empty progression and determining that never gets beyond the same principle of the abstract one. How *numbers* are further combined and separated depends solely on the positing activity of the cognizing subject. *Magnitude* is in general the category within which these determinations are made; it is the determinateness that has become an *indifferent* determinateness, so that the subject matter has no determinateness that might be immanent in it and therefore a *datum* for cognition. Cognition having first provided itself with a contingent variety of numbers, these now constitute the material for further elaboration and manifold relationships. Such relationships, their discovery and elaboration, do not seem, it is true, to be anything immanent in analytic cognition, but something contingent and given; and these relationships and the operations connected with them, too, are usually presented *successively* as *different* without any observation of an inner connexion. Yet it is easy to discover a guiding principle, and that is the immanent principle of analytic identity, which appears in the diverse as *equality*; progress consists in the reduction of the unequal to an ever greater equality. To give an example in the first elements, addition is the combining of quite contingently *unequal* numbers, multiplication, on the contrary, the combination of *equal* numbers; these again are followed by the relationship of the *equality* of *amount* and *unity*, and the relationship of powers makes its appearance.

Now because the determinateness of the subject matter and of the relationships is a *posited* one, the further operation with them is also wholly analytic, and the science of analysis possesses not so much *theorems* as *problems*. The analytical theorem contains the problem as already solved for it, and the altogether external difference attaching to the two sides equated by the theorem is so unessential that a theorem of this kind would appear as a trivial identity. Kant, it is true, has declared the proposition $5 + 7 = 12$, to be a *synthetic* proposition, because the same thing is presented on one side in the form of a plurality, 5 and 7, and on the other side in the form of a unity, 12. But if the analytic proposition is not to mean the completely abstract identity and tautology $12 = 12$ and is to contain any advance at all, it must present a difference of some kind, though a difference not based on any quality, on any determinateness of reflection, and still less of the Notion. $5 + 7$ and 12 are out and out the same content; the first side also expresses the *demand* that 5 and 7 shall be combined in *one* expression; that is to say, that just as 5 is the result of a counting up in which the counting was quite arbitrarily broken off and could just as well have been continued, so now, in the same way, the counting is to be continued with the condition that the ones to be added shall be seven. The 12 is therefore a result of 5 and 7 and of an operation which is already posited and in its nature is an act completely external and devoid of any thought, so that it can be performed even by a machine. Here there is not the slightest trace of a transition to an *other*; it is a mere continuation, that is, *repetition*, of the same operation that produced 5 and 7.

The *proof* of a theorem of this kind—and it would require a proof if it were a synthetic proposition—would consist merely in the operation of counting on from 5 for a further 7 ones and in discerning the agreement of the result of this counting with what is otherwise called 12, and which again is nothing else but just that process of counting up to a defined limit. Instead, therefore, of the form of theorem, the form of *problem* is directly chosen, the *demand* for the operation, that is to say, the expression of only *one* side of the equation that would constitute the theorem and whose other side is now to be found. The problem contains the content and states the specific operation that is to be undertaken with it. The operation is not restricted by any unyielding material endowed with specific relationships, but is an external subjective act, whose determinations are accepted with indifference by the material in which they are posited. The entire difference between the conditions laid down in the problem and the result in the *solution*, is merely that the specific mode of union or separation indicated in the former is *actual* in the latter.

It is, therefore, an utterly superfluous bit of scaffolding to apply to these cases the form of geometrical method, which is relevant to synthetic propositions and to add to the *solution* of the problem a *proof* as well. The proof can express nothing but the tautology that the solution is correct because the operation set in the problem has been performed. If the problem is to add several numbers, then the solution is to add them; the proof shows that the solution is correct because the problem was to add, and addition has been carried out. If the problem contains more complex expressions and operations, say for instance, to multiply decimal numbers, and the solution indicates merely the mechanical procedure, a proof does indeed become necessary; but this proof can be nothing else but the analysis of those expressions and of the operation from which the solution proceeds of itself. By this separation of the *solution* as a mechanical procedure, and of the *proof* as a reference back to the nature of the subject matter to be treated, we lose what is precisely the advantage of the analytical problem, namely that the *construction* can be immediately deduced from the problem and can therefore be exhibited as *intelligible* in and for itself; put the other way, the construction is expressly given a defect peculiar to the synthetic method. In the higher analysis, where with the relationship of powers, we are dealing especially with relationships of discrete magnitude that are qualitative and dependent on *Notion* determinatenesses, the problems and theorems do of course contain synthetic expressions; there *other* expressions and relationships must be taken as intermediate terms besides those *immediately specified* by the problem or theorem. And, we may add, even these auxiliary terms must be of a kind to be grounded in the consideration and development of some side of the problem or theorem; the synthetic appearance comes solely from the fact that the problem or theorem does not itself already name this side. The problem, for example, of finding the sum of the powers of the roots of an equation is solved by the examination and subsequent connexion of the functions which the coefficients of the equation are of the roots. The determination employed in the solution, namely, the functions of the coefficients and their connexion, is not already expressed in the problem—for the rest, the development itself is wholly analytical. The same is true of the solution of the equation $x^{m-1} = 0$ with the help of the sine, and also of the immanent algebraic solution, discovered, as is well known, by Gauss, which takes into consideration the *residuum* of $x^{m-1} - 1$ divided by m, and the so-called primitive roots—one of the most important extensions of analysis in modern times. These solutions are synthetic because the terms employed to help, the sine or the consideration of the residua, are not terms of the problem itself.

The nature of the analysis that considers the so-called infinitesimal differences of variable magnitudes, the analysis of the differential and integral calculus, has been treated in greater detail in the *first part* of this *logic*. It was there shown that there is here an underlying qualitative determination of magnitude which can be grasped only by means of the Notion. The transition to it from magnitude as such is no longer analytic; and therefore mathematics to this day has never succeeded in justifying by its own means, that is, mathematically, the operations that rest on that transition, because the transition is not of a mathematical nature. Leibniz, who is given the credit of having reduced calculation with infinitesimal differences to a *calculus*, has, as was mentioned in the same place, made the transition in the most inadequate manner possible, a manner that is as completely unphilosophical [*begrifflos*] as it is unmathematical; but once the transition is presupposed— and in the present state of the science it is no more than a presupposition—the further course is certainly only a series of ordinary operations.

It has been remarked that analysis becomes synthetic when it comes to deal with *determinations* that are no longer *posited* by the problems themselves. But the general transition from analytic to synthetic cognition lies in the necessary transition from the form of immediacy to mediation, from abstract identity to difference. Analytic cognition in its activity does not in general go beyond determinations that are self-related; but by virtue of their *determinateness* they are also essentially of such a nature that they *relate themselves to an other*. It has been already remarked that even when analytic cognition goes on to deal with relationships that are not an externally given material but thought determinations, it still remains analytic, since for it even these relationships are *given* ones. But because abstract identity, which alone analytic cognition knows as its own, is essentially the *identity of distinct terms*, identity in this form too must belong to cognition and become for the subjective Notion also the *connexion* that is posited by it and identical with it.

(b) Synthetic Cognition

Analytic cognition is the first premiss of the whole syllogism—the *immediate* relation of the Notion to the object; *identity*, therefore, is the determination which it recognizes as its own, and analytic cognition is merely the *apprehension* of what *is*. Synthetic cognition aims at the *comprehension* of what *is*, that is, at grasping the multiplicity of determinations in their unity. It is therefore the second premiss of the syllogism in which the *diverse* as such is related. Hence its aim is in general *necessity*. The different terms which are connected, are on the one hand connected in a *relation*; in this relation they are related and at the same time mutually indifferent and self-subsistent; but on the other hand, they are linked together in the *Notion* which is their simple yet determinate unity. Now synthetic cognition passes over, in the first instance, from *abstract identity* to *relation*, or from *being* to *reflection*, and so far it is not the absolute reflection of the Notion that the Notion cognizes in its subject matter. The reality it gives itself is the next stage, namely, the stated identity of the different terms as such, an identity therefore that is at the same time still *inner* and only necessity, not the subjective identity that is *for itself*; hence not yet the Notion as such. Synthetic cognition, therefore, has indeed the Notion determinations for its content, and the object is posited in them; but they only stand in *relation* to one another, or are in *immediate* unity, and just for that reason, not in the unity by which the Notion exists as subject.

This constitutes the finitude of this cognition; because this real side of the Idea in it still possesses identity as an *inner* identity, its determinations are to themselves still *external*; because the identity is not in the form of subjectivity, the Notion's own pervasion of the object still lacks *individuality*; what corresponds to the Notion in the object is indeed no longer the abstract but the *determinate* form and therefore the *particularity* of the Notion, but the *individual* element in the object is still *a given* content. Consequently, although this cognition transforms the objective world into Notions, it gives it Notion-determinations only in respect of form, and must *find* the object in respect of its *individuality*, its specific determinateness; such cognition is not yet self-determining. Similarly, it *finds* propositions and laws, and proves their *necessity*, but not as a necessity of the subject matter in and for itself, that is, not from the Notion, but as a necessity of the cognition that works on given determinations, on the differences of the phenomenal aspect of the subject matter, and cognizes *for itself* the proposition as a unity and relationship, or cognizes the ground of phenomena from the *phenomena* themselves.

We have now to consider the detailed moments of synthetic cognition.

1. *Definition*

First, the still *given* objectivity is transformed into the simple and first form, hence into the form of the *Notion*. Accordingly the moments of this apprehension are none other than the moments of the Notion, *universality, particularity* and *individuality*. The *individual* is the object itself as an *immediate representation*, that which is to be defined. The universality of the object of definition we have found in the determination of the objective judgement or judgement of necessity to be the *genus*, and indeed the *proximate* genus; that is to say, the universal with this determinateness that is at the same time a principle for the differentiation of the particular. This difference the object possesses in the *specific difference*, which makes it the determinate species it is and is the basis of its disjunction from the remaining species.

Definition, in thus reducing the subject matter to its *Notion*, strips it of its externalities which are requisite for its concrete existence; it abstracts from what accrues to the Notion in its realization, whereby it emerges first into Idea, and secondly into external existence. *Description* is for *representation*, and takes in this further content that belongs to reality. But definition reduces this wealth of the manifold determinations of intuited existence to the simplest moments; the form of these simple elements, and how they are determined relatively to one another, is contained in the Notion. The subject matter is thus, as we have stated, grasped as a universal that is at the same time essentially determinate. The subject matter itself is the third factor, the individual, in which the genus and the particularization are posited in one; it is an *immediate* that is posited *outside* the Notion, since the latter is not yet self-determining.

In the said moments, which are the form-difference of definition, the Notion finds itself and has in them the reality correspondent to it. But the reflection of the Notion-moments into themselves, which is individuality, is not yet contained in this reality, and therefore the object, in so far as it is in cognition, is not yet determined as subjective. Whereas, cognition on the contrary is subjective and has an external starting point, or it is subjective by reason of its external starting point in the individual. The content of the Notion is therefore a *datum* and contingent. Consequently, the concrete Notion itself is contingent in a twofold aspect: first it is contingent in respect of its content as such; secondly it is contingent which determinations of the content from among the manifold qualities that the object possesses in external existence are *to* be selected for the Notion and are to constitute its moments.

The latter point requires closer consideration. For since individuality, which is determined in and for itself, lies outside the Notion-determination peculiar to synthetic cognition there is no principle available for determining which sides of the subject matter are to be regarded as belonging to its Notion-determination and which merely to the external reality. This constitutes a difficulty in the case of definitions, a difficulty that for synthetic cognition cannot be overcome. Yet here a distinction must be made. In the first place, the definition of products of self-conscious purposiveness is easily discovered; for the end that they are to serve is a determination created out of the subjective resolve and constituting the essential particularization, the form of the concrete existent thing, which is here the sole concern. Apart from this, the nature of its material and its other external properties, in so far as they correspond to the end, are contained in its determination; the rest are unessential for it.

Secondly, geometrical objects are abstract determinations of space; the underlying abstraction, so-called absolute space, has lost all further concrete determinations and now too possesses only such shapes and configurations as are posited in it. These objects therefore *are* only what they are *meant* to be; their Notion determination in general, and more precisely the specific difference, possesses in them its simple unhindered reality. To this extent, they resemble the products of external purposiveness, and they also agree with the subject matter of arithmetic in which likewise the underlying determination is only that which has been posited in it. True, space has still further determinations: its *three-dimensionality*, its continuity and divisibility, which are not first posited in it by external determination. But these belong to the accepted material and are immediate presuppositions; it is only the combination and entanglement of the former subjective determinations with this peculiar nature of the domain into which they have been imported that produces synthetic relationships and laws. In the case of numerical determinations, since they are based on the simple principle of the One, their combination and any further determination is simply and solely a positedness; on the other hand, determinations in space, which is explicitly a continuous *mutual externality*, run a further course of their own and possess a reality distinct from their Notion; but this no longer belongs to the immediate definition.

But, thirdly, in the case of definitions of *concrete* objects of Nature as well as of spirit, the position is quite different. In general such objects are, for representation, *things of many properties*. Here, what we have to do in the first instance is to apprehend what is their proximate genus, and then, what is their specific difference. We have therefore to determine which of the many properties belong to the object as genus, and which as species, and further which among these properties is the essential one; this last point involves the necessity of ascertaining their interrelationship, whether one is already posited with the other. But for this purpose there is so far no other criterion to hand than *existence* itself. The essentiality of the property for the purpose of the definition, in which it is to be posited as a simple, undeveloped determinateness, is its universality. But in existence universality is merely empirical. It may be universality in time—whether the property in question is lasting, while the others show themselves transitory in the subsistence of the whole; or it may be a universality resulting from comparison with other concrete wholes and in that case it goes no further than community. Now if comparison indicates as the common basis the total *habitus* as empirically presented, reflection has to bring this together into a simple thought determination and to grasp the simple character of such a totality. But the only possible attestation that a thought determination, or a single one of the immediate properties, constitutes the simple and specific essence of the object, is the *derivation* of such a determination from the concrete properties of the subject matter. But this would demand an analysis tranforming the immediate properties into thoughts and reducing what is concrete to something simple. Such an analysis, however, would be higher than the one already considered; for it could not be abstractive, but would have to preserve in the universal what is specific in the concrete, unify it and show it to be dependent on the simple thought determination.

The relations of the manifold determinations of immediate existence to the simple Notion would however be theorems requiring proof. But definition is the first, still undeveloped Notion; therefore, when it has to apprehend the simple determinateness of the subject matter, which apprehension has to be something immediate, it can only employ for the purpose one of its *immediate* so-called properties—a determination of sensuous existence or representation. The isolation, then, of this property by abstraction, constitutes simplicity, and for universality and essentiality the Notion has to fall back onto empirical universality, the persistence in altered circumstances, and the reflection that seeks the Notion-determination in external existence and in picture thinking, that is, seeks it where it is not to be found. Definition, therefore, automatically renounces the Notion-determinations proper, which would be essentially principles of the subject matter, and contents itself with *marks*, that is, determinations in which *essentiality* for the object itself is a matter of indifference, and which are intended merely to be *distinguishing* marks for an external reflection. A single, *external* determinateness of this kind is too inadequate to the concrete totality and to the nature of its Notion, to justify its selection for its own sake, nor could it be taken for the true expression and determination of a concrete whole. According to Blumenbach's[1] observation, for example, the lobe of the ear is absent in all other animals, and therefore in the usual phraseology of common and distinguishing marks it could quite properly be used as the distinctive characteristic in the definition of physical man. But how inadequate such a completely external determination at once appears when compared with the conception of the total *habitus* of physical man, and with the demand that the Notion determination shall be something essential! It is quite contingent whether the marks adopted in the definition are pure makeshifts like this, or on the other hand approximate more to the nature of a principle. It is also to be observed that, on account of their externality, they have not been the starting point in the cognition of the Notion of the object; on the contrary, an obscure feeling, an indefinite but deeper sense, an inkling of what is essential, has preceded the discovery of the genera in nature and in spirit, and only afterwards has a specific externality

---

[1] Blumenbach, Johann Friedrich, 1752–1840, Professor at Jena; a pioneer in comparative anatomy and physiology.

been sought to satisfy the understanding. In existence the Notion has entered into externality and is accordingly explicated into its differences and cannot be attached simply to a single one of such properties. The properties, as the externality of the thing, are external to themselves; that is why, as we pointed out in the sphere of Appearance when dealing with the thing of many properties, properties essentially become even self-subsistent matters; spirit, regarded from the same standpoint of Appearance, becomes an aggregate of a number of self-subsistent forces. Through this standpoint, the single property or force, even where it is posited as indifferent to the others, ceases to be a characterizing principle, with the result that the determinateness, as determinateness of the Notion, vanishes altogether.

Into concrete things, along with the diversity of the properties among themselves, there enters also the difference between the *Notion* and its *actualization*. The Notion in nature and in spirit has an external presentation in which its determinateness shows itself as dependence on the external, as transitoriness and inadequacy. Therefore, although any actual thing no doubt shows in itself what it *ought* to be, yet in accordance with the negative judgement of the Notion it may equally show that its actuality only imperfectly corresponds to this Notion, that it is *bad*. Now the definition is supposed to indicate the determinateness of the Notion in an immediate property; yet there is no property against which an instance cannot be brought in which the total habitus, though it enables one to discern the concrete thing to be defined, yet the property taken as its characteristic shows itself immature or stunted. In a bad plant, a poor specimen of an animal, a contemptible human being, a bad state, aspects of its concrete existence are defective or entirely obliterated that otherwise might have been adopted for the definition as the distinguishing mark and essential determinateness in the existence of such a concrete. But for all that, a bad plant or a bad animal, etc., still remains a plant or an animal. If, therefore, bad specimens too are to be covered by the definition, then all the properties that we wanted to regard as essential elude us through instances of malformations in which those properties are lacking. Thus for example the essentiality of the brain for physical man is contradicted by the instance of acephalous individuals, the essentiality of the protection of life and property for the state, by the instance of despotic states and tyrannous governments. If the Notion is asserted against such an instance and the instance, being measured by the Notion, is declared to be a bad specimen, then the Notion is no longer attested by phenomena. But the self-subsistence of the Notion is contrary to the meaning of definition; for definition is supposed to be the *immediate* Notion, and therefore can only draw on the immediacy of existence for its determinations for objects, and can justify itself only in what it finds already to hand. Whether its content is *in and for itself* truth or a contingency, this lies outside its sphere; but formal truth, the agreement between the Notion subjectively posited in the definition and an actual object outside it, cannot be established because the individual object may also be a bad specimen.

The content of definition is in general taken from immediate existence, and being an immediate content has no justification; the question of its necessity is precluded by its origin; in enunciating the Notion as a mere immediate, the definition refrains from comprehending the Notion itself. Hence it represents nothing but the form determination of the Notion in a given content, without the reflection of the Notion into itself, that is, *without the Notion's being-for-self*.

But immediacy in general proceeds only from mediation, and must therefore pass over into mediation. Or, in other words, the determinateness of the content contained in the definition, because it is determinateness, is not merely an immediate, but is mediated by its opposite; consequently definition can apprehend its subject matter only through the opposite determination and must therefore pass over into *division*.

2. Division

The universal must *particularize* itself; so far, the necessity for division lies in the universal. But since definition itself already begins with the particular, its necessity for passing over into division lies in the particular, that by itself points to another particular. Conversely, it is precisely in the act of holding fast to the determinateness in the need to distinguish it from its other, that the particular separates itself off from the universal; consequently the universal is *presupposed* for division. The procedure is, therefore, that the individual content of cognition ascends through particularity to the extreme of universality; but now the latter must be regarded as the objective basis, and with this as the starting point, division presents itself as disjunction of the universal as the *prius*.

This has introduced a transition which, since it takes place from the universal to the particular, is determined by the form of the Notion. Definition by itself is something individual; a plurality of definitions goes with the plurality of objects. The progress, proper to the Notion, from universal to particular, is the basis and the possibility of a *synthetic science*, of a *system* and of *systematic cognition*.

The first requisite for this is, as we have shown, that the beginning be made with the subject matter in the form of a *universal*. In the sphere of actuality, whether of nature or spirit, it is the concrete individuality that is given to subjective, natural cognition as the *prius*; but in cognition that is a *comprehension*, at least to the extent that it has the form of the Notion for basis, the *prius* must be on the contrary something *simple*, something *abstracted* from the concrete, because in this form alone has the subject-matter the form of the self-related universal or of an immediate based on the Notion.

It might perhaps be objected to this procedure in the scientific sphere that, because intuition is easier than cognition, the object of intuition, that is, concrete actuality, should be made the beginning of science, and that this procedure is more *natural* than that which begins from the subject matter in its abstraction and from that proceeds in the opposite direction to its particularization and concrete individualization. But the fact that the aim is *to cognize*, implies that the question of a comparison with *intuition* is already settled and done with; there can only be a question of what is to be the first and what is to be the nature of the sequel *within the process of cognition*; it is no longer a *natural* method, but a method appropriate to *cognition* that is demanded. If it is merely a question of *easiness*, then it is self-evident besides, that it is easier for cognition to grasp the abstract simple thought determination than the concrete subject matter, which is a manifold connexion of such thought determinations and their relationships; and it is in this manner that we have now to apprehend the concrete, and not as it is in intuition. The *universal* is in and for itself the first moment of the Notion because it is the *simple* moment, and the particular is only subsequent to it because it is the mediated moment; and

CC

conversely the *simple* is the more universal, and the concrete, as in itself differentiated and so mediated, is that which already presupposes the transition from a first. This remark applies not only to the order of procedure in the specific forms of definitions, divisions, and propositions, but also to the order of cognition as a whole and simply with respect to the difference of abstract and concrete in general. Hence in learning to read, for example, the rational way is not to begin with the reading of whole words or even syllables, but with the *elements* of the words and syllables, and the signs of *abstract* sounds: in written characters, the analysis of the concrete word into its abstract sounds and their signs is already accomplished; for this very reason, the process of learning to read is a primary occupation with abstract objects. In *geometry*, a beginning has to be made not with a concrete spatial figure but with the point and line, and then plane figures, and among the latter not with polygons, but with the triangle, and among curves, with the circle. In *physics* the individual natural properties or matters have to be freed from their manifold complications in which they are found in concrete actuality, and presented with their simple necessary conditions; they too, like spatial figures, are objects of intuition; but first the way for their intuition must be prepared so that they appear and are maintained free from all modifications by circumstances extraneous to their own specific character. Magnetism, electricity, the various gases, and so forth, are objects the specific character of which is ascertained by cognition only by apprehending them in isolation from the concrete conditions in which they appear in the actual world. Experiment, it is true, presents them to intuition in a concrete case; but for one thing experiment must, in order to be scientific, take only the conditions necessary for the purpose; and for another, it must multiply itself in order to show that the inseparable concretion of these conditions is unessential, and this it does by exhibiting the things in another concrete shape and again in another, so that for cognition nothing remains but their abstract form. To mention one more example, it might seem natural and intelligent to consider *colour* first, in the concrete manifestation of the animal's subjective sense, next, as a spectral phenomenon suspended outside the subject, and finally as fixed in objects in the actual external world. But for cognition, the universal and therefore truly primary form is the middle one of the above-named, in which colour hovers between subjectivity and objectivity as the familiar spectrum, completely unentangled as yet with subjective and objective circumstances. The latter above all merely disturb the pure consideration of the nature of this subject matter because they behave as active causes and therefore make it uncertain whether the specific alterations, transitions, and relationships of colour are founded in its own specific nature, or are rather to be attributed to the pathological specific constitution of those circumstances, to the healthy and the morbid particular affections and effects of the organs of the subject, or to the chemical, vegetable, and animal forces of the objects. Numerous other examples might be adduced from the cognition of organic nature and of the world of spirit; everywhere the abstract must constitute the starting point and the element in which and from which spread the particularities and rich formations of the concrete.

Now although the difference of the particular from the universal makes its appearance, strictly speaking, with division or the particular this universal is itself already determinate and consequently only a member of a division. Hence there is for it a higher universal, and for this again a higher, and so on, in the first instance, to infinity. For the cognition here considered there is no immanent limit, since it starts from the *given*, and the form of abstract universality is characteristic of its *prius*. Therefore any subject matter whatever that seems to possess an elementary universality is made the subject matter of a specific science, and is an absolute beginning to the extent that *ordinary thought* is *presupposed* to be acquainted with it and it is taken on its own account as requiring no derivation. Definition takes it as immediate.

The next step forward from this starting point is *division*. For this progress, only an immanent principle would be required, that is, a beginning from the universal and the Notion; but the cognition here considered lacks such a principle, for it only pursues the form determination of the Notion without its reflection-into-self, and therefore takes the determinateness of the content from what is given. For the particular that makes its appearance in division, there is no ground of its own available, either in regard to what is to constitute the basis of the division, or in regard to the specific relationship that the members of the disjunction are to have to one another. Consequently in this respect the business of cognition can only consist, partly, in setting in order the particular elements discovered in the empirical material, and partly, in finding the universal determinations of that particularity by comparison. These determinations are then accepted as grounds of division, and there may be a multiplicity of such grounds, as also a similar multiplicity of divisions based on them. The relationship between the members, the species, of a division, has only this general determination, that they are determined relatively to one another *in accordance with the assumed ground of division*; if their difference rested on a different consideration, they would not be co-ordinated on the same level with one another.

Because a principle of self-determination is lacking, the laws for this business of division can only consist of formal, empty rules that lead to nothing. Thus we see it laid down as a rule that division shall *exhaust* the notion; but as a matter of fact each individual member of the division must exhaust *the notion*. It is, however, really the *determinateness* of the notion that one means should be exhausted; but with the empirical multiplicity of species devoid of any immanent determination, it contributes nothing to the exhaustion of the notion whether more or fewer are found to exist; whether, for example, in addition to the sixty-seven species of parrots another dozen are found is for the exhaustion of the genus a matter of indifference. The demand for exhaustion can only mean the tautological proposition that all the species shall be presented in their *completeness*. Now with the extension of empicical knowledge it may very well happen that species are found which do not fit in with the adopted definition of the genus; for frequently the definition is adopted more on the basis of a vague conception of the entire habitus, rather than in accordance with a more or less individual mark that is expressly meant to serve for its definition. In such a case the genus would have to be modified and a justification would have to be found for regarding some other number of species as species of a new genus; in other words, the genus would be defined by what we group together in accordance with some principle or other that we choose to adopt as unity; and in this case the principle itself would be the basis of division. Conversely, if we hold to the determinateness originally adopted as characteristic of the genus, that material which we wished to group, as species, in a unity with the earlier species would be excluded. This unsystematic procedure, which sometimes adopts a determinateness as essential moment of the genus and then either subordinates the particulars to it or excludes them from it, and sometimes starts with the particular and in grouping it lets itself again be guided by some other determinateness, gives the appearance of the play of a caprice to which it is left to decide which part or which side of the concrete it will fix on and use as its principle of arrangement. Physical nature presents of itself such a contingency in the principles of division. By reason of its dependent external actuality it stands in a complex connectedness that for it likewise is given; accordingly there exists a crowd of principles to which it has to conform, and therefore in one series of its forms follows one principle, and in other series other principles, as well as producing hybrids that belong at the same time to different sides of the division. Thus it happens that in one series of natural objects marks stand out as very characteristic and essential that in others become inconspicuous and purposeless, so that it becomes impossible to adhere to a principle of division of this kind.

The general *determinateness* of empirical species can only consist in their being simply *different* from one another without being opposed. The *disjunction* of the *Notion* has been exhibited at an earlier stage in its determinateness; when particularity is assumed as immediate and given and without the negative unity of the Notion, the difference remains only at the stage of diversity as such, a form of reflection that we considered earlier. The externality in which the Notion chiefly exists in Nature brings with it the complete indifference of the difference; consequently, a frequent determination for division is taken from *number*.

Such is the contingency here of the particular in face of the universal and therefore of division generally, that it may be attributed to an *instinct* of reason when we find in this cognition grounds of division and divisions that, so far as sensuous properties permit, show themselves to be more adequate to the Notion. For example, in the case of animals, the instruments of eating, the teeth and claws, are employed in systems of classification as a broad radical ground of division; they are taken, in the first instance, merely as aspects in which the distinguishing marks for the subjective purposes of cognition can be more easily indicated. But as a matter of fact these organs do not merely imply a differentiation belonging to external reflection, but they are the vital point of animal individuality where it posits itself as a self-related individuality distinct from its other, from the nature that is external to it, and as an individuality that withdraws itself from continuity with the other. In the case of the *plant*, the fertilizing organs constitute the highest point of vegetable life, by which the plant points to the transition into sex difference, and thereby into individual individuality. The system of botany has therefore rightly turned to this point for a principle of division that, if not adequate is far-reaching, and has thereby taken as its basis a determinateness that is not merely a determinateness for external reflection for purposes of comparison, but is in and for itself the highest of which the plant is capable.

3. *The Theorem*

1. The stage of this cognition that advances on the basis of the Notion-determinations is the transition of particularity into individuality; this constitutes the content of the *theorem*. What we have to consider here, then, is the *self-related determinateness*, the immanent difference of the object and the relation of the differ-entiated determinatenesses to one another. Definition contains only *one determinateness*, division contains determinateness *in relation to others*; in individualization the object has gone asunder within itself. Whereas definition stops short at the general concept, in theorems, on the contrary, the object is cognized in its reality, in the conditions and forms of its real existence. Hence, in con-junction with definition, it represents the *Idea*, which is the unity of the Notion and reality. But the cognition here under con-sideration, which is still occupied in seeking, does not attain to this presentation in so far as the reality it deals with does not proceed from the Notion, and therefore the dependence of reality on the Notion and consequently the unity itself is not cognized.

Now the theorem, according to the stated definition, is the genuinely *synthetic* aspect of an object in so far as the relationships of its determinatenesses are *necessary*, that is, are founded in the *inner identity* of the Notion. The synthetic element in definition and division is an externally adopted connexion; what is found given is brought into the form of the Notion, but, as given, the entire content is merely *presented* [*monstriert*], whereas the theorem has to be *demonstrated*. As this cognition *does not deduce* the content of its definitions and the principles of its divisions, it seems as if it might spare itself the trouble of *proving* the relationships expressed by theorems and content itself in this respect, too, with observation. But what distinguishes cognition from mere observation and representation is the *form of the Notion* as such that cognition imparts to the content; this is achieved in definition and division: but as the content of the theorem comes from the Notion's moment of *individuality*, it consists in determinations of reality that no longer have for their relationship the simple and immediate determinations of the Notion; in individuality the Notion has passed over into *otherness*, into the reality whereby it becomes Idea. Thus the synthesis contained in the theorem no longer has the form of the Notion for its justification; it is a connexion of [merely] *diverse* terms. Consequently the unity not yet posited with it has still to be demonstrated, and therefore proof becomes necessary even to this cognition.

Now here we are confronted first of all by the difficulty of clearly *distinguishing* which of the *determinations* of the *subject matter* may be admitted *into the definitions* and which are to be relegated to the *theorems*. On this point there cannot be any principle ready to hand; such a principle seems, perhaps, to be implied in the fact that what immediately belongs to an object appertains to the definition, whereas the rest, since it is mediated, must wait for its mediation to be demonstrated. But the content of definition is in general a determinate one, and therefore is itself essentially a mediated content; it has only a *subjective* immediacy, that is, the subject makes an arbitrary beginning and accepts a subject matter as presupposition. Now since this subject-matter is in general concrete within itself and must also be divided, the result is a number of determinations that are by their nature mediated, and are accepted not on the basis of any principle, but merely subjectively as immediate and unproved. Even in Euclid, who has always been justly recognized as the master in this synthetic kind of cognition, we find under the name of *axiom* a *presupposition* about *parallel lines* which has been thought to stand in need of proof, and various attempts to supply this want have been made. In several other theorems, people have thought that they had discovered presuppositions which should not have been immediately assumed but ought to have been proved. As regards the axiom concerning parallel lines, it may be remarked that it is precisely there that we may discern the sound sense of Euclid, who had appreciated exactly the element as well as the nature of his science. The proof of the said axiom would have had to be derived from the *notion* of parallel lines; but a proof of that kind is no more part of his science than is the deduction of his definitions, axioms and in general his subject matter, space itself and its immediate determinations, the three dimensions. Such a deduction can only be drawn from the Notion, and this lies outside the peculiar domain of Euclid's science; these are therefore necessarily *presuppositions* for it, relative firsts.

Axioms, to take this opportunity of mentioning them, belong to the same class. They are commonly but incorrectly taken as absolute firsts, as though in and for themselves they required no proof. Were this in fact the case, they would be mere tautologies, as it is only in abstract identity that no difference is present, and therefore no mediation required. If, however, axioms are more than tautologies, they are *propositions* from some *other science*, since for the science they serve as axioms they are meant to be presuppositions. Hence they are, strictly speaking, *theorems*, and theorems taken mostly from logic. The axioms of geometry are lemmata of this kind, logical propositions, which moreover approximate to tautologies because they are only concerned with magnitude and therefore qualitative differences are extinguished in them; the chief axiom, the purely quantitative syllogism, has been discussed above. Axioms, therefore, considered in and for themselves, require proof as much as definitions and divisions, and the only reason they are not made into theorems is that, as relatively first for a certain standpoint, they are assumed as presuppositions.

As regards the *content of theorems*, we must now make a more precise distinction. As the content consists in a *relation between determinatenesses* of the Notion's reality, these relations may be more or less incomplete and single relationships of the subject matter, or else may be a relationship embracing the *entire content* of the reality and expressing the determinate relation of that content. But the *unity of the complete determinatenesses of the content* is equivalent to the *Notion*; consequently a proposition that contains them is itself again a definition, but a definition that expresses not merely the immediately assumed Notion, but the Notion developed into its determinate real differences, or the complete existence of the Notion. The two together, therefore, present the *Idea*.

If we compare closely the theorems of a synthetic science, especially of *geometry*, we shall find this difference, that some of its theorems involve only single relationships of the subject matter, while others involve relationships in which the complete determinateness of the subject matter is expressed. It is a very superficial view that assigns equal importance to all the propositions on the ground that in general each contains a truth and is equally essential in the formal progress, in the context, of the proof. The difference in respect of the content of theorems is most intimately connected with this progress itself; some further remarks on the latter will serve to elucidate in more detail this difference as well as the nature of synthetic cognition. To begin with, Euclidean geometry—which as representative of the synthetic method, of which it furnishes the most perfect specimen, shall serve us as example—has always been extolled for the ordered arrangement in the sequence of the theorems, by which for each theorem the propositions requisite for its construction and proof are always found already proved. This circumstance concerns formal consecutiveness; yet, important as it is, it is still rather a matter of an external arrangement for the purpose of the matter in hand and has on its own account no relation to the essential difference of Notion and Idea in which lies a higher principle of the necessity of the progress. That is to say, the definitions with which we begin, apprehend the sensuous object as immediately given and determine it according to its proximate genus and specific difference; these are likewise the simple, *immediate* determinatenesses of the Notion, universality and particularity, whose relationship is no further developed. Now the initial theorems themselves can only make use of immediate determinations such as are contained in the definitions; similarly their reciprocal *dependence*, in the first instance, can only relate to this general point, that one is simply *determined* by the other. Thus Euclid's first propositions about triangles deal only with *congruence*, that is, *how many* parts in a triangle *must be determined*, in order that the *remaining* parts of one and the same triangle, or the whole of it, shall be *altogether determined*. The comparison of *two* triangles with one another, and the basing of congruence on *coincidence* is a detour necessary to a method that is forced to employ *sensuous concidence* instead of the

CC*

thought, namely, the *determinateness* of the triangles. Considered by themselves apart from this method, these theorems themselves contain *two* parts, one of which may be regarded as the *Notion*, and the other as the *reality*, as the element that completes the former into reality. That is to say, whatever completely determines a triangle, for example two sides and the included angle, is already the whole triangle for the *understanding*; nothing further is required for its complete determinateness; the remaining two angles and the third side are the superfluity of reality over the determinateness of the Notion. Accordingly what these theorems really do is to reduce the sensuous triangle, which of course requires three sides and three angles, to its simplest conditions. The definition had mentioned only the three lines in general that enclose the plane figure and make it a triangle; it is a theorem that first expresses the fact that the angle is *determined* by the determination of the sides, just as the remaining theorems contain dependence of three other parts on three others. But the complete *immanent* determinateness of the magnitude of a triangle in terms of its sides is contained in the theorem of Pythagoras; here we have first the *equation* of the sides of the triangle, for in the preceding propositions the sides are in general only brought into a reciprocal *determinateness* of the parts of the triangle, not into an *equation*. This proposition is therefore the perfect, *real definition* of the triangle, that is, of the right-angled triangle in the first instance, the triangle that is simplest in its differences and therefore the most regular. Euclid closes the first book with this proposition, for in it a perfect determinateness is achieved. So, too, in the second book, after reducing to the uniform type those triangles which are not right-angles and are affected with greater inequality, he concludes with the reduction of the rectangle to the square—with an equation between the self-equal, or the square, and that which is in its own self unequal, or the rectangle; similarly in the theorem of Pythagoras, the hypotenuse, which corresponds to the right-angle, to the self-equal, constitutes one side of the equation, while the other is constituted by the self-unequal, the *two* remaining sides. The above equation between the square and the rectangle is the basis of the *second* definition of the circle— which again is the theorem of Pythagoras, except that here the two sides forming the right-angle are taken as variable magnitudes. The first equation of the circle is in precisely that relationship of *sensuous* determinateness to *equation* that holds between the two different definitions of conic sections in general.

This genuine synthetic advance is a transition from *universality* to *individuality*, that is, *to that which is determined in and for itself*, or to the unity of the subject matter *within itself*, where the subject matter has been sundered and differentiated into its essential real determinatenesses. But in the other sciences, the usual and quite imperfect advance is commonly on the following lines; the beginning is, indeed, made with a universal, but its *individualization* and concretion is merely an *application* of the universal to a material introduced from elsewhere; in this way, the really *individual* element of the Idea is an *empirical* addition.

Now however complete or incomplete the content of the theorem may be, it must be *proved*. It is a relationship of real determinations that do not have the relationship of Notion-determinations; if they do have this relation, and it can be shown that they do in the propositions that we have called the *second* or real *definitions*, then first, such propositions are for that very reason definitions; but secondly, because their content at the same time consists not merely in the relationship of a universal and the simple determinateness, but also in relationships of real determinations, in comparison with such first definition, they do require and permit of proof. As real determinatenesses they have the form of *indifferent subsistence* and *diversity*; hence they are not immediately *one* and therefore their mediation must be demonstrated. The immediate unity in the first definition is that unity in accordance with which the particular is in the universal.

2. Now the *mediation*, which we have next to consider in detail, may be simple or may pass through several mediations. The mediating members are connected with those to be mediated; but in this cognition, since mediation and theorem are not derived from the Notion, to which transition into an opposite is altogether alien, the mediating determinations, in the absence of any concept of connexion, must be imported from somewhere or other as a preliminary material for the framework of the proof. This preparatory procedure is the *construction*.

Among the relations of the content of the theorem, which relations may be very varied, only those now must be adduced and demonstrated which serve the proof. This provision of material only comes to have meaning in the proof; in itself it appears blind and unmeaning. Subsequently, we see of course that it served the purpose of the proof to draw, for example, such further lines in the geometrical figure as the construction specifies; but during the construction itself we must blindly obey; on its own account, therefore, this operation is unintelligent, since the end that directs it is not yet expressed. It is a matter of indifference whether the construction is carried out for the purpose of a theorem proper or a problem; such as it appears in the first instance *before* the proof, it is something not derived from the determination given in the theorem or problem, and is therefore a meaningless act for anyone who does not know the end it serves, and in any case an act directed by an external end.

This meaning of the construction which at first is still concealed, comes to light in the *proof*. As stated, the proof contains the mediation of what the theorem enunciates as connected; through this mediation this connexion first *appears* as *necessary*. Just as the construction by itself lacks the subjectivity of the Notion, so the proof is a subjective act lacking objectivity. That is to say, because the content determinations of the theorem are not at the same time posited as Notion-determinations but as given *indifferent parts* standing in various external relationships to one another, it is only the *formal, external* Notion in which the necessity manifests itself. The proof is not a *genesis* of the relationship that constitutes the content of the theorem; the necessity exists only for intelligence, and the whole proof is in the *subjective interests of cognition*. It is therefore an altogether *external* reflection that *proceeds from without inwards*, that is, infers from external circumstances the inner constitution of the relationship. The circumstances that the construction has presented, are a *consequence* of the nature of the subject matter; here, conversely, they are made the *ground* and the *mediating* relationships. Consequently the middle term, the third, in which the terms united in the theorem present themselves in their unity and which furnishes the nerve of the proof, is only something in which this connexion *appears* and is *external*. Because the *sequence* that this process of proof pursues is really the reverse of the nature of the fact, what is regarded as *ground* in it is a subjective ground, the nature of the fact emerging from it only for cognition.

The foregoing considerations make clear the necessary limit of this cognition, which has very often been misunderstood. The shining example of the synthetic method is the science of *geometry* —but it has been inaptly applied to other sciences as well, even to philosophy. Geometry is a science of *magnitude*, and therefore *formal* reasoning is most appropriate to it; it treats of the merely quantitative determination and abstracts from the qualitative, and can therefore confine itself to *formal identity*, to the unity that lacks the Notion, which is *equality* and which belongs to the external abstractive reflection. Its subject matter, the determinations of space, are already such abstract subject matter, prepared for the purpose of having a completely finite external determinateness. This science, on account of its abstract subject matter, on the one hand, has this element of the sublime about it, that in these empty silent spaces colour is blotted out and the other sensuous properties have vanished, and further, that in it every other interest that appeals more intimately to the living individuality is silenced. On the other hand, the abstract subject matter is still space, a non-sensuous sensuous; *intuition* is raised into its abstraction; space is a *form* of intuition, but is still intuition, and so sensuous, the *asunderness* of sensuousness itself, its pure *absence of Notion*. We have heard enough talk lately about the excellence of geometry from this aspect; the fact that it is based on sensuous intuition has been declared its supreme excellence and people have even imagined that this is the ground of its highly scientific character, and that its proofs rest on intuition. This shallow view must be countered by the plain reminder that no science is brought about by intuition, but only by *thinking*. The intuitive character of geometry that derives from its still sensuous material only gives it that evidential side that the *sensuous* as such possesses for unthinking spirit. It is therefore lamentable that this sensuousness of its material has been accounted an advantage, whereas it really indicates the inferiority of its standpoint. It is solely to the *abstraction* of its sensuous subject matter that it owes its capability of attaining a higher scientific character; and it is to this abstraction that it owes its great superiority over those collections of information that people are also pleased to call sciences, which have for their content the concrete perceptible material of sense, and only indicate by the order which they seek to introduce into it a remote inkling and hint of the requirements of the Notion.

It is only because the space of geometry is the abstraction and void of asunderness that it is possible for the figures to be inscribed in the indeterminateness of that space in such a manner that their determinations remain in fixed repose outside another and possess no immanent transition into an opposite. The science of these determinations is, accordingly, a simple science of the *finite* that is compared in respect of magnitude and whose unity is the external unity of *equality*. But at the same time the delineation of these figures starts from various aspects and principles and the various figures arise independently; accordingly, the comparison of them makes apparent also their *qualitative* unlikeness and *incommensurability*. This development impels geometry beyond the *finitude* in which it was advancing so methodically and surely to *infinity*— to the positing of things as equal that are qualitatively different. Here it loses the evidential side that it possessed in its other aspect, where it is based on a stable finitude and is untouched by the Notion and its manifestation, the transition just mentioned. At this point the finite science has reached its limit; for the necessity and mediation of the synthetic method is no longer grounded merely in *positive* but in *negative identity*.

If then geometry, like algebra, with its abstract, non-dialectical [*bloss verständigen*] subject matter soon encounters its limit, it is evident from the very outset that the synthetic method is still more inadequate for *other sciences*, and most inadequate of all in the domain of philosophy. In regard to definition and division we have already ascertained the relevant facts, and here only theorem and proof should remain to be discussed. But besides the presupposition of definition and division which already demands and presupposes proof, the inadequacy of this method consists further in the general *position* of definition and division in relation to theorems. This position is especially noteworthy in the case of the empirical sciences such as physics, for example, when they want to give themselves the form of synthetic sciences. The method is then as follows. The *reflective determinations* of particular *forces* or other inner and essence-like forms which result from the method of analysing experience and can be justified only as *results*, must be *placed in the forefront* in order that they may provide a general *foundation* that is subsequently *applied to the individual* and demonstrated in it. These general foundations having no support of their own, we are supposed for the time being to take them *for granted*; only when we come to the derived *consequences* do we notice that the latter constitute the real *ground* of those *foundations*. The so-called *explanation* and the proof of the concrete brought into theorems turns out to be partly a tautology, partly a derangement of the true relationship, and further, too, a derangement that served to conceal the deception practised here by cognition, which has taken up empirical data one-sidedly, and only by doing so has been able to obtain its simple definitions and principles; and it obviates any empirical refutation by taking up and accepting as valid the data of experience, not in their concrete totality but in a particular instance, and that, too, in the direction helpful to its hypotheses and theory. In this subordination of concrete experience to presupposed determinations, the foundation of the theory is obscured and is exhibited only from the side that is conformable to the theory; and in general the unprejudiced examination of concrete observations on their own is made more difficult. Only by turning the entire process upside down does the whole thing get its right relationship in which the connexion of ground and consequent, and the correctness of the transformation of perception into thought can be surveyed. Hence one of the chief difficulties in the study of such sciences is *to effect an entrance into them*; and this can only be done if the presuppositions are *blindly taken for granted*, and straightway, without being able to form any Notion of them, in fact with barely a definite representation but at most a confused picture in the imagination, to impress upon one's memory for the time being the determinations of the assumed forces and matters, and their hypothetical formations, directions and rotations. If, in order to accept these presuppositions as valid, we demand their necessity and their Notion, we cannot get beyond the starting point.

We had occasion above to speak of the inappropriateness of applying the synthetic method to strictly analytic science. This application has been extended by Wolf to every possible kind of information, which he dragged into philosophy and mathematics— information partly of a wholly analytical nature, and partly too of a contingent and merely professional and occupational kind. The contrast between a material of this kind, easily grasped and by its nature incapable of any rigorous and scientific treatment, and the stiff circumlocutory language of science in which it is clothed, has of itself demonstrated the clumsiness of such application and discredited it.[1] Nevertheless, this misuse could not detract from the belief in the aptness and essentiality of this method for attaining scientific rigour in *philosophy*; Spinoza's example in the exposition of his philosophy has long been accepted as a model. But as a matter of fact, the whole style of previous metaphysics, its method included, has been exploded by Kant and Jacobi. Kant in his own manner has shown that the content of that metaphysics leads by strict demonstration to *antinomies*, whose nature in other respects has been elucidated in the relevant places; but he has not reflected on the nature of this demonstration itself that is linked to a finite content; yet the two must stand or fall together. In his *First Principles of Natural Science*, he has himself given an example of treating as a science of reflection, and in the method of such, a science that he thought by that method to claim for philosophy. If Kant attacked previous metaphysics rather in respect of its matter, Jacobi has attacked it chiefly on the side of its method of demonstration, and has signalized most clearly and most profoundly the essential point, namely, that a method of demonstration such as this is fast bound within the circle of the rigid necessity of the finite, and that *freedom*, that is the *Notion*, and with it *everything that is true*, lies beyond it and is unattainable by it. According to the Kantian result, it is the peculiar matter of metaphysics that leads it into contradictions, and the inadequacy of cognition consists in its *subjectivity*; according to Jacobi's result, the fault lies with the method and the entire nature of cognition itself, which only apprehends a connexion of *conditionedness* and *dependence* and therefore proves itself inadequate to what is in and

---

[1] For example, in Wolf's *First Principles of Architecture*, the *Eighth Theorem* runs: A window must be wide enough for two persons to be able to look out side by side in comfort.
Proof: It is quite usual for a person to be at the window with another person and to look out. Now since it is the duty of the architect to satisfy in every respect the main intentions of his principal (section 1), he must also make the window wide enough for two persons to look out at side by side in comfort. *Q.E.D.*

The same author's *First Principles of Fortification. Second Theorem:* When the enemy encamps in the neighbourhood, and it is expected that he will make an attempt to relieve the fortress, a line of circumvallation must be drawn round the whole fortress.
Proof: Lines of circumvallation prevent anyone from penetrating into the camp from outside (section 311). If therefore it is desired to keep them out, a line of circumvallation must be drawn round the camp. Therefore when the enemy encamps in the neighbourhood, and it is expected that he will attempt to relieve the fortress, the camp must be enclosed in lines of circumvallation. *Q.E.D.*

for itself, to what is absolutely true. In point of fact, as the principle of philosophy is the *infinite free Notion*, and all its content rests on that alone, the method proper to Notion-less finitude is inappropriate to it. The synthesis and mediation of this method, the *process of proof*, gets no further than a *necessity* that is the opposite of freedom, that is, to an *identity* of the dependent that is merely *implicit* [*an sich*], whether it be conceived as *internal* or as *external*, and in this identity, that which constitutes the reality in it, the differentiated element that has emerged into concrete existence, remains simply an *independent diversity* and therefore something *finite*. Consequently this *identity* does not achieve *concrete existence* here and remains merely *internal*, or, from another point of view, merely *external*, since its determinate content is given to it; from either point of view it is an abstract identity and does not possess within it the side of reality, and is not posited as *identity* that is *determinate* in and for itself. Consequently the *Notion*, with which alone we are concerned, and which is the infinite in and for itself, is excluded from this cognition.

In synthetic cognition, therefore, the Idea attains its end only to the extent that the *Notion* becomes *for the Notion* according to its *moments* of *identity* and *real determinations*, or of *universality* and *particular differences*—further also *as an identity* that is the *connexion* and *dependence* of the diverse elements. But this subject matter of the Notion is not adequate to it; for the Notion does not come to be the *unity of itself with itself in its subject matter or its reality*; in necessity its identity is for it; but in this identity the necessity is not itself the *determinateness*, but appears as a matter external to the identity, that is, as a matter not determined by the Notion, a matter, therefore, in which the Notion does not cognize itself. Thus in general the Notion is not for itself, is not at the same time determined in and for itself according to its unity. Hence in this cognition the Idea still falls short of truth on account of the inadequacy of the subject matter to the subjective Notion. But the sphere of necessity is the apex of being and reflection; through its own essential nature [*an und für sich selbst*] it passes over into the freedom of the Notion, inner identity passes over into its manifestation, which is the Notion as Notion. How this *transition* from the sphere of necessity into the Notion is effected *in principle* [*an sich*] has been shown in treating of necessity; the same transition also presented itself as the *genesis of the Notion* at the beginning of this book. Here *necessity* has the position of being the *reality* or *subject matter* of the Notion, just as the Notion into which it passes now appears as the Notion's subject matter. But the transition itself is the same. Here too it is only at first *implicit* and lies as yet outside cognition in our reflection; that is, it is still the inner necessity of the cognition itself. It is only the result that is for it. The Idea, in so far as the Notion is now *explicitly* determined in and for itself, is the *practical* Idea, or *action*.

B. THE IDEA OF THE GOOD

The Notion, which is its own subject matter, being determined in and for itself, the subject is determined for itself as an *individual*. As subjective it again presupposes an implicit otherness; it is the *urge* to realize itself, the end that wills *by means of itself* to give itself objectivity and to realize itself in the objective world. In the theoretical Idea the subjective Notion, as the *universal* that *lacks any determination* of its own, stands opposed to the objective world from which it takes to itself a determinate content and filling. But in the practical Idea it is as actual that it confronts the actual; but the certainty of itself which the subject possesses in being determined in and for itself is a certainty of its own actuality and of the *non-actuality* of the world; it is not only the world's otherness as an abstract universality that is a nullity for the subject, but the world's individuality and the determinations of its individuality. The subject has here vindicated *objectivity* for itself; its immanent determinateness is the objective, for it is the universality that is just as much absolutely determined; the formerly objective world, on the contrary, is now only something posited, something *immediately* determined in various ways, but because it is only immediately determined, the unity of the Notion is lacking in it and it is, by itself, a nullity.

This determinateness contained in the Notion and in the likeness of the Notion, and including within it the demand for an individual external actuality, is the *good*. It comes upon the scene with the worth of being absolute, because it is within itself the totality of the Notion, the objective that is at the same time in the form of free unity and subjectivity. This Idea is superior to the Idea of cognition already considered, for it possesses not only the worth of the universal but also of the out-and-out actual. It is an *urge* in so far as this actuality is still subjective, positing its own self, and not having at the same time the form of immediate presupposition; its urge to realize itself is, strictly speaking, not to give itself objectivity—this it possesses within itself—but merely this empty form of immediacy. Hence the activity of the end is not directed against itself in order to adopt and appropriate a given determination; on the contrary, it is in order to posit its own determination and by sublating the determinations of the external world to give itself reality in the form of external actuality. The Idea of the will as *explicitly* self-determining possesses the *content* within itself. Now it is true that this is a *determinate* content and to that extent something *finite* and *limited*; self-determination is essentially *particularization*, since the reflection of the will into itself as a negative unity in general is also individuality in the sense of the exclusion and presupposition of an other. Nevertheless, the particularity of the content is in the first instance infinite through the form of the Notion, whose own determinateness it is; and in this content the Notion possesses its negative self-identity, and therefore not merely a particular, but its own infinite individuality. Consequently the above-mentioned *finitude* of the content in the practical Idea is tantamount to the latter being in the first instance the not yet realized Idea; the Notion is, *for the content*, something that is in and for itself; it is here the Idea in the form of objectivity that is *for itself*; on the one hand, the subjective is for this reason no longer something merely *posited*, arbitrary or contingent, but an absolute; but on the other hand, *this form of concrete existence*, *being-for-self*, has not as yet the form of the *in-itself* as well. What thus appears in respect of form as such, as opposition, appears in the form of the Notion reflected into *simple identity*, that is, appears in the content as its simple determinateness; thus the good, although valid in and for itself, is some particular end, but an end that has not to wait to receive its truth through its realization, but is already on its own account the true.

The syllogism of immediate *realization* itself requires no detailed exposition here; it is altogether the same as the syllogism of *external purposiveness* considered above; it is only the content that constitutes the difference. In external as in formal purposiveness, it was an indeterminate finite content in general; here, though it is finite too, it is as such at the same time an absolutely valid content. But in regard to the conclusion, to the realized end, a further difference comes in. The finite end in its *realization*, all the same, gets no further than a *means*; since in its beginning it is not an end already determined in and for itself, it remains even when realized an end that is not in and for itself. If the good again is also fixed as something *finite*, if it is essentially such, then notwithstanding its inner infinitude it cannot escape the destiny of finitude—a destiny that manifests itself in a number of forms. The realized good is good by virtue of what it already is in the subjective end, in its Idea; realization gives it an external existence; but since this existence is determined merely as an intrinsically worthless externality, in it the good has only attained a contingent, destructible existence, not a realization corresponding to its Idea. Further, since in respect of its content the good is restricted, there are several kinds of good; good in its concrete existence is not only subject to destruction by external contingency and by evil, but by the collision and conflict of the good itself. From the side of the objective world presupposed for it, in the presupposition of which the subjectivity and finitude of the good consists, and which as a different world goes its own way, the very realization of the good is exposed to obstacles, obstacles which may indeed even be insurmountable. In this way, the good remains an *ought-to-be*; it is *in and for itself*, but *being*, as the ultimate abstract immediacy, remains *also* confronting it in the form of a *not-being*. The Idea of the realized good is, it is true, an *absolute postulate*, but it is no more than a postulate, that is, the absolute afflicted with the determinateness of subjectivity. There are still two worlds in opposition, one a realm of subjectivity in the pure regions of transparent thought, the other a realm of objectivity in the element of an externally manifold actuality that is an undisclosed realm of darkness. The complete elaboration of the unresolved contradiction between that *absolute* end and the *limitation* of this actuality that *insuperably* opposes it, has been considered in detail in the *Phenomenology of Spirit*.[1] As the Idea contains within itself the moment of complete determinateness, the other Notion with which the Notion enters into relation in the Idea, possesses in its subjectivity also the moment of an object; consequently the Idea enters here into the *shape of self-consciousness* and in this one aspect coincides with the exposition of the same.

---

[1] Baillie's translation, pp. 611 ff.

But what is still lacking in the practical Idea is the moment of consciousness proper itself; namely, that the moment of actuality in the Notion should have attained on its own account the determination of *external being*. Another way of regarding this defect is that the *practical* Idea still lacks the moment of the *theoretical* Idea. That is to say, in the latter there stands on the side of the subjective Notion—the Notion that is in process of being intuited within itself by the Notion—only the determination of *universality*; cognition knows itself only as apprehension, as the identity—on its own account *indeterminate*—of the Notion with itself; the filling, that is, the objectivity that is determined in and for itself, is for it a *datum*, and what *truly is* is the actuality there before it independently of subjective positing. For the practical Idea, on the contrary, this actuality, which at the same time confronts it as an insuperable limitation, ranks as something intrinsically worthless that must first receive its true determination and sole worth through the ends of the good. Hence it is only the will itself that stands in the way of the attainment of its goal, for it separates itself from cognition, and external reality for the will does not receive the form of a true being; the Idea of the good can therefore find its integration only in the Idea of the true.

But it makes this transition through itself. In the syllogism of action, one premiss is the *immediate relation of the good end to actuality* which it seizes on, and in the second premiss directs it as an external *means* against external actuality. For the subjective Notion the good is the objective; actuality in its existence confronts it as an insuperable limitation only in so far as it still has the character of *immediate existence*, not of something objective in the sense of a being that is in and for itself; on the contrary, it is either the evil or the indifferent, the merely determinable, whose worth does not reside within it. This abstract being that confronts the good in the second premiss has, however, already been sublated by the practical Idea itself; the first premiss of the latter's action is the *immediate objectivity* of the Notion, according to which the end communicates itself to actuality without meeting any resistance and is in simple identical relation with it. Thus all that remains to be done is to bring together the thoughts of its two premisses. To what has been already immediately accomplished by the objective Notion in the first premiss, the only addition made in the second premiss is that it is posited through mediation, and hence posited *for the objective Notion*. Now just as in the end relation in general, the realized end is also again merely a means, while conversely the means is also the realized end, so similarly in the syllogism of the good, the second premiss is immediately already present *implicitly* in the first; but this immediacy is not sufficient, and the second premiss is already postulated for the first—the realization of the good in the face of another actuality confronting it is the mediation which is essentially necessary for the immediate relation and the accomplished actualization of the good. For it is only the first negation or the otherness of the Notion, an objectivity that would be a submergence of the Notion in the externality; the second negation is the sublating of this otherness, whereby the immediate realization of the end first becomes the actuality of the good as of the Notion that is for itself, since in this actuality the Notion is posited as identical with itself, not with an other, and thus alone is posited as the free Notion. Now if it is supposed that the end of the good is after all not realized through this mediation, this signifies a relapse of the Notion to the stand-point occupied by it before its activity—the standpoint of an actuality determined as worthless and yet presupposed as real. This relapse, which becomes the progress to the spurious infinity, has its sole ground in the fact that in the sublating of that abstract reality this sublating is no less immediately forgotten, or it is forgotten that this reality is in fact already presupposed as an actuality that is intrinsically worthless and not objective. This repetition of the presupposition of the unrealized end after the actual realization of the end consequently assumes this character, that the *subjective bearing* of the objective Notion is reproduced and made perpetual, with the result that the *finitude* of the good in respect of its content as well as its form appears as the abiding truth, and its actualization appears always as a merely *individual* act, and not as a universal one. As a matter of fact this determinate-ness has sublated itself in the actualization of the good; what still *limits* the objective Notion is its own *view* of itself, which vanishes by reflection on what its actualization is *in itself*. Through this view it is only standing in its own way, and thus what it has to do is to turn, not against an outer actuality, but against itself.

In other words, the activity in the second premiss produces only a one-sided *being-for-self*, and its product therefore appears as something *subjective* and *individual*, and consequently the first presupposition is repeated in it. But this activity is in truth no less the positing of the *implicit* identity of the objective Notion and the immediate actuality. This latter is determined by the presupposition as having a phenomenal reality only, as being intrinsically worthless and simply and solely determinable by the objective Notion. When external actuality is altered by the activity of the objective Notion and its determination therewith sublated, by that very fact the merely phenomenal reality, the external determinability and worthlessness, are removed from that actuality and it is *posited* as being in and for itself. In this process the general presupposition is sublated, namely the determination of the good as a merely subjective end limited in respect of content, the necessity of realizing it by subjective activity, and this activity itself. In the result the mediation sublates itself; the result is an *immediacy* that is not the restoration of the presupposition, but rather its accomplished sublation. With this, the Idea of the Notion that is determined in and for itself is posited as being no longer merely in the active subject but as equally an immediate actuality; and conversely, this actuality is posited, as it is in cognition, as an objectivity possessing a true being. The individuality of the subject with which the subject was burdened by its presupposition, has vanished along with the presupposition; hence the subject now exists as *free, universal self-identity*, for which the objectivity of the Notion is a *given* objectivity *immediately to hand*, no less truly than the subject knows itself as the Notion that is determined in and for itself. Accordingly in this result *cognition* is restored and united with the practical Idea; the actuality found as given is at the same time determined as the realized absolute end; but whereas in questing cognition this actuality appeared merely as an objective world without the subjectivity of the Notion, here it appears as an objective world whose inner ground and actual subsistence is the Notion. This is the absolute Idea.

CHAPTER 3

THE ABSOLUTE IDEA

The absolute Idea has shown itself to be the identity of the theoretical and the practical Idea. Each of these by itself is still one-sided, possessing the Idea itself only as a sought-for beyond and an unattained goal; each, therefore, is a *synthesis of endeavour*, and has, but equally has *not*, the Idea in it; each passes from one thought to the other without bringing the two together, and so remains fixed in their contradiction. The absolute Idea, as the rational Notion that in its reality meets only with itself, is by virtue of this immediacy of its objective identity, on the one hand the return to *life*; but it has no less sublated this form of its immediacy, and contains within itself the highest degree of opposition. The Notion is not merely *soul*, but free subjective Notion that is for itself and therefore possesses *personality*—the practical, objective Notion determined in and for itself which, as person, is impenetrable atomic subjectivity—but which, none the less, is not exclusive individuality, but explicitly *universality* and *cognition*, and in its other has *its own* objectivity for its object. All else is error, confusion, opinion, endeavour, caprice and transitoriness; the absolute Idea alone is *being*, imperishable *life, self-knowing truth*, and is *all truth*.

It is the sole subject matter and content of philosophy. Since it contains *all* determinateness within it, and its essential nature is to return to itself through its self-determination or particularization, it has various shapes, and the business of philosophy is to cognize it in these. Nature and spirit are in general different modes of presenting *its existence*, art and religion its different modes of apprehending itself and giving itself an adequate existence. Philosophy has the same content and the same end as art and religion; but it is the highest mode of apprehending the absolute Idea, because its mode is the highest mode, the Notion. Hence it embraces those shapes of real and ideal finitude as well as of infinitude and holiness, and comprehends them and itself. The derivation and cognition of these particular modes is now the further business of the particular philosophical sciences. The *logical* aspect of the absolute Idea may also be called a *mode* of it; but whereas *mode* signifies a *particular* kind, a *determinateness* of form, the logical aspect, on the contrary, is the universal mode in which all particular modes are sublated and enfolded. The logical Idea is the Idea itself in its pure essence, the Idea enclosed in simple identity within its Notion prior to its *immediate reflection* [*Scheinen*] in a form-determinateness. Hence logic exhibits the self-movement of the absolute Idea only as the original *word*, which is an *outwardizing* or *utterance* [*Äusserung*], but an utterance that in being has immediately vanished again as something outer [*Äusseres*]; the Idea is, therefore, only in this self-determination of *apprehending itself*; it is in *pure thought*, in which difference is not yet *otherness*, but is and remains perfectly transparent to itself. Thus the logical Idea has itself as the *infinite form* for its content— form which constitutes the opposite to *content* to this extent that the content is the form-determination withdrawn into itself and sublated in the identity in such a manner that this concrete identity stands opposed to the identity explicated as form; the content has the shape of an other and a *datum* as against the form which as such stands simply in *relation*, and its determinateness is at the same time posited as an illusory being [*Schein*]. More exactly, the absolute Idea itself has for its content merely this, that the form determination is its own completed totality, the pure Notion. Now the determinateness of the Idea and the entire course followed by this determinateness has constituted the subject matter of the science of logic, from which course the absolute Idea itself has issued into *an existence of its own*; but the nature of this its existence has shown itself to be this, that determinateness does not have the shape of a *content*, but exists wholly as *form*, and that accordingly the Idea is the absolutely *universal Idea*. Therefore what remains to be considered here is not a content as such, but the universal aspect of its form—that is, the *method*.

Method may appear at first as the mere *manner* peculiar to the process of cognition, and as a matter of fact it has the nature of such. But the peculiar manner, as method, is not merely a modality of *being determined in and for itself*; it is a modality of cognition, and as such is posited as determined by the *Notion* and as form, in so far as the form is the soul of all objectivity and all otherwise determined content has its truth in the form alone. If the content again is assumed as given to the method and of a peculiar nature of its own, then in such a determination method, as with the logical element in general, is a merely *external* form. Against this however we can appeal not only to the fundamental Notion of the science of logic; its entire course, in which all possible shapes of a given content and of objects came up for consideration, has demonstrated their transition and untruth; also that not merely was it impossible for a given object to be the foundation to which the absolute form stood in a merely external and contingent relationship but that, on the contrary, the absolute form has proved itself to be the absolute foundation and ultimate truth. From this course the method has emerged as the *self-knowing Notion that has itself*, as the absolute, both subjective and objective, *for its subject matter*, consequently as the pure correspondence of the Notion and its reality, as a concrete existence that is the Notion itself.

Accordingly, what is to be considered here as method is only the movement of the *Notion* itself, the nature of which movement has already been cognized; but *first*, there is now the added *significance* that the *Notion is everything*, and its movement is the *universal absolute activity*, the self-determining and self-realizing movement. The method is therefore to be recognized as the unrestrictedly universal, internal and external mode; and as the absolutely infinite force, to which no object, presenting itself as something external, remote from and independent of reason, could offer resistance or be of a particular nature in opposition to it, or could not be penetrated by it. It is therefore *soul and substance*, and anything whatever is comprehended and known in its truth only when it is *completely subjugated to the method*; it is the method proper to every subject matter because its activity is the Notion. This is also the truer meaning if its *universality*; according to the universality of reflection it is regarded merely as the method for *everything*; but according to the universality of the Idea, it is both the manner peculiar to cognition, to the *subjectively* self-knowing Notion, and also the *objective* manner, or rather the *substantiality*, of *things*—that is of Notions, in so far as they appear primarily to *representation* and *reflection* as *others*. It is therefore not only the highest *force*, or rather the *sole* and absolute *force* of reason, but also its supreme and sole *urge* to find and cognize *itself by means of itself in everything*. Here, *secondly*, is indicated the *difference* of the *method from the Notion as such*, the *particular* aspect of the method. The Notion, when it was considered by itself, appeared in its immediacy; the *reflection*, or *the Notion that considered it*, fell within *our* knowing. The method is this knowing itself, for which the Notion is not merely the subject matter, but knowing's own subjective act, the *instrument* and means of the cognizing activity, distinguished from that activity, but only as the activity's own essentiality. In the cognition of enquiry, the method likewise occupies the position of an *instrument*, of a means standing on the subjective side by which this side relates itself to the object. In this syllogism the subject is one extreme and the object the other, and the former by means of its method unites with the latter, but in doing so it does not *unite with itself*. The extremes remain diverse because subject, method, and object are not posited as *the one identical Notion*; the syllogism is therefore still the formal syllogism; the premiss in which the subject posits the form on its side as its method is an *immediate* determination, and therefore contains the determinations of form, as we have seen, of definition, division, and so forth, as facts *found existing in the subject*. In true cognition on the contrary, the method is not merely an aggregate of certain determinations, but the Notion that is determined in and for itself; and the Notion is the middle term only because it has equally the significance of the objective, and consequently in the conclusion the objective does not merely attain an external determinateness by means of the method, but is posited in its identity with the subjective Notion.

1. Thus what constitute the method are the determinations of the Notion itself and their relations, which we have now to consider in their significance as determinations of the method. In doing so we must first begin with the *beginning*. Of the beginning we have already spoken at the beginning of the *Logic* itself, and also above, when dealing with subjective cognition, and we have shown that, if it is not made arbitrarily and with a categorical unconsciousness, it may indeed seem to involve a number of difficulties but nevertheless is of an extremely simple nature. Because it is the beginning, its content is an immediate, but an immediate that has the significance and form of *abstract universality*. Be it otherwise a content of *being*, or of *essence*, or of the *Notion*, it is as an immediate something *assumed, found already in existence, assertorical*. But first of all it is not an immediate of *sensuous intuition* or of *representation*, but of *thinking*, which on account of its immediacy may also be called a supersensuous

inner intuition. The immediate of sensuous intuition is a *manifold* and an *individual*. But cognition is thinking by means of notions, and therefore its beginning also is *only in the element of thought*— it is a *simple* and a *universal*. This form has already been discussed under definition. At the beginning of finite cognition universality is likewise recognized as an essential determination, but it is taken as a determination of thought and of Notion only in opposition to being. In point of fact this *first* universality is an *immediate* one, and for that reason has equally the significance of *being*; for being is precisely this abstract relation-to-self. Being requires no further derivation, as though it belonged to the abstract product of definition only because it is taken from sensuous intuition or elsewhere, and in so far as it is pointed out to us. This pointing out and derivation is a matter of *mediation*, which is more than a mere beginning, and is a mediation of a kind that does not belong to a comprehension by means of thinking, but is the elevation of ordinary thinking, of the empirical and ratiocinative consciousness, to the standpoint of thought. According to the current opposition of thought or concept and being it is regarded as an important truth that no being belongs as yet to the former, taken on its own, and that the latter has a ground of its own that is independent of thought. But the simple determination of *being* is in itself so meagre that, if only for that reason, there is no need to make much fuss about it; the universal is immediately itself this immediate, since as abstract it also is merely the abstract relation-to-self, which is being. As a matter of fact, the demand that being should be exhibited for us to see has a further, inner meaning involving more than this abstract determination; what is meant by it is in general the demand for the *realization of the Notion*, which realization does not lie in the *beginning* itself, but is rather the goal and the task of the entire further development of cognition. Further, since the *content* of the beginning is supposed to be justified and authenticated as something true or correct by its being pointed out in inner or outer perception, it is no longer the *form* of universality as such that is meant, but its *determinateness*, of which we shall need to speak presently. The authentication of the *determinate content* with which the beginning is made seems to lie *behind* it; but in fact it is to be considered as an advance, that is, if it belongs to philosophical [*begreifenden*] cognition.

Hence the beginning has for the method no other determinateness than that of being simple and universal; this is itself the *determinateness* by reason of which it is deficient. Universality is the pure simple Notion, and the method, as consciousness of the Notion, knows that universality is only a moment and that in it the Notion is not yet determined in and for itself. But with this consciousness that would carry the beginning further only for the sake of the method, the method would be a formal affair, something posited in external reflection. Since however it is the objective immanent form, the immediate of the beginning must be *in its own self* deficient and endowed with the *urge* to carry itself further. But in the absolute method the universal has the value not of a mere abstraction but of the objective universal, that is, the universal that is *in itself* the *concrete totality*, though that totality is not yet *posited*, is not yet *for itself*. Even the abstract universal as such, considered in its Notion, that is in its truth, is not merely the *simple*, but as *abstract* is already *posited* as infected with a *negation*. For this reason too *there is* nothing, whether in *actuality* or in *thought*, that is as simple and as abstract as is commonly imagined. A simple thing of this kind is a mere *presumption* that has its ground solely in the unconsciousness of what is actually present. Above, that with which the beginning is made was determined as the immediate; the *immediacy of the universal* is the same thing that is here expressed as the *in-itself* that is without a *being-for-self*. Hence it may indeed be said that every beginning must be made *with the absolute*, just as all advance is merely the exposition of it, in so far as its *in-itself* is the Notion. But because the absolute is at first only *in itself* it equally is *not* the absolute nor the posited Notion, and also not the Idea; for what characterizes these is precisely the fact that in them the *in-itself* is only an abstract, one-sided moment. Hence the advance is not a kind of *superfluity*; this it would be if that with which the beginning is made were in truth already the absolute; the advance consists rather in the universal determining itself and being *for itself* the universal, that is, equally an individual and a subject. Only in its consummation is it the absolute.

It is to be recalled that the beginning, which is *in itself* a concrete totality, may as beginning also be *free* and its immediacy have the determination of an *external existence*; the *germ of the living being* and the *subjective end* in general have proved themselves to be such beginnings and therefore both are themselves *urges*. The non-spiritual and inanimate, on the contrary, are the Notion only as *real possibility*; *cause* is the highest stage in which the concrete Notion, as a beginning in the sphere of necessity has an immediate existence; but it is not yet a subject that maintains itself as such even in its actual realization. The *sun*, for example, and in general all inanimate things, are determinate concrete existences in which real possibility remains an *inner* totality and the moments of the totality are not *posited* in subjective form in them and, in so far as they realize themselves, attain an existence by means of *other* corporeal individuals.

2. The concrete totality which makes the beginning contains as such within itself the beginning of the advance and development. As concrete, it is *differentiated within itself*; but by reason of its *first immediacy* the first differentiated determinations are in the first instance merely a *diversity*. The immediate, however, as self-related universality, as subject, is also the *unity* of these diverse determinations. This reflection is the first stage of the movement onwards—the emergence of *real difference, judgement*, the *process of determining* in general. The essential point is that the absolute method finds and cognizes the *determination* of the universal within the latter itself. The procedure of the finite cognition of the understanding here is to take up again, equally externally, what it has left out in its creation of the universal by a process of abstraction. The absolute method, on the contrary, does not behave like external reflection but takes the determinate element from its own subject matter, since it is itself that subject matter's immanent principle and soul. This is what Plato demanded of cognition, that it should *consider things in and for themselves*, that is, should consider them partly in their universality, but also that it should not stray away from them catching at circumstances, examples and comparisons, but should keep before it solely the things themselves and bring before consciousness what is immanent in them. The method of absolute cognition is to this extent *analytic*. That it finds the further determination of its initial universal simply and solely in that universal, is the absolute objectivity of the Notion, of which objectivity the method is the certainty. But the method is no less *synthetic*, since its subject matter, determined immediately as a *simple universal*, by virtue of the determinateness which it possesses in its very immediacy and universality, exhibits itself as an other. This relation of differentiated elements which the

subject matter thus is within itself, is however no longer the same thing as is meant by synthesis in finite cognition; the mere fact of the subject matter's no less analytic determination in general, that the relation is relation within the *Notion*, completely distinguishes it from the latter synthesis.

This is no less synthetic than analytic moment of the *judgement*, by which the universal of the beginning of its own accord determines itself as the *other of itself*, is to be named the *dialectical* moment. *Dialectic* is one of those ancient sciences that have been most misunderstood in the metaphysics of the moderns, as well as by popular philosophy in general, ancient and modern alike. Diogenes Laertius says of Plato that, just as Thales was the founder of natural philosophy and Socrates of moral philosophy, so Plato was the founder of the third science pertaining to philosophy, namely, *dialectic*—a service which the ancient world esteemed his highest, but which often remains quite overlooked by those who have most to say about him. Dialectic has often been regarded as an *art*, as though it rested on a subjective *talent* and did not belong to the objectivity of the Notion. The shape it takes and the result it reaches in Kantian philosophy have already been pointed out in the specific examples of the Kantian view of it. It must be regarded as a step of infinite importance that dialectic is once more recognized as necessary to reason, although the result to be drawn from it must be the opposite of that arrived at by Kant.

Besides the fact that dialectic is generally regarded as contingent, it usually takes the following more precise form. It is shown that there belongs to some subject matter or other, for example the world, motion, point, and so on, some determination or other, for example (taking the objects in the order named), finitude in space or time, presence in *this* place, absolute negation of space; but further, that with equal necessity the opposite determination also belongs to the subject matter, for example infinity in space and time, non-presence in this place, relation to space and so spatiality. The older Eleatic school directed its dialectic chiefly against motion, Plato frequently against the general ideas and notions of his time, especially those of the Sophists, but also against the pure categories and the determinations of reflection; the more cultivated scepticism of a later period extended it not only to the immediate so-called facts of consciousness and maxims of common life, but also to all the notions of science. Now the conclusion drawn from dialectic of this kind is in general the *contradiction* and *nullity* of the assertions made. But this conclusion can be drawn in either of two senses—either in the objective sense, that the *subject matter* which in such a manner contradicts itself cancels itself out and is null and void—this was, for example, the conclusion of the Eleatics, according to which *truth* was denied, for example, to the world, to motion, to the point; or in the subjective sense, that *cognition is defective.* One way of understanding the latter sense of the conclusion is that it is only this dialectic that imposes on us the trick of an illusion. This is the common view of so-called sound common sense which takes its stand on the evidence of the senses and on *customary conceptions and judgements.* Sometimes it takes this dialectic lightly, as when Diogenes the cynic exposes the hollowness of the dialectic of motion by silently walking up and down; but often it flies into a passion, seeing it in perhaps a piece of sheer foolery, or, when morally important objects are concerned, an outrage that tries to unsettle what is essentially established and teaches how to supply wickedness with grounds. This is the view expressed in the Socratic dialectic against that of the Sophists, and this is the indignation which, turned in the opposite direction, cost even Socrates his life. The vulgar refutation that opposes to thinking, as did Diogenes, *sensuous consciousness* and imagines that in the latter it possesses the truth, must be left to itself; but in so far as dialectic abrogates moral determinations, we must have confidence in reason that it will know how to restore them again, but restore them in their truth and in the consciousness of their right, though also of their limitations. Or again, the conclusion of subjective nullity may mean that it does not affect dialectic itself, but rather the cognition against which it is directed, and in the view of scepticism and likewise of the Kantian philosophy, *cognition in general.*

The fundamental prejudice in this matter is that dialectic has *only a negative result*, a point which will presently be more precisely defined. First of all as regards the above-mentioned *form* in which dialectic is usually presented, it is to be observed that according to that form the dialectic and its result affect the *subject matter* under consideration or else subjective *cognition*, and declare either the latter or the subject matter to be null and void, while on the other hand the *determinations* exhibited in the subject matter as in a *third* thing receive no attention and are presupposed as valid on their own account. It is an infinite merit of the Kantian philosophy to have drawn attention to this *un*critical procedure and by so doing to have given the impetus to the restoration of logic and dialectic in the sense of the examination of the *determinations of thought in and for themselves*. The subject matter, kept apart from thinking and the Notion, is an image or even a name; it is in the determinations of thought and the Notion that it *is* what it *is*. Therefore these determinations are in fact the sole thing that *matters*; they are the true subject matter and content of reason, and anything else that one understands by subject matter and content in distinction from them has value only through them and in them. It must not therefore be considered the fault of a subject matter or of cognition that these determinations, through their constitution and an external connexion, show themselves dialectical. On that assumption, the subject matter or the cognition is represented as a subject into which the *determinations* in the form of predicates, properties, self-subsistent universals, are introduced in such a manner that, fixed and correct as they are by themselves, they are brought into dialectical relationships and contradiction only by extraneous and contingent connexion in and by a third thing. This kind of external and fixed subject of imagination and understanding and these abstract determinations, far from meriting the status of *ultimates*, of secure and permanent substrates, are rather to be regarded as themselves immediate, as just that kind of presupposed and initial immediate that, as was shown above, must in its own essential nature [*an und für sich selbst*] submit to dialectic, because it is to be taken as *in itself* the Notion. Thus all the oppositions that are assumed as fixed, as for example finite and infinite, individual and universal, are not in contradiction through, say, an external connection; on the contrary, as an examination of their nature has shown, they are in and for themselves a transition; the synthesis and the subject in which they appear is the product of their Notion's own reflection. If a consideration that ignores the Notion stops short at their external relationship, isolates them and leaves them as fixed presuppositions, it is the Notion, on the contrary, that keeps them steadily in view, moves them as their soul and brings out their dialectic.

Now this is the very standpoint indicated above from which a universal *first, considered in and for itself*, shows itself to be the

DD

other of itself. Taken quite generally, this determination can be taken to mean that what is at first *immediate* now appears as *mediated, related* to an other, or that the universal appears as a particular. Hence the second term that has thereby come into being is the *negative* of the first, and if we anticipate the subsequent progress, the *first negative.* The immediate, from this negative side, has been *extinguished* in the other, but the other is essentially not the *empty negative,* the *nothing,* that is taken to be the usual result of dialectic; rather is it the *other of the first,* the *negative* of the *immediate*; it is therefore determined as the *mediated—contains* in general the *determination of the first* within itself. Consequently the first is essentially *preserved* and *retained* even in the other. To hold fast to the positive in *its* negative, in the content of the presupposition, in the result, this is the most important feature in rational cognition; at the same time only the simplest reflection is needed to convince one of the absolute truth and necessity of this requirement and so far as *examples* of the proof of this are concerned, the whole of logic consists of such.

Accordingly, what we now have before us is the *mediated,* which to begin with, or, if it is likewise taken immediately, is also a *simple* determination; for as the first has been extinguished in it, only the second is present. Now since the first also is *contained* in the second, and the latter is the truth of the former, this unity can be expressed as a proposition in which the immediate is put as subject, and the mediated as its predicate; for example, *the finite is infinite, one is many, the individual is the universal.* However, the inadequate form of such propositions is at once obvious. In treating of the *judgement* it has been shown that its form in general, and most of all the immediate form of the *positive* judgement, is incapable of holding within its grasp speculative determinations and truth. The direct supplement to it, the *negative* judgement, would at least have to be added as well. In the judgement the first, as subject, has the illusory show of a self-dependent subsistence, whereas it is sublated in its predicate as in its other; this negation is indeed contained in the content of the above propositions, but their positive form contradicts the content; consequently what is contained in them is not posited—which would be precisely the purpose of employing a proposition.

The second determination, the *negative* or *mediated,* is at the same time also the *mediating* determination. It may be taken in the first instance as a simple determination, but in its truth it is a *relation* or *relationship*; for it is the negative, *but the negative of the positive*, and includes the positive within itself. It is therefore the other, but not the other of something to which it is indifferent—in that case it would not be an other, nor a relation or relationship—rather it is the *other in its own self*, the *other of an other*; therefore it includes *its* own other within it and is consequently *as contradiction*, the *posited dialectic of itself*. Because the first or the immediate is *implicitly* the Notion, and consequently is also only *implicitly* the negative, the dialectical moment with it consists in positing in it the *difference* that it *implicitly* contains. The second, on the contrary, is itself the *determinate* moment, the *difference* or relationship; therefore with it the dialectical moment consists in positing the *unity* that is contained in it. If then the negative, the determinate, relationship, judgement, and all the determinations falling under this second moment do not at once appear on their own account as contradiction and as dialectical, this is solely the fault of a thinking that does not bring its thoughts together. For the material, the *opposed* determinations in *one relation*, is already *posited* and at hand for thought. But formal thinking makes identity its law, and allows the contradictory content before it to sink into the sphere of ordinary conception, into space and time, in which the contradictories are held *asunder* in juxtaposition and temporal succession and so come before consciousness without reciprocal contact. On this point, formal thinking lays down for its principle that contradiction is unthinkable; but as a matter of fact the thinking of contradiction is the essential moment of the Notion. Formal thinking does in fact think contradiction, only it at once looks away from it, and in saying that it is unthinkable it merely passes over from it into abstract negation.

Now the negativity just considered constitutes the *turning point* of the movement of the Notion. It is the *simple point of the negative relation* to self, the innermost source of all activity, of all animate and spiritual self-movement, the dialectical soul that everything true possesses and through which alone it is true; for on this subjectivity alone rests the sublating of the opposition between Notion and reality, and the unity that is truth. The *second* negative, the negative of the negative, at which we have arrived, is this sublating of the contradiction, but just as little as the contradiction is it an *act of external reflection*, but rather the *innermost, most objective moment* of life and spirit, through which a *subject*, a *person*, a *free being*, exists. The *relation of the negative to itself* is to be regarded as the *second premiss* of the whole syllogism. If the terms *analytic* and *synthetic* are employed as opposites, the *first* premiss may be regarded as the *analytic* moment, for in it the immediate stands in *immediate* relationship to its other and therefore *passes over*, or rather has passed over, into it—although this relation, as already remarked, is also synthetic, precisely because that into which it passes over is its *other*. The second premiss here under consideration may be defined as *synthetic*, since it is the relation of the *differentiated term as such to the term from which it is differentiated*. Just as the first premiss is the moment of *universality* and *communication*, so the second is determined by *individuality*, which in its relation to its other is primarily exclusive, for itself, and different. The negative appears as the *mediating* element, since it includes within it itself and the immediate whose negation it is. So far as these two determinations are taken in some relationship or other as externally related, the negative is only the *formal* mediating element; but as absolute negativity the negative moment of absolute mediation is the unity which is subjectivity and soul.

In this turning point of the method, the course of cognition at the same time returns into itself. As self-sublating contradiction this negativity is the *restoration* of the *first immediacy*, of simple universality; for the other of the other, the negative of the negative, is immediately the *positive*, the *identical*, the *universal*. If one insists on *counting*, this *second* immediate is, in the course of the method as a whole, the *third* term to the first immediate and the mediated. It is also, however, the third term to the first or formal negative and to absolute negativity or the second negative; now as the first negative is already the second term, the term reckoned as *third* can also be reckoned as *fourth*, and instead of a *triplicity*, the abstract form may be taken as a *quadruplicity*; in this way, the negative or the difference is counted as a *duality*. The third or fourth is in general the unity of the first and second moments, of the immediate and the mediated. That it is this *unity*, as also that the whole form of the method is a *triplicity*, is, it is true, merely the superficial external side of the mode of cognition; but to have demonstrated even this, and that too in a more specific application —for it is well known that the abstract number form itself was advanced at quite an early period, but, in the absence of the Notion, without result—must also be regarded as an infinite merit of the Kantian philosophy. The *syllogism*, which is also threefold, has always been recognized as the universal form of reason; but for one thing it counted generally for a quite external form that did not determine the nature of the content, and for another thing, since it progresses in the formal sense merely in the understanding's determination of *identity*, it lacks the essential *dialectical* moment of *negativity*; yet this moment enters into the triplicity of determinations because the third is the unity of the first two, and these, since they are different, can be in the unity only as sublated determinations. Formalism has, it is true, also taken possession of triplicity and adhered to its empty *schema*; the shallow ineptitude and barrenness of modern philosophic *construction* so-called, that consists in nothing but fastening this schema on to everything without Notion and immanent determination and employing it for an external arrangement, has made the said form tedious and given it a bad name. Yet the triteness of this use of it cannot detract from its inner worth and we must always value highly the discovery of the shape of the rational, even though it was at first uncomprehended.

Now more precisely the *third* is the immediate, but the immediate *resulting from sublation of mediation*, the simple resulting from *sublation of difference*, the positive resulting from sublation of the negative, the Notion that has realized itself by means of its otherness and by the sublation of this reality has become united with itself, and has restored its absolute reality, its *simple* relation to itself. This *result* is therefore the *truth*. It is *equally* immediacy *and* mediation; but such forms of judgement as: the third *is* immediacy and mediation, or: *it is the unity* of them, are not capable of grasping it; for it is not a quiescent third, but, precisely as this unity, is self-mediating movement and activity. As that with which we began was the *universal*, so the result is the *individual*, the *concrete*, the *subject*; what the former is *in itself*, the latter is now equally *for itself*, the universal is *posited* in the subject. The first two moments of the triplicity are *abstract*, untrue moments which for that very reason are dialectical, and through this their negativity make thmselves into the subject. The Notion itself is *for us*, in the first instance, *alike* the universal that is in itself, *and* the negative that is for itself, *and* also the third, that which is both in and for itself, the *universal* that runs through all the moments of the syllogism; but the third is the conclusion, in which the Notion through its negativity is mediated with itself and thereby posited *for itself* as the *universal* and the *identity of its moments*.

Now this result, as the whole that has withdrawn into and is *identical* with itself, has given itself again the form of *immediacy*. Hence it is now itself the same thing as the *starting-point* had determined itself to be. As simple self-relation it is a universal, and in this universality, the *negativity* that constituted its dialectic and mediation has also collapsed into *simple determinateness* which can again be a beginning. It may seem at first sight that this cognition of the result is an analysis of it and therefore must again dissect these determinations and the process by which it has come into being and been examined. But if the treatment of the subject matter is actually carried out in this analytic manner, it belongs to that stage of the Idea considered above, to the cognition of enquiry, which merely states of its subject matter what *is*, but not the necessity of its concrete identity and the Notion of it. But though the method of truth which comprehends the subject matter is, as we have shown, itself analytic, for it remains entirely within the Notion, yet it is equally synthetic, for through the Notion the subject matter is determined dialectically and as an other. On the new foundation constituted by the result as the fresh subject matter, the method remains the same as with the previous subject matter. The difference is concerned solely with the relationship of the foundation as such; true, it is now likewise a foundation, but its immediacy is only a *form*, since it was a result as well; hence its determinateness as content is no longer something merely picked up, but something *deduced* and *proved*.

It is here that the *content* of cognition as such first enters into the circle of consideration, since, as deduced, it now belongs to the method. The method itself by means of this moment expands itself into a *system*. At first the beginning had to be, for the method, wholly indeterminate in respect of content; to this extent it appears as the merely formal soul, for and by which the beginning was determined simply and solely in regard to its *form*, namely, as the immediate and the universal. Through the movement we have indicated, the subject matter has obtained for itself a *determinateness* that is a *content*, because the negativity that has withdrawn into simplicity is the sublated form, and as simple determinateness stands over against its development, and first of all over against its very opposition to universality.

Now as this determinateness is the proximate truth of the indeterminate beginning, it condemns the latter as something imperfect, as well as the method itself that, in starting from that beginning, was merely formal. This can be expressed as the now specific demand that the beginning, since it is itself a determinate relatively to the determinateness of the result, shall be taken not as an immediate but as something mediated and deduced. This may appear as the demand for an infinite *retrogression* in proof and deduction; just as from the fresh beginning that has been obtained, a result likewise emerges from the method in its course, so that the advance equally rolls *onwards* to infinity.

It has been shown a number of times that the infinite progress as such belongs to reflection that is without the Notion; the absolute method, which has the Notion for its soul and content, cannot lead into that. At first sight, even such beginnings as *being, essence, universality*, seem to be of such a kind as to possess the complete universality and absence of content demanded for a wholly formal beginning, as it is supposed to be, and therefore, as absolutely first beginnings, demand and admit of no further regress. As they are pure relations to self, immediate and indeterminate, they do not of course possess within themselves the difference which in any other kind of beginning, is directly posited between the universality of its form and its content. But it is the very indeterminateness which the above logical beginnings have for their sole content that constitutes their determinateness; this consists, namely, in their negativity as sublated mediation; the particularity of this gives even their indeterminateness a particularity by which *being, essence,* and *universality* are distinguished from one another. The determinateness then which belongs to them if they are taken by themselves is their *immediate determinateness*, just as much as the determinateness of any other kind of content, and therefore requires a deduction; for the method it is a matter of indifference whether the determinateness be taken as determinateness of *form* or of *content*. That a content has been determined by the first of its results is not in fact for the method, the beginning of a new mode; the method remains neither more nor less formal than before. For since it is the absolute form, the Notion that knows itself and everything as Notion, there is no content that could stand over against it and determine it to be a one-sided external form. Consequently, just as the absence of content in the above beginnings does not make them absolute beginnings, so too it is not the content as such that could lead the method into the infinite progress forwards or backwards. From one aspect, the *determinateness* which the method creates for itself in its result is the moment by means of which the method is self-mediation and converts *the immediate beginning into something mediated.* But conversely, it is through the determinateness that this mediation of the method runs its course; it returns *through* a *content* as through an apparent *other* of itself to its beginning in such a manner that not only does it restore that beginning—as a *determinate* beginning however—but the result is no less the sublated determinateness, and so too the restoration of the first immediacy in which it began. This it accomplishes as *a system of totality.* We have still to consider it in this determination.

We have shown that the determinateness which was a result is itself, by virtue of the form of simplicity into which it has withdrawn, a fresh beginning; as this beginning is distinguished from its predecessor precisely by that determinateness, cognition rolls onwards from content to content. First of all, this advance is determined as beginning from simple determinatenesses, the succeeding ones becoming ever *richer and more concrete.* For the result contains its beginning and its course has enriched it by a fresh determinateness. The *universal* constitutes the foundation; the advance is therefore not to be taken as a *flowing* from one *other* to the next *other.* In the absolute method the Notion *maintains* itself in its otherness, the universal in its particularization, in judgement and reality; at each stage of its further determination it raises the entire mass of its preceding content, and by its dialectical advance it not only does not lose anything or leave anything behind, but carries along with it all it has gained, and inwardly enriches and consolidates itself.

This *expansion* may be regarded as the moment of content, and in the whole as the first premiss; the universal is *communicated* to the wealth of content, immediately maintained in it. But the relationship has also its second, negative or dialectical side. The enrichment proceeds in the *necessity* of the Notion, it is held by it, and each determination is a reflection-into-self. Each new stage of *forthgoing*, that is, of *further determination*, is also a withdrawal inwards, and the greater *extension* is equally a *higher intensity*. The richest is therefore the most concrete and most *subjective*, and that which withdraws itself into the simplest depth is the mightiest and most all-embracing. The highest, most concentrated point is the *pure personality* which, solely through the absolute dialectic which is its nature, no less *embraces and holds everything within itself*, because it makes itself the supremely free—the simplicity which is the first immediacy and universality.

It is in this manner that each step of the *advance* in the process of further determination, while getting further away from the indeterminate beginning is also *getting back nearer* to it, and that therefore, what at first sight may appear to be different, the retrogressive grounding of the beginning, and the *progressive further determining* of it, coincide and are the same. The method, which thus winds itself into a circle, cannot anticipate in a development in time that the beginning is, as such, already something derived; it is sufficient for the beginning in its immediacy that it is simple universality. In being that, it has its complete condition; and there is no need to deprecate the fact that it may only be accepted *provisionally* and *hypothetically*. Whatever objections to it might be raised—say, the limitations of human knowledge, the need to examine critically the instrument of cognition before starting to deal with the subject matter—are themselves *presuppositions*, which as *concrete determinations* involve the demand for their mediation and proof. Since therefore they possess no formal advantage over the *beginning* with the subject matter against which they protest, but on the contrary themselves require deduction on account of their more concrete content, their claim to prior consideration must be treated as an empty presumption. They have an untrue content, for they convert what we know to be finite and untrue into something incontestable and absolute, namely, a *limited* cognition determined as *form* and *instrument relatively to its content*; this untrue cognition is itself also the form, the process of seeking grounds, that is retrogressive. The method of truth, too, knows the beginning to be incomplete, because it is a beginning; but at the same time it knows this incompleteness to be a necessity, because truth only comes to be itself through the negativity of immediacy. The impatience that insists *merely* on getting beyond the *determinate*—whether called beginning, object, the finite, or in whatever other form it be taken—and finding itself immediately

in the absolute, has before it as cognition nothing but the empty
negative, the abstract infinite; in other words, a *presumed* absolute,
that is presumed because it is not *posited*, not *grasped*; grasped it can
only be through the *mediation* of cognition, of which the universal
and immediate is a moment, but the truth itself resides only in
the extended course of the process and in the conclusion. To
meet the subjective needs of unfamiliarity and its impatience, a
survey of the *whole* may of course be given *in advance*—by a
division for reflection which, after the manner of finite cognition,
specifies the particular of the universal as something *already
there* and to be awaited in the course of the science. Yet this
affords us nothing more than a picture for *ordinary thinking*; for
the genuine transition from the universal to the particular and to
the whole that is determined in and for itself, in which whole that
first universal itself according to its true determination is again a
moment, is alien to the above manner of division, and is alone the
mediation of the science itself.

By virtue of the nature of the method just indicated, the science
exhibits itself as a *circle* returning upon itself, the end being wound
back into the beginning, the simple ground, by the mediation;
this circle is moreover a *circle of circles*, for each individual member
as ensouled by the method is reflected into itself, so that in returning into the beginning it is at the same time the beginning of a
new member. Links of this chain are the individual sciences
[of logic, nature and spirit], each of which has an *antecedent*
and a *successor*—or, expressed more accurately, *has* only the
antecedent and *indicates* its *successor* in its conclusion.

Thus then logic, too, in the absolute Idea, has withdrawn into
that same simple unity which its beginning is; the pure immediacy of being in which at first every determination appears to
be extinguished or removed by abstraction, is the Idea that has
reached through mediation, that is, through the sublation of
mediation, a likeness correspondent to itself. The method is the
pure Notion that relates itself only to itself; it is therefore the
simple self-relation that is *being*. But now it is also *fulfilled being*,
the *Notion that comprehends* itself, being as the *concrete* and also
absolutely *intensive* totality. In conclusion, there remains only this
to be said about this Idea, that in it, first, the *science of logic* has
grasped its own Notion. In the sphere of *being*, the beginning of its
content, its Notion appears as a knowing in a subjective reflection

external to that content. But in the Idea of absolute cognition the Notion has become the Idea's own content. The Idea is itself the pure Notion that has itself for subject matter and which, in running itself as subject matter through the totality of its determinations, develops itself into the whole of its reality, into the system of the science [of logic], and concludes by apprehending this process of comprehending itself, thereby superseding its standing as content and subject matter and cognizing the Notion of the science. Secondly, this Idea is still logical, it is enclosed within pure thought, and is the science only of the divine *Notion*. True, the systematic exposition is itself a realization of the Idea but confined within the same sphere. Because the pure Idea of cognition is so far confined within subjectivity, it is the *urge* to sublate this, and pure truth as the last result becomes also the *beginning of another sphere and science*. It only remains here to indicate this transition.

The Idea, namely, in positing itself as absolute *unity* of the pure Notion and its reality and thus contracting itself into the immediacy of *being*, is the *totality* in this form—*nature*. But this determination has not *issued from a process* of *becoming*, nor is it a *transition*, as when above, the subjective Notion in its totality *becomes objectivity*, and the *subjective end becomes life*. On the contrary, the pure Idea in which the determinateness or reality of the Notion is itself raised into Notion, is an absolute *liberation* for which there is no longer any immediate determination that is not equally *posited* and itself Notion; in this freedom, therefore, no transition takes place; the simple being to which the Idea determines itself remains perfectly transparent to it and is the Notion that, in its determination, abides with itself. The passage is therefore to be understood here rather in this manner, that the Idea *freely releases* itself in its absolute self-assurance and inner poise. By reason of this freedom, the form of its determinateness is also utterly free—the *externality of space and time* existing absolutely on its own account without the moment of subjectivity. In so far as this externality presents itself only in the abstract immediacy of being and is apprehended from the standpoint of consciousness, it exists as mere objectivity and external life; but in the Idea it remains essentially and actually [*an und für sich*] the totality of the Notion, and science in the relationship to nature of divine cognition. But in this next resolve of the pure Idea to determine itself as external Idea, it thereby only posits for itself the mediation out of which the Notion ascends as a free Existence that has withdrawn into itself from externality, that completes its self-liberation in the *science of spirit*, and that finds the supreme Notion of itself in the science of logic as the self-comprehending pure Notion.

SOME RECENT ENGLISH BOOKS
ON HEGEL

J. N. Findlay, *Hegel: A Re-examination*, George Allen & Unwin, London, 1968.

G. R. G. Mure, *An Introduction to Hegel*, Oxford University Press, Oxford, 1940.

G. R. G. Mure, *A Study of Hegel's Logic*, Oxford University Press, Oxford, 1950.

G. R. G. Mure, *The Philosophy of Hegel*, Oxford University Press, Oxford, 1965.

W. Kaufmann, *Hegel*, Weidenfeld & Nicholson, London, 1966.

GEORGE ALLEN & UNWIN LTD
London: 40 Museum Street, W.C.1

Auckland: P.O. Box 36013, Northcote Central, N.4
Barbados: P.O. Box 222, Bridgetown
Beirut: Deeb Building, Jeane d'Arc Street
Bombay: 15 Graham Road, Ballard Estate, Bombay 1
Buenos Aires: Escritorio 454–459, Florida 165
Calcutta: 17 Chittaranjan Avenue, Calcutta 13
Cape Town: 68 Shortmarket Street
Hong Kong: 105 Wing On Mansion, 26 Hancow Road, Kowloon
Ibadan: P.O. Box 62
Karachi: Karachi Chambers, McLeod Road
Madras: Mohan Mansions, 38c Mount Road, Madras 6
Mexico: Villalongin 32, Mexico 5, D.F.
Nairobi: P.O. Box 30583
New Delhi: 13–14 Asaf Ali Road, New Delhi 1
Ontario: 81 Curlew Drive, Don Mills
Philippines: Manila, P.O. Box 4322
Rio de Janeiro: Caixa Postal 2537-Zc-00
Singapore: 36c Prinsep Street, Singapore 7
Sydney, N.S.W.: Bradbury House, 55 York Street
Tokyo: P.O. Box 26, Kamata

HEGEL: A RE-EXAMINATION

J. N. FINDLAY

This book attempts a critical reinterpretation of Hegel's idealism and his dialectical method, and stresses their connection with many contemporary philosophical ideas and methods. It also seeks to give a comprehensive statement of Hegel's system, with sufficient clearness to be of some use to the layman, and enough detail to assist the student of Hegel's difficult writings. After three introductory chapters, dealing mainly with Hegel's notion of *Geist* (Spirit) and his notion and use of Dialectic, it covers the contents of the *Phenomenology of Spirit*, the *Science of Logic*, the *Philosophy of Nature*, and then deals with Hegel's Psychology, his theory of Law, Morals, the State and History, and finally with his treatment of 'Absolute Spirit' i.e. Art. Religion and Philosophy.

Professor J. N. Findlay is a South African by birth and a great-nephew of Olive Schreiner. As a Rhodes Scholar he did 'Greats' at Balliol, and has held University chairs in New Zealand (1934–44), South Africa (1945–48), King's College, Newcastle-upon-Tyne, University of Durham (1948–51) and King's College University of London (since 1951). He is the author of a book on Alexius Meinong, the Austrian philosopher (Oxford University Press, 1933) and of many philosophical articles. He for a time attended Wittgenstein's courses at Cambridge and was much influenced by his methods. His present philosophical interests extend in many directions, not all of them fashionable. He was President of the Aristotelian Society in 1955–6.

THE PHENOMENOLOGY OF MIND

G. W. F. HEGEL

'It is impossible to speak too highly of the limpid translation, and the editorial aids which light up this famous philosophical treatise.'

SECOND EDITION   *London Quarterly Review*

GEORGE ALLEN & UNWIN LTD